To Chris and Sarah,
Welcome to HIS Fields in
North Carolina —
John Curtis Ager

We Plow God's Fields

The Life of James G. K. McClure

by John Curtis Ager

Cover photograph of Dave Sharp taken by James G. K. McClure, III.
Cover and dust jacket design by Mark H. Suggs.

Library of Congress Cataloging-in-Publication Data

Ager, John Curtis, 1949-
    We plow God's fields : the life of James G. K. McClure / by John Curtis Ager.
    p.   cm.
    Includes bibliographical references.
    ISBN 0-913239-63-1 (hardcover : alk. paper)
    ISBN 0-913239-68-2 (paperback : alk. paper)
    1. McClure, James Gore King. 2. Farmers—United States—Biography. 3.
Farmers' Federation (N.C.)—History. 4. Agriculture, Cooperative—North Carolina—
History.   I. Title.
HD1771.5.M38A73   1991
334'.638'092—dc20
  [B]   89-17906

APPALACHIAN CONSORTIUM PRESS
Boone, North Carolina

The Appalachian Consortium is a non-profit educational organization comprised of institutions and agencies located in the Southern Highlands. Our members are volunteers who plan and execute projects which serve 156 mountain counties in seven states. Among our goals are:

Preserving the cultural heritage of Southern Appalachia
Protecting the mountain environment
Publishing manuscripts about the region
Improving educational opportunities for area students and teachers
Conducting scientific, social, and economic research
Promoting a positive image of Appalachia
Encouraging regional cooperation

The member institutions of the Appalachian Consortium are:

Appalachian State University
Blue Ridge Parkway
East Tennessee State University
Gardner-Webb College
Great Smoky Mountains Natural History Association
John C. Campbell Folk School
Lees-McRae College
Mars Hill College
Mayland Community College
N.C. Division of Archives and History
Southern Appalachian Highlands Conservancy
Southern Highlands Handicraft Guild
U.S. Forest Service
Warren Wilson College
Western Carolina University
Western North Carolina Historical Association

We Plow God's Fields
is dedicated to
my wife Annie McClure Clarke Ager
her mother, Elspeth McClure Clarke
and to the Forgotten Pioneers
of Western North Carolina.

Contents

Acknowledgments

Researching and writing a book is on the whole a solitary and lonely pursuit. And yet, you are dependent on a whole range of people for help. I have needed a large contingent of people to urge me on, to encourage the work. My mother, Mary Lucille Ager, my wife, Annie, my sons, Eric, Kevin, Jamie and Douglas, and my mother-in-law, Elspeth Clarke, have all been my primary encouragement team, and I am indebted to them beyond words. Debbie Aly, secretary to the McClure Fund, labored over her typewriter long and tedious hours for the benefit of this project. Buffy White agreed to subject herself to editing the manuscript, masterfully providing order in the midst of a whirlwind. The Trustees of the James G. K. McClure Educational and Development Fund, including James McClure Clarke, Reuben A. Holden, Dr. Harold Bacon, Mrs. Burnham Colburn, Martha Guy, Julian Woodcock, and Richard Jennings, patiently provided the funds and the time to complete this biography. Tom Eller of Warren Wilson College guided me through his word processing maze. John Murphy, Donna Kilpatrick, Doug Clarke, Franklin Sides, Donna Price, Susan and Chris Crosson and the Brown family (Ralph, Shirley, Clifford, Ben and Charlie) all kept the cows milked and the apples picked at Hickory Nut Gap Farm while I stole away to write this book. Finally, I am grateful to all my editors at the Appalachian Consortium, and to those who typeset and printed this book. In the end, it has been a community project, and how fitting that it should be.

Prologue

And for their sake I consecrate myself, that they also may be consecrated in truth. (*John 17:19, a favorite sermon text for Jim McClure*)

Describe Jim? That's difficult. He's tall & very well set up. About 5 feet 11 in his stockings & weighs about 170 pounds. He looks more like an Englishman or a Scotchman than an American & he wears his clothes the way they do—Tweeds and such likes. He has a very refined rather small head with dark hair & dark eyes that are very brilliant at times & with humorous lines about them. He has the most charming smile I've ever seen on any human being, and that's not merely the opinion of his prejudiced wife! He has regular features & a certain youthful almost childlike look to his face combined with an expression of immense strength & a curious concentrated vitality. He has a warm brown coloring that suggests an Italian . . . He has an extraordinary mind & a very real gift of expression, a singular intellectual quickness and a german thoroughness of investigation. He is one of the most original thinkers I have ever known & is wholly untrammelled by tradition. Added to that he has a humor & wit that is the joy of all who know him. This is written as much as possible with the eye of a cold outsider! (Elizabeth Cramer McClure to Martha Clarke, July 7, 1916)

This biography is a story of the life of one man, James Gore King McClure, Jr., and his vision for a better life in the mountains of North Carolina. At his prompting, and under his leadership, the Farmers Federation was founded in Fairview, North Carolina (near Asheville) in 1920. Out of his own determination and his superb organizing skills, he created a cooperative agricultural movement that began to shift the economy of Western North Carolina from one hopelessly beset with inertia to one that gave the farmers of the area new hope. The Federation organized markets, provided test trials for farm products, and upgraded breeding stock. For the first time in many years, farmers had money in their pockets and a legitimate pride in their production.

A name like James Gore King McClure seems made to be announced in a resounding bass voice, after which all mumbling and chit-chat would quickly subside into attentive silence. But though honor, respect and even power would eventually come to this man, they were won more with a smile and a cheerful remark than with an authoritarian presence. He was brought up, a minister's son, in the posh Chicago suburb of Lake Forest, Illinois, but was able to break through the narrow circle of this society to move easily among different levels

v

and conditions of humanity. He inherited a powerful Presbyterian vision as the descendant of staunch Scottish Covenanters, and was trained in theology and the rhythms of Protestant church work. He could challenge the complacency of a prominent New York City church with his message of the Social Gospel; and two weeks later, in shirt sleeves, challenge the mountaineers of the Bearwallow Baptist Church in Gerton, North Carolina, to take hold of their own lives, to consecrate themselves for the sake of their neighbors and their children.

Jim McClure always felt a thrill when he gathered together the varieties of people in his life. He possessed the gifts of charm and humor, and the ability to create an ambience of good feelings and warmth that brought individuals with little common ground in touch with one another. The man drew a kind of power out of a crowd, a spiritual power he returned in kind. Whether it was playing Santa Claus for the mountain children at his home, Hickory Nut Gap Farm, or raffling off a rooster to a wealthy dowager at the Waldorf Astoria in New York, he had a knack for understanding what it was in a situation that gave people a sense of ease, satisfaction and excitement. He knew when to be serious, and when a tense moment needed relief. His skills were human ones; and they brought into his life most of all many, many friends.

This is also the story of his wife, Elizabeth Cramer McClure, an extraordinarily sensitive woman who saw the rich colors of life with a painter's eyes, and who taught Jim to balance Calvin with Monet. Without her sense of proportion and beauty, Jim's work for the Farmers Federation would certainly have failed. She made a home for him, remodeling an old neglected inn and surrounding it with flower and vegetable gardens. There were the two children, Elspeth and Jamie, with their friends and cousins romping about the mountainside. It was the kind of place Jim McClure could both entertain his guests and really relax, and where he could find support and comfort in his spiritual struggles.

Elizabeth's portrait of Jim continues to greet his descendants and old friends in the dining room of Hickory Nut Gap Farm. One mountain woman who had grown up on the farm said every time she passed by it she just thought he was going to jump out and start talking to her. Elizabeth, an exquisite portrait painter, captured his gifts on canvas. It was with his famous eyes that she told with her brush of his "immense strength & a curious concentrated vitality." The eyes are determined and full of the adventure of a great vision of life. And his mouth, with a little smile, balances the Presbyterian hardness to portray the "humor & wit that is the joy of all who know him." Elizabeth showed how the mouth and the eyes complemented each other, in the portrait as well as in her marriage to him.

This man chose and articulated the highest ideals, and then doggedly pursued them. He had to struggle not only with the ingrown fatalism of the mountaineer, but with himself and the limitations his own culture imposed on him. Both he and his wife worked to enjoy and appreciate the incongruities of their lives. Their grace and good humor, though, did not leave them casual wayfarers. They were hard-working participants with and movers of the people around them, always ready to take a stand for progress and then to battle hard for its fulfillment.

It would be easy to say that these two people lived in an era when faith in progress supported them. It is true they had the backing of a dynamic American society that was making such economic strides that no problems appeared insurmountable, and yet was still old-fashioned enough to believe in an American destiny. But Jim and Elizabeth McClure faced the cynicism and hypocrisy that are always prevalent in human societies. The story of Jim's life is full of human hope and courage. He wanted his life to stand for spiritual excellence, not as a contemplative monk but as a man who was unafraid to dream that the Kingdom of God could be established on this earth and was willing to dirty himself trying to build it. His struggle was imperfect; not all of his projects were successful. The Farmers Federation itself died a suffering death. His life, like most, was filled with tragic elements that would haunt and discourage him. And yet he kept battling and fighting right up to the very end. Read this book to discover a great human spirit, the man baptized James Gore King McClure, Jr.

Chapter 1
The McClure Family

Grandchildren are the crown of the aged, and the glory of sons is their fathers. *Proverbs 17:6*

The memory of my Father is a constant inspiration to me—in every high and holy line. (*James Gore King McClure, Sr., to James Gore King McClure, Jr., October 6, 1928*)

The oldest room at Hickory Nut Gap Farm, the original log cabin in fact, was made over by Jim and Elizabeth McClure to be their study. The bookshelves were filled with his theological and historical works, with several shelves reserved for her art books, and volumes on landscaping, interior design and horticulture that were used for the transformation of the old inn. When there was a need for serious talk, the McClures retired to this study, closing the door behind them. Of all the rooms in the house, it was the one reserved almost exclusively for business matters and intellectual stimulation. It is no accident that Jim and Elizabeth hung above the old fireplace in that room an engraving commemorating a decisive development in Scottish history. Although these events occurred nearly 300 years earlier, they had such a profound effect and so powerful an influence on Jim McClure's ancestors that they were in large part responsible both for his desire to enter the ministry and his very presence in the United States.

The engraving is peopled with figures going about a most serious and, for some, painful ordeal. On the right, men of the nobility arrive on horseback amid aristocrats still wearing their swords and uniforms of command. No one smiles. On the left, a confident and stern-faced minister of the gospel shoves into the scene a small book, perhaps the hated Anglican *Book of Common Prayer*. The light, the outstretched arms and the faces all focus onto the center of the picture, where a simple country woman sits with an open Bible on her lap. Her face looks off into the distance with an expression of unnamed terror, because she understands better than all of the others that the consequence of this gathering will be war. And war, to the peasant mother, threatens her family most of all, because it brings along not only death, but hunger and disease as well. The year is 1638, and the Scottish Presbyterians are rising to oppose the ill-fated King Charles I and his Archbishop, William Laud. The specific issue is a decree that the Scottish church must use the Anglican prayer book. But the real issue is: who rules Scotland, the English crown or the Scottish Presbyterians? To under-

1

"The Covenanters," an engraving hanging over the fireplace of the study at Hickory Nut Gap, Fairview, N.C. Engraved from a painting "By His Most Obedient Servant George Harvey."

stand Jim McClure, it is important to know what his ancestors were doing and thinking at this time of crisis.

The Scots never developed an institution comparable to the English Parliament. But in order to root out the Roman Catholic Church, John Knox (1505–1572), leader of the Scottish reformation, had organized his Presbyterians into a powerful political force, one that was astonishingly representative of the different classes of its day. By the time Charles I assumed the throne, he was faced with a church body that wanted to rule Scotland, and he had to find a means to thwart it. The battle over the English prayer book was the loose thread that started to unravel Charles's rule, ending finally with his execution. The picture in the McClure study commemorates the renewal of the Scottish Covenant with God, and it bound each signatory to resist the authority of the Church of England and its royal promoters. English historian G. M. Trevelyan wrote: "The Covenant with God . . . embraced all ranks from the highest to the lowest. In every parish men signed it, weeping and lifting their right hands to heaven. When the Scots display emotion, something real is astir within them."[1] The Scottish resistance forced Charles I to call for the election of a Parliament to provide money for an army, setting in motion the famous struggle for power between that body and the English monarchy. When the dust had cleared, neither Oliver Cromwell nor the restored Charles II could abide a Scotland ruled by radical Presbyterians. Life was made increasingly uncomfortable for the

Covenanters. Some years earlier King James I, father of the ill-fated Charles, had created a plantation of Scottish settlers in Ulster, Ireland, sowing the dragon's teeth of sectarian hatred amongst the Catholic Irish. Some members of the McClure family left Scotland at this early opportunity, and were well established in Northern Ireland when the screws began to tighten on their Scottish brethren later in the century. A family letter describes the situation:

> It was towards the latter part of the seventeenth century that the Sloans with the McClures and Craigmiles were forced to take refuge in Ireland. As covenanting Presbyterians they were subject to severe persecution, and with their brethren in the faith they sought peace and safety in a land where they could worship God after the dictates of their hearts. Passing over from Craig in Scotland they found a resting place in the province of Ulster where the Presbyterians so largely predominated, settling in the County of Armagh; they there remained surrounded by sympathizing friends, enjoying the quiet they sought.[2]

One family story tells of a mother and daughter hiding in a load of hay being shipped across to Ireland. English soldiers sank their bayonets into the hay, but miraculously neither mother nor daughter was discovered, and they arrived safely. Through the fires of such adversity, a strong Presbyterian identity was firmly stamped on the McClure family.

At this point in the family history, individual McClure ancestors emerge. Archibald, Jim's great-grandfather, married Elizabeth Craigmiles. Her father, if family traditions are accurate, felt that this McClure boy was too lowly to marry the daughter of a famous military man. James Craigmiles, born Craig, was a member of the family that had emigrated from Scotland with the McClures during the seventeenth century. He had made a name for himself, in the literal sense. At the age of eighteen he enlisted in the British Army, and in 1759 found himself in the New World as a part of the siege of Quebec. In one of the most celebrated military paintings of the period James Craig holds in his arms the brilliant young General Wolfe as death overcomes him on the Plains of Abraham. Wolfe's watch and papers were delivered personally by Craig to the general's family, and for his heroism he was granted property and the suffix "miles" (Latin for soldier) was added to his name.[3]

With the passing of time, Ireland ceased to be a haven from persecution. It was also a poor land where an ambitious person had little hope of satisfactory fulfillment. Religious questions and questions of national identity were hopelessly tangled, as they are today, and the London government felt forced to limit the rights of citizenship to those people loyal to the Church of England. By law, both Covenanters and Catholics

> . . . could hold no public office, nor be married by their own ministers, nor bury their dead by their own simple rites, nor build churches, nor buy land, nor employ teachers except those of the Established Faith. Thus deprived by oppressive laws of every position of trust or honor, denied the liberty of

speech, the free exercise of conscience, together with the burdensome re-
straints of commerce and extortionate rents from their landlords, they began
to look toward America as another and a better home.[4]

The new American republic was attracting settlers who hoped to leave
behind both the politics of the Reformation and the poverty of Ireland. In 1801
the McClure family made the decisive break, and Jim McClure's great-grandfather, Archibald McClure, sailed for New York. James Craigmiles and his wife
joined their daughter and son-in-law and their children for the voyage to America. Another young couple went with them, for Archibald's brother John had
married another of James Craigmiles's daughters, doubly diluting his fine new
name with McClure blood. Mary McClure, sister to Archibald and John, was
on board as well. She was the crucial link in her two brothers' future, for she
had married and moved to America in 1794 and had returned to Ireland to see
her family and accompany them across the Atlantic. The whole McClure clan
was presided over for the trip by Mr. and Mrs. McClure, Sr., Jim's great-great-
grandparents. They all settled in the primitive manufacturing town of Hamilton
Factory near Albany, New York, where Mary's family lived.[5]

Sailing the Atlantic in 1801 was very risky, especially for the older members of a family group. The boats were cramped and the crossing took many
weeks. Tragedy struck the McClure voyage as yellow fever broke out on board,
and when they arrived in New York the port authorities refused to allow the
passengers to disembark until the disease had run its course. It must have been
a dreary wait on the edge of the New World. The older passengers suffered
terribly, and when the time came to set foot on American soil, only the old
warrior James Craigmiles was alive among the collective parents of Archibald
and Elizabeth. But despite the sorrows of death, these two entered the New
World that much less encumbered with the ties and responsibilities of their
former lives.[6]

But the doughty old James Craigmiles was apparently enough to deal with,
remaining with his two daughters and making a terrible nuisance of himself.
The habit of command rarely dies out in an army man, and how tempting it is
for the most forbearing of fathers (which the senior Craigmiles was not) to give
advice to his own children and sons-in-law. The tensions at home were perhaps
exacerbated by the treatment he received out in the streets of the town. A spirit
of Jeffersonian egalitarianism was sweeping the nation in 1801, and the common
folk failed regularly to tip their hats to him in passing. Elizabeth and Archibald
McClure must have been quite relieved when he decided to sail back to Ireland,
complaining all the way of the insolent Americans.

By 1808, Elizabeth and Archibald had five children. In 1810, Archibald
McClure died of a fever that had swept through the village. At his death,
Archibald charged his wife to see that the children "feared God and were
obedient."[7] The Presbyterian faith remained strong in this family. As each child
was ready, the parents made a trek to the town of New Scotland, the nearest

Presbyterian Church, in order to have them properly baptized. Religion and education were inseparable in this household. Archibald, Jr. told his own children later how he learned to read the First Psalm by the light of the fireplace as his mother spun yarn on her wheel.[8]

The widow Elizabeth was an industrious mother, and was able to support her family adequately. "Grandma McClure was a good manager . . . She kept boarders, she made yarn and knit much, she put down pickels [sic] for a family in Albany named Russell. She was especially successful in spinning shoe thread and made . . . from it enough to more than keep her children in shoes. She also made linen thread which was sold in Albany."[9] As the children were able, they helped their mother and grew up with the same industrious habits. The eldest son, James, went to Albany to be apprenticed to Mr. Russell, Mrs. McClure's "pickel" fancier. He owned a paint and glass store, and was so impressed with the work of James that when young Archibald was of age, on his fourteenth birthday, he too went to Albany to work for Mr. Russell. Archibald had been a sickly child, and was quite attached to his mother. She found it difficult to tell him straight that he was leaving home for good. She explained that the trip to Albany was to be a special birthday present, a holiday with his brother. She carefully gathered together his clothes and placed them inconspicuously in the wagon. Elizabeth Craigmiles McClure did her best to give him an ordinary goodbye, but as soon as he was out of sight, she sat down and cried.[10] Tradition handed down in the family tells of Archibald sleeping under the counter in Mr. Russell's store, and walking home to see his mother every Sunday, a fourteen-mile round trip.

Religion and education, as well as a gift for business, were yoked together in the McClure family. Mrs. McClure had certainly stressed these pursuits, and after only two years of Archibald's apprenticeship, Archibald and brother James went into business for themselves. They bought their own drug and paint firm in an Albany buzzing with money and big ideas. The Erie Canal had just been opened, and suddenly the town became the funnel for enormous wealth moving down to New York City. At the same time, young Archibald devoted himself to his own education by attending a Sabbath School his brother James helped to organize. Classes were held in a sawdust-floored carpenter's shop, and were designed to help those who worked the other six days of the week. This Sunday School was quite a controversial idea as many thought it a sacrilege against the sanctity of the Lord's Day. When the school tried to merge with the Second Presbyterian Church the issue almost split the congregation. Archibald himself saved the situation by convincing Mrs. De Witt Clinton, the governor's wife, to send her children to the Sunday School. Archibald McClure felt such gratitude to the school that for the rest of his life he worked to build up its resources and improve its services. He gathered together enough books to make a school library, an expensive aid to education in that era. Many of the poorest boys of Albany learned to read, write and 'cipher' at the Sunday School of the Second Presbyterian Church, hearing as well the gospel of Jesus Christ.[11]

Archibald married Susan Tracy Rice on May 22, 1833. She was a woman of such deep-rooted New England ancestry that she could trace five direct ancestors to the *Mayflower*. Her father had served in the War of 1812, and her mother had been William Cullen Bryant's first teacher. The poet honored her every year with a visit.[12] Susan had grown up in Washington, Connecticut, and loved to describe the visit there of the Marquis de Lafayette in 1825. The seven Rice children were perched on the fence along the road, each proudly displaying a new pair of shoes. The great hero spotted them in his parade through town, and made the grand gesture of giving them a personal salute.[13] Susan became a teacher like her mother, and went to Albany to accept a school appointment there. No one could have been more attractive to Archibald than a beautiful teacher, and happily his affections were well received by Miss Rice. They spent their honeymoon traveling along the Erie Canal to view the great wonder of New York, Niagara Falls.[14]

Susan and Archibald McClure raised a family of seven children in a prudent and sober atmosphere. Morning and evening prayers were an unvarying ritual of daily life. No liquor, smoking, card games or dancing were allowed at any time or in any place. Outside the home, the Second Presbyterian Church of Albany was the most important family focal point. With Archibald's business success, the McClure family's social position rose to a level of great influence in Albany. The mahogany dining room table, made for Archibald's family, became a gathering place for ministers, politicians and business leaders.

Archibald's success allowed him time to travel as well. He made one trip to the Illinois frontier to investigate a mission society project of his wife's. In 1847 he sailed for Europe, returning to the world his father had left almost a half a century before. On his return voyage, the link to the future of this story was almost broken. A terrible gale blew up. And as the ship began to toss about Archibald became gravely ill. A friend made during the passage, a prosperous New York City merchant named James Gore King, cared for him and nursed him back to full health from a state perilously close to death. Without Mr. King, our narrative would never have been, because it was after Archibald's return that Susan conceived a fifth child. On November 24, 1848, James Gore King McClure, the father of our hero, drew in his first breath and let out his first wail of greeting.[15]

Religion, education and business continued to blend and support one another in the McClure household, and young "Jamie" absorbed a balance of all three. For him to be a minister of the gospel, however, was the dearest hope of his parents. Archibald had been unable to study for the ministry himself, and looked forward to the pleasure of sending one of his own children into that honored profession, fulfilling a personal dream through one of his offspring. To that end, they dedicated his young life, continually praying that the living God would lead their son into His service.[16] After his near death at sea, Archi-bald undoubtedly felt a keen sense of gratitude toward his Creator. In any event, spiritual prompting affected young Jamie quite early. In later life he wrote:

Archibald McClure. The following note was written on the back of the portrait by James G. K. McClure, Sr.) "This portrait was painted in 1838 Frederck Fink (?) of Albany, N.Y.—when my father was 32. This was 10 years before I was born. The memory of my father is a constant inspiration to me in every high and holy line. He lived to be 66. His black hair was untinged. It was perfectly black."

The first distinctive religious experience that I recall was in 1858—when I was nine years of age. The revival which originated in the Fulton St., New York City prayer meeting in 1857 was a prayer meeting revival . . . The meetings held in Albany were largely attended, were very hushed, had scarcely any exhortation, but had much outpouring of the heart in prayer . . . Moved by the atmosphere of such meetings, I asked a group of boys of my own age to gather in my father's dining room—perhaps ten in all—and have a prayer meeting

Jamie McClure.

of our own . . . At that time boys of our age were not allowed to unite with the church—so we were virtually left to ourselves.[17]

Jamie McClure grew up absorbed in the collected wisdom of his Presbyterian heritage, and with the stature of a taut and wiry athlete. His physical prowess opened up for him the boys' world of baseball, which complemented the heavy doses of ecclesiastical training he received at home and at church. He was a happy and witty child, able to gain the confidence of his peers. His father sent him to preparatory school in Massachusetts and it was there, in the spring of 1866, that he made a firm covenant with God. He once wrote. "It was at Andover that I became a Christian . . . My whole life has been shaped by the decision there made." (James Gore King McClure, Sr. to Marion Cooper, November 15, 1902) During his vacation, he united with the Second Presbyterian Church of Albany.

> Fortunately three questions were not asked me. One was: "Had I experienced a precious hope?" Another, "Was I distressed for my sins?" the third, "Did I love God?" These were questions often in the air. Now the fact was that . . . I had not experienced anything "precious," I had not been distressed about my sins and I could not claim any such feelings toward God as my love for my mother. All these features were in due time to be the fruit of the Spirit-but I was just planted . . . Indeed I was rather irritated at God because I had felt forced to yield to Him and I initially said, "If you insist upon my being a minister, I will do as you say, but I don't want to . . . "[18]

After his spring vacation, he returned to Andover with the adulation of all of his parents' friends ringing in his ears. Before he knew it, he was in trouble and the headmaster had to suspend him from school for a serious breach of discipline. He had been attending a meeting of a theological society along with a ball-playing schoolmate nicknamed "Tompie." On the way home, a plan arose in some of the boy's minds to "egg" a particularly hated teacher. The final strategy was to:

> creep up the garden lawn and put the tick-tack* on the window, pull the string and when old B—— comes out we will throw our eggs at him and run. This was a turn in affairs for which I was not prepared. But Providence came to my relief. The boy next to me was tossing his egg up in the moonlight (he was a base ball player) when it slipped past his hand and fell upon the ground— whereupon I said to him, "Tompie, you can throw straighter than I can, you take my egg." Pilate like I attempted to evade responsibility for the scheme in which I nevertheless was a participator. The scheme worked well. Old B—— came to his front door, the eggs showered upon him and we disappeared.

The school authorities made a quick bed check, and the principal perpetrators

> were summoned . . . convicted and . . . suspended. What should the rest of the eleven do? In the spirit of . . . loyal allegiance we drew up a paper stating that we were equally guilty with the three . . . and presented it to the Principal, who simply said, "You may consider yourselves suspended."
> Here I was—just having united with the Church—and suspended! What shakings of heads now by the elderly people, instead of pattings on the back— if they could know. We were allowed to remain in Andover -and no word was sent to our homes. After a week of uncertainty we were summoned one by one to the Principal's office and were told that if we apologized in person to Mr. B——, we would be restored . . . I had learned the best lesson of my life.[19]

His deference to Tompie was all the more condemning because Jamie McClure was an outstanding baseball player in his own right. He eventually played on two semi-professional teams in Albany, the National Nine and the Albany Blues. Cousin Archie Bush, while playing for the Blues, is thought to have developed the first "curve throw."[20] Jamie went to Yale University in 1866, became the captain of the baseball team, and was third baseman when the team trounced Harvard 38–18.[21] Jim McClure, as his friends now called him, realized that baseball added a common touch to his reputation. He credited the sport for much of his success in influencing his classmates at Yale, because it broke down the stuffy image students might have had of the practicing Christian. He was chosen for the most prestigious secret society, Skull and Bones. At graduation, he was awarded the traditional giant wooden spoon as the most beloved man in the class. One professor, the distinguished Dr. Timothy Dwight, could testify to his personal appeal. He said, "I have not the command of

---

*The author was unable to ferret out the exact nature of the 'tick-tack,' but perhaps a more astute reader will understand.

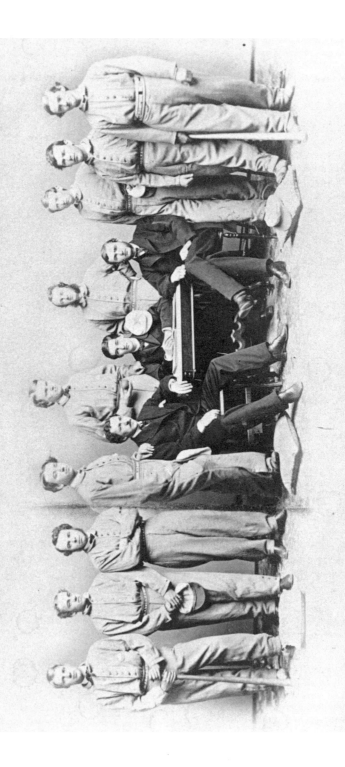

language to describe the position which he held in our class. Someone once divided the class into Lits and Pops. Jim was no mean scholar, attaining a First Dispute stand and enrolled in Phi Beta Kappa, but was pre-eminent in the latter class. No man in the class was more popular."[22]

And yet, Jim McClure maintained an active ethical vigilance against the moral laxity he saw sweeping the university following the Civil War. Heavy drinking had become a badge of manhood, and with all the fierce determination of his Covenanter ancestors, he fought what began as a one-man battle against the abominations of undergraduate life. He said, "My sense of responsibility led me to fight the drinking customs of the day . . . It was . . . a terrible grief to me to see . . . scores upon scores of my classmates drunk. The class ahead of mine was notoriously dissipated. Its leaders tried to influence the sentiment and practices of my class. Quietly but unceasingly I endeavored—in every possible way—to get ahead of those leaders and thwart them—much to their disgust and anger."[23] The confrontation on this issue was none too subtle. Some upperclassmen caught Freshman McClure and tried to force him to drink, " . . . but he resolutely kept his lips tightly shut and the whiskey poured over him."[24]

For four years Jim McClure exercised his sense of responsibility from the elected office of class deacon. That he took his duties seriously is clear by the testimony of a former underclassman:

> Dr. McClure . . . was perhaps the most prominent senior at Yale when I was a Freshman . . . While I naturally never spoke to him in college, I well remember that he called our class together near the end of freshman year and gave us a little talk urging us not to drink at all during Sophomore year and mentioning that liquor was never served in the successive fraternities of which he had been a member, an argument of much more force than can be imagined by one unfamiliar with the conditions . . . perhaps more than half the class, signed an agreement of compliance and I think observed it.[25]

Perhaps the life work of young Jim had been preordained by a pact made between his parents and God at his birth, and maybe he was dragged squirming and kicking against his will as he realized the moral force he was able to bring to bear on his contemporaries at Yale. In any event, when his college years were almost finished, he decided to attend Princeton Seminary. In pondering his decision, he credited the little boys' prayer meeting for opening " . . . the soil of the heart to seed thoughts and seed ideals that lay there quietly for ten years or more, and then the sunlight got down to them, and they felt the stirring of their life, and the boy decided to be a minister."[26]

Opposite: *The National Nine, 1865.* Players left to right: *Lansing, Sprague, Johnson, Server, Waddell, Ross (Capt.) Woolverton, Cantwell, McClure. E.W. Traw, V. Pres; W. Bruce, Jr. Scorer; E.C. Smith, Pres. Published by Churchill and Denison, Photographers, Albany, N.Y.*

☞ BASE BALL.—*National vs. Rivermont.*—
On Tuesday afternoon the National Base Ball
club of Albany, and the Rivermont club of this
village, played a match game on the grounds of
the latter club. A large number of spectators
were present, among them many ladies, who
viewed the contest with pleasure and interest.
The Nationals are a "crack club," and their
playing was very beautiful, and elicited the en-
comiums of every beholder. The Rivermonts
have been but recently organized, and having
had but limited practice, were not able to cope
with their more practiced adversaries, with any
hope of success. The Nationals are heavy bat-
ters, excellent fielders, swift runners, and spry
and active on the bases. They scored 113 runs
to the Rivermonts 15—beating them 98 runs.
We append the score below, which will give
our readers an insight to the game:

RIVERMONT.	O.	R.	NATIONAL.	O.	R.
Brinkerhoff, c.	2	3	Sprague, 3d b.	6	11
McDowell, p.	3	1	Bush, c.	0	15
Smith, Lew. s.s.	4	1	Ross, r. f.	2	15
Rogers, 1st b.	3	2	Waddell, p.	3	13
Strong, C. L. 2 b	3	1	Woolverten, s.s.	4	10
Strong, J. 3d b.	4	2	Lansing, 1st b.	3	13
Smith, L. l. f.	1	2	McClure, 2d b.	3	12
Rozell, c. f.	3	2	Ertzberger, l. f.	4	12
Courtney, r. f.	4	1	Johnson, c. f.	2	12
Total	27	15	Total	27	113

Innings...	1	2	3	4	5	6	7	8	9	
Rivermont.	0	2	0	5	0	4	0	1	3—	15
National.	2	32	7	9	23	8	0	14	18—	113

Umpire—Thos. Lloyd of Undercliff
Scorers—Messrs. Bruce and Scofield.
Fly-catches—National 13; Rivermont 7.
Time of game—3 hours and 10 minutes.

At the conclusion of the game, which ended
shortly after 6 o'clock, the clubs, with a few invited guests, repaired to Wood's Hotel, where
about 8 o'clock, the company sat down to an
excellent supper, provided by the Rivermont
club, for their guests. Vigorous appetites appeared to result from the exercise taken, and
amid the clatter of knives and forks, the monster Hunger was obliged to succumb. At the
close of the repast, several brief speeches were
made, and a number of songs given; all of which
tended to strengthen the bonds of friendship so
pleasantly begun. The Nationals are a body
of gentlemen, whose courteous demeanor, pleasant manners, and smiling, frank countenances,
won the esteem and respect of all. We wish
them that success in their present tour, which
their merits as ball players and gentlemen en-
title them to. Tuesday morning they played
with the Lorillard club of Rhinebeck, beating
them, we believe, 27 runs. Wednesday they
were to play at Cold Spring, with the Under-
cliffs; Thursday at Morrisania, with the Unions;
and Friday at Brooklyn, with the Excelsiors.

If Yale had been the scene of his moral battles, Princeton Seminary would be the seat of his intellectual struggles. He later admitted that for his Yale years "I scarcely recall the actual material of any book in any department of my four years—though I had the supposedly best books of the day and had teachers of wide reputation."[27] At seminary, he reined in his active social life in order to make up for lost time, and was able to master Hebrew and Greek and the philosophies of the day. Princeton Seminary in the early 1870s was being pulled back and forth by conflicting theological voices, but Jim McClure refrained from controversy, preferring to master the knowledge at hand in order to prepare himself for a life of service to whatever community the Lord entrusted to him.[28]

While he was in seminary, his father Archibald died of pneumonia. He never forgot how his father's influence had led him into the ministry. At the ordination of his own son, he reminded him: "At the time of the death of your grandfather, my father, two papers inscribed in his own handwriting were found in his private desk. One read, 'It is impossible to estimate the power of a completely consecrated life;' the other read, 'I have no greater joy than to know my children walk in TRUTH.' These two sentiments . . . speak of the religious earnestness of your ancestry."[29] Archibald McClure had taught his Sunday School class for forty years, bringing 111 new Christians into the church. The power of his consecrated life had its background in the Scotch-Irish ancestors who had suffered so much for their beliefs, and his example would inspire his descendants to do mighty works in their respective generations.

But mighty works begin one day at a time, and the Reverend James McClure left the heady atmosphere of academia for a small rural community of Christian souls in need of pastoral care and simple teaching. In 1874, the Presbyterian Church of New Scotland, New York, called the young graduate, and he accepted their offer.[30] Years before, Jim's immigrant grandmother had carried his father to the nearest Presbyterian congregation to be baptized, in this very same church. The new shepherd of the flock became a beloved member of the community, known to all by the endearment "Dominie," the Scottish and Dutch term for minister.

On at least one occasion, though, his youthful instincts betrayed his sense of pastoral duty. In a book of stories written for his grandchildren, he recounted the time that some of the young men of the congregation challenged him to a race. The winter snows were deep, and the evening service had just ended. The Dominie sped away in his sleigh, tearing along the country roads—to victory. Only then did he remember his promise to drive an older lady, one of the pillars of the church, home. She had remained forgotten on the church steps, wrapped in blankets, anticipating her drive in the young minister's sleigh.[31]

Despite such setbacks, the New Scotland Presbyterians hung onto their bachelor minister for five years. On November 19, 1879, he left his post to marry Phebe Ann Dixon, whom he had met just before accepting his first

Opposite: *Box score & story—National vs. Rivermont*

Rev. James G. K. McClure Bids Farewell
to New Scotland.

Never in the events of the past has a scene
been witnessed in New Scotland to compare with
that on the evening of Sunday, October 5th, at
the Presbyterian Church. Our dear pastor, Rev.
J. G. K. McClure, was to speak his farewell
words. Soon after five o'clock carriages began
entering the churchyard, and from that time on
the crowd came pouring in. At a little past six
o'clock the church was filled to overflowing. The
aisles were packed, standing room could not be
found in the vestibules, and enough were left
outside to nearly fill the church were it empty.
Every window was raised, and the window sills
filled with people, much to the discomfiture of
those who were crowding up to the windows
from the outside. One had only to glance at the
assembled throng, and the involuntary expression
would be: "Behold, how they loved him."

Newspaper clipping: Rev. James G.K. McClure Bids Farewell to New Scotland.

position in the ministry. He met her at his sister Grace's marriage to her brother,
Nathan F. Dixon. Their father was Rhode Island's Congressman.

Phebe Ann Dixon was a gentle, sensible person who never appeared agitated or ruffled no matter what the circumstances. She had been born to privilege. Living with her parents in Washington, and studying in New York, she remembered shaking hands with President Abraham Lincoln at a White House reception. Her grandfather had been a U. S. Senator during the Jacksonian era. Later her brother, Grace McClure's husband, would become a Senator as well.[32] In 1840, her grandfather wrote a prescription for greatness, while observing his colleagues in Congress:

> Since I have been here I have been more thoroughly than I ever was before
> convinced of what it is that makes great men. It is hard study—and intense
> application. The lawyers and members of Congress here work like slaves and
> no man at the present day can be favorably distinguished without it . . . John
> Q. Adams is up every morning at four o'clock—takes his walk—and then
> down to his work—he studies more than twelve hours every day of his life . . .
> any man of ordinary capacity can be great who will adopt that course of
> industry.[33]

Phebe Ann's own father was described as ". . . remarkably endeared to all
. . . people, old and young, far and near, on account of his ease of manners,
geniality of spirit and large generosity. He had the characteristic traits of the
Dixons largely developed, namely, benevolence, hospitality, frankness and
good fellowship."[34] Phebe Ann moved easily from the political realm to her life
as a minister's wife. She was quite accustomed to a home always open to visitors,

> **The McClure-Dixon Wedding.**
> At the residence of the Hon. Nathan F. Dixon, at the hour of four, Wednesday afternoon, his eldest daughter, Miss Annie P., was joined in marriage with Rev. James G. K. McClure, son of the late Archibald McClure, of Albany, the bridegroom being the brother of Mrs. Nathan F. Dixon, Jr. A very distinguished and brilliant party was present. One hour prior to the services, carriage after carriage rolled up the hill, while at 2:55 P. M., a special train from Stonington arrived, and on the arrival of the 3:15 express from Providence, many ladies and gentlemen also arrived. The bride was attired in a dress combination of white silk and satin, and in full dress style. Her ornaments were rich and brilliant. There were no bridesmaids. Messrs. E. Phelps Hubbard and C. P. Dixon, Jr., acted as ushers. Rev. Mr. Harris, of the Central Congregational Church, of Providence, officiated. Immediately after the ceremony and the congratulations of friends, the invited guests went out to a sumptuous collation. The bride's presents were almost endless in number and unsurpassed in elegance. The bridal party leave on the six o'clock express, to be absent a few days, when they return to pass Thanksgiving at home, and will sail for Europe on the 3d of December, in the Cunard steamer Scythia.—[*Providence Journal.*

Newspaper announcement of the McClure-Dixon wedding.

and felt comfortable discussing topics of intellectual breadth. She understood how much the ambience of one's home contributed to an effective ministry.

The union of the politician's daughter and the young minister was the talk of Westerly, Rhode Island, as the two clans gathered a second time for a marriage ceremony. A family story illustrates at least one conflicting tendency between the Dixons and the McClures. One of the McClures, less preoccupied than the others, noticed that many of Mr. Dixon's Washington friends made frequent visits to the private study. Pursuing the matter further, he discovered the dispensary of the young Reverend's most hated substance. "Mr. Dixon wanted neither to upset his . . . in-laws nor to let his old friends go dry. He was a politic man!"[35]

The honeymoon was to Europe and the Holy Land, a time for the two young people to soak up the sights and sounds of the Old World, while being able as well to devote themselves to each other. With a characteristic sense of the past, James took his bride to County Armagh, Ireland, in search of living evidence of his family's Covenanter past.[36] The marriage of these two people was a great union whose fruits would be a sense of purpose and great happiness. When James McClure was asked years later whether he might live his life over

Correspondence of the New York Observer.
AMERICA ABROAD.
BY REV. JAMES G. K. MC CLURE.

To cross the Atlantic and leave America entirely behind is to-day an impossibility. The traveller who sails away from his native shores with any such expectation has surprises in store for him at every point of his foreign tour. His heart beats lightly as he puts foot for the first time on European soil, and his eye brightens as he thinks that all that he is now to see will be new and strange. Scarcely has he reached his hotel at Liverpool before he opens his window to look out upon the street life of England's second commercial city. Right before him in this land which has sung the merits of its roast beef for centuries he sees a huge sign bearing the words, " American Beef," and he is forcibly reminded of the statement he has often heard, but never appreciated until now, that our Western cattle supply England's tables with their choicest joints.

"America A Broad."

again, he replied that he would rather not, because "Suppose that somebody should get ahead of me and marry my wife!"[37]

The newlyweds went west, to Illinois. The Reverend James McClure accepted a call from the Lake Forest Presbyterian Church. What had been a frontier when visited by his father was now, one generation later, a thickly settled and thriving state, with prosperous farms and a growing meat-packing industry. The city of Chicago was rapidly expanding, with its superb location as the hub of rail and inland water transportation. These two dedicated Christians stepped into the midst of a world of growing wealth (and materialism), and here they would raise their family and live out their ideals.

Lake Forest, Illinois, twenty-eight miles north of Chicago, had been founded by Presbyterians as a suburban experiment, on 2300 acres along high bluffs above Lake Michigan. The founders hoped to build a community where they could bring up children in a Christian atmosphere, uncorrupted by the evils of the city. Lake Forest College was established in the center of town to encourage faithful Presbyterian scholars. The Reverend James McClure accepted the call of the one church in this community. For more than twenty years he handled each controversy with such delicacy, and maintained such a broad-minded, ecumenical spirit, that when he left there was still just one church, despite the rapid growth of the community.

And it was not as though the sheep of his flock were mild-mannered and deferential. Some of the most powerful captains of industry moved to Lake Forest: the Farwells, the Armours, the Swifts and the McCormicks were only a few. Mansions were constructed, many to be used only in the summer. A swirling social scene came to life. And yet, amidst all the money and mansions, there was not a more respected and beloved man in the community than James G. K. McClure, nor a more cordial hostess than his wife, Phebe Ann. The charm, intelligence and integrity of these two influenced an entire town. James McClure was not afraid to stand up as he had done at Yale against the most powerful of men and demand excellence and virtue in Lake Forest. He took the leadership in routing the liquor interests. He could upbraid a church member, but most of all he was a sympathetic and understanding counsellor and friend. Perhaps his greatest contribution was issuing a call to manly Christian living and to "high ideals of daring" to young people growing up in the midst of wealth and culture.

James Gore King McClure, Jr. was born three years after his parents were called to Lake Forest. He shared with his sister Annie and three more children who were born later a great heritage reaching back to Scotland, Ulster, the Mayflower, New England and Albany. Religion had always been, for the McClures, the interpreter of life, and the boy would be taught about his family in that light. The great battle of each generation was a spiritual one. He was told of the Covenanters, the escape from Scotland, persecution in Ireland, the hardships of immigration to America, the Pilgrims' voyage, the struggles of his great grandmother McClure in Hamilton Factory, raising her five children to know the truth in spite of poverty, and of her son's devotion to his Sunday School. By adhering to the enduring principles of Christianity one could replenish and build up the spiritual stores on earth, and perhaps take a place among the family heroes. He learned the importance of developing a Christian character.

The power and influence a family can have over its members can be overrated, but in the case of the McClures, how can that be? They have been ardent Presbyterians as far back as the historian can see, and right up to the present generation. There has been faltering along the way, but those members who have remained faithful to the ancient Christian ideals have lived extraordinary lives.

1. G.M. Trevelyan, *History of England,* Vol. II, "The Tudors and the Stuart Era," (Garden City, N.Y.:1953), p. 177. (originally published in 1929)

2. Elspeth McClure, "The McClures," unpublished paper, no date, p. 3. The letter quoted was from Mrs. John McClure to Grace Griswold, March 26, 1900.

3. *Ibid.*, p. 6. Also found in *Archibald McClure and Elizabeth Craigmiles, his wife* (private publication, 1938), p. 3–4.

4. James Alexander McClure, *The McClure Family* (Petersburg, Virginia: Frank A. Owens, 1914), p. 15.

5. Elspeth McClure, "The McClures," p. 7.

6. *Op. cit., Archibald McClure and Elizabeth Craigmiles*, p. 4.

7. *Op. cit.*, Elspeth McClure, "The McClures," p. 11–13.

8. *Ibid.*

9. *Ibid.* Cited from William M. Clemens, *The McClure Family Records* (New York: W.E. Clemens, 1914), p. 3.

10. *Op. cit.*, Elspeth McClure, "The McClures," p. 14.

11. *Ibid.*, p. 19–20.

12. *Ibid.*, p. 24. Also mentioned in *James Gore King McClure* (Chicago: Lakeside Press, 1932), p. 27.

13. Christmas letter prepared by Katherine McDowell Rice, date unknown.

14. *Op. cit.*, Elspeth McClure, "The McClures," p. 25.

15. *Ibid.*, p. 30–33.

16. *Op. cit., James Gore King McClure*, p. 25–26.

17. James G. K. McClure, Sr., "Would I Do It Again?" *Cleric,* March 8, 1930.

18. *Ibid.*, p. 4–5.

19. *Ibid.*, p. 5–7.

20. *Op. cit.*, Elspeth McClure, "The McClures," p. 45.

21. *Op. cit., James Gore King McClure,* p. 29.

22. *Ibid.*, p. 31.

23. *Op. cit., James G. K. McClure, Sr., "Would I Do It Again?"* p. 10–11.

24. *Op. cit., James Gore King McClure,* p. 31.

25. *Op. cit.*, Elspeth McClure, "The McClures," p. 46.

26. *Ibid.*, p. 47. Taken from a piece written by James G. K. McClure, Sr., "The Autobiography of a Dining Table," Unpublished, p.9.

27. *Op. cit.*, James G. K. McClure, Sr. "Would I Do It Again?" p. 9.

28. *Op. cit.*, Elspeth McClure, "The McClures," p. 47.

29. James G. K. McClure, Sr., address given to his son James G. K. McClure, Jr. at the time of his ordination.

30. *Op. cit.*, Elspeth McClure, "The McClures," p. 48.

31. James G. K. McClure, Sr., *Grandfather Tells Some More Stories,* from "The Horse That Won the Race," (Chicago: The Lakeside Press), p. 1–9.

32. *Op. cit.*, Elspeth McClure, "The McClures," p. 51.

33. Senator Nathan F. Dixon, in a letter to Nathan F. Dixon, Jr. June 18, 1840. Found in a notebook of James G. K. McClure, Jr. dated November 1, 1910, p.61.

34. *Op. cit.*, Elspeth McClure, "The McClures," p. 52. Originally from *In Memoriam: Nathan Fellows Dixon* (Rhode Island; private publication, c. 1881), p. 15. First published in the Providence (R.I.) *Press,* April 12, 1881.

35. *Ibid.*

36. *Ibid.*, p. 53.

Chapter 2
Lake Forest

The man or woman brought up in . . . a home [of] self-sacrifice, trust and love . . . cannot help believing in mankind. He may be disappointed again and again but he knows that these qualities are real . . . (*James G. K. McClure, Jr., Iron River sermon, "The Family and the Home"*)

As I lay in my bed at night—[a] candle from mother's & father's room lighting [the] rafters—I w[ou]ld hear Father night after night pray, kneeling by Mother—"Oh God Bless these boys." (*James G. K. McClure, Jr., in his Santa Barbara notebook*)

Owners of country estates in Lake Forest spent Christmas much as the great land owners of England spend theirs each year, with family and friends and retainers about them. The arrival of snow on Friday night made the country more alluring than ever and a joy to the lover of outdoor sports. (*A newspaper clipping stuck in Jim McClure's Santa Barbara notebook*)

Lake Forest, Illinois, remains a quintessential American suburban town. The grass *is* greener, well-nourished, properly (and regularly) clipped. Driving through the streets of Lake Forest, one senses that here is a community of people who have won a great victory over chaos and disorder. Peeling paint, dirty children, weeds and broken-down cars seem to have been zoned beyond the town limits. Beautiful homes present the unmistakable appearance of confident success. The business world lies down the train tracks in another realm altogether: Chicago. The view from the commuter train window as it approaches the city speaks of the daily litany of social and political evils that churn constantly there. By contrast, Lake Forest appears safe, tranquil and comfortable.

Lake Forest occupies a two and a half mile bluff along Lake Michigan. The appearance of order has been imposed on an undulating terrain by skillful planners and architects. Deep ravines lie behind fine houses, allowing Lake Forest to retain most of its natural splendor. These ravines are a wonderful haven for children, who seem to prefer the disorder of the natural world to the order of their own lawns. The great lake is nearby, with all of its moods from calm to rage.

The Lake Forest of today is the creation of well-organized and powerful people who have worked hard through civic clubs and local political offices to build up their town. In 1856, a group from Chicago left the city by rail to picnic along the high bluffs of Lake Michigan. The train dropped them off in a wilderness accessible only by an old ox cart that wound around the ravines to a clearing in the woods. That clearing was the first improvement made by the Lake Forest Association. These men and women were interested in a project: to build a Presbyterian Seminary for the Northwest territories. Ironically, the project was spurred on by the promise of $40,000 from a Cincinnati brewery owner. When the money failed to materialize, the moral overtones of depending on such ill-gotten profits were not lost on those promoting the project.[1] In fits and starts, lots were sold and resold, homes and schools were built, and the church became the focal point of the town.

When James and Phebe Ann McClure moved to Lake Forest in 1881, the local economy was just sputtering along. Town real estate was moving slowly, and the old church, as the Dominie remembered, " . . . was not at all presentable. All along its side walls might be seen the impression made upon the paper by the heads that had leaned against it. . . . Its furnaces . . . heated the head but left the feet well nigh frozen . . . ; many times I have kept my overcoat on until I stood up to preach."[2]

A member of the Lake Forest ministerial search committee first remembered the name of James McClure in connection with the Yale baseball team, and that set into motion the train of events that brought him from the East. A group went to Albany to hear him preach, and he was subsequently invited to Lake Forest as a candidate. On his third Sunday, a member of the congregation gave him the first indication of his acceptance. ". . . Mr. Sylvester Lind, the Scotchman, perennial Mayor and general head of Lake Forest, met me in the aisle and said, 'And have you a lady?' 'Yes,' I said, 'I am a married man.' 'Well,' he continued, 'you may go your way back and get your lady, for I think we'll take you.'[3]

The Reverend McClure and his lady arrived in Lake Forest on September 16, 1881, during a torrential rain storm, and he later admitted, "We both were self-distrustful."[4] He was to be the pastor of the Lake Forest Presbyterian Church for twenty-four years. He knew the hidden difficulties of many of the residents, and with his quiet charm and strong leadership he set a moral tone that earned him enormous respect. As he saw it, that respect enabled him to move people towards Christian perfection, and to influence the entire life of the community. His wife, known to her friends as Annie, fulfilled her variety of roles with the same evidence and appreciation of God's grace as her husband. The work of a minister's wife is difficult. Mother and housekeeper, paragon of virtue in the community, and entertainer of an endless stream of guests are all duties of the post. Her husband's time is the property of the community, and his working hours are irregular. She is expected to be a leader in the church, and most every other civic organization. Annie Dixon McClure's capacity for work and her ease with people served her well in Lake Forest, and as the children began to come, served them well also.

On October 28, 1884, James Gore King McClure, Jr. was born into this place and this family. He was the second child, having left the chore of breaking

Lake Forest Presbyterian Church

PRAYER MEETING TOPICS

Jan., Feb., Mar., 1882,

Wednesdays (excepting Jan. 26th) at 7½ P. M.

JAN. 11.—THE SPIRITUAL LIFE A CONFLICT.
"We wrestle against spiritual wickedness."

JAN 18.—MAINTAINING OUR GROUND.
"Stand therefore."

JAN. 26.—TRUTH THE FIRST REQUISITE TO VICTORY.
"The girdle of truth."

Day of Prayer for Colleges.

FEB. 1.—RIGHTEOUSNESS AN UNASSAILABLE DEFENCE.
"The breast-plate of righteousness."

FEB. 8.—READINESS TO OBEY ALL DIVINE INSTRUCTIONS.
"The sandals of preparation."

FEB. 15.—TRUST IN GOD DISARMS TEMPTATION.
"The shield of faith."

FEB. 22.—GOSPEL HOPE THE SAFE-GUARD FOR THE IN-
TELLECT.
"The helmet of salvation."

MAR. 1.—GOD'S WORD THE WEAPON OF THE CONQUEROR.
"The sword of the Spirit."

MAR. 8.—PRAYER A CONSTANT NECESSITY TO VICTORY.
"Praying always."

MAR. 15.—VIGILANCE ESSENTIAL TO VICTORIOUS PRAYER.
"Watching thereunto with all perseverance."

MAR. 22.—CONSIDERATION OF OTHERS A MEANS OF
SAFETY.
"Supplication for all saints."

MAR. 29.—RESULT OF SUCCESSFUL SPIRITUAL CON-
FLICT.
"Strong in the Lord."

"Prayer meeting topics" from the Lake Forest Presbyterian Church, 1882.

in his parents to the vicissitudes of child-rearing to his older sister Annie. Not yet six months, on April 19, 1885, baby Jamie was baptized in the Lake Forest Presbyterian Church, the duties being performed by a minister who served in Canton, China.[5]

The town of Lake Forest grew up around little Jamie McClure. When his father first came the streets were unpaved, the fire department was unorganized, and there was only a small shopping district of five stores. By the time Jamie graduated from Yale, there were six times as many stores, city water and sewerage, and an excellent rail service to Chicago.[6] All of these accomplishments meant innumerable meetings of committees, and Dr. McClure was always sought out as a key figure in any undertaking. He first proved his determination when he made a great push to have a new church built.

Mr. C. B. Farwell was perhaps the wealthiest man in his congregation, and when the drive to raise money for the new church building was under way, Mr. Farwell sent a note to his minister saying he was not giving a cent as he wanted

to support the University exclusively. Jamie Jr. later wrote in one of his note-books, with obvious admiration:

> Father walked down the next Sunday before church and said, "Mr. Farwell I received your letter. Here it is. I want you to take it and tear it up." "Tear it up," answered C. B. "I never had a man talk to me like that." "Yes, I want you to tear it up" said Father—and he tore it up and later gave largely to the Church. Had he not torn up the letter and had he thought that Father had shown it to anyone that Mr. Farwell was on record so positively, he would have stood his ground for aye.[7]

In 1887, when Jamie was two and a half years old, the family moved to the Manse that was built along with the new church. The little boy was now firmly located for his childhood. Later on, when his father became president of McCormick Seminary, the congregation presented the Manse as a gift to the McClures, in order to keep them as a Christian influence in Lake Forest. After this extraordinary gesture of generosity, the McClures named the house "Gien Hame," Scottish for "given home."

As well as holding firmly to their religious principles and remaining dedicated to education, the best of the McClures have also been effective business-men. When Lake Forest University found itself in debt, the Board of Trustees called on Dr. McClure to become its temporary president. He promptly raised the money, and then returned full time to his church. In 1897 he was again installed as the president, remaining in office for the next four years. He not only wiped out the deficit, but also successfully followed through on a major building program.[8] All of the talk and stories of these projects surrounded young Jamie as he grew up, and as later events bear out, the son learned well.

The McClures made no pretense of their faith at home. There were five McClure children in all: Annie; Jim, Jr.; Harriet; Arch; and Nathan. They were surrounded by Christian teachings and habits, and were involved in church duties and the entertainment of numerous guests. Religion was a way of organizing life into a daily rhythm.

> Every morning in the Manse, family prayers were held and great petitions offered for those in the community in which we lived and for God's children everywhere, so that each child of the Manse felt an intimate relationship to the events of the day in households of joy and sorrow, in world conditions. Every Sunday afternoon at five o'clock Mother gathered the children about her for prayer. First she offered prayer asking God's blessing on Father, his work, the people of Lake Forest, and then praying for the missionaries in the home and foreign lands. In turn each child, according to age, followed with his petitions, so that . . . [Jamie] from his earliest days, could speak to God in the presence of others, and from his childhood days felt a deep interest in the people of every land and nation.[9]

Opposite, left: James G. K. McClure, Jr. Opposite, right: Annie and Jamie McClure.

Religion in the McClure home was a serious matter, where principles of character in the conduct of one's affairs were continually discussed and emphasized. Correct behavior first, then self-sacrifice, were held up as the marks of a Christian. But the Reverend and his wife were not harsh parents; self-sacrifice was not taught as a form of flagellation. To give oneself freely to help others was simply the law of grace handed down by the Heavenly Father, who gave his Son as a sacrifice to an undeserving humanity. By acting on earth as an agent of grace, one comes naturally under the spiritual care of the Deity, and as such one receives incomparable spiritual blessings. The real battle in life was an unseen one, within the hearts of men, fighting against selfish tendencies in hopes of spiritual regeneration. These teachings were an integral part of the heritage of each child in the McClure family.

The daily duties of the home fell on Mrs. McClure. She was no less a Christian than her husband, and because his time was so filled with duties, it was her influence in the early years that nurtured the children. From a pamphlet written about her, perhaps written by her husband, one learns that:

> She held stoutly to her [Christian] convictions but with persuasive gentleness. In her loyalty to high standards she made others aspire to them. She held an imperturbable mental serenity which was without coldness or aloofness. Although she herself was consistently efficient she was patient of the interruptions of others . . . she exercised tact without compromise and a diplomacy which sprung from a genuine interest in people. Her selfless, creative interest in other people characterized her in every waking hour. . . . With all her public responsibilities she still found time to foster for her own family an ideal Christian upbringing. She instinctively used methods of child training that many another mother struggles to learn from a book. Her techniques of Christian education were in practice what so much present-day religious training is in theory.[10]

Years later, she wrote her oldest son a compassionate note of support when he left home, revealing her tenderness and affection for her children:

> My beloved son,
> While you and Nathan are playing ball, I am writing a line which will, I hope, reach you on the steamer as you are starting. I have dreaded your going, for the joy of your presence with us again in the home, taking your place in the family life has been so great—that I have not known how I could get on without you. Today, that day of your acceptance God had filled my heart with more appreciation of the privilege for you of this year abroad and I shall try to feel glad that you are to go. You have been a great blessing to us all this year and a half, and I am sure that we are all the better, and stronger for your home coming. My thoughts and prayers will be daily with you . . .
> [You] may think of me as knitting early and late to get another necktie ready to send . . . I will also "en allons" (I do not dare promise more definitely) encourage the family in literary pursuits. . . .

Harriet McClure and her mother, Annie Dixon McClure.

Your devoted Mother, Annie D. McClure (Phebe Ann Dixon McClure to James G. K. McClure, Jr., April 29, 1909)

In the church, she made use of her natural talents as a mother to care for other children along with her own. She knew each by name, and taught them in Sunday School. At home, the Manse was open to all, without a tinge of reservation. And people came. Missionaries, visiting intellects, university students, members of the congregation and later any and all connected with McCormick Seminary. The table around which those varied people gathered came from the McClure house in Albany, where it had been used for the same hospitable purposes. Christmas often meant a sit down meal for thirty-three,[11] and for Thanksgiving:

> At dinner we had four students—later in the afternoon . . . fifty students and members of the Faculty families dropped in upon us for a cup of tea, for singing and for games. I am sure you will appreciate my statement that Mother, Annie and Harriet were quite wonderful in their ability at such a time. Everything moved off yesterday without the least suggestion of difficulty, and all the guests were happy. (James G. K. McClure, Sr. to James G. K. McClure, Jr., November 26, 1909)

There is evidence of at least one quiet Sunday in the life of this family:

> We had an almost undisturbed Sunday. We read, sang, attended services, listened to Annie's paper on the Passion Play, talked and went to bed. Perhaps it is selfish—but I trust not, to spend a day in this way. Our thoughts were on high themes, we were happy and we came to the opening of the week refreshed in heart as well as body. (James G. K. McClure, Sr. to James G. K. McClure, Jr., December 27, 1910)

While in Lake Forest, on many Sundays Dr. McClure spent the time between services making calls on members of the congregation. In his twenty-four years, the Dominie made 19,211 such visits (as he meticulously recorded), and one can only marvel at the amount of coffee and tea he must have consumed! He loved to take young Jamie along with him, both as a chance for father and son to be together, and as a way to soften the entrance into a parishioner's home. When he was old enough, Jamie would hitch up his Welsh pony Erma and drive his father in the buggy. The son could observe how his father, with a kindly smile and a remembered shred of information, would break down the barriers that separate people. To be able to make people laugh and feel at ease is a great gift, and it was perhaps on these visits that the young man learned these skills from his father. Humor was a means by which Reverend McClure could enter a home and relieve fears enough so he could really comfort or advise the people in his care. The son would later employ the same skills.

Jamie's first agricultural venture is revealed in a notebook he kept when

Note home from school, 1892.

he was eleven and twelve. He recorded an expense of $1.30 "For grit and powder, 50c for chicken feed and 15c for a poultry almanac." Maybe the business was in its early stages, but the only income evident is a mere ten cents for eggs sold. Much more profitable was his delivery enterprise. He charged fifteen cents an hour, and cleared almost $2.00 in July, not including the nickel he found. Golf was a large drain on his finances, especially when it cost him $1.25 to repair his broken driver. He did earn thirty-five cents for "cadying," but his golf bill ate that up. A nickel for "cracker jack," a penny for gum were his only apparent splurges, while a dime went to Sunday School and $1.42 for Christmas presents. The next year tennis balls show up as an expense, and the chickens had become a luxurious hobby: "exhibition coop, $1.50." The missionaries garnered a mere seven cents, which still might be respectable considering a twelve-year-old's sense of priorities. A recurring expense was his subscription to "Steady Streams," which was not a fishing magazine but a children's missionary society organized within the church, in which Mrs. McClure was quite active. It provides a good example of how church life affected the views of its young people.

The unrealized possibilities of the Sunday School was a thought constantly on the mind of the mature Jim McClure. During the Second World War, he proposed that the churches of America train their young people to go into the world in a Peace Corps-like venture. He reasoned that if Hitler could motivate his people for evil, why couldn't the church motivate theirs for good? His grandfather Archibald, who taught Sunday School for forty years (and was never once late!) had clearly made his mark on his descendants. Young Jamie joined Steady Streams at birth. The Victorian era was a great one for societies and clubs, and was also a period of intense missionary effort. What could be more natural than a club to develop in young people an appreciation for foreign lands and the work the church was doing there? Steady Streams also worked to inculcate the habit of Christian giving, and the song sung at every meeting was none too subtle on this point.

> Give, said the little stream
> Give, O give, give, O give!
> Give said the little stream
> As it hurried down the hill.
> I am small I know but wherever I go
> Give, O give, give, O give
> I am small I know but wherever I go,
> The fields grow greener still.[12]

At the April 1897 meeting, the subject was India, and the children were to describe an imaginary journey there. "Jamie McClure told of the trip to Benares, the holy city of India, and of the pilgrims they met there."[13] In time the boy would actually visit this city, and throughout his theological training he fully expected to enter the mission field. The spirit of Steady Streams was a vibrant reflection of the times, and that spirit made its mark on Jim. An old pamphlet from Steady Streams concludes with this version of a Mother Goose rhyme:

> Little Jack Horner
> Sat in a corner
> Eating a Christmas pie,
> While out in the cold,
> With hunger untold,
> He heard another boy cry.[14]

But Jamie McClure was a normal boy, and he did not spend all that much time worrying about the hungry people of the world. There were his hens, and his friends. And of course there was school, in his case the Lake Forest Academy. This letter to his mother, who was visiting her family in Westerly, Rhode Island, reflects his interests. "I hope you are safely at Grandmas ... I got a ninety five in my Algebra ... Yesterday I got three eggs and day before I got two ... 1 gave Papa a dozen eggs last night and he paid me ... We are having pretty good meals and Annie is very good to me. We miss you very much but under Annie's care we get along beautifully without you." A postscript from Annie, very suspicious of her brother's charm, is included. "I think Jamie must have added this last thinking I was to see the letter and that must be the reason for these compliments ... " (James G.K. McClure, Jr., to Phebe Ann Dixon McClure, February 12, 1897) Three days later he wrote again to his mother. "Jamie Fales sent for some white fantail pigeons and two pair came today ... I have been over at Judy's all the afternoon ... shooting paper wads ... Tell Uncle Nathan that my Wyandottes are laying a great deal better than the Leghorns ... Tonight Mrs. Holt sent over some ice cream ... " (James G.K. McClure, Jr. to Phebe Ann Dixon McClure, February 15, 1897)

𝕷𝖆𝖐𝖊 𝕵𝖔𝖗𝖊𝖘𝖙 𝕬𝖈𝖆𝖉𝖊𝖒𝖞

Report of *Jamie McClure*

For Year 1897-1898.

FIRST FORM.		THIRD FORM.	
Beginning Latin..	*G*	Cicero..........	*G*
English..........	*F*	Anabasis.......	*G*
Algebra.........	*E*	Greek Prose......	*G+*
U. S. History....	*G*	English..........	
English History...	*F*	German..........	
SECOND FORM.		French..........	
Cæsar..........	*G*	~~Physics~~..........	
Latin Prose......	*F*	Geometry.......	*E*
Beginning Greek..	*83*	**FOURTH FORM.**	
English..........	*G+*	Virgil..........	*G+*
Algebra.........	*94*	Iliad..........	*F*
Zoology..........	....	English..........	*G+*
Ancient History..	....	German..........	....
		French..........	
		Physics Chemistry......	*E*

Above 90, E for Excellent : from 80 to 90, G for Good :
from 75 to 80, F for Fair : below 75, P for Poor.
75 is passing mark.

_____*A. G. Miller*_____**Head Master.**

Report card, 1897–1898.

He may have learned to shoot wads at the Academy, because he gained a strong reputation there as a prankster. Years later he ran into two young men in Berlin, and wrote home that " . . . the strange looking one asked me if by any chance I . . . was the Jimmie McClure who used to disturb things at the Academy . . . " (James G. K. McClure, Jr. to his family, November 9, 1909). Under his picture in the Academy annual are the words: "James G. K. McClure, Jr.

has practiced his innocent little pranks upon the inhabitants of Lake Forest for fifteen years. He . . . is the youngest graduate of the Academy."[15]

He was in fact three or four years younger than most of the other seniors. Jamie McClure possessed an excellent mind and was a precocious student. His home life provided an extraordinarily rich blend of ideas and discussion, and his parents took a strong interest in their children's education. Jamie excelled in mathematics, but mastered the entire secondary school curriculum with only one mark below 80 percent. A good dose of Greek and Latin were considered excellent remedies for ignorance in that day. Jamie mastered, or in any event completed, translations of Caesar, Cicero, Anabasis, Virgil, Xenophon and Homer, all before he was sixteen. He commented, "Every morning at 9:45 o'clock we have to go to Little Bill's room to study Algebra. He said that he would give the best ones a little extra work: so this morning I started to work my examples for tomorrow and I did them pretty quickly, so he gave me another book to work the examples out of. They were awfully hard but I got ten" (James G. K. McClure, Jr. to Phebe Ann Dixon McClure, February 15, 1897). Jamie grew up breathing an intellectual air that promoted science as the means to solving problems, and this faith remained with him always. In his youth, he would take great pains to describe events with such precision that their meaning was often lost in the detail.

At his graduation ceremony, the commencement address of one John Harlow of Chicago made a lasting impression on him. At best, his memory of the speech made it sound hackneyed and predictable, but it expressed heroism and a life of purpose. To a precocious fifteen-year-old, that was enough. He reported: "John Harlow . . . told us that as we got on in life we must every so often go to the looking glass and face the man we saw there and ask him what he was doing with his life—whether he could respect himself, whether he was making any contribution to the rest of the world, whether he was helping the world; whether he was doing his part or whether he was wasting his life."[16] These words stuck with him, and there were to be periods of his life when facing that mirror was very painful. But always, he could count on the support and encouragement of his family.

Reverend and Mrs. McClure worked at their family life, made it the first priority of their marriage, and were rewarded with devoted children. And they in turn remained loyal to one another. The oldest, Annie, eventually married Dumont Clarke, a minister. He and Jim became great friends, and in time both would move to North Carolina to share in the work of the Farmers Federation. Jim's younger sister Hetty, or Harriet, had an exuberant personality that matched his. Whether in serious matters or in family pranks, these two siblings remained close. Archibald or Arch followed Jim to Yale and through divinity school, and always saw his older brother as a source of wisdom and honest advice. The two older boys corresponded often, debating weighty theological and philosophical issues of the day. In fact the entire family was quite comfort-

Seated, left-right: *James McClure, Jr., James G.K. McClure, Sr., Annie Dixon McClure, Nathan McClure.* Standing, left-right: *Harriet McClure, Archibald McClure, Annie McClure.*

able discussing matters of the intellect, a tribute to the broad-minded environment fostered by the minister and his wife.

Then there was baby brother Nathan, whom Jim adored. Nathan kept him up to date on the fortunes of the Cubs and White Sox, and in return Jim liked to take him out to the ball parks. Professional baseball in the early 1900s was thought by many to encourage the most boorish and uncouth of habits. How was a child to build up his character if his heroes were baseball players? But the sport had been a large part of Reverend McClure's life, and he was wise enough to realize that children hemmed in on all sides by petty rules could lead a suffocating existence. The playful and happy life of these children can be gathered from this excerpt from a wonderful letter Jim wrote to Nathan from Germany, where he was studying: " . . . [y]our fears of what I will do to you for pushing me off the raft are well grounded. I have not fully made up my mind what I will do to you . . . I am sorry to say that your life next winter will be a hard one. I have been practicing on German children and have made several boys and girls cry simply by looking at them . . . I intend to take one whole year to think up a fitting return for pushing me off that raft." He went on to tell Nathan of the circus he had attended in England, where he shook hands with the tallest woman in the world and watched elephants play cricket. Jim concluded with the remark, "The children in Paris seem to be a very happy set—in Ger-

Jamie's parents.

many I have not seen so many children, probably because I was preparing for next winter and they see me coming and hide in the houses." (James G. K. McClure, Jr. to Nathan McClure, 1910).

The raft incident undoubtedly took place on one of the family outings to Wisconsin. Dr. McClure's wealthy Lake Forest parishioners gladly offered their summer camps to the family for vacations. Pictures survive of Jim with his sisters and parents, all in the remarkable bathing garb of the era, posing self-consciously for the camera. The physiques of the family range from the lanky, angular style of the McClures to the more rounded, almost pudgy Dixon model. Without question, Jamie was on his mother's side in this matter. His oval, smooth face always made him look younger than his contemporaries. He joined sister Annie in this respect, but Arch inherited the almost Lincolnesque body of his father.

On one of these trips to Wisconsin, the two elder siblings, Annie and Jim, remained behind when the rest of the family returned to Lake Forest. From

Lake trip with family and friends. Young Jim McClure in the center, seated, parents standing behind. Jamie (left) with friends on a buggy.

Island Lodge, Lakewood, Wisconsin, the thirteen-year-old boy (apparently suffering a spelling relapse during the summer vacation) reported home that:

> Sunday, in the morning we had church in which we sang and Mr. Wheeler read a chapter from *In His Steps* as a sermon. In the afternoon Annie and I went off in the woods and read and Annie here a noise and there stood a *dear* it was awfully pretty but as soon as it saw us it turned and ran. At about five we all went out in the boats and joined them and sang.
> This morning Mr. Wheeler and I got up at five o'clock to go bass fishing, we fished 'till eleven o'clock leavig [sic] out breakfast but the fish must have been all caught for we did not get one. All the rest of the party started off for Boot Lake but only got so far as Bass Lake because some went one way and some another. (James G. K. McClure, Jr. to James G. K. McClure, Sr., August 29, 1898)

The book *In His Steps,* by Ralph Connor, is the story of a young man, quite popular in upper-class society, who makes the decision to become a practicing Christian, thus setting himself against his friends' standards of behavior. It had a lasting effect on Jamie, and he urged his children to read it in later years.

Jamie McClure, now beginning to be called Jim, graduated from Lake Forest Academy in June 1901. What to do with this lively young man next? His wise father knew that Yale College was not the place for a fifteen-year-old boy, and what could he do in a wealthy suburb like Lake Forest where everyone knew him as the son of their beloved minister? He spent some months at Lake Forest College, living at home, but apparently had little interest in his studies. Jim had a lot of Tom Sawyer in his nature, and he yearned to find out what life was like beyond the fringes of the circumscribed civilization of Lake Forest. There were tastes of wilderness on the family jaunts to Wisconsin, and yet life there dealt with the natural world from within the bounds of Victorian habits and decorum. There was no grit or struggle, and too much talk. And most of all, there were no Huck Finns, poor boys up against the real fight of life, with whom to join in comradeship on some great adventure.

Vigorous boys at the turn of the century all dreamed of going to one place, where life was down to basics and where what talk there was, was to the point and necessary. In 1902, Owen Wister wrote *The Virginian,* establishing the American cowboy on the pinnacle of the American Olympus of mythological heroes, and Texas was the home of the cowboy. In the spring of 1896 Dr. McClure had gone to the XIT Ranch in the Panhandle of Texas as a guest of the Farwells, who owned a part interest in it. He returned with stories and descriptions that were bound to excite the imagination of any young boy. The characters he met and the vocabulary they used did nothing to tarnish young Jim's dime-novel view of the cowboy.

Dr. McClure had kept a journal of this expedition. The XIT was then the largest ranch in the world, occupying as much land as several states. At first the Panhandle was thought to be virtually worthless. Rainfall was minimal. Very little grew except prairie dogs and coyotes. But after the cattle boom in the 1870s ranch land became more valuable. The people who lived on the XIT in 1896 were isolated and often lonely. A man's wife could go six months without seeing another woman. With such a thin population and a geography that attracted desperate men, there was naturally a law enforcement problem.

Into this world came the gentle Reverend. His guide was a Mr. Boyce, "a wonderful combination of activity, fearlessness, principle and purpose."[17] Spending the night with this man, he was shown several bullet holes where the Graham brothers, local cattle rustlers, had tried to shoot his host. In the ensuing melee, six-shooters blazed and one Graham and the sheriff died. The other Graham went to the "pen" and was eventually released. He was reportedly out to avenge the loss of his brother, aiming to ambush Mr. Boyce. "It is not much of a wonder that he carries a six-shooter with him when he is off on his wanderings," Dr. McClure wrote.

The minister went by buckboard more than 500 miles, camping out with Mr. Boyce who loved to wake up his citified guest with injunctions such as "Take up your bed and walk."[18] He met horse wranglers and watched a roundup. When the cook sang out, "Chuck is ready," he helped himself with the other cowboys. One of his favorite stories, often retold to his children in Lake Forest, involved meeting a local legend—Ira Atin.

> People had told me about a very brave fellow. Once two men had threatened to shoot him. They were standing close to him. Putting his hands in front of his chest as one catches a ball he said "Shoot and I will catch the bullet and throw it back." They shot, neither hit him . . . one dodged behind the corner of a building and the other under a wagon. They shot again. Then he drew. He shot through the corner of the building and hit one on the arm: then he shot under the wagon, got his man in the back of the neck and he dropped. Then the men came forward, apologized and said, "Ira, you are a better man than we thought."[19]

Near the end of his western trip the gentle minister was packed into a small room one night with some strange cowpokes.

> Somehow I could not sleep. The moon was still bright. It was past midnight when to my utter amazement what should appear in that doorway but a man. It was but an instant before he was down the steps. What did this mean I asked myself. He struck a match; he entered. The match woke the sleepers. They saw his face. "Is that you, Ira?" they said. "Yes." One rolled a little closer to his bed fellow and said, "here's room." In a few moments I was asleep.[20]

There was something in the independent spirit of these men that appealed to James G. K. McClure. Many years later he himself drove off two robbers from the house on Halsted Street in south Chicago, where the McClures lived while he was president of McCormick Seminary. As he and his wife lay sleeping

Jamie McClure, Jr., in front; Sister Harriet on right, standing beside brother Arch. Annie McClure stands behind little Arch. Others in photograph are unknown.

he was wakened by a light shining in his face and a voice telling him not to move. Leaping out of bed with a shout he rushed down the stairs after the fleeing intruders. They fired several shots as they ran, but miraculously missed. The bullets sank harmlessly into the walls of the stairway. He told his family afterwards he had never thought to be afraid.

When one of the Farwell brothers heard that their minister was wondering what his son could do until he was old enough to attend college, he immediately suggested the ranch in Texas. Young Jim, stimulated by his father's tales, enthusiastically embraced the plan. It was surely a dream realized, a chance to swap the refinements of Lake Forest for the sweat and leather of Texas.

A photograph remains of Jamie McClure as a child, and it says a great deal about his youth. He must have been eight or nine years old. His brothers and sisters are all bunched around him, their dour expressions reflecting perhaps the coercion that was applied to get them all into their clothes and before the camera. Jim sits cross-legged in front, with one hand holding the collar of the family pup, a marvelous little white dog with one black patch over its left eye. Jim's shoes are the high-laced variety, with the laces hooked to the proper tension. His socks disappear under his knickerbockers, and his knickerbockers disappear under a checked coat buttoned three times. Poking out from a Little

Lord Fauntleroy collar is his round Dixon head. A most stupendous polka-dotted bow tie dangles from beneath the collar. And on top of that head a small, curl-brimmed hat is perched, making either the head appear too big or the hat too small. The brim travels just over the eyes of our young hero, and already they are eyes of distinction. In later years, his eyes could sparkle when he was having fun, they could bear down on someone whose performance had come up short, and they could mesmerize the ladies. And so what else can be said for this picture of our hero? My bet is that hat, collar, tie, knicks and shoes all came ripping off before the photographer was halfway through dismantling his equipment.

The life of this boy would create a man of unusual instincts. He would grow up to be part theologian and part missionary, part cowboy and part intellectual. All of these tendencies were kept boiling by Jim's extraordinary pursuit of heroism. He wanted, desperately, for his life to stand for something great. He sought challenge, not as a businessman does, but more like the best of missionaries, who burn with desire to change people's lives. At age sixteen, he was anxious to taste the different diets of the folks of this world, and so with all the dreams of youth he headed west to be a Texas cowboy.

1. James G. K. McClure, "History of the Presbyterian Church," A pamphlet printed in April, 1905.

2. James G. K. McClure, Sr., "A grateful Review of his Happy Pastorate of the Presbyterian Church, Lake Forest, Illinois, as Presented on the Twenty-fourth Anniversary of the Pastorate" (Unpublished), Sept. 10, 1905. p. 8.

3. *Ibid.*, p.5.

4. *Ibid.*, p. 6.

5. Notation in the baby book of James G. K. McClure, Jr.

6. James G. K. McClure, Sr., "History of the Presbyterian Church, Lake Forest, Illinois" unpublished, 1905, p. 26–27.

7. James G. K. McClure, Jr., personal notebook, dated 1910.

8. James G. K. McClure, Sr., "History of the Presbyterian Church Lake Forest," p. 38.

9. Untitled pamphlet about the life of Archibald McClure, printed privately, 1931.

10. "An Appreciation," paper about Phebe Ann Dixon McClure (unpublished), no date.

11. James G. K. McClure, Sr., letter to James G. K. McClure, Jr., Dec. 27, 1910.

12. "For Auld Lang Syne: A Retrospective of Steady Streams," pamphlet printed in 1906.

13. *Ibid.*

14. *Ibid.*

15. Lake Forest Academy Annual, 1900, p. 125.

16. James G. K. McClure, Jr., sermon given at the Iron River Presbyterian Church, Jan. 1, 1914.

17. James G. K. McClure, Sr., "Among the Cowboys of Texas," unpublished, no date, p. 9.

18. *Ibid.*, p. 13.

19. *Ibid.*, p.56–57.

20. *Ibid.*, p.57.

Chapter 3

Texas

Please tell Father that the razor was a plumb good one and I thank him ever so much for it. (*James G. K. McClure, Jr., to Grace McClure, February 2, 1902*)

If you send off a young lad, already inclined to be Tom Sawyeresque, to live among cowboys, eat their food, and talk their talk, and then try to bring him back home, you have to expect some resistance. The benefits of life in Lake Forest are hard to dispute, but Jamie McClure wanted to taste a rougher and manlier world. He wanted to be on his own without the amenities a mother provides. Like most young men at the turn of the century, bronco busting, chuck wagons, chaps and cowpokes evoked for him the gritty, but nonetheless romantic world where coyotes, long-horned steers and wild horses squared off against courageous men. Jamie threw himself into that world, and when his allotted time there was over it was his love for his family, his sense of duty, and his father's persuasive ability rather than the attractions of Yale's intellectual and social life that convinced him to leave.

Young Jim McClure landed in Texas in November of 1901. He arrived at the Shoenail Ranch through a connection with a Presbyterian minister in Chicago. Word that he was coming came late, and without a letter of introduction he appeared to be just another greenhorn Yankee looking for a job. He was taken on and thrown in with all the other hands. He had to make his own way without the benefit of his father's introduction, which suited him just fine.

In later years Jim was always quick to say that at the start he was just plain lucky. It was probably at the Shoenail that a group of horses were corralled and Jim was asked if he could ride a bad horse. Not being constituted to say "No" in the face of a challenge, he said he could. One of the cowboys brought forward several noted buckers for the suburban greenhorn, one after another on successive days. He was told to "Thumb 'em and hang 'em in 'em," which means run your thumbs up the horse's mane the wrong way and spur him at the same time to irritate him. All these procedures Jim carried out, but still these broncos just trotted off with him. The days happened to be quite warm, Jim was a confident rider, and the horses were in no mood to act up. The greenhorn began to acquire a name for himself. They called him "Chicago Jim," and fortunately his reputation for riding a bad horse remained untarnished. He found himself well accepted in this new society.

In winter, there was time to become close friends with the other cowboys. Two fellows named Emory and Enoch became devoted to Chicago Jim and vice versa. He wrote to his family:

> Emory and I set traps. The next morning we went . . . [and] found nothing but a hawk in one and shot a few quail. . . . I shot a large Mallard duck. Wednesday was spent in fruitlessly hunting duck and getting about 10 or 12 quail. . . . Thursday for dinner we were going to have duck but the duck failed to materialize. . . . (James G. K. McClure, Jr. to family, December 1, 1901)

A few days later:

> Yesterday . . . we all went to town. Emery and I got a hair cut and ate a fine dinner at the hotel. I then got my saddle repaired. . . . We then watered some stock and the horses. . . . (James G. K. McClure, Jr. to Harriet McClure, December 10, 1901)

On the day following:

> After dinner Babe Owens, Enoch, Emery and myself went to West Pasture. . . . We rode nearly twenty-five miles during the afternoon. . . . Father's pants which I brought along have already given out completely at the seat. (James G. K. McClure, Jr. to Harriet McClure, December 11, 1901)

Perhaps it was a sign of his growing confidence that he dispenses for the first time with his childhood name and signs the letter, "Your devoted brother, James G. K. McClure, Jr."

Even though going to church meant a two-hour buggy drive to town, he often made the effort to go, even if he had only "womenfolk" for company.

> This morning Mrs. Craven, Miss Hempstead and I went to church in the buggy. They had no church at the Presbyterian or Methodist churches so we went to the Baptist. The church was full and the preaching was certainly queer. The house was so full that one old fellow sat on the carpet on the platform. The chairs had done give out. There were sure a right smart a people there.
>
> If you happen to have an extra razor. . . . I wish you would forward it by mail as my G. strings are about 1/2 inch long. Maybe that accounts for my weight. . . . The presents that you'uns sent were fine. . . . [I am] more thankful every day that I have such a fine Father and Mother and brothers and sisters. (James G. K. McClure, Jr. to James G. K. McClure, Sr., December 30, 1901)

Jim was trying out the language of his new buddies, and apparently ready to begin serious shaving (although the G. string terminology certainly is baffling!) Even more than his reference to needing a razor, however, it is his stated appreciation for his family that shows he was gaining a new perspective. When the child ceases to take his upbringing for granted, he is beginning to see himself in a new light.

Such a new perspective is often hardest for mothers to accept. Young Jamie dashed off a note to "My dearest Mother" on New Year's Day. She had sent him some cookies and a homemade plum pudding, and had inquired tentatively as to when he might return home. In this note, he revealed to her an astounding plan. "As to coming home I thought that I would spend the winter here and . . . start from here about the first of April with Emory and . . . ride home on horse back. The ponies cost about twenty dollars apiece and we could take a tent, bedding and a few cooking utensils on a pack horse. I think the best plan would be to tell fortunes on the way home and live as the gypsies do" (James G. K. McClure, Jr. to Phebe Ann Dixon McClure, January 1, 1902). He had a lifelong ambition to live for a time like a gypsy. He loved the exhilaration he felt when completely free and independent. The reaction of his mother to this idea was predictable, and somehow the idea was squelched.

It was the freedom of Texas, where the very geography breathes the word, that helped to mature young McClure. The pictures he took with Harriet's Kodak camera, which she loaned him for the trip, show a land so vast and flat that the barns and people look inconsequential. He loved to photograph friends, and his horses. "The picture of the single horse is Bob Short with my saddle on. My thumb got in the way and spoiled his head" (James G. K. McClure, Jr. to James G. K. McClure, Sr., February 5, 1902). Next to Bob Short in his album is a picture of a wildcat that was caught and tied up by one of the other hands. Another shows Jim posing on one of his horses, cutting a fine figure with a large cowboy hat, vest, boots and lasso. He loved to hunt coyotes, and wrote to brother Arch: ". . . we jumped a coyote quite near us. The dogs went after him on all fours and Ned and I right behind. Old Swapsie (a dog) caught him in about half a mile and the dogs just ate him up. He had Miss Dordy (another dog) by the upper jaw and swung her round and round but when she got loose she just tore at him. . . . It was fine" (James G. K. McClure, Jr. to Arch McClure, February 16, 1902). And to his poor mother he wrote, "Can you please ask Father to let me know how he got his coyote skins home and how much he paid to have them made into rugs" (James G, K. McClure, Jr. to Phebe Ann Dixon McClure, January 19, 1902). In a birthday letter, he undoubtedly scared her to tears with this story:

> Talk about your Buffalo Bill's Wild West Show, we beat it all to pieces Thursday. They brought up four broncos which had never had a rope on except when they were branded. We had been coyote hunting and when we got in we threw up for the first choice. I was the lucky number. . . . I chose a boy with a white spot on his face. . . . When we got back from feeding the cows and calves . . . I . . . saddled my bronco and rode him. We had to ride without bridles, simply with halters. Mine didn't do anything at first but shortly de- cided that he wished no more of me and pitched a little. . . . It felt very funny to ride all over the prairie totally unable to guide your horse. I had a short rope to quirt [whip] mine with and accidentally I hit him on the tail with it and he broke in two for a second or so.

We are each going to get three dollars when they are broken to saddle and bridle. (James G. K. McClure, Jr. to Phebe Ann Dixon McClure, February 22, 1902)

Jim McClure made his mark in this cowboy world as a bronco buster. Of all the challenges not involving a six-shooter, taming a wild horse earned the most respect in this society. It was a skill that took great courage, and one that Jim was justly proud of ever afterwards. He became friends with a bronco buster named George Young, and they teamed up to ride from ranch to ranch to break horses. They were paid $3.00 a head to "bridle 'em, saddle 'em and ride 'em five times." These horses, mostly four-year-olds, were herded in from the range where they had grown up in perfect freedom except for the terrifying experience of being branded as colts. Jim used the Kodak to record an excellent sequence of George Young, master broncobuster, saddling a bronco, mounting, riding through the first jump, and finally astride a subdued horse.

Jim's daughter remembers him telling her about their experiences:

... most of the cowboys hated to ride a bronc. ... He and George would take the broncs turn about, and at first it seemed to him that George always got the worst ones. After riding a particularly tough bronc the first time, George would sometimes have blood running out of his nose, mouth and eyes! Once ... they had finished all the broncs at a ranch and went in to get their pay. The boss said there was one bronc they had not yet ridden. My father was very tired and said he wouldn't ride it, but the boss was insistent. Finally my father said he would look at it. He went up to the corral and saw the horse standing exhausted at one side of the corral. He realized that it had just been driven in from the range by the cowboys and that it was exhausted. So he said he'd ride it right away. He soon discovered it was not a young bronc (four years old as they usually were) but a horse of about seven and probably an outlaw. But since it was so exhausted he saddled it right up and decided to ride it on the range rather than in the corral ... it just walked off quietly. Pretty soon a "norther" sprang up, as sometimes happened in Texas. At first he felt just a little puff of wind, then another and another. The temperature dropped twenty degrees in minutes, and the cold wind roared. The bronc pricked up its ears. It began to feel better and better. Then it started to buck. My father said he rode it from its ears to its tail, and it kept right on bucking. All the time he kept spurring the horse and sawing on the bit. At last the horse slowed down until its bucks were just crow hops and finally it stopped altogether. It was all bloody from the spurs and at its mouth, too. And my father rode the horse slowly back to the ranch. It was a rough business on both horse and man. This horse remained a tough one to ride. One day my father needed to go into town and decided to give the bronc a good workout. When they arrived at the town corral, the horse was terrified of all the wagons, men and buildings ... things it had never seen. My father tried to leave it in the corral, but the horse just put its head on my father's shoulder and followed him like a dog. After that the bronc never bucked with my father again. It was a regular pet, but no one else could ride it. It was a "one man horse." When my father went East some of his friends wrote him about that horse. No one could ride it and they sold it to a rodeo.[1]

Jim's success at this job was all the more remarkable as he had ridden very little more than old Erma back in Lake Forest.

The letters he wrote home spilled over with the ebullience of his new life. Sensing a potential problem, his father continually reminded his son that Texas was only a short excursion. He could not really escape the patterns laid before him and, although admittedly he was tempted, in later life he would be glad he had stayed on his ordained course. Son, like father, would attend Yale University. He needed to return to Lake Forest in time to brush up on his Greek and Latin, so he could pass the college's entrance exam. He kept pushing back the time of his return as far as he could. Early April became mid-May in his plans. " . . . I would just as soon stay until Annie gets home . . . about the first of July. That would give me from six to eight weeks to study, according to whether I got home on the first or middle of May. . . . 1 never appreciated my father and mother as I do now" (James G. K. McClure, Jr. to James G. K. McClure, Sr. March 2, 1902).

The appreciation was sincere, but comparing Greek and Latin to riding the range was to compare dreary duty with youthful freedom. At the Shoenail, one aspect of range riding revolved around water. In the winter, the ice had to be broken. In the early spring, a fascinating aspect of ranch life appeared with the hatching of the heel fly. During the first warm days, these flies would attack the cattle with such fury that the animals would rush into the nearest pond or bog for relief. But they tended to be so weak after the winter that they would get stuck in the mire and eventually die if they were not dragged out. Jim and his friends would ride the bogs looking for animals in such a state. The cowboys tied ropes from the pommels of their saddles to the cows and pulled for all their horses were worth. If they succeeded, they had to quickly release the rope from the cow—the cattle were so wild and mean that as soon as they returned to solid ground, they would as often as not turn and charge the cowboys. The animals that had died in the bogs were skinned on the spot. Jim reported, "Friday morning we rode the bogs and in the afternoon we tried to pull a cow out of the creek and finally had to skin her in the creek. My horse broke loose from her ten times, breaking the rope five times. We then found another cow bogged down but she went off all right" (James G. K. McClure, Jr. to James G. K. McClure, Sr. April 13, 1902).

His daughter remembers that he had one mean bronco whose buck had a twist that made it difficult to stay on. He decided to take this horse to bog camp with him so that he could ride it where the other hands wouldn't see him get thrown. Only his friend Enoch would be with him. The first time the horse threw him he landed in a briar bush, the second time he just missed the camp fire and the third time as he lay on the ground he saw the horse coming down at him to stomp him, which few horses will ever do. Jim drew back his fist and punched the wild one in the nose and the horse whirled away. The horse's fate is not known.[2]

The time was drawing near that Jim would have to go back to his preordained life, and he had not ridden a roundup. He learned that on the XIT Ranch this event was held early. He could take part and still get back in time to study for his Yale exams. On April 14, Jim left the Shoenail Ranch for the XIT. It was a sad parting, for the men and animals of that ranch had taken him a good distance towards manhood. Emery, Enoch, Oscar, Bob Short and many more would become part of the repertoire of adventure stories with which he would later entertain his friends and children. One he loved to tell was how the hands were loafing around in front of the fire one day, so bored they could barely keep their eyes open. A lively cowpoke thought he would have some fun, and grabbed a handful of bullets and tossed them into the fire. Grown men never left the prone position any faster.

A roundup on the XIT was an enormous undertaking. Yearlings were branded and made ready for the trip to Montana, where they would graze all summer and then be slaughtered for the Chicago meat markets. The ranch was the largest in the United States, approximately three million acres. Jim used Harriet's camera to record pictures of the men and their activities out on the prairie. Pictures survive of the men sitting around the chuck wagon eating breakfast; the men saddling up; Lee Landers on his horse Black Snake; Boss Moore and Old Joe. Jim loved to talk about how a man had to check his bed roll carefully before crawling out in the morning. It got cold at night and rattlesnakes often crawled in beside or under the sleeper for warmth.

Each cowpoke had a string of five or six horses, so that he could ride a fresh horse daily. When a large number of cattle had been gathered together to drive towards the rail head there was always the danger of a stampede. Several men rode around the herd all night keeping watch; for any strange sound, a roll of thunder or a sudden coyote howl, might start the herd running out of control.

Jim McClure understood the essential loneliness of the cowboy's life. His daughter remembers:

> He told me what a lonely life the men led, and that so many he met were always talking about how they would go back home and settle down when they were paid off in the fall. But in the spring most of them would show up again. It was the only life they knew. There was an old cowboy along on that XIT roundup who would sing at night before they went to sleep, "I ride an old Paint I lead an old Dan I'm goin' to Montana just to throw the hoolyan*."[3]

The song Jim remembered best was the "Cowboy's Prayer." He used to sing it for his daughter when he drove her to school. It went like this:

---

*A 'hoolyan' is a lariat or rope.

"Chuck Wagon," picture taken by James G.K. McClure, Jr., in Texas.

Last night as I lay on the prairie
And looked at the stars in the sky
I wondered if ever a cowboy
Would get to that sweet bye and bye.

I wondered then if I'd meet her
That mother whom God took away
And if in that bright land I'd greet her
Upon the last judgement day.

They say there will be a great roundup
When the cowboys like dogies will stand
To be cut by the riders of judgement
Who are posted and know every brand.

They say there's another great owner
Who's ne'er overstocked, that day,
He always makes room for another
Upon the last Judgement Day.

The trail that leads to those bright regions
Is narrow and dim, so they say,
But the road that leads down to perdition
Is broad and blazed all the way.

In the East the grey dawn is breaking
Heaven's thought from me take wing
The cattle from sleep are awaking
And into my saddle I spring.[4]

One can imagine the boy lying in his bedroll under the Texas stars listening to the old man sing. His daughter surmises:

> His experience in Texas certainly meant a lot to him and he did love to think about it all those many years later. I loved to hear about it, as he had taught me to ride and even though he often scared me because he rode fast and hard, I loved it. I tried hard not to show my fear because he was the kind of person you were desperately anxious to please.
>
> I think it was while working on these ranches that my father first really got to know men who worked on the land for what they had. I think it stayed with him all his life. He probably saw some of the same admirable qualities of independence and humor and ability to bear up under the hardships of life here in the North Carolina mountains.[5]

Texas also gave Jim tremendous confidence. He had earned the respect of men who lived an earthy, basic way of life. This life always afterward appealed to Jim. He did not throw away the cultural graces of his upbringing, but neither was he a prisoner to them. He learned to appreciate those segments of society that lacked the refinement of Victorian manners. He always loved the daring courage of the moment: challenge made him come alive. His friends in Texas were for the most part straightforward and unpretentious, and for those very traits they gained the admiration of young Jim McClure.

And I'm sure Enoch, Emery and George never forgot him either. He received a few letters later from the more literate of his friends.

> I imagine you had quite a time hunting and fishing last summer! Wish I could have been with you. But instead of that I was down here punching cows to beat thunder. . . . I traded off one of your main cowhorses the other day, "Old Splity." . . . Well next year during vacation come down and spend a month or two with us. . . . I am still in the race for County Judge with fair prospects to win out. Will send you my card. . . . (J.E. Moore to James G. K. McClure, Jr. October 8, 1902)

Another letter came from Oscar Ledbetter, the windmill man on the Shoenail Ranch. Jim always remembered a day when Oscar, driving a wagon and team of four mules, was persuaded to join the boys as they galloped by on a coyote hunt. Mules and wagon were flying over the prairie when they came to a hidden draw, a deep cut made by a small stream. The mules *really* flew, landing safe on the other side, leaving Oscar and the wagon in a tangle of broken traces and cuss words, but miraculously uninjured. Oscar wrote:

The barbecue was a howling success. . . . The boys had a good time. Old Mary Ann took it all out to Coxey's race mare. Old Will is all right, he is in gopher flat pasture getting fat. . . . Jim what about that fish story? It sounds— well-er like—just let it go. Jim I wish you could arrange to come down this winter as hunting is going to be fine. We have nine brand new dogs, that makes us nineteen so you see I will deal the coyotes misery this winter. Wishing you a bushel of pleasure. (Oscar Ledbetter to James G. K. McClure, Jr. August 23, 1903)

The course of Jim's life was scheduled to pass through Yale, and despite the pleasures of Texas, that plan remained unaltered. So he returned to Lake Forest in the late spring, by railroad and not as a gypsy, to review Virgil and Xenophon. That summer he attended the annual "Lake Forest Open-Air Horse Show." Serious riding there was English style. He must have thoroughly enjoyed leaning up against the ring and telling his stories about riding out West while the McCormicks and Swifts and Farwells pranced about winning ribbons. He did pass his entrance test to Yale, and by the fall of 1902 he had exchanged his Stetson and chaps for a bowler and cane.

1. Interviews with Elspeth McClure Clarke.
2. *Ibid.*
3. *Ibid.*
4. *Ibid.*
5. *Ibid.*

Chapter Four
Yale

You must think my chief pals when I was in college were sweeps and old clothes men—I suppose my name would sound unfamiliar to every professor in the place. (*James G. K. McClure, Jr. to Arch McClure, Fall, 1909*)

I once knew an old professor, who woke up one morning with ill health. By mistake, his wife brought in a barometer instead of a thermometer. When she pulled it out of his mouth, it registered "dry and windy." (*A joke Jim McClure used to tell when speaking.*)

Yale University at the turn of the century catered to young men of wealth and social standing. New money and old money were represented, but all had money nonetheless. The only notable exception were the sons of clergymen. Yale reflected the chasm between the social classes that had been yawning wider over the decades since the Civil War. It was one of the precipices from which the monied class overlooked the working class at a greater and greater distance. Shortly after the anthracite coal miners of Pennsylvania went back to work after one of the country's most devastating strikes, the university served to Jim and his classmates the following Thanksgiving dinner: "Grape Fruit Round Cut with Sherry, Blue Points on Half Shell, Salmon with Tartar Sauce, and Filet of Beef with Mushrooms, Turkey, Cranberry Sauce . . ."[1]

In 1902, a dynamic young American, Theodore Roosevelt, succeeded to the presidency after the assassination of William McKinley. Roosevelt began to push his plan for the Square Deal (the first of many "Deals" in this century), which in essence was an attempt to arbitrate fairly between the competing elements of labor and capital. In February of 1902, while Jim was still hunting coyotes and breaking broncos, Roosevelt told his attorney general to bring suit against the Northern Securities Company for violating the Sherman Antitrust Act. It was a dramatic break with the past, and signaled a new epoch in American politics now remembered as the Progressive Era.

The following May, when Jim was getting accustomed to Yale, the coal workers went out on strike, creating the largest work stoppage in the history of the country. For decades, labor unrest had threatened the United States as the social changes wrought by industrialization created pressures that upset the agrarian status quo of an earlier and simpler America. In every labor dispute to date, the federal government (if it became involved at all) put its weight directly behind the business interests. But in a precedent-smashing decision, Roosevelt called both sides in the coal dispute to come to Washington. He had become convinced that the mine operators were prolonging the strike and threatening the national welfare (coal was the principal source of energy and heat in this era). To further urge the owners along, he threatened to confiscate the mines and operate them with federal troops if they refused arbitration. By October the mines were reopened and the worst abuses had been rectified.

Despite his Dixon heritage, in 1903 Jim's political consciousness remained shallow. Roosevelt's Progressive Era would stamp a deep impression on him, educating him more thoroughly than the Yale Greek and Latin departments. He remained throughout his life a loyal Republican, even after moving to the Democratic South. But his Republicanism was in the style of Teddy Roosevelt: progressive, forward looking and full of energy. This Republican was no businessman's flunky, but a Progressive whose loyalties were with the downtrodden of America.

Jim's father was deeply loyal to his *alma mater,* and was quite sure that his years spent at Yale had helped to develop his strength of character and breadth of vision. He eventually sent all three of his sons to Yale, and returned yearly himself to celebrate the reunion rites with his friends of the class of 1870. There were still McClures in and around Albany, particularly Jim's Aunt Grace; and there were the Dixons in nearby Westerly, Rhode Island. Yale would be a homecoming for his sons. But during his first weeks at Yale Jim was very uncomfortable. He did not feel at home with these elegant young men from Exeter and Andover and the other prep schools. Like Yale and Harvard, these schools had been founded originally to educate the clergy, but now their main patrons were well-to-do industrialists and professional men. In later years he told his daughter laughingly that he felt totally out of place that first fall at college. Texas certainly hadn't lost its lure for Jim, and at least twice he was tempted to go back. The first offer came through a friend named Charles K. King, who wrote:

> . . . I have a letter from the owner of the *C* Ranch down in New Mexico where I learned the business, you know, and he wants me to send him a young fellow to learn the business and his ways and eventually take charge of his business and as he has a fine place and lots of cattle it is certainly a fine opening for any young man who would like the life . . . Please write and let me know what you think about it, Jim. Do not decide in a hurry, for he will wait if I ask him to . . . I believe it will mean a fortune in the years to come and it would take me just long enough to get there to accept it if I were foot loose . . .
>
> I write to you and thought of you simple because I like you most sincerely and because I believe you are just the sort of man he wants, honest, straightforward, true and obliging. I am not jollying you now, Jim, but merely enumerating the qualities I am positive you possess that will please him. . . .
> (Charles F. King to James G. K. McClure, Jr., November 14, 1902)

Then came a letter from another Texas friend, an "old nester." This was the Texan term for a comparatively small landholder, nestled in among the big ranches. The old fellow had taken a fancy to Jim, and had already asked him to come to live with him. Now he wrote that if Chicago Jim would come to help him run his place he would deed him half his land and cattle, and make the rest over to him in his will. Jim thought it over, but briefly, and wrote his father he was going to accept the offer and leave Yale for Texas, the place where a man's work made the difference and the people were not so layered with civilization. Dr. McClure did not write and he did not telegraph. He boarded the *Twentieth Century Limited* at once and appeared unannounced in Jim's room. The impulse for Texas was thwarted.[2]

In time, Jim realized the wisdom of his father in this matter. His years at Yale, while not marked by academic achievement, included contact with a critical mix of people and intellectual influences that bore great fruit later in his life. Yet, it must be said that his dream of a practical life, with cattle and chickens and earthy farmhands, remained part of the young man's makeup. His life would have to make room for that vision, too.

Jim speedily adjusted to the social mores of his classmates. As it had for his father, Yale meant a time to build character and make friends. The uneasiness of his first term soon disappeared, and more than any other aspect of his college career it was the solid coterie of loyal and devoted friends he made that helped him tremendously then and all through his life. Like his father before him, he took much more of an interest in the social and religious aspects of college than in academics. One acceptable scheme of attending Yale in 1902 was to get by with the daily recitations in order to take advantage of the myriad activities that swirled around the college. He constantly received notes from the Dean's office concerning academic problems, quite drastic ones in some cases, but they seem to have had little effect on the goings and comings of his daily life.

Jim was met on his arrival at New Haven by Mr. Franklin Dexter, one of his father's dearest friends. He wrote his sister Annie that he could see "Mr. Dexter's head and shoulders over the crowd at the train. . . ." He stayed a few days with the Dexters while purchasing furniture for his room, ". . . a Bed, Mattress springs, bureau, washstand, Toilet Set, desk, desk chair and cane chair for $50.22 . . ." (James G. K. McClure, Jr. to Annie McClure, September 24, 1902). Later on his father would become concerned about his son's ease with money, but he apparently made a thrifty beginning. Yale was a large, disorienting place. After a month, a little homesick thread creeps into a letter to his family.

> I can never thank you enough for these eighteen lovely years. Since coming here I have felt the meaning of life more than ever before. In the Dwight Hall [religious] meetings there have been some of the finest things said that I have ever heard.
> I hope that you will always remember that although I am a long ways off

yet I love you more than ever and I do wish that you could be here or better
still I be at home for a little while. Christmas will be here soon, however, only
eight weeks from tomorrow. As I write I suppose that you are both at Prayer
Meeting and that Annie is playing the piano. (James G. K. McClure, Jr. to
family, October 28, 1902)

Jim learned to love Yale, and threw himself into diverse aspects of the life
there. Most important of all for him was religion. He joined the YMCA, and
faithfully attended his class prayer meetings on Sunday after chapel. He told his
family that the Dwight Hall meetings of the Yale University Christian Association meant a lot. He was placed on the Freshman Religious Committee.

At a meeting of the Freshman Union, Jim debated the affirmative side in
the question, "Resolved, that Latin and Greek should not be required studies in
college." Despite the strident pragmatism exhibited by Jim in this debate, the
ancient texts still had to be faced daily, Monday through Saturday, by Freshman
McClure.[3]

Religious life and daily life at Yale were completely intertwined. The
current president, Arthur Hadley, was a political economist and the first president of the university who was not a clergyman. Among the class of people who
attended Yale, Christianity in one form or another was an expected part of one's
intellectual wardrobe. Academic regulations for the school included the following: for chapel, "students are required to occupy the seats assigned by the ushers
at morning prayers each weekday, and at the Sunday morning service. . . ."[4]
The idea implicit in these rules is that one of the principal responsibilities of the
college is to inculcate the habits of religion in the student body, and that in this
pursuit it had the approval of the wider culture the college represented. In the
name of student free choice, discomfort with religious coercion, and certainly
as the result of a more diversified student body, such rules have disappeared
on nearly all American college campuses today. Even back in his college days
though, Jim McClure felt a growing suspicion of a religion that was "expected"
and class bound. It should be, he thought, alive with ideas and truths that helped
real people in need regardless of their station in life, and that energized souls
with the immense spiritual power available to them. Protestant Christianity had
reached a zenith of sorts in 1902. It was a distinguishing mark of Northern
European and American culture, and world wide there were few who doubted
the power and influence of these Protestant countries. At Yale, Jim breathed the
air of this cultural confidence, and it was an obvious source of his optimism.
And yet he began to catch an occasional musty whiff that all was not so well
after all.

If the seeds of Jim's eventual revolt against the *status quo* were in the
ground in 1902, they showed precious little evidence of germination. He was
actually much more interested in football—Yale football at this time was national news. He became an avid fan of Yale sports in general, and his scrapbook
is packed with tickets stubs and sports articles. He was on his freshman football

team, but by the looks of the picture, everyone who went out made the club. There is no evidence that he ever played in a game, but he remained a touch-football enthusiast ever after.

Another freshman delight for him was sneaking into the junior prom:

> Monday night was the Prom Concert. Of course there was a terrible crowd of freshman striving to get in to their gallery. Everyone going in was searched but nevertheless lots of things were brought in. Thousands of these paper streamers were thrown, lots of confetti and lots of cards. We took balls of string and let down notes to the girls and they sent up flowers and notes and all sorts of things. (James G. K. McClure, Jr. to Phebe Ann Dixon McClure, February 4, 1903)

He collected many of the cards he mentions and pasted them into his scrapbook. One, with a slight political ring, went:

> Of the Prom Girls he thought he's a trust
> But the Freshman class on high
> Caught the pretty girl's eye
> And behold, all the fuss trust was bust.[5]

Since the college athletic teams were beyond his abilities, Jim made a habit of working out on the college track and helped to organize informal football and baseball games among friends. To better focus his body-building efforts, he submitted to a physical examination provided by the college. In nearly every way his body was approved by the physician, except for one glaring defect: a flat thorax! Remedies were referenced for him in a booklet, and whether or not he succeeded in adding some bulge to this area of his anatomy is a question left to other historians. He did help to organize a spring baseball game between his own Pierson Hall and White Hall. He wrote home, "Everyone has to be as poor a player as possible. . . . At present I am going to catch for the Pierson team" (James G. K. McClure, Jr. to Arch McClure, March 26, 1903). We will leave the gymnasium segment of Jim's Yale career with the admonition he received on the local regulations: "Attention is called to the following rules regarding lockers: Offensively soiled clothing must not be stored in the locker. The director will remove such clothing without notice."[6]

Academically, he averaged 2.50 his first term at Yale, an adequate but unimpressive score. In the spring, he developed a passion for the German language and at the same time made a friend of Joe Twichell, a devoted companion from that time on. He and Joe worked over the German together and made the effort to attend German language plays on campus. As a nation, Germany always fascinated Jim, so much so that he eventually studied at three German universities. It was a nation that was to thrust itself on his generation like no other. But despite this spark of interest, he wrote home that his second term scores would be worse if anything: "My dear Harriet: As to your questions I will reply as follows: 1st studies Very Poor, can't do very well this term. Started out poorly. Have been very busy with outside work. May get 2.35 if lucky." And to the eternal question, he replies: "Common food fair. Not starving." And as if to substantiate this fact, he adds, "Weight 149 lbs. last Friday" (James G. K. McClure, Jr. to Harriet McClure, May 13, 1902). Just how busy with outside work has he been?

> Monday afternoon I went out to the golf course and fooled around a little. In the evening I went out to Lake Whitney about ten o'clock with Joe Twichell. The moon was out and full and we got a canoe and paddled around. It was simply great. We are going out again tonight. (James G. K. McClure, Jr. to Harriet McClure, May 13, 1903)

> Monday six of us started out sailing about eight-thirty . . . We had a great time. We sailed down to the Thimble Islands where we got lunch and then started out again. The wind died down at half past two and we were becalmed until six. At six a strong wind sprang up and we arrived in port at eight o'clock. I had one of the best times I have ever had. (James G. K. McClure, Jr. to Phebe Ann Dixon McClure, June 3, 1903)

Good times evaporate into memory, but somehow those ancient tongues that bedeviled Jim so much forever loomed before him: "Thursday we had our Latin Examination. I think that I got through it all right" (James G. K. McClure, Jr. to Phebe Ann Dixon McClure, June 7, 1903). As our hero completes his freshman year, we see him as a fanatic sports fan, an endearing friend, a survivor of the ancient languages, and now out for the summer.

Along with obvious enjoyment of the entertainments at Yale, religion does appear to have been his central focus. Like his father he became a leader in his class in this sphere of college life. Before returning to Lake Forest, he attended the Northfield Conference. This was a prestigious annual gathering of student religious leaders from schools and colleges all over the Northeast. Bible classes, missionary projects, "Life Work meetings," and platform discussions all helped to bring out current topics of interest in the Christian community. There were also tennis courts, a river to swim in, and new friends to make. And even at a religious conference there were the inevitable pranks. Once the boys laid a trap for an irascible professor. They papered the walls of the hallway with flypaper, then shouted "Fire," and ran. Jim found himself charged up by this conference, and returned each year he was at Yale except his last, when a scheduling conflict prompted him and some others to organize a parallel gathering at a different time for those who could not attend Northfield.[7]

Jim McClure exercised his social conscience by helping with a local Boys' Club in New Haven that had just opened its doors. Teaching Sunday School there, he appears to have begun to try to break through the class barriers that separated him from so many Americans. One of his young charges wrote to him this touching but misspelled letter over the summer:

My dear James:

I received your letter Wensday . . . well Jemmie it is awful lonesome sence you went away all I do is to sit in my room and smoke my pipe and listen to the Katie did and katie didn't . . . be sure and write me long letters as I will be anxious to here from you.

Your Friend Patrick Cody.

(Patrick Cody to James G. K. McClure, Jr., June 31, 1903)

The Edwin Foote Boys' Club, with Jim's help, met with phenomenal success its first year. By December of 1903, a news article stated that it was "only ten months old and yet over 800 different boys have joined. . . . These working boys have contributed over two hundred dollars to meet the expenses of the club."[8]

Between the Northfield Conference and his last exam, Jim met his mother at Westerly, Rhode Island. For three generations the Dixons went to Washington to rule the nation, and naturally the habits of politics ran deeply in the family. A good portion of Jim's education took place around the dinner table in Westerly, where the great issues of the day were common talk, and where the talk itself was on the highest level. Pictures of the Dixon home give the impression of confident elegance. The position of the family was so well established in the community that any brash or pretentious additions would have been superfluous. A large, white clapboard structure enclosed an interior filled with a vast array of Victorian jumble. No corner was left unadorned, and no shelf or mantle left unladen with knick-knacks and objects of interest.

Jim had visited Westerly during the summers of his youth, and rather enjoyed a household oriented more toward pleasure than toward the Presbyterian Church. Trotting horses and a servant known as "Old Harry" were of special interest to Jim. The horses were an extravagant hobby of the Dixons. Old Harry was a black servant who resembled the faithful Southern house slave more than anything else. He and Jim were devoted friends, in the manner of an old man serving the family of the young man. One time, Jim and Harry decided to leave early to see the trotting races, and Jim wanted to be sure he woke up in time to get out of the house without waking anyone else up. He told Harry that there would be a string dangling down from his window, and early in the morning he was to yank it. Tying it to his toe, he dangled it out the window and went to bed. Early the next morning, Harry began to pull, and yank, and tug—and never let up. Jim was almost dragged from his bed, but managed to gain his balance in time to save his toe and to notify Harry that his efforts had been quite successful.[9]

Later in the summer of 1903, Jim enjoyed the pleasures of a resort in Oconto, Wisconsin. Several of his Yale friends were there, along with two lively young ladies, Helen and Martha. On the train back to Chicago, the two girls wrote Jim a crazy letter that appears to have been written by both girls at the same time, each alternating a sentence. The mood of the gathering can best be described by this correspondence: "At Oconto we needed a chaperon . . . I

NATHAN FELLOWS DIXON
OLD HOMESTEAD

was kept busy holding Martha from tackling the men who were making eyes at Helen. Martha is holding me, or the above would be erased . . . Helen's tears have soaked three handkerchiefs and has now begun on mine . . . Please try and think of us as being very grateful for having the best of good times . . ." (Helen ? and Martha ? to James G. K. McClure, Jr., August 13, 1903).

Two weeks before, Jim and his family helped to organize a picnic from the Lake Forest Sunday School that really does sound like fun. The usual games of the day, including sack races, lemon hunts, nail driving contests (for girls only!) and three-legged races, were successfully worked through, all culminating in a big baseball game. Dr. McClure played his old position of third base, while Jim pitched for the opposition. Jim's nine was reduced to eight almost immediately when Mr. Durand became "tired out in [the] first." In the fourth, Dr. McClure was injured, surely costing his team the game as Jim's pitching maintained the 4–3 win.[10] Jim had a naturally cheerful disposition, and there were few discordant notes to mar his college summers with family and friends.

Back at Yale in the fall, Jim proudly reported home that he had been elected class deacon, a position of great respect. "My dear boy:" his father wrote,

> I do not believe any word from Yale could have brought me more joy than the word of your election as a class deacon . . . As I look back on my own days in College it seems to me nothing tended to steady me and make me careful of my example and influences more than my sense of responsibility as a class deacon.
>
> I think the fellows look for a high type of life in their deacons, and however much they may joke about them, the fellows wish their deacons to be men whom they thoroughly respect. While preserving an attractive demeanor it is better for the deacons to err on the side of consistency rather than on the side of inconsistency. (James G. K. McClure, Sr., to James G. K. McClure, Jr., October 26, 1903)

Respect, though a cruder version, was also part of Deacon McClure's initiation into the Junior Society Psi Upsilon Beta. As described by the college press corps, the story ran:

> Junior Society Fun: How the Neophytes are
> Made to Recognize Their Humble Station
>
> . . ."Fagging" services are required of the candidates. This is a late revival of an ancient custom. Each man has a master to whom he is appointed for a certain period between his pledging and his initiation . . . He must wake him at a stated hour, prepare his bath, bring each morning a fresh boutonniere, his mail and his breakfast, if need be. He must walk behind his master in the rounds of the Campus, keeping a respectful four paces in the rear.
>
> There are other things the candidate for election must do. He may have,

Opposite, top: Dixon Home, Westerly, R.I. Opposite, bottom: *Old Harry*

perhaps, literary aspirations. In that case he may be asked to deliver an oration to the moon and in the highest flights of imagination he is interrupted with deprecatory remarks reflecting on his ability on all points, his truth and sanity. Passersby are frequently in doubt about the latter and have been known to take another street to avoid what seemed to them a real madman. Another trial for a literary candidate is to have him embrace a tree or post and murmur words of deep affection, while instructions such as these are shot at him from his tormentors. "Louder," "Take off that smile and stick it on the tree," . . . Soon the unfortunate man is shouting endearments to his wooden friend.[11]

Skits and short plays were a specialty of these "literary" societies, and during initiation week impromptu productions could be seen all over the campus. Jim saved for posterity a collection of instructions such as "Candidate McClure will be at 172 Farnum Hall at 8:40 3/4 p.m. . . . Do not reveal these instructions."[12] In the end, tormentors and tormented alike gathered for an initiation banquet that was held in the Hall of Beta, amidst Broiled Squab, Filet of Beef, Bisque Tortini and Cigars. Officially, the miserable life of the "fag" was over, and following dinner he was royally entertained by the older club members in dramatic productions such as *Beatrice, the Bovine* (A Bucolic, The Milky Way, In Two Tits and a Tatter). Jim was mentioned in the elaborate program as part of an "Entirely New Troup, Imported at Great Expense" that will next season present *Three Little Jades.*[13]

But if the absurd was given its hour upon the stage, most of the weeks and months were given to Latin and Greek. But Jim began to veer away from the slavery of the ancient texts, and to search out in academic nooks and crannies more up-to-date and scientific studies. Science, and its remarkable success as a method of discerning the workings of the world, had already drawn Jim very closely into its orbit. Much of his optimism about the future of the human condition, which was a distinguishing characteristic of his thinking, emanated from a strong faith in the ability of science to solve once and for all the problems that created strife among mankind.

Increasingly, Jim took courses in the social science department. Economics, the American Social Condition and Nineteenth Century Communities were all subjects a young progressive would find vital. He had a faith that the social scientists were on the brink of discovering how to "inoculate" society in order to eliminate human poverty. If the riddle of smallpox could be unraveled, why not the disease of hopelessness?

Slowly through time, Jim reconciled his faith in science and his faith in Christianity. He became a practitioner of the Social Gospel, a movement led by Walter Rauschenbusch, who preached the Holy Word as a means to bring about the salvation of society. In Rauschenbusch's vision, the minister was comparable to the medical doctor in his battle against physical ailments, except that the minister's goal was a healthy community. Public health, education, settlement houses, the fight to clean up crooked politics, YMCA's, and Boys' Clubs all became legitimate realms for the minister. At Yale, these ideas were still in their germination stage for Jim. His struggle with these two faiths is a fascinating dynamic that is the proper subject of his seminary years, yet it should be noted that as far back as his college days he was searching for a scientific base in the social science departments for his spiritual prompting.

As a part of the Yale religious community, he was given opportunities to speak before a variety of gatherings. "COMING: TWO YALE STUDENTS! Messrs. Banks and McClure . . . To address Young Men of New Britain, at YMCA Hall . . . General subject 'Standards and Tests.' A unique meeting for men only."[14] "Young Peoples Meeting, in observance of the Day of Prayer for Students. Address by James G. K. McClure, Jr. and Joseph H. Twichell of Yale College. . . ."[15] One of his speeches remains from this period of his life, and in it can be discerned an immature expression of the ideals he pursued throughout his life. Before the Yale YMCA he proposed:

> To show that men can live and do live at college a Christian life. To show that it is the only way to live here at school . . . We will only live once and now is the time to live an upright Christian life . . . Mr. X was living a careless, thoughtless life. Mr. Y had a purpose, a great desire to better mankind, he was filled with love . . . [U]nless we lead a Christian life, we will fail in the hour of trial. So let us be men, face the questions squarely, not be afraid of the man in the looking glass [remember him?] and live up to our best ideals. Let us strive to be like Christ-to love as he did . . . But what shall our ideals be? That is a question that puzzles man but it should not—Let's go back to first principles. Our ideals should be Christ. Now Christ is love. Therefore our ideals should be perfect love . . .
>
> We will take for instance the matter of drinking and see how this perfect love ideal would answer such a question. I want to drink and I say, can I drink in perfect love to my fellow man? If I drink a little will I cause another, a friend to stumble and fall? Is there danger of my drinking causing suffering anywhere? Reasonably I can't drink with the ideal of perfect love.[16]

On this final point, he joined up with a long line of his McClure forebears, and refused throughout his life to yield to the temptations of strong drink.

Jim McClure was never a mean-spirited fanatic, however. Like his father, he took a strong stand against alcohol but did not condemn or embarrass friends who used alcohol in moderation. He always enjoyed a party and the Helens and the Marthas adored him. He escorted Joe Twichell's sister Louise to his own class's Junior Prom. His dance card was full, forty-one dances in a row, alternating between the two-step and the waltz. During his summer at home, he had struck up a strong friendship with one of the several Elizabeths in his life. She was a spicy girl, and addressed a letter after the summer was over to "Simple Life McClure," an obvious jibe at the discussions the two of them had had about their personal aspirations.

> When you read this you will be rolling swiftly away from-shall I say "Home and Mother?" Don't forget "the girl you left behind you" nor how to make the

happy moments fly when we are together. It's an art any girl will appreciate and one which you have to almost as great degree as Louis [Douseman, Jim's friend and Yale classmate.] Perhaps if you see a great deal of him this winter you will catch on to his methods ... Don't do anything rash in the Helen Boyce line or the Louise Twichell region or the Nellie Lake direction until I reach the East so that I can bait fairly ... for you ... Also don't pick up any stray chickens but turn up in New York to greet me with some real sensible hen, a nice, old one ... I will announce my arrival in New York in some way or other and then I shall expect an immediate and insistent descent and that right early too.

I hope you have a pleasant journey, a corking trip (I am *so* glad there is no girl there to read aloud, drive and fish with you), a wonderful year and that you won't forget me or that I love you in the same old way. I am yours sincerely, Elizabeth manager general.

To heighten the mystery, she scrawls in the note. "I hope you can read between the lines as there is more to this than I dare say" (Elizabeth Waller to James G. K. McClure, Jr., no date).

Jim's remaining college years contained more of the patterns he had already established. He flourished in the Beta Club gag shows. His soft-looking face made him a natural for those dramatic parts hardest to manage at Yale in those days, the female ones. He pranced about on stage as "Sidewalk Sadie—The Swash of the Sewer," and in a photograph of the Beta Club members, he is found with some difficulty perched on the lap of a fellow member (next to another dressed as a gorilla), as pretty a belle as fashions of the period allowed.[17] (These fashions, quite cumbersome by modern standards, did a superb job of losing a male physique inside numerous folds and ruffles.) Glee club concerts, baseball games, summer trips to the lakes of Wisconsin and the Spring Regatta were only part of his normal round of activities.

Jim was sent as a member of the Yale religious community on a tour of boarding schools, in order to "Inform the boys about all phases of college life" and to "Attract them to the Christian life." He was given strict written instructions that included these admonitions: "Give a talk describing Yale life. *Emphasize the opportunities*...Get together informally the boys who are coming to Yale and let them ask questions ... This isn't a fussing tour ... so don't spend too much time in the company of the principal's daughter or anybody else's daughters. You're after the boys and ought to spend the time with them."[18]

On one such trip in 1905, he went to Washington, D. C. to see the inauguration of Theodore Roosevelt and then the next day spoke to the Quaker students of Haverford College. His theme was " ... to show [that] manly men can live [a] Christian life":

I want to talk to you today ... about the tests in our lives and the way to come out of them triumphant. Life is a series of tests.

... I want to tell you of two men who were in [the Iroquois Theatre fire in Chicago] ... One was a man of some sixty years. He escaped. A friend saw him the next day and congratulated him but he wanted no congratulations, he was absolutely ashamed of himself, had lost all his self-esteem. He thought that in his sixty years he had built up within himself a respect for women and helpless children that would have kept him from trampling down and pushing back helpless ones, as he must have done to escape. There was no more pleasure in life for that man . . .

There was another man at the fire who saw an exit which had two stairs leading up to it . . . He stationed himself beside it and handed out woman after woman, child after child. The fireman outside could see him helping them out, his clothes and hair aflame. Then he fell and somehow . . . he was gotten out . . . Think of the difference in the way these two men met their tests.[19]

Does Jim's speech sound simplistic? Do his examples of heroism smack of a morality melodrama, a Victorian tear jerker? Remember first of all that Jim is a college student, young and with a relatively limited experience. But more to the point, the sophistication of our own times has become a smoke screen. The smoke distorts moral questions by exposing their complexity without even asking, but what is right? This is a tendency to consider heroism passé, and mixed motives are assumed to be behind the purest of good deeds. Self-denial is perceived as limiting personal freedom, or worse, a repression that may cause, when one least expects it, an ugly psychological reaction. To pass off Jim's thoughts as naive, not the stuff of reality, is to deny the heroic possibilities of mankind. Sophistication is too often synonymous with cynicism. Jim spent his life searching for corruption; he wore no rose-colored glasses. Wrongdoers were meted out swift punishment when it was in his power to do so. And yet, he maintained his dream that, given encouragement and right understanding, and given the possibilities of the human will, everyone could raise himself or herself above the sinful state of the world.

If Jim *thought* life was a series of tests, he *knew* that college was. Daily recitation followed, in theory, daily preparation. For our hero, such a rule remained all too often in the realm of theory. He saved and carefully pasted into his scrapbook a collection of incriminating cards that circulated regularly from the Dean's office to Jim's mailbox. "Your work for the first term of Junior year was not satisfactory in Archeology, Rhetoric, English, Physics. Your attention is called to the rule, in accordance with which a student cannot be enrolled in the Senior class until he has satisfactorily completed 41 hours of class-room work."[20] "Your allowance of absences for the term was exhausted on Feb. 28. Since then you have been reported absent as follows: Soc. Sci., Feb. 28, Soc. Sci, Mar. 1, English Mar. 12, Soc. Sci March 12 . . . [the list goes on]. Over cuts involve failures. If you know any reason why the penalty should not apply to the above, please explain it promptly."[21] There seemed to be little self-discipline in Jim's own pursuit of knowledge at Yale, and how he came out unscathed is not known.

Horace Ferry, his freshman roommate and close friend from Lake Forest, telegraphed this mysterious message to Jim's father: "Jim tapped for Bones

DEAN'S OFFICE,
Yale College.

January, 10, 1905.

Your work for the first term of Junior year was not satisfactory

in Archaeology B3 (125) Rhetoric B2 (220)

English B10 (220)

Physics A1 (205)

*Your attention is called to the rule, in accordance with which a
student cannot be enrolled in the Senior class until he has satisfactorily completed 41 hours of class-room work.*

Truly yours,

Mr. McClure   WILLIAM MILTON HESS.

Dean's office card.

Congratulations."[22] Skull and Bones is the most prestigious of Yale University's
secret societies. Rituals, codes, special handshakes and oaths are unfailingly
honored by its members. Each initiate swears devotion to members past and
present, one of whom was Jim's father. Exactly who belongs to Skull and Bones
is held in strict confidence. The club meets in an eerie building in New Haven
with no windows. There were fifteen members of "Bones" in the class of 1906.
Jim considered his election to Skull and Bones one of the greatest honors of his
Yale years. He wrote in his diary, "Who would have ever thought I would have
been included among Yale's strongest men."[23]

Many of Jim's classmates maintained an exciting and expensive social life.
Jim did his best to keep up, and thoroughly enjoyed the round of weekend house
parties to which he was invited. If he missed a lot of classes, he also spent a lot
of money, and on this last point he touched one of his father's very few sore
points.

> My dear son:
> I hope your Norwich trip was happy and profitable, and I hope your boils
> are gone . . . I . . . enclose a New York draft for $150.00. I am unable to send
> you more at this time. It is only by being as careful as I can be, of every little
> expense in the way of a car fare or an extra paper, that I have been able to
> provide for my children as I have. This draft makes the amount I have handed
> you since Sept. 1, 1905 [7 months] $1163.50.

*Beta Club Photograph. Jim McClure can be found on the bottom right, sitting on a young
man's lap between the gorilla and the policeman.*

> . . . Unless you have pledged yourself to go to George Miller's this summer,
> I suggest you do not go. It really seems to me that it would be better for the
> fellows themselves if they called a halt to this running around. It is not fair to
> you—for it tends to develop thoughtlessness that may be akin to selfishness.
> (James G. K. McClure, Sr. to James G. K. McClure, Jr., March 23, 1906)

But it must be admitted that one trip would have had the approval of his
father. Jim was in charge of organizing all Yale men interested in going into the
ministry, and taking them to Hartford for a conference whose purpose was "To
present to those college men who are now deciding upon their life work, definite
and reliable information concerning the opportunities and work of the Christian
Ministry in this country."[24] Horace Ferry and Joe Twichell both went along.
Among the many speakers was the President of Princeton University, Woodrow
Wilson. Jim's father was a personal friend of Wilson's, and on at least one
occasion stayed in his home. Ironically, three weeks later, Jim brushed with
another future presidential candidate, the man who opposed Wilson in 1912.
Helen Hadley, the Yale President's wife, asked Jim "to be one of our ushers"
when Secretary of War William Howard Taft arrived to give a series of lectures
on campus.[25]

Before going to Hartford, Jim had decided to enter the ministry. It was a
natural decision arising out of his interests at Yale, his respect for his father,
and the McClure's Covenanter heritage. Jim's father, after reading his letter of
decision, mailed back a carefully composed message touching on thoughts that
were very much on his son's mind.

> First, I believe you can do and will do fine service in the ministry if you
> give yourself to it. Men like you are eminently needed—never more needed
> than now. The very fact of your going into the ministry will do good. It will
> encourage men like myself: it will point the way to oncoming boys and college
> fellows to do as you have done.
> The work of the ministry is so varied that in one way or in another I feel
> you will help the world very much.
> I do not say that the ministry is easy. It is not easy: it is difficult, very
> difficult. That is one reason why I think it should appeal to a man: it is a
> summons to his heroism. (James G. K. McClure, Sr. to James G. K. McClure,
> Jr., March 23, 1906)

Heroism is exactly the quality that attracted Jim into the ministry, and he
meant to give himself up to the Christian work that was the most taxing. The
young man, after four years of a plush Yale education, after sixteen years of
privileged suburban life in Lake Forest, wanted to devote the rest of his life to
mission work in China. Many an idealistic young man of this generation had the
same impulse. Rudyard Kipling and his white man's burden seemed reasonable
to the Western world before it was saturated with talk of the Third World and
imperialism, and surely the Peace Corps, albeit a more secular approach, is
guided by a similar missionary spirit.

Back in 1906, Protestant nations giddy with the sense of power and accomplishment were scrambling to collect parts of Asia and Africa like so many stamps. The heroes in this complex pr̶̶ ̶̶s seen from home, were the missionaries. Forsaking all the fruit̶ ̶gress in the Western world, they were seen as sacrificing their lives to teach a solid base of Christianity to people whose local beliefs had left them in cultural bondage. In fact, the missionaries were the cutting edge of a powerful Western European and American culture whose very success muted criticism. Missionaries were as varied as the myriad of Christian denominations and individual personalities they represented. Not only did they bring a new religion and culture to the four corners of the earth, they also brought back to their churches and missionary societies vivid reports of the foreign lands where they worked. The remarkable volume of cross cultural flow that occurred was unprecedented in the history of the world, and one has only to remember young James' church group, Steady Streams, and its hundred of thousands of counterparts to conceive of the impact that was felt. In any event, this comfortable world of Western domination began to fray at the edges early in the twentieth century. Woodrow Wilson himself, by including national self-determination as one of his Fourteen Points to end World War I, detonated the explosives that destroyed the basis of European colonialism.

Certainly genuine idealism was at work in the minds of many young Americans when Jim McClure was attending Yale. China and the life of a missionary were topics of discussion at nearly every conference and religious meeting he attended. He knew several people who went to China. For example, a college friend, John Magee from Pittsburgh, experienced a remarkable conversion as he walked down the corridor to his room. He was struck as by lightning, like St. Paul, and from that moment he determined to go into the ministry, and then to China.

As an undergraduate Jim corresponded with Warren B. Seabury, who had already graduated and was in the Chinese mission field. His letters came to Jim during his senior year and clearly had an impact on the young man's thinking. Mr. Seabury gave Jim an unheroic, somewhat homesick, but provocative picture of his role in China. "My dear Jim:" one letter began, "Can you stand a drip from an old missionary friend tonight? Brace up, it won't hurt long." These communications gave Jim, and also give us, an idea of the rewards of missionary work and an insight into the missionary's drive.

> . . . I returned last night from a trip up into the country with a mighty good friend of mine . . . Well this friend of mine although an Episcopalian is very human! He is one of the wittiest and drollest men I ever knew. We went up the Han River from which Hankow is named and . . . The more I see of these native cities the worse I think they are. People who have been in China always talk about the smells until you are tempted to think it more or less of a joke, But actually the odors from open drains, dirty corners, stale meat-shops, boiling fat, Chinese dye (one of the worst known to science!), "tonsorial parlors" etc., etc. is a rank catalogue of impossibilities! At the first you find

these cities interesting and novel but soon the novelty wears off and you take a full breath when you come out . . .

A good part of the morning we pushed along on the puffy little streamer . . . A village street is as Chinese as a city street, but it is if anything darker and meaner, rougher and more uneven. Up and down steps you have to go with houses above and below you. The mission hall was not large and Episcopal looking at all. Rude benches, horses such as carpenters use were all we had to sit on . . . We wanted to be alone but our Chinese hosts conceived it their duty to escort us and regarded our earnest protestations as only polite phrases . . . You notice two things in almost all your travels in typical China. One is that there are very few nice little nooks, a bunch of trees, a brook, a shady pasture. The trees are cut down; the brooks are dug out . . . for irrigation purposes; the pastures are grave yards on high land and fields for crops in lower land. Everything about you looks used for something. Another thing you noted sooner is that China is a very populous country for there seems to be no getting away from them. Chinese, Chinese everywhere. You sit down and they gather about you to ask you questions and discuss you but always to stare. A missionary over in Hankow said that his first idea of eternity came from a Chinese stare!

. . . I do really think that there is lots of room for men who see that they are not like other men, who feel that they are not pious and gentle souls, but who want to chip in somewhere and help. It is not only the natives with whom we must deal. There are plenty of foreigners here with whom much is to be done. And it seems to me that all the health and ability of body, all the social grace, all the mental vigour and breadth and all the spiritual desire . . . ruling a man in his devotion to the progressively revealed will of God can find no better field for exercise than China . . . The best things we do are done by bravely entering open doors. (Warren Seabury to James G. K. McClure, Jr., October 10, 1905)

. . . In your last letter you speak of the possibility of being a missionary. I had not known how you stood on the question although I had reason to think that you and your friends were considering the thing with care. It is a big question and no one can settle it for any one else. At Northfield and at New Haven one hears a great deal of argument and . . . if he is in earnest he studies it very carefully . . . He would like to know the joys of real missionary life as they really are but he would also give much to get a fair view of the trying features of life in these lands. I am going to mention a few of these harder features of life in China.

How would you like to live in a city of narrow crowded streets as all the Chinese streets are? Every time you go out people on every hand stop and gaze at you. If you enter a shop or stop to talk with anyone a crowd of curious, ignorant looking people gather about you asking you questions, feeling of your clothes and making remarks about you as if you were an inmate of the zoo . . .

How would you like to live among a people who are not trustworthy and not appreciative? . . . They do not tell the truth. They do not believe in each other. They don't trust you and they don't want you here . . . You are their guest but you are not a welcome one and you have to watch in every purchase . . . that they don't get away with two or three times as much as they have earned . . .

I will come closer home. How would you like to work in a mission with

whose members you are not in sympathy? They are older, they are very
conservative, they want you to do just as they irregardless of your tendencies
. . . There are those who come from different levels of society, coarse men
and women, critical, outspoken, ill natured perhaps . . . Upon you, the new
man, a lot of the work is placed which you regard as too much. . . . They might
be jealous of your ability or injured by what they regard as your feelings of
superiority.
    . . . Jim this may all sound pretty hard. You will find noble exceptions to
all of them. (Warren Seabury to James G. K. McClure, Jr., November 26,
1905)

The thoughts of Jim McClure were with Warren Seabury, and as graduation
approached China weighed heavily on his mind. Certainly Jim was no academic,
but he did graduate on time. Yale honored his father on the same day, awarding
him the degree of Doctor of Divinity. His sister Harriet came to dance with his
friends at the Senior Prom. It was a joyous and happy moment; songs such as
"Bright College Years" were belted out by the Class of '06. Others must have
grated a bit on the McClure ear, but were none the less part of the festivities of
these final days. Is it possible Jim Sr. and Jr. joined in enthusiastically on the
likes of "Here's to good old Yale, Drink her down" and "My comrades, when
I am No More Drinking?"[26] The class poem was written and read by James
Wallis of Dubuque, Iowa, who compared Yale to Camelot and his fellow classmates to young knights.

> But there is greater work
> We yet shall do, for we shall travel far, . . .
> To give the good here molded into us
> To needy places where we shall set up
> New Camelots.[27]

Even if the meter was heavy, in Jim's case the sentiments of Mr. Wallis were
truly prophetic. The class orator was Jim's close friend and fellow Bones member, Lee Perrin. In his commencement speech he said: "We are born to an
heritage of privilege and responsibility, an heritage which we may altogether
accept or decline . . . For our common foster-parent Society . . . requires where
she gives; and it will not answer that we have our talents laid up in a napkin."[28]

    That foster parent had given richly to those young men, and no one was
more keenly aware of this truth than Jim McClure. His father, now the president
of McCormick Theological Seminary, advised his son to put off China for three
years. He wrote:

> It may be that the very best thing you could do would be to come right here,
> take a room in one of the Seminary buildings, have your meals either at home
> or in a club and let us feel your presence and your aid . . . At the end of the
> year you would know clearly whether you desired to continue your studies for
> the ministry or not.
>   Of course this would involve . . . the surrender of many social opportuni-

ties. A man cannot do his professional study well and keep up a round of social
engagements at the same time. But I believe you would be happy. In due time
you would be interested and contented . . .

I love you very dearly, my boy—I do not mean to lean upon you too
heavily. (James G. K. McClure, Sr. to James G. K. McClure, Jr., March 23,
1906)

After graduation Jim was in charge of organizing a Yale Summer Conference at the Hotchkiss School, because the Northfield conference was scheduled
in conflict with activities in New Haven. Afterwards he was off to the St.
Lawrence River to join his Skull and Bones friends on Deer Island. One last
fling with his closest of comrades, and the Yale years were complete. He sailed
to Chicago with Louis Douseman on the steamship Northland.[29]

The summer of 1906 was a social feast for Jim, a final chance to gorge
before, if he followed his father's advice, his seminary studies would force him
to slim down his list of engagements. Chicago's North Shore during the summer
featured a spectacular series of fairs, with each community vying to outdo the
next. Lake Forest brought in American sharp-shooters and Japanese contortion-
ists for an open air vaudeville show. But it was in the town of Oconomowoc,
Wisconsin, that in 1906 the Chicago society crowd was most dazzled. A news
article reported that when it was over, " . . . the women who had toiled hard for
the success of the event . . . drew a long breath, and asked each other, 'Was it
better than Lake Geneva?' "[30]

One of these sighing ladies was a Mrs. J. H. Eckels, who had invited Jim
to be a house guest during the fête. She filled her large and splendid house that
weekend with privileged young people. Her daughter Phebe, along with a
friend, Charlotte Partridge, appear to have garnered the most attention. Jim
enticed Charlotte into a photography booth long enough to snap a souvenir
picture of the two of them staring intently into one another's eyes.[31] At the fête,
Mrs. Eckel's exhibit was an elaborate stage show known as the French Amusement Hall. Jim took turns as barker, a role for which he had a natural gift. For
his efforts he was awarded a card that read, "Jim McClure (The Handy Dandy
Man). And he Barked where ever he went (the Dog)."[32] His pitch went something like this: "Step right up, ladies and gents, and see the prize fight of the
century. Inside, the French Amusement Hall proudly presents an entire troup
of midgets, preparing this very minute to box for your entertainment." Or else,
"See the saucy Salvaggi five, who will bring to your unbelieving eyes an
acrobatic orgy that will confound the forces of gravity."[33] At heart, Jim McClure
was a showman, a promoter. Nothing could fire his vital forces more than a
crowd needing to be entertained.

This Oconomowoc Fair was a reflection of the vast wealth being made in
Chicago at the turn of the century, and the good ladies who worried lest the
town of Lake Geneva surpass them flaunted this fact. It was tagged the Billion
Dollar Carnival, because the net assets of the twenty families who backed it

supposedly exceeded that figure. A Chicago newspaper gloated, "never before in the west has so much wealth been represented in an outdoor entertainment."[34] A Mrs. Valentine spent $5,000 to build a German village that included an exact replica of an old Rhine River beer garden.[35] And yet, mirroring the rapid shift in the local economy, there were also awards for the best white onions, beets, potatoes and corn. Undoubtedly, Jim enjoyed it all, despite the conspicuous consumption and display of wealth. The $5,000 could have helped so many suffering people in China, or in Chicago for that matter. He was caught up in a world in which he was losing faith, and in due time this conflict would make a strong mark on Jim McClure's outlook. But to the residents of Oconomowoc, Wisconsin that summer of 1906, the burning question remained, was their fair really better than the one in Lake Geneva? The society editors in Chicago all agreed, "It was the special success of the summer . . ."[36]

Jim had every right, in that same summer of 1906, to feel that his own prospects promised a "special success." He had avoided (barely) burying his talents in the Panhandle of Texas, and Yale University had indeed offered him a great deal. He had thrived within the religious community. Everyone liked him, not least of all the young ladies. He enjoyed the friendship of the sons of the powerful families who attended Yale. He had been asked to join a small and select group, Skull and Bones, an honor that his father shared. The past and future members of this society had a continuing constructive influence in American Society. Years later many of them would help Jim finance his work for the mountain people of North Carolina. In his heart he was sure that idealism would yield the real treasurers of personal satisfaction, and time would show that this notion was right, but not before he endured a great personal struggle. After Yale and the festivities of summer, a period of austerity set in, and a gloom began to hang over his life that was not fully dispelled until after his marriage. He began this phase of his life in Scotland, the home of his ancestors, during the long nights of that country's dreary winter.

1. Scrapbook of Yale memorabilia made by James G. K. McClure, Jr.
2. Interviews with Elspeth McClure Clarke.
3. Yale Scrapbook.
4. Yale College Book of Rules, in the Yale scrapbook.
5. Yale Scrapbook.
6. Yale Scrapbook.
7. Yale Scrapbook.
8. Yale Scrapbook.
9. Interviews with Elspeth McClure Clarke.
10. Yale Scrapbook
11. Article in Yale Scrapbook.
12. Yale Scrapbook.
13. Yale Scrapbook.
14. Yale Scrapbook, March 13, 1904.

15. Yale Scrapbook, February 14, 1904.
16. Address by James G. K. McClure, Jr., to the Yale YMCA< no known date.
17. Yale Scrapbook.
18. Yale Scrapbook.
19. Speech made by James G. K. McClure, Jr., at Haverford Pa., March 5, 1905.
20. Yale Scrapbook.
21. Yale Scrapbook.
22. Telegram to Rev. and Mrs. McClure from Horace Ferry, no date.
23. James G. K. McClure, Jr. in his Berlin notebook, 1909.
24. Yale Scrapbook.
25. Yale Scrapbook.
26. Yale Scrapbook.
27. Yale Scrapbook.
28. Yale Scrapbook.
29. Yale Scrapbook, several photographs.
30. Yale Scrapbook, newspaper clipping, paper and date unknown.
31. Yale Scrapbook.
32. Yale Scrapbook.
33. Chicago *Evening American,* August 4, 1906.
34. *Ibid.*
35. *Ibid.*
36. *Ibid.*

Chapter Five

Europe: Edinburgh and Tübingen

> Well James my boy, you are about to start across the briny deep to take up
> the more serious forms of life and I only hope you find it as fine as you expect
> and the vocation just suited to you. (*Louis Douseman to James G. K. McClure
> Jr., October 2, 1906*)

The home to which Jim returned in the summer of 1906 was not the familiar
manse in prosperous, safe Lake Forest. His father, as president of McCormick
Seminary, now lived on Halsted Street, the border of Chicago's Little Italy.
Their home was not far from Jane Addams' pioneer urban settlement project,
Hull House. She had opened Hull House seventeen years before as a challenge
to all Christians " . . . to share the lives of the poor [and] express the spirit of
Christ." Jim's new surroundings must have reinforced the powerful pull he felt
toward meeting the needs of the less fortunate. Already he was questioning the
smug and class-ridden Victorian church, which appeared to him to dodge its
duties in an industrial climate bearing the ripe fruit of hate and violence. With
broad strokes, he began to rough in a mental picture of a reactionary religion
bent on maintaining the *status quo*, while feeding the oppressed a thin diet of
repentance, ladled out with large portions of bourgeois morality.

The plight of the American laboring class dwelt heavily on Jim's conscience. He often imagined himself denying his own position of privilege. These
attitudes led him inexorably into the political camp of Progressivism, a body of
opinion that encompassed a wide range of reform ideas that began to dominate
the American political and intellectual scene during these years. Republican
Theodore Roosevelt became the most visible leader of the movement. Indeed,
1906 was the beginning of the era of the "muckraker," a term coined by
Roosevelt. A muckraker was a journalist who was prone to explicit exposure
of corporate or political evils, and wrote in a style designed to create a wave of
moral outrage. The year Jim graduated from Yale, Upton Sinclair published his
book *The Jungle,* which spoiled an entire nation's taste for packaged meat by
portraying with graphic detail some of the common practices of the processing
plants of Chicago. Sinclair set the style, and following his lead exposes began
rolling off American printing presses. This intellectual climate of moral outrage
shaped Jim's impressions of politics and capitalism. Part of a new generation
rejected the dying spirit of the Gospel of Wealth for the hope of Progressivism.
While an older generation might still extol the pluck of Horatio Alger, the

favorite author of a series of success stories for boys, their sons and daughters began to question the smug theories of Social Darwinism and its proclamations about the "survival of the fittest" in a competitive society. The Progressives envisioned a new role for government, that of protector of the powerless and underprivileged. Laissez-faire politics came under heavy attack. "Trust-busting," political reform, concern for the rights of the working man, and even consumer protection came to life with the leadership of Theodore Roosevelt. In short, the Progressives believed that American government ought to purge itself of corruption in order to become a fair arbiter between the various power centers of a new industrial society.

But even while these new ideas were forming the outline of a value structure for Jim McClure, he could not resist the pleasures available to a young man of his position. The summer of 1906 was a string of grand parties and romance all along the North Shore. Perhaps he knew himself well enough to guess that for him to remain in Chicago at this time would prove disastrous to his growing sense of serious purpose. He decided not to enroll at McCormick Seminary that fall, but accepted instead a generous offer from Mrs. Cyrus McCormick, the inheritor of the vast reaper fortune and a member of his father's congregation. She offered to pay his way to Scotland, ancestral home of the McClures (and McCormicks!), so that he could study at New College, the theological school of the University of Edinburgh. Nothing could have appealed to "Madame" McCormick more than to send her beloved minister's young son back to his Presbyterian homeland to prepare for the ministry.

Jim left for Scotland by way of New England in the fall of 1906, accompanied by his two younger brothers, Nathan and Arch. They were keenly interested in all the stories and pranks of Jim's Yale years. They were interested as well in his decision to enter the ministry, in his theological views, in everything he said and did. The love within this family was never more evident than during these weeks before his departure for Scotland. In Boston they watched their White Sox fall to the Red Sox. In Westerly, they were embraced by the Dixons. Perhaps it was there that their father caught up with the three of them. He reclaimed the two younger sons, and later reported back to Jim:

> My dear boy:
> As soon as Nathan and Arch got out of your sight, Nathan pulled his hat over his eyes—to conceal his tears, and both he and Arch wept silently. I am lonely without you. The more you are with me the quieter we are together, the stronger I feel. I commit you to God . . . I have been up in your room and thought of you. (James G. K. McClure, Sr. to James G. K. McClure, Jr., September 22, 1906)

Several days later, he wrote again to Jim:

> Paul said to Timothy, whom he called "my beloved child," "I thank God, whom I serve from my forefathers in a pure conscience, how increasing is

my remembrance of thee . . . Suffer hardship with me as a good soldier of Christ Jesus." So I say to you. When I wake at night, I will think of you: when I do my daily work I will likewise think of you . . . You and I have many ties together. Yale is one, and Bones is another and now we may look forward to another . . . Every morning and every night your name will be on my lips before the throne of Grace. (James G. K. McClure, Sr. to James G. K. McClure, Jr., October 3, 1906)

From his mother came a package with pajamas and slippers " . . . and Annie sends the paper and envelopes . . ." (She had graduated from Wellesley and was helping her father as secretary). Every member of Jim's family sent an expression to him of his or her love. There was a feeling that Jim's status with them had changed; he was now severing his ties with them, leading the way for the others into the adult world.

These family love offerings arrived for Jim in Norwich, Connecticut, where he had gone to usher in the wedding of his Bones comrade, Grosvenor Ely. Both of Grove's parents had died, leaving him an enormous house and plenty of endowment. The wedding was one of those occasions Jim absolutely adored. There were all his friends, and an opportunity for frivolous entertainments that he more often than not devised. For his services as an usher, Jim received a wooden cane topped with a gold snake head. The night before the ceremony, the bachelor's party spilled out into New Haven, and the young graduates toured about "the upper part of town singing glees."[1] Louis Douseman had been unable to leave Wisconsin to come East and writes to Jim with obvious envy. Louis described the disillusionment he felt on returning home and trying to deal with his family's neighbors. Class divisions haunted America, and for Jim, having just participated in his friend's wedding, Louis's words must have made him pause and wonder about what illusions he himself might have to shed.

I have changed my ideas about things considerable since my home coming, as you are bound to do, and it isn't all such a cinch as I had hoped for as the ways of man [aren't] as noble as my acquaintance in the past has led me to expect . . . You ought to see me attending meetings of the Town Board on roads and surrounded by farmers, who have it in for me, as I force them to give up some of their old habits of making public thoroughfares of our land. It is rare sport but I almost had a fight at our last session—They surely are a dullheaded bunch who have to be taught a lesson sooner or later. (Louis Douseman to James G. K. McClure, Jr., October 2, 1906)

As the "knights" of Yale '06 returned home, anxious to recreate Camelot, contact with real people struggling to survive in a difficult world rapidly eroded their college ideals, bringing out the old defensive and snobbish instincts of class. Jim McClure had yet to be tested, but it would be the mark of the man throughout his life that he sought to maintain the Christian ideals of both his upbringing and his choosing. He learned to empathize with people of all layers and conditions of society. He considered it a human tragedy when a man left the high road of idealism to pursue a life of cynicism.

On October 6, 1906, Jim left the United States as a First Cabin Passenger on the steamer Columbia. He was sent off with a batch of telegrams from his family, friends and romantic interests (the last group skirmishing a bit over whose special friend he was!). Just before sailing, he squeezed in an automobile race on Long Island, the Third Annual International Competition for the William K. Vanderbilt, Jr. Cup, quite something to see in 1906. So our hero left this country, quite independent and with the spirit of great adventure. Great Britain in 1906 ruled much of the world, and was the cultural foundation for the English-speaking world. By comparison, Chicago was considered a crass metropolis somewhere west of New York, buried in the provincial hinterland of the United States.

The New College of Edinburgh was a very demanding theological institution. Enrolled there were some of the finest young minds of the Presbyterian Church, having endured a rigorous curriculum in order to earn the privilege of attendance. Jim's academic record was mediocre; he had concentrated on friends and fun. His grasp of Greek and Latin, World History, Literature, Philosophy and the rest was thin and confused. He had been preceded at the New College by another Bones man, Henry Sloane Coffin, who was destined to become one of the most influential men of his generation. Jim wrote to Mr. Coffin for advice, and received in return a list of his friends in Edinburgh and some kind encouragement. He was also preceded by his father's reputation as a leader in the American church.

On arrival he was greeted by the distinguished New College theologian, Marcus Dods, who knew and admired his father. He spent several days as a guest of the Dods family before settling into a room. By this time Jim was beginning to realize that his personal charm gave him the ability to persuade and move people. Perhaps he was getting overconfident of his ability. Dr. Dods sized him up quickly enough. According to family tradition, he wrote an American friend that "Jim McClure is the most charming and the most ignorant young man I have ever met."[2]

It was not long before Jim himself realized his abysmal ignorance in comparison with the serious and dedicated students in his class. He learned that for a McClure, especially a Presbyterian McClure, ignorance was a sin. You couldn't get by on charm alone. With characteristic zeal he began an all-out assault on his academic shortcomings. He loved to gather up his strength for a plunge into combat, and so he began by making a list of great books, those he felt constituted the essence of Western Civilization. He then determined to read a book a week until the list was done. He kept records of his progress, making it harder on himself by counting books of two or three volumes as only one completed work. Green's History of England, in four volumes, was a particularly arduous seven-day challenge. It was an endurance race of sorts; and he kept at it, with list after list, until 1913. He read in all more than 500 books, in

Marcus Dods, President of New College, Edinburgh, Scotland.

addition to the required reading for his courses. He polished off William James, Rudyard Kipling, John Fiske's *History of the United States, Huckleberry Finn,* Charles Dickens, Aldous Huxley, Ibsen, Dante, Bunyan, Balzac, and the list stretches on.

Jim's roommate in the dormitory was a young man named John Baillie. They became great friends and used to lie in bed at night making up lists such as "ten things I most dislike" and "ten reasons for not getting out of bed in the morning." Later on, John became a distinguished Scottish theologian and president of the New College. In his books there are a number of such lists, but in a much more serious vein.[3]

By December, Dr. Dods had come to appreciate Jim. He sent word back to the McClure home on his progress. "I think I cannot send you a Christmas card you will find more welcome than the thankful acknowledgement that your son has quite won the hearts of all members of our College. He is, I think, the most popular man we have had from the U.S.A. . . . His face captivates every-one and on acquaintance we find it is lived up to. . . ." But he went on to say he was unsure about Jim's decision to leave the dormitory in order to live in an urban settlement house in the Cowgate, a tough section of Edinburgh. He wrote with resignation that he "Certainly . . . will see a good deal of institutional church work" (Marcus Dods to James G. K. McClure, Sr., December 11, 1906). "Institutional church work" was putting it mildly.

The weekly routine of the Pleasance Street Settlement House included mothers' meetings, Bible classes, Sabbath services, Lads' Club, a Savings Bank meeting (to teach profligate Scotsmen a little thrift), classes for sewing and music, and something called the Band of Hope, which might have been a program for alcoholics. The purpose of this mission was to involve members of the local community in a daily routine that would break the old patterns of self-destruction. A new culture of Christ was provided to replace the general culture of vice that operated in the neighborhood. Pleasance Street was an area of the city so densely populated that Jim could count fifty-five families using the same doorway across the street from the mission, in a structure not over four stories tall. He noticed that the people's physical growth was stunted by their poverty. He remarked later in a sermon that he had " . . . never met a man taller than 5'7" living in the Cowgate."[4] Jim was looking face to face at the alcoholism that is endemic to Scotland, a cultural sickness that surely influenced the determination of his own family's choice of abstinence.

On Saturday evenings Jim walked along the streets with Warden Symington, who was in charge of the mission. He was a great big man with a shock of red hair. The two of them walked along breaking up fights. Symington would catch hold of one man and Jim the other, and they would forcefully jerk them apart. Once they went up to the second floor of a tenement to stop a fight. A "Bobbie" was ahead of them, and the warden disapproved of his behavior. He picked him up and dropped him out the window.[5] Drunks, prostitutes and brawls were a part of the routine. These drunks remained for Jim a symbol of the fantastic possibilities of human hypocrisy. He said later, "In Scotland, I have heard some of the finest talks on religion and temperance from men who were drunk."[6] Mr. Symington left the employ of the mission during this time. At the farewell party, Jim received two playing cards, the King and ten of hearts, as a memento. The warden signed them, and inscribed this message to Jim: "May this be the only card of this kind you handle unless to destroy."[7] Evil for these Scottish Presbyterians of 1906 was not a matter left open for debate.

And so the young idealist from Yale came face to face with the scourges of an urban society. Many a young man in such a situation retreats hastily back into the safety of academia, allowing fatalism and cynicism to grow up from within to crowd out his former hopes for a finer world. Jim McClure took his walks in a world where brutality and anger had to be dealt with quickly and confidently. Forever afterwards he remembered the Pleasance Street Settlement House in a quaintly fond way, as an exciting time of testing when he became engaged in the problems of the lives of people outside the confines of the college. He discovered he had a taste for this work, and that neither his courage nor his ideals were easily shaken. Unlike his friend Louis Douseman, he did not change his ideas. Jim thrived on excitement and liked to think of himself as courageous and persuasive enough to wade into other people's problems.

Scattered through Jim's diary are many entries referring to his work with the Settlement House. On one of those interminable Scottish winter nights he wrote " . . . out with the Warden . . . quiet—one woman's purse stolen-awful sight—women drunk with children—pity."[8] A few weeks later he noted,

"Brought a poor boy home—gave him 4d. . . ."[9] He celebrated Washington's birthday by skipping all his classes in order to attend the trial of one Pougrate, who was "condemned and hung by Shaw, the hangman."[10]

Despite Jim McClure's curiosity about the sensational, the routine of these days in Edinburgh rotated about the daily class meetings with his seminary professors. The winter term began on January 8, 1907 with a controversial address presented by Dr. Dods, castigating the gathered group of Highlands ministers for laziness. Jim must have felt a little uneasy himself. His own academic diligence remained an unproved commodity. The Yale good-times habits were hard to extinguish. Worrying about his little vices, he confessed to a lapse in personal purity; he smoked "10 sigs" the week following Dr. Dods' sermon. Other entertainments included the companionship of two young ladies, a Miss Simpson and Dorothy Lowe. He entertained the latter on horseback, no doubt exhausting his repertoire of bronco-busting stories. Jim also received several visiting friends. With one, Frank Dodge, he spent the day talking and sight-seeing, walking up to Holy Rood, the ancient seat of Scottish royalty, and becoming so absorbed in conversation at one castle that they remained late into the night "til we were thrown out." He enjoyed several day trips to nearby towns of interest. He returned in a rush from Aberdeen in order to read *Pilgrim's Progress* to a group of children. For sports, there were field hockey and rugby. His seminary "ruggers" challenged the "Established Church" to a match. He belonged to the local Theological Society, where he read a paper on Tolstoy.[11]

Jim McClure allowed himself to be pulled in many different directions. He had an appetite for adventure and excitement, something he rarely found in theological classes or books. From 9:00 a.m. to noon each day, he attended the classes of each of his three professors. The educational methods were formal, but the small size of the faculty and student body allowed for an intimate learning environment. There were regular teas with the professors, where a student could launch out on a tangent or clarify a theological point. These classes and assignments Jim pursued with a sense of duty, not pleasure. He often discovered delightful reasons why he might cut a class from time to time, especially those of a Dr. Martin. Exams were scheduled for late March, and by Jim's own admission he had as yet not mastered the rigors of academia. On March 21st, he "Sat a poor exam in Dogmatics . . ." and four days later admits that he "Cut [a] poor figure in exams. . . ."[12]

Jim was never particularly concerned with church dogmas anyway. The study time he lost he turned to advantage in travel around Scotland. He tried to see as much of the country as he could. For one jaunt, an agreeable young Princeton man joined him for a tour of Loch Katrine and Loch Lomond, and on "up to Rob Roy's cave. . . ."[13] By the end of March, after his exams, he announced in his diary that the Scottish time was running out. "Hate to leave Edinburgh—very happy days—Everyone too kind!" Well, not everyone, for he goes on to say that he made a farewell stroll in the moonlight "up Carlton Hill—lots of bad people."[14]

Dr. Dods closed the session with another address, summing up the theological thicket in which Jim McClure now found himself. Jim greatly admired Dr. Dods, for both his intellect and his persuasiveness. Jim would mourn his death within the year. Dr. Dods had endured throughout his career the theological fads of his generation. He explained to Jim and his classmates that the unsettled condition of church dogma was an opportunity for the young men listening to him. He said, "It was in a time of transition such as this, when every old belief was called in question and when the traditional moorings were sunk, that men felt their need of guidance and the expert found his opportunity. When all things were fixed and ready to take their shapes, the hand that could form the mould had the control of the new world."[15] Jim left New College with many friendships and a growing theological curiosity. Dr. Martin signed his diploma stating that "Mr. J. G. McClure Jr. B. S. had been a student in this College during Session 1906–7; is much esteemed both by the Senatus and by his fellow students; and is recommended hereby to the kind offices of the authorities of the University in which he proposes to study during the summer."[16]

The University he chose was located in Germany, the country that had so fascinated Jim McClure at Yale. Germany was the center of the theological controversies of the day; the very place where Dr. Dods' "new moulds" were being shaped. The force and power of science, in the German universities more than anywhere else, were at work to "demythologize" and "modernize" a Christian creed that had for so long viewed the cold objectivity of the scientific method as a threat. Jim McClure, having caught the excitement of these struggles, and having a natural predilection for the rational as opposed to the revealed nature of Truth, was drawn to Germany.

The Seminary of the University of Tübingen was founded in 1537 amidst the theological revolution of the Reformation. It was established as Protestant, and has remained a leading theological center for Protestant thought. The town of Tübingen lies in the southwest corner of Germany, within about sixty miles of both Switzerland and France in the old political region of Württemberg. The seminary had maintained its revolutionary vigor into the twentieth century, and was widely known for the number of brilliant professors working there in an attempt to demythologize Christianity. Rudolf Bultmann, who became most skillful in the science of form criticism, and Paul Tillich, who devised a comprehensive existential theology and had a considerable intellectual following, were Tübingen students and Jim's contemporaries. Bultmann labored throughout his life to unravel the mystery of the "historical Jesus" by carefully trying to discern and remove the various layers of myth surrounding him in the Biblical testimony. Paul Tillich based his theology on a synthesis of culture and faith. Both these men were looking for a new, firm basis for faith, in order to revitalize the churches with a meaning that did not try to side-step the scientific method of inquiry. Jim McClure came searching for a religion that would energize people and societies as well, so that a transformation could begin that would usher in a new era, a real earthly Kingdom of God. He was ready to plunge ahead and

Postcard from T. Zieglar, July 4, 1907.

to get his hands dirty, but he needed first to find a message that he could both believe and act upon.

Jim's letters from Tübingen sounded a variety of themes, and were read with interest around the dinner table on Halsted Street.

> . . . [Tübingen] is about the most beautiful place I have ever been in—right in the midst of the Swabian Albes . . . We could see the Hohenzollern Castle. The hills and small mountains are wonderful and we walked through valleys and through Pine Forests and it really is wonderful.
>
> Also for theology it seems that I have chosen very fortunately. There are about 300 theological students here . . . However I am the first American student—they say.
>
> Today . . . I attended two lectures without understanding a word . . . I wish the family could all see me thrashing about in this unutterable language. I never expect to understand a word. (James G. K. McClure, Jr. to family, May 1, 1907)

> Talk about silent people. Your boy has not opened his lips to speak for five days . . . Since last writing nothing of importance has happened except the forgetting of three German words which I thought I knew when I came here. Also Mother will be pleased to know that as yet no German students have challenged me to a duel . . . (James G. K. McClure, Jr. to family, May 2, 1907)

The German language remained a puzzle to Jim at Tübingen. This blocked his comprehension of the theology he was studying. Despite his afternoon efforts with Joe Twichell at Yale, attending lectures on Kant and Hegel in German was a great trial to him. Philosophy is subtle enough in one's native tongue, and so Jim appears to have taken to doodling. His notebook is full of fanciful caricatures half man-half beast, no doubt satirizing his proud and serious German professors. He became quite lonely in Tübingen, and treasured letters from home. From Nathan he received this peppy note: "3 cheers for the cubs . . . Wright me soon . . ." (Nathan McClure to James G. K. McClure, Jr., December 10, 1906). Arch follows up with a more concrete summary of the baseball situation. "The Cubs are still eight games ahead of New York . . . In the American League, Cleveland, Detroit and Philadelphia in that order are right at the Sox heels" (Arch McClure to James G. K. McClure, Jr., July 16, 1907).

Dueling was the honored sport of the German aristocrat. Face scars were for many the prerequisite for respect. Sunday afternoon duels were a fine spectator event in Tübingen, and Jim was unable to keep himself away. "[I] walked out . . . to get a look at duelling. Butted in but students very polite . . . Blood flowing freely."[17] Jim was always drawn towards excitement, whether Cubs baseball, Yale football or German duelling. While Jim watched one of these duels, a contestant lunged at his opponent, neatly severing one ear. The lost appendage dropped to the ground, and was immediately gobbled up by the victim's pet hound, who had been waiting in the wings.[18]

In another episode, Jim was entertaining his American friend Charlotte Partridge. Her family had come to Germany on a European tour. Jim and Charlotte were sitting in a small garden cafe in Heidelberg. There had just been a heavy summer rain shower. Tables were set up outside, protected from the storm by a canvas awning. As awnings are prone to do, it bulged this particular afternoon with the water that had collected during the shower. Jim and the girl were happily preoccupied with each other's company. Into this lovely garden scene marched a haughty Prussian officer. Perhaps the world of man has never created a personage that could exude such a sense of superiority, such contempt for others, or such excessive pride, as the Prussian officer. The mien of such a man grated against the democratic ideals of the young American, and anyway he had a fine girl to entertain. He was seized by a reckless impulse. Canes were in style in the Germany of this day, and Jim surreptitiously reached up with his and pushed the nearest bulge in the awning at just the right moment to drench the officer. A moment later, the joke became a little hollow as the officer sent a message to Jim demanding a duel; after all, a proud man's honor had been thoroughly debased in a public place and the local codes demanded an opportunity to redress. A foolhardy joke had now placed Jim in a serious predicament. According to the duelling code, the man challenged had the right to choose the weapon, the time and the place. Jim returned a note to the Prussian, accepting the challenge under the following conditions: as for weapons, one could use only his fists; as for the time, it was to be right away; and as for the place, it was to be behind that very garden cafe. Jim McClure had shrewdly chosen a "duel" no German of honor could abide. Brawling was too undignified, and the Prussian declined.[19]

Charlotte's family invited Jim to join their entourage. It was for him a glorious reprieve from his studies and his loneliness. He wrote home, "Charlotte Partridge wrote me this morning that they would be in Munich on Sunday—so will I. Though—this for father—I will return to Tübingen without a pfennig and hold a record breaking fast until reimbursement comes" (James G. K. McClure, Jr. to family, late April, 1907). Charlotte made life gay for Jim again. They went to vaudeville shows, rowed on ponds, ate pastries for breakfast, and drove about in an automobile Mr. Partridge had hired for the family's use. Jim's diary gives a lively account of his movements. Motoring through Germany, he and Charlotte

> . . . saw everything in Wurzburg and ate two sausages in that half hour . . . Ch[arlotte] and I drove madly thru town . . . We got to Frankfort in time for lunch—after lunch we drove over town and through it . . . [At Wiesbaden] Mr. Partridge and I arose at 5:30 the next morning . . . and had a hot mineral bath. I felt gouty before but the bath put me on my feet again. We then drove to the Rhine and embarked on a capacious boat and took the trip down the Rhine—it was simply wonderful—descriptions do not touch the real thing with a long bamboo pole . . . Koln [Cologne] at 5:00 said goodbye . . . did not relish it.[20]

One picture that has survived of this episode shows Charlotte under and behind a large and discrete veiled hat, with Jim peering cheerfully from beneath a handsome bowler.

It might seem surprising that Charlotte should turn up in Germany, but in fact Europe was fairly swarming with Jim's friends. Between Edinburgh and Tübingen, he ate dinner with "Bill" Coffin, and went to Buckingham Palace with Frank Dodge. Russell Cheney met him in Paris, and then who should appear but Charlotte's rival, Phoebe Eckols. Jim and Phoebe did their driving in Paris, on the Bois du Bologne and in the shadow of the Pantheon and Notre Dame. After Phoebe left, Agnes Booth arrived in town. It was as if the powers of American society were making a special effort to entertain the lonely seminary student. The Booths invited Jim to join them for a chauffeured tour of France. From Chartres to Orleans to Tours, and on and on they went; chateaux, dungeons, cathedrals and the finest French cuisine, with dominoes after dinner, for a week of luxury. They breezed back to Paris in time to catch Madame Butterfly. Sadly for Jim, the ". . . Booths start for England [and I] almost went with them."[21]

But Jim's friends in Paris had by no means been exhausted after the departure of Agnes Booth. There was a fine bunch of his Yale buddies there, and he drove around with them in a Mercedes taking in more sights, including the tomb of that most famous of all Frenchmen, Napoleon Bonaparte. In 1907 Europe had become a wonderful American playground. If the Old World was exporting its masses "yearning to breathe free" to the New World, the new was returning tourists who had "struck it rich" in America, returning in part to discover their own backgrounds, and also to brag a little about their success and their country.

After some weeks of language difficulties back at Tübingen there was a holiday. In late May Jim and Otto Berlin, a German student, planned a walking tour in the nearby Black Forest. Jim looked forward to playing the gypsy. He carried along a little concertina, and accompanied Otto's singing to pay for supper and lodging. Otto wished to learn English and Jim expected to learn German. But Jim found that he missed the comforts of the more lavish tours in the automobiles of his lady companions.

> I am at present . . . situated in the worst hotel in the world . . . We climb up to our room on a ladder.
> You would die if you could see me on my tour with the German student. We left Tübingen yesterday morning . . . and travelled by train to Freudenstadt—on the train we travelled fourth class—rather we bumped over the rails fourth class . . . We each carry a pack on our back and in said pack besides clothes for the journey we carry a loaf of bread and a Big Wurst which we eat for lunch.
> Yesterday he tried to tell me the love story of his life, showing me a picture of his loved one. I however understood almost nil and tried to put in intelligent ejaculations.
> Yesterday we walked 61 kilometers—a breath taker for me—but I pulled in at night ahead of the student . . . after this I will never think of falling in love. (James G. K. McClure, Jr. to family, May 19, 1907)

At Lake Constance, on the Swiss border,

> The German student left for Munich and I heaved a large sigh of relief . . .
> This whole journey—some 400 miles and seeing all these things cost me just $13.00 which I think is about as cheap as such journey was ever made . . .
> (James G. K. McClure, Jr. to family, May 24, 1907)

Although at the time this walking trip certainly seemed difficult, Jim remembered it with joy in later years when telling his adventure to his daughter.

On returning to Tübingen, Jim McClure began again the struggle to comprehend the contortions of philosophy and theology in a language he did not understand. To make matters worse, his professor was a Hungarian named Haring, who lectured on material straight out of his book *Dogmatik*. Jim doodled through his lectures and then went back to his room to try to figure out from *Dogmatik* what the man had been saying. He had to look up nearly every German word, moving at the glacial speed of about a page an hour. "Fearful stuff" he called the professor's writings. He decided German lessons would help him, and so employed a Fräulein Oeler to teach him the language each afternoon. Soon afterwards, he felt as if he had made progress. "[I] Understand

Scheel and was delighted." But he was still puzzled about *Dogmatik*. "After three hours [I] did not understand Haring."[22] Slowly the Fräulein helped him improve his German conversation, and he was able to make more friends and join in informal meetings with the professors and students. Professor Haring presided at one such gathering, and Jim brags a little about his temperance: "The students all sit around a table with beer, cigars and water—note this last as it is quite unusual at such an occasion—and hand in questions to the Prof. and a discussion follows" (James G. K. McClure, Jr. to Phebe Ann Dixon McClure, July 7, 1907).

There was a strain to his life here in Tübingen, excepting his interludes with Miss Partridge and Miss Eckols *et al.*, that began to eat away at his health. He naturally possessed great nervous energy that needed a constructive outlet. He was determined to master theology, and at the same time week after week he added to the growing list of outside reading in the notebook he had begun in Edinburgh. The stress of his work, the loneliness of being in the midst of people whom he barely understood, and the confining style of student life began to have a physical affect on him. He found it difficult to digest regular meals, and throughout June and July he often subsisted on a diet of bread and milk. He decided to play tennis regularly, in order to benefit from proper exercise. But tennis tended to aggravate his knee, which he may have damaged when climbing in the mountains of Craig while in Scotland.[23] Beginning in Tübingen, a dark cloud of illness began to build up over Jim McClure, which he would be unable to shake off for many years. He decided with hindsight that perhaps the strain of trying to push himself academically, plus the personal problems any young man faces, plus all his difficulties in adjusting to Germany added up to a damaging burden. Jim McClure did not possess an academic temperament; he was a man of action who believed that theory was useful as a starting reference, but had to be followed up in a practical way for courage and persistence to achieve results.

A man's youth, however long it may last, needs to be a testing time, where one probes the limits of endurance and capacity. Jim McClure discovered at Tübingen that he had limits. He found it hard to be happy without friends. He discovered, eventually, that he could learn a great deal from study but could never lose touch with life and become completely absorbed in books. The magic of the man was his ability to inspire people with his personal attributes, from street urchins in Edinburgh, to chance acquaintances on the street, to the loyal cadre of friends he maintained throughout his life. People in the flesh, not in the abstract, inspired him to selflessness and Christlike acts. And although he was eventually able to stretch his understanding in order to master the thorniest of intellectual difficulties, academic pursuits rarely provided him with as much spiritual lift and inspiration as did personal contact with a single struggling man or woman. In Edinburgh and especially in Germany, the strict academic regimen stifled the more natural interchange among people that he had enjoyed at Yale. His father had warned him that this might be the case, and that he should nonetheless steel himself to the task. But without his friends, Jim found it hard to see much purpose in what he was doing. And so he complained about the "stiffness of German social intercourse."[24]

Beyond the frustrations of his daily life, Jim McClure was also beginning to grapple with difficult theological questions. In Germany he began to see beyond the cheerfulness of his immature idealism, and to face the rooted depths of human misery. Was the Christian message, perhaps, really a simple crutch, an opiate to soothe the world's pain? He wrote to his mother that " . . . the more I see of the world, the more the surface layer vanishes and the sorrow and burden-bearing and strength underneath become evident" (James G. K. McClure, Jr. to Phebe Ann Dixon McClure, July, 1907). Sorrow and inner strength are the stuff of religion, and even though it took him an hour to decipher a single page of each German tome, he was beginning for the first time to face the real religious battles that were raging within the souls of men and women at this time.

Fred Henderson, a Scotsman from New College, was one soul with whom he kept in intimate contact during his time in Tübingen. This man's letters were an indication to Jim of his personal gifts, and speak of the intellectual milieu of the period. Fred wrote:

> I don't suppose you know and perhaps I am making a mistake in telling you but I know you must have better friends and people you love far more than me—still all the same I am going to tell you that there is no one else I know that I love in quite the same way that I love you. You don't feel the same way towards me and I can't expect you to. But Jim man you have got a tremendous power in your personal influence and not only for your own sake but for the sake of all of us whom your life touches you must keep holy, keep close to God. "For their sakes I sanctify myself." . . . We'll have a rare good time in heaven when the wrestling is over . . . (Fred Henderson to James G. K. McClure, Jr., February 24, 1907)

These two men, like many of their age and class, talked a great deal about healing society; they both were fascinated by the world of the working classes that functioned so close at hand, and yet so out of reach. Fred wrote on his way to an Asian mission field:

> Dear Jim,
> I have been looking at the steerage passengers and I think it wouldn't be at all a terrible experience after the first three days . . . Of course I haven't seen the sleeping accommodations or the grub but just watched their games on the cargo hatch and with the Arabs who came aboard to sell things off Suez. The net result of all which discussion about steerage is not that I am to go steerage all the way back or go out of my way to take a special steerage trip but that if the only way to do anything that I ought to do involves travelling steerage then that will rather spice the doing of it than prevent it. (Fred Henderson to James G. K. McClure, Jr., March 10, 1907)

There is a comical aspect to this young missionary peering over the deck at the poorest passengers, but it serves as a poignant reminder of the artificial barriers in this class-ridden society. For all their naivete, young men like Jim McClure and Fred Henderson were seriously uncomfortable with the compartments that limited social intercourse.

Fred and Jim were dedicated "self-improvers" as well, and worked out a set of duplicate cards in order to concentrate better on their spiritual battles. Fred suggested an amendment in one letter. "About these duplicate cards of ours: What do you say to inserting for Sunday 'to get rid of self-consciousness.' I think we . . . are quite sick of ourselves in that line. . . ." He goes on in his letter to discuss the practice of the Sabbath day, contrasting Jim's more modern and casual approach to the common practices of Scotland: ". . . [Y]ou don't know the Scotch tradition about Sunday and the feeling that lurks in every Scotchman's heart that he ought to be uncomfortable on Sunday when he is not in church or reading the Bible . . . you are emancipated from all that Jim but I am not sure that I envy you. That dear old Scotch Sunday has got into my blood and qualified by sincerity and humanity it still . . . seems to come nearer the ideal than any other I know" (Fred Henderson to James G. K. McClure, Jr., March 10, 1907).

From one of Jim's American friends whom he had just seen in Paris, Mary Kay Waller, he received a letter that illustrates once again Jim's powerful influence over people:

> . . . I feel as if I ought to apologize for the cynical nasty mien I showed in everything that night at Dorothy's . . . I've been working on so many problems, that my mind is settled on a wheel, and instead of facing the real facts fearlessly, I've hidden my defeat in cynicism. Way down deep I do believe in sincerity, in absolute simplicity which is really only the direct expression of the universal in us—of all that is noblest in us-of God . . .
>
> Whatever we believe, we can always be honest in living up to the very best in us. That is what you are starting out to do now, Jim, and to think, in your very decision, you have grown—you seemed older . . . more manly the other night—and I am wishing you all the courage, all the strength which it takes to be true to one's highest self . . . I am proud of your friendship. (Mary Kay Waller to James G. K. McClure, Jr., 1907, exact date unknown)

One of Jim's closest Skull and Bones friends, Hugh Wilson, sounded the very same theme. Jim McClure, if he did not know anything else, knew that his friends looked to him for advice, and as an example. Hugh Wilson later became the American Ambassador to Nazi Germany, the last before the Second World War. He wrote to Jim McClure in 1907:

> I have always said that to my knowledge no man had ever influenced my character one way or the other, but now I shall have to take it back and say that I am a decidedly better man for having had that talk with you. Not so much better, as changed, having a greater pleasure in things beautiful, in music

and poetry that I had been gradually shutting off from myself by a wall of materialistic selfishness ... You see, Jimmie it was the sight of you and analysis of how high and spiritual thinking combined with unselfish living had changed the boy fond of the good things of life into a man of reason and power that set me to realizing how little my nature had grown in the same period of time, and how small was a spiritual increase compared to the intellectual of the last year. Thank you, Jimmie for all such realizations and let me believe that this will help a little to heal up the pain in your heart that I saw you carrying away from Paris with you. (Hugh Wilson to James G. K. McClure, Jr., May 13, 1907)

John Magee, who became a missionary to China and who had served with Jim as class deacon at Yale, echoed Hugh Wilson's comments: "Hugh said last night that you had had a tremendous influence on him, more so than any other man. The change that had come over you was so wonderful. He said he had gotten more materialistic before he saw you than ever before in his life ... It certainly was a splendid tribute" (John Magee to James G.K. McClure, Jr., June 19, 1907).

These letters were heady praise for a young theological student, and must have encouraged Jim enormously during a difficult period of his life. Surely his friends were telling him that his chosen field matched his gifts. He finished the term at Tübingen, leaving on July 20 with a diploma inscribed for one "Jacobus McClure." He then met up with John Magee and Lee Perrin, their class orator, for a tour of Europe. He sent his trunks on to Paris and carried a few belongings in a small canvas sack, a gypsy traveller once again. He made his first visit to Worms to pay homage to Martin Luther, the man who had changed the history of the West and shaped the Christian views of Jim's Scottish ancestors.

John Magee arrived in Paris in a dismal frame of mind, dampening the impulsive spirits of the other two. The three of them meandered about Switzerland, lazily absorbing the scenery from Lucerne to Geneva. Then, for a brief period, Jim left his friends and made a breathless tour of northern Italy. This was typical of his constant push to get the maximum dosage of sights and sounds. He rejoined them in Paris and departed for Chicago in mid-September, 1907.

The remaining years of Jim's seminary career involved learning the rudiments of his trade. The faculty of McCormick Seminary trained him in all phases of Presbyterian theology, church history, apologetics and the meaning of the Gospel. He wrote sermons, and tried to deliver them properly. He wrote papers on social and ethical questions, including one on the world of the Chicago saloon. In 1909, Jim was ready to return again to Germany, and studied there at the universities in Jena and Berlin. He was now comfortable with the habits of scholarship, and understood great chunks of the philosophical masters, in both German and English.

1. *Norwich Evening Record,* September 27, 1906.
2. Interview with Elspeth McClure Clarke.
3. *Ibid.*
4. James G. K. McClure, Jr., "The Social Crisis," sermon given March 22, 1914, Iron River, Michigan.
5. Interviews with Elspeth McClure Clarke.
6. James G. K. McClure, Jr., "The Social Crisis," sermon given March 22, 1914, Iron River, Michigan.
7. The cards were found in a scrapbook kept by James G. K. McClure, Jr.
8. Edinburgh diary, March 1, 1907.
9. *Ibid.,* March 22, 1907.
10. *Ibid.,* Feb. 22, 1907.
11. *Ibid.,* various entries.
12. *Ibid.*
13. *Ibid.*
14. *Ibid.*
15. Marcus Dods, closing address, Edinburgh, March 1907.
16. This diploma is among the papers of James G. K. McClure, Jr.
17. Diary entry, July 18, 1907.
18. Interview with Elspeth McClure Clarke.
19. *Ibid.*
20. Diary, various entries.
21. Diary, no date.
22. Diary, no date.
23. Diary, June 7, 1907.
24. Edinburgh diary, March 23, 1907.

Chapter Six

Unsystematic Theology

... Here lies the danger of every young man—that he will make a choice
which will stunt him, will dwarf him, will choke down all these high yearnings
of his youth and will land him at fifty high and dry and wizened with parched
tongue on some sandy, hot island, while the heroes of the race have safely
gone on far beyond. (*James G. K. McClure, Jr., untitled sermon written while
attending McCormick Seminary 1908*)

My religious views are so different from [the] Presbyterian that I doubt of
the board's accepting me. (*Letter to L. B. [Lucy Blair?], November 21, 1909*)

I must devote more time in the morning to prayer—to fixing in my mind the
reality and omnipresence of God . . .
Matter is so near; the interest in details . . . so absorbing; pleasure is . . .
so alluring; the seen world is so explainable and seemingly sufficient that
unless I start out in the morning by fixing in my mind the deeper interpretation-
the seeing of God in everything—l am apt to lose him altogether . . . (*Liverpool journal, 1909, undated entry*)

Last Sunday evening I visited a Pietist Hour—you know of the Pietist
movement—and I was very much impressed. The German theology needs a
good airing and hanging on the line and beating . . . (*James G. K. McClure,
Jr., to Phebe Ann Dixon McClure, end of July, 1907*)

In the autumn of 1909, Jim McClure found himself for a second time
steaming across the Atlantic for Europe. The conviviality and adventure of an
ocean voyage gave Jim great opportunities to make friends and discuss the
issues of the day, but he was not returning for pleasure. Instead, he was trying
to rediscover the theological glimpses he had seen before, and find out if they
held answers to his questions. He was dissatisfied with the conventional doc-
trines of McCormick Seminary, and he had not forgotten how his intellect had
been stirred and challenged in Edinburgh and Tübingen before. Now he needed
to go back to Germany, where a new and disturbing theology was being formu-
lated.

Already the American Social Gospel movement, which made service to
one's fellow man the criterion of one's religion, was influential in Jim
McClure's theology. But he wanted to know why a man should devote his life
to such service. What was the compelling drive of Christianity? He was simply
dissatisfied with the traditional catechism of responses. He felt he must probe

deeply for himself. He sought ideas that would send him with abandon into battle, with a fierce determination and reckless confidence that could upset the lethargic world around him. Jim McClure dreamed heroic dreams of a conquering youth who with logic and energy might sweep away the evils inherited from the past. It was a posture he would never abandon, although the experiences of life would temper his energy and increase his wisdom.

As he plunged into his studies he was at first overjoyed, and wrote in his journal:

> Never, in all my life, until this fall have I been able honestly to thank God for anything for I had never been thankful for my existence. I am now beginning to realize what it means to exist—an incomparable thing . . . It is like a small boy gaining admittance to a circus tent and there is no comparison with the outside—and I would lie on my belly on the tent ropes, or perch under the tiers of seats or lie on my face under the tent skirts-simply for the fact of figuring among those present . . .[1]

In this enthusiastic frame of mind he began to dig out the answers to his religious questionings, to find a theology that inspired action. It hardly seems possible that the Yale sports buff and gay blade of only three years before could write in his notebook, "If a man is to study theology he should master Thomas Aquinas and the Aristotelian logic . . . He should grind his nose on the Scholastic grindstone."[2] This intelligent young man, fired with an inborn determination to serve his fellow men, was about to run head on into the great controversies that marked off modern Protestant thinkers from conservatives in 1909. On what authority could answers to the problems of existence be based? Was the Bible the holy, inspired word of God, or was it simply a random collection of ancient documents, full of wisdom but carrying no supernatural authority and meaningful only in its historical context? Was Jesus divine or simply a man of outstanding compassion and nobility after whom men could pattern their lives? Could a man ask a personal God in prayer to intercede on his or anyone's behalf, or was such hope the folly of presumption? Was a belief in immortality essential to Christian doctrine? Where could a Christian fit in the new scientific explanations of the world? Science and religion seemed to be deadlocked in a struggle for men's minds. Was man's sinful action a grief to God and a cause for guilt to the man who had sinned? Or was sin only an expected, and therefore acceptable, falling short of the ideal?

Armed with the logic and reason of the pedagogues of Jena and Berlin, Jim joined with his German mentors in questioning the core concepts of Christianity. After studying the work of two orthodox theologians Jim wrote in his notebook, "Seeberg and Kaftan emphasize again and again that theology has as its one ground the Bible and ethics has as its main ground the Bible. This is as conservative theology must hold to—but however gallant it may be to remain on the sinking ship—there comes a time when it is better to row calmly ashore."[3] The "shore" he rowed to was the firm ground, so he thought, of the scientific method, so widely acclaimed as the solution to all questions in the early twentieth century. Scepticism, logical reasoning, controlled data, hypotheses and conclusions were helping to unlock many of the great mysteries of the physical universe. To many people it seemed that religion, which was often attended by tradition and superstition, blocked the march of scientific truth.

While studying in Scotland, Jim had been much impressed by a book written by a Scottish minister, Henry Drummond, called *Natural Law and the Spiritual World*. Drummond outlined a plan for using scientific law in personal Christian development. One instance was the theory that a spirit, like a plant, begins to decay if it is not growing. Jim felt it was possible to end what he considered the fruitless struggle for supremacy in the battle for human progress between the devotees of religion and those of science. He wanted to bring the two great forces together; to maintain his belief in reason and the scientific method while enlisting the powerful theological arguments that would move humanity closer to a world of perfection, to the Kingdom of God on earth.[4]

As he continued to question Christian tenets, Jim demythologized Jesus Christ in the same fashion that he cut through the authority of the Bible. He asked himself the question, was Jesus unique, different from the rest of man? Writing in his journal, he replied:

> . . . modern thought answers in the negative—for to help us, Christ must have lived as we did; must have been one of us—and modern thought has no use for a God who is out of touch with the world . . .
>
> When we come to the Divinity of Christ—I do not see that believing Christ divine has advantages while believing him human has great advantages.
>
> The work supposed to have been done by the divine Christ—forgiving sins and presenting eternal life-we no longer look at as done in this way.
>
> God should not need to send his son to show his interest in the world and in each individual . . .
>
> The death of a holy man caused by sin, would strike the lowest note in our scale of values—and the divine element added could strike no deeper note. Here then the last advantage of attributing divinity to Christ vanishes.
>
> To make such a lot of the acceptance or non-acceptance of the belief that Christ is the Son of God seems absurd because it is merely a figure of speech, an analogy. It is only in humanity that we know anything of a relation between Father and Son—and we are simply using this human analogy in connection with God. We have no reason to think, that God has a "Son"—we simply mean that God seemed to be in an especially close relation . . . that the nearest men of his day could come to describing it was to say it was the relation of Father to Son.[5]

One might want to ask Jim the question, if Jesus Christ was a mere man, what is there to preach? After reading several rather contradictory entries in his journal, I believe he would have vehemently objected to the adjective "mere," and carefully reapplied "divine" to describe Jesus as he did on one page from his Berlin notebook.

> But by saying that Christ is not God I do not say he is not divine, or [that he is] a mere man. I say he is not God simply because the word God represents a being of powers and of an existence which Christ does not claim to have and of which he has no need of being.
>
> Christ was certainly more than a mere man—to call him mere man does injustice to his character—therefore I use the word divine. Here comes out a great deal of misunderstanding about words. As far as I can see there are two possibilities. Christ was a mere man or more than a mere man—a or b, but b I call divine. (I believe that people who call him a mere man but a perfect man . . . stand on the same ground.)
>
> Christ is not God, and never assumes that he is-always distinguishing himself and God—for God (as the word means to me) expresses both the character and Being of God whereas Christ claims only to represent his character . . .[6]

Here one can see Jim trying to stake out new theological ground for his "modern" Christianity, but reluctant to throw out the terminology that had served the church so well. In his use of words like "divine" he forced the language, redefining words so that he could continue to use the traditional religious vocabulary. In a moment of honesty, he looked forward to being able to dump the whole load of archaic Christian terminology. He wrote: "The next great convulsion of society will be a revolt against language. It is absurd to suppose that a language formed when man's idea of himself and nature were primitive can content the man with a more definite knowledge of himself. . . ."[7]

But Jim was doing more than stretching the meaning of words. He was trying to reconcile what was thought to be a scientifically determined universe with the Christian religion. He was always a forthright thinker who asked direct questions and expected from himself and others an honest response. Knowledge for him would always be based on reason. Facts were to be laid out straight, and firm conclusions drawn from the evidence.

Thus he was puzzled when one of his professors, Herr Weniberg, postulated that scientific sceptics were able to question, to peel back the layers of truth, until the whole philosophical basis for any knowledge was destroyed. Facing such existentialism, Jim pondered in his notebook:

> Is knowledge possible? This question is forced upon me by the uncertainty of my relation to the external world. I must investigate and see what this relation is and if knowledge at all is possible, for knowledge is the basis of my action . . . I think I perceive a thing-but when I investigate I find that the thing is to me colored, hot, hard, etc., i.e. that it is only its qualities that I perceive and these qualities only exist in my consciousness . . . The thing itself I cannot discover-its nature is absolutely unknowable.
>
> Does the thing externally exist then? All that I think I know of it I find to be a product of my own consciousness . . . What proof have I that my knowl-

edge even of this subjective world is true—that the logical forms under which
I try to formulate it are true? None.

And then he wrote, "I am simply *convinced*."[8] And convinced he remained,
although these thoughts may have disturbed him deeply at the time. No American devotee of pragmatism could be dragged into an intellectual hole of nihilistic
despair for long. The Texas bronco-buster would not dwell on the essential
nature of a pin stuck in his hand, debating whether the pain was real or subjective. He had larger questions on his mind.

His younger brother Arch, to whom he was very close, was at Yale,
thinking of entering the ministry himself. The two young theologians enjoyed a
rich correspondence. Jim replied to Arch in one of his letters from Germany,

> I am glad you sent the questions . . . In the first place in all my answers
> remember two things. First-that I do not know any more about these things
> than you do—except as I have thought more about them—and Secondly—no
> other man who ever lived does either. We have to decide things each for
> ourselves and we [have] as good a chance at solving them as Solomon. One
> thing we always must be—that is—we must be honest in our thinking; and no
> matter how true other people say a thing is, if it is not true for us we must
> never say it is true for us. (James G. K. McClure, Jr. to Arch McClure, Fall,
> 1909)

Jim's Covenanter ancesters might have argued with him over his modern
ideas, but his sense of personal integrity and tenacity in the defense of his beliefs
would have struck a sympathetic cord. He wrote in the same letter:

> "Why did God make the world? Which I can not answer nor can anyone else
> . . . we must not think of God as creating the world out of nothing, i.e. saying
> Presto and there the world is . . . I do not think of God as making the world—
> but of God as existing and so the world necessarily existing, too."

Perhaps it is unfair to take such scraps from Jim's notebook and letters,
presenting only a cursory view of his answers to these questions. But it is
important to understand some of the thoughts that were troubling him. Jim
continued in his letter to Arch:

> Your 2nd question—is why God made the first mortals so imperfect that
> they sinned? The answer follows partly out of my answer to the first. We think
> of God as the infinite and perfect being. Now as the existence of the world
> follows naturally from the existence of God so it must be perfect. For out of
> perfection only perfection could follow and God is not limited by anything.
> You see the way I have always judged the world before recently is this—I
> have myself set a standard and when the world and men fall short of it I have
> said . . . they sin . . . I used to condemn [the world] because it fell below my
> idea of what it was meant for—Now I say that I do not know just what God's

purpose is but the world as it is must be perfect. (James G. K. McClure, Jr. to Arch McClure, Fall, 1909)

A naturally perfect world is a beautiful proposition, but Jim McClure was quick to condemn much of what went on in it. He, along with many others of his optimistic generation, was tempted to follow the lead of thinkers like Hegel and Marx, believing that mankind was progressing, evolving, towards a harmonious and perfect world. Darwin's theories implied that biology was moving from a simple state, a primitiveness, to complexity, towards a more perfect adaptation to the environment. As Jim concluded his letter with a firm statement of his belief he moved further and further from the concept of a personal God and closer to the rather ethereal notion of a spirit moving in all things. Yet he was firm in his belief in a God of some sort.

> An atheist is either irrational or insane. No man who looks at the world and man honestly and clearly can deny that there is a power behind things which is superhuman. We call it by many names: "the Great First Cause," the "Absolute," the unknowable . . .
> And the progress that this power has wrought out during the last 100,000 years is incomprehensible. From the brute to man, from savage, barbarian, from primitive to civilized man—until we feel that some day we shall be as gods. The reason we hear the outcry that mankind is growing worse is that the crier has tied his eyes to the moment and to the backward or stagnant or outworn tendencies of the present—such a pessimistic utterance is silly in the extreme. The world, and man cannot help advancing. And advance has now become so rapid that we can see it with the naked eye.[9]

If progress appeared inevitable to Jim, he never thought it would be automatic. Our species, in his view, must struggle for every inch of collective improvement.

> That brings me to the historical appearance and development of man. The Genesis account is the way the wandering Hebrews thought men were created and started on their development. Today we think a little differently. In the process of the upward development the animals appeared and then the animal man and he kept developing. To develop man must struggle and keep struggling to develop this nature in him . . . The nature of man demands that in every choice, he choose right. This [is] man's free will. The idea of sin is one which was brought in by people . . . who thought God's plan was that no one should ever fall short of their better nature . . . and so when they fell short they said . . . you have sinned . . . (James G. K. McClure, Jr. to Arch McClure, Fall, 1909)

He explained his understanding of personal sin this way:

> If man is to progress he must have an ideal and if his ideal is sufficiently high, if it is higher than his attainments, he must at various moments fall short

of its realization. For these acts of omission and commission—these fallings short—he should feel sorry but not letting them discourage him, he must press on again toward the goal . . . Our relation to our ideal is forming our character—and the long and persistent striving toward the ideal creates in us a character that is, as virtue, its own reward.[10]

By trying to soften the sting of sin, and thus minimizing the burden of guilt, Jim lost the powerful image of a divine Father sorrowing over his lost children. He admitted as much in his notebook.[11] But he felt it was important to lead people toward attainable ideals rather than have them dragged backwards by being constantly reminded of their failures.

He was constructing his cosmos by radically departing from the traditional Christian view, moving, like many other theologians of the era, out into the borderlands between Christianity and pantheism. The pantheist sees God less as a personality or mind, and more as an essence that pervades all of reality. In most forms of pantheism, all matter, all nature, is indistinguishable from God. Jim wrote in his notebook while trying to sort out these conflicts: "That brings me to . . . believe in a God who permeates and is the Universe . . . But it is a personal pantheism—which although a contradiction of terms expresses my meaning. God comes into relation to me in everything . . . Father, mother, friends, acquaintances, things I see, handle, this pen with which I write-everything in fact."[12] But if God permeates all creation, and is the universe, how can evil exist? What becomes of personal sin when each person is a part of the God-essence?

Even as Jim was pondering all these perplexing questions with the intention of becoming a Christian leader, he was also questioning the institution of the church. Martin Luther, whom he greatly admired, attacked the Catholic church for, among other things, acting as a barrier to the personal relationships between men and their Creator. Now the time had come, Jim thought, to extend the theological frontiers of personal freedom once again. He feared that the modern Protestant denominations were once again damming up struggling humanity's communication with the Diety.

A blurring of God's personality and the need for each person to work out his or her own salvation with only an impersonal essence places a heavy load on the strength and accuracy of the individual conscience. While recovering from a knee operation with his relations in Liverpool, Jim wrote in his journal:

My creed—as I hastily write it out—is something like this—and I find it differs very much from the creeds behind most of the sermons that I hear.

I believe that there is an intelligent power outside myself—which I will call God. The universe is an expression of God and every single thing that happens to me each day, whether it be from nature, from human beings or in my thought realm—is God expressing himself to me. All these things constitute my relation to God, which will thus be seen to be a personal and uninterrupted one (comprising everything which happens to me, which I do, or that I think.)

The purpose working out in the Universe and in me in particular is beneficient [sic.]. [This purpose] I call the Will of God. The working out of this purpose is the very best thing for us as a race and as individuals —in fact in no other way can we answer the end of our existence, i.e. be happy. It is therefore the best thing for us as a race and individuals to do the Will of God. Our only means of doing the Will of God . . . is to follow unreservedly the dictates of our conscience enlightened by as much education as is possible . . . (We are never able to see far ahead into the program of the eternal purpose—for us all that is possible is to see a step at a time—but we can always see this one step.)

. . . Believing that God is good, I am confident that if I do His Will, everything that happens to me will be the very best thing for me. This includes weather . . . all relations of Nature to me . . . all words spoken to me, all chance acquaintances, accidents, disappointments—in fact everything that happens to me. "All things work together for good to him that loves the Lord . . ."

All these things become expressions of God to me-it is impiety to fear anything that may happen to me in the Universe and it is impiety to complain of or seek to elude anything . . . for which I am not personally responsible.[13]

Although Jim did not consider the Bible infallible, he did see it as a great source of inspiration and help, a record of men and women struggling to understand the source and purpose of life. So Jim McClure concluded that "Nothing in the Bible is true for the mere reason that it is in the Bible . . . But the authoritative value of the Bible lies herein that it speaks deeply and truly to the conscience."[14] Here was a young man who believed in action, but was trying desperately to understand the roots of Christian belief in a modern setting. In the process he dove into the murky philosophical waters that have drowned many a young idealist.

Rigorous academic pursuits and Jim McClure would never become comfortable companions, yet in the fall of 1909 he felt a sense of progress in his efforts to cope with the esoteric thoughts of theology and philosophy. His self-imposed regime of long nights of study had overcome most of the academic deficiencies first noted by Marcus Dods of Edinburgh three years before. Moreover, he had mastered the German language, both as a scholar and in the tea rooms. He now found himself plunging into the philosophical abyss, trying to formulate a comprehensive theology that would give him the freedom and confidence to go out into the world and act, and at the same time dovetailed with his sense of pragmatism. In his later life, of all of his beliefs, he felt most certain that nothing could be more debilitating than knowledge without action. There must have been a subconscious undertow, even here in Germany, that all of his study, all of his time and energy pursuing academic goals, might be quite useless to him later on. Such a cross-current might have added to his sense of strain during this time. He wrote in his notebook:

In talking with the students of Philosophy here ... They seem to think that Psychology and Philosophy are ends in themselves whereas they exist and should be studied and taught simply to enable a man to act more wisely and rightly. The proper business of men is acting, doing. And these men who can talk glibly of the different schools and viewpoints of philosophy and can logically maintain, fairly well, a certain system—and yet do not realize that the proper business of philosophy is to better the actions of men, have not begun to know what they are about; they are interested and entangled merely in forms as were the sophists in the day of Socrates and do not even know that they are ignorant . . . Descartes's quote should be "I act therefore I am . . ." [Instead of "I think, therefore I am."][15]

Berlin University marked the end of Jim's seminary training, and it was there that his theological views began to germinate a confident and distinctive view of man, his Deity and the condition in which he is found in this world. His views contrasted sharply with his father's, allowing Jim the sense of independence a young man needs. For three years he had thrashed about in the theology of the day, questioning, evaluating and making tentative solutions. In Berlin, an order grew out of the conflicts, a balance that fitted with Jim's sense of reality. At Berlin, the culmination of his education was a powerful, almost mystical sense of discovering the Truth. His friends and family followed him along in his discovery, especially his father, who never found it difficult to discuss such matters with his son. He decided to write to his father a letter on prayer. "Warn Father that his letter is temporarily in dry dock at the 41st page," he wrote to his mother (James G. K. McClure, Jr. to Phebe Ann Dixon McClure, July 1909). The letter was not only a summary of his new vision, but also a declaration of independence.

In 1902, Jim's father had published a book entitled *Intercessory Prayer: A Mighty Means of Usefulness*. It is a serious step for a son to reject a central tenet of a loved and revered father. Perhaps that is why Jim's letter ran on so long— seventy-two pages. In essence, Jim explained in this epistle that he did not believe in the usefulness of intercessory prayer. "God's will towards his creatures is perfect," he wrote, "and therefore cannot be increased by a prayer of man's." He felt that " . . . the whole content of prayer is in the expressing of our yearnings, hopes, purposes and desires to God, and in his presence correcting what errors have crept in, 'what flaws may lurk'" (James G. K. McClure, Jr. to James G. K. McClure, Sr., August 22, 1909).

One such "lurking flaw" took Jim to his knees in prayer. Being twenty-five, and living in the near monastic conditions of the university of that day, besides being very handsome and attractive, Jim naturally enjoyed the friendship and even adulation of many young women. For most of September 1909, he was incapacitated after a serious knee injury. With typical exuberance, he had leaped over a tennis net to congratulate his opponent, only to find himself unable to walk, and suffering from terrible pain. He had torn a ligament, breaking the blood vessel that passed through his knee. Blood filled up the knee cavity, making it stiff and very sore. When it failed to improve, he went to stay with some Dixon relatives in Liverpool, and had an operation.

Recuperating in the household of his "Cousin Lilly," he found himself surrounded, in his helpless state, by a number of kind and adoring young women. One of them wrote to Jim's parents afterwards, "I made it . . . my study to surround him with comforts and am constantly devising fresh plans which I think will help his amusement" (Jim's nurse to Phebe Ann Dixon McClure and James G. K. McClure, Sr., name illegible, no date). His parents visited him in England at this time, and his mother especially seemed much concerned about his health. Perhaps she sensed that his mental state was not easy. Jim's father wrote to him:

> During all our married life I have never seen your mother cry so much and so hard as when she held your flowers in her hand, kept her eye upon Liverpool where she was leaving you and let her grief find its relief in tears . . . Surely you have been blessed with a good mother and whatever experiences of disappointment in humanity you may have, her beautiful spirit is to be your life-long comfort. (James G. K. McClure, Sr. to James G. K. McClure, Jr., September 1, 1909)

After a month of being surrounded by comforting lady friends, Jim trudged sadly back to Germany. Back in Berlin, he attempted to befriend "an innocent German girl," inviting her to go somewhere with him. He was flattened by her rejection, and in the evening wrote with a penitent tone that "We cannot act the same everywhere that was right at the nursing home and all right at Cousin Lilly's where I was known—but not here. The woman was right to refuse."[16] The little incident lay heavily on his mind, and he composed this prayer soon afterwards:

> Oh God—Forgive me that so often I have let impure thoughts creep into my mind and dwell there—and not made a more spirited effort to throw them out. Enable me to act toward every woman that I meet or am thrown near in the whirling vortex of this great city as I would have my mother and sisters acted toward—remembering that the courtesy of a stranger must differ from that of an acquaintance . . . Impure thoughts . . . soon allow me to do the questionable thing, to do something or say something not because it is right or necessary but because it . . . has the added zest of a little impure excitement. Help me Oh God this winter in this great city and alone . . . [17]

As well as striving to give his best to his studies, Jim strained to realize ideal behavior, to achieve the perfection of a complete harmony with the purposes of the Creator and Sustainer of the Universe. In that pursuit, he honestly tried to admit his failures. No matter how taboo a subject might be, he wanted to expose it to the light of reason with the detached air of the scientist. Nothing should be allowed to remain in the shadows, gathering superstitions and misconceptions like dust in a cobweb. The Victorian bugaboo of sex he treated with a remarkable frankness, all the while trying to maintain an ideal attitude. In his Berlin journal he wrote:

Knowing only of the young man's problems, I should say that the most difficult problem the young man has to solve is his relations to women—the keeping of his . . . actions, his motives and thoughts pure. This problem too I should say to be the fundamental one of Society—as long as we are under earthly conditions these two classes of beings, males and females, will exist. And seek to hide the problem we do, speak of it in undertones or not at all; ignore it; cover it up etc., it keeps popping its head up and I am deceived unless history shall find that it is the fundamental whetstone of human existence.

In young men it takes all sorts of forms running up the scale from the mad, blind rush for sexual intercourse with any young woman and at any price, thru the more refined gratifications of the passions, through impure and smutty talk, impure thoughts and here rising to a higher plane, but still the same basis, the thought of marriage as the "sunnum bonum," [highest good] not looking beyond it, the filling of the mind with the thought and talk of marriage and thus closing the mind to any higher ideal than a happy marriage . . .[18]

And later in Liverpool he added:

The reason for sexual morality is that a man can not scatter his affections and have deep and true affections for any one person. For this reason, the man who in his youth has scattered his affections will not have deep enough feelings for his wife to enable him to carry through the sacrifices that true married life means and will mean. The man who holds aloof is building the foundations deep and strong for the love of one woman.[19]

If the most difficult battle of the young man is his relationship to women, worries over career choice must rank a close second. In 1909, Jim felt the call to serve mankind as a Christian, but he was questioning his earlier idea of going to the mission field in China. Clearly Spinoza and Hegel would not be much use. Such thinking, which influenced Jim and many of his well-educated, modern contemporaries, chilled the fire and zeal needed to convert the Chinese "heathens." He wrote to his college roommate and childhood friend Horace Ferry:

I cannot imagine on what ground I could ever have a reasonable longing to go to China unless it were arrant adventure which we outgrew at 12 years . . . [A]s to trying to take our forms of theology to China, that I consider absurd . . . And as for this pitying wail that goes up and the mentioning of the hardships well as you say life is pretty much a scrap anyway and we might as well fight it out where the thing is thickest and we will have to take our gloves off . . . [Life] only lasts 3 score years and ten, and [what a waste] if we wear Jaeger underwear 4 score and . . . are not winded yet nor sweating . . .[20]

Jim sought neither arrant adventure nor warm underwear to insulate him from the battles of life. He dreamed of becoming a great leader of men, and he did not expect it to be easy. Realizing that God had given him extraordinary powers of influence and persuasion, he struggled to conquer even small weaknesses and become a model of Christian ethics. Keeping a close watch on his actions he confessed his failings to his Lord:

> Oh God! . . . [I]nstead of loving display, *putting myself forward, seeing to be noticed, being loud or eager in speech,* and bent on having my own way . . . help me to be content, nay, to rejoice in being made little of, to perform what to the flesh are servile offices . . . not to argue, not to judge, not to pronounce censure . . .
>
> Oh God . . . increase my humility . . . forgive me for striving so for the good opinion of others, for aiming at effect; for thinking too much of my personal appearance—and above all—to which I am a slave—to little deceits, in expression and act, by which I plan to raise myself in the opinion of others . . . [21]

He had read Benjamin Franklin's *Autobiography* when he was laid up with his knee, and he was an enthusiastic believer in the old patriarch's theories on the ability of individuals to control their habits. Many scholars think that Franklin wrote with tongue in cheek to cash in on the American fascination for self-improvement, but Jim McClure took Franklin at his word. He was always looking for ways to improve himself, and jotted down these notes after witnessing a "heated discussion between two ear-splitting Germans":

> The cock-sure and assertive attitude that many people, especially men, have is an attitude which hinders communion of spirit, rouses unconscious hostility, is the opposite of persuasive, keeps the owner of the attitude from further enlightenment, is apt to lead him in to absurd positions and is on the whole an attitude more suited to a bar room than a home . . . Benjamin Franklin's idea was better. He found this assertive method in discussion not so valuable as the humbler, so he dropped such words as "absolutely," "without a doubt," and substituted "It appears to me" and "I consider" etc. Neither does loudness of talking seem so effective as a regulated pitch. [22]

On his own, Jim discovered the best way to draw out a stranger, to charm him from his isolation. He had mastered this technique, and it is wonderful to see his humor in the midst of all of his serious philosophizing:

> What a man carries in his pockets, how he carries his money, what sort of a hat he wears, what he likes for breakfast . . . how he keeps up his socks, the way in which he likes to recreate, whether it be to talk, to read, to ride, to run, to sleep, how he sits when by himself, with shoes on or slippers, how many hours he sleeps, these are all of great interest to a man, his dog, his horse, his knick-knacks in his house, especially if he has some pet little thing made, or labor-saving device invented by himself, his garden, his chickens, on all these things will a man warm up, especially perhaps on the dare-devil pranks of his youth. [23]

As he developed his personal gifts, Jim also struggled to create for himself a powerful new vision of what his service to humanity ought to mean. And his answer continued to harp on the heroic, a self-perfecting model of personal sacrifice. After absorbing the philosophy of Spinoza, he was plainly becoming a theological elitist. He questioned all theological systems and formulas, and cast the bulk of humanity, who accept the current view of life without questioning, into the role of the mindless. Jim was determined to find his own system. He was sure that his education, and intellectual quest for honest truth, had raised his religious sensibilities way above those of most men and women. He refused to compromise his sharp critique of the Christian church. Being an idealist, he saw around him little evidence of a world being redeemed by the sacrifice of the Son of God. He drew away from his earlier optimistic view that the world was rapidly improving.

> Has Christianity been such a great success as it is sometimes spoken of as being? Take a rapid survey of it at present . . . we could scarcely call South America, Russia, Spain and Italy Christian countries . . . with our Protestant ideas . . . We must hesitate to brand France and Germany Christian countries. England, Scotland and North America seem to have more religion than any [other] country, yet the existence [of] drink, war, discontent, worry, restless striving for money, class divisions, will not warrant us in calling these Christian countries . . . There must be something wrong with the religion which has made such slow progress. Impurities must have become mixed with it.[24]

Then he writes on a more positive note:

> Whether I believe in God or not my words do not show truly, only my life. I have met a few people whom I can plainly see believe in God . . . some people really have believed in God enough to give their whole lives, their money, their home, their friends and everything to Him . . . All philosophical, theological, scientific discourses, proofs and writings concerning religion I believe to be merely concerning the outworks of Christianity and to be of comparatively little worth. *The only unanswerable argument for Christianity is a Christian life.* And it is the one persuasive and influential argument. In my life the arguments for Christianity that have really affected me are Christian lives—Mother, Father, Dr. Dods, Fred Henderson, and John Magee.[25]

In spite of his theological differences with his father, Jim certainly felt a deep admiration for him, and thought his example was worthy of emulation. But once more he described his discomfort with the *status quo:*

> What makes me doubt religion is the way it is lived—so many professors of religion and so much preaching of love of one's neighbor and the good Samaritan—and yet the brotherhood of man, nothing but a phrase, no reality in it—men everywhere striving for themselves . . . the brotherhood of man seems ages off . . .
> How the love of humanity and battleships come into the same scheme is

absolutely ununderstandable to me ... The patriotism which limits one's neighbors to the inhabitants of one's own land and sees in every other nation a possible and already armed enemy is un-Christian. How can an Englishman cherish at first sight the feeling of love for a German with a subconscious knowledge on both sides that each is armed to the teeth? How can the universal brotherhood of man come when each nation looks out of its own feathered nest over a fringe of guns and pikes?[26]

Five years later, a gruesome answer to Jim's question came as the Great War bled Europe of its vision and vitality. He felt such a natural affinity for people, with all of their idiosyncracies and problems, that he truly was baffled by the powerful forces of hate that seemed to divide nations and set people at each other's throats. What about the brotherhood of man? Was it just a pretty idea? Jim knew better. Of one thing he was sure, that the moral idea of Christianity can best be seen in a person's life rather than in any doctrine he might hold. He remained convinced that all theology was of little use unless it transformed people, and unless it contained the power to use a man like him to change others.

What Jim hoped to find in theology was not so much a neat intellectual solution that pleased his sense of order, but a powerful, motivating vision that could sweep people together into action, giving their lives purpose and meaning. Jim was sure that meaning in life came more out of doing something positive than out of believing the right dogmas. Christianity had been a powerful force in history when it inspired people to sacrifice themselves for spiritual ends. Jim wanted to weld this Christian spirit to the progressive historical forces he felt gathering strength around him.

But as he prepared to go back to the United States and seek out a place to serve and lead his fellow men, a serious problem was developing for him. His health was going seriously awry. Indigestion and severe headaches were beginning to plague him. Was his demanding philosophy of self-sacrifice and perfectionism to blame, or perhaps his rebellion against the tenets of the church and his father? Or was he just exhausted by too many late nights of study, neglect of physical exercise, and a hard play schedule when he did take time off to be with friends? In any event a man who sought the heroic virtues of self-sacrifice and moral action was to spend the next ten years of his life in virtual bondage to his health problems, with only brief periods of reprieve. How did he keep his faith through this long, difficult period? How did he regain his balance and become an instrument of God's purpose?

His daughter, Elspeth McClure Clarke, knows that he had gained a deep faith in God's unfailing help by the time she was growing up. Certainly he was no longer trying to achieve his goals unaided. Again and again he stressed to his children and in his sermons, "I can do all things through Christ which strengtheneth me" (Philippians 4:13). "Fear not, for the Lord thy God is with thee whithersoever thou goest" (Deuteronomy 31:6). "He who doeth the will shall know the doctrine" (John 7:17). Perhaps this was the verse that finally made sense of all the theological conflicts and confusions. The simplicity of Jesus' invitation, "Follow me," would again become clear to him. In all his daughter's recollection he was a vigorously healthy person.[27] But for some time after these intense theological studies Jim was not well, and his illness was difficult to diagnose, difficult to treat, and, most of all, difficult to live with. But these years were not wasted, frustrating as they must have been. How often does adversity work to strengthen the characters of great men and women?

1. James G. McClure, Jr., "Berlin Journal," 1909. Most entries in this journal are undated.

2. *Ibid.*

3. *Ibid.*

4. Henry Drummond, *Natural Law and the Spiritual World.* (London: Hodder & Stoughton, 1883).

5. Berlin Journal.

6. James G. K. McClure, Jr., from a set of miscellaneous theological papers, 1909.

7. James G. K. McClure, Jr., note written in his notebook on German Psychology, 1909.

8. *Ibid.*, November 29, 1909.

9. James G. K. McClure, Jr., "God," paper written at McCormick Seminary, 1908.

10. James G. K. McClure, Jr., Liverpool notebook, 1909. Most entries in the notebook are not dated. Exceptions are noted.

11. *Ibid.* The entry reads "one thing I seem to lose—namely the personal sorrow that each sin causes God . . ."

12. Miscellaneous theological papers, 1909.

13. *Ibid.*, September 29, 1909.

14. Liverpool notebook.

15. Berlin journal.

16. Liverpool notebook, September 29, 1909.

17. *Ibid.*

18. Berlin journal.

19. Liverpool notebook, December 18, 1909.

20. *Ibid.*, October 24, 1909. The journal entry appears to a copy of a letter sent to Horace Ferry.

21. Berlin journal, October 27, 1909. Italics in the original.

22. Liverpool notebook, October 1, 1909.

23. *Ibid.*

24. Liverpool notebook.

25. Miscellaneous theological papers, this section inspired by a walk with John Baille, June 13, 1909.

26. Liverpool notebook.

27. Interviews with Elspeth McClure Clarke.

Chapter Seven
Affliction

Oh God in whose goodness I try to believe—enable me, as I have come home discouraged and with every hope apparently blighted and with no light at all for the future, to accept this lot in which I am with sturdy cheerfulness and determination. Give to me courage, Oh God, to persist in those ideals and hopes and aims of conduct which I believe to be for the world's good irrespective of the hopelessness in which they seem to involve my own future. Oh God, help me to give Thee a willingness to do and accept whatever is meted out to me . . . confident that Thou who inflictest the pain will at the same time and even more surely dole out strength and patience to bear it.

Forgive me that my heart has been heavy and even bitter and that I have added to others burdens by talking about my own—And now God, give to me patience to wait and to cause others to wait and courage Oh God how I need it! to persist in believing and acting on the belief that it is grandly and altogether worthwhile to live wholly for Thee—

Amen

(James G. K. McClure, Jr., personal notebook begun November 1, 1910, entry made May 12, 1911)

Jim McClure returned home to Chicago early in 1910, in order to fulfill the requirements for graduation from McCormick Seminary. He graduated in the spring, finishing his formal education at the age of twenty-five. He had had the advantage of a comfortable and stimulating home life, and the educational opportunities of seven institutions of higher learning, including some of the world's most highly renowned. He had met the challenges of Texas, New Haven, Scotland and Germany. He possessed a natural charm and leadership ability, qualities that made him ideally suited for his theological vision. In short, he was a dynamic young man, well-motivated, with the ability to work and to bring energy and enthusiasm to projects. At twenty-five, it was high time for him, according to his own precepts, to act, to put his knowledge to work for the benefit of mankind.

Then how to explain the years from 1910 to 1920? The years between twenty-five and thirty-five are often the heart of a successful man's career, and yet Jim McClure spent more time in those years playing golf than preaching his gospel. His only position of responsibility was a ten-month pastorate at the Iron River Presbyterian Church. For the most part, he traveled about visiting friends. He fished in the lakes of Wisconsin, played golf in lavish Santa Barbara, rode burros in Arizona, helped to build his sister Annie's home in Vermont, and

101

made a mad dash around the world on Mrs. Cyrus McCormick's money. He also ushered at numerous weddings.

It is a curious interlude in the man's life, and the one firm explanation for what happened is illness. His knee was mending slowly, but it was never a serious obstacle for him. The problems were physical, but with psychological origins. There were the apparent digestive difficulties that first cropped up in Tübingen. But the complaint that sapped his drive involved severe headaches, migraines perhaps. The exact nature of his malady is not discernable, because Jim McClure was never a complainer, and mentioned his problems rarely and without detail. What is more important is how he and his family diagnosed the source of his trouble. Everyone agreed on this point, that Jim McClure suffered from mental strain, overwork, trying to do more than is possible given the circumstances. In November of 1910, Jim's father wrote to him:

> Our hearts are with you by day and by night. I want you to carry as free a spirit as possible to be such that your mind may be without burden and your body without strain. Let us take it for granted that months must pass before you are in condition to take up the work you desire. In the meantime let us believe that our lives are planned by God and that some wise and helpful result is to be the outcome of these present days . . . Always know, my boy, how precious you are to your mother and me, and how I rejoice in you.
> Affectionately,
> Father
> (James G. K. McClure, Sr. to James G. K. McClure, Jr., November 4, 1910)

In retrospect, Jim himself traced the origins of these difficulties back to Edinburgh. Trying to keep up with his daily lessons, piling on extra reading to compensate for his academic gaps, and taking on responsibilities at the settlement house had been more than he could manage. He had allowed for too little relaxation in his life, he surmised. Jim had been determined to test his capacities, to find out just what the powers of his will could accomplish. But the record of his theological years does not indicate that his life was all work and no play. There were all the interludes with his lady friends and the gents of Skull and Bones in Europe. While much of his training took place in the familiar confines of Chicago's McCormick Seminary, perhaps there was an added strain in attending classes where one's father is president. Jim did have a rather restless mind, one that suggested many more worthy projects and deeds than one person can carry out. And he did tend to follow up these notions, throwing himself behind ideas and over-volunteering himself without regard for the limitations of time and energy. He was always happiest when lost in some enterprise or other, and found it difficult to pace himself, to quit rushing long enough to relax, especially during these early years. And yet, only those people who knew him best even noticed these tendencies. He also worked hard to present himself as a relaxed and affable young man. No one ever thought of him as nervous; he rushed on his own time.

As a young man, Jim McClure imagined the joys of the solitary, simple life, not realizing how ill-suited his temperament was for Thoreau-like contemplation. Just after graduating from seminary, he managed Mrs. Cyrus McCormick's country residence on White Deer Lake, Wisconsin, and during a quiet moment there he wrote:

> . . . character is the only thing in the world worthwhile . . . and to this end [I should be] guardedly simple. That motor cars, clubs, fine clothes, expensive and luxurious food are things which only seem to have a high value—and but blind us to the simple virtues . . . [They are] not only a great drain on character but a soil in which a great character can hardly grow . . .
>
> Let us realize that with simple food, with plain clothes, with quiet retired living—we can best grow in character and our lives will become fuller and we can best serve mankind . . . corn meal mush instead of caviar.[1]

Jim McClure was a man who appreciated the simple pleasures of life. He would rather wear his coat out, and then ink the worn places, than be stylish. But Jim McClure could never be happy leading a "quiet retired" life, contemplating the activity around him. He was a man of action who would much rather conduct the music than listen to it.

There were spiritual links to Jim's afflictions of 1910 that may help to understand them. His belief in a theology of perfection allowed for no relief from his own indiscretions. He would grieve over his faults, feeling quite guilty when his quick mind inflicted a sharp rebuttal to someone else's pet ideas. He wrote in his diary:

> Oh God . . . Keep me from jumping to conclusions, from thinking that I understand the point of another before he is half thru explaining or even half begun; keep me from nervousness and irritation at what seems to me the obtuseness of people, and the slowness with which they understand, and the slowness with which things happen in the world. Help me Oh God to be calm, and tranquil and very patient with all people and all things and in disappointment and most of all with myself.[2]

Jim moved home again for brief periods of time, but felt the discomfort of being supported by his family and surrounded by his friends, all of whom were busily organizing their own families and careers. He spent a lot of time with his youngest brother Nathan. The two of them liked to hitch up old Erma to her cart, drive to the lake shore, and go swimming on a hot summer day in Lake Forest. He used to treat Nathan to a day at the ball park, rooting for the Cubs or White Sox. In June of 1910, Jim drove up to Prairie du Chien to usher for Louis Douseman's wedding. Hugh Wilson joined him for the trip, and the two of them would have been quite a vision on the rural roads of Wisconsin in their Packard.

The following fall, Jim packed himself off for the Territory of Arizona,

Jim McClure, Jr., at White Deer Lake, 1910.

thinking that the climate there would help to cure him. Foster Rockwell, of "Yale '06 and Skull and Bones," was trying to make it there as a rancher. The dry winter weather of Arizona, along with the physical work of a ranch, held out for Jim much better prospects than being confined at home during the blizzards of Chicago. And besides, he had always enjoyed Foster's companionship, and admired his football prowess as the quarterback for Yale. The Dominie supported the move as well, and made a point of writing his son regularly during this difficult period for him. Dr. McClure understood Jim, knowing that his impetuous temperament was his own worst enemy. He watched his son struggle; he saw his energy and impatience cause great frustrations, and felt the need to caution him about building up unreasonable expectations.

... I often feel how little is accomplished that is actually worthwhile. However, there must have been in Christ's life very many days—and perhaps years, where the advance appeared to be very small, if it could be detected at all. . . . Wherever I went in the East affectionate inquiries were made concerning you. You certainly have an abundance of warm and devoted friends who believe in you . . .

Keep as free a heart and mind as possible and be a vegetable. (James G. K. McClure, Sr. to James G. K. McClure, Jr., November 22, 1910)

If matters do not progress by the middle of January, we will try to work out some new scheme. I fancy that you may not be able to do much but virtually loaf for some months to come. I am not at all discouraged about you. We will get the better of this trouble in due time. It is pretty hard on a temperament that likes to act quickly to be obliged to go through this prolonged process of delay, and I feel great sympathy with you in the delay. Still let us expect that in due time patience shall have its perfect work . . . (James G. K. McClure, Sr. to James G. K. McClure, Jr., December 7, 1910)

As Christmas approached, the Dominie continued to encourage his son, to look for God's purposes in the present difficulties, and to maintain reasonable expectations for recovery.

The word from Drs. Billings and Haven does not discourage me. Mr. David Fagan thinks you are doing as well as could be anticipated and he expects that some further time will elapse before all is right, and then he expects it to be permanently right . . .

Mother and I are seeking all possible light as to your immediate future . . .

Yesterday I preached in Evanston on the words "God who commanded the light to shine out of darkness." For several years I have been thinking of how God takes the dark periods of our lives and makes them conducive to our good—causing light to spring out of darkness. It is wonderful how many people have been stopped in their desired courses—by hindrances to themselves or their homes—and how later they had reason for thanking God for their dark experiences . . .

So let us be brave and hopeful, and walk the pathway of the present as gently as possible, and steady ourselves by believing that the outcome of it will be to the good of God's world.

This morning I went to the minister's meeting. Dr. Shailer Matthews of Chicago University made a searching and thorough address on the subject of the religious need of today, and he ended with the idea that . . . the supreme need is in Christian people (so called) denying *themselves,* taking up *their crosses* of human helpfulness and *living* Christ's life of self-sacrifice for one's good. I thought of you and our conversation during the summer, many times as he spoke. (James G. K. McClure, Sr. to James G. K. McClure, Jr., December 19, 1910)

Between one letter and the next, events back in the McClure home took a surprising turn. A young seminary student had begun to direct his affections towards Jim's older sister Annie. He was in truth determined to pass successfully through the Victorian courtship maze and emerge arm in arm with Annie McClure. The Dominie described the scene at home.

> As Annie has sent you word a young fellow has appeared on the scene, Dumont Clarke, a Princeton University man, with a partial Seminary career at Auburn and Union, a gentleman and a consecrated man, and it looks as though he had taken Annie and would some day carry her off . . . Annie will accompany me to New Haven . . . and then go with me to New York—where she will see Mr. Clarke's family and they will see her. If all then seems favorable, I fancy that an engagement will be the outcome.
>
> This is the most sudden and overwhelming thing that has occurred in our family life. It has taken dear Mother off her feet. She has not been able to sleep. At the same time she likes the fellow and feels that the affair is all right—as I do.
>
> To think of *Annie* in such a situation is well nigh ridiculous . . . The fellow is quiet and unassuming—but he went straight at Annie and told her his love, and took her breath away—and I should judge that he has got her.
>
> I suppose it devolves on me as the father to ask all proper questions of the young man and also *about* the young man—this I am trying to do . . . (James G. K. McClure, Sr. to James G. K. McClure, Jr., February 1, 1911)

A week hence, Dumont himself relays the message to Jim that the proper questions had been asked, and he in turn had given the proper replies, and that all parties therefore concurred in his proposal of marriage to Annie McClure.

> Dear Jim,
>
> Well—yes—brother Jim! You don't know how eager I am to meet you. For its all settled now! . . . I am very fortunate . . . God has richly blessed me in giving me your dear sister.
>
> When David Lusk told me, out in Madras, India of a certain Jim McClure— a friend of his in Edinburgh; I little thought of the relationship that was in store for us . . . And now that these eventful weeks have gone by I feel as though I know you almost as familiarly as . . . 'brother' Jim! For we have much more in common than simply our affection for, and our relationship to Annie! We have ideals and purposes in life, that, nourished and strengthened in atmospheres much alike, are, I doubt not almost identical. The religious life of Yale and Princeton is of that healthy type that, together with other opportunities and environments we have both experienced—and accidental resemblances (I was taken for you one day at the Seminary!)—it would seem that we could be chums right off. Lets try anyway! . . . Annie may have told you of the break down from which I suffered . . . then after my year in India I had another bad time of it—Well I know what you're going through and I *feel* for you . . . (Dumont Clarke to James G. K. McClure, Jr., February 9, 1911)

These two men did find more in common between them than their break-downs, and an enduring friendship grew up that would bear fruit later in their lives. Meanwhile, though, Jim remained through the winter at the R & R Ranch in Arizona, his social possibilities limited by the flux of his own spirits and the great expanses of desert. Jim helped to organize a softball game with some of the local ladies, snapping a picture of everyone out amongst the sage brush. The ladies look quite peculiar amidst all their ruffles and bows, bending down in the desert and awaiting their chance to make a play over to first base. And then there was a Mr. Reeves and his sister, whom Jim met on a burro trip across the arid country along the Salt River, through Tortilla Flats to Fish Creek. It was so dry that a drink of water for either man or beast cost five cents. Jim was cooking some biscuits one night, and maybe bragging a little about his days as a bronco-buster, when the Reeveses appeared. They were invited to join the expedition for dinner. Mr. Reeves looked like a down and out prospector— a loner dogged by failure. His long drooping mustache gave a theatrical look that was more than matched by his sister, who was wearing a funny straw hat with the front of the brim pinned up. Jim noted in his log of the trip, "Camped by the roadside near Mesa—completing the outfit we entertained Mr. and Miss Reeves at dinner."[3]

The daily rhythm of the R & R Ranch revolved around young Rockwell's vision of a successful ranch in an Arizona desert. There were to be orange groves and lemon groves, rose bushes, grape arbors, olive trees and a large commercial hay operation. Jim claimed to have planted 221 rose bushes in one day out there. He and his old friend had plenty of time for talk, and Jim loved to hear Rock's stories from the inside about the Yale football team of his day. Jim loved sports because he admired struggle and the spiritual cohesion that develops among the members of a successful team. He wrote down in a note-book he kept in Arizona some of the anecdotes that Rock told him, fascinated by the techniques of successful leadership these stories illustrated.

Jim returned to Chicago in June of 1911, in time to help with the preparations for Dumont and Annie's wedding. The family chose Lake Forest and the Presbyterian Church for the ceremony. Eighteen hundred admirers squeezed into the sanctuary. "One of the largest weddings ever celebrated on the north shore . . ."[4] chirped a social reporter, a fine tribute to the love for the McClure family in Lake Forest. One news article describes the crowd as " . . . a long line of solidly massed humanity on the streets leading to the church."[5] The reception afterwards was held on the grounds of the old Manse, "Gien Hame," just across from the church. "As Mr. and Mrs. Clarke hurried across the lawn after the reception to their carriage, a dozen or more children were waiting to say good-bye to the bride, and she stopped to kiss every one of them."[6]

The newlyweds invited Jim to join them in Manchester, Vermont, where they were planning to build a home. So Jim went East, after leaving Dumont and Annie to themselves for a respectful period of time. Manchester might be the essence of Vermont; it lies between two long ridges amidst the Green

Jim McClure at the R & R Ranch in the territory of Arizona.

Mountains, just underneath the focal point of the village: Mt. Equinox. White-spired churches, red barns, maple syrup, rocky brooks and glorious fall foliage all appear to be divinely arranged to entice people away from the distractions of urban worldliness to the "Walden Pond" of New England simplicity. And besides, there was a fine golf course in Manchester. Jim's Uncle Will McClure had been hooked by the town and lived out his life there, fly fishing for brook trout in defiance of his family's stern work ethic. Jim came to help build his sister's new home, but Manchester was destined to play a much larger role in his life than mere carpentry, for another young Lake Forest resident often returned to her family's ancestral homeland in this very same Vermont valley.

But carpentry was the trade at hand, and it was a good one for a young man whose mind had been too long absorbed in the philosophical battles of the day. Rafters and joists yield much more easily to the queries of mankind than do questions of eternity. A day's work produces the kind of physical fatigue and the palpable results of progress that are a wonderful antidote to the scholarly life. And Jim always enjoyed helping someone. He and Dumont grew to be good friends, close friends, just as the latter had predicted.

Jim made Manchester his home base through most of 1912, making intermittent excursions to meet friends and relatives around New England. He and Dumont were working on April Fool's Day that year, and both of them needed only the smallest excuse to pull a practical joke. Dumont slipped into the workshop the night before to take all of Jim's tools and nail them down to the bench. The next morning, after a great deal of prying and laughter, the working day settled into a routine. But all through the day Jim was scheming to top Dumont's prank. That evening, Jim left the house to take a short stroll and in the meantime Dumont received a telephone call from one of the great characters of the village. Bill Tuttle was something of a mad inventor, a prospector of patents hoping to strike riches and glory. "Mr. Clarke, I have a terrific idea I want to talk with you about. With a little backing, we will both become rich. Can I come over to talk with you right now?" Dumont tried to brush him off politely, but the persistence of the inventor won out, and soon he appeared in the doorway. The two men sat down to discuss the inventor's idea: a system whereby the headlights of an automobile were connected to the steering rods, so that when the driver turned a corner, the lights turned as well. Dumont listened politely, inwardly groaning at the nuisance of having to put up with this man. As incredible as it may seem, the "inventor" was none other than Jim McClure, who had mimicked the neighbor so well that, as the story goes, Jim left that night still undetected.[7]

The Clarke's new home was finished and ready to dedicate on July 4, 1912. It was christened "Sa Du Ja Dit," an acronym of the names of the principal builders including "Du"mont and "Ja"mes. Everyone was invited to visit and explore it on Independence Day. There is an old photograph of Aunt Kitty (Will McClure's wife), looking stiffly from the porch with the young married couple. Her coachman and carriage await her pleasure in the background. Uncle Will was no doubt off fishing on the Fourth. Another picture shows Annie and Dumont, Jim, Arch, Hetty and Nathan in greatly relaxed poses, together with their parents, enjoying one another's company on the new porch.[8] Jim's parents always made great efforts to bring the family together, to the extent that Hetty was brought home from boarding school the year Jim returned from Germany so that the entire clan could be under the same roof for a last brief time.

Moving on from Manchester, Jim and his family went to Castine Island, Maine, for a vacation together that included walks along the rocky coast and plenty of golf. Jim and Dumont had played quite a bit in Manchester, and in fact golf seems to have been a sport Jim pursued throughout this time as a remedy for his difficulties. Jim helped organize a tournament at the Castine course for late August, although there is no evidence he won any prizes. There is a wonderful picture of him entertaining three beautiful ladies with his accordion.[9]

Curiously, a golf game was one of the few situations in America at this time where the different classes came into informal contact with one another outside the home. Many a gentleman understood the working class world solely through the eyes of his favorite caddie. Jim noted a report from Dumont and Annie's "man." He had a wife and four children, and was forced to caddie because work was scarce. Judging by his tips, he took home between $1.50 and $4.00 per day. Jim responds to these facts with a sense of outrage that began to grip him during these years. "[It is] distressing to see men caddying at Manchester. [It is an] indictment of [the] industrial system when a man at a decent employment can find no work and goes caddying and has money thrown at him."[10]

Jim McClure tried to break through the barriers of class to become interested in the lives and potential nobility of the tradespeople who surrounded him. He collected short anecdotes to prove to himself the worthiness of the working class men around him. "The Larned's chauffeur worked like a Trojan . . . and would take no tip. The caretaker, a fine looking young chap, pushed the car with me 200 yards and would take nothing. . . ."[11]

Jim McClure was more and more drawn during this period to the Social Gospel. He read and quoted the works of the two men most prominent in the movement, Washington Gladding and Walter Rauschenbusch. Simply put, these men advocated a Christian socialism. They hoped to use the power of religion, and religious terminology, to transform society. The Kingdom of God was a fully realizable state of social perfection, in which class differences and antagonisms would disappear. In effect, the labor agitator could lie down safely with the capitalist. The emphasis shifts from individual sin to social sin, whereby the actions of one person can demoralize the entire community. In the Social Gospel vision, Jesus becomes the greatest reformer of all times, enlisting tax collectors, prostitutes and fishermen together into an organization that threatened the entrenched class structure of first century Palestine. With the death of Jesus, the movement did not die but took on the mighty Roman Empire with little more than a belief in the brotherhood of all men. Martyrs died as a sacrifice to their vision of an ultimate Peace on Earth. It was Saint Luke's "The Acts of the Apostles," full of examples of an early church that practiced a form of socialism, that most inspired advocates of the Social Gospel.

In reading Rauschenbusch's Social Gospel manifesto, *Christianizing the Social Order*, Jim checked and underlined this stirring call:

> To become fully Christian the Church must come out of its spiritual isolation . . . It has often built a soundproof habitation in which people could live for years without becoming definitely conscious of the existence of prostitution, child labor, or tenement crowding. It has offered peace and spiritual tranquility to men and women who needed thunderclaps and lightnings. Like all the rest of us, the Church will get salvation by finding the purpose of its existence outside of itself, in the Kingdom of God, the perfect life of the race.[12]

Like many members of the American elite, he felt strong twinges of guilt about the unequal distribution of wealth in the United States. In looking for scapegoats, he found the same ones everyone else found, and then some. Here is a compendium of his thoughts on some of the social and political questions of the day:

Alfred Hamill [a Lake Forest neighbor] told me that all the great Banks of Chicago [and] New York . . . break the law continually and knowingly . . .

This country is in the hands of a few men, i.e. Rockefeller controls most of the large banks in New York and Chicago. When a man attempts to initiate a new business, he applies to the banks for funds. The Bank officials—being to a certain extent figureheads, ascertain whether the Rockefeller interests are willing that the new business start up—if they agree to loan the money they do it on condition of the control of the new business. By this system the whole country is held in a few hands.

[Mr. Ambrose Cramer, Jim's future father-in-law, on corruption in the Chicago city government.] 'Hinky Dink' sends a ton of coal to every needy widow, tides over all men out of work; pays for funerals, etc. in his ward with the money he secures from legislation. Should an honest man win from him once he would surely lose at the next election—for Hinky Dink by these kindnesses would have secured the allegiance of the voting majority . . . no track or switch can be laid in Chicago without paying the council—no tracks laid in the state without paying the legislature . . . the most serious feature is the growing disregard of the Sabbath.

I do not see how a man with a family of 5 can spend more than $10,000 a year without committing grave social wrong.

Father thinks the country needs a whipping.

The idea that the method of life is "the survival of the fittest" furnishes the excuse to advance their own interests, perhaps ruthlessly and at the expense of the good of the whole body of humanity. This phrase is a catchy one and a popular one and yet it supports an entirely erroneous idea.

All my friends give me this excuse for not going to church (for none of them go) "I get nothing out of it." That is very true and I grant it. But I feel that that is but one half of the question and I should reply "What do you give it?" We must realize that we are the privileged class-have had education and the culture and breadth which are only possible thru wealth and our attitude toward the . . . church . . . as a means of affecting the community, should not be "What can I get out of it?" but "What can I give it?"

Imagine the treatment Jesus would receive, should he enter a first class hotel in any great city . . . He would probably be ejected without ceremony. Whereas the most immoral, debased man, with his pockets lined, arriving in a touring car and swaggering in with a chorus girl would be bowed to by every bell hop.

> These large hotels are one of the culture nests of artificial values—character counts for nothing—money for all . . . (Of course this is too sweeping for kindliness . . . the bell hops are working for dying mothers; the old lady in No. 17 thinks of the long hours of the maid and brushes her clothes herself . . .)[13]

The Social Gospel, in Jim's view, condemned the old vices of drinking and dancing as strongly as the Presbyterians traditionally had done. His prom stand-bys, the two-step and the waltz, might be safe enough, but he became concerned about new dances corrupting the working girls of America. He saved a New York *Times* article that expressed his outlook, and conjures up images of this lost world.

Influence of Social Follies

> The manner in which lax conduct in high social circles can influence the humbler to evil practices is somewhat alarmingly shown in . . . the investigation of some new kinds of fashionable dancing which have been made by the Committee of Amusements and Vacation Resources of Working Girls. The "turkey trot," the "grizzly bear," and other dances, so called, which are merely developments of terpsichorean extravagances . . . have been taken up this season to diversify fashionable dancing. They are not lively, and whatever may be done with them, in the way of artistic modification, in polite circles, they were originally intended to be indecently suggestive.
>
> The working girls get them from good society. They were not introduced into the popular dance halls directly from the lower depths, the unspeakable places where they constitute one form of joyless diversion. Because it is noised abroad that at a "coming out" party of a daughter of good society the "slow rag" or the "tango argentino" were danced, those grotesque posturing must, perforce, be imitated in the Saturday night dances of the poor girls . . .[14]

Such a quaint world America was in 1911. Will there ever be a "Committee on Amusements and Vacation Resources of Working Girls" again, or an article on "Social Follies" and the "grizzly bear" in the New York *Times*? At the height of the Progressive flood tide, the mood of the country was a paradox. On the one hand, the muckraking spirit searched out evil, corruption and self-interest in every level of American life. But the national mood was basically optimistic, with a strong "can do" spirit riding high. Exposure, along with the legion of committees, would rout out the blemishes within the country. Confidence in the democratic faith was strong. In 1912, one of the more remarkable of the nation's elections took place. Two Republicans (Taft and Roosevelt), sought re-election, thereby splitting their constituency. As a result, the nation elected Woodrow Wilson, the first Democratic president since Grover Cleveland. Stern and moralistic, Wilson became an apt symbol of the era, taking his views of a world based on Christian principles to the Treaty of Versailles. Never before had an American president received so much attention or been so influential on the world stage.

And never before had the mood been right for the prohibition of liquor. Evidence of the evil of alcohol is never hard to find, and the hope of the Progressive movement coupled with the self-denial of World War I produced the Great Experiment. Jim McClure's position had been staked out long before. In his haphazard study of the working class, he came up with this particular case to add weight in the general Temperance struggle:

> Nels Hanson, whose funeral was held on August 20—was 23 years old, and after spending an evening at Waukegan, was killed by a Northwestern train. He was intoxicated. A great deal of drinking is done by the young [working] men of Lake Forest.
> . . . The liquor is secured by getting some man . . . who is out of a job for the day to go to Highwood or North Chicago for the stuff. [Jim's father had kept it from being sold in Lake Forest itself.] Whiskey is the beverage and it is drunk straight.[15]

Temperance supporters have the reputation for being fundamentalist crusaders, popularly pictured as ax-wielding females who are naive enough to think that the sins and ills of mankind can be laid almost exclusively at the door of one substance. Jim McClure, and there must have been many more like him on this issue, was not of that ilk. He believed that it might be possible for mankind to perfect itself on this earth, and that for this reason alone alcohol should be removed from the list of demoralizing temptations. He wrote a paper while at McCormick on the saloon trade in Chicago, and pointed out how these institutions gave away free sandwiches to the working men who patronized them during the lunch hour. The enticement of the free lunch, Jim reasoned, was more than enough to bring "straight" men into a "crooked" place. Conviviality and relaxation soon worked its magic to draw even the strongest men into the habit of drink.

> To these saloons, in winter, the men must come at noon hour. They must have a warm place to eat their lunch in. The saloons supply the place—they offer to the cold ignorant men warmth and free lunch, but in return the men must fulfill the one condition attached—they must drink. If the workman does not drink he is put out in no time. Right here is where the man starts on his slide. On the cold days he will drink more to keep warm—he will seldom thereafter drink less. He will cash his pay checks at the saloon—there is no other place. The saloon-keeper gets a grip on his throat and gradually tightens it . . .[16]

There must have been quite a number of reformers such as Jim McClure to join up with the more fanatical Temperance adherents in order to pass the Eighteenth Amendment.

But as the tides of Temperance were rising, Jim struggled with his own weaknesses, his own character. He wanted to feel in tune with God's progress, to have his natural inner impulses match the high ideals of his thoughts. On January 26, 1911 he wrote down this remarkable prayer:

> Oh God, give me too some surety and conviction that this whole process of development and progress that thou art engineering on this earth . . . has . . . a benevolent purpose toward each individual . . . And as time goes on enable me more and more to understand how these two purposes are one. Make me to feel this personal relation to Thee and to feel, too, that the daily doings of even the most obscure of us all, the cooks and the ditch diggers and lazy Mexicans, is of importance to Thee and really matters in Thy plan for the whole.
>
> . . . Help me to dignify all men in their own eyes.
>
> And now God, give to me enduring patience that I may accept this long period of inaction with a cheerfulness, tho not boisterous, [that] may infect all those with whom Thou dost throw me with the conviction that after all and at bottom life is tremendously worth while. . . .[17]

To truly appreciate and empathize with the "menial" class (and the lazy Mexicans!) for a man with Jim's education and Lake Forest upbringing took a great deal of rethinking, and reshaping, of his behavior to fit the ideal. The habits of class ran deep. Jim wanted desperately to feel real love for all of mankind, and he tried to follow that ideal with each individual he met. Whenever he traveled, he had the conviction that the person sitting next to him was sent by God, and it was his duty to encourage that person in some way. This attitude made life for him a wonderful carnival of surprises, and indeed the uplifting effect his personality had on many, many people became one of the living fruits of his life. Again he prayed:

> Oh God, who art so silent that I forget thee, and who art so all pervading and so necessary that I take thee as a matter of course—forgive me that I live so much for the sake of cutting a figure in the eyes of those people who are about me. Forgive me that I give a real value to artificial standards and aim to be thought well of by the rich man or the successful man than the good man and by Thee. Forgive me that I flee . . . to artificial standards and lean to them rather than stand on our common humanity. Help me—Oh God! to feel toward and to act toward each man as a man and as a child of all loving source— Forgive me that I retire within the walled city of social position, good clothes, friendship with those in power or of money rather than stand in the open plain of simple manliness and uprightness and honor. Forgive me that I am . . . unwilling to appear to be on the losing side or to be outdated. Give to me more common sense and prudence and keep me from so recklessly and heedlessly rushing into things. Forgive me for talking so much.[18]

With all the energy, wit, and intelligence within him, he did find it difficult to control his tongue. He wrote: "Oh God . . . Help me to keep my mouth shut on all derogatory remarks and all remarks that may in any way strain or smudge another's honor, or diminish the esteem in which he is held or he holds himself."[19]

Out of this period in Jim's life came a thorough search from within of his impulses and pretenses that would never have been possible had he been in China, say, building up a school or hospital. His father had told him how often God teaches those people who are receptive during their weakest moments. Jim's friends were out in the world, pursuing a variety of successful ventures that built up their self-esteem. Jim had nothing to fall back on, no accomplishments he could point to and say to himself, I have achieved something worthy of the world's praise. The courage of St. Paul, who like Jim suffered debilities during his ministry, was an inspiration to him. Paul's single-minded adherence to the highest standards, the Apostle having been shown on the road to Damascus how much his life was based on artificial standards, produced in him a beautiful character of strength and courage.

Jim McClure was facing a dilemma that has troubled Americans since the beginning of the industrial revolution. On the one hand, the efficiency of machines and business practices has created enormous amounts of wealth along with the possibility of material subsistence for all. But the drive that produced such wealth was fueled to a large extent by the desire for personal power, influence and a sumptuous way of life. Jim, like many of his contemporaries, wanted to infuse the American business spirit with selfless Christian virtue in order that "society" might be saved.

In 1912, Jim returned from Manchester to the elegance of Lake Forest. Even if he felt strong yearnings for a simple life, how could he turn down a free trip around the world backed by his generous benefactress Mrs. Cyrus McCormick, widow of the inventor of the McCormick reaper, and a member of his father's congregation? She had taken a special interest in Jim, and worried about his present difficulties. Perhaps the ocean air and the variety of the world would work a special cure, and show him at the same time the wide variety of Christian mission work. Mrs. McCormick loved Jim as she loved his father. She was perhaps the richest widow in America, and thoroughly Presbyterian. Her hearing was almost gone by this time, and so she carried her silver ear horn everywhere. Being a doughty old woman, she liked to wield her horn as something of a weapon. If someone bored her, or she did not approve of what was being said, she laid down the earpiece to return to her silent world, leaving the speaker noticeably embarrassed. Young Jim was never boring, and he was full of wonderful ideas she approved of, and so he maintained ready access to her horn. A trip around the world might indeed clear up his troubles, and how much he enjoyed travelling! Jim found a friend, Bob Dangler, who was likewise in the mood for travel. In fact, the two of them left the day after Bob heard the plan, on New Year's Day of 1913.

To travel in Asia and the Middle East just prior to World War I was to see the last rays of twilight of the European colonial order. In August of 1914, the empires of Europe's most powerful nations began to unravel. Colonial competition was a major source of tension that lay behind this tragedy, and by 1918 the colonies began to hope for an end to European domination. But in 1913 Asia was still part of the old order, and Bob and Jim could travel amongst Christian missionaries hard at work, European administrators firmly in control, and Western businessmen confident of their markets. A Yale graduate could expect to see a world that, to a large extent, "his people" managed.

The first stop was Honolulu, in this day a pristine town managed by the United States for the benefit of its navy. Then it was on to Japan. Jim thoroughly enjoyed life on the steamships. He and Bob played baseball on deck, and Jim became the master of ceremonies for a day of activities. His knee held up as he won the one lap race around the boat, and his stomach likewise as he beat back all opposition in the Bun Eating Contest.[20] Throughout his trip, Jim had lists of family contacts to visit and look up. He wrote home from aboard the Japanese ship *Shinvo Maru:*

> We left Kobe yesterday noon, and coming thru the Inland Sea, are on the way to Nagasaki which we should reach about noon today. We have just passed the place where the Japanese destroyed the Russian fleet.
>
> I enjoyed my stay with Mr. Learned. He was in high spirits, gave his classes a day off and kept me trotting from morning to night. He wanted me to tell you that the Japanese have a custom of retiring about 55 or 60 years of age, handing over their duties to their sons and spending their days in meditation and writing poetry. He wants you to come to Kyoto for the poetry end of it . . .
>
> The best thing about my trip thus far is that tho I have been doing a good deal in Japan I feel none the worse for it. (James G. K. McClure, Jr. to James G. K. McClure, Sr., January 26, 1913)

Like many young men, Jim became fascinated by the institution of the Geisha girl in Japan. He talked with a Dr. Schwartz about them, and recorded what he learned in his notebook.

> Geisha girls are girls trained to entertain by singing, dancing, conversing. They are used by Japanese men in giving dinners, even in their homes. They are kept by some person . . . and let out.
>
> As to their morality they all have their price, tho the tea houses in which they dance are not houses of prostitution, they can be taken to a house across the street or someplace after their performance. Dr. Schwartz considers Geisha the greatest influence impairing the purity of the Japanese home.[21]

On to Shanghai, where Jim and Bob were only two of the many "Sons of old Eli" who attended the annual Yale dinner. Such a comfortable world in which to travel! In Hong Kong, Jim met up with one of his old friends from Germany while crossing the street, and Bob Dangler immortalized the moment with his camera. The superstition and poverty of China he discovered to be as rampant as he had expected. He thought the Chinese were foolish to think that they needed firecrackers to let the local god know someone was needing attention. Chinese beggars were a part of any American's view of the country, and Jim recorded the following incident:

> [I saw] a mob of some fifty of the dirtiest, toughest and most ragged individuals I had ever seen, lying in the sunshine of the street. I asked the missionary whom I was with what that filthy crowd was. "Why," he replied, "they are professional beggars. They travel together with a leader and start down a street, the leader going into a shop and asking the proprietor for a handout. If the proprietor is reluctant or stingy he points to the crowd outside and if the proprietor refuses to come across he beckons to the gang and they pour in and wreck his store. They work the city systematically, working each street every couple of months."[22]

Jim concluded that Christianity was the factor that made Western society different, that made helping the helpless a virtue. In China and throughout Asia he noted great numbers of suffering people and almost a complete void of compassion. "It is only under Christian civilization that we have hospitals . . . I found that in China if a coolie is injured in the streets he is left there or finally hauled off much as we would haul off a sick horse. . . ."[23] Soon the trenches of the Western Front would remind Jim and his contemporaries that barbarism lay just below the surface of European civilization as well.

After Hong Kong, the two travelers boarded a ship that would eventually land them in India. Bob Dangler wrote to Harriet McClure about Jim's colonial appearance. "Just docking at Manila in glorious sunshine—flags flying and band playing. Jim is looking like a prosperous planter in helmet and pongee suit" (Bob Dangler to Harriet McClure, February 6, 1913). They visited a rubber plantation at Kuala Lumpur and McGregor's Lumber Yard in Rangoon, with the main attraction at the latter being an elephant handling teak logs. A Miss Starr was very much in evidence during this phase of the excursion. The countries came and went so fast that Jim rarely broke beneath the superficial colonial view of this complex world. He returned with comments such as "The Burmese do not make soldiers . . . The Burman is indolent, the women industrious. . . ."[24] He was horrified to find people bathing regularly in a river infested with man-eating crocodiles. One had been killed and its stomach found to be full of the bangles of his victims. Because of a fatalistic religion, Jim wrote in his notebook, "the natives in the neighborhood of a man-eating crocodile continue bathing in spite of the losses in their ranks, looking upon it as fate."[25]

Bob and Jim maintained their fast pace of sight-seeing in India. Two days at each stop seems to have been the maximum time allotted. Their itinerary took them to Calcutta, Darjeeling, Benares, Agra, Delhi, Bombay, Bangalore, Madras (where they visited Eli Yale's son's grave!). To sister Harriet, Jim sent a picture of the gruesome funeral pyres along the Ganges River at Benares, the city he had visited years before in his imagination for "Steady Streams." "Knowing your moribund taste I send this postal" (James G. K. McClure, Jr. to Harriet

The Harbour, West.

Feb 9/13

Just docking at Manila in glorious sun-shine — flags flying & band playing. Jim is looking like a prosperous planter in helmet & pongee

Hongkong. The trip from Hongkong was absurdly smooth. We're having a wonderful time & call good wishes from Bab

McClure, March 3, 1913). And with similar grim humor, he sent to Annie and Dumont the message that "We have seen the Towers of Silence and the vultures who polish off the Parsees . . ." (James G. K. McClure, Jr. to Dumont Clarke, March 7, 1913). He and Bob made a pilgrimage to Bangalore, where Dumont Clarke had worked as a YMCA secretary and had done so much to raise money for a new building. There they found the new YMCA just completed. Dumont had asked Jim to bring with him the original scale model that had been made of clay, which he did, through all the vicissitudes of the remaining trip. It was packed in a big, bulky box, most unsuited to the gypsy life of Jim and Bob. But Jim wanted to do this favor. When he presented it to Dumont proudly, and opened the box, the clay model had been reduced to rubble!

In between the Taj Mahals and the Mt. Everests, Jim did have a chance to meet and talk with a young Indian "of one of the lower castes" who had picked up some English. "He asked me about caste in America and I told him the story of Lincoln. He frankly would not believe it. His ambitions, his possibilities, his future, his hopes were circumscribed . . . Nothing could call forth the best in that man."[26]

Jim's insatiable curiosity aroused his interest wherever he went. Questions about carpentry and queries about religion tumbled about in his mind, and wherever the language barrier could be circumvented, out they came. Bob wrote to Arch McClure that "Jim is very busy righting the wrongs of the Orient" (Bob Dangler to Arch McClure, no date).

The trip served to buttress Jim's faith in America and in Christianity. A Miss Richardson, whom he met at an archeological dig in Egypt, told him another story to support this faith. A Turkish foreign minister worked with her father in the diplomatic community of Athens, Greece. One day he ". . . received an order from the Sultan to return to Constantinople. He was afraid to return for the Sultan had a habit of ordering those not in his favor home and having them dropped overboard en route. He wanted to return hoping that he was to be promoted to Secretary of State . . . He went home and was never heard from again."[27] In Egypt, family acquaintances like the Richardsons continued to take in and entertain the two young men, and Jim made a noteworthy trip to Luxor on the back of a camel known as Will Taft.

The final and certainly inevitable leg of this grand tour was through the Holy Land. In 1913, Palestine was on the eve of becoming the political thorn it has remained ever since. A few years later, in 1917, the Balfour Declaration was signed by the British to enlist Jewish support for World War I. This pact was the first great victory of the modern Zionist movement to reclaim Israel for the Jewish people. Jim visited a backwater land full of donkeys, Arabs and a preponderance of religious shrines. After landing in Jaffa, Bob and Jim made their way to Bethlehem. The next day they rented a pair of donkeys, and slowly

Opposite: Postcard to Harriet McClure from Bob Dangler, February 6, 1913.

made their way along a Jericho a road not much different from the one Jesus had walked 1900 years before. They enjoyed a picnic lunch at Elisha's spring and an afternoon swim in the Dead Sea.[28]

Jerusalem yielded up its list of familiar sites: the Mount of Olives, the Garden of Gethsemene, and the Via Dolorosa. At Jacob's well they ran into 900 Russian pilgrims who had walked from their motherland. These people fascinated Jim, all the more so because he witnessed their simple joy as they attained the object of so great a trek. At the same time, he was disheartened by the way they were gypped out of their meager savings by unscrupulous Arab souvenir sellers. In Nazareth, Jim and Bob become acquainted with two pretty English ladies, the Misses Tassel, and that eventful day ended with the four of them praying together on the roof of the hotel.[29]

The Misses Tassel appeared again just over the border in Syria, where Jim and Bob had been touring the pagan ruins of Baalbek. Three Hellenist temples, one each to Jupiter, Bacchus and Venus, contrasted in Jim's mind with the more subdued Christian and Jewish sites to the south. Damascus, "the Pearl of the Desert," which was the city Paul entered after his dramatic conversion, was just about the end of the trip. It was a Grand Tour of the world in five months, and what can be said for it? First, it was a conventional trip with a predictable itinerary. From the Taj Mahal to the Wailing Wall to Chinese beggars and the pyramids, Jim McClure saw what was expected. There was nothing in this trip to shake his basic faith in the views of Protestant Christianity or in Western superiority, the American variety in particular. His admiration for foreign missionaries, with whom he almost invariably stayed, was heightened. One of his last visits on the trip was to the Syrian Protestant College (soon to become the American University) in Beirut (Lebanon was then a part of Syria). He was visibly impressed with the work there; American churchmen and American money were educating about 900 local students each year in the school's program. Jim yearned to be a part of such a work. The mission field that eventually captured him was found nowhere along the itinerary of this trip; in fact, it lay only a long day's train ride from Chicago. Yet the quaint habits of the people, the rigors of life, and the primitive nature of the society there could match almost anything he had seen in Asia.

Jim returned to America on the *S. S. Cretic,* from Naples to Boston. He sailed first class, and greatly enjoyed the company of several gentlemen traveling likewise. He took an engaging picture of a Mr. Dunn, a Mr. Hammand and one Marziale Sanchioni; the accoutrements of class in this photograph are all too obvious, from attire to pose, and remind us once again of the clean lines of social status that existed in this world. The young Indian who asked Jim about caste in America would have been even less likely to believe the Lincoln story had he been able to sail on the *S. S. Cretic* in 1913.

Jim remained in New England, going directly to Dumont and Annie in Manchester with his bulky box. After the shock of opening the box for Dumont, and finding nothing but dust, he told the details of his trip. One of his favorites was the time he and Bob were accosted by bandits. The family memory is somewhat vague on the exact nationality of these men, but they seem to have found our young hero on a mountain top somewhere, possibly the volcanic Mt. Etna of Sicily. How did Jim McClure handle the prospect of being robbed by dangerous natives of a foreign land? He challenged them to a jumping contest. If Bob and Jim could outjump the two bandits, they would go free. If not, the bandits could have their fair share of the Americans' loot. Well, as unbelievable as this story sounds, Jim's bad knee held up, and the wan Bob Dangler gave it all he had; the bandits were beaten fair and square and went home empty-handed.[30]

The Manchester crowd all returned to Lake Forest in time for the June marriage of sister Harriet. Douglas Stuart was the groom, a very upright and capable business executive who would in time rise to be President of the Quaker Oats Company. During the Eisenhower administration, he would serve a successful stint as the U. S. Ambassador to Canada. The wedding occurred on June 10, 1913, and the surviving pictures show a wonderful scene of a baseball game on a Lake Forest lawn. One of Harriet's and Jim's close friends, Marian Farwell, was playing third base while wearing a Quaker costume in honor of the bridegroom's business affiliation. The Stuarts hired a special train to bring their South Side Chicago friends to Lake Forest. Since the size of "Gien Hame" was restricted, "the wedding tea was served on the lawn, where pretty girls in lingerie dresses, flower hats and gay colored silken coats poured tea at beautifully decorated tables."[31] Jim ushered, and helped to escort one of Harriet's best friends, the lovely Elizabeth Cramer, among the rounds of society during this occasion. She was to return to France shortly thereafter to pursue her artistic aspirations which, fortunately for Jim, were interrupted by the events of August 1914.

For Jim McClure, the days of restlessness were almost over. He was now feeling well enough again to take on responsibilities. For three years he had traveled about, to Arizona, to Vermont, around the world, with uncounted side trips. He was desperate to engage himself in the world, to try out his abilities, and yet his nagging health difficulties had kept him back. In August of 1913, a letter came to Mrs. McCormick from a small mining town in Michigan. She had helped the writer find a pastor six years before.

> At the present time I am located at Iron River, Michegan [sic] at which point we have a church consisting of about thirty-five members.
> Iron River is situated in a district where large ore deposits have been made recently, the opening up of which has brot [sic] one a boom phase, causing the influx of a large number of families, and the church is desirous of getting in touch with these people. (Unknown writer to Mrs. Cyrus McCormick, August 30, 1913)

Mrs. McCormick recommended Jim McClure for the position, and truly it was a situation ideally tailored to fit a young purveyor of the Social Gospel. Iron River was a rough mining town, with immigrants pouring in for jobs. Rapid growth and the strain of absorbing many different national groups had left any previous sense of community in a shambles. Crime and alcohol were common problems. Great distrust among the immigrant groups, exacerbated by a babble of languages, created enormous tensions. Jim understood the role of the church to be a great force for civilization, and in Iron River he had his chance to start practically from scratch. In November, the Iron River *Reporter* announced that the "Rev. James G. K. McClure, Jr. of Chicago arrived here yesterday and will become the pastor of the Presbyterian Church ... Rev. McClure is a young unmarried man. He is a graduate of Edinburgh, Scotland, and McCormick seminaries and also of Yale University ... He is a pleasant and genial young man and comes to his new charge highly spoken of."[32]

Jim's three and a half years of convalescence were over. They were not wasted years. New influences and experiences became a part of his life. Arizona, Shanghai, Vermont and Nazareth ceased to be simply names to him. He had learned the rudiments of carpentry, and met hosts of new people. But his efforts had been scattered and undirected, and his life remained nearly all potential with very little yet accomplished. The Iron River pastorate fitted him well, and yet his strange and debilitating malady lurked in the background. Friends and family, and Jim himself, wondered whether 'the cure' was complete.

1. James G. K. McClure, Jr., "Stray notes" journal, 1910.

2. *Ibid.*

3. *Ibid.*

4. Newspaper clipping from June 28, 1911, saved by James G. K. McClure, Jr., paper unknown.

5. *Ibid.*

6. *Ibid.*

7. Interview with Dumont Clarke, Jr.

8. Family photograph album

9. *Ibid.*

10. James G. K. McClure, Jr., 1910 personal notebook, entry dated January 2, 1911.

11. *Ibid.*

12. Walter Rauschenbusch, *Christianizing the Social Order,* (New York: MacMillon, 1912), p. 464.

13. 1910 notebook.

14. "Influence of Social Follies," New York *Times,* January 5, 1911.

15. James G. K. McClure, Jr., Lake Forest Notebook, 1910.

16. James G. K. McClure, Jr., "The Saloon Question in Chicago," unpublished paper.

17. James G. K. McClure, Jr., notebook begun on November 1, 1910, entry dated January 26, 1911.

18. *Ibid.*

19. *Ibid.*, entry dated September 4, 1911.

20. James G. K. McClure, Jr., scrapbook of his trip around the world.

21. James G. K. McClure, Jr., Loose-leaf notebook.

22. James G. K. McClure, Jr., "Rackets and the Public," unpublished paper written in the early 1930s for the Pen and Plate Club, (Asheville, NC), p. 1–2.

23. Loose leaf notebook.

24. *Ibid.*, entry dated February 23, 1913.

25. *Ibid.*

26. James G. K. McClure, Jr., "Has Democracy Achieved Its Economic Purpose?" an unpublished paper presented to the Pen and Plate Club, Asheville, NC, 1926.

27. Loose leaf notebook.

28. Loose leaf notebook and the Scrapbook of the trip.

29. *Ibid.*

30. interviews with Elspeth McClure Clarke.

31. Newspaper clipping, June 11, 1913, paper unknown.

32. Iron River *Reporter*, November 14, 1913.

Chapter Eight

Iron River

No one disputes that the forces of good in the world, with their divisions into denominations, are inefficiently organized. So inefficient are they that tho we have millions of members in our churches, each with a professed belief in the brotherhood of man, the organization of these millions is not able to translate their ideals into action. It is as if into a giant hopper, the church people were pouring their ideals of brotherhood, their hopes for a better world, their money, their prayers, their work, their time. And out of the hopper instead of a society permeated by the spirit of Christ . . . comes a thin stream of prayer meetings, of exhortations & of accomplishment.[1]

I mean never by word, look or sign to show my discouragement. Further, no matter what happens I will see life thru & see it thru handsomely & graciously. Further I mean always to appear to be and to be content with my lot & full of quiet courage—no matter what the Lord calls upon me for. (Inserted by James G. K. McClure, Jr. into a notebook he kept while in Iron River)

Iron County, Michigan, is an aptly named district that lies on top of one of the world's finest mineral deposits. The ore extracted from the Mesabi Range of Michigan's Upper Peninsula has been a major component of the growth of the American economy in the twentieth century. In 1913 the town of Iron River was a rollicking, boozing, boom town, spawned by the growing appetite of the American steel industry. In a year's time, the demand for Mesabi ore would soar, and much of it would be shipped to France after having been fashioned into implements of war: bayonets, artillery, helmets, and even the barbed wire that was rolled out along the trenches of the Western Front. But to see Iron River's connection to that bloody future, or its connection to much of anything else in 1913, took an act of imagination. The place was remote, and its inhabitants for the most part were a rude collection of men and women drawn together by the wages of the mining industry.

The raw nature of life in Iron River was the precise quality that drew Jim McClure into service there. He wanted his ministry to be an act of social healing, a building up of a town and its inhabitants. He saw the opportunity to establish the ideals of Christian civilization among a people who were suffering from its absence. Rather than coming to soothe and comfort, Jim McClure came to Iron River as a general leading his congregation into battle. He intended to renovate the spiritual life of all the inhabitants of the town and better align it with his concept of the Kingdom of God.

The elders and deacons were impressed with the young man's sense of purpose, and so the church issued a formal call to Jim McClure: "The Congregation of the First Presbyterian Church of Iron River, Michigan, being, of sufficient grounds, well satisfied of the ministerial qualifications of you, Mr. James G. K. McClure, and having good hopes from our past experiences of your labors, that your ministrations in the Gospel will be profitable to our spiritual interests, do earnestly call and desire you to undertake the pastoral office in said congregation . . ." (Board of Elders of the Iron River Presbyterian Church to James G. K. McClure, Jr., October 28, 1913). The church promised to pay him $1,000 a year, and to allow him a four-week vacation.

His call to Iron River was followed by his ordination as a minister of the Gospel of Christ. In the McCormick Seminary Chapel, Dr. Andrew Zenos, Jim's former teacher, issued him his charge. Jim's father prayed for the fruitful guidance of his son by the supreme Lord of creation, and then everyone sang a most appropriate hymn, "Faith of our Fathers."[2]

Working and on his own at last, Jim gathered up his belongings and left his family. He found the church itself to be a simple structure, with bare grounds without any flowers or shrubs. Houses crowded right up to the church building, which was a plain white clapboard box with a large and rather ill-proportioned steeple. His congregation was made up of the leaders in the local mining industries, the owners and engineers. The only other Protestant congregation of any consequence in Iron River was the local Methodist Church, which had about as many members as the Presbyterian congregation. The bulk of the working class families, excepting the Scandinavians, were left to the two Roman Catholic churches, one of which was Polish.

Jim intended to cross all of the barriers that divided the people of Iron River, from religion to language to social class to national origin. He would minister to the entire town. He chided in his first sermon the businessmen in his congregation, demanding that they follow him across the social chasm on a mission of Christian duty. On November 16, 1913, twenty-nine members listened as he outlined his purposes in his first message to the church:

> As several of you know it was with some hesitation that I decided to offer my name for the consideration of this congregation, for as I looked around on the Sunday which I spent here the tasks confronting this church seemed so large, the town growing as it is and indifference in the community to the deeper values of life so strong and militant that it seemed to me that considering my lack of experience in the ministry, the whole work was more than I should attempt. I was strongly drawn to the work, however, and I felt that, as I had explained my limitations and emphasized my lack of experience, and endeavored to make that clear, that if you felt that I could be of service to this church and community I should like to come.

Top: *Iron River Presbyterian Church, Iron River, Mich., photographed by James G.K. McClure, Jr.* Bottom: *Train ticket to Iron River.*

This morning I want to speak in general terms about what I come here to try to do.

In the first place, I come here not to do certain things, I do not come here to attempt to run anyone's business ... l was born and brought up in a community of business men and they were fine, strong, self-reliant men and I have always had a great respect for business men and men engaged in the actual affairs of life. In those spheres you men are experts. Almost all the young men with whom I have grown up have entered some form of business or the law.

But there is one thing, in connection with the business world, that is a burden on my heart and I expect I shall frequently mention it and speak of it and that is my hope that the business world may be permeated by the spirit of Christ . . . the fact remains that the principle upon which business is based is not that of the strong helping the weak and it is the great task of our generation to attempt to re-generate business-to have business permeated from top to bottom with the spirit of Christ and that is a task before those of us who are businessmen.

. . . I do not mean to . . . interfere with anyone's individual responsibility or conscience.

. . . in all matters of conduct, I shall not interfere with your personal decisions . . . such as dancing, theatre-going, keeping Sunday, card playing.

. . . I mean to hold before you the highest ideals. . . . A church, anywhere, to be of any use at all must be a working church—and it must be working for the community. Every member must be doing something. It is more important that a member of the church do something than that he believe something. Do not think of the church as a place of retreat, a place in which you can escape the trials of the world and the strenuousness of life. The church is not a place for tired men and women.[3]

The die was cast that Sunday. If Jim wanted a working church, then its pastor would be required to exert himself to the very limits of endurance. He would have to overthrow the accepted notion that a minister rode a pretty soft ride, and earn respect first of all as a man of action, and secondly as a man of vision. With no home or retreat of any sort, it would be hard for him to resist filling each day, all day, with some useful activity. He had to prove himself to these people, and do it by making an impact on the community. The question was, how much stress could he maintain before his old symptoms returned?

Jim's father and mother visited him about two weeks into the work. The Dominie understood the strains of his own profession, and what can happen to overeager young ministers. Moreover, he knew his own son's personality, and so cautioned him to learn to pace his life.

. . . Annie, Dumont, and Arch are eager to hear every possible word about you and your church.

. . . Now my dear boy, let me say:

I. Try to be as calm in your mind as possible: "Study to be quiet" is Scripture.

II. Don't try to make matters move too hastily
"Hasten slowly" is a good motto for you and ___ work.

III. Make your sustained health a matter ___ purpose, plan and persistency"—Get to your room and lie down—and *not think*.

IV. Persuade Mrs. Young to let you remain where you are for the winter. I will pay the bill. Fix up your bedroom in the Manse and when she wishes your room, you can go to the Manse for a night or two.

V. I see the limitless opportunities and demands that are sure to come to you. Conserve your strength. *Visiting is killing* to nervous peace, to intellectual development and to spiritual power. A call counts for more in many instances than a long visit.

VI. You are answering to all that my heart could possibly wish. You are a noble man, you are doing noble work—and I am perfectly content. *Only—Be careful not to overdo.*

Let *time* be an element in your power. You made us very happy every minute we were with you. Our tender and abounding love is yours.

Father

(James G. K. McClure, Sr. to James G. K. McClure, Jr., December 15, 1913)

A week after receiving this advice, Christmas would come to this frozen community. Jim was determined to bring the spirit of brotherhood into his church, to fill it with as diverse a group of people as Iron River could provide. At the same time, he would sorely miss the great joy of being with his own family at home, a very special time for him each year. He set out throughout the town and surrounding countryside, knocking on the doors of strangers and persuading them to come to the Presbyterian Church for a fine Christmas service. His famous powers of persuasion worked their magic, and on Christmas the church began to fill up with the most remarkable variety of people. As the regulars and the newcomers began to settle into the pews, a palpable sense of uneasiness began to settle over the congregation. Feigning nonchalance, people began gazing about the church, wondering whence all of these people had come. It was the kind of scene Jim McClure adored. He was a master at breaking down the barriers between people, cutting through the suspicion and creating a joyful and friendly ambience. After the service, he rushed about thanking the newcomers for making the effort to come, and introducing them among the regulars. He had a knack for remembering names, and for remembering some small item of interest to dispel an embarrassing silence; and soon, almost singlehandedly, he created that Christmas among a group of men and women very strange to one another, a wonderful feeling of conviviality and Christian brotherhood. The event was a grand success, and the Presbyterian Church in Iron River afterwards became a growing body of believers.

Back home on Halsted Street, gathered around the McClure table that same Christmas Day, Jim's family prayed for his well-being and then sent some letter paper around to everyone, to cheer up their missing member.

My dear boy:

We are all gathered around the family dining table, Mother, Annie and Dumont, Harriet and Douglas, Arch, Nathan. . . . and myself. We think and speak often of you. We have wished for you a thousand times today . . .

[Harriet writing] Dinto [Nathan] and Doug are upholding the 'arty appetite club'; D. Clarke is trying a good deal of his pleasantries much to the annoyance of his wife, who claims that she "doesn't talk as much as she used to." Whereat the whole table burst into a shout of acclamation.

[Annie writing] The above is not literally true. Nothing that Dumont does annoys me, as you well know. We are having a grand Christmas but we do miss you every minute. The baby (Dumont, Jr.) has had a wonderful day, enjoying all his gifts with true delight. We wonder where you are celebrating— and how many attractive ladies are looking at your "melting eyes"—I must close as Douglas simply can't wait to put his sentiments down—

[Douglas Stuart writing] This has been a great Christmas . . .

[Dumont Clarke writing] I am following in the foot-steps of a great man, you see so I shall shine only by reflecting glory. Dumont Jr. is just sighted and havoc ensues—so there is no chance for more or greater thoughts. (McClure family to James G. K. McClure, Jr., December 25, 1913)

In Iron River, the winter that followed Christmas was as harsh and cold as it always was. Like everyone else Jim pulled his driving blanket right up over his nose when he drove about. The physical suffering of the local inhabitants was exacerbated as the demand for ore slackened, and the mines began to close down. Yet, what glory there was must have shined off the young minister Jim McClure, for he persistently worked to alleviate any hardships that came to his attention, physical or spiritual. The boom town atmosphere of Iron River seemed to break down the bonds of self-restraint, and Jim had to face squarely the ugly faces of sin. Of his nine Sunday School teachers, three had had sisters or a daughter "ruined." In one month alone twenty-one cases of rape were brought to his attention. One girl had to leave Iron River for the second time to abort her illegitimate child. One man, Kilkollins " . . . had slept with every cat in the county." His wife was almost raped by her uncle, but she tore up his face with hair pins. She eventually hired a girl with syphilis for $10 to sleep with Kilkollins so he would contract the disease, and she would have grounds for divorce. With unflagging energy, Jim waded into the midst of these problems, doing what he could.[4]

During the winter of 1914, widows were being turned out of their homes for the lack of $5 in rent. Young children roamed about town with no place to go but the saloons for a little excitement. The local Catholic priest was hopelessly corrupt, getting drunk with his housekeeper and carrying on with little girls at church picnics. At church suppers, after liberal doses of wine, the priest would urge girls to dance the jig on the table. The local Polish community tried to have him removed, but according to Jim's notes the priest bribed the bishop and had the leader of the movement put into an asylum![5]

Jim McClure took on the town's business. He once smelled a whiff of corruption in the local school system, and stood up at a public meeting to grill the Superintendent and bring to light the duplicity of his policies. He helped to found the Iron County Welfare Association, whose purpose was to abolish the "Liquor Traffic" and to prevent "Immorality and Vice." To the surprise of everyone, saloons were voted right out of the county. That spring, Jim spearheaded a drive to build and equip a playground and ball park. Bats and balls were purchased, and teams organized. Jim brought in a gymnastic exhibition, to inspire the local children on how to use the new parallel bars and spring boards. He realized that the life of any community revolves around shared activities, and that sports were a great deal healthier for the morals of the young than hanging around idle.[6]

Jim's mission to Iron River fulfilled his ambitions; here was a place where his Godly training could be put to work, rooting out sin and bringing people together in a more holy and less suspicious environment. Here he could minister to an entire town instead of a single, well-established church. By his own reckoning, he set himself up as a model of high character and self-sacrifice. He wanted to drag this grimy little mining town a little closer to paradise, and he knew that his influence could make a difference only if he remained above reproach. Not unlike Moses leading his ungrateful people about the Sinai desert, he was determined that no amount of grumbling would dissuade him from his purposes, and no amount of sin would force him to compromise his adherence to the moral commandments. How long can a man endure such a life? His heroic outlook masked the loneliness of his role.

In February of 1914, in the middle of that awful winter, Jim showed himself to his parishioners as a man who was obsessed with perfection, and consequently was unhappy with anything less in himself. Jim's ministry in Iron River was largely a matter of preaching the highest of ideals, and then setting himself up as an example. In a sermon, entitled "The Mastery of the Will," there were no biblical references and God was a distant and somewhat fuzzy concept. One's ultimate faith, Jim explained, rested solely in the individual will. Sin and human frailties were too easily accepted; instead, through the exercise of will weakness was to be rooted out. "We make the universe we live in," he told his congregation. "If we determine to live as if God is good and as if men are the children of God we will find that true. If we determine to live as if God is a lie and all men are liars & deceivers we will find that true." He advocated a " . . . systematic training in Mastery of the Will. . . ."[7] He concluded by saying that "The man who will call upon his will, with God's help, can keep from doing wrong because . . . he brings his will into battle & creates a victory." In these ideas, and in Jim's natural inclination, there was very little room for him to follow his father's advice, to find a time and place to rest and relax his mind. He began to have headaches again, but tried to ignore them.

During the following summer, he threw himself into a campaign to draw immigrant families out of the Catholic fold. Most of the miners in Iron River were a part of the pre-World War I exodus from Southern and Eastern Europe. Like most old-stock, Protestant Americans, Jim was appalled by the behavior of these men and women, and felt the Catholic Church was in large part to blame. He saw his mission to Iron River as a chance to influence the ideals of these Catholic workers and their families, almost none of whom attended his church. The Presbyterian Board of Home Missions was interested in Jim's efforts among the immigrants as well, and advised him that summer to make an informal census of the town, partly to answer specific questions and partly as a pretext for meeting and talking with these people. Jim was advised: "In your canvas I hope you will find some way of ascertaining what your people are thinking about. It is not adequate simply to say that so many people are Roman or Greek Catholic. What do they think of the church? Are they loyal to it? What is their affiliation with socialism?"[8]

"Socialism" was a scare word to the businessmen in the Iron River Presbyterian Church, filled as it was with the specter of violent labor unrest that a small mining town could ill afford to endure. But Jim thought these businessmen worried too much about their profits, and too little about the welfare of their workers. He told them so in a sermon called "Unsparing Helpfulness," and challenged his congregation to work out a plan to raise the moral level of the local Slavic people and to alleviate some of their grievances. The businessmen must be examples of Christian charity, or else "American standards will inevitably be sucked down by those Southern European standards—as a drowning man sucks down a rescuer-unless we raise them artificially to our level."[9]

But by the time Jim McClure proclaimed "Unsparing Helpfulness" from the pulpit, he began to face the prospect of leaving this work behind. He had not followed his father's advice, and now all of the old troubles with his health began to creep in and incapacitate him. In October he took a leave of absence, hoping to rest up and return. Two months later he officially resigned, with this letter. "After thorough examination by and careful deliberation with specialists it appears that there is no possibility of my immediate return to the pastorate. I feel further that a longer postponement of decision would be unfortunate. It is with sorrow and disappointment that I herefore tender my resignation of the pastorate . . ." (James G. K. McClure, Jr. to the Iron River Congregation, December 9, 1914).

It was with very similar emotions that the congregation accepted his resignation. They responded with a resolution, adopted unanimously.

> Rev. McClure, in a period of less than one year, completely won the hearts of the people of Iron River. He impressed everyone with his sincerity, cordiality and common sense.
>
> . . . Under his care the work prospered greatly, as may be judged by the fact that forty-eight new members were received, and a large increase was made in the number of adherents . . .
>
> As a leader he drew both the weak and strong to him and called forth the best they had to give. We were drawn by his enthusiasm; we were held by his tact, and helped by his teaching.
>
> But Mr. McClure was a pastor to the community rather than to a single church. That an enterprise was for the public welfare was sufficient for it to claim his interest. He adapted himself strikingly to the peculiar needs of this community, holding firmly to his convictions, yet cheerfully admitting room for difference of opinion. He saw good in every man and in every creed. His numerous small acts of attention and kindness bound him to scores of the young and the mature. He seems to try not so much to find perfect men as to make better men. He regarded every man's conscience as sacred. In many cases he won the loyalty of those who naturally would have opposed him.

Top: *Gymnastic show brought to Iron River by Jim McClure.* Bottom: *Newspaper announcement.*

In letting Mr. McClure go we feel that our Church and our community has suffered a great loss. We wish him God-speed in his future life and work.[10]

The ways of the Lord are indeed inscrutable, for in a year's time that future life and work would take on an entirely new look for Jim McClure. But for now, all was the gloom of his ill-health with only the letters of his former parishioners to cheer him up. Gustavus R. Waeber wrote:

It is difficult for me to express our feelings of regret and loss that your resignation has brought forth among us all. The hope of your returning to the Iron River pastorate has been with us at all times and our prayers have been for your speedy return, for we felt that we needed you here . . .

It is we who have to thank you for the seed you have planted within us; altho your work at Iron River was only begun, I am convinced that it will have its lasting influence, marking the time when this congregation took its first steps toward a practical Christianity. (Gustavus R. Waeber to James G. K. McClure, Jr . . . Exact date unknown)

A Mr. William H. Seldon wrote this rather personal note, offering as well a sure cure for his troubles:

We miss you, and while we miss your presence and influence at all times, we miss you particularly Sunday evening at crackers and milk . . .

I felt that you were working very hard last summer, and perhaps carrying too great a burden, but did not discover that it was affecting your health, in fact thought quite the reverse was the case, and that you seemed to become more vigorous under the pressure of hard work.

Now I am going to prescribe a remedy, which I believe cannot fail to restore you to health, which is a summer spent in our Michigan woods, getting just as near to nature as possible . . . (William H. Seldon to James G. K. McClure, Jr., December 20, 1914)

One of the mine owners, Herbert Fisher, wrote Jim:

Your resignation came in the form of a shock I assure you and the loss of your presence in this community was a real loss.

I personally knew right along that I owed you a lot for the influence on my life and my family's, but I did not know how much that same influence had been to the whole community.

I seldom go anywhere but what you are spoken of, and they seem so anxious for your welfare.

Even tho you were here but a short time the people of Iron River will never forget you and the master you served. . . . (Herbert Fisher to James G. K. McClure, Jr., February 16, 1915)

Although Jim never returned to take up his post in Iron River, he never forgot his friends there either. He continued to send money to the Welfare League long after he had moved away, and that summer he sent one of his coats to the minister in the neighboring town, Reverend J. W. Helmuth, who wrote him back:

Your letter came stating that I was to be the recipient of a frock coat and vest. In due time they arrived and I put on the coat and we all delighted to think you sent me so good a coat and made so well and such excellent fabric . . . I moderated the congregational meeting when they acted upon your resignation. Your letter when read made a great impression upon the people, and when I asked for statements from different persons bearing on the resignation, it was hard for them to speak. . . . (J. W. Helmuth to James G. K. McClure, Jr., June 28, 1915)

Of all the letters he received from Iron River, one, more than the others, indicated to him that he had sown the seeds of Christian life there. George Terrill, a high school student, wrote Jim that spring:

Dear King:
Last Wednesday night I appeared before the Presbyterian Session to join the
church on confession of my faith . . .
I will have to be a good boy after this, which I am afraid I will find a hard
thing to do altogether. But "one and God is a majority." (George Terrill to
James G. K. McClure, Jr., March 13, 1915)

Iron River was an aborted start for Jim, but he did have a chance to try out
some of his ideas. He saw himself as a crusader, not only making his church
and Iron River a better community, but also trying to prove that religion still
had a role to play in modern society, that Christianity could lead mankind
forward. Many people, including Jim, thought that the institution of the church
was a reactionary force, retarding progress by thwarting science. Jim wanted to
disprove this view. He preached in Iron River, in January of 1914, elaborating
on the Apostle Paul's vision of the church as a body with many parts (Romans
12). Forty-two parishioners came to church that morning, and listened as Jim
preached "Is the Church Necessary in Modern Society?"

You hear often criticisms of the Christian church and disparaging remarks
about the church, remarks pointing to the idea that the church has finished its
task and is becoming impotent. When I was studying for the ministry in
Germany comparatively alone and with time for thought, I asked myself the
question, "Is the church necessary in society today?" And after withholding
my judgement for months and considering the question from all sides, I came
to the conclusion that it was absolutely necessary today.

He reviewed at some length the direct and indirect good done by the church
in history, and attributed " . . . much of all that is brightest and best in our lives"
to the influence of the church. Then he turned to the present. He quoted a judge
who claimed that he had never tried and sentenced a youth who was a church
member and attended Sunday School. The judge went on to say:

The influence for good of the modern church is greater than the church's
influence ever was before. The church has grown amazingly as the world's
wisdom has increased, all statements to the contrary notwithstanding . . . I go
about a good deal to the men's clubs of the churches, to deliver addresses upon
one topic or another, I find their membership to be made up, not of milk and
water youths, and doddering old men with a foot each in the grave and nothing
to live for on this earth, but of energetic, fine young chaps of all ages, among
them always, the best men of the neighborhoods in which the churches are
located. . . ."

Having established the present moral influence of the church, Jim turned to the
future. He said,

Even if the church had had no past and were not existing at present, I believe
that some such organization would be absolutely necessary for the future. We

are in the midst of a vast historical movement . . . The organization of society is being called to the bar of judgement and being confronted by its sins. We are in a period of flux . . . We are in a position to inject into the organization of society, the spirit of the brotherhood of man. . . .

He argued that, in order to establish the brotherhood of man, sweeping social changes would be necessary, and the church would have to be involved in making those changes take place. He talked about the redistribution of wealth, "making a simpler life the fashion," and the importance of helping the laborer see the importance of his contribution to society as a whole. In defense of the poor, he said:

People often tell us that the poor are poor through their own fault, and [the] rich [are] rich through their own efforts, and one can cite instances enough of shiftlessness keeping men poor and industry making men rich to seem to prove this. But it is not true. There are any number of hard working, faithful, industrious men who are poor through no fault of their own and any number of comparatively worthless men rich through no fault of their own.

He talked then about changing society through the efforts of "regenerated individuals, whose wills set justice above profit and policy, and whose vision is not warped by the desire for wealth." He urged the businessmen in his congregation to be seekers after justice, who will bring this "social gospel" to their business decisions, and so change society. He called for unity among Protestant Christians to accomplish this task. Then he concluded with this call to the church, which expresses the ideal he longed to see in the church throughout his life:

The amount of power that a church has depends on the amount of self-sacrifice that goes into it and there lies before us, the possibility, by each one sacrificing time or pleasure, of making this church a great power in the community and in the lives of every one who comes in touch with it.[11]

Although Jim McClure left his mark on the Iron River Presbyterian Church, he was not able to achieve its perfecting as he had hoped. Nor did he ever, as it turned out, hold the position of pastor in a church again. But he did have an influence on many churches in another part of the country. Before he could continue his life, however, he had to overcome the strange debility that crippled his work. Was it in fact his approach to that work that was the problem? Did he fight so hard against imperfect behavior in himself that eventually his emotional and physical equilibrium was destroyed? He had to find answers to these questions before he could go on to the active life he desired more than anything.

1. James G. K. McClure, Jr., Berlin notebook.
2. Church Bulletin for the ordination service, among the papers of James G. K. McClure, Jr.

3. James G. K. McClure, Jr., sermon given at Iron River (Michigan) Presbyterian Church, November 16, 1913.

4. Iron River notebook.

5. Iron River notebook.

6. Iron River notebook, including a photograph showing the Iron River ballfield.

8. Letter to James G. K. McClure, Jr., from The Board of Home Missions of the Presbyterian Church, signed W.P. Shriver, August 10, 1914.

9. James G. K. McClure, Jr., "Unsparing Helpfulness," sermon given at Iron River Presbyterian Church, September 27, 1914.

10. Resolution passed by the Congregation of the Iron River Presbyterian Church, December 29, 1914. Found among the personal papers of James G. K. McClure, Jr.

11. James G. K. McClure, Jr., "Is the Church Necessary in Modern Society?" sermon given at Iron River Presbyterian Church, Sunday evening, January 11, 1914.

Chapter Nine
Elizabeth Skinner Cramer

Painting should be an accompaniment to life—it should be a means of stimulating the imagination and spiritual side of human beings to further development, and at its greatest epoch this is what it has always been. (*Elizabeth S. Cramer to James G. K. McClure, Jr., February 28, 1915*)

Since I have known you, I have somehow been "born again." (*Elizabeth S. Cramer to James G. K. McClure, Jr., March 2, 1916*)

In the summer of 1914 two unconnected tragedies conspired to bring Jim McClure and Elizabeth Cramer, daughter of a successful Chicago businessman who had been studying painting in France, back to their homes in Lake Forest. Jim returned from Iron River, discouraged and distressed over the breakdown of his health. In October, 1914, he requested an indefinite leave of absence from his duties as pastor from the Board of the Iron River Presbyterian Church. The work of preacher, pastor and town reformer had broken him again. By all accounts his efforts had been effective, and he was much beloved and respected by his congregation, but something remained terribly out of balance in his life. His old maladies flared up again, leaving him incapable of sustained work; so he was forced to leave the only church he would ever have under his care.

That same summer Elizabeth Cramer was in France, busy painting. She had set up a household in the little village of Trépied with her friend and "chaperone," Miss Martha Clarke. The German attack on France effectively spoiled her dreams of intense artistic efforts. Trenches, mustard gas and casualties soon took hold of the popular and serious imagination alike, and art ceased to be the passion of Europe for some time to come.

Elizabeth had been back and forth to France for several years. She was brought up in Lake Forest, the daughter of wealthy businessman Ambrose Cramer, and Susie Skinner Cramer. Elizabeth's mother had been known in her youth as a brilliant conversationalist, and was the favorite of Chicago society.[1] Elizabeth's grandfather was Judge Mark Skinner, an important figure in the development of early Chicago. The Skinners were from New England, having been prominent in early Vermont history.[2] The Cramer ancestors were from the Church of England settlements of Southern Ireland under Cromwell. Ambrose's great grandfather had come to Virginia in the 1700s. Ambrose grew up on a plantation, and watched the family fortune crumble during the Civil War. After a stint at the Naval Academy in Annapolis, he came to Chicago to recoup that

Elizabeth reading on her lawn at Rathmore.

fortune, and succeeded. The family moved to Lake Forest in 1896, when Elizabeth was eight. Two years later, her mother died. This was a tremendous loss for Elizabeth and for her younger brother Ambrose, Jr. When Elizabeth was thirteen, her father remarried. His new wife was Isabelle Corwith McGennis, who had a daughter around Elizabeth's age, also an Isabel. These two girls became dear friends. As Elizabeth grew up she remained very close to her maiden aunts, Elizabeth and Frederika, the adoring older sisters of her mother, Susie.

The Cramers were members of Lake Forest Presbyterian Church, and moved in the same circles as the McClures. They lived in a large brick house, "Rathmore," on the bluff above Lake Michigan, with a ravine beside it winding down to the lake. Elizabeth wrote a small book, which her father had bound in green leather, about the children's daily adventures called *Life on the Bluff*. Elizabeth and Isabel were inseparable friends of Harriet McClure, Jim's sister, throughout their school years in Lake Forest. It was through this friendship with Harriet that Elizabeth eventually met Jim.

Opposite, top left: *Elizabeth Skinner Cramer. Opposite, top right: Elizabeth with her father, Ambrose Cramer, and her brother, Ambrose, Jr.* Opposite, bottom: *Elizabeth swinging; brother Ambrose sits on ground at left (holding bow), with an unknown companion; step-sister Isabel at right.*

Elizabeth.

Elizabeth had early shown a talent for art. As a little girl she had been
delighted at winning a contest in St. Nicholas Magazine (until her mischievous
brother Ambrose pointed out that the shadows of the pine trees in her drawing
were slanted towards each other). At St. Timothy's School near Baltimore she
and Isabel suffered under the petty regulations of a traditional boarding school,
but her artistic ability continued to develop. Then, through a program of Miss
Wheeler's School in Providence, Rhode Island, she was able to spend a summer
painting in France. A small group of girls lived in Giverny, on the Seine, right
next door to Claude Monet, who was then in his eighties. Elizabeth and Mildred
Burrage, from Portland, Maine, watched him paint in the field beside his garden. He would set up eleven canvasses in different positions around a hay stack,
then move every fifteen minutes as the light changed.[3]

Elizabeth Cramer's pursuit of art was no mere whim of a grown-up school girl with nothing better to do. She had ability and she took her artistic education very seriously. Her father sent her to study art in Paris. There she imbibed the air of Impressionism, studying with an American impressionist, Richard Miller, who had earned a fine reputation in his day. Her considerable talent grew and developed. Her companion in art, Mildred Burrage, was equally dedicated. Both these young women felt that the techniques of painting were based on a firm philosophical foundation, or they were based on nothing at all. Mildred was a vivacious and active person who pursued her intellectual sources with something of a vengeance. A lively interaction of ideas grew up between her and Elizabeth, and greatly stimulated the latter's curiosity. An example of Mildred's scope of ideas is evident in the following letter, bringing in as well Jim's friend and fellow Skull and Bones man, Rev. William Sloane Coffin. ". . . Mr. Coffin thinks we have gone back to where the Renaissance began in the 13th Century. Then men broke away from the Byzantine and Oriental standpoint and tried to accomplish realism—and that has been done—so now we are to go back to the East to get 'the record of a spiritual impressionism' . . ." (Mildred Burrage to Elizabeth Cramer, January 8, 1909). Elizabeth felt a spiritual kinship with these Asian artists, who were seeking in nature a perfectly balanced beauty, but she and Mildred, like other artists in France, were still trying to comprehend the artistic revolution brought about by the Impressionists.

In the meantime, Elizabeth had fallen in love with France: its people, its language, its landscape, its "influences." Lake Forest must have seemed to her crass and rather showy, a place where time had not been allowed to deepen and enrich either the look of the landscape or the thoughts of the people. Ambrose Cramer, like most of the men, enjoyed discussing business. Although that particular topic bored Elizabeth, her father's financial successes helped to pay for her French sojourn. In 1913 he helped her buy a lovely little house in the village of Trèpied near Etaples-sur-Mer, a noted artistic community. She invited an older friend, Martha Clarke, to live with her. Mildred Burrage and another young American artist, Julie Turner, planned to join them. Miss Clarke, affectionately known as "Wiggy Wags" or "Wiggy," came from Antrim in Northern Ireland. She was well educated but had limited financial resources, and she lived with the American girls and one or two friends as a companion, teacher and chaperone. The exact relationship is lost in the mists of the conventions of the time, but the fact of their mutual admiration was clear enough from their letters. Elizabeth began to correspond with her before the Trèpied house was purchased, in the winter of 1913 when the Cramer family was touring Italy. She collected great quantities of postcards to send back to Wiggy in France, with comments such as these: "Don't you think this fat angel is a darling? . . . It's the nicest thing in all St. Peters I really think, and it's tucked away in the vestry . . ." and "These little monks are such darlings that I had to send them to you! Do you suppose Fra Angelico's contemporaries ever did look like these two little ducks!" (Elizabeth Cramer to Martha Clarke, winter of 1913)

Elizabeth's lovely world of Fra Angelico's monks and fat angels exploded with the first shells of the Great War. Trèpied was located in the northeast corner of France, just across the channel from England in the old province of Picardy. Centuries before, Flemish immigrants had brought the cloth trade to the region, and enough prosperity and foreign influence to tempt other powers of the region to try to pry it loose from the French. Since the Hundred Years War, this area had been a small splinter in a larger bone that has been fought over constantly. In August of 1914, with Elizabeth and Wiggy having just settled in, the Kaiser began his sweep through Belgium, just shy of Trèpied, with the most superb war machine the world had yet seen. Her prior concerns, such as planting and managing the little garden in her yard and trying to remove the "horrid" concrete walk, a job her brother Ambrose, who was travelling in France, had promised to do for her, became irrelevant in the face of these events. Ambrose, nicknamed Pedro, made a mad dash for Trèpied to help his sister leave the country. Her mother's indomitable maiden sisters, Miss Elizabeth (Bessy) and Frederika (Freddy), were visiting their niece, staying at a nearby inn. This little American society in France was caught by surprise, and the swirling excitement that ensued quite thrilled Elizabeth. She described in a letter to her parents the series of events that led to their escape to England.

> Here we are safe & sound in London . . . It was absolutely impossible to get any reliable information at Etaples. A week ago . . . nobody even dreamed of such a thing as war. Everybody knew of course, about the Austrian-Serbia business but absolutely nothing else was known . . .
> When the news of Germany's ultimatum came we gloomily decided that we should probably have to leave . . .
> Saturday morning everything was quiet as usual . . . We all went bathing . . . & the only indication of anything out of the way was the long line of people in front of the Banque Adam cashing money. We all had a hilarious lunch together at noon & I went over to Paris-Plage where Aunt Bessy and Aunt Freddy were staying to have dinner with them. At four O'clock came the sudden news that the men were to mobilize at once. A trumpeter rode through the streets reading the proclamation & inside of two hours the men were leaving for the front. The waiters in the hotels left instantly—in the Casino the head-waiter came in and said that he was very sorry but he "could serve no more tea." There was no excitement & no noise.
> . . . [the] Aunties and Miss Clarke and I decided we had better go in to Etaples & find out what was happening at the Mayor's office. We managed to cram into the little tram that ran into Etaples in company with countless men who were leaving at once for the army. It was then only 6 o'clock & the order for general mobilization had come at four & the men were already on the way. It was unbelievably swift. They all seemed eager & ready & one man said "Well if it had to come this is the best time." Ever so many of the men in the little tram car looked as though they had just come from their work in the fields; their clothes were tied up in handkerchief bundles & they had not even had time to change their working clothes . . . we tried to get a wagon to take us back to Trèpied but there were no men left to drive the horses. Finally we

Left: *Elizabeth*. Right: *With brother Ambrose in Southern France, ca. 1913.*

did manage to find an old, old man who took us home. Nobody yet believed there would really be war. Everybody insisted that the mobilization was merely a precautionary measure . . .

We were told Sunday that "foreigners" would not be allowed to leave until they had seen the mayor of Trèpied Monday afternoon. That of course meant the loss of another day. We spent all Monday trying to close the house & pack up a few things . . .

In the afternoon the mayor told us that we could not leave France without a pass-port from Arras which might take from two to three weeks to secure. He also said that no tickets would be issued on the railway to Boulogne as the trains would be needed for the troops . . . All this had come about in one day-it seemed simply unbelievable. "All I can do for you" the mayor said, "is to give you permits to stay in Trèpied in order that you may not be seized as suspicious persons." Well we got our permit anyway and then I tell you we got busy. Somehow or other aunties had been able to get hold of a motor & truck . . . There were no men left to drive but they managed to secure a woman chauffeur. We determined to motor to Boulogne then & there & see what we could do about leaving for England. That afternoon the order had been published for the mobilization of all motor cars & horses on Tuesday so that if we didn't get away that day goodness knows when we ever should . . . We left Trèpied at four o'clock for Boulogne & were stopped several times by armed soldiers. You can't think how exciting it was—it didn't seem real for a minute & everybody said that we should never get through. The railroad tracks were guarded by soldiers & all the river bridges, but there was no excitement, only a kind of fierce determination to kill the Germans.

At Boulogne there was the most fearful crowd of people on the docks I have ever imagined. There was a frightful crush & at times it came near to panic. We all got separated from each other & from Ambrose who was buying the tickets & we were nearly squeezed to death. I don't know how Aunties ever survived . . . Some how or other Miss Clarke managed to find Ambrose with our tickets & in turn she found each one of us. Once we had our tickets we could at least try to get on board. The crowd pushed and jammed so that we were perfectly unable to find each other & the first thing I knew poor Aunt Freddy in a half fainting state was pushed up the gang-way by two officials & onto the ship. After a long time we saw Aunt Bessy pushed on. Then after an interminable interval I squeezed up to the entrance. A French soldier grabbed me by the arm & said "Vous etes anglaise." I said "no"—whereat they pushed me back & said "you can't get on without a passport."

I was only conscious of being perfectly enraged and as soon as I could, I bobbed up again & tried to get by the French soldier but he pushed me back again in the same way. Ever so many people were being turned back & I couldn't imagine how aunties had succeeded. Finally I managed to go up a third time & when the officer told me I couldn't get on I told him he'd just have to let me on & that if I wasn't English I was at least part Irish & that I would keep turning up until he let me on . . . The officer looked at me hard & finally said "Laissez passer les femmes" with which they shot me up the gang-way . . . when Pedro [Ambrose] turned up he said he'd gotten on by dint of his beautiful British accent acquired at Cannes! Poor Aunt Bessy and Aunt Freddy had looked so ill that the officers had been obliged to hustle them on . . .

It was a thrilling sight going across the channel. The full moon shone through masses of jagged clouds & the great line of French battleships absolutely dark—without a light anywhere about them was beyond measure impressive. Tremendous searchlights played up & down the harbor & through the sky seeking for the enemy's airships.

. . . The next night, about one o'clock, we were awakened by the most tremendous shouting & singing. "God Save the King," "The Marseillaise," "Britons never, never will be Slaves" & the most tremendous hurrahing & shouting. War had been declared between Great Britain & Germany.

At present Pedro is moving heaven & earth to get passage to America . . . it's a cheerless thought to feel that we may be blown up by indiscriminate German mines on the sea or captured by one of their warships! . . . Yesterday evening Pedro & I saw Lord Kitchener come out of the War office. The crowd around the war office were beside themselves with enthusiasm. The cheering almost made me want to fight too! . . .

I wonder if in America you have any idea of how thrilling it is here. (Elizabeth Cramer to her parents, October 25, 1914)

Ambrose secured, with much difficulty, reservations on a British ship, the *Royal George.* When he brought the good news back to his ladies, Aunt Bessie flung up her hands and recited, "Down went the *Royal George,* With all three hundred men!"

The Aunts refused to go on such an ill-starred ship. The earliest passage that Ambrose could find was for October, so he and Elizabeth went over to

Ireland to visit their Cramer relatives in the tiny sea coast town of Castle Townshend, County Cork. The Coghills and Somervilles had been living there since the mid-eighteenth century. Sent originally to help maintain order amongst the "wild Irish," they lived in sympathy and harmony with them. Edith Somerville's books on Irish country life were just receiving acclaim in England. There Elizabeth met her cousin, Sir Kendall Coghill, veteran of the Crimean War and the Indian Mutiny. He had the power to hypnotise and used it to save suffering in the primitive hospitals at the front (even for amputations!) In Ireland she also met people who accepted fairies as a part of life, and she read *Dracula* in a lonely tower room in the Coghill family's rambling stone edifice, Glenn Barahan. The Cramer entourage finally sailed back to America on the S. S. *Olympic,* surrounded by the uncertainties of war.

After docking Elizabeth hurried back to Lake Forest, looking forward to her old room at "Rathmore," the family home. Her friend Harriet McClure was now the wife of Douglas Stuart, a smart young businessman who worked for Quaker Oats. Harriet was beginning to take on the responsibilities her parents had raised her to accept. Among other things, she served on the board of directors of the Day Nursery, a child care center in Chicago. Working women brought their children to the nursery to be cared for during the day. Harriet thought if only the place could be made less drab, what a wonderful improvement that would be. With her old friend Elizabeth home, she knew just the artist to take on the project. The board voted to provide the money, and Elizabeth accepted the job. Later in October of 1914 she wrote to Wiggy, who had remained in France to guard the house and work as a volunteer nurse:

> What do you suppose? I have a lovely job at last. You've heard me speak of the Day Nursery I'm sure. Well Harriet McClure asked me if I wouldn't decorate it right off now & of course I am only too delighted. It's a large room where the poor women leave their kids while they work . . . I had Hetty & Douglas Stuart & Jim McClure to dinner & we all had a really charming time. (Elizabeth Cramer to Martha Clarke, October 29, 1914)

A week later, Jim McClure again appears at the dinner table with Elizabeth: "Saturday I went . . . to spend Sunday with Harriet Stuart & her husband. Jim McClure & I were the only guests. Jim had come down from Iron Mountain (where he has a church) for a rest, and we all had a delightful old time visit" (Elizabeth Cramer to Martha Clarke, November 5, 1914). That particular occasion ended abruptly when brother Ambrose called with an urgent message that Aunt Bessy, on a trip, had been admitted to a Washington, D.C. hospital and required immediate surgery. Ambrose asked Elizabeth to go right to her Aunt's bedside. Jim McClure volunteered to drive her to the train, " . . . so I packed my bag and went as far as Evanston with Jim where I caught the 3:39 train . . ." (Elizabeth Cramer to Martha Clarke, November 5, 1914).

Aunt Bessy recovered fully from her operation, and Elizabeth returned home again. But something quite momentous had taken place. The little trip to the train station proved to be a most propitious event. Elizabeth wistfully recalled a year later her feelings that day in a letter to Jim. "I have just remembered that this coming Sunday a year ago we were at Hetty's and poor Aunt Bessy was suddenly laid in the dust and you were so nice & friendly about helping me to get off. Do you remember sitting on the bench in the sun at Evanston waiting for the Lake Forest train to come in, and talking? A year can sometimes be a very long time" (Elizabeth Cramer to James G. K. McClure, Jr., October 29, 1915).

And so it was to be. By early December she began to suspect that Jim was showing her special attention. She wrote to Wiggy, who was the confidante she did not have in her kind but distant stepmother, that she dreaded his "getting such ideas in his head," for she considered him just an old friend of rare charm and interest. One of the signs of Jim's interest was his persistence. If she declined an invitation he asked her again. He invited her to go with him to the Art Institute in Chicago. He sent her articles and books. She wrote to him " . . . I like being poked up and I am immensely grateful to the person who does it and a mere 'thank you' is not at all adequate to the occasion" (Elizabeth Cramer to James G. K. McClure, Jr., December 15, 1914).

Jim stimulated her thoughts in the religious realm, and it was perhaps at his suggestion that she read a book called *The Inside of a Cup*. She reviews it for Wiggy, revealing a good deal about herself at the same time:

> It is not in the least a "work of art," or literature either, for that matter, but it is the best interpretation of modern Christianity that I ever read anywhere and you *must* read it . . . I nearly burst with joy when I found a good many of my own "heretical" views being trumpeted forth as the essence of Christianity . . . The minister in it is very much like my unorthodox clerical friend Jim, who informed me yesterday that he meant to do his level best to rid the Church of "outworn doctrines" and "archaic forms" & that he thought the creeds ought to be thrown out root & branch! I like reformers & I like fighters & anybody who can do that . . . is both. (Elizabeth Cramer to Martha Clarke, December 9, 1914)

Again she wrote to Wiggy:

> My parson friend comes to see me all the time & we converse on the most revolutionary topics. I have a feeling that he will end up by being "unfrocked" but he's just the sort of man the churches need and I don't think he'd stop at anything, but the poor dear has got a dreadfully hard row to hoe in the face of all the old Presbyterian members of the session & the stick-in-the-mud formalists who rule the church boards. He has so much real charm, and is such a favorite socially that it is extraordinary to find such single-mindedness and virility besides. (Elizabeth Cramer to Martha Clarke, December 16, 1914)

Meanwhile, Jim's doctors advised him to spend the winter in a more agreeable climate than Chicago. He was urged, in fact, to give his famous single-mindedness a good, long rest. His cousins, the Sages, were more than happy for him to visit them at their Santa Barbara home, so after Christmas he decided to make his move to California. With such a long absence from Lake Forest imminent, he thought he had better clarify matters with Elizabeth, known among her friends as Siddy. How painful for even the most courageous and charming of young men to broach the subject of love. There had been a heavy fall of snow and he came for her in a cutter, a one-horse sleigh, and they drove all around the McCormick's ravine. "The vivid moonlight on the trees was a sort of fairy land," she wrote to Wiggy. Jim only asked her if she was engaged to anyone? When she said "No," he was silent for a long time and then said, "Well the first thing for me to do is to get well quick." No more was said about the subject, but Elizabeth told Wiggy she thought Jim felt he could not ask her to marry him as long as he was ill and could not support her. She continued:

> I think I told you that he'd broken down this fall and had been obliged to lay off . . . Jim is one of these ardent tremendously interested people who go until they drop & never consider themselves. He has had a church at an awful place called Iron Mountain—miners & such likes & he boarded at a drummer's hotel & not only ran the church all alone but tried to do an awful lot of social work in the town, besides, amongst the 'Bums' and the bad lot. The consequence was he had to resign the church which was a blow.

She felt that he would probably ask her to marry him when he returned from California in April and admitted:

> I like him immensely, we both have a good many crazy, socialistic ideas about things which make us extremely congenial and I admire him very much . . . I'm not in love with him but then I don't really know him—it's been years and years since I've really seen him as we've both been away— but it is perfectly possible that if he were very much in love with me & made me feel it—it might—in time—create that feeling in me. I don't want to be in love with him because I want to be free to do nothing but paint & live with you . . . so I'll fight against it, if that feeling ever should come. (Elizabeth Cramer to Martha Clarke, January 4, 1915)

Jim McClure's removal to Santa Barbara marked off a breathing space in his affections toward Elizabeth. He needed not only to get well, but also to be sure the healing process was providing a permanent cure. He and Elizabeth thought almost continuously about one another, their future together, and the obstacles and uncertainties that plague all romances. They were both mature adults who could articulate and often even understand their personal feelings. The social labyrinth they had to negotiate in a proper Victorian courtship insured a slow pace to their romance, and their ages and temperaments reduced even further the chances of an impetuous decision.

In California, Jim did manage to achieve one victory of sorts. Never before, or afterwards, did he play golf so well. On what must have been a glorious winter's day at the Santa Barbara Country Club, Jim achieved a "select score" of sixty-six, seven strokes under par.[4]

The slow pace of Jim's present life gave him time to wonder, not only about Elizabeth, but also about many other issues that touched his life. He kept a rambling notebook of thoughts and ideas, allowing us to peer into his concerns of 1915–16. The physical debility that kept flaring up caused him the greatest worry, because until he could overcome this problem, none of his other dreams would ever be realized. He found great solace in the gospel of Luke. There he found a Jesus with a "spirit of abandon, insouciance, gaiety, recklessness . . . [who] based everything on [an] unrestrained life of spirit & full speed ahead-. . . Do not bother about what you are to eat or drink: God clothes lilies, he will clothe you. . . ."[5] Jim sought just this vision of Christian freedom in his life; he felt that Christ's life was a beautiful example of a man divorcing himself from anxiety, letting himself become a perfect instrument of God's will and ceasing to care about the material preoccupations of the world. If only he could achieve this freedom, his mind and body would stop rebelling against his desire to carry out God's will.

Jim also wanted to lead a rebellion against the spiritless and dreary practices of the Christianity of the day, which he felt dammed up its potential.

> Religion must be lively . . . The Man in the pulpit must realize that he is trying to inject into life a force more powerful than any other. A lively force, that will turn a man inside out, change him, drive him, carry him thru the mud of life & thru a long distance run . . . The Organist should play hymns jig-time . . . I do not believe Christ would have boasted about his family tree & ancestors as many do today. He probably would have hidden the fact & tried to make good himself . . . If Heaven is what it is often cracked up to be, a lead pipe cinch, etc. I do not want to go there until all the misery & wrong is removed from the world. I would prefer living in the worst hell hole in the slums & trying to make it better. . .[6]

And yet, there he was surrounded by the luxuries of an exclusive resort, where everyone was " . . . going about as if life was a soft snap—motors, golf, idleness."[7] He moaned about the expenses of his hostess, Mrs. Sage, who thought nothing of spending $4,650 to rent a private railroad car in order to tour America, while that same winter many wage earners were without work and their families were hard pressed to feed themselves. "Mrs. Sage is as kindly, generous, dear old lady as you can find—she means to do the right thing, on the other hand, men & women are starving."[8] Clearly, Jim felt great discomfort in his own social position. At times he wished he could have been a nameless urchin pitting himself against all the evil forces of the day without a good name and comfortable friends to fall back on. He saw the "difficulty in a place like Lake Forest where no one is an out & out worker of evil . . . in Iron River the saloons & saloon keepers drew a sharp line—children were brought up to feel they must fight the saloon. Life is a battle & they lined up. The Saloon element would knock their blocks off in a dark alley, if they opposed."[9]

In the Progressive Era Jim saw himself as a rebel, both by temperament and by choice. He threw his weight in with the reformers who want to overturn the established social order, and yet he recognized the tendency in himself and those like him to " . . . throw out the baby with the dirty water. . . ." He went on: "Certain individuals are born rebels—grow by rebelling, by taking the opposite side. This is the way the world keeps from stagnating, by the introduction continually of these people. They have a divine office. But they are in danger of rebelling negatively. They must take it upon themselves to rebel constructively—to better what they see is wrong . . . We need rebels, & should welcome them but their lot is a hard one—construction is harder than destruction."[10]

Even though Jim leveled broad attacks against Victorian piety, in some of his prejudices he was out of step with the most progressive of his brethren. First of all, the literary trend towards realism and naturalism chilled his emotions, in part because they pictured man in a determined world helplessly hemmed in by forces beyond his manipulation. He much preferred the Victorian morality play, shoe-shine boy to bank president, over the stories of Dreiser and Norris and writers of their ilk. He wrote, "Many 'realistic novels' are not true to life; they simply see things without the vision. The vision is more real than the thing itself."[11] He always felt that novels, and later movies, were a wonderful vehicle to raise the hopes of men and women, to give people a lift and encourage them to work hard for a better world. But when a book or a movie left one in despair, he felt progress was thwarted. Jim also found it difficult to tolerate the Roman Catholic Church, a long standing McClure position.

Back in Chicago, Elizabeth Cramer was intent on her work at the Day Nursery, locking horns with her own sense of social responsibility. She was desperate to inspire the little children of the Day Nursery, and their parents, with the same joy in beauty that meant everything to her life. The murals she painted there would eventually win great acclaim for Elizabeth. By January, the basic designs were worked out. The average size of the three works was to be ten feet by seventy-six inches, quite a large space for a painter to fill. The pictures were to be based on three nursery rhymes: "Jack Sprat and his Wife," "Mary, Mary, Quite Contrary" and "Curly Locks, Curly Locks, Wilt Thou Be Mine?" Elizabeth sent this general description of the designs to Wiggy. "Little figures against a balustrade . . . with an occasional pillar now and then, big vines sweeping down across the skyline & distant country that you look off at with winding rivers, trees & little villages. It's more fun than a goat . . ." (Elizabeth Cramer to Martha Clarke, January 12, 1915). Behind all of her effort was a new vision of the purpose of an artist, a vision very much influenced by her talks with Jim McClure.

> Isn't it funny how the minute you begin to do anything with an eye to using
> it for the good of other people that thing at once becomes immensely interest-
> ing and worthwhile in itself. It seems as though we had to relate our lives or
> rather what we do with our lives to the people about us & just as soon as we
> do that, things become really thrilling. It's so queer & that was what was &
> is the matter with so many painting people—they don't connect their "life
> work" with the needs in the world about them. (Elizabeth Cramer to Martha
> Clarke, January 26, 1915)

These "decorations" were Elizabeth's connection to the world about her.
The patrons of the Day Nursery were the Chicago tenement dwellers so much
on the Progressive mind. Elizabeth was sure that beauty in itself, no matter how
imperfect, would move people emotionally, encourage them, and give them
hope and new vision. By placing these pictures in the daily world of all these
mothers and their children, the power of beauty might help to lift up their lives.
The more cynical thought she was wasting her time, hoping to make silk purses
out of the rabble of Chicago.

> . . . People have said to me that they think it is practically a waste of time to
> spend so much time & effort on things that are going up in a place "where they
> won't really be appreciated." "Something else not requiring nearly as much
> effort would please them just as much" the old wheezes say. It makes me so
> mad but I understand what is in the back of their minds. They are thinking of
> the replicas of Greek statues & the Braun photographs of Italian paintings &
> all that sort of thing that the "uplift" people are always putting around settle-
> ment walls. Of course those things don't mean much to the people. It's not
> because the "masses" don't appreciate & want beauty it's simply that beauty
> expressed in terms of Greek goddesses & Italian renaissance ladies is simply
> unintelligible to them—before everything else it's "queer" to them. It's the
> interpretation of a life & epoch that Westside Chicago can't figure out at all
> . . . I am convinced that the masses always respond to beauty when it reflects
> or interprets what they can understand.
>   I've tried to keep this in mind in painting these decorations & by Jiminy
> they are so awfully simple & obvious & everydayish that the little North
> Avenue children really like them & enjoy them and so do the North Avenue
> mothers & aunts . . . I'm sure that the "masses" in America don't get beauty
> enough. They're just crazy for it & by gum I *don't* think I'm being foolish or
> quixotic. (Elizabeth Cramer to Martha Clarke, 1915)

Jim encouraged her in the work and Elizabeth's justification of it, telling her
she had discovered the very reason to paint. He went on to explain that by
catching a sense of the beauty in these pictures, these "Westside people" would
be in direct contact with Christ's spirit, thus raising their ideas and vision of
life's possibilities.
    In her return letters, she loved to describe her efforts at the Day Nursery
and her thoughts for Jim.

I am up to my ears in the Day Nursery pictures . . . We [a friend who had painted with her in France, Julie Thompson, was helping her] pasted huge sheets of butcher's paper together & then carried them in bodily to the Day Nursery where we tacked them to the walls and drew the designs as they were to be, right onto the paper. We spent three fervid days of climbing step ladders and falling off of them and swallowing clouds of ancient Day Nursery dust that we had disturbed from its hallowed resting place on the top of picture moldings and doors . . .

The Day Nursery Playroom is a miserable narrow high room that gives you the impression of prison walls and it has been a most interesting proposition to make it seem wider and lower by the use of certain lines and masses. The children persisted in swarming about the step-ladders a large part of the time and narrowly escaped complete annihilation but their excitement was something unbounded and all sixty filled the air with criticism, enthusiasm, and . . . instructions as to how we might improve our labours. In spite of threats and cries of rage from me on the stepladder, they played London Bridge with joyful abandon, right under it, & then, with a Biblical precedent to guide them, they impersonated Sampson and struggled to bring down the roof by grappling with the pillars of my support. I was mindful that the jawbone of an ass had once laid low the Philistines . . . Next day, Julie and I in the proverbial "wiser, sadder" frame of mind crawled out of bed before dawn and made much headway at the Nursery before the arrival of the sixty Dreadnaughts! . . . (Elizabeth Cramer to James G. K. McClure, Jr., January 24, 1915)

In a month's time, Elizabeth wrote to Jim about more of her ideas. "The dreadful part about ideas is that half the fun of getting them is sharing them with somebody else . . ." she said. The letter continued:

Our things for the Day Nursery are slowly progressing but the hardest work is about done & I shall go off to California with a free mind. I've found out all sorts of things about painting. I told you that for a long time I had had a sneaking fear that the business of going off into a pleasant corner & painting two foot square "pictures" was never going to mean much to anybody. Once or twice I said this to people who I thought might help straighten me out but they always looked so astonished that I finally decided that it was no use that I never *would* find out why I felt the way I did. No other painting people seemed at all bothered that way excepting a girl with whom I had worked a great deal off & on—a very special friend [Mildred Burrage]. Then all of a sudden, last Spring, we . . . found out for ourselves that art was never worth anything except when it was related to life; that painting was only vitally important & significant when it was an actual factor in the spiritual development of the race. The trouble with us was that what we had been doing was artificial and meaningless. We spent all our time doing ladies under trees and at tea tables or painting landscapes that had a certain amount of charm. Our things were reasonably presentable & they gave the people who saw them a certain momentary emotional thrill but that was absolutely all. We had never used our minds a moment in the whole process; we were perfectly satisfied to express a mood rather than an emotional truth, . . . It isn't so much the *subject* that counts in art as it is what you may discover *in* the subject that is significant

& universal & worthy of being recorded. Everything in the world is an expression of the Spirit one way or another, I suppose, & in painting it's up to you to find that out & put it down whether the subject is an Annunciation or a polo game. Painting should be an accompaniment to life—it should be a means of stimulating the imagination & spiritual side of human beings to further development, and at its greatest epochs this is what it has always been. In the thirteenth & fourteenth & fifteenth centuries artists realized that they were just as important and necessary as plumbers are now. They realized that it was their business to make life more beautiful & more significant to the people about them & they got right to work & did it . . . There's just as great a need for art now as there was then but very few artists are supplying this need.

The trouble is they devote all their time to doing clever stunts; or to getting an emotional effect of sun & shadow, or to painting a mood. That's why our art exhibits are such fearful bores for the most part. You go to them in search of bread & you receive a stone. You give a few admiring gasps at somebody's clever "realism" or somebody else's "interesting brushwork" but after all you come away with a dissatisfied, disappointed heart! It is very rare that you come away with a feeling that your spiritual eyes have been opened, that you have responded to somebody's revelation of a great truth. You almost never feel, after a dose of this sort, that life is tremendously worth living. That all this should be so is very bad business. The proof of the pudding is, perhaps, that on the other hand, the average human being cannot go into a Gothic cathedral without being carried quite out of himself,—he cannot see the Greek temples at Paestum and go away unchanged,—he cannot see a Botticelli fresco in an old convent, or a drawing by Holbein, or a statue by Rodin without being convinced that the life of the Spirit is the only thing that matters in the end . . . If these things that we're doing for the Day Nursery mean anything, they ought to mean a lot! The decorations, if they are any good, should make the children realize- unconsciously—that there is an order & a beauty and a joyfulness in life that is greater than anything they have yet come in contact with. They ought to create an impression that, were they to analyze it, would make them dissatisfied with dirt and evil and conscious of a better order of things somehow attainable. Of course, to these little mites, the decorations will be primarily amusing—that is all, I suppose, that they will be directly *conscious* of, but nobody can be really amused without being interested & to be interested is to be open to many influences. Of course our things are bound to fall a long way short of doing all this, . . . [but] perhaps the next time I do a decoration, it *will* have a creative influence.

Mildred & I are just bursting to do a Sunday School, —white walls & big decorative panels from the Parables or the Life of Christ set in the walls, and blue flower pots with pink geraniums in the windows & queer little blue chairs for the children to sit on. Don't you think it would be nice & don't you think the children would have a different feeling about Sunday School in a room like that? One could do the Parables in a very simple, human appealing way . . .

I was immensely interested in what you said about substituting the word Life for God in some of the New Testament sayings. It is extraordinary how revealing such a change can be. A year ago for many reasons, I was all tangled up and I wasn't sure whether there really *was* anything to work for. But now I know what Christ meant by "the Kingdom of God" and as you once said, just because "God needs man's help," human life is significant when it is expressed in terms of service.

When you realize that Christ impressed it upon his hearers that perfection is attainable & that all one's efforts should be directed to such an end, it puts a new meaning into life. But when I was a child, I was taught the dreadful gloomy doctrine that no matter how much you strive for perfection around you in this world it was no use really because you were merely "human" & Christ was "Divine"—and yet; you were to go on trying just the same . . . This is a very long queer letter for me to be writing to you but we did talk about these things and somehow or other my inky tongue has pursued an unbridled course. That A.C.C. [her brother] letter paper was so inviting (fortunately the supply has come to an end!) It has such a leisurely expansive air! You can't help being conversational on paper like that whereas my variety is the tall, crabbed species that spells moderation & sedately chaperones your pen! . . .

Sincerely, 'Sid' (What a funny stubby name! I feel apologetic for this document. I had no idea of its length!!) (Elizabeth Cramer to James G. K. McClure, Jr., February 28, 1915)

This author makes no such apologies, and is only grateful that the A.C.C. stationery held out as long as it did. Jim McClure was becoming involved with a remarkable woman.

By a stroke of good fortune, Elizabeth and her family were leaving in a week's time for a trip out West, and Santa Barbara was on the itinerary. Leaving a slowly thawing Lake Forest for the sunshine of California, the Cramer entourage included Aunts Bessy and Freddy and young Ambrose. For Jim McClure, it would mean a short rendezvous with Elizabeth, and he looked forward to the visit with all of the expectations and fears of a young man in love. Perhaps his golfing scores began to balloon upwards as he began dividing up and filling in the time she would be with him, wondering exactly what activities would please her the most. Fortunately, Jim was the sort of man with friends scattered everywhere, and right nearby he had one who was a painter! The Cramers were all house guests of their cousins the Bakers, who claimed a spectacular view of the Pacific Ocean in one direction and the mountains in the other. To Wiggy, Elizabeth sent her confidential report on the fruits of Jim's efforts:

In about five minutes Jim is coming for me in his motor to go up to Russel Cheney's studio to see his paintings. Do you remember hearing Mildred speak of him? . . . He is also a great friend of Jim's . . . We had such an entertaining time the other night. The children plus the Reverend James have been planning a concert for weeks. Isabelle & young Grace Meeker [who had sparked a romance with Elizabeth's brother Ambrose] being the star performers on combs, Mary Baker on a concertina & Jim the master of a dreadful instrument called a "humanatone" that he manipulated somehow with his nose! Ambrose & I were drawn into the thing so I got a cheap fiddle down town & Ambrose took the part of Orchestra leader . . . It was very amusing & absurd; the night of the performance the "artists" were all asked to come dressed to dinner, so I roughed & curled my "short" hair until it stood out around my head like a regular German Genius. Then I wore my black goggles & Father's evening coat, collar & shirt. I was a sight! But I did look the part even to the legion of honor button. It was a huge joke because I sat next to Mrs. Sage (Jim's cousin) at dinner & she was so surprised she pretty nearly went under the table. Naturally she had a lively curiosity as to what I was like & when she was introduced to "Monsieur Jaques Thibaut" a wild mass of . . . terrier hair & black goggles, I wish you could have seen her face! (Elizabeth Cramer to Martha Clarke, March 17, 1915)

Monsieur Thibaut and her Cramer clan ended their short visit, leaving Jim to himself and his golf. They went off to view some more of the wonders of California, as her next letter to him reveals.

Dear Jim,

After several days of intense enthusiasm in the Yosemite Valley, we are back again in San Francisco. We spent most of four days driving behind a bouncing stage and eight horses. It is an amazing place. Everything was somehow on a superlative scale. The "Big Trees" are the most extraordinary things in the world & it is all I can do not to give you detailed accounts of just how high & how thick they were . . .

I do hope your head isn't bothering you,—I have somehow a feeling inside me that you should not write long letters even to a very appreciative lady friend, for I know what a fatiguing business it is when you are not feeling up to the mark. These, sir, are sage words . . .

What you said about the possibility of really attaining perfection had a very special meaning because in your case it was backed up by actual experience. It must have been a thrilling kind of life to make those Iron Mountain people realize just what they were up against,-but every now & then I keep thinking how did you do it,—how could you always give them what they demanded,- how could you so interpret their own needs when the intellectual stimulus in a place like Iron Mountain must have been very slight, very meagre? How could you do it! All this is very personal but when we passed through the dreary little Kansas towns with their hideous frame houses and their dingy streets I tried to imagine myself living in just such a place,—it was a kind of test after all our conversations,—and somehow or other every bit of self confidence seemed to leave me and I had a dreadful feeling that in spite of everything I had said, six months in such a place would use up every thought, every worth while emotion I had ever had & that in a little while I would be going about with a dead spirit in a living body. Because, if you give & give to people and nothing in the way of spiritual or intellectual stimulus comes back to you why how can you go on living? But perhaps the answer to all that is again in Christ. When He said, over & over again, "The Kingdom of God is within you" isn't it simply making a definite amazing statement that the life of the spirit can after all be best renewed from within; that prayer, in the highest meaning of the word is a source of eternal life to the spirit,—that in seeming to lose all, one gains everything? I don't know; when I said something like this to you a little while ago you said that you too were dependent on outside stimulus. And yet, one thing is certain. Christ, who possessed one of the richest minds the world has ever known, lived in surroundings that demanded all of him that gave him almost nothing in return. The people he came in contact with had for the most part simple untutored minds. The poverty and sordidness about him must have been immeasurably alive. Nothing in the life of Christ seem to me more significant testimony than that. (Elizabeth Cramer to James G. K. McClure, Jr., April 11, 1915)

With what beautiful encouragement Elizabeth Cramer gathers up the threads of Jim's life into a poignant sermonette. She too worships the hero Jesus of Nazareth, who effortlessly waded into the sordidness of first century Palestine without obvious encouragement and cultural sustenance. Could it be that the kingdom within, the power of the Almighty, might sustain one in the desert of poverty? Or maybe there is nourishment after all, a world "immeasurably alive." Both Jim in Iron River and Elizabeth at her Day Nursery were seeking answers.

For Jim, the practical question remained, "How can I 'lose my life' to the gospel, and yet remain healthy?" He had to solve this riddle, not only to carry on his work, but to propose marriage to Elizabeth. As she left California, Jim's spirit—the health of his spirit—weighed heavily on her thoughts as well. Was the California cure working its magic? When would he be able to come back to be with her? She writes to Miss Clarke about the present state of his malady, going on to outline some of the thoughts the two of them had been sharing.

He is better—but he said that he wasn't as much better as he had hoped to be . . . Older people shake their heads & say "he ought to leave the ministry & take up something less absorbing & less taxing" but he won't hear of it. He is confident that once he is well again he can go back to his job, & it is a job that he is perhaps peculiarly fitted for because he has a fine mind, a rare quality of charm & sympathy & an ability to meet people on their own ground. At heart he is a reformer & a radical but he has much tact & a way of looking at *every* question from many sides. At Iron Mountain parish . . . he lived in a perfectly crazy sort of way. He had a room in a drummer's hotel & ate there with all sorts of people & he worked like a dog every minute to change social conditions which in a mining town are apt to be pretty bad. He said himself that the people he was up against were the kind who felt that a minister had an easy berth & an easy job & that the only way he could get a hold of them was to work harder than anybody else. That he did with the result that at the end of ten months he was knocked out. What makes me hopeful however is that he has never been to a real nerve specialist & they are bound to give a treatment that is different even from that of the best general practitioner.

In the meantime we are both the richer for a friendship that is very real & very stimulating—a friendship that is based on a community of ideas & that is constantly opening up new paths in many directions . . . [Jim] thinks that humanity will get rid of poverty just as it has freed the world from the Plague & from certain other horrors & that once this is done, the "Kingdom of God" will come far more swiftly. But charity is never going to do it. Charity is only a poor substitute for justice & love. (Elizabeth Cramer to Martha Clarke, March 29, 1915)

Springtime in Chicago drew Jim away from the eternal summer of California, where his homemade "cure" had produced only a meagre improvement. He decided to take a more professional approach toward better health. He found a sanitarium in New York State, the Jackson Health Resort, that held out hope for a full recovery. There could not be a resolution of the romance until Jim's health began to respond to treatment, and any uncertainty was enough of a reason for Elizabeth to try to keep the condition of her private affections as secret as possible. Before leaving again, Jim slipped out to Lake Forest and left a small gift at the Cramer residence, Rathmore. He wanted to let her know that his intentions remained serious, and she, in turn, writes back in her most assuring style:

There are blue violets in the woods. The wild crab-apples are in bloom and the blue sky behind the pink blossoms is the most beautiful thing in the world. This evening the maid brought me your flowers—I wonder why you sent them. I remember so well the first ones you brought me—pink sweet peas & some little stray white flower that had an indescribable haunting fragrance. I was so surprised when you brought them to me; it was a cold winter day & the dear things made me remember Spring & all the joyful moments that come with Spring. We went for a long walk afterwards and all at once I knew that you were not like anyone I had ever known. There was a strange little joyful song in my heart all that evening—"Here at last is someone who regards life as a high adventure. Here is a man who has dug down below preconceived opinions & old prejudices and who is willing to stake his life on his beliefs." It meant more to me than I can say. Ever since my mother died I had been searching & questioning & sometimes giving up on the fight & just drifting with the tide, then last year all at once I began to feel that at last I was on the right track, that the light ahead was from God & that the business of life from now on was to keep on this road. After so many years of following blind trails & beating about in pathless woods it meant a peace that could not be put into words. And then came that walk with you; the water was a strange magic colour, indescribably beautiful. I remember how delicate & lovely was the tracery of the black twigs against the sky. We talked of ordinary commonplace things and then on the way home when it was dusk you talked on the things you believed in. I said almost nothing but all the time in my heart I was saying "does he know how much it means to me to hear these things?" It wasn't so much the things that you said though these things illumined my own life but it was that *you* should have said them. Can I ever make you know what that meant. It meant that something gallant and brave and adventurous had suddenly revealed itself as the very essence of one man's life. And this man would perhaps some day be my friend—one of those rare precious friends with whom one is permitted to share the life of the spirit. I wonder if you felt at all any of the intense eagerness & the amazed happiness that could find no adequate expression in my words to you? After you had gone I sat still for a long time & thought of all the things you had said. I was proud, in a curious personal way that you had not given in or accepted the beliefs & conventions of the society that claimed you; that you had been too honest to accept belief before you had earned the right to take it. There is something tremendously exhilarating in what you had done. I wanted you to know that I felt this but there were no words to tell you. (Elizabeth Cramer to James G. K. McClure, Jr., May 18, 1915)

Jim McClure left Chicago two days after receiving this message from Elizabeth. He was determined to overcome his disability, but restless determination was also a source of his difficulties. At the Jackson Health Resort, he would be under the direction of doctors who assured him that cases like his came through their doors all the time. Jim's new "cure" consisted of great quantities of fresh air and water. The air was breathed playing more golf; he bathed daily in the hot mineral springs around which the sanitarium had been built. He wrote Elizabeth that after so many baths, he was bound to emerge as either a sea lion or a tadpole. The doctors wanted him to rest and forbade reading; he was somehow to slow down the torrent of ideas that swept through his mind. He did hire a Mrs. Steele to read aloud to him, otherwise the ennui of this life would have been unbearable. To his mother he wrote that "My days pass without much variation. Today I indulged in a hair cut . . . Mrs. Steele . . . finished Cortez some time ago, then read accounts of various other Spanish explorers in America . . . Golf every other day has been my program" (James G. K. McClure, Jr. to Phebe Ann Dixon McClure, exact date unknown). Mrs. McClure herself arrived to help break the monotony, perhaps on her way to Rhode Island, a trip she tried to make every summer. Indulging in a little 'cure' herself, she had come to comfort her son, and give him the confidence he needed to see his recovery through to the end. Jim kept careful records of all his considerable expenses, and somehow fought back the notion that was a basic part of his view of life: a thirty-year-old man not pulling his own weight in the working world was draining the resources of his family and the pool of wealth of the society at large.

Another sinking notion that must have crept into his mind from time to time concerned the distance between him and Elizabeth. Despite all the letters, there was no formal agreement between the two of them. She was a most eligible young lady, and disastrous scenarios of successful suitors replacing him were a natural condition of his tenuous circumstances. The romance had reached a plateau. But she and Jim still continued to enjoy a rich intellectual relationship, despite the distance between them. She wrote him after a dinner party when she had sat next to a gentleman who considered Christianity

> . . . morbid, reactionary, most injurious in its effects on the world. He also said that he would never have anything to do with any clergyman because "all clergymen were either fools or hypocrites." I said that I personally knew two who were neither—yourself, Sir, & an Irish friend, whereat he very amusingly asked, to my secret indignation, "were they good looking?" I regretted bitterly that I could not tell him that you were both as homely as a rhinoceros! . . . I couldn't understand at first why such a very clever man should so utterly misunderstand the teachings of an extraordinarily keen-minded revolutionary

> like Christ . . . After I had thought about it a while it seemed to me that
> Christianity to him meant bondage & ceremony & hypocrisy & an emphasis
> on doctrines that are based on assumptions rather than on fact and behind it all
> Crusades & Albigensian wars & all the hundred & one inquisitions & horrors
> that have been perpetuated in the name of Christianity, and that living in
> Europe one feels perhaps with added force. He has mixed up Ecclesiasticism
> with Christianity, I feel sure. He condemns the fire that warms his house
> because of the smoke that fills his eyes. And yet he is so sincere & so intolerant
> of shams . . . The last time I saw him he said "Never *believe* anything, you
> only *know*." I thought about that & then I had to admit that while he had a
> remarkable intellect, he had no imagination whatever, & that after all civiliza-
> tion has only progressed when people *were* willing to trust their imaginations
> . . . I wished for a glib tongue every time I saw him instead of my own
> stumbling possession! (Elizabeth Cramer to James G. K. McClure, Jr., June
> 2, 1915)

A week later, her thoughts return to painting.

> . . . I suppose the whole "raison d'etre" of art depends on whether you think
> beauty is necessary in life or not and that is something that almost everybody
> would answer in only one way. Perhaps it is because real beauty is something
> that possesses a life giving quality,—it somehow or other renews your spirit
> and everybody wants *that*...Everybody wants beauty—it seems always to
> quicken your sense of being alive and that means happiness and peace and a
> blessed conviction that you are really necessary in the scheme of things. The
> people who live in the hideous dreary parts of Chicago just flock to the Art
> Institute Sunday afternoons hoping that they will find what they lack there . . .
> I used to think that people's souls couldn't develop in sordid hideous surround-
> ings but I know now that I was wrong. Spiritual development comes from
> within but beauty is an incalculable help because it keeps your spirit alive.
> (Elizabeth Cramer to James G. K. McClure, Jr., July 2, 1915)

Elizabeth Cramer loved the reveries of a carefree afternoon, when her
imagination could be loosed without constraint to stumble over some new inspiration. She told Jim, "I feel envious of tramps. They have no possessions to
chain them down. They can go comfortably out in the sun & smell the . . .
flowers & lie on their backs and watch the clouds making patterns of themselves
while all the time the affluent Mrs. Jones & Mrs. Smith are angrily cleaning
their silver or making new chair covers" (Elizabeth Cramer to James G. K.
McClure, Jr., July 5, 1915). Relaxation never came easily to Jim. He always
thought of one more chore that needed doing, remaining uneasy until the
thought was followed by the accomplishment. Elizabeth's quiet nature, her
insistence on late afternoon strolls, her constant thrill at finding new and unexpected scenes of beauty all brought into Jim's life a new dimension of experience that protected him from his own nature. Jim's life in the summer of 1915
was in flux, and slowly but carefully he and Elizabeth learned about each other.

The events that followed their marriage would alter his aspirations, his daily habits and his geographical allegiance.

The doctors of Dansville were already telling him to stay away from the ministry for a few years. In one of Elizabeth's letters to Wiggy she mentions that " . . . the Dansville man says he will be cured but that he cannot go back to the ministry for two years & that he would have to do something that keeps him out of doors. It is cussed luck & he thinks now of getting some land in South Carolina or Georgia & as he says digging himself in" (Elizabeth Cramer to Martha Clarke, August 20, 1915). The Jackson "cure" was taking a long time. He spent the summer and most of the fall there, except for a brief sojourn in the backwoods of Michigan. "Jim is up in the Michigan woods," Elizabeth reported to Wiggy. "Poor dear he's rather cast down. He wrote me the other day that he would have to give up writing me until he gets the better of his head. The doctors say he will surely be cured but that he will have to be outdoors & live a quiet outdoor life for the next *two* years which he says has upset all his plans" (Elizabeth Cramer to Martha Clarke, August 25, 1915).

In another letter, she explains to Wiggy the diagnosis of Jim's difficulties. "It seems that they think that for some years he has forced the blood into his brain through overwork & study & that in doing so the blood vessels became dilated & lost their elasticity so now they're trying to get it back again & I rather think he's there for all summer." And then to Jim again:

> Of course you mustn't write letters to people until your head is quite well again, I said as much to you before, young man.
>
> Isn't it splendid that your Dansville doctor has discovered the reason for your headaches. That is so encouraging because of course it is only a question of time now before you are quite over. I'm so glad you've decided to take his advice about leading some kind of outdoor life for two years or so . . .
>
> In two weeks I expect to wipe the last remaining paint stains off my shoes and start for Manchester. How nice that there is a possibility of seeing you there— . . . (Elizabeth Cramer to James G. K. McClure, Jr., August 30, 1915)

Manchester, Vermont held out great possibilities for Jim and Elizabeth. The Green Mountains in the early fall put on one of the natural world's most miraculous events, "The Foliage Season." Jim did indeed plan to visit Manchester. He was to stay with Annie and Dumont in the house he had helped to build. Elizabeth's home base would be the stately and rambling Mt. Equinox Hotel, where she resided with the aunties, Bessie and Freddy, who were often seen strolling down the shaded marble sidewalk in long white dresses.

She wrote to her confidante, "Jim is staying with his sister . . . I'm afraid, Wiggy darling, he is nicer than ever. My aunts adore him . . . The poor thing is nearly dying of ennui because he can't look at a book and he adores reading" (Elizabeth Cramer to Martha Clarke, September 27, 1915). With both Skinners and McClures in the surrounding countryside there was a constant round of social obligations for both of them. But despite Elizabeth's expectation of a month of companionship with Jim, he abruptly cut his visit short, returning to the sanitarium a frustrated young man unable to see himself a marriageable prospect. She was stunned by his departure. She wrote to Wiggy:

> . . . We went on some long, long walks & climbs & the time just flew by. Tuesday we took lunch with us up Stratton Gap . . . He told me then that all his best hopes had gone smash, that the Dr. said he wouldn't be really well for six months & that he was going back to Dansville the next day. I was so surprised I nearly fell off the log into the ravine below because, only the day before he had been planning for us to go up Equinox and over to Roaring Brook & goodness knows what all. I tried to appear as though it were perfectly natural for him to be going though I knew that his original intentions had been to go back to the Sanitarium in November but he seemed so dreadfully upset that I didn't ask any questions. "You see," he said, "the trouble with me is I've got congestion of the brain; that's the long & the short of it. The doctors say it's a very common thing but that it takes time to cure & that I'll have to come back here for the rest of winter." He started to say more but he stopped short & after that we both of us tried to forget all about it—and we did I think. We talked & talked & finally as it seemed about lunch time Jim looked at his watch & found it was 3:30 & there we were at the top of the mountain with our lunch way at the foot of the mountain. It was too absurd for words but there were so many things to talk about that the time had fairly rushed by. When we finally did get back to our lunch it was five o'clock & pitch black before we started home. We had motored over the stoney field . . . just below the mountain & it was a delicious black night with huge shooting Northern lights in the sky. Going back I behaved as though his departure next day were the most natural thing in the world. "I'm sure you'll feel a lot better Jim after this second Dansville bout," said I in my most commonplace tones. He didn't answer at first. Then he said right out flat, "It isn't that I really have to go back to Dansville tomorrow but I can't go on seeing you any more until I'm perfectly well,—so I've *got* to go away. As far as my head goes I'm feeling pretty fit; —its been pretty stiff work to keep from saying anything to you," he added. That was all but of course I knew what he meant. He won't ask me to marry him, he won't even tell me that he cares about me until he's a well man. If he did, I don't suppose any longer that I could give but one answer. I might even be a bold & brazen hussy & do the proposing myself if I were not afraid that it would only make him feel worse about it all & be totally ineffectual. With all his charm & his gentleness he is perfectly immovable when he makes up his mind. Apparently he thinks that it would be dishonorable to ask me to marry him & to even tell me he cared about me while he is out of a job & ill, & I suppose he felt that it was an impossible situation to go on seeing me day after day without speaking of what was uppermost in his mind. There was nothing else for him to do but go, but it has been hard on us both. . . .
> (Elizabeth Cramer to Martha Clarke, October 3, 1915)

Annie and Dumont, like the Aunties, were doubtless hoping the match was being made on the hike up to Stratton Gap. When darkness closed in, his brother-in-law Dumont decided that either Jim had proposed, or they were lost, or most likely they were both engaged and lost. He organized a search party, setting forth to meet the straying couple with lanterns, and when they met them both smiling and in good spirits, he was even more sure of the results. Later he queried, "Well Jim, did you ask her?" It was of course the very worst of questions under the circumstances, and even Jim could not hold back a gruff reply.[12]

In two letters to Wiggy, Elizabeth wrote:

> He sent me yesterday a perfectly *huge enormous* box of lilies of the valley & orchids. I never had so many flowers from anybody in my life. They filled four or five huge vases & I felt like a debutante . . . I didn't open the box for ages because it was huge I thought it contained my clothes from the wash & I almost passed out when I opened it and saw the flowers. I feel as though the sender had vanished. I had a little note from him when he reached Dansville but he was unable to write oftener than once a month as writing brings on the pain in his head. I don't write either . . . It's the deuce . . . The time seems awfully long & next spring seems a hundred years off. . . . (Elizabeth Cramer to Martha Clarke, October 16, 1915)

> The Aunts are *horribly disappointed* that he is gone & totally mystified. They think of course that he simply overdid here. I don't know what in the world his sister & her husband think! Of course they know that he likes me & I'm afraid they think I've calmly turned him down & sent him packing like an unconscionable flirt. The Aunts, dear things, are so amusing. They do nothing but descant on Jim's charms & they would almost burst with joy if I *should* marry him. Aunt Freddy keeps telling me how fond she is of him & what a thoroughbred he is & how much charm she thinks he has, though she adds quite frankly that she doesn't agree with him in all his ideas. Dear Aunt Freddy, she and Jim are poles apart when it comes to theology & a number of other subjects! I'm writing all this dearest because . . . I just have to talk about it to somebody. (Elizabeth Cramer to Martha Clarke, October 3, 1915)

Jim and Elizabeth must have been central figures amongst the parlor gossips that fall, and when he pulled out of town so abruptly, theories of cause and effect rattled around Manchester. Elizabeth remained with the aunts at The Equinox for her allotted stay, missing Jim terribly.

The leaves of Vermont turned brown and dropped. The smell of them burning filled the late afternoon air after the men had come home from work. It had been a year since Jim, Harriet and Doug Stuart, and Elizabeth had dinner together at Rathmore. Time in Manchester passed very slowly for Elizabeth and her letters to Jim were fewer and attempted to rejuvenate some interest in theology. It seemed that the six more months at Dansville would be a year. Jim wrote her to explain.

> The thing that has been at the bottom of my mind & that has been bothering me for a long time is not so much the getting fit but the ability to *stay* fit & do heavy strenuous work. I knew all along that I was apt to go at things too

hard and in a way that might use me up again, so I asked this man (Dr.
Gregory) could he do this for me. He is a direct sort of a chap & his answer
rather staggered me, "Not unless you remain here a year." I've decided to
settle down & see the thing through. . . . (quoted by Elizabeth Cramer in a
letter to Martha Clarke, November 26, 1915)

She absorbed the latest setback while visiting her artist friend Mildred
Burrage in Kennebunkport, Maine. By late November, it was time to return to
Lake Forest. She planned to spend the weekend in New York City, and then
on to Chicago and home. On the train from Kennebunkport, she wrote Jim about
the Burrage household and the little town. Doing her best to set an encouraging
tone, she told him: "You're a regular 'brick,'—I feel like saying a lot more but
I won't! Of course the only thing for you to do is to stay on at Dansville . . . A
year seems an awfully long time when you first think of it but even *two* years
wouldn't be long if it meant that you were going to come out with sound health.
Do stay a full year where you are" (Elizabeth Cramer to James G. K. McClure,
Jr., November 22, 1915).

Elizabeth checked into the Martha Washington Hotel, a prim establishment
that advertised itself as "The only hotel in the world exclusively for women."[13]
She received there an urgent message from Jim that he was coming to New
York and wanted to see her. She left him this message at the front desk:

Dear Jim,
    I feel turned topsy-turvy,—a few days ago it seemed as though I should not
see you again until I had achieved white hairs & a cap, and now,—here you
are!
    Will you meet me at the Plaza—in front of the news stand near the elevators
& across from the main desk, about half-past three this afternoon? It is too bad
for you to have this trip down town for nothing but I am obliged to keep an
appointment with the oculist this morning and it is apt to be a longish performance. Rather than keep you waiting in this odious place [the Martha Wash-
ington] I shall take you at your word & name the Plaza instead, as I have
appointments in that neighborhood. Besides, I somehow hate to think of asso-
ciating anything nice like you with this smug bourgeois spot! The drawing-
room resembles a dental "parlour" and the "lady guests" all wear white waists
with stiff collars & seem to be concealing curl-papers under their hats! Ugh!
Why is Respectability always so uninviting! This seems to be the one place in
New York where the lone spinster may stay without offending Madam
Grundy. You are a bright prospect and after 3:30 I am bound by no ties. The
Plaza is near the Park so we can go for a walk therein & throw peanuts at the
monkeys, or take a bus-ride, or just retire to the Plaza drawing room & talk . . .
    I have a sort of an idea that this is all the result of a Thanksgiving dinner &
that I shall presently wake up & find that you are not coming at all. (Elizabeth
Cramer to James G. K. McClure, Jr., November 27, 1915)

At the Plaza hotel a remarkable scene unfolded. Impediments fell away,
and the romance of Jim McClure and Elizabeth Cramer found its freedom.

Without hesitation, he asked; and she accepted. A flood of the rarest joy swept over them both. They rushed out and hired a horse and carriage. Jim told the driver to keep going around Central Park until told to stop. Afterwards, they returned to the Martha Washington, a most ironical setting for the newly engaged, and he proceeded to scandalize the patrons with his obvious affections towards Elizabeth. She laughed and called him a "shameless creature," and recalled later that " . . . you so disturbed that respectable, open-mouthed old lady in the corner . . . and you a properly brought-up young man!" (Elizabeth Cramer to James G. K. McClure, Jr., December 14, 1915) She was as guilty as he of course, and they were both utterly unconcerned about the rest of the world. All that mattered was that the waiting and uncertainty were over, their engagement had begun. What had happened to change the situation so quickly?

> My own dearest Wiggy,
> . . . I wrote you a hurried tiny line two days ago to tell you that your indifferent celibate Pigie was actually going to marry Jim McClure . . . You see when the Dr. told him he would have to stay on for a year he said he just couldn't bear it, that he couldn't sleep for thinking of me & that he knew all the good he got there would be nullified so he went to Dr. Gregory & told him he just couldn't bear it living away from me, & not speaking and that Dr. Gregory had somehow *got* to help him. With that, Dr. Gregory sprang from his chair, grasped him by the arm and said, "Why, why, *why* didn't you tell me all this at first! Why the best thing you can possibly do is to get married. You'll be all right in no time. You are well *now*. It's only to insure your *remaining* well that I said you must stay here a year. Why you'd be *far* better off married. You'd recover your staying powers more quickly & there is absolutely no question about it's being the best thing to do!" Jim said that he brought up every possible objection and that the Dr. just bowled them over one after one. Jim said it took him just twenty minutes after that before he telegraphed me thinking I was still at the Burrages and—you know the rest. Of course Wiggy darling he will not be able to do any work for two years and he will have to live very quietly. But he has a small income—a *very* small one & considerable money put by, & so we can get married anyway. We shall always be frightfully poor . . . Anyway it's much more exciting to marry a poor person with ideas than a rich one with none & then there's always my money for emergencies though he declares that he will never touch a penny of it . . .
> We don't know where we shall go & what we shall do. Jim's idea is to rent a little place somewhere in the mountains of Carolina or Virginia perhaps with the option of buying it at the end of two years & then keeping it as a "retreat" for vacations & things like that when he was busy with a parish. When he gets well he'll probably take a parish in the slums because he said that for all he knew he would always pick out poor & unfrequented districts but it's a grand good adventure & I can cut my coat to fit my cloth even though it may be a bad job at first. (Elizabeth Cramer to Martha Clarke, December 1, 1915)

Earlier in the same letter, Elizabeth had told Wiggy:

... his whole life seems to be permeated & filled with what Matthew Arnold calls "The Power not Ourselves." I never thought I should find anybody who could somehow make my own life so much larger & freer & with it all so full of humor & lightness. I am a very lucky person Wigywag darling. A curious thing is that ever since I have known him I have had the feeling of being tremendously stimulated & yet immensely peaceful—there was no effort no striving after anything, just a curious sense of being recreated within. I knew after Christmas last year that nothing but this inevitable end was possible but I wanted to think it out clearly & consciously. (Elizabeth Cramer to Martha Clarke, December 1, 1915)

And in yet another letter:

... It isn't that Jim is brilliant or extraordinarily clever either. I don't know what it is exactly. I've known men who were very much cleverer. I think one reason that I like him so much is because he is so unconscious of himself as it were; he's such an odd mixture of impulse and reason and he's a very eager person only he's almost more eager for other people than he is for himself if you know what I mean by that. And then he always trusts people & expects the best of them and he consequently always gets it. (Elizabeth Cramer to Martha Clarke, winter of 1915)

Other people have commented on Jim McClure's personal qualities, but no one ever described them better than Elizabeth. Here was a woman who could match Jim's intellect, slow down his "impulses," help him to notice the beauty around him that he might otherwise rush past. Elizabeth Cramer was the perfect match for Jim McClure—intelligent, sensitive, fun-loving, and willing to share a life of intellectual and literal adventure.

1. Clipping of article from Chicago newspaper, 1916, found among family papers.
2. Pamphlet on the Pierrepont family genealogy.
3. Interview with Elspeth McClure Clarke.
4. Jim's scorecard, found among his personal papers.
5. Santa Barbara notebook, February 20, 1916.
6. Santa Barbara notebook.
7. Santa Barbara notebook.
8. Santa Barbara notebook.
9. Santa Barbara notebook.
10. Santa Barbara notebook.
11. Santa Barbara notebook.
12. Interview with Dumont Clarke, Jr.
13. Hotel slogan printed on a piece of letterhead found among family papers.

Chapter Ten

Marriage

> So long as our lives individually strive to embody the spirit that comes of God, our souls seeking renewal always in the source of all life must then meet, and of necessity become one, since in God there is no separation. (*Elizabeth Cramer to James G. K. McClure, Jr., February 8, 1916*)

> I thought of you in the middle of salad tonight . . . about made everyone else in the dining room look as gray and uninteresting as oysters. (*Elizabeth Cramer to James G. K. McClure, Jr., January 23, 1916*)

If Jim and Elizabeth's courtship had meandered and lingered through a difficult course, the end came in a rush. Now they would have several months of engagement to savor their joyous new status. Before their rendezvous in New York, queries and doubts had often piled up in their minds like afternoon thunderheads on a hot summer's day.

Elizabeth had not always been sure that she was ready to become Jim's wife, characteristically because she worried that she, an artist, might hinder his work as a minister. The conventions of the day portrayed the artist as a free-spirited rebel, especially if the artist was a woman and had left the confines of America to pursue her craft in Paris! There could not have been more distance between that image and the one reserved for the wife of a minister, who was expected to radiate prim virtue, to be in all matters reverent and uncomplaining, to participate in the endless talk of missionary societies and sewing circles, to raise her family according to the rules of the Victorian Age, and to entertain the steady stream of visitors that were a part of her husband's job. If the pastor's wife was not a "paragon of virtue" the parish would not accept her, and this would make her husband's life extremely difficult. Elizabeth had been thinking about all this before she and Jim were ever engaged. She had written to her confidante, Wiggy, her doubts about being able to fit into a minister's life. Now she rejoiced to find her worries evaporated in the sunshine of Jim's optimistic view of her future role.

> . . . But way back in my mind is still the thought of those ladies in the Tuesday afternoon Benevolent Society who will raise their eyebrows when they meet your wife in a paint-apron—perhaps, I thought, I can coax them all into wanting the Sunday School "done up," and I *know* I could teach a Sunday School class! There are quantities of things in the Bible that I should just love talking about to a lot of youngsters and it would be so satisfying to have a free

fling. I read "Jonah" the other night to Corwith [her half-brother] & Susan [a cousin who was living with the Cramers] and we all three almost burst with excitement. Poor Jonah was so human & so able apparently and so "temperamental" & he was dealt with so promptly! I never knew there was any more to him than the whale! . . . (Elizabeth Cramer to James G. K. McClure, Jr., December 6, 1915)

After receiving a letter from Jim on the subject of her art, she wrote to Wiggy:

The beautiful part Wiggy darling is that he feels just the way I do about painting—he has all sorts of awfully interesting ideas about it & he says that he just couldn't endure it if I had anything to do with the details of church work & that the only thing he wants is my cooperation in the spirit—just what you said Wiggywag. He insists that I go on painting & says that I will mean just that much more to him if I do. You can't think how relieved & happy I feel. . . . (Elizabeth Cramer to James G. K. McClure, Jr., December 1, 1915)

And to Jim she wrote:

. . . If you by any chance *had* said that you wanted me to paint because it was temperamentally a way of living that satisfied me, I should have been so low in my mind that I could never have done a stroke of work thereafter. Of course it *is* a way of living in which I find much happiness but that is not the reason for adopting it. The reason is because it is simply a means to an end and the end is never anything but the Kingdom of God. I will never forget how absolutely joyful I felt when you suddenly made me see it all in this way. I had only the most scrappy little glimpses of it, I could never get everything into focus. I lived in a hundred different ways and they were all more or less detached. I was always having glimmerings but the glimmerings were somehow unconnected & then, all of a sudden, after a conversation we had out in the studio one late afternoon, in front of that old stove, everything suddenly shifted and fitted into place. [She was recalling a day at Rathmore during the early months of their courtship.] It was the most extraordinary experience. All the loose ends seemed somehow caught up, and ever since, every idea or experience or sensation I have ever had has somehow or other fitted itself onto the piece; it was like a pattern that you slowly evolved. Formerly I had quantities of colors all jumbled together, all valuable in themselves, but confused. Then you came along & I suddenly got a clue that I hadn't had before & ever since then I have known that if I kept at it long enough, I could always fit the pieces on where they belonged and the pattern would be always growing and growing . . .
You can't think how I felt on that "stove day" after you had gone home. I had never, I think, been so happy or so peaceful & at the same time so thrilled through & through. I felt as though I had been hitherto walking along a road with a high wall on either side and above the wall were the tops of trees & birds & now & then roses climbing down the sides. All of a sudden, it was as though the doors in the walls had opened and I could henceforth whenever I wished go into those lovely gardens and then I looked in all directions there were vistas

leading everywhere. It was all just like that. For a long time I only wanted to stay outside and look in. After a bit I went inside—and always there was you. My Dearest,—do you know, have you any idea what it all meant? (Elizabeth Cramer to James G. K. McClure, Jr., December 14, 1915)

Jim, of course, had been terribly concerned about his health, but the doctor at Dansville had now assured him that if he married Elizabeth and lived and worked outdoors for a couple of years he would be as strong as ever. The decision reached that day in the Plaza Tea Room transformed their lives. For a few days they kept the joyful secret between themselves and Jim's brother Arch. Jim was staying with him at Union Seminary, where Arch was studying for the ministry, so he was in on the engagement from the beginning. Then Jim and Elizabeth went to visit the Skinner Aunts, who were staying in New York, and they rejoiced with them.

Elizabeth returned to Lake Forest and the painting of the Day Nursery murals and made preparations for the wedding, and Jim went back to Dansville, but little must have seemed the same for them. The larger questions had been resolved, but there were other tensions and differences that would have to be understood. After all, both had been living independently for some time and inevitably there were points of view and habits that would have to be questioned and thought through before their marriage. The two of them had a future to be sketched in, for one of the remarkable circumstances of this marriage is that despite their ages (Jim was 31 and Elizabeth almost 28) basic decisions such as their livelihood and where they would live were virtually undetermined.

Jim thought it best to remain quiet and away from Elizabeth, making a brief appearance during the Christmas season for a proper announcement and a round of entertainment. The result of this separation is a daily stream of letters to him from Elizabeth. Through these letters she and Jim shared their inner thoughts and worked out their differences. It is a loss that Jim's letters have not been found, but by Elizabeth's replies we can learn much of what he was thinking.

Their first duty was to inform their family and close friends. Discretion in these matters was important; the right people had to hear the news in the right order, so that no one would be miffed at being left out.

Dear Jim,

I have told Isabelle & Father and Mother . . . and the rascals *say* they were not surprised! Though Father admits that he thought "nothing was going to happen." The dear things are immensely nice about it all and full of little jokes and much affection. They think a great deal of you—more than you have any idea of—and as for Isabelle, she nearly burst with satisfaction . . . Father is already full of ideas as to a "retreat" and insists that he knows of one already that is promising—an old, very old house 15 miles from the Hot Springs, where there is, as you know an excellent golf course . . . I only mention all this to show my parent's immediate enthusiasm. He already has us housed! . . .

Dear, there are no words to tell you all I feel. The thought of you is like a light shining where once there was only darkness, like a strong wind that blows suddenly through a room long closed, like flowers springing up in April among the winter leaves. The dear remembrance of you fills my heart. My cup runneth over. The fervor and the joy that quicken my days are only equalled by the peace that comes of a mutual understanding, by the love that purifies and restores.

God bless you my Dearest all my life.

Elizabeth (Elizabeth Cramer to James G. K. McClure, Jr., December 1, 1915)

Dear Jim:

How much I liked your letters to Father & Mother. They were such splendid straight sincere letters—so beautifully written & so free from anything that was cheap or lacking in dignity . . . What you said in them about me touched me more than I can ever tell you. As for Father, he & Ambrose both said that if they had chosen from all the men they knew for me they could not have chosen differently. That is a great tribute Mr. James G. K. McClure because the above mentioned gentlemen are inclined to be extremely fussy and over-critical! I like to think of something I read once. "Through such souls alone God . . . shows sufficient of his light For us in the dark to rise by."

****

Dear Light in my darkness illuminating countless ways that hitherto seemed somehow all obscured, my heart is yours utterly. . . . (Elizabeth Cramer to James G. K. McClure, Jr., Dec. 6, 1915)

Arch McClure rushed a letter off to Elizabeth as soon as he understood the news was out.

There is no one that I love quite as I do Jim—no one whose life and character I respect more. He has done far more for me in opening my mind to truths I hadn't seen than I can ever repay; and then his own life has been one of such amazing and unfailing cheerfulness during all the months of his waiting for strength that he is a constant inspiration to me . . . In fact it always makes me want to be better just to be with him . . .

It certainly did surprise me to have him appear in New York, and to have the whole thing happen almost under my very eyes. And it did delight me to see how happy he was and to know that you had made him so. (Arch McClure to Elizabeth Cramer, December 1, 1915)

Soon after the news reached McCormick Seminary, Jim's father wrote to Elizabeth.

. . . I make humble but joyous confession that I have hoped for a long time that you and Jim would care for one another. I never have spoken to Jim about the matter for it seemed too sacred to be mentioned . . . again and again I have told his Mother of my great wish. I have the truest respect and the tenderest affection for you. There is no girl I have ever seen whom I would be so glad to have Jim marry as yourself. My confidence in you is absolute, my admiration for you is perfect. (James G. K. McClure, Sr. to Elizabeth Cramer, December 6, 1915)

Jim's mother had written promptly exclaiming her support.

> This morning's mail brought us, from Jamie, a letter telling us a secret that seems almost too wonderful to be true . . . you are, of all the world, the one I would most rejoice to have as Jamie's choice for his life companion, and I know that since he saw you in New York, he has been happier than ever before in his life. (Phebe Ann Dixon McClure to Elizabeth Cramer, Dec. 3, 1915)

Elizabeth wrote to Jim: "Such dear letters from your Mother and Arch and Nathan—I didn't know how they might feel about it and my mind is immensely relieved. I have such a proud feeling, Sir, when I think that you are considering me with some affection! . . ." (Elizabeth Cramer to James G. K. McClure, Jr., Dec. 6, 1915).

Jim wrote to his sister Harriet and her husband Douglas Stuart, ending with "Tell Dudley [Doug's nickname at that time] he must decide whether to come in his shirt sleeves or his bath gown to Sid's and my wedding for I will have to be wearing his cutaway—" (James G. K. McClure, Jr. to Harriet Stuart, Dec. 1, 1915).

Jim's sister Annie Clarke wrote, "Our only regret is that it didn't happen here in Manchester, where we felt that we gave you every opportunity" (Annie McClure Clarke to Elizabeth Cramer, Dec. 7, 1915). And then from Dumont, "Perhaps . . . you will tell us that the atmosphere of a stone in Manchester did have some part in helping a man whom we love to win you to the decision we think is so beautiful" (Dumont Clarke to Elizabeth Cramer, Dec. 8, 1915). Elizabeth's artist friend, Mildred Burrage, wrote that she wept for joy when she received the news in her family's Kennebunkport, Maine, home (Mildred Burrage to Elizabeth Cramer, December 8, 1915).

Elizabeth found it hard to concentrate on her murals at the Day Nursery in Chicago. She wrote Jim:

> . . . Such a job as the Nursery is,—my thoughts go way off and the part of me that paints somehow gets along as best it can. If there were any real composing to do I should hang a sign up & inform the public that the person who worked therein was temporarily deceased. To have to paint apple trees & toys when every thought is running your way is a form of mental discipline that is unequalled. I do disastrous things—paint eyes red and apple blossoms blue . . .
> Dear Thing, good night—Siddy
> (Elizabeth Cramer to James G. K. McClure, Jr., December 3, 1915)

Four days later she wrote again:

> Dearest,
> The only natural easy thing to do is to write, -everything else I do with one hand as it were in a very lame fashion—all of which goes to show you that I am in a bad way . . .

Tonight I dined . . . to the tune of scrambled eggs & muffins, & there was
I eating them with much composure when suddenly I remembered that I had
no idea whether, when it came to Sunday night suppers, *you* would have a taste
for onions or alligator pears! (Dreadful things, those last!) . . . [She would
soon find out that he liked boiled eggs and crackers and milk.]
. . . I told Corwith [her half-brother] today about you and me. First I made him
guess. He launched the most incredible and disturbing conjectures that forced
me to enlighten him with all possible speed, and *then*, his surprise was unbounded. "Well," he said reflectively, "I'd forgotten about *him*, you see."
(Elizabeth Cramer to James G. K. McClure, Jr. Dec. 7, 1915)

Later she wrote that Corwith had told her one morning that Jim might never
marry her after all. "Mr. McClure might change his mind before January first.
It's a long ways off, you know." Elizabeth feigned scorn and laughed at Corwith
but he continued solemnly, "Still, Tibbits, you will admit that it is quite possible." Elizabeth added to Jim, 'Ponder and reflect, young man! Youth is hot-
headed and rash and there are yet twenty-two days in this month for mature
reflection . . ." Elizabeth Cramer to James G. K. McClure, Jr., Dec. 9, 1915).
In several letters she told him how she pretended that his "ghost, as the Irish
say," would come in to sit by her bedroom fire of an evening and how she
looked forward to this. Thinking of their walk in Central Park after Jim's
proposal and her acceptance in New York, she wrote:

When I think that only a week ago we were walking in the park in all that
amazing fog and darkness with the shining Plaza glittering behind the trees! I
love to think of that. Always, always, the park is there full of peace and
thoughts that are apart, and around on every side is the roaring hungry city
with all its enterprise & struggle and effort.
It was like that, I think, when you talked to me & said the little things that
made me think you really cared. It was the first time that I had ever known the
real meaning of peace. All life must somehow mean a desperate effort, but
that at the heart of it there should be peace & serenity and a joy that was
somehow not of this world was something that transcended all experience.
Only a little over a week ago what sober guarded creatures we were. And I
was none too sure that you would even want my frequent letters! Now, Sir, I
am pleasing myself. It is a relief to write long pages about nothing at all.
(Elizabeth Cramer to James G. K. McClure, Jr., December 7, 1915)

Two days later she wrote:

My Dearest,
The first of January seems further off than ever, —I almost believe that
time is going the other way & that we're slipping back again into November
. . . I have a sort of a feeling that when you do come I shall wait until you are
within sight of a window & then I shall promptly hide in the cellar. You seem
such a safe distance off just now that I feel I can write you all kinds of rubbish,
if you were here, I should never run on in such a fashion—I should always be
looking out of the tail of my eye to see whether you are astonished or dis-

mayed, and when I see you again after all the nonsense I am always writing you, I shall feel very red and stiff and inclined to disappear. I shall probably call you Mr. McClure & shake hands politely and ask after your health and you'll have to begin all over again, if you still like me! Have you ever noticed that there are some people you like very much in Winter whom you can't abide in summer? and vice versa? I'm not sure whether you've had a real square all-around look at me, or not . . . Besides, you've never seen me at Breakfast. I, at any rate never like anyone before eleven o'clock and until at least twelve I always wear my hair slicked tight back and never speak of anything but the thermometer or why Gustave hasn't fixed the furnace. This is all in a burst of honesty that might never again come back so I'm hurriedly writing it down while it lasts. Also I always wear my shell spectacles at least half the day and I sometimes waste a terrible lot of time picking out tunes with one finger while the maids are dusting and I have an old blue skirt that I love & that everybody else hates because it somehow has a tendency to drop in the back no matter how much I hitch it up. I feel sure, now, that I am going to be quite made over & that I shall never lose any more handkerchiefs or door keys if you still continue to like me, BUT,-I saw in the paper the other day that "marriage does not change the individual" which is a sobering thought and one that urges me to bid you reflect! What, just what if you should get a church in which your parishioners . . . demanded a competent, efficient, capable, executive wife!!!!

1. I am not competent.
2. I am never efficient
3. I am not capable
4. I am not executive

(Elizabeth Cramer to James G. K. McClure, Jr., December 9, 1915)

Jim remained in Dansville until just before Christmas. When he arrived at the Lake Forest Station he was greeted by Rathmore's butler. Jim's physique came to inhabit the spirit that had been visiting Elizabeth every evening, and presumably he did not need to search the cellar to find her. The season of 1915 was the gayest yet at Rathmore, because not only had Jim and Elizabeth agreed to marry, but young Ambrose was ready to announce his engagement to Grace Meeker. She was a member of Jim's Santa Barbara "band," and had been featured in the previous spring's *Vogue* magazine. Both couples decided to announce their intentions on New Year's Day, but beforehand they enjoyed all the social events of the season, pretending to keep the well-known secrets. Jim returned to Halsted Street on Christmas Eve, to spend his last holiday as an unmarried son in his family's household. As he drove out of Rathmore that night, he found Elizabeth concealed behind the stone gate that served as the entrance to the estate. There they parted, after exchanging affections and written messages, the latter to be read on first arising Christmas Day. Elizabeth and Jim were savoring, with all of the literary accoutrement, the fruits of their romance.

According to the firm rules of the day, Jim and Elizabeth and Ambrose and Grace acquired a new status on January first. The double engagement of Susie Skinner's children made quite a stir in Chicago when it appeared in the Society pages. Elizabeth wrote a eulogy on Jim to Wiggy, who was still holding the fort in the Trèpied house, surrounded by war: ". . . I feel so natural & so happy & so comfortable with him & never have a single fear or worry or anxious thought about the future with him which apparently is almost unheard of with an engaged young person!! . . . People seem to be very pleased about it everywhere & I just go about on air . . . Jim is as honest as you . . . I can't say more than that & he has the loveliest sense of humor & can be as much of a goat as Ambrose! . . ." (Elizabeth Cramer to Martha Clarke, Jan. 1, 1916)

A flood of congratulatory notes poured in on Jim and Elizabeth after their engagement was made public—some two hundred altogether—and they add up to a great crescendo of support. One sad young man, who had tagged doggedly after Elizabeth, wrote in a defeated tone, "I feel absolutely no bitterness toward you" (John W. Brown to Elizabeth Cramer, December 16, 1915). Her cousin, Mark Skinner Watson, had come from Chimney Point, Vermont, to work on the Chicago *Tribune*. He was a promising young newspaper man and they had had great fun together. From his letter it is easy to see why he became a noted columnist.

> Possibly your Aunts have told you that I received your letter and read it with keen excitement the very day after you wrote it instead of three or four weeks later as you had expected. Thus, for four days I carried with me the mighty secret, restraining the impulse to show an unsuccessful suitor's vengeance and tell the *Tribune* all about it . . .
>
> Also I've been hoping particularly that I might see you and tell you face to face how happy I am that you are happy . . . But [you are] rather inaccessible, particularly to a youth who still finds his hours of freedom better suited to owls, nightingales, bats and deeds of darkness, rather than to young ladies who now, if never before, must be exceeding prim.
>
> Prim? Ah me. How can we again have a spree at the Blackstone, followed by "Tristan" or Mr. G. B. Shaw . . . How unless then be added Jim and, and, and, —why, of course, my own fiancee! The only trouble is that the poor thing is non-existent . . . And you will continue nice and agreeable, even though married. Please.
>
> . . . my very best congratulations and as near a prayer as a heretic can come.
> . . . (Mark Skinner to Elizabeth Cramer, Jan. 4, 1916)

A friend identified only as Beth wrote a sharp commentary on the same social conventions of the time that troubled Jim and Elizabeth:

> Many time and aft have I heard the familiar name of Jim McClure mentioned, and I feel as if I knew him well. And your letter—which, I hasten to assure you, did *not* resemble the Ladies' Home Journal—assures me beyond any doubt that that fabulous creature, a nice modern saint with all the latest improvements in brains, and the courage of his convictions, exists after all . . . I'm not very fond of the cloth, as a rule, but I'll hand it to anyone who can live and work in Iron River . . . and return with a sufficient sense of perspective to encourage his future wife to go on beautifying the world with mural

decorations. Most reformers look at you with a wild gleam in their eye and say "How dare you be happy when children are starving?" . . .

I can't imagine anything more fun than your slum existence. No, I'm not sentimentalizing for the occasion. Ever since I grew up I've wanted to do just that-discard every non-essential and concentrate on the things that really ought to be done, instead of—oh, sending cards to every fool who invites you to tea. Goodness, what a relief! No clothes, no social stunts, no more servants than you need, no more food than you want to eat. And all the time there is in which to do the interesting things. Please, may I come and visit you and see how it's done? Because some fine day, when I'm fifty, or so, I may be free to do the same thing, and I want some pointers meanwhile . . .

. . . how glad I am that you're not marrying anything even resembling a stockbroker! When my friends' husbands are "in business" I go and dig the grave of any human sympathy we may ever have had. Thank goodness for a socialist for you . . . ! You always needed one, anyhow, by the way; it will do you pounds of good. (Beth [last name unknown] to Elizabeth Cramer, December 26, 1915)

There were peons of praise for Jim from classmates and fellow members of Skull and Bones at Yale, including a prophecy from John Magee, now a missionary in Nanking, China. He wrote, "I'm sure your coming into Jim's life at this time will mean a very great deal to him in every way and that he will now be in the way of gaining completely his normal health" (John Magee to Elizabeth Cramer, Jan. 13, 1916).

Just before Jim was to go south for a little more rest with Annie and Dumont and their new son, Dumont Jr. at Daytona Beach, a tragedy leveled the high spirits of Rathmore. Elizabeth's step-sister Isabelle and her husband, Donald Ryerson, lost their little son. Jim was asked to conduct the funeral services. Elizabeth had always been very close to Isabelle, and Donald and Jim were friends as well. But the wedding plans had to go on. While Jim was keeping a safe distance in Florida resting with his sister's family, Elizabeth's father sent his adored daughter off to New York with her step-mother on a shopping "bat." From the Biltmore Hotel she wrote to Jim:

. . . New York should always be visited a deux. I only feel half a person! If only it were last November, but all the same I'm glad it isn't, because I am just fifty one days richer than I was then and the last two weeks have been worth six ordinary ones besides . . .

This afternoon Mother and I surveyed various silver services and I am now sleeping on two as the saying goes, —it is not as simple as buying a Hudson [automobile] but nevertheless vastly absorbing. How I wish you were here! Only half of me looks at things—the other half is at home trotting around with you, sir. Father is presenting me with the most galumptious petticoats and suchlikes. I shall never want to put a dress on at all. Such fine feathers! . . . (Elizabeth Cramer to James G. K. McClure, Jr., Jan. 19, 1916)

Your little book of treasures is such a joy. I read a bit of it every night. Here is a quotation that you wrote January 1906—"for those children of God

to whom it has been granted to see each other face to face and to hold commun-
ion together and to feel the same spirit working in both can never more be
sundered though the hills be between. For their souls are enlarged for ever
more by that union and they bear one another about in their thoughts continual
as if it were a new strength." That is it, isn't it, Dearest? (Elizabeth Cramer
to James G. K. McClure, Jr., January 20, 1916)

Elizabeth settled on her silver service, and frequented several New York antique
dealers looking for suitable furniture for her new household, slum parish or not.

Dearest—such a place as this is to get ideas about things! I'm just *full* of the
house furnishing variety . . . I go around to all kinds & varieties of shops so
as to see everything going, and if you don't have a nice house, Mr. James G.
K. McClure Jr., my name isn't mine own! I've penetrated antique shops of all
varieties and entered "Decorator's Parlours" with a brazen air of intending to
buy everything and leave with nothing, and my notebook & my head are just
crammed full . . .
    You will love the silver service. It has the most extraordinary dignity and
simplicity. Just to have tea out of it is a privilege . . .
    This [the Biltmore Hotel] isn't a bad place & you have a room with a bath
and three meals for $3.00 a day. From the front windows you look out over
the roof tops at that beautiful Madison Square Garden Tower and down below
are some nice old red brick houses. At night I hear the boats as the river is
just back of us & it makes me think of our ferry ride. I can shut my eyes and
remember every inch of it. Dearest Thing, if I were going to live in a cave in
South Carolina and eat acorns and frogs, if you were there I should be just as
happy as I am now—the automobile and the silver service . . . don't make any
difference at all, somehow. They are just like the holly tissue paper and the
red ribbons that tie up ones loveliest Christmas present. . . . (Elizabeth Cramer
to James G. K. McClure, Jr., Jan. 25, 1916)

Elizabeth's buying spree brought to light one of the tensions between the
prospective mates. The whole question of the correct use of material possessions
in one's life had been an early philosophical link in the romance. Both agreed
that conspicuous consumption, buying for show, material self-indulgence and
the like were rank sins that many of their own class were guilty of, and suffered
spiritual difficulties as a result. The irresponsible rich, they were both sure,
flaunted their wealth and thus aggravated class tensions, and were in fact mo-
nopolizing the resources of the world to the detriment of nearly everyone else.
Elizabeth had grown up in a privileged household, but the material objects that
appealed to her did so because of their beauty, a spiritual quality of the greatest
importance to her. She felt that her gift was to create an ambience of beauty
that would surround her and those she loved, and that furniture, dresses, silver
services and flowers were her means to that end. Such an environment, touched
with the divine, lent itself to spiritual development. Jim, on the other hand, was
as thrifty in all ways as the reputation of his Scotch forebears would indicate.
His habits, like his father's, were built around the premise that one should be

most careful in managing whatever financial resources one had. The more surplus money there was in one's budget, the better able a person would be able to support worthy projects. In short, Jim felt that spending money in excess of need was pure and simple selfishness. Jim would have to increase his vision of "need" to include Elizabeth's urge for beauty. As she explained to him:

> It seems to me that it is an impossible thing to go on living with people simply on a basis of material interests—meals and dinner parties and hats and servants and railroad tickets and sports. It's terrifically wearing to keep up a close personal relation of that sort particularly if you've ever known what the other thing means. That's what's at the bottom of so much unhappiness in married people's lives. Often the only things that two people have in common are material interests and the difference of sex. Of course that can only result in material dissatisfaction and I suppose, under such circumstances, it simply goes to show all over again that the life of the spirit must be shared or the material expression of it can have no real meaning. That's another thing that neither the church nor school ever touches on. (Elizabeth Cramer to James G. K. McClure, Jr., Jan. 23, 1916)

But in her next letter she asserts the importance of owning material things that are beautiful.

> If we go off & live in some starving place . . . why then there will be much *more* reason for our acquiring essentially *good* possessions, because in such a place, the need for sharing such things is so terribly felt even though people there may not be really conscious of it. With our knowledge of beauty and how it can be used, we've *got* to use every means we have to bring people in touch with it. If we have nice furniture (and by that I don't necessarily mean *costly* furniture) and surroundings that are poles removed from their horrible lace window curtains & "bird-eye maple" furniture & red velvet rockers it will mean a lot, I know. We can create a house that will express, through its self, law and order and proportion and repose and aliveness-all those things that you will be constantly opening people's eyes to in what you *say*. *I* want equally to open people's eyes to it in what they *see*. And that's what's the trouble with all modern painting right now, It tries to give you a "thrill." . . . (Elizabeth Cramer to James G. K. McClure, Jr., January 27, 1916)

In her struggles to conceive of a sensible attitude where her art and the needs of the "masses" could meet, she met a figure from across the social gulf, who gave her more to think about. The maid came in to clean her hotel room.

> . . . a huge, strapping, coarse, kind, sort of a woman & she appalled me by seizing upon the remains of my lunch & gobbling them up!—horrid cold remains they were, too,—salmon & cold vegetables and the bitterest kind of strong tea that I couldn't touch. She said apologetically that she was hungry because the hotel didn't give the "help" enough to eat. Then I asked her later on if she liked pictures & her eyes just shone, & her whole manner changed when she said that she did.

I never can get away from the "poor" somehow or other! . . . After the chambermaid had departed, I had a violent reaction . . . and I almost hated my silver service when I thought of that woman's need of food. At such a time, I feel like chucking "art" entirely and going out & handing forth bread line tickets or working for a better wage system! But I *know* that this is mere emotionalism & I *know* that such a state of mind is unintelligent. The "poor" need bread for their souls as well as for their bodies and a silver tea service . . . is something they should have access to in their lives and it is only a millstone around your neck when you aren't willing to share it. Some of the poor *think* that they resent ownership by the upper classes of a silver tea service . . . but it isn't really the fact of *possession* that they resent. It's the attitude of mind that they resent (but they aren't developed enough intellectually to see that this is so), the attitude of mind that assumes that beauty and culture are the special, private privilege of the rich. But if you become one of them in spirit and make them feel that you insist on having your own surroundings beautiful because you feel that beauty is a necessity of life & something to be *shared* and experienced by all who want it too,—why then I'm sure their resentment would disappear. (Elizabeth Cramer to James G. K. McClure, Jr., Jan. 28, 1916)

If Elizabeth struggled with her higher views of silver services, she knew Jim to be the most frugal of men with himself, but very generous to others.

Dearest, I look at all your pictures & none of them look like the same man. So many different people propped up on my bureau and every one of them you . . . There is the you (and such a cuke this one is!) that rolls on the rug with Percy [the Cramer dog] & Corwith and ties poor unoffending Chum [the Cramer cat?] up in a [sic.] overcoat! Then there is another one that buys me velvet overshoes for bad weather and insists upon my going to bed early. (Dear thing, what a nice man that one is!) Then there is another that pulls the Aunts legs every now & then (to use an outrageous old expression) and another one that carries a horrible old german bag around (the same man that does that inks the bare places on his black coat), and still another that always looks as clean as a whistle and has the nicest kind of hands. Then there is a specially dear one that treats me as an equal & that tells me about things & that takes it for granted that I won't shirk facts even if they are hateful ones . . . (I love that one—he always gives me a kind of strength that I never had before.) And then there is another you that reveals to me a far wider more beautiful and significant life than I ever before imagined could come to any one. (Elizabeth Cramer to James G. K. McClure, Jr., Jan. 29. 1916)

Art was Elizabeth's passion. She sought to understand life and apply what she learned through her art, and to understand other people through theirs. While in New York, Mildred Burrage came down from Maine and the two of them called on Claude Monet's daughter and her family, whom they had known in Giverny.

Yesterday . . . we had tea with the Butlers. Mingie [Mildred] & I knew them very well in France and it took me straight back to Paris to meet them again.

Mrs. Butler is Monet's (the French impressionist) daughter & she's very French & very much powdered & rouged & made up but with such a generous kind heart. I like her immensely. Mr. Butler was a friend of Stevenson and Will Low and St. Gaudens & all that 1880 crowd in Paris. He's an extraordinarily handsome man with huge black eyes and much charm of a certain sort. They have two children —Jimmy & Lilli about 25. Lilli is a fascinating little thing with an oriental kind of beauty and Jimmy is a straight, thin, lean youth with real ability if he could only be gotten on the right track. He got in with the post-impressionists in Paris & while he has an awfully honest mind he still sees things from their standpoint and turns out the most awful things just like his father -reds & blues & terrible violent greens. (Elizabeth Cramer to James G. K. McClure, Jr., January 30, 1916)

Before leaving New York, she returned to the Plaza Hotel.

. . . Mingie & I fell in with an older friend . . . and in a burst of extravagance I took them to lunch at the Plaza.

Such seemly conduct on my part, Mr. McClure, all the time I was there. Never a suggestion of my shady past! O I glance with a furtive eye at the waiter to see if he recognized my purple suit but being a man of infinite tact & discretion he looked the other way. What a bold brass monkey you were! I can see that scandalized waiter now rushing off to tell all his dear friends the latest "spice." And there wasn't anything hesitating or apologetic about you either! Ach, such a man!—(dear thing, how I love him for all his bold ways—perhaps —between you and me—the bold ways are just an added reason.)

After lunch, Mingee & I parted company . . . I wanted to be alone.

It was a dully gray afternoon. The street was full of dirty snow, and a raw penetrating mist blew in from the river. I passed the little church where we went together that Sunday morning in November and because you seemed very near, I went inside.

It was dark and quiet and peaceful. Away off in a distant part of the church a man was talking to some coloured people and after a time the service ended, & the people left.

I sat there a long time. Never before, I think, have I been so conscious of all the joy and blessedness that has come to me through you.

I had your precious letter with me—the one you wrote last Thursday & I read it again and again with increased joy and tenderness and humility and I thought of New Year's Eve & of all that you had said to me that evening when we were alone together in the little room. I can never forget your words nor the sincerity & pureness of heart that shone in your dear eyes.

"For their souls were enlarged for evermore by that union"—the quaint words of the old quotation in your little book come back to me always.

I thought of all the things we had talked of together. I tried to realize anew what marriage must mean—marriage in its deepest, truest sense; union of heart & soul & body through mutual longing to be more nearly one with God in order to further his purposes here by whatsoever means are possible.

So long as our lives individually strive to embody the spirit that comes of God, our souls seeking renewal always in the source of all life must then meet, and of necessity become one, since in God there is no separation. That which is you and that which is I must then perforce unite and become eternally part of one another just as two rivers meeting, henceforth mingle and become one stream that continues on its way until it is merged in the great sea . . .

I stayed a long time in the church. After a while people came in and a later service began. A choir of little boys sang the *te Deum,* & everything in me responded to that magnificent glorious chant, "Oh Lord in Thee have I put my trust, let me never be confounded." (Elizabeth Cramer to James G. K. McClure, Jr., February 1, 1916)

Elizabeth Cramer was a deeply sensitive woman, and there would be times when confusion overtook her, but always she maintained ready access to her emotions. She felt deeply, but understood that emotions are the steam that runs the locomotive, but the driver must control them firmly or the engine will run away. She felt deeply, but had the self-discipline to control her feelings. Such a rich interior life was the source of her perceptiveness. If mankind is unique in the scheme of creation for being "life aware of itself," she experienced a high degree of this essential trait. She half-apologized for her last letter when she wrote the next day:

I have a sort of an idea that I wrote you a terribly serious epistle last night . . . it was just the result of being happy, I suppose. Because I didn't feel a bit long faced inside when I wrote it, even though it undoubtably *sounds* that way! I *hate* solemn people & I'm not one myself, truly I'm not. But in my "early youth" (and I'm ashamed to say occasionally now thus well along in years,) I used to retire to a secluded corner & indulge in a private outburst of tears whenever I felt really happy through and through . . . Another shocking tendency in your future bride is an inordinate desire to laugh at funerals. I always think of the most absurd and comical and outrageous incongruities even though inwardly I may be touched to the heart. (Elizabeth Cramer to James G. K. McClure, Jr., Jan. 27, 1916)

She accepted her own inward emotional conflicts, and in the same way that she hated "pure emotionalism" in art, and she was bothered by feelings within her whose meanings she could not grasp. She never wanted merely a frothy emotional "experience."

Despite Elizabeth's serious thoughts, new subjects of a more mundane nature were beginning to creep into her letters. She picked up volumes on the science of Victorian household management, and bravely began to wade through them.

. . . I'm reading valuable tomes of what day you sweep & what day you wash & which day the maid claims as her own! It seems that "system is a great thing but not system at the price of family comfort." If your husband likes to write in the library from ten to twelve it seems that you are not to disturb him with a broom. I grow daily more and more enlightened!

Dearest what you say about living perhaps among Mountain [folk] might be an awfully interesting thing to do. With a hot water bag and overalls we could be comfortable anywhere. (Elizabeth Cramer to James G. K. McClure, Jr., February 1, 1916)

On her way back to Lake Forest, Elizabeth decided to visit the Jackson Health Resort in order to discuss with Dr. Gregory the care of her prospective husband. To her unconcealed delight, the doctor ordered a wonderful carefree existence for the newlyweds.

> What a thoroughly likable man that doctor is. He talked to me for a good three quarters of an hour & I sat back in the chair & listened with all my ears & now & then asked him a question. He was as direct & definite as could be and he talked straight from the shoulder . . . there was no question whatever but that you could in a course of time take up your work again & do eight hours hard concentrated work everyday, PROVIDED . . . you were willing to give those overworked brain cells of yours absolute rest from thinking for a good *long* time (two years or perhaps three, say I) . . ."He's got to do nothing but *play*," Dr. Gregory said—"Just have a good time & refuse to feel responsible about anything or anybody. He must remember that the *one* thing for him to do from now on is to let everything else go & just have a good time because only in this way can he give the blood vessels & capillaries in the cerebellum a chance to renew themselves.."..Anything that requires direct intellectual effort on your part, Mr. James Gore King, is hotly denounced. Just mere surface exchange of ideas between you & me when you feel them cropping up inside you of their own accord . . . But any deliberate concentration on an abstract problem . . . is tabooed . . .
>
> In other words, my Dearest, you are to turn into a good healthy Bromide, agree with everybody and let everything disturbing . . . roll off your back . . . You're just to tend chickens & plant a garden & now & then make a piece of furniture if it so pleases you sir, for your wife to paint alarming colours. And the rest of the time you're to cultivate all your faculties of enjoyment; *think* what fun it will be—all the delicious sensations that come from seeing apple blossoms against an April sky—late spring afternoons & the fresh odour of wet brown earth-strawberries for breakfast out of doors —white "pinks" in the moonlight on a summer night—golf balls & green turf—the comforting fragrance of bon-fires in the autumn-picnics in the woods when you can lie all day on your back under an oak tree & watch the chipmunks & the clouds—. My goodness me, I can hardly wait. (Elizabeth Cramer to James G. K. McClure, Jr., February 9, 1916)

Back home again, Elizabeth continued to retrace some of Jim's past. She went to Chicago and stayed on Halsted Street with the McClures for a short while. Mr. McClure gave her a tour around the seminary, and then invited the faculty over for dinner to meet her. Many of these men had taught Jim, and she said, "They all eyed me with immense curiosity & were extremely cordial & I was hugely interested as it was wholly unlike any party I had ever been to before. Your father was superb! He mixed them all up, made them all so pleased with themselves & kept things going in a way that was simply astonishing" (Elizabeth Cramer to James G. K. McClure, Jr., February 11, 1916). The McClure social gatherings were much more intellectual and academic than the usual Cramer ones, and Elizabeth was quite intrigued by the contrast. In this new world, she was delighted by Jim's mother.

To my great pleasure I sat next to your mother at dinner. She gave me a darling little tea cup—a beauty-such a charming design.

I truly love Mrs. McClure. I don't know of anyone who in every single thing she does or says always shows such distinction and graciousness and charm. It is just a joy to be with her—it gives me a curious impersonal kind of pleasure just to see her & hear her talk—it's a little bit the delight one always gets from contact with essential beauty. She has the most exquisite sense of proportion—l always feel with her that she is an artist through and through and by an artist I mean, in the real sense of the word, a person who understands proportion. (Elizabeth Cramer to James G. K. McClure, Jr., Feb. 11, 1916)

The Cramers, Annie McClure Clarke, and the Aunties all pitched in to help Elizabeth prepare for her wedding. There were parties and showers, presents to receive, and silver sorting with brother Ambrose in the treasure trove of Rathmore's attic. Her dressmaker made great demands on her time. "Marriage apparently is akin to dying!" she wrote to Jim, "I am as neat & well arranged & tidy as though I were about to make a sudden but graceful departure from this dark world . . ." (Elizabeth Cramer to James G. K. McClure, Jr., Feb. 21, 1916). "I feel that marriage," she wrote four days later, "is in the same class with Plagues, Fires, Floods and other pestilences in that it effectively sweeps away the debris of years and is something that only the fit survive" (Elizabeth Cramer to James G. K. McClure, Jr., Feb. 25, 1916). Aunt Bessy and Aunt Freddy were as excited about the event as Elizabeth, and they were in charge of the lists of family friends who were to be notified. "Between us, we seem to have close on three thousand acquaintances. Aunt Bessy & Aunt Freddy have been simply invaluable as 'Collaborators.' They seemed to know by instinct whether people had died or taken unto themselves new husbands or departed for good & all to unknown parts" (Elizabeth Cramer to James G. K. McClure, Jr., March 1, 1916). Many nights, Elizabeth went into Chicago to stay with the Aunts at their house on Rush Street. She could not resist describing the comedy scene that unfolded there at bedtime, every night. "The aunts have just finished 'going the rounds.' The tremendous nightly affair of 'locking up' is at last over. Aunt Bessy has performed her regular nocturnal ceremony of looking under the beds to see if any burglar could be spied timidly crouching, & peace has at length settled down" (Elizabeth Cramer to James G. K. McClure, Jr., February 29, 1916). The Aunts wanted to be sure their house was neat before they went to bed because, as they told Elizabeth, the doctor might have to be summoned in the night!

Meanwhile, Jim remained at a safe distance in Florida. His life moved at a leisurely pace, and included long walks with his young nephew Dumont, Jr. along the beach. He took the time to investigate the marvel of the age, the Ford automobile, this one owned by the Clarke family. Elizabeth wrote him that "It is too splendid to think of all that you have done in the garage! It was so like you, my Dearest, to want to do it. I *love* to think of you grubbing round under motors covered with oil & dirt and looking like a mechanic yourself. I told

Father what you were doing & he was *enormously* pleased" (Elizabeth Cramer to James G. K. McClure, Jr., March, 1916). Jim spent a lot of his time reading, pondering, re-reading and replying to Elizabeth's letters, one every day. On his last day in Florida, he received her final offering.

> My dearest,
> What do you suppose! The future Mrs. James G. K. McClure is about to have her portrait painted! . . . I feel more than ever as though I were about to depart this earth & the portrait seems part of the last obsequies!
> It is such a strange feeling—this business of packing up all ones belongings & all at once leaving the old life behind. In a way, it's a wrench, & I never thought it would be I who have been such a rolling stone these many years . . . to know that you are freely and voluntarily leaving behind you much that is dear & cherished, is to experience a very poignant emotion. Sometimes it's even a bit overwhelming. A state of mind that savours of absurd & hateful tears brought about merely by the sight of . . . [brother] Pedro's hat, or the look of the lake from my window in the morning. When this happens, I remember how funny I must appear & this makes me laugh, but that little devil of a Hob-goblin Memory, comes & perches on my back when I least expect him, & then I'm forced to seek a private corner and a comforting pocket handkerchief. It's *ridiculous* in anybody who has been away from home & about the world as much as I have! It's wholly inconsistent in a "sensible party" who is truly rejoiced to be shaking the dust of Lake Forest off her feet! Nevertheless, such is the case. We are so bound, in spite of ourselves, by what has been. We feel so sure of ourselves, so independent of the past; yet when the time comes we cannot break away without paying the price. The Past rises up in us—insistent, ironical & tender; it is relentless & pursuing . . .
> I know, too, that some of our possessions can be truly gained only when they are finally lost; my dear people here, this old place with its cherished memories, all that my days here have meant, are now truly mine in a way that they never were before. In leaving them I have found them again . . .
> Dearest, these long waiting days are nearly over. Your letters have meant more to me than I can ever tell you. Because of all that you have written me, I have come closer to you than ever before. I am so glad that it was possible for us to write one another. . . . (Elizabeth Cramer to James G. K. McClure, Jr., March 6, 1916)

This particular letter continues on in a most adoring, personal way, but it is time to draw the curtain of discretion. Elizabeth Cramer has arrived to give Jim's life form and meaning, proportion and beauty. Her perceptions and vision will fill the rest of this book, just as they filled and enriched Jim's life.

Their wedding was held March 29, 1916, at Rathmore. It was small and quiet because Mrs. Cramer's mother had died recently. "If there were only some way of 'working in' your famous brown hat," Elizabeth mockingly wrote Jim, "I should be entirely satisfied. Perhaps it could be suspended from above like a cardinal's hat in a cathedral. And you might carry the ring in that terrible green woolen bag" (Elizabeth Cramer to James G. K. McClure, Jr., March 4, 1916). But the Cramers and the Aunties remained in firm control, and the

A small and extremely quiet wedding service was that of Miss Elizabeth Cramer, the daughter of Mr. and Mrs. Ambrose Cramer of Lake Forest, and James G. K. McClure Jr., which took place yesterday before the members of the two families and a few friends at "Rathmore," the residence of the Cramers in Lake Forest. The service, at 4 o'clock, was read by Dr. James G. K. McClure, the bridegroom's father, who is president of McCormick Theological Seminary, and former pastor of the Lake Forest Presbyterian Church. Mrs. Donald F. Ryerson, a half sister of the bride, was matron of honor, and Archibald McClure, the bridegroom's brother, was best man. The bride wore a simple robe of ivory white satin with garniture of Venetian lace and carried a bouquet of lilies of the valley. Mr. and Mrs. McClure left immediately after the wedding for a trip South and probably will be in Lake Forest upon their return, although their plans are rather indefinite.

Wedding announcement, March 30, 1916.

wedding was a picture of decorum. Dr. McClure performed the ceremony, Isabelle was her sister's matron of honor, Jim's brother Arch was best man. Elizabeth described it for Wiggy, still in France.

The wedding was very small . . . We were married in the library in a niche opposite the fireplace and just before it was time the sun came out & just illuminated everything. It was *lovely*. I had a white satin dress made with *huge* panniers on either side & a funny little pointed waist & a fichu of my mother's rose point applique lace that she had on her wedding gown—it *was* a pretty dress Wiggy dear, if I do say it. Only a very few Lake Forest friends like the Thompson's & Farwells & McCormicks were there—we didn't even have invitations issued so you see what a quiet affair it was . . .

Wiggy darling I'm so very happy, you can't think how dear & good & considerate Jim is to me. At the end of a month I shall be totally spoiled and we are such huge friends Wiggy wag & I somehow feel as though I had been married years & years . . . It's the real thing Wiggy dear. . . . (Elizabeth Cramer to Martha Clarke, April 6, 1916)

The circle of the beautiful courtship of Elizabeth Cramer and Jim McClure was complete. With indefinite plans they went south, allowing the promise of adventure and odd circumstances to rule their days. Their marriage would prove to be a strong foundation on which to build a new and remarkable life together, one that even Elizabeth's vivid imagination could not have foreseen.

Chapter Eleven
Hickory Nut Gap Farm

Mere possessions don't interest me a bit but possessions that can be used to create surroundings that will express the best understanding of beauty that one has, becomes a rarely worthwhile undertaking and one that is worth immense effort. Why? Because a room or a house "furnished" with this principle back of it means something added to the collective beauty of the world and is another way to bring people in contact with the spirit of perfection. And as the Collective Beauty of the world grows, just so the Spirit of God is increasingly revealed. *(Elizabeth Cramer to James G. K. McClure, Jr., January 24, 1916)*

Mr. and Mrs. McClure will go south on their wedding trip. They are undecided as to where they will reside . . . and for how long a time they will be away. *(The Chicago* Daily News, *March 29, 1916)*

There is much to be said, if one marries at thirty-one, for being thoroughly unoccupied with and disconnected from the distractions of the world for a time. Although both Jim and Elizabeth had been involved in their own pursuits and adventures, the circumstances of their courtship helped to wipe clean any commitments one would have expected of two such vibrant individuals. In the spring of 1916, the only given in their lives was their marriage. And from that point of departure, all else had to be added, consciously and together, one item at a time. It was, as Elizabeth would have said, a "delicious situation."

They were not particularly pressed for time. They had a sufficient joint income to keep themselves afloat financially, and they had the admonitions of the doctors from Dansville to let life flow lazily around them until Jim's recovery was complete. The circumstances could not have been better arranged for the new couple, and it seems clear that during this time of adjustment both individuals were fortified and strengthened by the union of each other's habits and daily conduct of life.

The honeymoon was to be a blend of spring in Appalachia, the new Hudson automobile, and an adventurous "gypsy life." Jim suggested to Elizabeth, when he was still in Daytona, that they have the Hudson shipped to Asheville, North Carolina; and that they roam about the mountains camping out, or staying in small inns and in general being completely incommunicado from their former lives and acquaintances. Elizabeth's response was enthusiastic.

I just adored the idea of sleeping out, fine nights a la belle etoille! It would be such a joyful thing to turn into gypsies! I've always envied them, their

ability to go to bed by the road! And as you say, it would be so easy to manage
with good warm blankets and some rubber things (and a pillow or two—you
wouldn't object to my having a pillow, would you my own Dear!) (Elizabeth
Cramer to James G. K. McClure, Jr. February, 18, 1916)

I can hardly wait to turn into a gypsy! It's such a joy to be marrying
somebody who likes to do haphazard out of the way things! I should hate the
idea of a tent, but a bed on the ground is something I've always pined after. I
quite agree with you that it is better to "go slow" at first. It will take us a little
time to get a financial grasp on just how much living expenses are going to
work out . . . Besides it will be much more fun to go to little inns & boarding
houses than to go to big hotels. All my days I've been going to big hotels &
it would be so stupid to go on doing it now. We'll get a lot more out of the
little places & it will be immensely interesting. Once in a blue moon or so we
can stop off at a sporty hotel just to see the people & hear a band. I so love to
think of the frying pan & a bed out of doors. I've got an old jaeger sleeping
bag, maybe it would be a good thing to take along? (Elizabeth Cramer to James
G. K. McClure, Jr., February 19, 1916)

. . . I'm so rejoiced that you like doing queer things & that you like stopping
off at queer places. Let's always keep on doing queer things all our days! I
don't care if I never see a bathtub again . . . All my days I've had a gloomy
fear that if I ever did get a husband he'd be eminently respectable & sober and
anxious to do everything a month in advance and, oh my goodness me, all our
days we'd jog along in one little rut with never a turning to right or left.

Now you are not at *all* respectable, James Gore King. More than that, you
are not at all "careful" or "anxious" or cautious and I love you more than
tongue can tell . . . You've given me such a nice comfortable feeling of space
about me too; I feel as though I could stretch up in all directions & there would
be no restraining bars anywhere.

To go back to the alluring topic of gypsies, do you remember Stevenson's
"Night Along the Pines," in the Travels with a Donkey? And the lines in it
from an old play?

> The bed was made, the room was fit,
> By punctual eve the stars were lit;
> The air was sweet; the water ran;
> No need was there for maid or man,
> When we put up my ass and I
> At God's queer caravanserai.

Do you remember what Stevenson says? "Night is a dead, monotonous
period under a roof; but in the open world it passes lightly with its stars &
dews & perfumes . . . What seems a kind of temporal death to people choked
between walls & curtains is only a light & living slumber to the man who
sleeps afield . . . And to live out of doors with the woman a man loves is of
all lives the most complete & free . . ."

How does this affect you, Sir? When I read it & think of you, it is almost
as though I were with you now. (Elizabeth Cramer to James G. K. McClure,
Jr., February 22, 1916)

Elizabeth's literary imagination easily transformed Stevenson's donkey into the Honeymoon Hudson, as incongruous as her gypsy vision must have appeared in that sleekest and shiniest of new cars. To the mountain people of Western North Carolina, they would have appeared in 1916 as nothing less than strays from a world of wealth unimaginable. But they were by no means the first of their kind to appear in the region. Asheville, North Carolina in 1916 had earned for itself quite a sporty reputation, and catered to some of the wealthiest citizens in the country. George Vanderbilt's colossal home, Biltmore House, was located just south of town. E. W. Grove invested part of his patent medicine fortune in the Grove Park Inn, one of the most well-known and respected hotels in the United States. During the summer season, Asheville glittered with many of the same kinds of people and gatherings with which Elizabeth and Jim had grown up.

But just beyond the glitter, there was a population of mountaineers who, for the most part, were left untouched by the Industrial Revolution. Cash was scarce, and Hudson automobiles were cause for comments. Out beyond the local markets of towns like Asheville, there was almost no way to sell crops, and as a result great populations of people lived a subsistence style of life based invariably on a big garden, a few hogs, wild meat, berries and edible plants. It would be to these men and women, with their strong religion, self-sufficient habits and ability to work, that Jim and Elizabeth would devote their lives. And it was on their honeymoon that they became acquainted with this peculiar region; and they never left.

The plan of the honeymoon was of course to have no plan. But they were required back in Lake Forest on April 12 for young Ambrose's wedding, and they returned for two weeks to take in all the festivities surrounding that event. Elizabeth described it to Martha Clarke: "Jim and I spent two hectic weeks at home alternately visiting the aunts, the McClures & Rathmore. We spent all our free moments boxing up various possessions . . ." (Elizabeth Cramer McClure to Martha Clarke, April 28, 1916). Jim's father again performed the ceremony, while Jim ushered. Afterwards, they fled south again, this time to look seriously for a farm to rent as a temporary home to speed Jim's recovery.

They began again in Asheville, where they had left the Hudson, and headed west into the Sapphire Country near Brevard, North Carolina.

Dearest Wiggy,
We have been camping out in the mountains having the finest time in the world but far from the post! I wish you could see us! We are honeymooning with no plans whatever; we just move from day to day. Jim has concocted the greatest sleeping bag you ever saw which is a bed all "made up" and ready to pop into. It is encased in black oilcloth & stands up in the bag like a fat black sausage! Then Jim has devised a box which hinges onto the side of the car and carries all our provisions & food, it's famous! And we look highly respectable but are really wandering gypsies. (Elizabeth Cramer McClure to Martha Clarke, May 17, 1916).

One morning they awoke to find themselves surrounded by curious little boys in overalls, which made dressing a bit of a problem. Sometimes they stayed in country inns. Wiggy learned from Elizabeth: "We are just having the time of our lives. We spent Sunday with an old lady in Morganton who lives in an old, old house & who gave us the most delicious food while two ancestral portraits looked down on us from the wall. Tuesday night we slept at a farm and were royally entertained. There were box hedges growing in the front yard that the farmer's mother had planted 60 years ago and some quaint old furniture within . . ." (Elizabeth Cramer to Martha Clarke, June 21, 1916)

Their plan was to find a small country place to rent so that they could take time to find a farm to buy. They kept looking, but saw no place that suited, until one day they were driving along the old turnpike road that led from Asheville through the little town of Fairview and across a valley toward the mountains. They began the ascent of the Hickory Nut Gap, historically one of the most important passage ways across the Blue Ridge. As the Hudson's gears groaned under the strain of the steep and rough road, Elizabeth and Jim looked up to see a large weather-beaten house nestled under the mountains at the top of a long, sloping pasture. Slowing the car, Elizabeth and Jim both gasped, "That's the place for us!" The old inn, in its unique situation, appealed to their sense of drama and history. But of course they had to have a closer look, and who could say that the inhabitants had any notion of selling?

Jim and Elizabeth pulled up to the house, and found the owner was an elderly gentleman of about eighty whom everyone called "Judge" Phillips. His title signified nothing but the respect of his friends, perhaps earned by his success in persuading his young ward of eighteen to marry him. Her mother, at some age in between, rounded out the Phillips household. Undoubtedly Jim cheerily thrust his hand out to the old gentleman and said, "My name is McClure, and this is my wife, Elizabeth."

Jim McClure was famous for his charm and he must have been especially persuasive that day. He and Elizabeth were given a tour of the place, and at some critical juncture of the visit the old Southern 'judge' and the young Yankee minister disappeared into a room of the house to talk business, man to man. Elizabeth and the young wife were left in each other's company on the porch. The girl broke down and sobbed on Elizabeth's shoulder, begging the newcomers to buy the house so her husband would move back to town and she could leave her solitary rural existence behind. Elizabeth used to say in later years she wondered why one bride should be in such a hurry to move in when another was so anxious to move out![1]

Mr. Phillips said he would consider Jim's offer of $6,000, and the McClures headed for Virginia where Ambrose Cramer was anxious to have them settle. "For three sporty days," Elizabeth wrote Wiggy, "we went to the Homestead, which is the swagger hotel here" (Elizabeth Cramer to Martha Clarke, July 7, 1916). Then they moved to a more modest *pension de famille* and

Top: *Sherrill's Inn; photograph taken by the McClures circa 1917.* Bottom: *Smokehouse/ stockade located at Sherrill's Inn.*

continued their search. But nothing they saw in Virginia compared with the old inn at Hickory Nut Gap. Elizabeth described it for Wiggy:

> ... & it has been ... because of its commanding position, a genuine land-mark. It is 45 minutes en auto from Asheville on a fine motor road & just two miles & a half from a little village called Fairview. It has an altitude of 2700 feet so you can imagine how fine the air is & it is just at the crest of one of the Blue Ridge ranges with a most superb view across the valley at the mountains in the distance & at the little town lying far below. There are 50 acres of bearing apple trees—2500 trees so the present owner tells us, & superb old oak & chestnut trees on the grounds; wide porches, the finest spring you can imagine flowing so freely that it can be piped to the house by gravity & the loveliest little cement lined "springhouse" for keeping milk & butter etc. cool. Then there is a big farm & a dairy & a huge vegetable garden. Of course the house is just the simplest kind of an old southern wooden farmhouse un-painted, but it has a great deal of atmosphere & is by far the most distinguished place around Asheville,-or indeed of any we've seen. It could be made fasci-nating with very little expenditure & it has a wonderful all year round climate & is so near to Asheville that you could run in for lunch or golf or anything else. Then there is an R.F.D. right to the door & in summer (I'm not certain about winter) a regular motor service twice a day past the door into Asheville. It would be a simply wonderful place to live in. We've made the owner an offer of renting it for two years, we are putting in a bath & furnace & making some minor changes with an option of buying it for $6,000 at the end of that time. Jim thinks that the apple yield alone will pay the tenants salary & the general upkeep, so we feel sure that old Judge Phillips will never accept our offer but they say he wants cash so there is just a chance so, though it's a very slim one indeed. . . . (Elizabeth Cramer to Martha Clarke, July 7, 1916)

When the McClures returned to Asheville they discovered that a catastro-phe had struck in their absence. On Sunday, July 16, 1916, the worst flood ever to hit the region swept away millions of dollars worth of investments and a considerable number of human lives. The damage was not confined to the flood plains. Many a mountain cabin came tumbling down the hillside as the over-saturated soil slid off its rock base. It had been a grim Sabbath in the mountains, and Jim and Elizabeth must have been shocked by what they saw. But they were desperate to hear from the Judge, and despite the fact that no automobile had been able to drive to Fairview since the flood, Jim loaded up a shovel and with characteristic determination made his way. All the bridges were washed out, but by careful driving and a lot of shovelling he was able to ford the creeks and reach Sherrill's Inn. The results of this meeting were recorded in the Buncombe County deed books for August 10, 1916. Both husbands and wives signed the lease agreement giving the McClures approximately sixty-five acres, and the house, with an option to buy in two years for $6,000. In lieu of rent, the McClure's were to " . . . install in the residence of said property a heating plant and bathroom." Soon after, Jim and Elizabeth rented eighty acres contiguous with the property, for $100 over two years, and with the option to buy it all for $900.[2]

It is a testimony to the vision of Jim and Elizabeth that they saw the potential of this neglected and dilapidated landmark. Elizabeth, with her high standards of decorum, was taking on a new home that was unpainted and served by an outhouse. Old pictures show a drab building situated on a landscape strewn with boulders, as if pigs had been allowed to root right up to the threshold. Neighbors later commented to the McClures that Mr. Phillips was so lazy that when someone came to buy apples, he would stick his head out of a window and tell them to go pick their own and leave the money on the doorstep. The room that became the McClure study had been used by the Judge to store hams in ashes, and was in fact the original log cabin, built around 1800. His method of curing hams was to cover them with ashes, and Jim and Elizabeth had to wheelbarrow out nine loads of dirt and debris to even find the floor. The project they undertook together to redesign, repair and landscape this property is alone worthy of praise. It has remained a landmark in Western North Carolina, providing to date a 'home place' for four generations of McClures and Clarkes.

Despite the short term of white settlement in Buncombe County, just over a century when Jim and Elizabeth moved in, their home half-way up Hickory Nut Gap already claimed a rich heritage of history and legend. A man named John Ashworth first bought the land for a shilling an acre, in "the XXXIst year of independence" (1797).[3] The following story gives the flavor of the times: On a frigid winter night, the Ashworth family was huddled around their enormous fireplace, built big enough for the "old woman" to roast a whole pig. On this particular night, a starving wolf pack began to howl and moan just outside the cabin door. Mrs. Ashworth's husband was away, perhaps in the lowlands buying salt and other necessities, and so the responsibility of protecting the family fell to her. She grabbed the poker and placed it in the fireplace until it glowed red hot, and then she thrust it out under the door. One wolf bit at it, and burned his mouth so severely that the others smelled cooked meat. Another wolf snapped at the smell of burning flesh. A vicious fight broke out within the pack and soon they all ran off howling with hunger and pain.[4] The first structure John Ashworth built on his place was a log fort, which was later used as a smokehouse. The building still stands, and is thought to be the oldest standing structure in Buncombe County. He believed the Cherokee enough of a menace to cut rifle slots in the thick, square poplar logs, so that he could fend off an attack if necessary.

In 1834, Mr. Ashworth sold out to Bedford Sherrill, a stage coach driver. Sherrill married Molly, the daughter of the owner of Flack's Hotel in Chimney Rock, a village on the other side of the mountain. A new era in the mountains came with the construction by private companies of turnpike roads. One such road was built over Hickory Nut Gap to connect Asheville to Rutherfordton and points to the south and east. Mr. Sherrill secured the contract to carry the mails along this route, and to Tennessee on the northeast run. His "Albany Coach" could carry nine passengers inside and more on the top. He was an enterprising man, and could see the possibilities of his home becoming a tavern and inn. So when he bought it, he built a long two story addition onto the cabin, with plenty of room to put up travellers. The fifteen miles from Asheville to his inn were about as much as a traveller could endure in a day over the roads of that era.[5]

Within eight years, Bedford Sherrill was out of debt and pushing his business in new directions. He dropped the mail route, and began to sell goods to travellers and the local farmers. Records remain of the transfer of such items as cloth, shoes, coffee, tobacco, spices and brandy. Everything from horses to guns to castor oil was peddled at the inn. The farmers would usually pay for these goods in corn. In fact, a remarkable economy grew up in Buncombe and Henderson Counties in pre-Civil War Western North Carolina, as merchants used the turnpikes to drive great herds of swine across the mountains, to be sold to the plantation owners of South Carolina and Georgia. The trade built up to around 175,000 hogs a year, plus a number of turkey, sheep, mule and horse drives to boot. Bedford Sherrill worked hard to attract travellers away from the more popular Buncombe Turnpike to the Hickory Nut Gap road, with enough success to set up his own "stand," or temporary stockyard, to feed the hogs and drovers for the night.[6]

The stage coach continued its route through the mountains during most of the Nineteenth century, adding some colorful details to the history of the inn. As the stage began its slow journey up the mountain, the driver would blow a long horn, sounding it as many times as there were passengers on board. Up at the inn, Mrs. Sherrill listened and could judge by the horn just how much food she needed to prepare for supper. When the coach arrived, Mr. Sherrill would offer apple brandy to the weary and jolted passengers, and his slave boy would take the horses down to the barn. The guests would be shown their rooms, which were small cubicles reached by passing through the rooms in front. But travelling in those days provided few comforts, and there was always the tap room, where apple brandy, corn liquor, and sometimes strawberry wine and grape juice were available.[7] Many distinguished guests stayed for the night at Sherrill's Inn, including members of the wealthy plantation families from the South where malaria threatened during the summer. In October of 1857, Governor Andrew Johnson of Tennessee signed the guest register, the same man who went on to become President of the United States after the assassination of Abraham Lincoln (and was nearly impeached). The signature of Millard Fillmore appears the year before, when he would have been president, but it has not been authenticated and may have been penned by a school girl practicing her handwriting.[8]

The Civil War brought chaos to the mountains. Local sympathies were divided, but once a young man had enlisted, his loyalty was fierce. The topography provided cover for the whole range of common criminals, deserters and renegades that grew up along with the disturbances of the war. Bedford Sherrill was a slave owner, and his sympathies lay clearly with the South. Toward the end of the war, a General Palmer brought a detachment of Union soldiers through Hickory Nut Gap, and they stayed at Sherrill's Inn.[9]

Family stories of the Yankee soldiers' visit survive among Sherrill descendants. Word must have raced across the gap of the troops' approach, for the family had time to hide a gold watch or two on a ledge in one of the great chimneys, and to hang the hams in the thickness of the wall in the log cabin room, hanging Mrs. Sherrill's hoop skirts on pegs to cover the new carpentry. When the soldiers arrived the commanding officer rode his horse right onto the porch to demand lodging. There was a trap door to the basement in the floor. With bated breath the family watched to see if it would give way, but the hinges held. When a slave girl was frying eggs for the soldiers' breakfast next morning, one of the six Sherrill daughters took off her stockings and shook them over the pan exclaiming, "Those Yankees can eat the dust off my feet and they'll think it's pepper!"[10]

After the war, the Sherrills sold out to a Mr. Lee from Tennessee, who was fleeing persecution by the Union sympathizers of that region. Jim Walker (known as "Tight Jim") eventually took Mr. Lee to court, trying to prove that he had had him arrested and thrown in a Confederate prison in Richmond. Mr. Lee's troubles never seemed to cease. When he tried to market the "Woman's Friend and Steam Washer" and the "Genuine Improved Common Sense Sewing Machine," his only comment for the failure of his enterprise was that "The people here seem very cautious." He tried to attract the old drover traffic again, but the economy of the plantation South lay in ruins, drying up the hog market. So in 1874 Mr. Lee gave up, sold the place back to the Sherrill family, and left the country.[11]

The Sherrills re-established the inn in their name, and entertained travellers from Asheville on the way to tour the gorge on the other side of the gap. When the railroad was completed in 1880, the town of Asheville experienced an economic boom, and was well on its way to developing a reputation for "salubrious air," beauty, wealthy summer tourists, and tuberculosis sanitariums. The little town of Fairview grew up, and travel across the Gap increased. At the same time, visitors began to expect more comforts than an old inn could offer. The Sherrills sold out again, this time to a Captain Spangler, who in turn sold out to Old 'Judge' Phillips. He had worked the place for about ten years when Jim and Elizabeth drove up in the Honeymoon Hudson automobile.

The newlyweds saw life as an adventure, and the purchase of this old inn with its romantic history was characteristic. No doubt their relatives back in Illinois were somewhat taken aback, but soon a fine traffic of Lake Forest visitors began to make their way to Hickory Nut Gap and they, too, were quickly charmed.

Elizabeth was ecstatic. The house had history and good architectural lines,

66-34

No. X 51

ASHEVILLE, N.C. Oct 4 191 8

THE BATTERY PARK BANK

PAY TO THE
ORDER OF H. T. Phillips

Twenty nine hundred and nine + 18/100 DOLLARS

$ 2909 18/

James E. K. McClure Jr

and the location was a rare confluence of superb natural beauty, picturesque buildings and enormous potential for improvement. There were even ghosts to remind the McClures of the past!

Dearest Wiggy,

Do you remember that in my last letter I wrote you all about the place near Asheville that had once been an old inn..? . . . He accepted our offer & we take possession the 15th of September. It is a simply ideal place for us . . . We are planning to move out to the Fairview Inn on Monday to take up our quarters there as there will be a good deal of red tape with regard to leasing the house . . . Then, as soon as the owners move out we will put in a furnace & a bathroom etc. & paint the house . . . Such apple trees, Wiggy darling, & such quinces! When you come to see Pigie you will have to put up loads & loads of jam & preserves! Just you wait till you see the fruit on the place & the lovely spring & oh such fine mountain air. You will get so fat when you come that you will have to buy all new clothes. I shall need your advice badly about planning the garden. If you ever get time to, send me a plan of the Trèpied flower borders & I will try & duplicate it here—it would be such fun. (Elizabeth Cramer McClure to Martha Clarke, August 5, 1916)

Our place here is just a dream, darling, and some day we will be sitting [you] . . . down on a wide porch with a whole stretch of superb mountains out in front. Then dear, you'll be set down to a table full of country food & after that tucked into bed (perhaps a four poster) with a fire in the grate & a warm comforter over your toes & you'll sleep as you haven't slept in years . . . In no time you'll be just as fat as butter again & you'll forget all about this cruel war . . .

In the meantime here we are at this charming little inn 2½ miles from the house & we shall probably be here until Christmas as there are a lot of little things that we have to do to the house & Jim has to take them slowly. Ever since we arrived here he has been so much better as he sees nobody & just rests & keeps out[side]-The doctors don't want him to make any social effort so I don't think we will be able to have any guests—even family 'till next summer anyway & perhaps not till autumn. But he is getting on so splendidly I am very happy . . . We've decided to call our place "Old Tavern" because that's what it once was. How do you like the sound? It sounds cozy don't you think? (Elizabeth Cramer McClure to Martha Clarke, August 20, 1916)

For the next several months, Elizabeth and Jim managed the repair and remodelling of "Old Tavern." They also began interviewing for a man to be in charge of the farm and a couple to help out with the work. By mid-November, Wiggy received this report:

We have got the steam heating system almost in, at Old Tavern, & we're going to have the finest water system that was ever anybody's, I truly believe.

Opposite: *One of Mr. McClure's payments to Mr. H.T. Phillips for Hickory Nut Gap Farm.*

The source of the spring is about 300 feet above the house on the side of the
mountain & the loveliest purest water will come running down to the house
that you ever tasted. Our altitude is equal to the top of Mt. Equinox in Manchester so you can see how high we are & how good the air is.

. . . We are more and more delighted with the place-it is superbly situated
with a magnificent view, & all sorts of old stories center about it. We have had
the house painted white & are lining the inside with beaverboard —painting it
& panelling it with moldings. We can't afford to do but 3 of the rooms this
year but it will be all the more fun doing a little at a time. I long for you to see
it. The windows have little panes of glass that are all rainbow colours from
age. (Elizabeth Cramer to Martha Clarke, November 10, 1916)

Amidst all the projects going on about the house, and purchasing the
property, and hiring on help, Jim McClure had to spend money as he never had
before. Ever after his Yale days, he had worked to be as careful with money as
he could. He felt strong resentment towards "conspicuous consumption" and
felt great satisfaction in walking through Germany for almost no money at all
and in inking the bare spots on his winter coat. His dreams of being a gypsy,
or of going back to Texas and working with the old nester until he died, were
the direct result of his attitude that real freedom came when one was no longer
dependent on money. However impractical such a dream would be as a way of
life, Jim McClure always remained unable to spend money merely to increase
his own comfort. As a goal, he wanted to live for under $3,000 a year.

On these issues, Jim and Elizabeth had some working out to do. No spend-
thrift herself, she did love the objects of life that were beautiful, and these were
invariably expensive. All of the silver that flowed their way delighted Elizabeth,
but bothered Jim. There was no great battle here, but merely a sore point that
says a great deal about each of these people. In putting together the pieces of
their household, the ways and means of spending money had to be faced.

It was during the engagement that this issue of wealth was first broached.

Dearest Thing:

I know you wish you were marrying a pennyless creature! I'm sorry my
blessed Dear to be depriving you of all such opportunities! But there's no use
pretending you are marrying a lady without a red penny to her name. Facts are
facts & they have to be accepted and the old idea that a husband must pay all
the expenses & assume all the financial burden in marriage has always seemed
absurd & conventional & irrational.

It isn't any question of a man's growing "flabby" either as you said to me
once so long as he keeps true to his own highest purposes. Jointly, we shall
have an income of $8,000.00 a year. If you were the sort of a man whose
standard of life consisted of giving "sporty" dinner parties and keeping a
footman & generally taking things easy there would be some truth in what you
say about a man's becoming "flabby." But you know you're not that sort &
you never could be. And it doesn't matter a row of brass beans which of us
has the most money. What's yours is mine and what's mine is yours, that's all
there is to it & its not right to make any difference . . .

You can't think my Dearest, my darling Jim how dreadfully it would make me feel if you refused to let us together use *all* our money, *mine* as well as yours. If you did otherwise it would be to live on an artificial basis. What earthly difference does it make that by some curious accident of life I happen to have a little more money than you? The fact that I am a woman should not for one moment have any bearing on the case. The only thing that is to be considered is that we lose no single opportunity to use *all* the money we have to the best possible advantage in God's world. It may be in buying furniture, it may be in getting you a new coat and it may be in doing over a church or in financing some social scheme or in buying me a hat. It's the principle that matters every time.

I *insist* upon figuring always in all our living together on the basis of an $8,000.00 yearly income & not on the basis of a $3,000.00 income. Then . . . if we choose to run a very simple establishment, it will be because we feel that such action is in accordance with our attitude towards life & our social beliefs and *not* for what would be an artificial reason—namely the assumption that we couldn't *afford* more inasmuch as we only had $3,000.00 a year.

I am as anxious as you are to try to run our house on $3,000.00 a year, but I am only anxious to do so because, just now, we have decided that $3,000.00 a year "establishment" best expresses our attitude toward life. I should never for a moment be willing to do so if I thought that it was because we were going on the assumption that we had only $3,000.00 a year to spend; that would be insincere because it would be dealing with an unreality. If our living expenses are kept within $3,000.00 a year we shall simply have to use the remaining $5,000.00 for the best purposes known to us; it might be for a pool in the garden, it might be for a sea voyage, it might be as a boost to somebody who was down and out, it might be to get a church going; *all* these things perhaps, and it goes without saying of course that we should always want to put some by for the inevitable rainy day & that the "ten percent" to the Lord seems a cold way of measuring out his money & that it would just have to go any way because we couldn't help ourselves.

It seems to me, the only thing to remember is that you & I have been brought together to more adequately serve God's purposes & that if incidentally we have *money* it's simply up to us to use it to the fullest capacity & to accept life as it has come to us & use it.

I tried to say all this to you once before but somehow I couldn't. I didn't think you were taking a square look at things. If you don't agree with me you can tell me why when you get back & then we'll talk it over. (Elizabeth Cramer to James G. K. McClure, Jr., February 21, 1916)

Elizabeth's thoughts here were not the last word on the matter, but without a doubt there were to be times when Jim McClure would be mighty glad to have some of her family money to tide him, his family and the Farmers Federation over some tight places.

One such place came early. Just after paying out so much money for the farm and its restoration, and then hiring the first wage earners, Elizabeth became ill and had an internal cyst removed. The bills began to pour in. The two of them moved back into Asheville and were staying at the swanky Manor Inn when Jim wrote to his sister Harriet: "You will be startled at the luxurious look of this

letter heading but you will be more startled to see Siddy & Jamie reach Lake
Forest in rags and overalls respectively, hounded by creditors and with a lean
and starved look . . . E. is getting on famously . . . but it has been a very severe
financial jolt to the McClures and they will be groggy for several months"
(James G. K. McClure, Jr. to Harriet Stuart, October 31, 1916). Elizabeth
related her version to Jim's mother:

> We hope to go back to Fairview early next week and I am eager to see how
> they are getting on at the "farm." Just now the countryside is gorgeous . . .
> "The operation" was more trying for Jim than for me—I really believe. The
> poor dear lost ten pounds but he will soon get them back. He is really much
> better than he was when we were first married but he has not yet much
> endurance & so is still obliged to go very slow . . . I think "the farm" & its
> various out of door healthy activities are already doing him much good. . . .
> (Elizabeth Cramer McClure to Phebe Ann Dixon McClure, November 1,
> 1916)

The McClures decided to remain in town as the Fairview Inn was not
heated. By December the work on the house was nearly completed and Elizabeth
wrote to Wiggy describing how the place was looking. They were only completing three rooms downstairs.

> . . . the house is really going to be fascinating. It is all painted now with green
> blinds (like Trèpied's) and the roof is a nice gray. Then inside, we are pan-
> elling the walls in the dining room & living room with strips of moulding and
> it will then be all painted a lovely old ivory white. The little hall is in the oldest
> part of the house together with Jim's study, so we have left it just as it was &
> have painted the old walls cream colour. There are two little ancient doors in
> the hall with old, old iron latches & hinges such as they used to have 100 years
> ago. You go up a step & one of these doors opens into Jim's study. There are
> huge hand hewn beams running across the ceiling & there we are staining an
> old one walnut & polishing with wax . . .
> We have engaged two such nice coloured people, a man & wife who
> together only cost us $8 a week(!) & who will do all the work about the house
> & in the garden. Our "apple man" too arrived Monday & has started pruning
> the old apple trees. He is named Davidson & has been superintendent of two
> State Test farms besides having an agricultural education to boot so we hope
> that he will make a financial "go" of the place. We are putting a good deal of
> cash into it all as we're so anxious to have the place pay in a couple of years.
> We really think it is one place in a thousand! (vain creatures!) We are putting
> up a nice little house for Davidson, down in the lower pasture & we also have
> to put up a little one-room servant house right near the back of "Old Tav-
> ern."..so you see we have our hands full. We've built the tenant house so that
> it looks as old as the rest of the place. The roof has a fine sway & the place is
> built along old time lines so its quite in keeping with the rest . . .
> The country life down here is really more like the Old English Country Life
> than anything . . . I just adore this country. There is really nothing in Europe
> more lovely . . .

Tomorrow we plan to motor out to the place & spend the day taking our picnic lunch. It is such fun & we both love superintending the work . . . We have a fine road & *such* a drive. (Elizabeth Cramer McClure to Martha Clarke, December 7, 1916)

The black couple, Esther and John Shorter, soon became the heart and soul of Hickory Nut Gap life. Esther died quite young, but John remarried. His new wife Mathilda Shorter, a plump young New Orleans girl, took over and stayed to raise the grandchildren. John Shorter had grown up in Fairview, and was a highly respected man for his fine character and his working skills. He had a cheerful heart and fine bushy mustache. James Davidson's first appearance was brief, as he was drafted into the U. S. Army during World War I. After the war, he returned to the farm and in time married a lovely young red-head named Virginia, adding another valuable member to the community.

Elizabeth and Jim traveled to Chicago for Christmas, returning to North Carolina laden down with purchases for their new home. Elizabeth enjoyed so much thinking through the problems of interior design and making discoveries in shops of items that suited her exacting criteria. They returned to their Old Tavern in February, still unable to move in. In the latter part of the month, Jim and Elizabeth began to keep a diary together, jotting down short notes of their activities for the day. Often they would also include endearments to each other. Added to her father's nickname for her "Blos," and Wiggie's "Pigie," Jim added his own nickname for Elizabeth, "Petie." For her part, she addressed Jim as "Cricket." The first entry was a momentous one: February 27, 1917, "Esther & John start in with us." On March 12, 1917, the house was finally ready for habitation. Esther and John had worked hard to create a livable situation, but it certainly did not match the elegance of Rathmore. That March day was not a glorious one in the mountains. As Jim and Elizabeth motored along the highway from the Fairview Inn, it was pouring a chilly March rain and the gravel road was turning into mud. At the foot of the mountain, the Honeymoon Hudson bogged down for good. Jim trudged out into the weather and found John. Full of good cheer, John harnessed up his yoke of oxen, hitched them to the Hudson, and, with perhaps some happy thoughts about the superiority of animals over machines, dragged the automobile up the mountain.

In his daily activities, Jim still had to go slowly. He and Elizabeth had the wonderful opportunity to picnic and take walks together and investigate the mountain landscapes they had purchased. More than that, they could both make decisions, and both plan and dream about the future of the farm and of their own lives. At this stage, the future remained outlined roughly this way: Jim would recover his health, seek a "call" in a church, and they would leave Hickory Nut Gap as a smoothly functioning business in the charge of Mr. Davidson. They would return for vacations, but it was not envisioned as a permanent home. In fact, they had only leased the property, and could have turned it all back over to Judge Phillips if other opportunities had come along.

But slowly, the work, the money and the dreams the two of them enjoyed together, not to mention the very real charm of the house and mountains, worked their magic. If they had been forced to face the facts, they might have even admitted that they had found their home. Once Elizabeth planted her gardens, the die would be cast. Even though Jim's daily activities were slowed down by his debilities, the important elements of his life were rapidly fitting together. Within the span of two Marches, 1916 and 1917, Jim had both married and moved into his permanent home, having relocated both himself and his wife to completely unexplored territory. And little did he realize that in a few years time he would create an organization that would have as large an impact on this mountain region as perhaps any in its history. When Jim's father wrote him back in 1910 that so often the tragic times in one's life are seen in retrospect as the key turning points towards a new plan and purpose for that person, Jim perhaps shrugged off the idea as merely loving encouragement. But his father was correct. How else could events have conspired to bring together Elizabeth Cramer, Hickory Nut Gap, the mountaineers of North Carolina and Jim McClure?

1. Interview with Elspeth McClure Clarke.
2. Buncombe County Deed Books, Book 208, p. 435.
3. Old Deed located at Sherill's Inn.
4. Elspeth McClure, "Sherrill's Inn and the Development of Buncombe County," Unpublished paper, p.7.
5. *Ibid.*, p. 9–10.
6. *Ibid.*, P. 10–11.
7. *Ibid.*, p. 12–14.
8. Old Registers found at Hickory Nut Gap.
9. *Op. Cit.*, "Sherrill's Inn and the Development of Buncombe County," p.25-26.
10. Interviews with Elspeth McClure Clarke. This story was told to Mrs. Clarke by a member of the Sherrill family.
11. *Op Cit.*, "Sherrill's Inn and the Development of Buncombe County."

Chapter Twelve
Farmer Jim

This week Jim has sold four pigs, purchased 4 ducks and a calf and sold large quantities of stuff to the hospital . . . in Asheville. His sales for the month of August are already over $200. (*Arch McClure to Harriet Stuart, August 22, 1918*)

Since the Aunts installed a "cabinet de toillette" off the Green Room upstairs it is really not at all bad so we now have ample room for guests with a little country squeezing. (*Elizabeth Cramer McClure to Harriet Stuart, September 13, 1918*)

Our visit was a memorable one. I feel that Elizabeth and Jamie live in an enchanted country, it is so beautiful. The mountains, the wonderful growth and variety of trees and shrubs, all make a real fairy land. Mr. McClure and I are delighted with it all.
The house under Elizabeth's transforming genius is a gem in its rare setting. I wonder at all that has been accomplished.
As to Elizabeth's housekeeping abilities, it is indeed amazing. Such order and system in her household, such delicious viands, the table so perfect in every particular, I must see you soon, and then talk it all over with you. How Elizabeth manages it all, through Esther and Eliza, I do not know. She certainly succeeds in inspiring them to do their best. As to the shelves filled with those shining jars of fruits and vegetables, all prepared under Elizabeth's directions, words fail me to express my amazement, and admiration. I do not wonder that "Town and Country" celebrates her skill. (*Phebe Ann Dixon McClure to the Misses Skinner, October 9, 1918*)

In the spring of 1917, the ghastly pall of World War I still hung over the Western World. The excitement and patriotism of those early days when Elizabeth watched Lord Kitchener emerge from the war office amidst cheering crowds had been replaced with the issuing of endless lists of grim statistics and numbing casualty lists. The Russian Empire was beginning to disintegrate under the weight of the war. As the McClures moved into their new home, the Tsar had abdicated and a moderate democratic government under Aleksandr Kerenski was searching for some formula on which to base its rule. Elizabeth expressed the American satisfaction with Russian democracy when she wrote to Wiggy, "Isn't it superb news about Russia. It is truly one of the few good things that have come as a result of this war. It should greatly aid the cause of the allies" (Elizabeth Cramer McClure to Martha Clarke, April 20, 1917). But as the apple trees bloomed that April at Hickory Nut Gap, the Germans were sending the fateful sealed train containing the communist "bacillus" in the person of Nikolai Lenin across the border to infect the already weakened Russian body politic. At the same time, America was preparing to enter the war. On April 2, 1917, Woodrow Wilson expressed the idealism of the American people when he explained his reasons for declaring war. He said, "The world must be made safe for democracy. Its peace must be planted upon the tested foundations of political liberty. We have no selfish ends to serve. We desire no conquest, no dominion. We seek no indemnities for ourselves, no material compensation for the sacrifices we shall gladly make."[1]

Despite Jim McClure's dogged opposition to American involvement in the war, he was moved by Wilson's words of idealistic purpose. One can imagine him bringing home the Asheville newspaper, and excitedly calling Elizabeth into the study to read her the speech. She had always suffered with her old French neighbors. She would argue with her more pacifistic husband that the war was a struggle against the German spirit of mechanical brutality. Before they were married, in 1915, she wrote him that when the cathedral of Reims was leveled by the Germans, she recoiled in horror that such beauty could be so quickly destroyed, and it confirmed her suspicions that the German government opposed the very ideal of beauty she held dearest. She also wrote to her father about it, and he wrote back that although the Cramers were of German stock, they claimed the ancestral homeland of Southern Germany, and not that of the militaristic state of Prussia.

Wilson's message of self-sacrifice and a united effort to win the war could not have been better designed to put a zealous spirit into Jim McClure. Here he was, living on a farm, and what the nation needed was food, enough to feed the allied armies and all those left behind without a breadwinner. Herbert Hoover was placed in charge of the home front, and was so successful in appealing to the nation's patriotism that there was never a need for ration cards. The popular sentiment was:

> My Tuesdays are meatless,
> My Wednesdays are wheatless,
> I'm getting more eatless each day.
> My coffee is sweetless,
> My bed it is sheetless,
> All sent to the Y.M.C.A.[2]

World War I was all out war, and by 1917 it was clear to nearly everyone that the winning side would be the one whose economy could be mobilized to produce the necessary food, arms and supplies. Russia, with its immense stores of raw materials, was about to withdraw altogether, but not before the German army had captured the Ukrainian bread basket. France and Britain had been bled almost dry by 1917, and morale was beginning to slip. The Germans prepared one more large thrust at Paris, to break through before the United States forces could arrive. But in the end, as much as her soldiers, it was the strength of America's industrial economy that won the war. Moreover, it was Woodrow Wilson's statement of high principles that allowed his country to rally so strongly behind the effort.

The call for production of foodstuffs made a serious farmer out of Jim McClure. He wrote to Harriet during the summer:

> The food shortage seeming so acute, and not being able to do anything else, we decided to get the remaining land that the old Judge had and which was lying idle & useless. We are now engaged in making plans for its temporary and future use and enjoying it vastly. As time goes on our specialties will be orchards & beef cattle, but the next year or so we may raise considerable grain.
> . . .
> Except for the car, oxen are our sole means of conveyance & work & we use them to plough, cultivate and every other farm activity. (James G. K. McClure, Jr. to Harriet Stuart, June 11, 1917)

Elizabeth wrote to Wiggy in France:

> Everyone here is of course occupied with the war. Many of the young men in Chicago have already enlisted. Ambrose has gone into some sort of clerical work to do with the Navy . . . We are very busy planting extra crops as that seems to be the great necessity this year . . . We've planted about 4 acres . . . in beans for the allies besides various other crops such as corn & wheat. (Elizabeth Cramer McClure to Martha Clarke, May 27, 1917)

Her father kidded them when news came to Rathmore that they had purchased more land to aid the war effort. "Darling Blos," he wrote, "So you Hickory Nut Gap people are land Barons and deliciously short of cash. Well, 'Ya can na be baith grand and comfortable'" (Ambrose Cramer, Sr., to Elizabeth Cramer McClure, August 8, 1917; quote from J.M. Barrie, *The Little Minister*).

Ambrose Cramer's curiosity had already brought him down to North Carolina to see just where this idealistic minister had taken his "Darling Blossom." Elizabeth wrote to Wiggy, "Mother & Father & Corwith came down for a few days . . . Father just had the time of his life walking about and giving advice. We really have a perfectly beautiful old place & *such* a view of the mountains . . . I think it was really far nicer than they had anticipated. It really is quite a place, Wiggy dear, & in 10 years if we are still in the land of the living & still out of Debtors' prison it ought to be a beauty" (Elizabeth Cramer McClure to Martha Clarke, May 27, 1917).

Jim hired James Davidson, an agricultural graduate of North Carolina State, to manage the farm because he was an experienced orchardist. He was promptly drafted into the U. S. Army, but returned in 1918. Mr. Davidson was not only an able farmer, but also had the knack of leading the work force with a minimum of tension. Jim himself enjoyed the men who came to live on his farm. He found their mountain ways both fascinating and exasperating. He wrote to his parents that March:

> We have a new hand working for us. He moved in on Tues. with a wife and three children—using our oxcart for the moving—and reported for work on Weds. with a wife & four children at home—mother & daughter doing well. He is quite pleased with himself & feels that he moved just in time.
> . . . if we do not go broke should make a good showing with our crops. We plan to plant so much that they will have a hard summer caring for it—but I feel relieved to have three men we can depend on & not have to chance picking up day labor. . . . (James G. K. McClure, Jr. to his parents, March 17, 1917.)

Elizabeth had never cooked a meal, although in later years she became as talented a cook as she was a painter. In her report to Wiggy she listed the latest acquisitions, and described the routine of her typical day.

> We have had to buy a pair of mules & two oxen-we also now possess 3 cows & 3 pigs and two calves so you see our livestock is increasing—not to mention chickens . . .
> You said you wanted to know how we spent our days. In the morning by 8 o'clock breakfast comes, rumbling up on a dumbwaiter. Then after breakfast I attend to our room & bathroom, make the beds & generally tidy up. Jim stays in bed until after lunch & I spend the morning doing all sorts of things from painting chairs & tables to arranging flowers. After lunch we both snooze for an hour; then Jim gets up & goes down to the porch & we read or write. After tea we go for a little stroll & then comes supper. Once in a great while we go over to Fletcher & call on friends there but as a rule Jim sees nobody.
> He overdid a little this Spring in the interest of making over the place, so now I am very strict with him so that he will be well enough to go to Manchester in September to visit the Aunts. . . . (Elizabeth Cramer McClure to Martha Clarke, July 16, 1917)

This letter reminds us that Jim McClure was still a long way from full recovery. His daughter Elspeth finds it hard to believe this schedule after knowing the vigorous and tireless man her father became. It was somewhere between his after lunch snooze and tea that Jim sat and wrote down the ideas that bubbled through his mind. Prior to Wilson's declaration of war, he had taken a strong stand against American involvement. Back in 1914 he had written a letter that was published in the Chicago *Tribune* under the heading "Faith in Mankind." In it, he suggested a radical departure from traditional dependence on military strength.

> We can wipe out our coast defenses, reduce our navy to a police force, and say to the world that the day of force has passed, as we in 1775 said the day of autocracy is past . . .

If we adopt a policy of non-resistance we proclaim once more and out loud our faith in all mankind.[3]

Jim never shrank from challenging the basic presuppositions of any cause or concept, and rather enjoyed his provocative nature. His brother-in-law, Dumont Clarke, was equally devoted to Christian ideals in his own way and according to his own temperament. He was a determined leader in the peace movement during and after World War I, and Jim admired especially the way Dumont made a personal sacrifice to back his beliefs. Long before the war he had been given a number of shares of stock in a company that manufactured submarines. Prior to August 1914, the stock price languished at around $15 a share. When war broke lose, the price naturally leaped upwards. Dumont told Jim of his dilemma, a man preaching world peace growing rich off the war. Most of his friends told him not to worry, that he should not miss a chance like this to make easy money. As the price rose, Dumont felt more and more guilty. At $115 a share, he sold out. The money realized, $19,000, was sent to missions set up to relieve suffering caused by the war. That particular stock continued to rise in value, eventually reaching its apex at $530 a share. Jim wrote in his notebook that Dumont was "Very glad he sold when he did for [he] fears if [he] had gotten so much for it, he would have thought of other things he could do with the money & not had [the] resolution to give it all away. Even as it was [he] caught himself looking at [the] papers to see how [the] stock was rising & felt [the] beginnings of demoralization."[4] But Jim and Dumont encouraged each other's ethical decisions, trying to make their own way of thinking conform better with the notion of the coming Kingdom of God.

After the declaration of war Jim joined in support of his country's struggle against the German state, at first reluctantly and then with enthusiasm. Actually the conduct of war fascinated him, and the leisure of his convalescence gave him the opportunity to study events as they unfolded. What interested him most was the self-sacrifice demanded of the soldier, and of the whole country as well, and how people willingly joined in overwhelming support. Why was it that war commanded so much unity and obedience, and most people at the front enthusiastically accepted the extra burdens? Why could not men and women learn to pursue the vision of the Kingdom of God with a similar attitude of single-minded selflessness? Peace and world harmony were much worthier goals than victory in war. Ironically, Jim McClure was quite heartened by the American response to war, and he became convinced that the same power of morale could be kept strong when it was over, to rebuild the world on firmer foundations. That summer of 1917 he wrote in his notebook:

The right attitude toward mankind, is, I am sure, something like this—That millions of men have a longing & a vision of an ideal state of society. This ideal might with ease be developed into the ideal of the Kingdom on earth. Further, millions of men are willing to make enormous sacrifices for this idea, i.e. the millions of men, & of others at home, too, who are willing to sacrifice in the present war.

The great need then is to work out the means of bringing this ideal state of society & explaining it definitely.[5]

Jim continued to wrestle with these thoughts, trying to develop them in a workable and practical alternative to war.

This frightful monster, Prussianism, with all its loathely characteristics, suddenly unclothed itself and attacked an unbelieving world, a world not willing to believe & not able to conceive such barbarism still possible . . . It sardonically & efficiently violated everything that the long labors of idealists had made sacred.

It had to be opposed immediately, there could be no delay. Many & many a man was torn between the ideal which he dimly felt that he saw in the life and death of Jesus, the way of love and reliance solely on spiritual power and on the goodness & divinity latent in mankind; and the old and tried method of armed resistance . . .

The decision had to be made at once . . .

But there can be no doubt that it was not Christ's way. Christ grew up at a time when the whole hope of his nation was in the Messiah who was coming to lead the people by force into freedom & security . . . Christ chose . . . a different way. He put his sole reliance on the spiritual forces latent in the hearts of mankind . . . With no resistance he allowed himself to be battered & killed by brutal, coarse, densely unspiritual men. There can be no doubt that he discarded physical force as an inferior method.

And astonishing as it seems there can be no doubt of the success of his method. The very sacred belief that he wanted to give mankind, that each individual was capable of infinite spiritual development, that he was of the same nature as God himself . . . that very belief commenced to spread. As it spread it commenced to recreate mankind. Force never has been able to prevail against it. Rome, by force, attempted to exterminate the Christians . . .

The offenders (Germany et al) . . . are going to continue living in our world &, as the distances grow shorter, cheek by jowl with us. Shall we have a continual thorn in our flesh or shall we have a well wishing cooperator & helper. Our problem is how to make the offender into a co-operator. And this is where force fails . . .

The German is going to keep on living & right in our world, rubbing shoulders with us. Our problem is not to exterminate him but to make him our co-worker, our helper . . . We can do that only by spiritualizing him. And there is but one way to do that. It is not by talking, or writing . . . It is by living it ourselves; by the power of life (or example) . . .

It happened to Christ. He recognized the futility of a tirade against force, or a wordy spiritual propaganda when he was tried. He went ahead, simply living his life staking his all on the spiritual possibilities in mankind and let them try and kill him . . .

It takes nerve, it seems impossible, a joke almost, absurd, but Christ took that very sort of a chance—and God stood by him.[6]

All this time Jim kept plugging away at farming, but often he overworked, and his old physical troubles would flare up again. He was unhappy with the slow progress of his recovery and decided to consult again with a doctor who had offered him hope for recovery the previous fall. He and Elizabeth went first to Manchester, where the fall foliage was still bright, to see the Skinner aunts. They enjoyed many of the old haunts of their courtship days without being pursued by the gossip of friends and relatives. In November they went down to the little town of Stockbridge, Massachusetts, in the Berkshire Mountains, to submit to the care of the remarkable Dr. Austen Riggs. Elizabeth described the situation to Wiggy:

> Here we are . . . for a few days with the Aunts on our way to Stockbridge, Mass. for two or 3 weeks where Jim will take a "cure" with Dr. Riggs who is supposed to be quite a wizard in these respects. He looked Jim over last September & said that his case was as definite as typhoid or a broken leg & needed similar definite treatment. Jim was not making the fast progress he wished to make, so we are going north for a few weeks. I myself am in the best of health as usual—fairly bouncing. (Elizabeth Cramer McClure to Martha Clarke, November 18, 1917)

Dr. Austen Riggs had been a successful physician in New York City when he contracted tuberculosis in 1908. He moved to Stockbridge to recover, and there had the leisure to reread the philosophy of William James. He also filled his hours by working with his hands: building ship models and constructing his own bows and arrows. He took up "clog dancing," a curious Appalachian folk style, and he fenced and drummed along with Sousa marches. It slowly dawned on him that the satisfactions of such activities were a wonderful antidote to "modern life," and he prescribed similar pastimes as therapy for his patients.

When a patient first came to talk with him, he would ask, "Why have you come to me?" Invariably the reply would be something like, "Because I want to get well, Doctor, I want to get well!" "That," Dr. Riggs would reply, "doesn't interest me. *Why do you want to get well?*" Austen Riggs understood human life to be an interaction between one's intellect and one's environment. If a person was struggling along, it was because he had made a poor adjustment to that environment, or because the environment itself was faulted. Since there was little Dr. Riggs could do to alter the conditions of a person's situation, he worked to understand how an individual had adjusted both psychologically and philosophically to his environment, and then tried to improve that adjustment. He was forever quoting Justice Oliver Wendell Holmes around the sanitarium, "The great purpose of life is to live it," then adding the corollary, "Happiness . . . is only a by product of successful living." He believed that the body and mind were indivisible, but that the mind or intellect must always take the lead in the adjustment process. His stated theory was: " . . . a person functions on four levels, the reflex, the instinctive, the intelligent, and the ethical . . . The elements of mood and temperament complete the picture of an individual. The individual plus his environment . . . equals adaptation or maladaptation. Out of the latter rise the problems loosely catalogued as 'nervous,' the psychoneurosis sometimes so elaborately cloaked by resulting physical ills."

Dr. Riggs worked almost exclusively with men and women of social position. He found that the first step was for them to overcome their inhibitions enough to admit that their breakdown was something other than self-indulgence or worse, incurable insanity. Jim's cure, like everyone's, began with a frank talk. Dr. Riggs continued these interviews, trying to learn in what way the patient was out of line with his world. In the meantime, the cure consisted of working with one's hands in the shop in therapeutic activities. In short, the Riggs treatment was an educational process that emphasized "balanced living, with work, play and rest all in proportion . . ." His only advice was to accept reality, accept life as it is. "Nervousness is not a *disease* but a *disorder*...simply a maladjustment on the part of an otherwise perfectly sound, essentially normal person, and therefore it is *avoidable*." He preached his own ten commandments:

1. Neither run away from emotions nor yet fight them. Accept them as the wellsprings of all action. They are your automatically mobilized energies. Force these energies into the channels of your choice . . . it is like guiding spirited horses.

2. Be efficient in what you do. Do not drive your tacks with a sledge hammer. Find out how easily you can do things well, and take pride in such skill.

3. Do one thing at a time. Only thus can we practice concentration. I do not mean that violent over-dramatization of effort, but the gentle art of controlling the attention.

4. Make clean-cut practical decisions, subject to change in the face of new facts or additional knowledge.

5. Do not accept hurry as a necessary part of modern life. Quality of work, not quantity, spells success, and quality is destroyed by hurry.

6. Worry is a complete circle of inefficient thought whirling about a pivot of fear. To avoid it, consider whether the problem in hand is your business. If it is not, turn to something that is. If it is your business, decide it is your business now. If so, decide what is best done about it. If you know, get busy. If you don't know, find out promptly. Do these things; then rest your case on the determination that, no matter how hard things may turn out to be, you will make the best of them—and more than that no man can do.

7. Keep work, play, rest and exercise in their proper relative proportions; not only in the space of decades, but year by year, month by month, week by week, day by day.

8. Shun the New England conscience. It is a form of egotism which makes a moral issue of every trivial thought—

9. When a decision has been reached, when something has to be done, waste no time in "getting up steam"—just do it.

10. Do not criticize your part in the play, study it, understand it, and then *play* it, sick or well, rich or poor, with faith, with courage, and with the proper grace.[7]

Dr. Riggs' philosophy of treatment spoke to Jim's problems. He had been struggling with his temperament, one that certainly resembled "spirited horses," and needed to be told how important a balanced life was: "work, play, rest and exercise." "He seems to be benefiting Jim already," Elizabeth wrote Wiggy, "& [he] assures him that he will come out on top—all of which is very good news. Jim is really in very good shape most of the time, but he is eager to get back all his old endurance & vim so we are here to hurry things up" (Elizabeth Cramer McClure to Martha Clarke, December 4,1917). They remained in Stockbridge through Christmas. Jim includes a progress report in this "thank you" to Harriet, who often supplied him with new suits and had sent him one as a Christmas gift:

> I only fear that when the doc sees me sporting all the grandeur, he will murmur "some fellah," and double his bill . . .
> I am progressing famously and in about 10 days we are going to Andover (to visit Annie and Dumont) for my trial trip. The doc sends his patients out on a trial trip & then they return to report to him.
> After that we will rush for Hickory Nut Gap— . . . The Aunties & Siddy each gave me a Hampshire sheep—I am most anxious to see them. (James G. K. McClure, Jr. to Harriet Stuart, December 26, 1917)

The visit to Andover, where Dumont Clarke was serving as school chaplain, went well. Elizabeth's next report to Wiggy continued to be optimistic. "Jim is getting on wonderfully. He is better than he has been in years. Isn't that fine?" (Elizabeth Cramer McClure to Martha Clarke, January 1, 1918). A few weeks later she reported, "Here we are back . . . for what we think will be only a short stay. We have been in Andover 10 days staying with Jim's sister on a sort of trial trip & Jim fared unbelievably well. He didn't take a single rest, even, except for the orthodox Sunday nap and did just what he liked. It is wonderful to see him so well again" (Elizabeth Cramer McClure to Martha Clarke, January 27, 1918).

And finally, Elizabeth relays the message to Wiggy that "Here we are, mon chere, on our way back to the farm from Stockbridge. Jim is *wonderfully* well but the doc wants him to remain at the farm another year" (Elizabeth Cramer McClure to Martha Clarke, February 11, 1918).

Jim and Elizabeth left Dr. Riggs' sanitarium on the eighth of February. The short interlude with Dr. Riggs made a dramatic difference to Jim McClure. Somehow, those private meetings and all the therapy in between helped him to finally take control of the illness that had plagued him for eight years. Throughout the rest of his life, Jim gave Dr. Austen Riggs the credit for freeing him from his malaise.

They were home at Hickory Nut Gap on the twentieth, settling back into their routine. The "Riggs cure" seemed to be holding, except for a few mild warnings, and Jim did his best to balance his life better with equal doses of work and play. Mr. Davidson was in the Army, and Jim slowly took on more of an active role in managing the farm. As Elizabeth mentioned to Wiggy, the household was still enduring life on a wartime footing.

> Everyone here in America is trying to think up substitutes for meat, wheat & sugar & the housewives are busy delving into cookbooks. I wish you could hear me talk about corn breads & wheat products! I made a poster a short time ago representing a beautiful lady feeding a pig with a stout soldier standing by. It read KEEP A PIG IN THE BACKYARD!
> Hoover says "a pig is worth more than a shell in winning the war." . . . We hope to put up 500 quarts of vegetables & fruit this summer so I shall be busy! (Elizabeth Cramer McClure to Martha Clarke, January 27, 1918)

Jim set his production goals quite high for 1918: "three to four thousand bushels of corn, two hundred bushels of wheat and rye, one thousand bushels of apples, five hundred of potatoes and fifty pigs . . . pretty good for a farm that has been producing nothing to speak of for years past!" Elizabeth noted. Three more hands were hired, and Hickory Nut Gap began to hum with life. The two Yankees became totally immersed in the farming ways of the mountains, and their new home began to be the scene of a remarkable cultural interchange. For Jim and Elizabeth, the summer of 1918 was their true baptism into an Appalachian world. A fascination for the people caught in the mountain backwaters began inexorably to overcome these two. They became consumed by a desire to throw their idealism, their leadership and their very lives in with them, in order to create a new economic and spiritual basis on which everyone could enjoy the fruits of modern civilization. A look at the diaries of the learned minister and his artist wife give a graphic picture of the education the mountaineers provided for the McClures during 1918, when they returned from Dr. Riggs' Sanitarium. Sometimes one made the entry, sometimes the other:

> March 7 E[lizabeth] spent a furious day cleaning the dairy. Clad in a raincoat & perched in the rafters she used the hose with such effect that she nearly took the roof off.

> March 8 E. spent another terrific day wrestling with the old kitchen. After dinner [we] went together down to [the] Sumner tract where Sinclair was ploughing & Mr. Nix, John Settle & Zeb MacAbee were clearing. Pisgah [Mountain] had "broke out" [in fire]. Mr. Sumner letting it out, when burning over his land. The three mentioned as clearing, went to the North of the fire and headed it off.

> March 9 While E. still wrestled with the remains of the old kitchen & John [Shorter] assisted by Mr. Nix & John Settle performed the ceremony known as "hog killing." . . . Home to find Petie [Elizabeth] worn & haggard cranking the churn with her teeth set, after 3 hours at hard labor the butter did not come.

> March 11 Zeb MacAbee hired on at $32.00 per month . . .

March 13 Registered sow & boar from Mr. McCoughlin arrived. Boar got out at Biltmore but Porter [MacAbee] who was "in for a ride" saw it & it was captured.

March 16 Mr. Sinclair drilled 9 1/4 bu. [of] oats in bottom . . . Raspberries, gooseberries & currants planted.

March 21 Wild orgy of house cleaning. The army posted all over the house & every five minutes stage coach & bustle in new location. Hay loft & upper orchard only refuges.

April 11 Our own ham for supper & it was delicious.

April 14 to church 1 hr. late but still heard 35 minutes of ghastliness. Wrote article "Is Peace Possible?"

April 15 The pet polished my article. Dispatched article to New Republic.

April 20 Article returned by New Republic.

While Jim labored over this article it was beginning to look as though the Allies were going to win after all. He took one more crack at trying to resolve the issue of war. Although the editors of *The New Republic* chose not to publish it, a copy remains in the family archives. The article reveals not only what he thought on this issue, but also how he approached all such problems.

Is Permanent Peace Possible?

Permanent peace in the world is possible. The one condition of our attaining it is that we refuse to be denied it . . . Wishing and hoping will not bring this to pass. It will be more difficult of accomplishment than the defeat of Germany.

So long as the nations of the world have sovereign and supposedly equal power, there is bound to be war. Each nation is a law unto itself. Each nation, therefore, will have recourse to arms when it considers the grievance or the prize sufficient. At any time this may bring on a general war. No sovereign nation could brook interference on a point of national honor or national aggrandizement.

To each nation its own government is the ultimate and highest authority. We shall have in the world, then, several highest and ultimate authorities. Any one who knows anything at all of human affairs realizes that sooner or later these ultimate authorities are bound to clash. Nothing can prevent future wars if we adhere to this old basis. No league of nations would ensure peace—for it is merely a league of equal nations and no ultimate and mobile authority has been created.

The only possible basis of permanent peace is to have one ultimate and highest seat of authority; and this must be a mobile authority, created, freely granted, and controlled by the people of the nations themselves. This would insure permanent peace.

Such a plan can be actualized by an international parliament or congress. The people of each nation would elect representatives ... The number of representatives might be proportionate to the number of literate voters in the various countries. The capital of the world would be situated at the Hague or Constantinople or any such satisfactory place. Let me call to mind that the distance in days travel in 1775 was longer between Boston and New York than it is now between New York and London; San Francisco is capable of closer communication with Constantinople than Charleston then was with Philadelphia. The details of such a plan present no insurmountable difficulties and it is our one and only hope. There is no use deluding ourselves, or building our structure on 19th Century hopes. Unless we, the people of the world, voluntarily create a representative international authority, we are fighting in vain.[8]

The war was much more than an intellectual puzzle for Jim. He and his wife had spent a considerable part of their lives in Germany, France and England, and they wondered often about their friends remaining there. Nathan McClure enlisted in the Army, and Ambrose Cramer served in the Navy and as a French translator and administrator overseas. Jim himself was called up by the draft, but when he reported for his physical, he had such a bad case of poison ivy that they flunked him.[9]

In spite of these disappointments Jim kept working steadily on the farm and in the community.

April 30 1st meeting [of the] Hickory Nut Gap Farm Co . . . Mr. Davidson, Mr. Sinclair, & John Shorter assembled in my study & I outlined the plan . . . [This was a plan to allow the farm workers to share in farm profits. It was later given up because profits just did not materialize.]

(Elizabeth) May 5 Bearwallow Baptist Church "Choir is all tore up." Old man wanted to "Get shut" of his collection money. Grand revival hymns! Cricket [Jim] referred to as "Brother McClure." Hateful turkeys are hatching.

(Jim) May 10 —rounding up sow that got out . . . a Mr. Williams desired a night's lodging for his party, appearing about 9:30 & was hesitatingly refused.

May 12 . . . 58 minute service on "Unbelief & Everlasting Torture."

May 17 Went to meet Hetty [Stuart] & Grace [Cramer, wife of Ambrose] both delighted with country. Took them over Beaucatcher [Mountain] . . . Quite impressed with place and views . . .

May 18 Mr. Dalton's, mail carrier's, first trip in Ford—displacing mule.

May 19 another ghastly sermon.

May 20 Gracy ploughed. Hetty churned.

May 21 Africa [a sow] brought 6 pigs.

May 22 Africa lost 2 pigs——one strayed another crushed. To Asheville . . . bearing John Settle on his matrimonial errand. After errands were taken by Hetty & Grace to lunch at Grove Park. Home via Fletcher . . . Ran into mud on Cane Creek Road & girls much agitated by skidding.

May 24 graphophone moonlight party . . .

May 27 Motored & climbed to top of Chimney Rock . . . picked 10 qts. of strawberries.

May 29 Canning bee lasted 'till 9:30 p.m. —owing to misfortunes — spinach & chard & beets canned.

May 31 . . . bull calf . . . was down. We worked in Herculean manner all morning—dosing him with whiskey . . . the cow . . . died.

June 2 Anna [Esther's mother] arrived & took Eleazer [a young household helper who was John's niece] dissolved in tears home to hoe corn—conference with Anna lasted until we had to rush for the mules to go to Bear Wallow Church—tires being flat.

June 9 At 1 a.m. started to rain & up again & with lantern got Australia [another sow] & offspring into dynamite crib [for shelter].

June 15 Sent in 24 quarts [of] cherries & got 12 1/2 qts. = $3.00 & for 5 doz eggs $1.75. Brought car back with a bill of $73.00.

June 17 anointed turkeys with oil Petie saved a chicken by warming on the hot water bag.

June 19 Supper at [the] Bandanna Tea Room & to a screaming movie "A Dog's Life" Charlie Chaplin— Forgot the tires at the movie & started for Mrs. Heywoods 7–9 tea at 8:45 p.m. Burned up the road till puncture came—finally arrived at Mrs. Heywoods about 9:20.

The resources of good health gave Jim the freedom not only to push along his plans for the farm, but also to begin tentatively to act on behalf of his community. He and Elizabeth organized a local chapter of the Red Cross before the Germans surrendered. Since the war still seemed far away it was a little difficult to raise money for the Red Cross in such a poor area, so a fair was organized in the Bat Cave section, which was over the mountain from the inn. Jim always loved a big community get together, and threw himself into this Red Cross Fourth of July affair with wonderful enthusiasm. On July 3rd, the Red Cross supplies of 300 pounds of ice and 15 gallons of ice cream arrived at Hickory Nut Gap at 5 p.m. and were transferred to a wagon. Mr. Davidson, farm manager, Mr. Sinclair and John Shorter started at once for the Esmerelda

Inn, some ten miles over the mountain in Bat Cave, causing great excitement along the route. Next day Jim started at 8 a.m. with the Pet, household helpers Mary and Pete, and Croaker [or Croak, a farm worker] on the running board, bringing more supplies. A huge crowd bought lemonade, cider, ice cream, cake, cookies, apples, peaches and buttermilk, and the successful event cleared $70.00. Not even a puncture on the return trip could dim the joy of the participants.

Jim discovered early on that he, like his father, had a knack for raising money for a worthy cause. He sold Liberty Bonds throughout Fairview, which took him inside the homes of many of his neighbors.

Once the neighbors found out that Jim was a preacher, and an educated one at that, he began to receive invitations "to bring the message" to several of the local Baptist congregations. Jim relished the idea, and made use of the opportunity the rest of his life to preach his gospel of progress. The Sunday after the Red Cross picnic he was invited by the Bearwallow Baptist Church. He warmed up his neighbors that day by describing the old mountain circuit riders, who were called not to a particular church but to a community. "Don't just help out the saved among you, but go out and minister to everyone in the community," he told them.

> We can not only help the poor, but we must remove poverty. We must so build up our soils, & breed up our stock so that we remove poverty . . .
>
> Only when we got to thinking it was Christ's work to prevent boys & girls from getting liquor did we start the liquor bus[iness] on the toboggan.
>
> There are two choices before us—the life of selfishness or the life of service. The life of selfishness dries up the sources of vitality of the comm[unity]: it stunts development & paralyzes the comm[unity]-
>
> The life of service liberates. If you live among men as one who serveth you will find that you are setting free the life of the community & creating the life of God in other men. "He who loseth his life shall find it."[10]

The title of this sermon was "The Sin of Aachan." Jim McClure felt it was one of his most popular, and he reworked it many times for different churches. The text was from Joshua, the sixth and seventh chapters, which deal with the battle of Jericho. The walls of Jericho had just fallen, and the city was on the verge of conquest by the Jewish nation. Yahweh ordered the city destroyed, but would condone no looting in order to maintain the religious purity of the people. " . . . [K]eep yourselves from the things devoted to destruction . . ." lest trouble be brought down on the camp of Israel. But Aachen was tempted by all the wealth he discovered in Jericho, as well he might after having spent his entire life in the desert. He was eventually caught, but not before the morale of the Jewish camp was poisoned by his selfish act. It is an anecdote perfectly suited to Jim's notion of social sin.

Jim McClure wanted to introduce a new concept of sin into the mountains. The old idea he called "a selfish view of sin." Many country preachers continually hammered on the idea that specific acts, such as swearing or drinking, no matter how secretly performed, would be discovered at the judgement day by the Lord God Almighty. Jim wanted people to see that drinking and swearing, and a whole multitude of other selfish acts, had an immediate impact. Your friends, neighbors and relations all were demoralized by your sin. Moral weakness would be caught like the influenza, and passed about the community. The truth about sin, as Brother McClure told it, was that selfishness endangered the strength of the entire community. He liked to tell the story of an American soldier in France who drank up the entire ration of water for his company, bringing down on himself the hatred and derision of his fellows. "They knew his breach of discipline endangered their lives. . . ." Sin was not simply a mark in the "Black Book on high." "Think of yourself as owing, not owning, all you have . . . Much of what you have [is in] trust . . . If land . . . think of generations to come and build it up." When one realized the debt owed to those who came before, one also understands that the conduct of one's present life will leave a legacy for future generations. Jim then exhorted the members of the congregation to serve one another, in honor of the past and to prepare for the future. "Believing does not mean anything unless put into action." Jim argued that the instinct to serve one's friends and neighbors emanated from the Holy Spirit, and to dam it up, to leave it unfulfilled, would block off the source of true satisfaction and happiness. Service, in Jim's scheme, covered a broad range of helpful activities, from building pure water systems to keeping scrub bulls from siring new stock. A man pursued God's purposes when he worked to eliminate the breeding areas for typhoid fever, built better schools and roads, and brought electricity into the community.

On the practical side, Jim's parents were coming to visit soon and the old inn must be made ready.

Aug. 1 The cursed pigs are rooting up the whole lawn.

Aug. 10 Great Cleaning up—barns, barnyard & house in preparation for coming of Mother & Father [McClure].

Aug. 12 Passing thru Biltmore with enormous load—found Pete & Mary with 4 nieces and nephews stranded. Somehow packed them in.

Aug. 16 Nathan & Arch arrive. Nathan looking very fine in his new [Army] uniform. [They were soon followed by Dr. and Mrs. McClure]

(Elizabeth) Aug. 18 All went to church & heard the dreary Dr. Loache preach his best effort. Dr. McClure requested to preach in the evening . . . Dr. preached to quite a little gathering.

(Elizabeth) Aug. 19 Dr. & Mrs. McClure leave. Felt sad to have them go.

Aug. 24 Cow choked on an apple.

(Elizabeth) Aug. 25 Nearly driven to distraction & boredom by the terrible effort of Dr. Loache; a most unchristian man! Resolved not to attend any longer.

Sept. 11 . . . threshed 46 1/2 bu. [of] wheat, 15 rye, 18 oats & 1 barley.

Sept. 13 Sent wheat to Alexander's mill & they said it was the best wheat they had had brought in.

Sept. 14 — 12 a.m. to 1 a.m. I arose & made a sally after hunters.

Sept. 18 molasses being made, Fin [Sinclair], John Shorter & Foy Wall at the evaporator, John Settle with Red & Brown hauling cane—& W. B. Morgan, Croak & Zeb [MacAbee] stripping & cutting cane.

Sept. 19 Molasses started at [the] crack of dawn. By noon [the] cane was stripped & cut and 50 gal. was made by 8 p.m.

(Elizabeth) Sept. 23 Black Monday! Eleven hands failed to appear that were due to pick apples. Poor Cricket deeply gloomy. Esther & Iola depart for the circus via very late mail man . . . The poor coloreds return in the evening—unable to get into the circus!

Oct. 8 Finished picking apples—totalling 125 bbls. [Barrels] . . . Started [grain] dryer this day & it did twice catch on fire & we are feeling sullen at the Demonstrating agents for getting us into it.

Oct. 9 Influenza 'a raging . . .

Oct. 13 Rumor that Germany has unconditionally surrendered.

Oct. 19 — . . . made chairman [of the] Transportation Local Influenza Committee — 2000 cases in Asheville.

Oct. 25 In bed all day to prevent sore throat developing . . . The Pet read me the sinister, bloodcurdling, terrifying & fearful *Dracula*.

Oct. 27 Still housed with sore throat . . . spent the day reading with the Pet, writing & swatting flies . . . swatted 61 in dining room & study, 16 in pink room, 54 in pantry & over 700 in kitchen.

Nov. 1 —Evening enlivened by a great rat hunt-finally John & I secured the burly victim . . .

Nov. 2 Just before noon George Sherrill appeared, out of his head. I put him to work in my overalls & jumper, but he soon left for other parts leaving his coat behind & promising automobiles to us all—stating he had invented a steel cat to catch rats.

Nov. 11 PEACE.

The Great War finally ended in the fall of 1918, or rather the fighting paused for twenty years, resuming in 1939. In countless ways the world was never quite the same again. When the armistice was signed in November 1918, Jim could feel the country relax. Self-discipline and sacrifice dissipated, and the American people hungered for a "return to normalcy." The stage was set for the frenetic and worldly Roaring Twenties. Jim was left wondering why the same people who were willing to sacrifice even their lives for victory over the Germans had little interest in working for peace. "Is Permanent Peace Possible?" he asked again, and then watched as even Wilson's much less radical idea of a League of Nations was rejected by his countrymen.

Jim McClure hoped he could inspire the people in his area to maintain the sense of self-sacrifice and what he called the "thrill of common purpose" that the nation had developed while fighting the Central Powers, and re-direct the energy to fighting poverty. In the little churches he spoke of the satisfactions that most Americans felt enduring the privations of the home front. "Soldiers of Christ arise . . . Put money into community purposes as you did into $50.00 Bonds— War [wants] to tear down— Get . . . at [the] idea of building up."[11] These were noble ideas. Jim McClure would put them into action when he founded the Farmers Federation, but for most Americans, the Roaring Twenties were anything but an era of self-sacrifice.

He became a different preacher than he had been in Iron River. Up there, he had composed weighty messages more likely to impress his professors than his parishioners. In North Carolina, his delivery became more extemporaneous, his sermon notes more sketchy. He included humorous anecdotes that he collected from his friends, little stories that perked up his listeners and helped to lighten the message. It was a step away from his somber Calvinist tradition, a step toward the lively style of the mountain preacher, and it gave his sermons the impact needed to move people.

Certainly the lives of Jim and Elizabeth McClure had been changed since the beginning of the Great War. Four years before, the two of them were rather distant acquaintances whose ambitions were carrying them in two different directions: she into the French artistic circles and he into the social ministry of the Presbyterian Church. Now they were married and living on the side of a mountain in the midst of the Southern Appalachians. In August 1918, Elizabeth and Jim learned something wonderful and become aware that their life together might mean more even than the challenges of their household and their mutual friendship and respect. After bustling the often-present Aunties off on the train, they visited their doctor, ". . . who confirmed our judgement and forbade motoring." Two weeks later Elizabeth broke the news to Wiggy.

> Now then for some thrilling news which is to be a secret dear darling until the end of October anyway. We are expecting a small McClure about the middle of March. Can you imagine *me* mere de famille! I can't!!! Anyway I am enormously well—I have no disagreeable symptoms that apparently people

usually have & really I can't believe anything is going on at all. However the doctor who is a very excellent one says that everything is very normal & I look just as I did 3 months ago so its hard to believe at all, at all. (Elizabeth Cramer McClure to Martha Clarke, August 26, 1918)

She held out another few weeks before sending the word northward, charging Hetty to strict confidentiality. "This is for your special private ear—how would you like being Aunt to a little new McClure—about the middle of next March? Do you suppose it will preach or paint? I already have grave fears as to its future." (Elizabeth Cramer McClure to Harriet Stuart, September 13, 1918)

Life at Hickory Nut Gap during the following fall and winter revolved about the expectations of the new arrival. Elizabeth's movements, according to the custom of women of her station in that day, were severely circumscribed, but the pace of life at the farm went on.

Nov. 15 —Mr. & Mrs. Cramer come.
Nov. 18 — . . . Mr. Cramer and I went hunting . . . getting 9 quail a.m. & 4 in p.m.

Dec. 12 [replanting of boxwoods in front of the house] . . . all hands going without lunch & getting 8 of 9 to our place after dark where we unloaded aided by the famous efforts of Zeb [MacAbee] . . . The Pet thrilled.

Dec. 20 Brought Alec Huntley back from Asheville where he had sold his potatoes for $1.00 per bu. I should think the farmers would quit.

Dec. 23 The Pet working hard on Santa Claus suit.

Dec. 24 . . . A roaring morning, getting Xmas presents, trees etc., seeing about George Sherrill & with much embarrassment even purchasing nighties for my Pet.

Dec. 25 Santa Claus appeared and gave presents to those assembled-to wit Ben & Maggie Owenby & their 3 offspring, Christine, Gertrude & Almer, Baxter & Minnie Owenby & their offspring Geneva & Otis, Katy Sinclair & Porter & Homer, Belle McAbee & Hattie Pearl, Porter & Annie May . . . Ice Cream & cake served, Cricket superb as Santy—great delight amongst crowd. [the last addition by Elizabeth.]

With nearly the whole farm crowd on hand for a Christmas celebration that was to become a tradition at Hickory Nut Gap, one can see what a cast of characters was around to educate Jim and his wife, to show them how life was led back in the mountains of Western North Carolina. During these years, Jim McClure learned what the mountain family battled against. His education was a practical one; the economics and sociology involved the lives of real people in the community as well as on the farm. He learned how enduring and tough these people were, and he discovered endearing traits as well: the earthy humor, patience and religious faith that made them survivors. He also discovered what happens when a society can afford only the most meager of schools, and how ignorance can become an accepted part of the culture. Not all the mountain men and women were ignorant, or humorous, or religious, or even welcoming to a stranger. Some were utterly poor, and others relatively prosperous. But Jim knew, having grown up where he did, that the economic life in Fairview, and elsewhere in the region, lagged well behind the rest of the country. He had an idea that if the people could make a little money, the spiritual reservoir that lay backed up in the mountains could be unleashed and great works could be accomplished.

As the winter progressed Elizabeth, who had to curtail her usual activities, took on the project of copying a picture of Jim's Grandmother Dixon. Jim rather irreverently commented in the diary, on the completion of the portrait, that she had succeeded in "making a decent looking old lady of her . . ." (January 9, 1919). He continued to read and ponder such subjects as the future of Christianity, democracy and the United States. The country did seem to be in the grip of a very disagreeable judgement of some kind, whether demonic or divine, in the form of an influenza epidemic. Death was not at all an uncommon result of the virus, and so when it swept up into the coves of the mountains, Jim wanted to do all he could to protect Elizabeth. John Shorter fell ill, and he was immediately quarantined in his home. By the end of January, the strain of the winter, the flu, and the ennui of pregnancy finally overrode all objections, and the two of them decided to move into Asheville for a few days. "Both feeling somewhat drab & determined to have a spree at the Manor—started for Asheville . . ." (January 25, 1919). Even though "Fear of the 'flu' kept us from church" (January 26, 1919), they were stimulated nonetheless by their new surroundings and companions. Elizabeth notes in the diary that "Cricket talks late with various lobby loafers" (January, 1919). The interlude at the Manor helped to dispel for a time the gloom of winter, but the diary reveals that tempers may have been short on through February.

Feb. 6— . . . selected all chickens for execution & then they all got out . . .

Feb. 16—Went to Bear Wallow . . . to preach on Zaccheus & found no one there . . .

Feb. 21—Esther sent up word that she was sick & feared it was the flu . . . her temp . . . was only 101°-but sloshed down to Fairview—not a light anywhere—& roused the Dr. who prescribed in a flannel night shirt. [This was Dr. Cicero McCracken, who took faithful care of the sick of Fairview for many years.]

Feb. 24 Esther in a rage at finding her dishes washed separate from the others in the Old Kitchen because of the "flu"—[She] departs . . . John depressed. Petie incensed.

March followed February, and with it came a heightened sense of expectation. Elizabeth's parents arrived just before the presumed time of arrival, and close on their heels, "Wiggy" appeared to take command. The latter had retained for Jim a somewhat mythical existence up until the moment she appeared in the flesh. All in all, Jim fared rather poorly in these last days, quite overwhelmed not only by his role as a prospective father, but also by the amount of entertainment required by all the guests. The Cramer's train arrived on March the tenth, and Elizabeth notes in her diary that "After lunch rush to station to meet Father and Mother who appeared just as we were pulling up" (March 10). Elizabeth and Jim, the Cramers including their son Corwith, who was about thirteen, and Martha Clarke (Wiggy) were all waiting together for the baby at the Grove Park Inn, Asheville's finest resort hotel. The waiting usually took the form of golf, for those so inclined, and for three days Jim tensely entertained his father-in-law and young Corwith on the hotel course. On March the 18th, Jim's patience wore thin. "After leaving Azalea I drove fast & furiously over the rough roads— the strain of paying for 3 rooms being too much . . . dined at the G. P. Inn & bored to death by the movies" (March 18).

Late the next night, however, all was different; the long wait was about to end. "The dear Pet soon after lights were out finding signs multiplying we decided to move to the hospital. Miss Clarke was summoned . . . Fetching 3 dishes of ice cream & with Miss Clarke's birthday cake we had a fine party. [It was] a most gorgeous moonlight night so we determined on a joy ride part way up Sunset [Mountain] before interning in the hospital at about 12:30 a.m." (March 19).

The exact role of the moon in such cases is, shall it be said, mysterious. But by the next morning, its power had worked a magic, and the redoubtable Dr. Charles Millender delivered a fine baby boy, James Gore King McClure, III. It was March 20, 1919. He was tucked away in the bathroom because the baby ward was befouled by influenza.

For the young minister, not really so young anymore, the birth of the first child confirmed, as it always does, the miraculous nature of life itself. For a man who had fought through volumes of theology, the birth of his son was a supremely religious moment. He fell in love with Elizabeth all over again, as they both bathed in the joy of the birth of James Gore King McClure, III. The day after, Jim wrote, "The Pet progressing famously & looking as if she was at a party. Her color was good as ever & she looked most beautiful" (March 21). Two days later, he wrote: ". . . Took Miss Clarke up Sunset—Then to see the dear Pet looking perfectly beautiful . . ." (March 23).

The baby boy was given his father's name, a name that went back to grandfather Archibald's near death on shipboard years ago. Born with the finest of Presbyterian heritages, this child would grow up to be as stubbornly principled as his Covenanter ancestors. But as a baby, all of that history was less important than the motherly attentions that surrounded him. Even his imposing name was temporarily discarded, and the child became known simply as

"Punie." Weights and measurements were important tools for child-rearing in that day, and by all accounts young James grew slowly. Mother and child remained in the hospital for nearly a full month. Elizabeth had not been allowed to even sit up for nine days. Four days after that, she was carefully lowered into a wheelchair for her first venture away from the bed. Jim always admitted that he belonged to the "slow and easy" school of childbirth, a remarkable contrast to the way children were born amongst the tenants on his farm.

Jim was busy entertaining his in-laws and supervising work at the farm, but he made daily visits to the hospital, bringing stories to entertain Elizabeth. There was her young half-brother, Corwith, who was depressed by his freckles, and unmercifully teased by Jim about his interest in the young ladies at the Grove Park Inn. On the day after the baby's birth new cattle arrived at the Biltmore Station and he drove the Cramers over to see them, finding "Croak attached by a long rope to the biggest cow & being yanked hither and thither . . ." (March 21). Mr. Cramer was always greatly interested in the farm.

With these cows Jim created probably the first registered herd of Herefords in Western North Carolina, which he hoped might prove an encouragement to purebred breeding in the region. Ever since his days in Texas he had yearned to raise cattle, and to raise them right. Yet, despite his farm work and the birth of a son, and even though he was slowly sinking his roots into his adopted region, Jim McClure was still unsettled in the spring of 1919 about his own future. By now, Jim was well and able to cope with a full work day again. Moreover, the war was over and with it went, to Jim's way of thinking, the justification for pouring his efforts into farming. James Davidson had returned to take up his post as manager, and the place could be safely left in his capable hands. It was time, then, for Jim to pursue his goals as a minister.

He began scanning for possibilities. Just prior to the armistice, he considered working with the YMCA in Europe, in a war-related capacity. He had informed the powers of the Presbyterian Church that he was looking for a position, and with Elizabeth still in the hospital he made a dart up north to inquire about the position of minister at the Lafayette Square Presbyterian Church in Baltimore. While there, he wrote his minister brother Arch about the trip, who replied:

> Your letter from Baltimore quite took me by surprise. I didn't know you really had a line on Baltimore —but am awfully glad you have. It will be great to have you back preaching again. Would you take a church this Spring or are you going to wait until fall? . . . Any church that hasn't sense enough to give [you] a call . . . must be made up of a set of dominoes. It's lucky for me that my congo can't hear you or they would fire me immediately & call you. (Arch McClure to James G. K. McClure, Jr., April 15, 1919)

Jim preached twice at this church, but felt as if his "reception was lukewarm at best." " . . . Not a sign of cordiality before & but 3 handshakes after [the] service. Ibid in the evening—about 35 out. . . ."[12]

Jamie McClure and his father's Hereford bull, "Foundation."

So he returned home again and spent another summer as a farmer. He threw himself once more into a bond drive, as vice chairman for Fairview township, selling Victory Bonds to help finish paying for a war already won. In two weeks, he turned in $10,000 from this rural district. As a founder of the Fairview Community Club, Jim worked hard to sell shares to bring telephone service to Fairview. He had a definite talent for talking people out of their money when the cause was right: by midsummer local telephone service became a very real possibility, with forty-nine people taking stock.

Along with Victory Bonds and telephones, Jim, began organizing another effort that in retrospect stands out as a completely new beginning, not only for those who benefitted personally, but also for Jim himself. Clearly, the momentous nature of this occasion was not felt by either Jim or the others. He notes in his diary, in matter-of-fact style, that on April 19, 1919, he " . . . went out to [a] meeting at Fairview to organize farmers. Many women present, when I had thought it was to be entirely men. After much hot airing from women, decided to organize. . . ." Elizabeth adds the " . . . following officers were elected. Cricket, Pres., S. J. Ashworth, vice-Pres, Luther Clay Sec." The Fairview Federation of Farmers was launched! By May third, the group was officially organized and under way.

Jim McClure always believed that the best way to fathom the divine purposes of the Creator was one step at a time. The first step of the Farmers Federation was halting and tentative, but in time, in a short time, it would change forever the opportunities for farmers in Western North Carolina. The remainder of the summer and fall, he kept busy with the wide variety of activities that came his way. All the while he must have been wondering what form, what direction, his life was to take. Such a proposition is difficult enough for a young man, but Jim McClure was well into his thirties, with growing responsibilities, and as yet his dreams to spread the Social Gospel remained unfulfilled. But Hickory Nut Gap was certainly an enviable location to sort through such doubts, especially with a new son, a steady stream of visiting friends and relations, and a wife as lovely as Elizabeth.

Among the visitors were the Misses Skinner, come to view their darling niece's new son. In their long white linen summer dresses, they were determined figures on the porch or in the house. There was soon a confrontation with Wiggy, who had been firmly running the show since her arrival. Amidst the ups and downs of command between the three powers, little Jamie continued to thrive and Jim was barely able to find enough time to prepare a sermon to be given at the Asheville School for Boys.

> The Reverend James G. K. McClure, of Fairview, preached to the Graduating Class on Sunday, May 25th. His sermon, based on the text, "What seest Thou?" was a strong, forceful appeal . . . He analyzed the attitudes of different people—those who spurn the vision entirely, those who fail to see it, and those who are willing to act on it—and impressed the School with a sense of individual duty.[13]

But the rivalry between the visitors must have told on him. Elizabeth noted on June 23: "Cricket with his old trouble again." However he was soon well and back in the fray.

> June 28— . . . Great washing of Rex & Bowser [their dogs] & Lysoling porch to rid us of plague fleas . . .

> June 29 — to a Singing Convention. Great gathering of mountaineers.

> July 1—To town at 7:30 with 20 bu. potatoes & Miss C[larke] . . . Grove Park which was to have taken 10 bu. I unloaded etc. & 2nd Steward saw me & in a 2nd class way told me he wouldn't take them, as he had waited all preceding day for them, etc. and I had promised [he said] to bring them in day before.

> July 21—A.M. to O. F. Settles—whole sprightly family on deck Big talk with O. F. & his mother—Lola studying Sunday School lesson on porch.

Mr. O. F. Settles lived at the head of the Bud Owenby Creek in a "holler" between 'Tater Knob and the shoulder of Little Pisgah Mountain. Jim and Elizabeth carried little Jamie to see the family. Perhaps Jim was hoping to arrange a trade with Mr. Settles, which was later completed, giving the Settles family some of Jim's land on the highway in exchange for the Settles' land that adjoined the main farm. Jim asked Mr. Settles if he ever found his location lonely. Mr. Settles replied that he liked it "cause if anybody comes to see me I know they *really* want to see *me,* or they want *somethin'* " (July 21). This visit may have been the beginning of the long connection between the McClures and the Settles. Clinard Settles worked for Jim and Elizabeth and their children from the time he was fourteen until his death sixty-eight years later. Other members of the family, John Scott, Dorothy, McKinley, and Lola, were all faithful helpers at various times.

In August the McClure family came together for the important Presbyterian rite of baptizing James Gore King McClure, III. What a delight it must have been for Jim to have his parents and his brother Arch come for a good visit. It seems likely that Jim and his father and minister brother had many discussions of Jim's possible future. Jamie III was properly baptized in the Presbyterian way by his grandfather, using water he had brought from the River Jordan, sprinkled from a small silver christening cup that had been used for the baptisms of all three James McClures. The senior McClures and Arch returned home, and Jim and Elizabeth prepared to interrupt their life in the Southern Appalachians with an excursion to Vermont and Lake Forest, which would include time for Jim to survey the opportunities for returning to the ministry. If the world beyond Western North Carolina wanted to make a claim on them, this long vacation would be its last chance to make a pitch. The preparations for this trip, with baby, were formidable. A black travelling nurse, Effie Thomas, was hired. The day of departure, September third, was a

> Furious morning by all—John taking in early load of trunks—all hands finally getting packed into the 2nd load . . . & off for Biltmore, ice box and all. We swarmed onto the train, about eight . . . assistants helping us with our thousands of bundles—then commenced a journey unparalleled in crowdedness. The ice box, Puny, the Pet, myself & some 16 bags & boxes were cramped into the drawing room—The Pet banging her head whenever she turned around & Miss C. & Effie forcing their way in & out constantly. . . . (diary. September 3)

The little party arrived safely next morning in New York to spend two days. Elizabeth and Jim ate lobster and blue fish only to find Puny "very loud with colic" when they returned to their hotel room. Next day there was "a permanent for the Pet" and dining and dancing at Churchill's on Broadway, amidst many street speeches from striking actors. Then they joined battle again to get the luggage on board the train for Manchester, where they were welcomed by the indomitable Aunties and Ambrose and his wife Gracie.

Autumn in the Green Mountains! They remained on into October, and apparently Jim, "Bowser" (Ambrose), and Dumont agreed that the finest vantage point from which to enjoy the colors was out on the golf course. Jim and Elizabeth slipped away for several little day trips together, leaving Puny with Effie. Jim preached two sermons, and made one noteworthy trip down to Williamstown, Massachusetts. There a cousin of Elizabeth's, Parmalee Prentice, had single-mindedly set out to study the secrets of improving the genetics of plants and animals. Mount Hope Farm, because of the work of Mr. Prentice, became an agricultural magnet for progressive farm leaders, and although Jim did not yet know it, that was what he was about to become. He was thrilled enough with the work going on at Mount Hope in 1919, noting the "Painstaking attempt to improve existing stocks of poultry, potatoes, corn, [&] small grains. . . ."[14]

Church work, not agriculture, still seemed to hold out the greatest prospect of service for him. In the midst of the Vermont vacation he and Elizabeth went to New York. A large and prestigious Presbyterian church on Fifth Avenue was looking for a minister, and Jim had been asked to a dinner in Englewood, New Jersey, where the search committee from New York City could look him over unobtrusively. He and Elizabeth left Vermont on October the tenth. Elizabeth described the next morning in New York:

> Cricket spent morning cooped up in his chamber . . . writing prayer & sermon . . . Petie makes frantic effort to buy hat. Decides on one chez Mme Florette. Consults time. Late!! Frantic rush to meet Cricket in front of Scribners. Cricket denounces hat!! Frantic rush back to Mme Florette's. Old straw resumed. Great Flurry. Terrible crush in tube owing to ferry boat strike. Missed Englewood train. Despair! Petie very low. Catch next train & arrived only 12 min. late. Met by Powersy [their host] . . . much worried as to the need of dressing for supper. Decided in the negative. Sharply inspected during meal . . . The evening reasonably successful but extremely trying.[15]

The next day they attended the morning service at the Englewood church, and in the afternoon Jim returned to New York to speak at the Vesper Service. Elizabeth described the occasion: " . . . Slim congregation. Cricket a 'false note' in the 'well valeted church.' Refused to wear a gown. Scarcely probable that he was liked. He jarred them & was anything but soothing in his discourse. . . ."[16]

Their guide to the church, an enthusiastic gentleman, did gymnastics later in the anteroom on the red carpet to "get his blood up." Jim's blood was already up. He did not shrink from preaching a fiery message of social responsibility to these wealthy Presbyterians. Later he compared this church to a beautifully carved chest that was empty inside. "Religion is so well valeted . . . [there] that the real thing is suppressed. Elder came to me & told me aft[er the] service [that] they tried to make a quiet, beautiful vesper service—(I disturbed them, made them uneasy—they hated it, it offended them, seemed in bad taste.) . . . Everything in such good form in [this church] & good form so worshipped that . . . good form for good form's sake is committed."[17]

Following the vesper service in New York, Elizabeth and Jim went by train to Passaic, New Jersey, where Jim preached at the evening service of the First Presbyterian Church. The printed program welcomed Jim to the pulpit. "He is a son of Dr. McClure, the President of McCormick Seminary and it is hoped our people will make the effort to come out and hear this message." His sermon was titled, "Service: I am among you as one who serveth."[18] In the diary, Elizabeth again tersely writes of Jim's reception there: "Cricket again made a scene at the Passaic Church . out wearing the gown. [He] preached a thrilling sermon on service. Powersy muttering to himself that 'he had 'em all stirred up.' Petie proud . . . No idea at all what impression we made."[19] The next morning, Jim apparently felt little need to exercise restraint, and Elizabeth chides him a little in their diary (Oct. 14): "Cricket a bit bold & loud at breakfast— . . . ruined his chances by announcing at breakfast that he had once been thought to have had a brain lesion! In New York, he talked over an Englewood proposal as well as the possibility of being secretary of the Yale-in-China mission."[20] The next day, after a very difficult excursion into the strongholds of comfortable Christianity, they rode the train back to Vermont to be reunited with their son.

From Vermont, Jim and his entourage travelled westward to Lake Forest. The journey was full of personal possibilities for Jim. He was seeking his own "highest and best use" in the battle to make the world conform to his specifications for the Kingdom of God. Somehow, though, agriculture stayed foremost in Jim's mind. In Chicago, he visited the stockyards and was given a tour by Louis Swift, one of the chief buyers for the Swift family's meat company. He rode on horseback through the 20,000 head that were being held ready for slaughter and found himself talking over agricultural possibilities with men he knew to be knowledgeable in the field.[21] He also searched around for a water-powered electric generator to set up at Hickory Nut Gap and electrify his home and farm. That may have been the pretext for him to go to Detroit to visit Henry Ford. But clearly, he went also to test out on the great inventor a vision for a mission to the Southern mountaineers. He wrote in his diary:

> Nov. 6— . . . started for Dearborn for 11:30 appointment . . . Ford took me through [the] tractor plant, showed me water wheels & said he would send for, test & send me [a] Pelton wheel—said my scheme for Mt. farmers was the best scheme he had brought to him—To lunch with him . . . table of about 12 . . . Very stimulating clean cut, capable idealists . . . Then sent around in a Ford to Blast Furnace, Body plant [old Eagle plant] & motor works where 3500 per day are being turned out & 240,000 behind in delivery.

The rest of his time in the Chicago area revolved around pleasant social occasions, particularly the pleasures of showing off his new son to Hetty and Doug Stuart and other family members and friends. There were "big Pow-wows" with Doug and Mr. and Mrs. Cramer on the church and religion. On one late evening of talk, "Mr. C. making stealthy trips to [the] dining room or den & returning more loquacious each time."[22] The day before he and Elizabeth were to return home, he received a job offer that momentarily unbalanced him.

"To town at 10:30 much messed up by offer of job for 3 mos. to convert Presbyterian Churches of Chicago to social G[ospel] & no chance to speak of it to the Pet . . . Decided to turn down offer."[23]

That night at dinner with his parents, Jim's father sensed his son's agitation, and after he and his wife said their final good byes, he sat down to pen a special letter of encouragement to him.

> My dear boy:
> I did not say anything special to you as you left the house tonight. Let me now say that I love you very much, I am happy in you, I believe your life is telling and will tell for great good in the world. I rejoice in your marriage and I feel quite sure that you are doing right in starting back to your home.
> Mother and I are grateful to God that we could have had you and Elizabeth and the baby boy with us so much as we have had; and we rejoice that on this special night the gathering about the table had so many of our dear ones . . .
> Your mother is no usual woman. She has made a very sweet and blessed home for us—these beautiful years.
> May you get back to a restful condition of heart and be ennobled to meet your duties and responsibilities in a brave, patient and sustained way.
> . . . There is a very. very great work to be done in our world for God, and only God's grace can be sufficient for us!
> Tenderly, Father
> (James G. K. McClure, Sr. to James G. K. McClure, Jr., November, 1919)

The next morning, Jim, Elizabeth, Puny, Effie and the well-travelled ice box were all hustled to the Chicago train station and "Seen off with a rush by the Aunties." Their journey was slowed by a railroad strike, but two days later they all "Reached Asheville about noon . . . John came for us . . . & a beautiful drive home."[24]

Hickory Nut Gap, after two and a half months, *was* both beautiful and— most importantly now—home. Their two dogs came barking out to greet them as the familiar putter of the Honeymoon Hudson rounded the curves up the mountain. For two and a half months they had been singing the praises of their mountain country, telling tales about the local people, and describing the projects begun on the farm and house. That sort of conversation has a way of building loyalty, and they had surely convinced themselves, if no one else, that Western North Carolina was now their home. But what to do? Did Jim really want to spend the rest of his life puttering about the farm? What was to become of his career in the ministry? Could he be so bold as to direct his energies outside of the church into a farmers' federation? All of these questions ran about in his head that fall, as did the very basic question of how to support his growing family. His farm income was not even paying the expenses yet, and it rankled him to even consider living off of his wife's income. And yet, he and Elizabeth both dearly loved their adopted homeland, along with all the peculiar ways of its inhabitants. There was certainly a great work crying out to be accomplished

Elizabeth and "Puny" at Hickory Nut Gap.

in these mountains, and Jim held it to be a basic tenet of his personal faith that when a man threw himself in with God, the material details would fall into place.

Remarkably, considering his jarring performance at the Fifth Avenue Church, he received a call to become the minister there. Although we can find no formal record of this, his daughter Elspeth was told of it by her father, along with a caution not to mention the name of the church. Perhaps the search committee felt their congregation *needed* stirring up. In later years, Jim told Elspeth that he and Elizabeth decided he should accept. Then a little group of members of the farmers group Jim had founded that spring, hearing the rumor that Mr. McClure was leaving the mountains to go back to full time preaching, arrived at Hickory Nut Gap. The somber delegation, headed by Mr. Luther Clay, asked him to stay and help them. Jim and Elizabeth thought it over and decided to stay, a decision they never regretted. Jim McClure pledged his support to those men, and continued to work with them until his death.

But how could he begin to help these people? Jim's cumulative experience in agriculture and business were minimal at best. The mountain economy, especially outside of Asheville, was so stagnant that almost no one could even imagine what could be done to generate profits. There was no industry, no single cash crop, little investment money, and the people practiced, on the whole, a simple, superstition-ridden form of subsistence agriculture. Local farming was so inefficient that most of the food for the city of Asheville was shipped in by rail. Furthermore, the mountain farmers were reluctant to take advice from outsiders; too often they had been made to feel ashamed of their backwardness. They were a proud and independent people, exhibiting the traits of their pioneer forefathers. Unfortunately, though, game in the woods was getting scarce, the land was wearing out, and there was almost no market for the scrub produce and meat that was being grown on these farms. Jim wondered whether his organizational skills could make a dent in these problems.

What he knew about the mountaineer he had learned from those who lived on his farm or close at hand in Fairview. He constantly found himself caught up in the daily problems of both his own tenants and others in the community. People trusted his judgement and knew that he was always willing to help a neighbor out.

> Nov. 20—P.M. to Fairview to talk with Old Man Morgan relative to making his will—he asking my advice as 5 of W. B.'s children not his own . . .

> Nov. 21—After lunch [a] visit from O. F. Settles, with Lola heavily on his mind. Lola having become enamored of a 40–50 yr old Pegram woman.

> Dec. 2—Stopped at Uncle Mouse Freemans on [my] way home—Myrtle Bell & her new husband there—Asked Uncle Mouse what his son-in-law's name was & he replied "Let me see. Its Boyd isn't it—yes its Boyd" Was introduced to him by Myrtle Bell & found his name was Baird.

> Dec. 16—Up mt. looking for moonshiners on Rocky Point—the tip having been given me that Emory was operating near that Point. No sign of him . . .

> Jan. 5, 1920 — Zeb Nix told me he had been awakened the evening before by Bud Owenby's boys who had requested him to come & see to their sister who had cut her throat by falling on a nail. Zeb said that "he jumped out of the bed & run into my cold clothes" & found the wound bleeding badly but he stopped it. How I asked? By stuffing it with cobwebs—Where did you get the cobwebs? From the rafters, lots of them there.

The rhythms of life in the Southern mountains were a constant revelation to Jim and Elizabeth. They were fascinated by the dialect, and the endless strings of colorful sayings that helped people to understand their lives. Jim especially was genuinely appreciative of the mountain singing styles, and loved to attend the local shape-note conventions to hear family quartets sing the old-fashioned gospel songs. The quaint habits and ideas of the mountaineers were only a part of the culture that, at its best, produced men and women of strong character and determination. Very few people with Jim's background bothered to look too far below the surface of these people; the hillbilly stereotype was to most a perfectly workable model for understanding them. But while Jim was not blind to the defects within the mountain community, neither did he overlook the strengths. He had grown up in the midst of the business miracle of Chicago, and he knew that sound business organization was effective. Could he create such an enterprise in partnership with mountain farmers, and begin building up a firmer economic foundation on which to construct better churches and schools, better homes, and more opportunities for the coming generations? By 1920, Jim McClure had set his mind to just such a task. He had the support of his wife, and the full energy of a man whose health problems were behind him.

His trip up north had soured him on the prospects of a more conventional career in the ministry, and just after Christmas of 1919, he wrote down his thoughts on the church as he saw it.

> I am convinced that there is something essentially wrong with Christianity as organized today . . .
>
> I have at times thought, tho more often I have doubted, and I have always hoped that the church could be saved—feeling that it would be a shame to waste a great organization that had a hold & means of access to and opportunity to utilize so great a number of the best human elements in this country or Europe. But as I find the church continuing to be blind to and to be neutral to the great movements for the liberation of the Spirit, i.e. the labor movement, science, the increase of machines, the fight of the workers for control, the mastery of the machinery of civilization, the forcing of that nature & of commerce & industry to serve mankind & not enrich the few, the unbrotherly distribution of wealth & of political life . . . I have come to think that the church must be left aside, just as the R. C. church was at the Reformation, and that the time has come when the movement toward the development of the Spirit is hindered, more than it is helped by the church.
>
> The church is so unshaken in its allegiance to a system of metaphysics & to various forms & traditions. Christ found that organized rel[igion] was so taken up with forms & metaphysics & traditions & inhibitions that it hindered the development of the spirit more than it helped it.
>
> Luther found that organized rel[igion] was so taken up with forms & metaphysics & traditions & inhibitions that it hindered more than it helped . . .
>
> We are a race capable of great spiritual achievement, capable of arising and accomplishing things, capable of sharing the life of God, of controlling nature, of controlling the affairs of mankind so that brotherhood is produced (not a war & poverty) and we are not told these things, but our eyes are turned to unessential setting up exercises of rel[igion], to . . . quaint beliefs in heaven & to a strange assortment of metaphysical guesses. The church can not prevent us from sharing the life of God, developing our spirits, but they will have to be revolutionized or pushed aside in the doing of it.[25]

When the ink had dried on this manifesto, Jim McClure's own doubts were behind him. He wanted to carry out God's work in Western North Carolina. Perhaps, as a reporter once wrote of him in the old New York *Sun,* "Jim McClure was a minister who went wrong." But his wrong turning turned into the greatest single hope for a better life among the farmers of Western North Carolina.

1. President Woodrow Wilson, speech declaring war, April 2, 1917.

2. A popular verse at the time, cited in Bailey and Kennedy, *The American Pageant,* Sixth Edition (Lexington, Massachusetts: D. C. Heath, 1979) p. 680.

3. James G. K. McClure, Jr., letter to the editor, Chicago *Tribune,* November 28, 1914.

4. James G. K. McClure, Jr., brown notebook.

5. James G. K. McClure, Jr., 1917 notebook, dated January, 1917.

6. James G. K. McClure, Jr., brown notebook.

7. Donald C. Peattie, "Dr. Austen Fox Riggs" (An Atlantic Portrait), "The Atlantic Monthly" 168 (2), August 1941, pp. 200–207. All the general information and quotes from Dr. Riggs are from this article.

8. James G. K. McClure, Jr., "Is Peace Possible?" unpublished paper, submitted to *The New Republic* in April, 1918.

9. Interview with Elspeth McClure Clarke.

10. James G. K. McClure, Jr., "The Sin of Aachen," sermon given at Bearwallow Baptist Church, July 7, 1918.

11. *Ibid.*

12. Diary, April 13, 1919.

13. From a clipping out of the Asheville School for Boys newspaper, May 25, 1919. Found clipped in the McClure's diary.

14. Diary, September 25, 1919.

15. Elizabeth McClure, diary, October 11, 1919.

16. *Ibid.,* October 12, 1919

17. James G. K. McClure, Jr., personal notebook, October 13, 1919 (pp. 59-61).

18. Program from evening service, First Presbyterian Church, Passaic, NJ, October 12, 1919.

19. Elizabeth Cramer McClure, diary, October 12, 1919.

20. Elizabeth Cramer McClure, diary, October 13, 1919.

21. James. G. K. McClure, Jr. diary, October 21 and 23, 1919.

22. *Ibid.,* November 2, 1919.

23. *Ibid.,* November 13, 1919.

24. *Ibid.,* November 14 and 16, 1919.

25. James G. K. McClure, Jr., 1919 notebook. Written December 28, 1919 after attending the Fairview Church.

Chapter Thirteen
Farming in the Mountains of North Carolina

Dear Sirs:

The problem of the farmer must be seen from many angles before the composite and true solution can be arrived at . . .

All these . . . farm people manage to exist by working every member of the family, commencing with the child of five or six. The women are worked, literally, to death. The men work 12 hours a day and have no time for leisure or improvement of any kind. The housing conditions are worse than in the slums. In many a house in our section when the "flu" hit us there have been ten sick at the same time in a one room house and in three beds.

Farm produce has never yet brought a price high enough to warrant the replacing of the soil elements sold off in the produce . . . and farming has truly been called mining. The nitrogen, the potash and the phosphorus have been sold off the land from the Atlantic right through to the Pacific as the wave of pioneers has swept westward . . .

When he [the farmer] sees another demand for a raise from some Union, supported by the journals of opinion, and probably favored by the Government, he feels that he will have to pay for it. He fears the freight will be raised all along the line and he will pay the freight. He is beginning to feel sore. He is realizing as a farmer said to me the other day "the farmer doesn't control anything." (*James G. K. McClure, Jr., letter to the New Republic*, February 23, 1920)

James McClure had found his congregation. Scattered about a picturesque mountain terrain, in cabins built alongside clear creeks and amongst the wild laurel and rhododendron, lived one of the nation's least prosperous peoples. Jim's "church" members raised their big families in the timeless methods and habits of the subsistence farmer; at least most of them did. These men and women were of the purest Anglo-Saxon stock, frozen into a kind of permanent frontier existence. These people were an embarrassment to the race, some would say, who by their failure disproved the theories of racial superiority so beguiling to the age. So they were ignored, or worse, caricatured. The moonshine jug with a few X's on the side, the long, lanky frame, a felt hat with a feather stuck in, and of course the Kentucky rifle, mostly to be used on "revenuers" or some other brand of "furriner," were the stock props.

Most of the mountaineers in 1920 *were* independent; they rarely lived together in towns, for the simple reason that there was little commerce or

Mountain couple in Western North Carolina, 1920s. (McClure Fund Photograph Collection.)

industry to bring them there. Those who owned land lived on it. Land meant wealth, freedom and independence, or so their forefathers thought when they left England. Mostly though, in 1920, it meant taxes, hard work and a bare survival. Most of these mountain families were poor; poor at least in the way wealth is usually measured.

Jim noticed, too, a weary, disheartened look on the faces of his neighbors, and decided there was a spiritual poverty among the people, a poverty of hope. He saw it in the faces of young mothers, prematurely wrinkled from the burdens of the endless cycles of child-rearing, many of whom married in their early teens to escape the confines of their own parents. Jim always remarked that it was the faces of these women that had haunted him; he felt that he ought to try something to help them and their children. When he visited a farm, he always liked to calculate how far away the water supply was from the house, and multiply the distance by twice a day and then by 365 days in a year to estimate the miles that woman walked carrying water.

He also was disturbed by the message of hopelessness he heard in the churches. Twice on Sunday, and once on Wednesday, the best of the mountaineers attended church, and were fed on a steady diet of heaven and hell. The former was certainly going to be a lot better than the latter, but in the midst of the descriptions of everlasting torture and eternal bliss came the idea that the

present life on earth was so corrupted by sin, and the forces of Satan so power-ful, that it was an illusion to think that man could possibly improve his lot. It was best just to come on down to the old-fashioned altar and get yourself some fire insurance before it was too late. Look forward to the joy of heaven, they were told, when the misery of this life will be over. "Don't you hear the bells now ringing? Don't you hear the angels singing? Tis the glory hallelujah Jubi-lee!"[1] Jim McClure cringed in the face of this theology of hopelessness, and often came home enraged by the sermon.

> To the Fairview church with the Aunts & the Rev. Blackburn preached on the second coming . . . with a chart showing the dispensations etc. Perfectly aw-ful. E. & I were nearly wild. The man spoke from conviction for the first time. [He] said, "I do not despise education, do not despise movements for bettering conditions. These things are all right but the world can not be bettered that way-the only way is by the second coming which is immanent!" It seemed terribly wicked to exploit the aspirations of those people in that fruitless way.[2]

Jim despised the religion of resignation. But in more reflective moments he would have admitted that real opportunity was so absent in the mountains that few people could imagine life being any different. Aspirations were better left until after death, until after the testing period was complete, as fruitless an attitude as that may be. For them, living was strictly a matter of survival.

But life in the mountains did have its compensations, in spite of, or maybe even because of, its meager contact with the industrial revolution going on all around. These people were in no way homogenized by the forces of American culture. Speech in the mountains was a unique blend of coarse and earthy description, flecked with words and pronunciations more at home in a Shake-spearean play than the twentieth century United States. These people were the direct descendants of those who sat in the one-penny seats at Shakespeare's Globe Theater, and howled at the antics of Falstaff and his cronies. The speech of the isolated mountaineers had not been exposed to influences from the out-side. The place names in Western North Carolina reflect the variety of influ-ences that worked on the culture. The Cherokee Indians left a strong legacy, not only with place names like Tuckasegee and Nantahalla, but with a wide-ranging knowledge of plant and animal lore that the Europeans adopted. The plants and animals themselves were often chosen as labels, from Hickory Nut Gap to Rattlesnake Knob. From Jackson to Madison to Clay Counties and from Franklin to Democrat to Jefferson, politics left its imprint on mountain geogra-phy. The Bible (Mount Pisgah, Shiloh), the classics (Faust, Sparta), and even Greek mythology (Mars Hill, Jupiter) were popular place names. In at least once instance, a local name has entered the national language: the term bun-

Opposite: *Washing day in Western North Carolina, 1920s. (McClure Fund Photograph Collection.)*

combe or "bunk" derives from a label applied to the speeches of a particularly
long-winded member of Congress from Western North Carolina. Ferguson
Mountain, just behind Jim and Elizabeth's home, was named for the losing
British general at the Battle of King's Mountain during the Revolutionary War.
Most of all, the names in the mountains reflect the hardships, the prejudices,
the curiosities, and the humor of the inhabitants: the Devil's Elbow, Nigger
Skull Mountain, Good Luck, Loafer's Glory, Burntshirt Mountain, Cold Ass
Mountain (sanitized to "Cold" by the cartographers), 'Tater Knob and Licklog
Creek are only a few graphic examples.

If one wanted to hear the poetry and literary talents of the mountaineers in
1920, one sought out perhaps a gifted Preacher on Sunday, the old country store
on a cold winter's day, or best of all, the schoolhouse on election day. If the
preacher burned your ears for sinning, the pot-bellied orator or politician would
likely cuss you to death. There was usually quite a struggle between the sacred
and the profane, between the abstainers and the drinkers, between the honest
and the dishonest, the hardworking and the worthless. Often it was the woman
who dragged her family to church, while her husband stood outside chewing
tobacco or worse. In any event, everybody appreciated language, and the man
who could tell a good story was a popular man indeed. Rattlesnakes, panthers,
chicken thieves, whiskey and even the old Deluder, Satan himself, made frequent appearances in the mountain tales.

Yet many of these same men and women were hard pressed to write their
own names. Illiterate people hindered progress; Jim McClure's support of local
education ran parallel with his hope to bring profits to the mountain farmer. A
man who could not read would forever cling to the old ways, fear new ideas and
find it hard to embrace progressive programs. Even before he started promoting
the Farmers Federation, Jim attended the school meetings in Fairview to try to
find a way to improve local education. On one occasion, when a meeting was
to be held at the nearby Pleasant Grove School, to discuss consolidating with
the more modern one in the center of Fairview, Jim's progressive ideas were
so feared that an opposing faction tried to prevent him from attending by felling
a large tree across the road, blocking the way for his Hudson. But anyone who
really knew him knew that it would take more than one tree to discourage Jim
McClure. He arrived on foot, and when he stood up to speak, he looked into the
crowd and saw all of those wrinkled faces of the young women staring back at
him. He said later that he had resolved that evening to devote his life to those
women, their farmer husbands, and most of all to the new generation of children
who might otherwise inherit the same life of drudgery as their parents.

Once Jim had resolved to act, he immersed himself in the economics of
American agriculture. In order to understand the work of the Farmers Federation, it is important to try to grasp at least the primary threads of this subject,
one that has been of great discomfort to the American body politic throughout
the twentieth century. The "farm problem" is as old as civilization. Agriculture
is the most vital of topics, not only because it is the source of man's food, but

Young girls hoeing corn on steep mountain land in Western North Carolina. (McClure Fund Photograph Collection.)

also because all the rest of society must rest on its foundation. Throughout the ages, until recently, virtually everyone spent all of his time working the soil. Civilization, which first appeared in the irrigated river valleys of Mesopotamia and the Nile, was (and still is) impossible without a food surplus that frees up a portion of the population from the toil of farming to specialize in a skill or profession. The growth of towns and cities is dependent on the countryside for food. In fact, there are so many religious, social and economic ramifications within the subject of agriculture that its history is easily the most important component in understanding man's past and present.

The American present in the agricultural history of mankind is so remarkable that scarcely anyone could have predicted it. That so few people can feed so many is a fact whose true significance is scarcely appreciated. There has been no American revolution to equal the changes in agriculture that this country has pioneered. The rapid process of change also has caused its inevitable share of side effects and social dislocations. Even today, the prospects for a new wave of agricultural miracles lies just behind the exciting research into genetic engineering, but at the same time the difficulties of overzealous pesticide use, monoculture and soil erosion make one pause to wonder about the benefits of progress.

The pace of change in agriculture picked up after the Civil War as new machinery and techniques began to appear. The source of the McCormick fortune was the marvel of the age: a mechanical reaper that virtually replaced the scythe, an implement that had been used for more than 10,000 years. As one agricultural historian explained, " . . . Production and marketing functions began to peel off the farming operations. Farm machinery and implements became more productive and more complicated, and had to be produced . . . in factories."[3] Farming itself became specialized. Transportation, marketing, processing and supplying for the crops took many of the tasks of previous generations of farmers elsewhere. Wise capital investment became the key element of success, and debt the common cause of personal disaster. The social and economic ramifications of these changes created an understandable sense of loss of independence, and independence was perhaps the strongest value of the family farmer. All of the uncertainties found expression through organizations such as the Grangers and the Populist Party. Writers like Frank Norris, and later John Steinbeck, wrote movingly of characters crushed between invisible economic forces that seemed more evil for their impersonality.

These forces are now rather well understood. In the parlance of the economist, farm prices are extremely inelastic. It has been shown that to increase per-capita food consumption by 2 percent required a 10 percent decline in *retail* food prices, which translates to a 20 percent decline in *farm* food product prices. In other words, "Farmers are at the crack end of the price whip."[4] The " . . . face of market demand is precipitous: supply the market with a little more than it will take and the extra amount tumbles over the edge of the glacier and sells for a price at the bottom of the precipice. However, not only does the extra amount sell at a price at the bottom . . . but *all* the products sell at . . . [that] price. . . ."[5]

Outside of the vagaries of export, there is only one way for the market demand for American food to increase: more Americans. People might substitute roast beef for hamburger, or wine for milk, but there is a real limit to the total bulk one person can eat. A product manufacturer, on the other hand, can continually dream up new gadgets, stimulate demand for his goods with advertising, and try to manage supply to avoid over-production. Even then, the company has the advantage of being able to manipulate the price to stimulate customers. The farmer has no control over his price; he looks in the newspaper and takes what is offered, or leaves it and hopes for an improvement the next day. The total demand for food will not budge even with the best advertising, although people can be convinced to shift items on their grocery lists. Furthermore, over-production in the agricultural sector is very difficult to prevent, and as has been shown, is the worst enemy of the farmer. He, as one individual, will borrow money to buy a new tractor and machinery. He then needs to reap the biggest return possible to pay his bills. The new machinery increases his productivity, but when the increases are multiplied across the country, oversupplies are almost assured. Through price supports, allotments, market advice, and even paying farmers not to plant, the federal government has erected a rather byzantine structure to try to cope with this problem. The results are controversial at best.

During the years that Jim McClure began farming in North Carolina a milestone in American agriculture slipped by almost unnoticed.

> The farm economy crossed a great divide during 1910–20. Farm employment increased in every decade up until that one and thereafter declined . . .
>
> Output per worker jumped unpredictably before 1910; after that it skyrocketed . . .
>
> Something fundamental to or about farming in the United States changed between 1910 and 1920. Before then the national farm plant grew and developed by territorial expansion and an increased number of farmers. After 1920 it continued to grow, but in a new way; it grew through capital formation, the adoption of new and improved practices and technology, and improved management.[6]

The number of farm workers and the amount of acreage under production actually declined after 1920, despite the increasing production. The marginal family farms went out of business, and the surplus agricultural labor moved to the cities. "The traditional approach to farming—son learning from father and farming as his father and grandfather had before him—had crumbled slowly during the nineteenth century, and was shattered completely during the 1920s by the gasoline engine, the tractor."[7]

During the early twenties, when most of the American economy was decidedly upbeat, the agricultural sector plunged into an early depression. Several economic forces collided, conspiring together to glut nearly every commodity market. First of all, the preceding two decades had been lush times for the farmer. From 1900 to 1910, farm prices increased 40 per cent. The large influx of immigrants helped to push up the national population 21 percent while farm output jumped only 4 percent. The next decade was even more profitable. Output still lagged behind population growth, but much more dramatically. World War I opened up the enormous European markets to a continent too preoccupied with war to grow its own food.[8] Two decades of rapidly rising demand stimulated agricultural production in the United States. New equipment, new techniques and better management were all pressed into service to supply the customers. The addition of the tractor meant that several acres previously tilled to feed the draft horses and mules could now be used to grow food for sale. When the war ended, however, the Europeans began to seal off their home markets and American agriculture immediately found itself overproducing. "After World War I, farm prices fell sharply . . . That decade was not a happy one because so many farmers paid the price—business failure—for the land speculation of the preceding decade. But conditions could and did get much worse. The relation between population and farm output became decidedly unfavorable to farms during the unhappy 1930s: the population growth increased only 7 per cent and farm output 11. The consequence once again was tumbling farm prices and badly depressed farm incomes."[9]

Jim McClure's dream was to bring cash to the mountain farm by integrating the region's farming resources into the national agricultural system through the introduction of modern agricultural methods and a strong marketing effort. As it turned out, he picked the worst possible moment to try to plug in: for two decades that system remained ill, some thought terminally so. The year 1920 began favorably enough, but "Twelve months later prosperity had evaporated and farmers were confronted by the worst agricultural depression they had ever known."[10]

The short-term factor that kicked off the decline was the post-war deregulation of several spheres of the economy that had been managed by the government during the war crisis. The de-control of railroad freight rates, the end of the War Finance Corporation, and the elimination of government wheat supports all had a direct bearing on agriculture. To cope with the post-war inflation, the Federal Reserve Board pushed up interest rates, which cost the farmers in higher interest payments. The long-run effects, however, were what kept agriculture on the ropes. Foreign orders for American grain immediately went slack and prices plummeted. Two decades of prosperity had built up the cumulative agricultural productive capacity of the nation to levels domestic consumption alone could never sustain. From June to December of 1920, agricultural prices slipped an average of 40 percent.[11] Disaster had struck, and the torturous relationship between farm interests and government policy began to heat up in earnest. Jim McClure launched the Farmers Federation in the midst of this crisis. It may have been in large part because of his determined effort that the Federation survived these early years, but truly the mountain farmers had been in such perpetual depression for so long, and were so isolated from the national economy anyway, that the problems of Iowa or Kansas made hardly a ripple in Western North Carolina.

But the sharp drop in prices did create momentum across the country for cooperative agricultural movements. Joseph Knapp, an authority on the subject, wrote: "The year 1920 produced a veritable explosion in cooperative activity that brought a doubling of cooperative marketing business within five years. A combination of factors contributed. Most important was the severe post-World War I depression which led to chronic agricultural distress in the face of general business recovery. The depression awakened interest in cooperative marketing as a means of restoring farm prosperity, and it gave birth to a strong demand for monopolistic commodity marketing cooperatives that could control farm product prices.[12] The impetus, then, was for the wheat or tobacco or cotton growers to band together to sell their product as one seller, and command a higher, monopolistic price. This is known as selling on a "commodity basis." The difficulty with this kind of a program is the great discipline required of individual members not to create a break in the monopoly price. Cartels are notoriously unstable.

One remarkable man worked tirelessly to promote this system among the different commodity associations in the United States. Aaron Sapiro started organizing in California with the prune and raisin growers. Later, almost by chance, he found himself in Mobile, Alabama, in April 1920 at the annual meeting of the American Cotton Association. Even though his name was not on the program, Aaron Sapiro took that meeting by storm. Under his direction, a National Cotton Exchange was organized to sell, warehouse, finance and transport cotton. Sapiro next turned to both the flue-cured and burley tobacco markets, both of which were reeling because of price drops in 1920. The momentum of his ideas increased rapidly throughout the agricultural community. His theory included these requirements: organization on a commodity basis [rather than by region], democratic control by the members, long term and binding contracts, orderly and businesslike marketing, and the control of a sufficient proportion of the entire crop to dominate the market.[13] Jim McClure was well aware of Sapiro's activities, and tapped into his sense of mission and enthusiasm. But, unfortunately for Western North Carolina, there was no commodity with which it could compete in the national market, and so the Farmers Federation by necessity had to organize on a regional, not a commodity, basis. Moreover, Jim McClure was interested in more than economics. He wanted the mountain people to build for themselves a rural civilization based on the highest of spiritual values, so to him the marketing of farm produce was really only the means to an end. In time, the weaknesses in "Sapiroism" began to overshadow the movement, and by about 1925 it had lost its fervor.[14] Mere market power had been unable to combat the problem of over-production, and without coercion the monopolies became difficult to maintain. Yet Aaron Sapiro was one of the most remarkable and influential men of the history of the American cooperative movement, and his efforts created a favorable climate in which many such organizations thrived. The Farmers Federation was one.

In Western North Carolina, over-production, monopoly power and modern technology were concepts as alien as if the region occupied a forgotten corner of the Himalayas rather than the Appalachians. Larger than several states, the region the Farmers Federation eventually served was sliced and criss-crossed with mountain ranges more formidable and extensive than any others east of the Mississippi. Along the rivers and creeks the soil could be rich and fruitful, but more often, especially on the more rocky upland farms, it had been exhausted by short-sighted farming methods Jim McClure always likened more to mining than agriculture. The more one climbed the hillsides, the more the soil thinned out, and yet in 1920 many an Appalachian family survived on a farm perched overlooking the most prosperous bottom lands in the valley. Cash on these marginal farms was the scarcest of commodities: it was hoarded to pay taxes, and to buy a little salt and sugar. At Christmas time, a Florida orange and a big dinner was about all a child could hope for.

In 1920 there were no reliable cash crops in the mountains. The railroad brought the local farmers into competition with the more efficient, quality oriented farmers elsewhere in the United States, with the result that even the small population centers in Western North Carolina were fed to a large extent by farmers outside the region. During the early years of the Farmers Federation, the composite picture of mountain agriculture was bleak. If one traveled about in the 1920s, the visual evidence of one run-down farm after another would have been convincing enough. But in 1928, the governor of North Carolina received a "Report of the Tax Commission" that substantiated, with a series of grim statistics, how thin the economic base of life in the mountains was. The Commission studied 281 mountain farms from Jackson, McDowell and Ashe Counties. These farms were chosen to represent the actual diversity of the area as closely as possible, and then were studied by economists in great detail. One can only imagine what comic scenes developed when these representatives of academia invaded the mountaineers' home turf. For certain though, the farmers were given a great opportunity to pull pranks on the city folks, and for years afterwards the best of them were told and retold around the wood stove on a cold winter's day. There was no sport in the mountains better than aggravating invaders. One also wonders how anyone representing a tax commission could maneuver around at all. But the data rolled into Raleigh, outlining the shocking truth that agriculture in the mountains was not only providing little income, but in fact represented negative profit. As meager as the farmers' capital investments were, they were producing on average a negative return of –$192 or –3.4 percent. There were no incentives, clearly, to increase production by buying machinery, or more land, or even a better mule. Agriculture was simply a strategy for survival, the only option available outside of the logging camps. Discounting the unpaid wages of the farmer and his family, the average cash income for these mountain farmers in 1927 was $86 a year. Eighty-six dollars before taxes translated, when spread amongst the farmer's large family, into bare feet, homespun clothing, and a psychology of hopelessness that bothered Jim McClure more than anything else. Many farms, especially in Buncombe and Henderson Counties, were no doubt much more prosperous than these figures indicate, but on the other hand there were many farms where the $86 would have been a boom year.[15] It is no wonder that men turned to moonshine, for cash and consolation. How powerful the vision of that heavenly "city of gold" described by the preachers must have appeared when compared to the drab realities of life in this world.

In the starkest of contrasts, the city of Asheville glittered during the twenties as an earthly "city of gold," with a tempo that never skipped a beat throughout the Jazz Age. It was condemned by the local Baptist ministers as a magnet of vice and temptation. Wealthy patrons flocked in to enjoy the pleasures of the climate and the comforts of some of the most luxurious resort hotels in the United States. It was the town and the time of Thomas Wolfe. Asheville had earned the renown of the rich and famous, and became for a time their summer playground. George Vanderbilt had moved in earlier, to give the town one of the most monumental expressions of the gilded age anywhere in the country, the chateau known as Biltmore House. He also constructed the little town of Biltmore, with an integrated architecture of red roof tiles and stucco, to house and maintain the artisans who built the house and other employees of his estate. If the Vanderbilts represented a dying age during the twenties, Zelda and Scott Fitzgerald were the most notorious, the most frenetic harbingers of the new. And they too brought their show to Asheville. But if Asheville was enjoying its historical moment in the sun, those who lived in the countryside couldn't have cared less.

The local farmers could only sell perishable goods such as milk, butter, cream, fresh vegetables and fruit to this elite population. The railroads had created the Asheville boom, bringing in and taking away 250,000 visitors a summer,[16] and they also brought in the high quality food these visitors demanded. The choice meats, produce, eggs and potatoes that suited this clientele were not being grown by the mountain farmers. Ignorance and lack of capital meant that even the lucrative local market was being eroded away by outside farmers who bought quality seed and standardized breeds and practiced improved farming techniques. Even though potatoes are a crop well-suited to Western North Carolina, the guests at the Grove Park Inn preferred that their roast beef be complemented with a big baked potato from Maine, and therein lay the challenge before Jim McClure.

The same railroad that brought down potatoes from Maine also supplied the mountain farmers with fertilizer, lime, seeds and implements. But these farms were comparatively small, and lacked bulk buying opportunities. Buying supplies usually meant a day lost driving behind the old mule to the local feed and seed store. These stores themselves usually sold a low volume, and were often poorly stocked in a region plagued by notoriously poor roads. So the farmers paid dearly for what few agricultural supplies they could afford to buy. Selling produce was equally inefficient. The wagon was hitched up again and driven into the town square. In Asheville, the usual market was around Pack Square, and the farmers would spend the day with their load, haggling with the customers, swapping tales and chewing tobacco. It could be a pleasant day away from the routine of farming, and a chance for father and son to explore the delights of urban life. But all too often the journey home was spoiled by the meager return a year's work brought to the man and his family. It seemed as if every farmer picked his beans or dug his potatoes the same day, and nobody wanted to haul his load back home again. Towards the evening, when the farmers were ready to leave, the market tilted in favor of the buyers, first one farmer and then another would sell out for a pittance, reducing the value of his labors to almost nothing. Jim McClure ran up against the same problem. He combatted it by lining up his buyers ahead of time at hospitals and hotels, and endeavoring to grow a superior product. If he could not find his price, he brought the load back home. But he discovered early on that inferior products marketed in a haphazard fashion had almost killed and buried any profit in mountain farming.

Mountain farmer plowing with a matched pair of horses. (McClure Fund Photograph Collection.)

Prior to 1920, there had been at least two healthy spells of farming in the mountains, especially in Buncombe and Henderson Counties. An excellent turnpike road was built in 1827 that connected Tennessee, Kentucky and Western North Carolina with markets in Charleston and Augusta. Upwards of 170,000 hogs ambled through on this and other roads before the Civil War destroyed this commerce. It took bushels of corn to feed these animals each evening, stimulating such a demand that a surprisingly large number of slaves were purchased as laborers in areas near the road. After the war, from roughly 1870 to 1890, a flue-cured tobacco boom brought cash to the mountains. Curing barns in the countryside and warehouses and factories in Asheville sprang up like mushrooms in the rich soil of tobacco profits. Mountain leaf was popular as the wrapper for cigars, but, by the turn of the century, the introduction of cigarettes along with competition from Eastern North Carolina ruined mountain tobacco markets. Jim McClure helped to bring tobacco culture (and cash) back into the mountains during the Twenties, with the introduction of the Burley variety. Unfortunately, the intensive culture of both corn and tobacco during the Nineteenth Century, without the means or knowledge of the use of proper fertilizers, had left many of the farms with lifeless, eroded soil, creating a further challenge for the Federation.

Jim McClure was not the first man to attempt to organize the farmers of

Traveling the roads of Western North Carolina. (McClure Fund Photograph Collection.)

Western North Carolina, although he was by far the most successful. In 1873, the Grange movement had three chapters in Buncombe County.[17] As was the pattern elsewhere, though, the Grangers became discouraged when their over-blown expectations could not be realized, and the meetings sank into mere conviviality.[18] The shrill political ideas of the Farmers Alliance vocalized the next wave of discontent. That group's strong stands in favor of better education, self-government at the county level, an increase in the amount of money in circulation (the silver issue), higher farm prices, and regulation of the railroads by the government were later co-opted by the likes of the populist orators Tom Watson of Georgia and "Pitchfork" Ben Tillman of South Carolina. In North Carolina, the Farmers' Alliance went political in 1890. Many of their candidates were elected to the General Assembly, and this woke up the entrenched and complacent Democratic Party. But the Alliance's "farmers' legislature" failed to solve the financial problems of North Carolina despite its free-spending ways. As Theodore Saloutos explained in his book on farmer's organizations, it was because the rhetoric did not match the reality. "Alliance, instead of realizing that they, as farmers, were becoming the victims of sweeping economic changes to which they would have to make radical adjustments, preferred to believe that they were the victims of a money-mad society . . . The Alliancemen were simply stumbling in the dark in search of a working formula that would put more of the earnings of 'productive toil' into their pockets, and they called this formula 'cooperation.'"[19] The final wave of farmer protest and organization came through the efforts of the Farmers' Union, which derived its intellectual suste-

Mountain boys thinking about hoeing corn. O.T. Ashe's boys on the left, with Tom Anderson's boy on the right, Shooting Creek Section of Clay County, June 7, 1946. (McClure Fund Photograph Collection.)

nance from the free spirit of the Progressive Era. When Jim arrived in Buncombe County, there was the vestige of the Union locally, and a pathetic cooperative store near Fairview in Oakley.[20] Much of the appeal of the Farmers' Union came from the fascination with secret rituals and "bawdy horseplay." Many joined out of simple curiosity, just to learn the secrets.[21] Despite the ineffectiveness of these three organizations, the Grange, the Alliance and the Farmers' Union did help to encourage progressive agricultural techniques. But, as each wave came and went, as leaders rose and fell, enthusiasm was replaced by suspicion and cynicism. In the South, racial tensions tended to blunt the ability of these groups to make a political impact. For example, the Alliance was completely destroyed when the Democratic Party began preaching race hatred, thwarting the efforts of the Alliance leaders to unite the power of black and white farmers in North Carolina.

Jim McClure began selling stock in the Farmers Federation in the midst of the memories of all those failed attempts to help the farmer. A sharp gambling man would have given him long odds on success. The three organizations that preceded him all had a wide base of national support, and yet each died as the bloom of enthusiasm wore off. He was attempting to create a business over a rather large geographical area with an abysmal transportation system, among farmers with a high rate of illiteracy whose agricultural practices lagged far behind the competition's. The Federation was to be a boot-strap, self-financed organization in a region that was extremely cash deficient. He would have insufficient operating capital, no well-established outside market for crops, and himself as president, a man more knowledgeable about theological trends in Germany than agriculture in Western North Carolina. Moreover, the last time he had worked hard, his health had broken down within ten months. The very thought of a Yankee preacher, and liberal one at that, coming into the mountains and organizing a group of people who had little more than their own sense of independence to be proud of, seems in retrospect a preposterous scheme. How could he possibly hope to create a business out of thin air that would not only pay its own bills, but also pay dividends to its members? How could such an organization expect to survive the first little adverse business ripple? Undoubtedly many discouraging remarks were made both to Jim and behind his back about his scheme to help the mountain farmers by the bankers in Asheville and the residents of the hollows out in the countryside. But Jim's mind was made up; his course was set. He believed that men and women who dared to dream great visions were given the strength and support of the Lord God Almighty. With his own mind firmly committed, he could persuade people to believe in the impossible. For more than forty years the Farmers Federation served as an agency of change in Western North Carolina, as a cutting edge of progress. It became the great work of its founder and long-time president, reflecting his ideas and his urge to serve mankind until his death in 1956.

1. "When They Ring the Golden Bells," copyright 1887 by Dion DeMarbelle. Used by permission of the John Church Co., owners of copyright. Found in the Church Hymnal, (Cleveland, Tennessee: Tennessee Music and Printing Company, 1951), p.294.

2. James G. K. McClure, Jr., diary, June 13, 1920.

3. William W. Cochrane, *The City Man's Guide to the Farm Problem* (Minneapolis: University of Minnesota Press, 1965), p. 3.

4. *Ibid.*, p. 81.

5. *Ibid.*, p. 85.

6. *Ibid.*, p. 26.

7. *Ibid.*, p.27.

8. *Ibid.*

9. *Ibid.*, p. 28.

10. Joseph Knapp, *The Advance of American Cooperative Enterprise: 1920–1945* (Danville, Illinois: Interstate Printers and Publishers, 1973), p. 5.

11. *Ibid.*, p.6.

12. *Ibid.*, p. 3.

13. *Ibid.*, p. 7–9.

14. *Ibid.*, p. 74–75.

15. "Report of the Tax Commission to Governor Angus Wilton McLean," authorized by the 1927 General Assembly, Raleigh, 1928.

16. Talmage Powell, "Asheville: An Historical Sketch," Doug Swaim, editor, found

in *Cabins and Castles: The History and Architecture of Buncombe County, North Carolina*. (Asheville, N.C.: Historic Resources Commission of Asheville and Buncombe County, 1981), p. 43.

17. John Ager, "Buncombe County: A Brief History," in *Cabins and Castles* . . . *Op Cit.*, p. 22.

18. Theodore Saloutos, *Farmer Movements in the South, 1865–1933*, (Lincoln, Nebraska: University of Nebraska Press, 1960), p. 41.

19. *Ibid.*, p. 88–89.

20. Interview with Guy Sales.

21. Op Cit., Saloutos, *Farmers Movements* . . . , p.87.

Chapter Fourteen
The Farmers Federation

The greatest agricultural possibilities of the mountain country, indeed, can only be realized through the growth of the co-operative movement. Until the farmers of a neighborhood far from market join in some definite co-operative undertaking . . . the efforts of the individual farmer will fall far short of their desert, no matter how excellent his method."[1] *John C. Campbell*

[Jim] is still running the "Federation of Farmers" which has many ramifications & it seems too funny that he, a "town" man, should be President of a Farmers' Concern. (*Elizabeth Cramer McClure to Harriet McClure Stuart, January 12, 1920*)

By the spring of 1920, the Fairview Farmers Federation was duly organized and incorporated under the laws of North Carolina, and by the next fall it had grown so fast that the "Fairview" in the name had to be dropped. Suddenly, Jim McClure became surrounded by an organization that required all of his energies, all of his intellect, and most of all, every ounce of his famous charm. At times he dragged the Federation along as a dead weight in impossible circumstances, and at other times he just did his best to keep up with the momentum. After all the years of frustration, Jim McClure was back to work. He was satisfying his deepest convictions with an energy that infected those around him. The Farmers Federation was on the move, and so was James Gore King McClure, Jr.

Fourteen years later, Jim reminisced about those early days at the annual meeting of "The New York Farmers," a group of wealthy gentleman farmers.

We started in 1920 and had a little meeting in a log cabin, when we had a committee of five of these mountain farmers. We had the organization meeting in a log cabin where the family could not go to bed until after we got through with our meeting, because there was just one room with the beds in it. At this meeting we decided to put up a shed on a side track, which we were to put in ourselves. We have since put up two additions on this shed. We started in with one manager. At first we thought one of the directors would open the building on a Tuesday and another on Saturday, but we decided to risk employing a manager by the month. Within six weeks we had to have an assistant and within another six weeks we had to have another one. Then the movement began to spread.[2]

Despite the romance conjured up by this log cabin meeting, the most important of these early gatherings probably took place in Tom Nesbitt's modest frame house in Fairview. Mr. Nesbitt was a farmer who milked a few cows and raised a few crops to peddle around Asheville but like most farmers at this time he made a meager living for all his efforts. Around his fireside the members of the Federation took the courageous step to launch themselves as a business enterprise.[3]

In 1920, when the Farmers Federation was organized, there were no special laws set up in North Carolina under which the cooperative could be created, so these men incorporated under the general business laws of the State, and became a cooperative through their by-laws. These by-laws followed the Rochdale plan. The Equitable Pioneers of Rochdale, England, were a group of unemployed weavers who in 1844, with twenty-eight pounds, began the first consumers' cooperative. The weavers, like the farmers of Western North Carolina, were worried about the cost of their supplies, and so pooled their buying power to reduce their costs. The two distinguishing features of the Rochdale system were the financial structure and how voting power was organized. First of all, everyone who joined, no matter how many shares of stock he or she owned, was entitled to one vote. The usual corporate law is one share, one vote; but in a region where cash was scarce and suspicion of "big money" people was rampant, "one man, one vote" avoided disputes over control of the organization that could have blown the Farmers Federation away in the first discouraging wind. The second Rochdale fundamental incorporated into the Farmers Federation determined that all supplies were to be sold at prevailing retail rates. At the end of the year, after all the expenses were paid, each member would be given credit for his or her share of the profits, based on the quantity of business done during that period of time. Some profits were held out to be distributed to the stockholders, and some were plowed back into the organization. The Rochdale system of co-operation was created to serve its members, not make a profit. But its finances were based on sound business methods.

Jim McClure was elected President of the Fairview Farmers Federation, and although he offered to resign in favor of someone else near the beginning, he was always re-elected by the directors until his death thirty-six years later. At the first meeting a neighbor, S. J. Ashworth, was elected Vice President, and G. L. Clay was chosen as Secretary-Treasurer and Business Agent. Jim McClure believed in involving as many people as possible in an organization, so that they would feel interested and responsible. He wanted the work done for the Federation to be meaningful, to give those involved a feeling that their efforts promoted an enterprise of high purposes, of God's purpose. Jim McClure's notions were based as much on the Apostle Paul's description of the "body of Christ," where each member contributed his God-endowed gifts for the consecration of the whole, as they were on the modern business practices that had surrounded him in Lake Forest. He worked to pull in as many hands, feet and mouths as he could, and in those early days of the Federation he cajoled the strongest men of each of Fairview's districts to be on the Finance Committee. Added to the officers, then, the following men were appointed to solicit subscriptions of stock: Boyce Miller of Laurel Bluff, Ottis Briggs of Cane Creek, Henry Garren of Pleasant Grove, John B. Merrill of Brush Creek, Albert Reed of Gashes Creek and R. T. Merrill of Gap Creek.

On June 19, 1920, the directors decided that the Federation should print up a news sheet to promote its ideas, and chose Winslow Freeman as its first managing editor. This publication grew with the organization, and was itself a powerful agent for change in the region. Community news, recipes, morale boosting, constipation remedies and great quantities of hard-nosed agricultural information were the staple of the Farmers Federation *News*. To a region starved for reliable information about proven farming techniques, the *News* was influential beyond measure.

Volume 1, No. 1 of the *Fairview Farmers' News Sheet,* was published July 15, 1920. Jim McClure wrote most of the editorials, and his first is a wonderful expression of his enthusiasm and the early spirit of the Federation.

HELP YOURSELF

Every one knows that the farmer is up against it, and the farmer knows it better than any one else . . . He cannot help his children at home because he cannot offer them what they can get under the shadow of the big smokestacks . . .

There is a great deal of talk about helping the farmer. That kind of talk does not accomplish anything. The only man who is going to help the farmer is the farmer himself. The farmer has got to save himself, and what is more, he can do it.

The one and only way that the farmer can help himself is to control the price of his product. At present the farmer does not control the price of the stuff he produces, and until he does control it he will never be safe. As a step toward controlling what we produce, we plan to put up this warehouse on the Fairview siding. It can help every man in this section. It has great possibilities, but it can only do us good if we all stick to it. We have a chance now to help ourselves get ahead, so let every man in this section put his shoulder to the wheel and keep grunting.[4]

This first project of the Federation was to build a warehouse along the railroad near Fairview, in order to sell supplies and handle crops. Stock (at $50 per share) could be "bought" by helping to build this structure, and so the first *News Sheet* issued:

A CALL FROM THE FOREMAN

The Federation of Farmers of Fairview have completed plans for the warehouse which they are planning to build at the Fairview siding.

They are hoping that each farmer in the township will take at least one share of stock in the warehouse. These shares may be bought with material at market ·prices or by labor. The material may be delivered at the siding or at Fairview. Labor is required to extend the siding and to build the warehouse.

"Goodbye Forever"—cartoon in the Asheville Citizen, *July 5, 1924.*

    The prices: Muscle men, $3 per day
teams, $5 per day
Material at market prices as follows:
One set switch ties.
120 cross ties, first class
4 pieces 6 × 8, 10¼ feet long . . .

The *News Sheet* also urged readers to:

SET YOUR ALARM FOR AUGUST FIRST

    . . . We have arranged with the railroad to furnish the labor for all the work on the siding. They will furnish a foreman who will boss the job. This will give a chance to all the muscle men and all who can tap a spike on the head to earn a share of stock or at least make a running start toward a share . . .

FINANCING THE WAREHOUSE

A day or two after this paper reaches you the members of the finance committee will start around to solicit subscriptions. BE READY FOR THEM.

We will have to pay for three car lengths of track and for moving the switch. Two of these car lengths will be beside the warehouse and one will be for loading directly from wagons or trucks. We will also have to pay for our warehouse and having working capital in addition.

Stock can be taken in either one of three ways: (1) By full payment in cash, or by check. If it is possible, take your stock in this way, for we have to make a deposit of eight hundred dollars with the railroad company at once and we will need a substantial sum for the warehouse and working capital.

(2) Stock may be taken in work or materials. . . .

(3) Stock may be taken as outlined in the plan by the payment of ten dollars down and giving your note for the balance, which shall be paid out of your profits before any cash profits are returned to you.

Every farmer in this section should be able to pay ten dollars down in cash, or in materials or labor and so obtain the benefits of this cooperative enterprise.

One fifty dollar share is the minimum required to become a stockholder. It is expected that those who will do more than a minimum business . . . will take from two to four shares . . . This project cannot go through unless many of us make a sacrifice in the present for future advantages. The only rule that we have made is TAKE ALL THE STOCK YOU CAN AND THEN SOME.

LOOK OUT, FARMERS!

Don't let this opportunity slip through your fingers! If we farmers in this section will all go into this warehouse proposition and do our business through it, we can control the entire output of this section. "Now you've said something." We can write to companies with which we want to do business to meet our terms and they will. The united selling and purchasing power of the territory which feeds into this siding is great. We will never get any advantages from our power if we remain individual buyers and sellers . . .

WHAT IS WRONG WITH THE ASHEVILLE MARKET?

The other day with potatoes wholesaling for $4 and retailing at from $6 to $7, a Rutherford farmer came into the market and sold a few bushels at $2. The whole market dropped right down.

The trouble is with us farmers and not with the market. The farmer who sells his produce at less than what it costs to produce it plus a fair profit is robbing all the rest of us. As far as the writer of this article knows, no Northern potatoes are shipped into Asheville until September. The Western North Carolina farmers supply the market and in addition 100,000 summer visitors. The market will pay what we ask if we all stand together. If the farmers of Western North Carolina only knew it they could hold the summer market right where they wanted to.

. . . We must work toward all standing together or quit the farm.[5]

The *News Sheet* continues discussing potatoes, specifically THE FEDERA-
TION POTATO, that soon will be narrowed down to two varieties, with strict
specifications to make the grade. Cabbages are mentioned, along with Mr.
Clifford Shuford's "decision to launch upon the sea of matrimony at some future
date" with an unmentioned accomplice. Finally, Jim McClure described THE
PLAN, the by-laws of the Federation based on the work of those Rochdale
weavers.

Many of the ideas on which the Federation was based came from a remarkable young man who became something of a legend in Southern agriculture and
the cooperative movement. With zeal and common sense, he promoted modern
agriculture and farmer's cooperatives as the editor of North Carolina's own
magazine, born with the Farmers Alliance Movement, *The Progressive Farmer*.
The young man's name was Clarence Poe, and he spent his lifetime formulating
practical solutions to the problems of the Southern farmer. Naturally, he and Jim
became friends. But before they met, Jim knew Clarence Poe from his book
How Farmers Co-Operate and Double Profit, which Jim used as a blueprint for
the Federation. For example, Poe made these comments and suggestions in his
book:

> Agricultural co-operation on the whole . . . means simply that the farmer
> must take control of all phases of his own business . . .[6]

> [They] . . . may adopt the best marketing system on earth, but they must
> also do better farming or lose out in competition with other sections.[7]

> [One system for robbing the farmer. Your product is shipped off and when
> the report comes back it might read] . . . market glutted since you started your
> shipment; prices all off, . . . [or] Your shipment reached us in bad condition;
> will command only one-half or two-thirds regular market price." And in such
> cases, what redress has the small unorganized trucker? He cannot afford to
> make a trip to New York or Buffalo or Chicago, . . . to see whether the report
> is correct or not. He must take what is offered.[8]

> No sort of movement for rural co-operation or for the development of a
> greater rural civilization can win large success unless it recognizes and makes
> room for the country woman; and it is also true that the man will never
> organize the women.[9]

Against all odds, the early years of the Farmers Federation saw an organization take root and grow like the most persistent of weeds, in a soil few thought
could support life of any sort. Jim's wife encouraged him at home, but the early
enthusiasm of the local farmers in Fairview was crucial to the Federation's
growth. The work of raising sums of money through stock sales, promoting the
ideas in new sections of Buncombe County, and soon enough in new counties,
fell to a very hardworking group of men who followed Jim's leadership. These
men volunteered to spend time away from their own farms to serve the Federa-

"Watch Us Grow!" September 23, Farmers Federation News.

tion. In addition to the farmers of Fairview who have already been mentioned, some of the early "strongmen" behind Jim McClure were Church Crowell of Enka, a former state legislator, and Allan Coggins, "the mayor of Bee Tree," both graduates of the University of North Carolina. S. C. Clapp of the State Test Farm at Swannanoa, North Carolina, and C. C. Profitt, agricultural extension agent for Buncombe County, also helped.

With the second issue of the *News* in November 1920, the Federation had grown to 150 members, and could boast a substantial warehouse along the Southern Railroad tracks between Fairview and Asheville. The roll call of members that appeared in that issue represented the first time most of these men and women had ever seen their names in print. These members read the *News* with great interest, and learned the grim truth that just at the birth of their organization, the bottom was dropping out of American farm prices.

HAMMER THE FARMER

Right now you can see the process of hammering the farmer going on. Prices are coming down. The papers are carrying big headlines every day. There is a strong campaign on to hammer down the cost of living. As usual the heaviest blow falls on the farmer. Wages are not going down and we are all glad to see them stay up. But the farmer's wage has been driven down lower than any other thing. The farmer's wage is the price of his potatoes, his apples, his cabbage, his cattle, his cow, and the farmer's wage is being reduced 50%. . . .

Hollering and grumbling will not, however, do us any good. If we want relief, we farmers will have to get it ourselves. And we already have here in this section the beginning of relief, the point of the wedge . . . The warehouse and siding is our best chance. To make this proposition go we will have to get behind it and stay there. We will have to be patient with it. It is a baby and will have to be nursed along for some time. Give it two or three years. Don't expect it to set the price or to sell produce at fancy prices yet awhile. Don't expect it to be able to handle everything right at once. Give the Federation time to grow and the officers time to learn the ways.[10]

Clearly, Jim wanted the members to keep their expectations in line with realistic prospects. He preached solidarity and discipline to his stockholders, knowing full well that soon enough the beauty of the new bloom would begin to fade in the face of unrealized expectations.

THROW AWAY A NICKEL ONCE IN A WHILE

Don't lose that dollar because you can't see it for the nickel in your eye. Throw away the nickel and pick up the dollar.

When some one offers you cottonseed meal cheaper than the Federation is selling it and you think you can save a nickel, just remember that dollar. You know what cottonseed meal sold for before the Federation got its first car and sold it for $2.50. The Federation brought the market down, and every man in this section is getting the advantage of it.

If someone cuts under us a nickel or a dime and you only see the nickel and quit the Federation to buy from him, just remember that if the Federation is put out of business the price will jump right up again. You will save your nickel but lose your dollar.

Stick to the Federation. Glue to it. It has saved this section hundreds of dollars on fertilizer and meal already. And remember that you get your profits back at the end of the year.

STICK TO IT! GLUE TO IT! TRADE WITH IT! IT IS OUR BEST AND ONLY CHANCE.[11]

Not only did Jim McClure have to worry about the price of cottonseed meal and the defection of members, but in order for the Federation to survive, he had to find some way to market the products of Western North Carolina. In 1920, these products lagged behind other parts of the country in quality and standardization. From potatoes to hogs to chickens to beef cattle to string beans, the mountain farmer invariably grew crops from inferior seed or bred animals of poor genetic quality. Then, the cash starved farmer under-fertilized, or under-fed what he was raising, often using methods long ago discarded as inefficient or counterproductive in other parts of the United States. Right from the beginning, the *News* emphasized standard breeds and quality products. There were articles each month covering all aspects of farming, written by a wide range of experts. From the beginning, Jim McClure preached his message of agricultural excellence. The theme of uniformity was hammered by the editors of the *News* month after month, "Beg, Borrow or Steal A FEDERATION POTATO," and "GET A RED HOG" (Duroc-Jersey) were typical headlines.[12] Jim McClure had taken it upon himself to educate an entire region in modern agriculture, and slowly the results began to appear. Always the tone of the advice was clear and sharp, but not condescending. Information came in the form of new hope, with a heavy dose of enthusiasm.

MR. BUNCOMBE COUNTY FARMER, YOUR OPPORTUNITIES ARE UNLIMITED IF YOU WILL STOP THE LEAKS

With a CLIMATE excelled by no other in the world, and a soil that is naturally rich in all the plant food elements . . . you should certainly be one of the most progressive farmers in America . . . You should have modern home conveniences, with good schools, good churches, good roads, and other things that go to make country life more pleasant and wholesome.

The system of farming and marketing that you have used in the past has not yielded you a good living . . . Your profits have been leaking through the following channels:

First—You have let about 33% of your cultivated soils become sick and die . . .

Second—You are growing scrub stock, which is not profitable . . .

Third—You have been planting poor seed.

Fourth—You have not been pruning and spraying your orchard, and as a result your fruit is not marketable . . .

Fifth,—perhaps the greatest leak has been your system of marketing. You have hauled your products to market, unstandardized and ungraded, and took what the market offered you, which was often less that the cost of production. This is the most difficult leak to stop, but you can stop it by joining your neighbors as a member of the "Farm Federation."[13]

BUNCOMBE COUNTY FARMER ROBBED

A New York man and a Pennsylvania man recently turned a neat trick on a Buncombe County farmer. In February and March when broilers were bringing about a dollar a pound they came down here and slipped away with all the dollars from the big hotels and hospitals right under the Buncombe farmer's nose. The Buncombe County farmer did not realize he was being robbed. He acted as if he was sandbagged; he was not conscious of his loss.[14]

Thanks to the Federation, the leaks and the thefts began to subside. By November 1921, a second warehouse was built on the other side of Asheville, beside the railroad tracks at Craggy. By January 1922, the farmers of North Buncombe had rented their own warehouse at Stony Knob. Each of these efforts required an enormous amount of groundwork by Jim McClure. He had to organize the stock sales, set up the meetings, and keep everyone's enthusiasm from sagging. He had a genius for organizing meetings, mixing enough entertainment to bring the crowds out with enough hard facts to get his message across. He showed movies and stereopticon pictures. At one open meeting held in Fairview in the summer of 1921, a leading citizen of the community, Federation director John Baxter Merrill, was put on trial for (1) Putting in a bushel of undersized potatoes on a Federation contract; (2) Selling the Federation truck one ounce of buttermilk in a pound of butter; (3) Selling the truck an egg with age on it.[15] Nearly 1,000 people turned out to see this mock trial.[16] During one of these early meetings Jim McClure brought in his first string band, and ever afterwards he knew that there was nothing like the sound of the banjo and the fiddle to bring together the mountain folks. Guy Sales, who came to work for the Federation during the summer of 1922, recalls this first Federation string band. About twenty-five farmers were gathered in downtown Asheville, and Jim McClure asked young Sales if he knew of any music that could be brought in quickly. Across the street was a drinking and gambling establishment, and Guy replied that he thought there were some musicians inside. The teetotaling Presbyterian minister did not hesitate; he wanted musicians, sober or drunk. Guy Sales found his men inside, engrossed in a poker game, and talked them into coming to the meeting. "But you'll have to wait til we're done with this game," they said.[17] Jim McClure could always feel the pulse of a crowd. To his sister he wrote:

> The interest in the meetings has been rolling up like a snowball and we have been accumulating performances until we are putting on as fine a show as the rural districts have ever had. We have a five piece string orchestra which accompanies us, a moving picture outfit and a Delco Light plant and such worthies as the Chairman of the County Commissioners and other politicians have joined our moving caravan. The crowds turn out at every point, the string band alone being enough to draw the crowd. One more meeting remains and then the wee small hours will know us no more. (James G. McClure, Jr. to Harriet McClure Stuart, February 25, 1922)

The entertainment was a crucial element in the education of the mountaineer. Jim explained his methods as part of a slide presentation on the Federation:

> We have some subjects to talk about with our farmers that are very dull in many points of view, like spraying. When a farmer has worked all day in the fields, and particularly when he can't read and write, a lecture on spraying is pretty tough on him. It is hard to get them to come out to a lecture on spraying and if they do come, most of them fall asleep. So we decided to give subjects

of that type with the aid of clowns. We have the Farmers Federation clowns. We always have the old-fashioned fiddling and people come out to the meetings. This clown here [he is showing slides] is the superintendent of the State Test Farm. He can shout out a spray formula at the top of his lungs about forty times during the evening. We are getting them sold on the idea of spraying. There is the opportunity to get away with a lot of jokes, which make a hit. The clowns will come on with a hand-spraying machine and one of the clowns will take another's hat off and pick up a large bug from under the hat and spray it and it will drop dead on the floor. A few jokes like that popularize the idea of spraying.[18]

Could the Farmers Federation survive as a business? Trying to raise capital from struggling farmers in order to sell their crops in a sagging market might seem to be a foolish waste of time. Yet each year, the Federation sent out to its stockholders, both preferred and common, dividends of 6 percent. Most years, members were also paid a dividend of 5 percent of the amount of business they did with the Federation. But the Federation was cramped by the problem of how to raise money for capital improvements. For several years Jim convinced the membership to allow the Federation to keep the 5 percent dividend on business, in order to build up financial strength. Teaching men to vote against money in their pockets was not easy. Yet even these measures provided only meager funds. In the summer of 1921 Jim and Elizabeth were in New York, and he asked the Russell Sage Foundation for money to help the Farmers Federation expand. The request was turned down.

In November, the Federation faced a severe financial crisis. Jim notes in his diary that he and Elizabeth went into town together in the pouring rain to meet with Church Crowell, an active director. "... [H]ad to get $2000 more for Fed & felt bank closing in on us. Do not know where next cash will come from. Met at Proffitts [early leader who helped to edit the *Federation News*] at 11— Lunch with ... Dr. Grove [who] took 2 shares. ..."[19] Dr. Grove was the builder of the Grove Park Inn, and a millionaire from the profits of his patent medicine tonic, Fletcher's Castoria. He became an enormous supporter of the Federation in this early period, but his two share purchase on this occasion put only a small dent in the $2,000 debt. So three days later Jim McClure went back to the bank, and drew a rather humorous picture of himself seeking out a loan. "Dressed up in old black suit, with a shine, & jaunty air entered the Bank and breezed thru an interview securing promise of a line [of credit] to 15000 [dollars] with Battery Park [Bank]."[20] Next he tried to talk Buncombe's wealthiest citizen, Mrs. George Vanderbilt, into donating to the Federation. The entry for July 8, 1921, reads: "Fruitless call on Dr. Wheeler hoping for entree to Mrs. Vanderbilt for $2000.00. ..."[21] How he got an introduction is unknown, but in October he made this entry in the diary: "Petsie and I to town, shopping about. At 4:30 with quavering hearts slipped thru the Vanderbilt gateway ... Stopping in front of Mrs. V's we made a pass at the main entrance, which was barred, & doubled barred. Retrieving ourselves we rang at the proper place . . . Entering had a very pleasant tea with Mrs. V. & Cornelia [her daughter], holding our own. . . ."[22]

This was the beginning of Mrs. Vanderbilt's considerable interest in the Farmers Federation. Jim McClure quickly realized that the Farmers Federation would never be able to satisfy his visions for Western North Carolina if he relied only on the money of the farmers themselves. The Federation's first task was to try to renovate the economy of the region, but that was only to provide a sound basis to build up other areas of life. The educational system of the mountains was woefully inadequate, and would remain so until there was a tax base from which to draw and people who properly appreciated the importance of the endeavor. He supported vocational education in the high schools, and wanted to set up his own Federation Training School that would give promising young farm boys some technical training. He worried about the little country churches, too. He saw them propagating ignorance, fear and superstition; in short, a blighted vision of the possibilities of life. Hymn books, preacher's salaries, Sunday School literature and building repairs were almost always beyond the means of the little congregations. Jim McClure felt strongly that the cornerstone of American civilization was the little country church. When these churches suffered, the American dream of freedom and prosperity took on a tarnished look. So in the back of his mind he wanted to work out a scheme to strengthen the religious institutions of Western North Carolina. Moreover, he wanted to be able to test new crops and procedures, to try out ideas to see if they might fit into mountain agriculture. But none of these visions could be realized without outside money, and in fact he was strapped even to pay the promotional expenses involved in the geographical spread of the Federation. In March 1922, he made a loud plea in the *News* for financial help. "Wanted: A Promotional Fund! Requests are coming in to the Federation from other sections and counties to come and help them organize. We have to reply that we cannot do it as we have no one to send."[23]

Jim had some success building support in Asheville by the sale of stock. His early contact with Dr. E. W. Grove bore fruit when, in the summer of 1922, Dr. Grove offered to buy $5,000 in stock if $15,000 worth of the same could be sold in Asheville. "He thinks Asheville should be aroused to helping the Federation get financed and so made the offer. We already have $20,000 paid in but the more it [the Federation] grows the more capital we need" (James G. K. McClure, Jr. to Harriet McClure Stuart, July 2, 1922). The next issue of the *News* announced the proposition, and quoted the letter Dr. Grove had written to Jim McClure: "This is an investment that promises to pay dividends not only in the form of interest, but in the form of the development of the life of Western North Carolina."[24] In the next issue, Jim could proudly announce that "Asheville clinches Dr. Grove's offer. In three weeks from its opening the campaign to sell Federation stock in Asheville closed, having been oversubscribed $1900. Thus the provision on Dr. Grove's offer to take $5,000 worth of stock has been met, and the working capital of the Federation doubled."[25] The next year Dr. Grove made the same offer, and the goal was met in only three days. Clearly, Jim McClure had won the faith of the local business community. Then in 1925, Dr. Grove again made an offer, this time $25,000 if the community would take $75,000 worth of stock, an enormous sum that would give the Federation great strength. Jim McClure threw himself into the campaign to raise money, lining up some of the influential citizens of Asheville, and doing joyous battle. The results were astounding and thrilling for Jim McClure. " . . . [I]t is something out of the ordinary for a community to contribute over $165,000 to an undertaking where the returns will be largely measured in improvement of rural life, encouragement of better farming methods and good-will between farmer and city dweller."[26]

The good will of the Federation drew in Mrs. George Vanderbilt as well, and the McClures came to enjoy the festivities of the Biltmore House after the trepidations of their first visit. Mrs. Vanderbilt was intensely interested in farming, and as early as 1922 was commended by the *News* for her financial support of the County Extension service.[27] At about the same time, she and Jim appeared at the podium of the Civitan Club, one of Asheville's leading civic clubs, with the Federation's own Mr. Clay of Fairview, for a farmers' luncheon. In a letter to his sister Hetty, Jim described the event as "quite an affair. The Asheville businessmen each asked a farmer to attend. Mr. Clay led off the batting list and made a tremendous hit by telling an apt story and ending up in three minutes. Mrs. Vanderbilt attended the luncheon and followed me up, being given the fourth or clean up position on the batting list" (James G. K. McClure, Jr. to Harriet McClure Stuart, May 14, 1922). Her batting record is left incomplete, but she in fact became one of the Federation's principal local supporters, buying quantities of stock and encouraging her own Biltmore Dairy to join up.

Jim's sister Hetty and her husband Douglas Stuart were contributors during these crucial years. In response to a contribution, Jim wrote to Hetty: "You are a brick-the letter with $300 enclosed was received with the wildest acclamations. The Federation will have to raise a statue to the Stuart family" (James G. K. McClure, Jr. to Harriet McClure Stuart, May 14, 1922). Douglas Stuart was an executive for Quaker Oats Company, and helped the Federation by providing them with feed at a reasonable rate. Moreover, he sent down a variety of experts to help educate the mountain farmer. On one such occasion, this report appeared in a letter to the Stuarts:

> We have had with us during the past week the celebrated expert of the Quaker Oats Company, Mrs. Florence Forbes, and we have kept her busy with meetings afternoon and night and demonstrations during the morning hours. The Quaker Oats Company furnished moving pictures exposing all the inner secrets of the poultry kingdom and placing the modest, unsuspecting hen entirely in the power of the onlooker. The hens in this country from now on will have to forswear their life of ease and get down to Full-O-Pep and shelling out the hard boiled egg.

For these meetings the Federation provided a string orchestra that made the most staid citizens and matrons shuffle an involuntary foot. The week is always a little wearing on the participants. My good wife if she attends any meetings after the first has acquired a nasty habit of falling asleep and losing control of her center of gravity. This necessitates a body guard who constantly shoves her back into an upright position. (James G. K. McClure, Jr. to the Stuarts, April 20, 1922)

Through these early years, Jim kept his sister and brother-in-law informed on the progress of the Federation, and through these letters one can read some of his thoughts and a great deal of his enthusiasm.

The Federation announced its dividend for the year 1921 . . . We had a good year and will pay 6% on paid up stock and 5% on business done. This is quite a dividend and everyone is pleased. We also will add about 1500 dollars to our surplus fund. Our business keeps growing at a good pace and with our third warehouse opening up in a few days it keeps us moving lively. Our main difficulty is lack of capital as with almost all joiners coming in on the ten dollar down plan the total is not large. Our volume of business is quite large for the amount of capital we have, and I am trying to invent some way of increasing our working capital.

So endeth this chronicle and with love to each and every member unto the third or fourth generation. . . . (James G. K. McClure, Jr. to the Stuarts, February 19, 1922)

The Federation is still growing and leading us a merry dance. Our great and crying need is for more capital and yesterday we were all elated because $840.00 came in. Every Saturday the solicitors report their success during the week and $840 is our high water mark . . . We are now turning over our capital twice a month and this takes frenzied finance as well as all our capital is tied up in buildings and equipment. (James G. K. McClure, Jr. to the Stuarts, March 19, 1922)

The Federation keeps moving along and yesterday we indulged in a Reo speed wagon. This makes our delivery equipment consist of a ton and a half truck, a one ton speed wagon, a one ton Ford truck, a half ton Ford truck and a Ford passenger car.

On Thursday I addressed a great and high spirited crowd of Rotarians and received a free lunch for my efforts, which is more than I have received for my vocal efforts in many a long day. (James G. K. McClure, Jr. to the Stuarts, May 21, 1922)

. . . The Federation keeps coming along strong though I hear that at any time the tide may set in the other direction and I may be run out of the county. The populace are very fickle. Yesterday our 600th stockholder plunked his money down. (James G. K. McClure, Jr. to the Stuarts, July 23, 1922)

Those who have recently been among us will be interested to know that we had our proposed meeting of the Federation on Friday and authorized an issue of $500,000 Common stock and $250,000 Preferred, the first issue of $50,000 Common Stock being already subscribed. The same evening a meeting was held at Mills River, which is one of the sections contributory to Fletcher and the people decided to erect a warehouse at Fletcher . . . The redoubtable Mr. Crowell will move his seat of operations to Fletcher next Monday and start to burn up the country. The Federation now has a balance in banks of over ten thousand and bank presidents openly flirt with it. This bank account will soon be raided by the Q[uaker] O[ats] Company who takes our money as fast as we gather it together. (James G. K. McClure, Jr. to the Stuarts, August 27, 1922)

The opening of the Federation Warehouse at Fletcher on Wednesday was a conspicuous success. All County officials from both Henderson and Buncombe Counties were present and a big crowd of ordinary citizens. The affair went off peaceably. A car of Quaker Oats Feed arrived the day before the opening and the sacks made excellent seats for those who drank in the flow of Southern oratory. Fourteen speakers mounted the rostrum, seven before dinner and seven after dinner, and seldom has such a feast of wit, wisdom and exhortation been poured upon an audience. The crowd, replete and somewhat jaded broke up about four thirty. The capacity of the mountain farmer for successfully absorbing hot air is only equaled in the annals of America by the attendants at the early camp meetings where three and four hour sermons were successfully weathered before and after dinner. The crowd here breaks up, looking slightly gassed and with somewhat sagged jaws but otherwise apparently none the worse. . . . (James G. K. McClure, Jr. to the Stuarts, January 21, 1923)

Jim's jaws may have sagged a bit that week too when his hustle was foiled by Asheville's new "speed officer."

The week has seen me caught in the toils of the law. The attached clipping will explain one fall from grace. ("McCLURE TAXED BY NETTLES LAW: HIS HURRY COSTS HIM HEAVY FINE James G. K. McClure, famous in Farmers Federation circles, is a hustler. But his hurry cost him in the neighborhood of $60 today when he ran afoul of the enactment of that other friend of the farmers, Harry L. Nettles, chosen from the rural precincts to give the agriculturists an even break in the state's legislative halls. McClure is the second man to be brought before Judge Wells under the Nettles Act . . . for speeding on Biltmore Avenue.

The farmers' organizer has a boy's band, of which he is particularly proud, under his direction. He was anxious Tuesday afternoon to transport the juvenile musicians from one part of the county to another and he made no denial of that fact when arraigned. He thought he was going about 40 miles an hour when Lawrence Trexler, speed officer, drove his motorcycle behind him and trailed him . . . The policeman was sure 50 miles was the registration.

Regardless of who was nearer right as to the speed's computation, the Nettles bill was broken, and Judge Wells announced there was but one thing for him to do: Impose a fine of between $50 and $500 for going over 30 miles an hour . . . there was no indication that any lives were endangered by McClure's driving.") The others were two suits instituted by a woman who lost her head and ran into one of the Federation trucks. I was served with

papers on two counts by this woman and had to wage legal war before the magistrate. Our truck was not in the least to blame but in spite of this judgement was found against us on both counts . . .

Tomorrow I start on a flying trip to St. Petersburg, Florida to have an interview with Dr. Grove [who was helping arrange financing for the growing Federation]. . . . (James G. K. McClure, Jr. to the Stuarts, February 18, 1923)

The week of the Quarterly meetings is a fearful thing. One of our number seems to fall from grace every round. Last time I had my police court experience and this time our fiddler had the misfortune to get in a fight and sentence was imposed on him for three months on the chain gang . . . However in spite of this occurrence the round was a howling success. Crowds attended our meetings everywhere, local jokes were developed and a spirit of great jollity prevailed . . .

My muffler dropped off last night and I came home at 1:30 a.m., the car roaring like a lion. All along the road people moved uneasily in their beds thinking that Rumbling Bald (a local mountain known to experience earthquake tremors) had "broke out" again. (James G. K. McClure, Jr. to the Stuarts, May 20, 1923)

Clearly, with all of the work Jim McClure faced he loved the Federation and the mountain families it served. On a daily basis, however, the success of the Federation depended on each warehouse, and how well each manager treated his customers and ran his business. In the mountains, a man or woman would "trade" with the store where he or she felt at ease and welcomed. Customers felt strong loyalties to their shopkeepers, and often if a man left one store to work in another, he took those loyal to him along. Jim McClure quickly grasped these mountain habits, and tried to supply his warehouses with men not only capable of running an efficient operation, but also with personalities that attracted customers. The old Fairview siding was his first experience in learning how to manage a successful store, and several suggestions survive from notes he sent to R. T. Merrill, the manager there and the first employee of the Farmers Federation.

Private Attention R. T. Merrill
Suggestions: for use in running the Business.
(1) Spend some time in studying how to organize the force to best advantage. Give certain men certain responsibilities, i.e. one man to sweep up the first thing every morning, another man the responsibility for the outside picking up, another man the duties of shipping clerk, etc. (2) Make a list of wet day and slack time jobs such as sewing up torn sacks; putting up Growing Mash in ten pound packages etc . . . (5) Keep lists of everything. By this I mean lists of those who want lime, potatoes, prospects for stockholders, growers of vegetables etc. Our business has reached the stage where it has outgrown the

Opposite: *Directors of the Farmers Federation, 1923–1924. Left to right: S.C. Clapp, director; G.L. Clay, Secretary-Treasurer, James G.K. McClure, Jr., pres.; R.C. Crowell, vice pres.; Claude B. Wells, director.*

possibilities of the memory and we will have to make more and more use of lists.[28]

Ride hard after old collections and get security or something for the accounts . . . Keep the clerks on their toes . . . Put up signs to help move things.[29]

One of the most successful store managers in the Federation system was Bill Francis, who took over the Hendersonville warehouse. His affability was a sure drawing card, and he remembers with fondness the men swapping stories around his pot-bellied stove, leaning over from time to time to "let fly" with a perfectly aimed projectile of tobacco juice into his sand pit. He understood well that the Federation store had to serve a social role, or fail altogether as an enterprise. On the business side, he recalled that managing debt was always difficult. The nature of agriculture includes borrowing on supplies, seed, tools and machinery in the spring with the promise to pay when the harvests came in next fall. To the credit of the mountain farmers, despite the long periods of hard times, Bill Francis never had much trouble collecting his debts. "I did have to go in early to work for a while and milk a herd of cows grazing out behind the store, when a man failed to pay up." Bill Francis remembers his first store in Tryon, organized to serve Polk County. "The back of Polk" has always been a producer of moonshine, and he recalls the big selling items there were sugar, shorts and yeast. To serve his customers, "we would deliver in the middle of the night to keep out of the Revenue Officer's way."[30]

The Hendersonville stock drive began in the spring of 1924, and when the new warehouse was completed it meant that the Farmers Federation had six warehouses located throughout the two most prosperous mountain counties, Henderson and Buncombe. All were built in four years by money raised locally, during an era of depressed farm prices. The Hendersonville *News* stood behind the drive, cajoling the local businessmen to support the enterprise.

> The financing of the Farmers Federation appears to be on the last lap of its journey in Hendersonville. The businessmen let the farmer get the jump on them and it was difficult to catch up.
>
> The campaign and the Federation should serve to knit businessmen and farmers, the city and county, closer together.
>
> For years we have heard Hendersonville civic bodies discuss ways and means of helping the farmer. The first real opportunity has arrived and Hendersonville though slow to move has measured fairly well up to the most singular opportunity ever presented it. Our efforts will give the farmer more confidence in us. He has been shown that the businessmen have his problems at heart.
>
> But we must not pose as philanthropists. We have given the farmer nothing. We have made no real sacrifices. We have helped him on his journey to more profitable agriculture but in this we could assume a very selfish attitude, knowing that when the farmer has money to spend the business man is to get a good share of it.

Top: *Fairview Warehouse of the Farmer's Federation;* Bottom: *Early Federation truck hauling milk and cream.*

Next comes the opportunity of the farmer to produce more with assurance
of better markets. The time has come for him to change his ways, plant and
cultivate more scientifically and use both county agent and Federation to every
possible advantage.[31]

Hendersonville proved to be a strong link in the Federation chain, and by
1925 James McClure could boast a total sales of nearly a million dollars a year.
The fifth anniversary issue of the Federation *News,* August 1925, told of the
rise of the Federation in an article by an admirer.

And so the rise of the Farmers Federation reads like a fairy story. Just five
years ago the organization was a small group of neighboring farmers in
Fairview township.

Today the Federation is the progressive farmer element of Henderson and
Buncombe Counties. . . .

Madison, Jackson, McDowell and Haywood counties may soon feel the
touch of the Federation.

The rapid growth and development of the Farmers Federation owes much
to its guiding spirit. In fact, the tireless efforts, the sacrifices and steady nerve
of James G. K. McClure, Jr., have weathered the ship over rough seas to easy
sailing.

In the handful of farmers at Fairview, five years ago, Mr. McClure was the
guiding spirit. Today and every day since the first handful of farmers cast their
lots together, he has had his strong hand at the wheel.[32]

On the front page of this issue was a picture of "The six-story fireproof
warehouse on Roberts Street, Asheville."

It was here that the Federation sought security behind walls of steel and
concrete . . . now housing the marketing department, the executive offices, the
Federation *News* office and the poultry department.

This modern building costing around $75,000 has become Asheville's trade
center for the farmer. On busy days trucks and wagons line the street for some
distance on either side of the Federation building.

At one time during the tomato season in 1924 so many farmers brought their
tomatoes to the Federation at one time that traffic became hopelessly blocked
for over an hour, and it required a traffic officer to straighten out the traffic.[33]

Jim McClure was very proud of this building, a tangible result of his
unselfish devotion to his vision. He went to Roberts Street every day. In some
of the excess warehouse space, he stored his wife's very soul, all of her finest
paintings. Aunt Frederika's priceless furniture and family heirlooms were all
on Roberts Street, protected from catastrophe by steel and concrete.

The third morning after Christmas 1925, the weather in Western North
Carolina was a bitterly cold 0° F. Those who braved the elements to obtain a
morning paper were greeted with large headlines across the front page. "HALF

MILLION DOLLAR FIRE IN DEPOT SECTION. Farm Federation and Three Other Buildings Are Complete Losses. Wintry Weather Handicaps Force of Firefighters," The article continued, " . . . The Farmers Federation . . . also lost heavily, several carloads of beans, much poultry and several hundred turkeys being burned . . ."[34]

The next week, Jim wrote to Hetty and Doug:

> . . . We have been through quite a week. Last Sunday morning word was brought that the Marketing Department was burning down, and on rushing in to Asheville I found the condition of affairs that is shown in the attached newspaper . . .
>
> As good luck would have it we were buying out the wholesale produce business of Hayes-McCormack on Jan. 1st. These people were one of the largest wholesale concerns here. I got hold of them last Sunday afternoon and arranged to take over their stock and building Monday morning so that we were open for business with a fairly complete line at seven o'clock Monday morning and we have done over $5,000.00 worth of business this week at our new quarters.
>
> We could not get to our safes until Friday afternoon, as the wreckage kept burning and was badly piled together. The safe from my office we found with one side out from its fall and everything burned completely up. The office safe was intact but when opened everything in it was so charred as to be practically undecipherable. My safe contained the records of the stockholders, now over two thousand and also the subscription cards from our last summer's drive . . . You can imagine what a mess it will be to adjust.
>
> The worst personal feature of the loss was Aunt Freddie's furniture, every bit of which was stored in the warehouse and every bit of which was destroyed. This included all the portraits, letters, laces, papers, trunks and furniture of every kind.

It is almost incredible to find no mention of the loss of Elizabeth's paintings. It speaks to the kind of person she was. Certainly she made an immediate decision to say nothing about her private loss. Jim continued to Hetty and Doug:

> We had a total of $46,500.00 Insurance which has been admitted by the Adjustor . . . We had a considerably higher proportion of insurance than the owners or occupants of the other buildings, as every one had considered the building semi-fire-proof and thought that even if a fire started it would not go far without being controlled. The insurance companies had just made us another cut in our rate a few weeks ago.
>
> The loss will be a heavy one but we will try to win it back in a couple of years. We had a Directors meeting yesterday and decided to rebuild at once. . . . (James G. K. McClure, Jr. to the Stuarts, January 3, 1926)

Never a mention was made by Elizabeth of a loss so personal that her inner grief must have touched her deepest chords of despair.

Dearest Hetty,

. . . Poor Jim is simply engulfed in affairs. The fire was a horrid blow as
everything was running so smoothly & of course this means months of bother
and extra work. Nobody understands what in the world caused the fire as there
were only a few coals in the furnace when they left the building on Saturday
but that night was a fearfully cold one & there was a terrible wind, so much
so that the wretched watchman whose job it was to patrol the building every
hour never appeared at all! If he had been on the job, of course it would never
have gained headway . . . However, the Federation opened up promptly on
Monday morning not having lost an hour of business & has been going at their
usual full steam ahead ever since with more business than ever before. None
of the other three burned-out concerns have done a single stroke since the fire
. . . (Elizabeth Cramer McClure to Harriet McClure Stuart, January 8, 1926)

Jim McClure was deservedly proud of the ability of the Federation to
reopen the day after this terrible burn-out of the central warehouse; adversity
never numbed him, but always stimulated his energies and boosted his determination. The probable cause of the fire was determined to be bananas. In the
basement there was a room with straw on the floor where all the bananas were
stored, and kerosene stoves were used to keep this area between 75°F.and 80°F.
in order for them to ripen properly.[35]

The Federation recovered rapidly, and by the beginning of the Depression,
had strengthened itself for the economic doldrums to come. By its tenth anniversary in August 1930, the cooperative could boast a growth in the poultry business from $5,000 annual return the first few years to more than half a million
dollars.[36] The first chickens were boiled in an old black pot in front of the
Fairview Warehouse. By 1930, a special railroad car moved through Western
North Carolina, stopping at regular intervals to purchase poultry. In a later
speech in New York, Jim McClure recalled the early effort of the Federation to
create a poultry market in the mountains using a railroad car.

. . . We ran the enterprise at a loss for three years because the tonnage was
never great enough to make the car pay . . . We had a great deal of excitement
working up interest in the first car we shipped. We went all through the
mountains and held meetings and the car was ordered and the farmers at each
station brought in their poultry and finally the car was started rolling to New
York.

Well, I don't know whether you gentlemen know the poultry business in
New York. It was my first experience with it. We shipped the car up here and
about three days later the telephone rang and I thought static had broken loose
all the way from Asheville to New York. I have never heard a more excited
telephone conversation in my life than there was on the other end. This gentleman assured me—I could see his hands moving—that this was the worst car
of poultry he had ever seen, there had never been anything like it come to New
York, it was just terrible . . . I looked into the matter and I found that our
people, who have much sporting blood, had taken this opportunity to get rid

of their defeated game roosters and other poultry of that kind. Now, the game rooster is not a particularly toothsome thing to serve on the dinner table.[37]

More "toothsome" were the vegetables grown and canned in Henderson County. Jim McClure reasoned that the only way to encourage farmers to grow vegetables on a commercial level was to be able to assure them that the Federation could buy all that they grew. The only way that assurance could be made was to set up a cannery, so that the vegetables could be preserved during slack marketing times. In the early years, canning apparatus was fitted onto a truck and driven to the various farms. The rig was given by Henry Ford and stimulated such production, especially of tomatoes, that a large-scale, permanent cannery was eventually built by the Federation. Henderson County became well known for produce, even to the present day. The cannery could not pay a high price, but it could accept an unlimited quantity. Jim explained in the *News* that the farmers had learned it was "better to sell 1000 bushels of tomatoes for 60¢ per bushel than 10 bushels at $1.50."[38] He always hoped to be able to supply Florida with tomatoes during the late summer, and Bill Francis remembers once, when he was managing the Hendersonville warehouse, being sent south with a load of two hundred bushels of green tomatoes. He recalls with a laugh travelling up and down the state looking for a buyer. Even in the hot Florida sun those tomatoes would not turn red.[39]

The Federation continued to push for sales of its original concern, the Irish potato, and added the sweet potato as a sideline. Irish potatoes were rolling out of the mountains by the train load, and by 1930 Jim McClure could claim that the Federation had paid out over $600,000 for that humble tuber. Down in Rutherford County, where sweet potatoes were perfectly adapted to the soil and climate, the Federation built a curing plant to keep them off the market at harvest time in order to enjoy better prices during the winter. This experiment was a successful venture of the Federation and sweet potatoes proved to be a wonderful cash crop for the farmers of that section of the mountains. Apples, corn, wheat, mountain rye, and almost anything else the farmers could raise were sold by the Federation, and simultaneously the men and women of the North Carolina mountains were learning scientific agriculture and good citizenship.

In the latter part of the nineteenth century, a flue-cured, yellow leaf tobacco, used primarily to wrap cigars, enjoyed many boom years. Asheville became a large tobacco marketing center, and warehouses sprang up along with curing facilities and small processing factories. But during the 1890s the demand petered out. Jim McClure knew that in Kentucky burley tobacco had become a fine cash crop, and he reasoned that his mountain farmers could do as well. Jim got experts from the Department of Agriculture to analyze the area. They found it was well suited for tobacco. In 1926 he began promoting the idea, and 4,500 acres of mountain land were devoted to the "noxious weed" by 1930. Most of it was grown in Madison County, where the land was so rugged little else could be raised profitably. In 1930, the directors of the Federation voted

Mountain farmer with his tobacco. (McClure Fund Photograph Collection.)

to raise $2,500 to build a tobacco warehouse in Asheville. This building made money for the Federation in the years to come, and burley tobacco has been the most dependable cash crop in Western North Carolina ever since.

The more the Federation rolled along, gathering momentum, the more new projects Jim McClure's fertile imagination conceived for the region. But there was just not enough investment capital locally to finance them all. In 1927 he began to fit into the puzzle of the Federation the final pieces of his organizational scheme. It occurred to him that the people he had left behind to come to the southern mountains, the wealthy men and women of the northeastern cities, would be interested in the plight of the mountain men and women. He was a member in good standing of an American elite that controlled the strings of a capacious purse. Moreover, he knew the minds of those men and women, their prejudices and their ideals. He possessed the personality, the sincerity, the speaking ability and the handsome features to present the problems of the people he was trying to help in a most appealing way. He hit on exactly the right phrase for these men of the business world who valued independence and individualism—"Helping the mountain farmer to help himself." Jim McClure would draw together people with his charm and wit, with his genuine concern for his mountain neighbors and with his gift as a speaker. With a little book to note pledges, he would head off for the cities of the North each fall. The "campaign" was a battle plan for altruism.

In time, his skill at raising money gave him the freedom to pursue many of his more expansive ideas to improve life in the mountains. That money, held today in the James G. K. McClure Educational and Development Fund, is still at work educating hundreds of mountain young people each year in technical institutes, nursing schools, colleges and universities throughout the state and helping rural ministers to further their education. The creation of this development fund must be considered one of Jim's great achievements.

The "Educational and Development Fund of the Farmer's Federation, Inc." [the original name] was begun in 1927 to provide money to launch new ideas and programs. As he pursued this work Jim discovered, or was discovered by, a most remarkable man. Arthur W. Page, the son of the Ambassador to England, Walter Hines Page, came to Asheville to speak at the Rotary Club. His speech emphasized how important "cranks" were in pushing forward ideas and programs most thought unreasonable or impossible. After the address, Jim's friend Dr. W. P. Herbert went up to Mr. Page and said, "I know a 'crank' who thinks the mountain farm can make money." Off to Fairview went Arthur Page, and a partnership resulted that grew in strength in both personal friendship and good works accomplished. Arthur Page's father was a North Carolina native and journalist. Too progressive to be accepted in his home state at the end of the nineteenth century, he headed north, became editor of the *Atlantic Monthly* and was named Ambassador to England by President Woodrow Wilson. He worked vigorously for his vision of an Anglo-American position of world leadership, even trying to thwart President Wilson's neutrality rules prior to American intervention in World War I. He often wrote of the possibilities for the South. His book, *The School That Built a Town,* was an inspiration to Jim McClure, especially as it stressed the importance of giving a chance to the mountain woman. Nurtured by his father's ideas, Arthur Page felt strong ties to North Carolina and a strong conviction that America's purest population of Anglo-Saxons needed assistance to bring themselves more in line with the prosperity of the other brethren of their race.

Back home in the mountains Jim McClure kept these money-raising efforts in the background. He never wanted to make his friends in the Federation feel that they were objects of some sort of charity. To those in the cooperative who knew about and appreciated what their president was doing on his trips it all seemed at times to be a new wrinkle on the old game of "skinning Yankees." Hendersonville manager Bill Francis laughs and gives what was no doubt the prevailing potbellied stove opinion in his store, when he said that Jim McClure would take "two or three of these cross-eyed boys, a banjo or two, and come back with thousands of dollars."[40]

One of his first fund-raising efforts took place in the ballroom of the Colony

WHAT

WE ARE DOING ABOUT THAT

MOUNTAIN FARM

PRELIMINARY 1928 REPORT

EDUCATIONAL AND DEVELOPMENT FUND

OF THE

FARMERS FEDERATION

ASHEVILLE, N. C.

DECEMBER FIRST - 1928

Club in New York City. The announcement read: "The New York Womens
Committee of the Farmers Federation of North Carolina cordially invites you
to spend an afternoon with the North Carolina Mountaineers." Ballads were
heard, and a movie shown with the unlikely title "Stark Love." The invitation
contains sketches of the popular symbols of mountain life: a log cabin, a spinning wheel, the long Kentucky rifle and an old grist mill. The sketch of a wild
boar seems to be stalking the names of the women listed inside, names familiar
in American history for their power and influence: Roosevelt, Vanderbilt, Coffin, Gerry, Root and, of course, Page. Mrs. Henry P. Davison was the original
chairman. She worked tirelessly to help Jim raise money for many years. By
1928, she won publicity in all of New York's major newspapers, and "Stark
Love" was replaced by the live drama of a Miss Lucile Laverne. The Evening
Post described the centerpiece of that year's campaign:

> Mrs. Henry P. Davison, whose time is taken up almost entirely by multitu-
> dinous charities, of which the general public has no conception, heads the
> women's committee of the educational and development fund for the Farmers
> Federation . . . which is sponsoring the revival of "Sun-up," the play of the
> Southern mountaineers, at the new Lucile Theatre . . .
>   The first two performances . . . will be special benefits. Miss La Verne,
> who has become deeply interested in the lives of the mountaineers, will give
> a large share of the profits of the engagement to further the constructive work
> that is being done. Mr. James G. K. McClure, Jr. president of the Farmers
> Federation, Inc., has been in New York some weeks engaged in the undertak-
> ing of raising funds to develop the tremendous possibilities of the agricultural
> resources of the Southern mountains and is meeting cordial interest.
>   There are 450,000 of the finest pioneer stock of America living in the
> mountains of North Carolina and yet their standard of living is today probably
> lower than that of any similar group of people in the United States. The
> Farmer's Federation, an organization of mountain farmers, started seven years
> ago with the purpose of changing this condition by means of finding and
> creating markets. Limited in its finances, this organization is pointing the
> way, but cannot as yet take care of the situation.[41]

The revival of "Sun-up" was a smash hit, and helps to point out the
fascination felt in the North for the folk of Appalachia. One reviewer, Pierre
de Rohan, described the show:

MISS LA VERNE SUBLIME IN 'SUN UP' REVIVAL

> Set in the backwoods fastness of the Carolina hills, the play turns its search-
> ing spotlight on the households of the Widow Cagel, her son Rufe and their
> neighbors, the Todds.
>   Widowed by a revenue officer's bullet, Mom Cagel is a sworn enemy of the
> law, and is puzzled and resentful at Rufe's willingness to obey the ukase of a
> draft board.

Previous pages: *Early promotional material for the Educational and Development Fund.*

But Rufe has had 'larnin.' He can read a little, and write after a fashion. Of course, he believes France is 'somers 'bout 40 miles t'other side of Asheville,' and that 'Huns' is but a nickname for the Yankees his father fought against in '63. . . . [42]

New York had its own vision of mountain life, and Jim McClure found enough worthy people there to listen to him, and contribute to the Fund. He could tell stories and entertain his contributors with tales of the mountaineer. The Fund spread to other cities: Philadelphia, Pittsburgh and Detroit. His own enjoyment of the "victories" of the campaign show through often enough, as he kept his family informed of his movements. To Hetty he wrote, "Well-my dear-I have had good luck this day-the engagement with Edsel Ford which I lost by staying that extra day in Chicago I had almost despaired of as he has been in New York . . . , but I saw him today and he came on our committee & also subscribed $10,000.00. Doesn't that make you giddy?" (James G. K. McClure, Jr. to Harriet McClure Stuart, exact date unknown).

If Jim McClure ever allowed himself the opportunity to reflect back over the first ten years of the Federation, "giddy" would have been an appropriate emotion. Against all adversity—dismal farm prices, unscientific agricultural techniques, lack of working capital, an independent-minded population, transportation difficulties, and the disastrous fire on Roberts Street—he prevailed. By 1930, the Federation was financially strong and just beginning to tap resources in the North, and to expand operations into new areas of mountain life. Jim McClure's dream of ministering to a region rather than just a church had been fulfilled by the Farmers Federation, and with all of the hard work and responsibilities he shouldered his physical difficulties did not flare up again. The compensation Jim McClure received must have been spiritual, because for the first seven years he received no salary for his efforts and thereafter his pay was only nominal. He wanted to fight this war for the people, to serve the men and women of Western North Carolina. He once explained his ambitions in a speech to potential contributors in New York, and he never wandered from the purpose here expressed. "I am quite a crank, as I think you can see, on trying to develop people's self-help," he said. "I believe that the way to cure real want is to stir people's ambition and stir it with something definite in mind whereby they can really attain that ambition."[43]

And so it was that the Farmers Federation offered opportunity and hope to the farm families of Western North Carolina, and the sense of purpose for which Jim McClure himself had been striving.

1. John C. Campbell, *The Southern Highlander and His Homeland* (New York: Russell Sage Foundation, 1921) p. 257.

2. James G. K. McClure, Jr., speech on the Farmers Federation given September 10, 1935. In "Proceedings of the New York Farmers, 1934–35 Season," New York, 1935, p. 9.

3. Interview with Miss Ora N. Nesbitt.

4. James G. K. McClure, Jr., "Help Yourself," editorial, *Fairview Farmers' News Sheet*, July 15, 1920.

5. Selected passages from the *Fairview Farmers' News Sheet*, July 15, 1920.

6. Clarence Poe, *How Farmers Co-operate and Double Profit* (New York: Orange Judd Co., 1915), p.23.

7. *Ibid.*, p. 62.

8. *Ibid.*, p. 117.

9. *Ibid.*, p. 129.

10. "Hammer the Farmer," *Farmers Federation News Sheet*, November 1920.

11. "Throw Away a Nickel Once in a While," *Farmers Federation News Sheet*, November 1920.

12. Headlines, *Farmers Federation News*, March 15, 1921.

13. "Mr. Buncombe County Farmer . . . ," *Farmers Federation News*, March 15, 1921.

14. "Buncombe County Farmer Robbed," *Farmers Federation News*, June 15, 1921.

15. *Farmers Federation News*, June 4, 1921.

16. *Farmers Federation News*, February 1922.

17. Interview with Mr. Guy Sales.

18. *Op Cit.*, "New York Farmers," p. 15.

19. James G. K. McClure, Jr. diary, November 19, 1921.

20. *Ibid.*, November 22, 1921.

21. *Ibid.*, July 8, 1921.

22. *Ibid.*, October 13, 1921.

23. *Farmers Federation News*, March 1922, p. 4.

24. *Farmers Federation News*, August 1922, p. 1.

25. *Farmers Federation News*, September 1922, p. 4.

26. *Farmers Federation News*, October 1925, p. 4.

27. *Farmers Federation News*, June 1922.

28. James G. K. McClure, Jr., memo to R.T. Merrill, March 15, 1922.

29. James G. K. McClure, Jr., memo to R.T. Merrill, April 14, 1922.

30. Interview with Mr. Bill Francis.

31. Hendersonville *News*, March/April 1924 (exact date unknown).

32. Farmers Federation *News*, August 1925, p. 1.

33. *Ibid.*, p. 6.

34. Asheville *Citizen*, December 28, 1925, p. 1.

35. Interview with Guy Sales.

36. Farmers Federation *News*, August 1930, p. 2.

37. *Op Cit.*, New York Farmers, p. 10.

38. James G. K. McClure, Jr., "Cannery Acreage Signing Up," Farmers Federation *News*, April 1930, p. 4.

39. Interview with Mr. Bill Francis.

40. *Ibid.*

41. "Mrs. H.P. Davison Heads Committee Sponsoring Benefit," New York *Evening Post*, October 15, 1928.

42. "Miss La Verne Sublime . . ." New York *American*, October 27, 1928.

43. *Op Cit.*, New York Farmers, p. 16.

Chapter Fifteen

Hickory Nut Gap in the Twenties

"... [I was] greatly surprised to have a Pierce Arrow appear in [the] barn-yard." (*Diary, October 29, 1920*)

"I ain't goin' to clean your young 'un's dirty britches no more." The parting words of a mountain neighbor as she left the employment of Elizabeth McClure. (*Interview with Mrs. B. S. Colburn*)

The old Sherrill's Inn, perched just on the Buncombe County side of the Blue Ridge, enjoyed a renaissance during the twenties. Not only did Elizabeth and Jim continue to renovate the house and its environs, but they also brought in a new order of social life. Jim's Federation work made it an important focal point for various encounters and entertainments. For her part, Elizabeth joyfully pursued her vision of beauty. Flower borders, boxwood hedges, flowering shrubs, spring bulbs, grape arbors and John Shorter's vegetables all thrived under her caring eye and energetic hand. There was an upstairs maid and a downstairs maid, a cook and a nurse for the children, but Elizabeth herself was the flower gardener. She was not a harsh taskmaster, but the housework was to be done efficiently and correctly. She might put on a white glove looking for dust, even taking samples from the recently installed electric light bulbs. She considered her thoroughness to be an example to the mountain women working for her. Beyond the inner circle of house servants were the farm hands, many of whom lived in houses on the McClure property that had to be built and maintained. She wanted these simple frame structures to blend in with the rest of the buildings on the farm, and even went to the extent of a planned sag in the roof on a new tenant house to give it a look of age. The men, women and children who inhabited these dwellings were typically mountaineers without land, many of whom spent their lives moving from farm to farm with their large families. For Elizabeth, who possessed a kindly spirit of *noblesse oblige,* there were always births and measles and petty disagreements to sort out. She never wanted to appear condescending. A neighbor's comment, "I like Mrs. McClure. She's so common," startled Elizabeth, until she learned that "common" meant not putting oneself above anyone.[1] But it was hard for her not to be appalled by many of the unhygienic habits common in the mountains.

The patterns of life at Hickory Nut Cap were determined by the intermingling of two distinct and rather incongruous cultures. But the mix took hold in a wonderfully rich way, in part because the brittle formality of Lake Forest had

View of McClure home from the driveway.

already been tempered by a strong dose of the Social Gospel. While the ways of the mountain people frequently exasperated Jim and Elizabeth, the reverse was just as true. What could fancy city folks know about farming and gardening in North Carolina anyway? Elizabeth's drive for perfection must have been viewed as frivolous by the more pragmatic tenants. Her standards had to be met, even if it left her laborers grumbling about the extra work. In fact, she quite admired her tough neighbors at Hickory Nut Gap, who knew how to make do with almost nothing; and in turn they came to admire her and her ways. Elizabeth became a vision of elegant civility to the farm women, at least most of them.

Jim McClure relished the inevitable incongruities that popped up from time to time on his farm. He was a story teller, and took with him wherever he went an entertaining collection of anecdotes. These proved most useful in engaging the interests of his northern patrons. One of the real characters among the farm hands was Zeb McAbee, who never could quite make sense of the ways of the McClures. During the early years when help was plentiful, each afternoon, with guests or alone, Elizabeth had tea. She particularly liked to dress up for this ceremony; to bathe and put on a long gown to signal the end of the working day. One afternoon during her tea break, Zeb was sent up to the big house on business, and was rendered quite speechless by the appearance of Mrs. McClure. He returned to the barn shaking his head, and confided to one of the other hands, "I don't believe Mrs. McClure had quite finished dressin'."[2] On another occasion, old Zeb came up to borrow some vinegar. Elizabeth asked him, "Well Zeb, how much do you think you need?" He replied, "Oh, 'bout three or four gallon, I reckon'." "But Zeb, why so much?" "My old woman has got the rheumatiz, and I want to give her a bath."[3]

Whether the pickling of Mrs. McAbee was carried out or not, Jim and Elizabeth enjoyed learning about the country cures. Once in a while, an employee would turn on them seeking revenge, and then the humor was more macabre. For a short period of time during the twenties, Esther and John Shorter left Hickory Nut Gap to work their own land and care for Esther's mother Aura. Elizabeth struggled to find replacements for them. The position was a difficult one, not only because Esther and John had been so devoted, but also because it required that both a husband and wife work and live alongside Mr. and Mrs. McClure. One couple, the Babbs, were hired during this period and Elizabeth thought them quite suitable at first. She described them to Aunt Freddie as " . . . most promising. However one never knows and time will show but they seem very nice people and are most eager to please" (Elizabeth Cramer McClure to Frederika Skinner, May 14, 1923). Time did tell on the Babbs, and they had to be let go. A few weeks hence, complaints began to surface about the taste of the spring water piped into the house. An investigating party was organized, and found a dead sheep floating in the spring, a parting gift left by the Babbs.[4]

A more tragic story involved Emory McAbee and his family. Emory's farm was a losing battle, and about the only cash he raised was by "stilling" white corn liquor. Jim would sometimes get wind of one of Emory's operations back on his property, and try to search him out. In 1922, the revenue agents caught up with him, and he was subsequently thrown in jail. Jim took a special interest in the case, first going up to check on his wife and her children. On May 30th, he found "Mrs. Emory McAbee . . . with 4 children (oldest 8), two cows, molasses, corn meal for 3 days & flour for 6, and without one cent, facing a year without her husband."[5] Emory worked through the summer on the chain gang, but was returned to his jail cell in the fall suffering from fits of insanity. Jim "visited Emory McAbee in his bleak, bare room at the Jail and found him out of his mind—Puzzled conference with [the] Commissioners as to what to do—"[6] He served out his term, and was returned home still suffering spells of madness. He would get the idea that there was oil leaking out of the ground on Ferguson's Peak, the mountain behind the McClure's house, and every so often he would have a "fire fit" and set fire on the mountain in an effort to get rid of the oil.

The newcomers to the country side of life never failed to respond to the local calamities around them. When Porter Sinclair, from over the mountain in Gerton, shot himself accidentally while crossing a fence on a hunting trip, it was Jim McClure who volunteered to go to town to buy the coffin. He recorded in the diary in September 1920, "To town with Mr. Huntley for [a] coffin for Porter—[We] were run into by [a] Canadian soldier in a Ford who was going [the] wrong way on [a] one way St. To police court . . . each waiving damages . . . To undertakers—cheapest coffin $90 & [I was] assured [there were] no cheaper [ones] in town—To Police Capt. & with him to another undertakers and got one for $35. To Gerton . . . picking up a lovely aster wreath the Petsie had made."[7]

Bargain coffins and aster wreaths were visible expressions of Jim and Elizabeth's conception of their role as mountain neighbors. The sharp lines of social class were a part of this world, too, despite their easy ways and ability to pierce its walls with acts of kindness. Jim and Elizabeth wanted to be friends, but they did not want to compromise what they understood to be the superior quality of their upbringing. Part of their role here was to maintain the highest ideals of manners, beauty and virtue in order to exhibit before the local folk the fruits of progressive Christian civilization. And yet, Jim and Elizabeth could never be smug aristocrats on their mountain, lording it over their neighbors in Fairview. They might have accepted the superiority of their own values, but they knew too that these values came out of a training and education that was handed to them as the result of the struggles of former generations. The Farmers Federation and Elizabeth's pursuit of grace and beauty at Hickory Nut Gap were both meant to initiate the same respect for civilization that infused their own lives with purpose. Jim and Elizabeth tried to drop the social barriers between people without dropping their high standards of personal behavior and their impatience with shoddy work.

In organizing the little society of Hickory Nut Gap, they tried to put into practice their ideas of social justice. The Federation was organized as a cooperative in order to involve the people emotionally and financially in the work. It was an organization to be owned by the farmers themselves. In the same way, Jim set up the Hickory Nut Gap Farm Company to involve the workers as participants in the business rather than hired hands. Company meetings were held to decide farm procedures. Shares of stock could be earned or bought. The first such meeting occurred in April 1918 in Jim's study. James Davidson, the farm manager, was present, along with John Shorter. The proposal was made by Jim, and the company was duly formed.[8] Two years later, Elizabeth notes in one of her letters a new development in the Company. "Jim is enormously busy as ever. There are six renters this year in addition to the men working by the year so he is deep in contracts and shares. Last week the Hickory Nut Gap Farm Co. was incorporated so Jim is now actually trying out his scheme for letting all the hands have a share of the business. It is an experiment but so far it seems to be working" (Elizabeth Cramer McClure to Harriet McClure Stuart. January 12, 1920).

A month later, however, a financial cloud hung low over Hickory Nut Gap, and the experimental mood of January was just about to evaporate when the Valentine's Day mail arrived. "Big conference with the Pet about finances-both very depressed, decided to cut everything—both very low—Decided to write and try to sell Rathmore [Although Mr. Cramer still lived in Rathmore, he had given it to his two children. Presumably, Jim and Elizabeth were here considering selling their share in the house to someone else within the family.]—Mail came with letter giving the Pet and Ambrose Mrs C[ramer]'s share of her mother's estate—Enormous relief."[9]

Jim had overcome his qualms about spending his wife's inheritance. Not wanting to draw a salary from the Federation, he reasoned that her money was enjoying its highest possible use by providing indirectly for the benefits of cooperative farming in Western North Carolina. After the Valentine's Day financial scare, Jim sat down and made a thorough inventory of his and his wife's financial records. Their assets were considerable, mostly in the form of Chicago area real estate. In all, the annual income from rents and securities was just under $8,000, a sizable sum in those days. This money was sufficient for the management of Hickory Nut Gap Farm in 1920, and the other assets gave Jim the power to borrow more money in order to increase the size of the farm and make necessary improvements. Financial security also gave him the freedom to take an active part in community affairs.

Jim McClure continued throughout the twenties to preach his gospel of hope and courage to any gathering his schedule would allow, and to join in the leadership of worthy organizations. In 1921 he became a member of the Civitan Club, one of Asheville's leading service groups, and became its president in 1926. The local country churches continued to invite him to their simple pulpits, and he continued to preach the words of social salvation. "The blighting curse of country folks is jealousy, backbiting, distrust & gossip . . . Drive off evils as your fathers fought Indians,"[10] he told the congregation of the Fairview Baptist Church. Jim was quite fond of these country congregations. He liked the informality, the enthusiasm and especially the robust singing that was so full of the spirit of the mountains.

> Dear Hetty & Doug,
> This is a fifth Sunday with all the attending excitement in the mountains. Though a pouring rain set in at daybreak we repaired at eleven to "Emmas Grove" where plans were afoot for a "Singing" and in spite of the deluge found a house packed to overflowing. Singers from far and near had foregathered. I had the privilege of doing the exhorting. The crowd was large, three sitting on the preacher's seat as I was on my feet, two worthies leaning against the pulpit and one brave fellow in a bright green sweater standing at the foot of the pulpit savagely eyeing the crowd. The singing was exceedingly good. Dinner was served on the grounds during a break in the storm and Siddy plied her basket through the crowd with all the abandon of a street vendor. (James G. K. McClure, Jr., to the Stuarts, April 29, 1923)

Jim's specialty was the graduation speech. "Go out with courage and seek God's highest purpose for your life," he said on many different occasions and in many different ways. His light-hearted description of this particular event, written to Hetty and Doug, belies the seriousness with which he worked to relay his message to the young graduates: ". . . I had the chance of a lifetime to give tongue on the flapper problem which seems to be the most vital subject now before the public. The affair was the Commencement of Fassifern, a girls school at Hendersonville, with some twenty of the much discussed graduating. The thermometer was down to fifty and a cold wind blowing and the girls in the most summery of costumes so I let them down easy . . ." (James G. K. McClure, Jr. to the Stuarts, June 4, 1922).

These girls were the daughters of old families from Charleston and other southern cities. Jim was stumped by some of their names. He pronounced Miss Huger (U-gee) as Miss Hugger and Miss Talifaro (Tolliver) exactly as it was spelled, causing considerable giggling in the audience. One young lady was afraid she would not graduate. Her diploma slipped under the table and when her name was not called she fainted dead away![11]

The message delivered at the Fassifern School for Girls was likely to have stressed the same themes as the following example of Jim's oratory, delivered at the Asheville School, amidst calmer proceedings: "Behold I show you a mystery-a spiritual world. [The] hosts with you are stronger than the hosts against you . . . Seek ye first His Kingdom, and all the forces of the Universe will be behind you and the Lord God himself will be back of you to guide your fighting arm."[12] Jim made these speeches a call to heroism and self-sacrifice, and he always guaranteed self-fulfillment in return, knowing from experience that this was no vain promise.

Despite the puritan temper of many of his exhortations, Jim's life was filled with fun and the love of great entertainment. He and his charming wife became popular participants in the grand social life of Asheville in the twenties. During the summer "season," evenings were as gay as anywhere in the country. Celebrities of one kind or another were commonly present for these parties. The competition for prominence among the leading hostesses was keenly felt, even though it was Mrs. George Vanderbilt who held the keys to social respect. When one was invited to the Biltmore House, it meant acceptance by the highest powers in the realm. Jim and Elizabeth broke through to the top during the 1923 season. He feigned loneliness for his farm hands while describing a gathering one night at Mrs. Vanderbilt's mansion. "We have been quite gay this week as on Friday night we went to a dance at Mrs. Vanderbilt's and Siddy and I had the good luck to be seated at supper at a small table with our hostess, the Spanish Ambassador and wife, the governor of North Carolina, the Head of the U. S. Secret Service and two other notables. I felt ill at ease without the companionship of Zeb Nix and the other worthies. However we had a very gay evening" (James G. K. McClure, Jr. to Harriet McClure Stuart, July 8, 1923).

The widow of Biltmore House was eventually wooed by and married to Senator Peter Gerry, and thereafter she wasn't in Asheville as much. During the Christmas Season of 1925, however, she and the Cecils of England, members by marriage of her family, filled up Biltmore House again for a festive round of parties.

Senator and Mrs. Peter Gerry [the former Mrs. Vanderbilt] came down for the holidays and have given us quite a gay week. On Tuesday night we dined at Biltmore House with the Cecils House party and Senator and Mrs. Gerry and the next night we again dined with the Gerry's and attended a gypsy dance at Biltmore House which was the best party I have ever attended. Jack Cecil's older brother, wife and son were part of the house party and spent three weeks before the dance painting the cellar of Biltmore House. They painted scenes of every description around the walls, mainly taken from the Russian Chauve Saurie and had all kinds of gypsy atmosphere such as cauldrons and pots and glowing fire under them all around. As usual Siddy had the best costume of the evening. She is acquiring a great reputation along that line and everyone now expects her to set the standard. She had a guitar and I carried the old accordion which made a great hit. (James G. K. McClure, Jr. to the Stuarts, January 3, 1926)

The following summer, at the height of the season, they attended one of the year's most famous parties.

Friday night the Bachelors Club staged their annual fancy dress ball. It was about the most entertaining affair I have ever attended. It was staged this year in the form of a circus. There were pop corn stands, pink lemonade booths, hot dog stands, shooting galleries and some twelve side shows. Before entering the circus grounds guests had to go to the Bank of Buncombe and get fake money. Each side show had a barker and ticket taker. It gave great scope to the local talent to shout themselves hoarse and the whole business was great fun. I had the pleasure of barking for the Fortune Teller. Some four or five hundred were present and the costumes were very good and very amusing. (James G. K. McClure, Jr. to the Stuarts, August 29, 1926)

Asheville society provided for Jim and Elizabeth a close facsimile of the familiar world of their Lake Forest upbringing. The mountains had not isolated them from the people and the parties, the clubs and activities to which they were accustomed. Their fifteen miles of distance from the town and their deep involvement in the lives of the mountain people provided for them a rich blend of characters from both worlds. The two of them would never have been able to lead conventional, predictable lives. But neither could they turn their backs on their own heritage. Jim and Elizabeth cultivated many friendships that enhanced their lives and were useful to the work of the Federation. They were able to balance themselves quite uniquely between the customary world of Asheville, and the new mountain world of Hickory Nut Gap.

Their close friend and physician, Dr. Pinckney Herbert, descendant of the famous South Carolina Pinckneys, and his wife Frances, shared with the McClures an interest in the lives of the mountaineers. Dr. Herbert spent much of his own time and money serving these people, who could never have afforded decent medical care. Frances Herbert, a member of a grand old Virginia family, remembered first meeting Jim and Elizabeth back in 1916, when both couples were renting cottages near the Manor Inn in Asheville. With great wit and eloquence, she explained that the two women would forsake the accustomed grandeur of their respective youths to lead the comparatively "sketchy" lives necessary in the mountains. "But of course, we did it for love!"[13] Frances and Elizabeth became great friends. They helped to found the French Broad River Garden Club, an active group of ladies who not only "studied beautiful and useful plants, but also took real and effective interest in local conservation issues. As a leading figure in the 'French Broads,' Elizabeth helped to satisfy her own curiosity and stimulate the interest of others in the secrets of the botanical kingdom. As an affiliate of the Garden Club of America, Elizabeth greatly enjoyed exchanging ideas with other gardeners at regional and national meetings. She wrote articles on the medicinal herbs of the southern mountains and on the care of boxwoods for the Garden Club of America *Bulletin*. Perhaps her greatest contribution was a series of slides of mountain wild flowers. She and Ewart Ball, a talented Asheville photographer, roamed the area to get shots of flowers growing on dripping rock ledges or by sunny streams. This was before the days of color photography, so Elizabeth sent a plant of each variety in full bloom to New York by any trusted hand that was going up at the right season. There two expert ladies painted the slides in exactly the right shades. The slide show was rented to garden clubs all over the country until all expenses were paid.

Unfortunately for us all, Elizabeth found little time to paint in the midst of her duties at Hickory Nut Gap Farm and in the community. She told her daughter Elspeth years later that when she began a painting project she became so absorbed that she couldn't keep her mind on the daily routine. She said she became what the Scotts call "hag ridden," that is, carrying a witch on your back who won't get off until your project is finished. But Hickory Nut Gap Farm became her canvas, where she painted with the colors and shapes of the natural world. The gardens she created attracted many gatherings and luncheons during her tenure, and she greatly enjoyed sharing the place she loved so much and worked so hard to make beautiful.

The Herberts and McClures became friends for life, raising their children together and enjoying their mutual companionship. Frances Herbert was one of the first people who drove out to see the "Old Tavern" in 1916, and recalled that "It looked like the wrath of God."[14] The Herberts customarily came out to Hickory Nut Gap for quiet Sunday outings. Everyone would carry a "pocket lunch" and hike back into the mountains to find a peaceful creek bank or glade. They would all return in time for the McClure's traditional sparse Sunday night supper of crackers and milk and soft-boiled eggs.

Relatives on both the McClure and Cramer sides also made surprisingly frequent visits to Western North Carolina. On one occasion, in 1922, a large contingent of McClures including the family patriarch were on hand when word reached the farm that brother Arch had become the father of his first son. Jim described the scene to Hetty as the news spread about the house.

This morning the embarrassed voice of Western Union gave us the great news of the arrival of Archibald, Jr. The word spread through the house like wildfire. Mother and Dinto [brother Nathan] on the porch, Father in my study, Siddy in her room with Louise [Nathan's wife] upstairs, . . . were moved to immediate and delighted—ejaculations. We all went to church wreathed in smiles. At the Fairview church Father preached and completely dispelled the cloud which had hung heavy upon him since the worthy brother had denounced the theological Seminaries and especially the heads of theological seminaries two years ago.

Yesterday we took a spin to Spartanburg and Greenville and return[ed]. Father set foot upon South Carolina soil, a state in which he had never been. The day was perfect for the run and after we got out of the mountains we went through the cotton fields for miles. We had breakfast at home and had dinner at home, and between these meals traveled 180 miles in the 6 year old car [the Honeymoon Hudson!]. At times we reached a dizzy speed but to Mother we never went fast enough, and she always felt that we might have gone a little faster. . . . (James G. K. McClure, Jr. to Harriet McClure Stuart, August 20, 1922)

Nathan McClure, known as "the General" for having been in the American army during World War I, especially enjoyed his time on the farm, and pitched in with great enthusiasm. He had always admired Jim immensely, and felt satisfied when he could please him. Nathan, his wife Louise and little son (whom everyone called "Nainie") spent most of that summer with Jim and Elizabeth. In Jim's correspondence with the Stuarts, he described how much Nathan became involved in his projects:

Yesterday Louise, Nathan and I accompanied by John and a colored organizer left in the morning for Rutherford County where we attended a meeting of colored farmers who had up for discussion the subject of forming an auxiliary to the Farmers Federation. The meeting developed along the lines of a revival, hymns, prayers, Amens and Hallelujahs were interspersed at the proper moments and we all got well roused up. Even Nathan rose from his seat and made a speech. Needless to say that after such a warming up the auxiliary was formed. (James G. K. McClure, Jr. to the Stuarts, June 25, 1922)

The General is becoming the chief back door figure of Asheville. He has a way with him that makes his peaches and plums irresistible to the housewives and stewardesses of Asheville, Black Mountain and other nearby centers. I do not know how I could have made it this summer without him. (James G. K. McClure, Jr. to the Stuarts, July 23, 1922)

The General is keeping up his back door popularity and moving stuff off the farm in hilarious fashion. This last week he started to sell off my calves as the price of veal got up high. He is now taking Nainie with him on his trips to act as "side kick" or to "scotch" for him . . .

Zeb Nix was up yesterday to borrow three dollars which he gives me his bond he will repay when the General engages his hog for him. (James G. K. McClure, Jr. to the Stuarts, August 6, 1922)

Monday was a sad day In the chronicles of Hickory Nut Gap Farm. Father and Mother first entrusted themselves to the uncertainties of railroad travel and an hour and a half later Nainie, heavily guarded by his parents stepped boldly "into a Pullman, shaking the dust of Buncombe County from his trilbys. It was a grievous day for the natives. Zeb Nix arrived at 5:30 a.m. and knocked at my door . . . to fare well Nathan who had sold his hog for him so well and on Wednesday as I took up The Generals route in Asheville and environs I found every back door flag at half mast. . . . (James G. K. McClure, Jr. to the Stuarts, August 27, 1922)

The following spring, Hetty and Doug themselves came down, only to discover that Jim's Federation work had taken its toll on his golf game. Jim wrote, "As a final parting shot Hetty did me up on the Biltmore Forest Golf Links, and though beaten by a woman, I will say for her that she displayed a brand of golf seldom seen in these parts, holing out fours and fives with the regularity of [a] hardened pro" (James G. K. McClure, Jr. to Doug Stuart, August 8, 1923). The Cramer clan were avid golfers as well, as were most residents of Lake Forest. Ambrose Cramer, Sr. purchased for Jim a charter membership at the Biltmore Country Club, which opened on July 4, 1922. Membership in this readily accessible course, Jim joked, might have unforeseen consequences.

"Mr. Cramer has made E & myself members so I expect that I have seen the last of my wife & I am now planning an extra room in which to house the probable golf trophies. If Siddy should ever put her mind on the game I believe we would all lose her" (James G. K. McClure, Jr. to Harriet McClure Stuart, April 20, 1922).

Ambrose Cramer, Sr. took a lively interest in the life of his daughter and son-in-law, and was quite generous in helping to pay for projects that were beyond their reach. He offered to renovate the old inn by building a large addition to add a bedroom and make over the kitchen. The work was completed, following the advice of Ambrose, Jr., the family architect, and the result was a success that not only satisfied the needs of a growing family, but blended so well with the old structure that the entire effect of the house was greatly enhanced. Mr. and Mrs. Cramer became so enchanted with Western North Carolina that they bought a home in the new residential town of Biltmore Forest, which was growing up around the Country Club golf course.

The Skinner aunts, Bessie and Freddie, were also frequent visitors, along with their nephew, Ambrose, Jr. The Aunties contributed a new upstairs bathroom and many more touches of civilization to the old house. Ambrose, Jr., [Bowser], came regularly to Hickory Nut Gap to visit his sister and Jim.

Along with the relations, who were certainly curious about how one managed to live in rural Western North Carolina, many other travelers of various distinctions and peculiarities passed through Hickory Nut Gap. The old house, just as if it were still an inn, successfully brought together all sorts of these guests. Family members, odd visitors, employees, tenants and broken down automobile owners all became part of a group of people that could scarcely have been thrown together anywhere else on earth. Jim McClure loved this great mixing of people, at least most of the time. Genuine characters, such as this ancient specimen, seemed to be drawn to the place. "This day we were called on by an aged colored gentleman who said he was 114 years old . . . He was an old slave, is a relative of John Shorter's, and told us great tales of the old days. He remembers when the Indians were moved out of this country to their reservations which was sometime ago [about 90 years]" (James G. K. McClure, Jr. to Harriet McClure Stuart, July 2, 1922).

If the old men talked, the young boys worked. Jim and Elizabeth made a point to hire many of the children living around the farm for odd jobs around the house. Lawrence Huntley remembered his boyhood at Hickory Nut Gap with great sentiment, and credits the McClures with providing him with a strong moral example that influenced his life enormously. He usually worked alongside John Shorter and under the direction of Mrs. McClure. In the summer, he kept the grass clipped and the gardens weeded. In the winter, the wood box always needed refilling as the fires kept up a fearful appetite for wood. Lawrence recalled what it was like to work for Mrs. McClure. "If the work you did didn't suit her, she would say: 'Oh, I can hardly believe my eyes: that's the finest work in the world. Let's change it that way to see how it looks.' It had to be right . . . She had the prettiest garden in front of the house. If any weed got in there, I had to get her out." And for Lawrence, working with Mr. McClure "was just like a boy working for his father . . . He sent me off to school . . . [and] bought me a baseball glove. He'd take me with him everywhere he went. . . ." John and Esther Shorter stand out in his memory for their kindness to him. "Esther was in charge of the kitchen. She could really cook . . . [Each] night, [for] an hour or two . . . Esther would school me in my lessons." Two sisters, Minnie and Freenie Early, worked as maids during this period, and Lawrence remembers joking around with them. "John put me up to run and kiss 'em, kiss them girls-then take off. Fight you just like a dog . . . It would tickle John—that great big old fat belly—I can see him—would just shake all over." John also taught Lawrence to drive, in nothing less than the old Honeymoon Hudson. That automobile " . . . was something unusual . . . to be around here," and it sure made him feel proud for his friends to spot him sitting in the driver's seat.[15]

Lawrence Huntley's most vivid memory began with a squirrel hunting expedition:

Olson Sumner was a boy about my age. He was the one that caused that scar in my head right there. [And quite a scar, or really indention, it is!] We were after a ground squirrel in a hollow log and he was at one end of the log; we were splitting it, and I was at the other end with an ax. We were splitting that log to get the ground squirrel out . . . and I stooped down to pick a chip up, . . . and the point of it [the ax] hit me . . . Mrs. McClure—that was the first place I went. My shoes were full of blood—I mean it really bled. And

Mrs. McClure, she dressed it. Mother put soot in the cut to keep it from
bleeding, and the doctors "raised the dickens." . . . It split the skull. It's a
wonder it didn't kill me.[16]

Lawrence Huntley's parents boarded the first farm manager, James
Davidson, with them as long as he was a bachelor. The farm manager occupied
a position of authority in the hierarchy on the farm, and was the daily operator
of the business. James Davidson woke up with the rooster crows each morning,
and began the day by milking the cow. Jim McClure liked to run down and talk
to him during this chore if there were any pressing problems to size up. After
breakfast, at 7 a.m., all hands gathered at the barn. Here, the tasks of the day
were explained and divided up, and the working day began.

When James Davidson married, a new house was built for Lawrence's
family, who left the farm soon afterwards. They were replaced by another set
of Huntleys, David and Nannie, who remained on the farm for years and years.
Mrs. Davidson can recall these early patterns of life with a vivid eye for detail.
It was the Shorters, John and Esther, who again stand out. Esther, or Eddie,
would take little Jamie out for long walks every day. "She always carried a
hymn book, and sang wherever she went." One of her favorites was the song
"Life is Like a Mountain Railroad." She also had a predilection for praying out
loud as she wandered along. "Once little Jamie asked her, 'Who are you talking
to, Eddie?' and she replied, 'I'm just talking to the Lord, Honey.' A few days
later she caught him muttering to himself, 'talking to the Lord.'" Mrs. Davidson
said that the two old oxen that belonged to John and that had first pulled the
Hudson up the mountain back in 1916 went by two names. To Mr. and Mrs.
McClure, they were "Red" and "Brown," simply because John could never
bring himself to tell them that really their names were "Hell" and "Fire."

Mrs. Davidson remembers as well sitting on her porch and watching the
wagons coming over from Rutherford County on their way to Asheville. The
halfway camping spot was just across the road from her house, and there the
teamsters would unharness their horses, build a little fire and fry up some
fatback, corn bread and beans. The farmers were usually in groups of three or
four, so that on the return trip, when they were carrying their money, they would
be less likely to be robbed by thieves along the way. She recalls these wagons,
many of them covered, passing through in the fall of the year carrying their
harvests and hopes for the year. Mr. McClure would often stop and hear what
these men had to say around their campfires, and if there was something suspicious about them he wouldn't hesitate to send them on their way. But he would
usually let the farmers stay, especially if they showed some interest in the
Farmers Federation. These were the people he wanted to help.[17]

Elizabeth and Jim were gradually putting the old house into shape. There
was a room behind the living room with windows looking out to the mountains
across the valley, which had not yet been renovated. The idea of recording life
at the old inn on the walls of this room had been in Elizabeth's mind.

They had the register of guests of the Inn starting in 1850. Each had unknowingly bid against the other to get them as a Christmas present (Jim had won). Elizabeth could visualize the travellers coming through the gap: judges, political figures like President Andrew Johnson, who was Governor of Tennessee at the time of his visit; travelling ministers; hog and cattle drovers; fancy Charleston folk on their way to Flat Rock to escape the summer heat of the lowlands. She listened to the stories of neighbors who remembered the stage coach days, which had lasted well into the nineties, and studied historical records and drawings to get the make and measurements of the coach that was used. She began to piece together the visual remnants of the past—the past and present were not far removed from one another in this isolated region. As scenes slowly began to take shape in her mind, she started the "cartoons," or preliminary drawings in charcoal, directly on the beaverboard panels of the wall.

She knew the loose impressionist style she had studied in France was all wrong for the scenes of mountain life she envisaged. She wanted the panels to look like English water-color wall paper; yet oil paint was the medium she preferred to work with. To express the simplicity of life in the mountains she settled on a realistic, genie style, each little group of figures presenting an anecdote of life at or near the inn. To her credit she resisted including the stereotyped moonshiner with his still. She wanted to paint the more enduring themes of the mountains. She worked with oils, but used a medium that flattened the finish to resemble water color.

An old gentleman who had worked at the inn as a boy, catching chickens and chopping wood, took up the position of special adviser to the artist. He spent hours sitting in the doorway between rooms, making suggestions as Elizabeth painted and spitting tobacco juice a good ten feet into the living room fireplace. At first each spit made her nervous, but she soon learned that he never missed. Panels were planned for three sides of the room. One by one she filled each with life and motion—bear hunters, rattlesnake killers, pretty young gentlemen guests trying feebly to push the coach out of the mud she knew so well. She painted animals: bears; deer; razor back hogs; chickens; and in the foreground, the exquisite mountain wild flowers. She learned the type of coach used by Bedford Sherrill and wrote for pictures and measurements to the Boston Museum. She checked the details of costumes for accuracy. Only the dashing white horses, with bobbed tails and flowing black manes, were an imaginative touch that, along with the flowing contours of the local mountain peaks, unifies the diverse panels.

Jim reports in the weekly epistle of his family that "Siddy made a brave start at painting her panels but the collapse of the household put a sudden stop to that activity" (James G. K. McClure, Jr. to the Stuarts, March 19, 1922). By the first of April, Jim returned from a trip to find that ". . . the Pet had done a lot on the first panel & had painted the wheels of the coach red."[18] Jim tried to help her, not with mere praise but as a rather harsh critic. She writes in her diary that "Cricket [was] displeased with my mountain. Have to find some way of doing it more in the feeling of the period."[19] She struggled through her next session. "Spent an awful day trying to paint the mountain like an old fashioned one. Nearly killed me."[20]

In the first panel on the east wall, she painted the primeval forest. The scene depicts the moment of climax for a hunting party of Cherokee Indians. A pair of bucks and a doe are leaping out of the underbrush at the same moment that two strong braves draw their bows. Behind a rock outcrop hide the main body of men, watching expectantly as the scene unfolds. Moving to the right, the middle scene is a view of the courtyard behind Sherrill's Inn. The spring-fed dairy, the old smokehouse and the inn itself are all arranged to best display the architectural lines of the buildings. The smokehouse is thought to be the oldest structure standing today in Buncombe County, and the only one left constructed with the rifle slots needed in the event of an Indian attack. In the center of the picture, emphasizing its importance and grandeur, is the stage coach itself, a true copy of the one that traveled through Hickory Nut Gap. On its side the words "Sherrill's Flying Cloud" are painted. Four white horses with docked tails are being unhitched for feeding and watering while the coachman with his top hat leans back to have a word with a gentleman unloading a trunk. To the right of the coach, two men with coonskin caps carry in a bear cub they have just shot, flanked by four hunting dogs leaping up and running around the carcass. In the recesses of the scene, a little boy trying to lead a pig by a string tied to its hind leg is being dragged around the courtyard while a man slops a hog near the house. And there are other figures going about their business, old and young, all amidst the spring blossoms of the fruit trees. The scene, like the others, portrays the variety of the mountains, especially the variety of people.

On the same wall, further to the right, is a portrayal of an historical event. A small contingent of Stoneman's cavalry, with their blue union uniforms, is riding up the gorge toward Sherrill's Inn. Chimney Rock Mountain rises up in the background. These Union soldiers were coming to pacify Buncombe County, whose citizens on the whole had been staunchly loyal to the Confederacy. They set up their headquarters in the inn before moving on to Asheville.

Moving to the south wall of the room, the "Flying Cloud" begins its ascent up the mountain to the inn. One gentleman, riding with the driver, blows a horn, an old tradition on this line. The number of blasts will give Mrs. Sherrill the count of the travelers that day, and she will still have time to add more food to the table if necessary before the coach can "pull the mountain." Nearby, next to the road, a mountaineer and two well-dressed city men gather around a coiled rattlesnake, shotguns in hand. The mountain man looks distrustful of the city fellows' aim. Elizabeth has added to this panel many of the flowers that are her joy, including the rhododendron Maximum in full bloom.

On the west wall, the central panel is flanked on either side by two separate groups of travelers passing through the Gap. On the left, four covered wagons, each pulled by a team of oxen, lumber up the grade, preceded by a herd of hogs being kept in line by a mounted drover and a young boy. Wagons such as these were still to be seen in the early twenties passing by Jim's and Elizabeth's home. On the right panel, a mountain family has once again pulled up stakes and is on the move, a surprisingly common occurrence in the mountains. Two mules pull an overladen wagon, while members of the family either ride along or walk beside the entourage of people and animals, which includes a flock of sheep and two leashed hounds.

The central panel of this grouping represents another masterpiece of anecdote, full of characters and action. "The Flying Cloud" has just pulled to a halt in front of Sherrill's Inn, and as the passengers unload their jolted physiques, their mountain host comes out to greet them with a tray of "cordials." The painting is full of little touches of mountain life: Mrs. Sherrill's fine bonnet, a quilt drying on the roof, a little boy fruitlessly chasing after a chicken (the chicken drawn by Jim because he thought Elizabeth's was not running fast enough!), bees streaming in and out of the old-fashioned bee skeps, and a pretty young maiden with a billowing skirt and dainty parasol shyly being introduced to two nattily dressed young dandies. A boy holds the horses as they stamp and paw, eager to get to the barn after the long pull up to the inn.

These paintings are among the very few that remain as a testimony to Elizabeth's extraordinary talent. Her vision in these panels indicates a great deal about her attitudes; she loved the common poses and activities of life around her, its variety, humor and essential beauty, if only one took the time to see it. These pictures show her gifts as an artist, her ability to compose scenes that are both balanced and beautiful, and yet alive with activity. It speaks too for her appreciation of all people, high and low, her uncommon mountain neighbors along with her dandified friends from town. These pictures are a secret treasure of the Southern Appalachians, bringing together a time, a place and a gifted artist.

By May, Jim proclaimed to Hetty and Doug that "Siddy has her second panel almost completed and the room is going to be a wonder" (James G. K. McClure, Jr. to the Stuarts, May 21, 1922). By the fall of 1923, the word was out that a unique project depicting mountain life had been created by Elizabeth McClure, and Jim described in his distinctive manner the reception of these panels by the local critics. "We had quite a day yesterday for Cornelia Vanderbilt spread the news of Siddy's pictures on her return home & the Vanderbilt house party then commenced to arrive in relays during the afternoon. I plan to charge admission & also to wear a guard's uniform & stretch out an itching palm as sightseers depart" (James G. K. McClure, Jr. to the Stuarts, no date).

The autumn of 1922 marked not only the triumphant completion of Elizabeth's "painting fit," but many other changes in her life. Her second child was growing within her, while at the same time she felt the loneliness and melancholy of being without Jim, who was away on a long and difficult errand. Her brother Ambrose had been suffering through some personal and marital difficulties. He and Grace had been living in France while he worked on his architectural degree at the Beaux Arts in Paris, and with Jim he returned there to work through his problems. Jim's long absence was a sad and lonely time for Elizabeth, but produced more of her moving literary expressions of love. She and Aunt Freddie, little Jamie and Esther, all went up to New York to see Jim and a very depressed Ambrose off for France.

Dear Cricket & Bowser off for France . . . As the ship sailed slowly off I rushed to find a tall coloured porter who could hold Jamie up in the air to wave at Daddy . . . Auntie [Freddie] quite cheerful & [I] felt most cheerful myself to realize that Ambrose had really left & with my darling to cheer & strengthen him (Can't help worrying about that letter to G[race]). Jamie it seems raised the dickens while I was downstairs, yelling, & saying he didn't have to behave now [that] Daddy was gone . . . I miss my darling terribly & find myself thinking of him almost continuously. I hope he is sleeping well tonight & that [Ambrose] is more cheerful. There is an occasional fog horn sounding & it makes him somehow seem near! (October 16, 1922, New York City)[21]

. . . longing for Cricket & anxious as to how things are going. Hope he will think to send me a cable with some hint. (October 19, 1922)

Another lonesome night without Cricket. I miss him more every single night. Bowser's letter so pathetic but there is one line in it that makes me hopeful. (October 20, 1922)

Such a lovely autumn day, almost hot, with here & there cosmos, dahlias, chrysanthemums in bloom & such lovely subdued colors in the leaves. How I wish Cricket could see them. The mountains are just the way he loves them . . . I would have given anything to have been with him, to see all that lovely French land again for the first time together after so many years away. It is very hard not to hear from him—if I could only have letters he would not seem so far away . . . I kept thinking of Cricket & Bowser & Paris & longing to know how things were with them. It is very lonesome without Cricket & gets worse all the time! . . . (October 29, 1922, Asheville)
. . . a letter from that dearest Cricket telling me everything I wanted to know . . . His letter was *such* a comfort & delight & Ferderkins [Aunt Freddie] was greatly heartened & cheered by all he said about the Bowser. . . . (November 3, 1922)

On November 7, when election day arrived, Jim was still away and Elizabeth had the opportunity to exercise her new privilege at the polls. Her response to women's suffrage is quite curious, considering her family's political interests and her own independent life before her marriage, but it was still a new responsibility.

Mr. Davidson called . . . it was voting day. Very much irked at the thought of voting but felt that perhaps Cricket would want it . . . Cast my vote (after first calling Mr. P_____ on telephone to ask if there was any specially good man I should vote for) & Just put my mark on a straight

Republican ticket. Also voted for increase in pay for legislators. Hurried back home after first having dispelled the usual crowd that had gathered about Puny. (November 7, 1922)

Despite Jim's and Elizabeth's flirtations with socialism prior to the Great War, by the time of Calvin Coolidge they were both safely in the Republican camp, and there for good. Jim had voted for Warren G. Harding and his "return to normalcy" in 1920, as did Elizabeth in what would have been her first chance to vote.

The next evening Elizabeth wrote:

Spent evening sorting Cricket's mail & systemizing it. Miss my darling terribly but had the joy of finding a letter from Rouen in today's mail & 2 postcards. The Rouen letter took me right back to that thrilling old town. Cricket sounded in the letter exactly as though he had been affected by it in just the same way I was when I first saw it. I am counting every hour to my dearest's return. I miss him every minute & his dear letters are such a comfort. (November 8, 1922)

Next day, with the woods filled with dry leaves, their neighbor Emory McAbee had one of his "fire fits." Elizabeth described the scene.

This has been a day of excitements. Rushed out to post a letter early & smelled smoke. Clouds of it pouring over Ferguson & Rocky Point. Smoke pall descending all over [the] mountain. [I] learned . . . that a bad fire was raging in around Emory McAbees & was part on our land. They thought Emory had let the fire out . . . Mr. Davidson had sent hands up to fight the fire, but Mr. Early [who was there shingling the garage] feared wind & thought if it got going nothing could stop it. I felt much worried . . . Flew down to the barn and interviewed Mr. Davidson . . . Men came down about noon from fighting [the] fire. [They] had been obliged to start some sort of back fire about halfway up the mountain to head [the] fire off & some fire back of Rocky Point along [the] Ridge I believe. [I] felt that [the] danger had been averted. Mrs. Huntley came over about 9 & said that a lot of our timber had been burned a short time ago in one of Emory's crazy fire fits . . . It seems that Emory had built a fire . . . one day & Mrs. McAbee according to Mr. Davidson was terrified of him . . . Mr. Merrill . . . told me to tell Mr. Davidson that he had seen the sheriff in town & sent him out that afternoon & that Emory had been taken off. [I] Arranged with Mr. Davidson about sending some one up tomorrow to see about Mrs. Emory . . . Very "jumpy" this evening. Queer sounds in the cellar & disturbing noises. Scared of everything. Thank goodness only two more nights without Cricket. (November 9, 1922)

It was high time for Jim to come home! Elizabeth met him at the train in Biltmore on his return from France. As she rushed to embrace him he hastily warned her back. His suit and overcoat pockets were bulging with antique octagonal plates, each with a different French scene—his present after his long absence. Seven years later, the "Bowser" episode culminated with a surprise twist. Jim and Elizabeth were summoned to Washington to witness his second marriage, to Mary Meeker, his first wife Grace's younger sister.

While Jim was away, Esther Shorter felt a need to go home and take care of her old mother. The trip to New York as Jamie's nurse had been difficult for her, and despite all her virtues she could be rather temperamental on occasion. She was a proud and sensitive woman and had a bad heart that perhaps made her quick to anger. After six years of devoted service, in November 1922, there was "Much hurried packing & the two [Esther and John] . . . departed for good. No tears shed but such general good feeling."[22] Soon afterwards Esther died and John returned to the farm to remain a loyal pillar of the establishment until his own death in 1955.

Elizabeth struggled to find a replacement for Esther, with her second child expected in a few months. A nurse was hired, known simply as "Hawkins." With such a name, one would expect a military sort of figure. Elizabeth explained to her Aunt Freddie that "Hawkins is . . . more powerful than ever and I am sighing with contentment. She talks through her nose & squeaks & Jamie is beginning to talk just like her but she is such a tower of strength I could not manage without her for the present, anyway" (Elizabeth Cramer McClure to Frederika Skinner, June 29, 1923). Hawkin's powerful tendencies eventually overreached Elizabeth's bounds, when she learned that the woman had thrashed Jamie with real vengeance when the family was away. Elizabeth fired her on the spot and took over the nursing duties herself.

Soon after Jim's return from France preparations got under way for the birth of Elizabeth and Jim's second child, expected early in 1923. Childbirth brought out the most cautious instincts in Jim and Elizabeth, which is only to say that the lives of mother and child were given the highest value. But the contrast with today's recuperation schedule is startling. The whole family moved into Asheville in mid-January to be nearer the hospital. With the arrival of Wiggywags (Martha Clarke), all signs of the imminence of the great event were present. Yet, in all the correspondence, the exact nature of the details of the appearance of the new baby is discretely avoided, as if to mention childbirth itself was a bad omen that somehow might threaten the new life. In such a manner, Hetty and Doug, and the rest of the family, were kept informed.

> We plan to move to 306 Chestnut St., Asheville on next Thursday where we will be installed at the boarding house of Miss Elizabeth Bernard. It seems a most comfortable establishment. We plan to put Jamie in kindergarten so he may not grow up a social recluse. (James G. K. McClure, Jr. to the Stuarts, January 14, 1923)
>
> Our entourage moved into Asheville for the season . . . we are now awaiting the dinner gong before marching in to dinner . . .
>
> Jamie is proving a great mixer and already has an intimate acquaintance with every fellow boarder. He has introduced himself to them in whatever role he happened to be playing at the moment so that there is great confusion as to

Esther Shorter and Jamie McClure.

his name, some calling him George, some Tobey, some Mac, some Jinks and some Uncle Wiggly. (James G. K. McClure, Jr. to the Stuarts, January 21, 1923)

Letters and telegrams from all the readers of this weekly have put me in very close touch with you all this week. I can plainly see that the surest way to get a reaction from my faithful readers is to send out telegrams similar to the ones dispatched last Sunday night.

Elizabeth and Elspeth are doing famously. I have just come from the hospital where I said Goodnight to the pair of them. Dr. Millender is highly pleased with them both and says he has not had a patient do so well in years. Elspeth has been on her good behavior and everyone is charmed with her. Elizabeth will keep right on at the hospital for some time, in fact we are planning for a stay of four weeks, for we are exponents of the slow and easy school. We will have to be thrown out of the hospital as we were last time before we take the plunge into the cold hard world.

Miss Clarke is taking the most beautiful and loving care of the pair and it
is a piece of rare good fortune to have such a devoted friend. (James G. K.
McClure, Jr. to the Stuarts, February, 4, 1923)

Elspeth's cold hard world out at Hickory Nut Gap would be the same rich
blend of aristocratic values mixed with strong democratic intentions that marked
off the struggles of her parents. It would be a world of cooks and maids, and
the tough mountain children who were also growing up on the McClure farm.
Her world would include the great cast of characters that called Jim and Elizabeth McClure their friends. It would also include a membership in the wider
McClure clan, so aptly explained by the Dominie just after his granddaughter's
birth.

My dear Elizabeth,
I am just as proud of you as I can possibly be. I rejoice with all my heart
in the birth of little Elspeth. She has a very big place in my love already, and
the place grows bigger every day. How wonderful it all is, that a life comes
to us, and it isn't a stranger at all—it seems perfectly at home—as though it
belonged to us—and we love the life devotedly from the instant of its arrival!
I never have felt all this so much, as since word came that Elspeth was here.
Yesterday I spoke of this to Arch . . . and Arch said that this is exactly the way
he feels.
Well, Elizabeth, you always were a queen in my judgement (and it is a
sober, thoughtful but enthusiastic judgement) and now you are more a queen
than ever. If that husband of yours . . . is not proud of you and doesn't say
that you are the dearest, . . . loveliest woman in all the world, I will not believe
he is in his right mind.
Please put that question to him—and let us know what his condition of mind
is.
Grandfather McClure
(James G. K. McClure, Sr. to Elizabeth Cramer McClure, January 31, 1923)

The Dominie's wife, Annie Dixon McClure, wrote happily that the arrival
of Elspeth "completes the round dozen of our grandchildren" (Phebe Ann Dixon
McClure to James and Elizabeth McClure, January, 29, 1923).
Elizabeth's father took the opportunity of Elspeth's birth to sing again the
praises of his own daughter. "Darling Blos," he wrote, "We received the splendid news . . . Now you will know like myself the joy of having a daughter. If
your daughter brings unto you one half the love and affection and dearness of
my daughter. she will fill your life with happiness, and never give you a thought
save congratulations for a name. You and Jim can settle that, but do not call her
after local peaks or Hickory Nut Gap" (Ambrose Cramer, Sr. to Elizabeth
Cramer McClure, January 29, 1923).
"Elspeth" was neither peak nor gap, but a Scottish name that suited Elizabeth. Neither was the little child encumbered with a middle name, even if it
meant passing up the opportunity to honor a relation. Elizabeth's painting

friend, Mildred Burridge, welcomed the child with this exuberant return telegram. "Your telegram received with flourish of Trumpets Cornets Hauteboys Bassoons Bass Drums Triangles Display of Fireworks Pine Wheels Skyrockets Roman Candles Embrace Elspeth fondly for me I long to see her Am Telegraphing from St. Frances Hotel gaily decorated in her honor."[23]

The formality of "Elspeth" fell away to "Elfie," and that became the family name of their little girl. Jim McClure was keenly aware that each child was born into this world deeply in debt. There were the debts of history: political freedom, religious tolerance and scientific progress. There were the family debts: the struggling Covenanters, the trekkers of the new world, the hardships and the successes. All of these circumstances placed little Elfie in a distant world unlike the one her neighbor children knew. Jim wanted his progeny to grow up aware of these debts, and aware that the process must continue. His view was that the real leaders of each generation were those men and women who followed their highest calling, sacrificed their own pleasures for a better world. And, as the theory went, self-sacrifice would yield self-fulfillment.

The rock on which Jim and Elizabeth raised their children consisted of these same heroic virtues and strivings. Service was held up before them as the highest calling of life. Education was the cornerstone of ability. Like all parents, the McClures wavered between mercy and justice, but the values themselves were clear-cut and unassailable. Certain activities, such as card playing of any sort, were forbidden. Of course, this encouraged the youngsters to hide away in closets to play an illicit game of Lindbergh cards. From birth, Jamie and Elfie were carefully monitored so that their intellectual progress could be nurtured. But they were not lock stepped through youth, especially with the opportunities of a mountain farm. Besides, Jim and Elizabeth were too much fun to let their Victorian habits grind down the frivolous nature of youth. But these two children did grow up to be disciplined, each in his own way. Jamie was a seeker of truth, who would not abide sloppy thinking in either man or child. Elspeth, the more literary of the two, tried hard like her parents to appreciate people, to overlook the faults in others, and to stand ready to help them along.

Little Elfie and brother Jamie grew up in a changing world. Henry Ford's mass produced automobile revolutionized transportation during the twenties and ending the picturesque wagon trips through Hickory Nut Gap. Even back in the mountains of North Carolina, a surprising number of cars and trucks were on the road. Around Fairview, Jim McClure was known as much for his Hudson automobile as he was for founding the Farmers Federation. The fascination for the mechanical miracles of Detroit struck the farm boys of the mountains deeply. The big switchback curves going through Hickory Nut Gap became, and continue to be, the scene of dramatic automobile crashes. One of the earliest occurred back in the spring of 1922 when Elizabeth was painting her panels, and gives some indication of the carefree attitude that overtook a group of people with a flivver and a little gas money. To Hetty and Doug, Jim wrote,

> This day opened with a crash on the road at 6 a.m. which proved to be a party of young riders turned over in a Ford. On extrication none proved seriously hurt. How they do it in a Ford I fail to see unless Henry has some special arrangement with the special Saint detailed on motor accidents. This party drove straight over a bank turned completely over, all ended up in or under the car and none seriously hurt. The party had been out all night and slumber had gotten the better of them. (James G. K. McClure, Jr. to the Stuarts, May 26, 1923)

New cars meant new roads, and in 1923 the state began to pave the old sand road up the mountain with concrete. If there were great hopes for a fine road in the future, the present driving conditions were absolutely atrocious. Elizabeth described to Aunt Freddie the process of road building during the early twenties.

> . . . *never* have I imagined anything much worse than the sand clay road. It is ploughed up in great tracts & the mud & stones & ruts something incredible. They say that [they] are going to start the cement work on the 15th of June starting at the Fairview bridge & working toward Asheville. A camp of 25 men are located at the very top of the Gap where they are quarrying rock for the macadam part of the process & the stone crushing. They have to pay us so much a square yard of rock & will be there perhaps a year, so we shall get something out of it, anyway. Jamie is of course tremendously excited. (Elizabeth Cramer McClure to Frederika Skinner, May 26, 1923)

Little Jamie was fascinated by machines. He was four years old now, and loved to run down the pasture to watch all the road building activity. Men and mules worked together hauling rock and driving drag pans. Building a road by hand was a laborious project, but many a man worked whatever political pull he had to get hired onto the crew. The men and animals camped on the job during the week, going home only on the weekends. A few shacks were built to accommodate the workers. One crew of laborers was made up of all black men, and they loved to sing to while away the hours. Young Jamie was leaning up on the fence watching this particular group one day, utterly lost in fascination by the implements and processes of this working outfit. The negro gang fell into a slow rhythmic song to match their work, but one prepared especially for the little McClure boy. Jamie's presence was carefully monitored from the kitchen window up the hill; he suddenly turned and raced up towards the house crying. He was met quickly and comforted by his mother. When he calmed down, he explained. As he listened to the workers singing in spiritual rounds, he had suddenly caught the words of the chorus that ended each verse: "Little white boy, sittin' on the fence. Ain't got nothin' to do."[24]

The prospects for a new road worried Jim. The engineers were keen to eliminate the numerous switchback curves, cutting through an entirely new route. Jim dreaded the further desecration of his farm, as the road had already been changed several years before. He traveled down to Raleigh to plead his

Left: *Baby Elspeth, Elizabeth, and Jamie McClure, 1923.* Right: *Jamie and Elizabeth in the garden below the house, June 1923.*

case in the matter, and returned with the good news that "The decision to have the new road come up following the old road has greatly eased our minds" (James G. K. McClure, Jr. to Harriet McClure Stuart, July 8, 1923). The same road is still in use, and the picturesque curves provide today a scenic route for the tourists who can be seen almost year round enjoying picnics and taking pictures of each other as they travel through Hickory Nut Gap. But the work back in the twenties was painfully slow, and by late fall of 1924, Jim was thoroughly exasperated by the lack of progress. He wrote, "We are in the depths of misery over our road. It will be next June before the wretches are through and meanwhile we are hundreds of miles from town on a wet day" (James G. K. McClure, Jr. to Harriet McClure Stuart, November 4, 1924).

Throughout this period a whirlpool of activity swirled about Jim McClure: problems like the new road, the management of his farm and the Federation, and increasingly, the appointments that give public men and women even more duties. At the same time, in the eye of the storm, his family was growing up. Despite the demands on his time, Jim could always arrange to be with his wife and children. Like his own father, who had taken him along when making pastoral calls, Jim loved to take Elspeth and Jamie with him on his jaunts into the countryside. They loved the excitement of all the Federation activities, and children make a wonderful topic of conversation in a crowd of strangers. When they were older, Jim McClure would work them into the entertainment. Most of all, he wanted his children to be nurtured by the same rich Christian tradition and idealism of his own youth.

Jamie was in many ways a difficult child to raise. He was extraordinarily intelligent and was for four years an only child in a large household that must have seemed to him set up to revolve around his needs. There were no children with his background at Hickory Nut Gap, and he grew up a self-assured and completely fearless child. Jamie McClure inherited his father's strong tendency to question the comfortable assumptions, and he did not hesitate to speak up to correct his own contemporaries, or even his elders, if he became convinced that they were wrong. Perhaps it is fair to say that he was as "cranky" as his father, but had not as a boy acquired Jim's tact as a counterbalance. One Sunday, Jim preached a sermon at the Fairview Church. Surprisingly, his keen son was paying close attention to the message, and when the word "demolish" turned up, he immediately demanded a satisfactory definition. With great warmth, Jim explained that he would have to pause to clarify this point with a member of the congregation.[25]

Jamie's forthright nature and precocious intellect, fed by an endless curiosity and stimulated by his parents' wide interests, added to his courage. At three, while in New York City, Aunt Freddie and Elizabeth took him to the Bronx Zoo. His mother described the expedition in her diary. "We got a gorgeous Pierce Arrow to come for us at 9:30 . . . Jamie adored the park & especially the monkey, laughing immediately at their antics. In the Elephant house the keeper took an immense fancy to him & before the envious eyes of other astonished children took him behind the separation and let him feed the elephant hunks of bread. Jamie was very bold & Delighted the keeper by not being afraid."[26]

Jamie's quick mind made it difficult for him to hold his tongue among his friends, and he rarely felt the same ease with boys his age that had so distinguished his father. He spent a lot of time with adults, and was perhaps more comfortable in their presence. Usually he possessed a courageous soul, but a Halloween Party given in Asheville by the Perry family would have been a test for any child.

> Puny and I taxied over to the Perrys stopping on the way for a pillow case in which to array Puny at the Palais Royal. Puny [was] terribly interested at the prospect in store. We arrived at the Perrys and found several other little spooks waiting on the steps— Puny somewhat reluctant to descend when he saw them but clutched my hand & we entered boldly. We all wended our way to the barn where with many ghostly noises each child was ushered singly into the dark barn. They all seemed to enjoy it though Puny *again* clung to me like mad & when we got inside was somewhat terrorized by a shaking corn stalk (colored man concealed within) as the children's shrieks of excitement *were* rather appalling. The poor lamb started to weep but when he realized it was all fun he laughed & shouted with the rest though he stuck to me like a leech. The children bobbed for apples in a big tub which again he declined to participate in explanation of which he said "there is no room for Jamie" & when we played

another game in a circle he declined to come in the middle because "there was too much of a crowd." I was rather ashamed of him but considering that it was his first party he did pretty well & looked like a little Prince. When it came to refreshments to my horror I saw him wash down a ham sandwich with three cups of cider & crunching salty almonds & cake & candy! I knew he would be sick & after he got to bed tonight a doleful voice summoned "Mummy"—I rushed him to the cabinet & all his supper upchucked! Poor little darling—[27]

The following spring Jamie was big enough to hike with his father to the top of Ferguson, the mountain behind the house. Jim recorded the event. "Jamie and I climbed Ferguson's Peak this afternoon. I carried him on alternate stretches and we had a grand afternoon, getting a view from South Carolina to Tennessee. Jamie was much troubled because he thought the Peak was in the sky and on getting to the top found the sky was still out of reach. He also marvelled that the mountain went down on the other side."[28] At about the same time, the curiosity of the little boy overtook him, and he disappeared completely from under the watchful eyes of his nurse. "At noon Puny can not be found— Dragnet out & report comes in that about 10:30 he had appeared in bottom & been sent home on Mr. Ben Nesbitt's wagon—Following up this clue . . . I drove to Gerton & on foot to the saw mill when we found the fellow gay as a lark & having had a glorious time with Mr. Nesbitt."[29]

Jim and Elizabeth's progressive notions made them at first reluctant to spank Jamie. But one night he refused to stay in bed despite all the cajoling and stern lectures his parents could muster, and so his father finally "Had to paddy whack Jamie as he was unmoved by any other force of punishment & got out of his bed by night & by day when supposed to stay in—He was greatly startled but reformed at once."[30] Two weeks later, Jim tried a more innovative disciplinary tactic. "Jamie has suddenly become very unruly, getting out of bed on all occasions . . . but my impersonating the Sheriff and having him formally summoned, sentenced and immediately dealt out a summary punishment, we seem to be getting the upper hand of him without drawing upon ourselves any of the rancor that a child should feel for a stern parent. The Sheriff and the writer are two distinct persons" (James G. K. McClure, Jr., to Harriet McClure Stuart, April 16, 1922).

Jamie grew up as a boy filled with ideas and projects, stimulated by his life on the farm. One of his first contacts with the animal world, however, taught him the value of prudence and caution. "Jamie has twice been butted by the sheep, each time being knocked off his feet and his dignity seriously hurt, as the second time it occurred he was trying to placate another sheep by sprinkling her with his water pot. He now moves through the pasture heavily armed with a stick with which he hopes to successfully defend himself" (James G. K. McClure, Jr. to the Stuarts, April 22, 1923). At five years old, he became consumed with the mysteries of egg laying. "Jamie is delving into everything on the farm and his questions are legion. He has succeeded in taming a rooster and secreted him in his closet a few nights ago. Hoarse crowing from this closet about 6 a.m. startled the sleeping household. Jamie had secreted him in the hope that he would lay an egg for breakfast and as he failed to do what was expected of him, Jamie asked me at breakfast 'Why don't roosters have egging powers?'" (James G. K. McClure, Jr. to the Stuarts, January 5, 1925)

Jamie's father, in the pose of Saint Nicholas, thrilled his own children and all the children on the farm at Christmas. The first performance of the day was scheduled strictly as a family affair, and was described here by the impersonator himself. ". . . Santa himself appeared at five o'clock on Christmas Eve. All the family were on hand to meet him dressed in fancy dress. Mr. Cramer as a naval officer, Aunt Freddie as an 18th Century lady, Miss Patterson as the Queen of Scotland, Jamie as a white rabbit and Elfie as a Gainesborough child. The event was the most happy one" (James G. K. McClure, Jr. to Harriet McClure Stuart, December 27, 1925). The following day, Santa made his public appearance for the benefit of all the children living on the farm. Despite the season, ice cream always provided the glorious finale to this occasion. "After [Christmas] dinner we turned and again sped back to Hickory Nut Gap where Santa Claus again appeared to the startled tenants. Ben with his seven children and Zeb with his seven held the family attendance records. As this is the closed season for bathing down here it took some days to air the room out" (James G. K. McClure, Jr. to the Stuarts, January 4, 1925). The McClure Christmas was Elizabeth's production. Presents, for her family and the tenant children alike, were judiciously chosen and wrapped with the exquisite taste of an artist. She made the season special at Hickory Nut Gap, and all with an effortless appearance.

An appearance of another kind occurred when Elspeth was just six. A legendary and famous disembodied creature appeared to Ben Owenby's daughter Christine, who was helping at the house.

> Christine, Ben's oldest daughter . . . came out of the Dairy, where she had been pouring the milk and started for the house when she heard someone stumble and looked up and there was a 'hant.' She was dressed "in an old timey sweep tail white dress and her black hair hung in ringlets to her waist." She walked across the court yard and melted into the old kitchen chimney!! This was at once taken as a sign that something was going to happen. The next day Ben was taken with acute appendicitis and rushed to the hospital!! (James G. K. McClure, Jr. to the Stuarts, February 3, 1929)

Elizabeth was familiar with spirits from the time she had spent with her Somerville relatives in Southern Ireland and always enjoyed discussions about them. She vowed it was old Mrs. Sherrill herself who banged doors or knocked on windows on windy nights. Her daughter Elspeth would have found it easy to believe in these spirits, for she loved the kingdoms of the fantastic. Her brother was more interested in machines and airplanes.

Although Elspeth found it easier to play with the farm children than her brother did, he was the leader of the group. When she grew older, she resented

Ker Boone, a farm resident, oversees the harnessing of his dogs for Jamie and Elspeth McClure, July 1925.

her nickname "Elfie" because she wanted the Boone children to think she was tough (Mr. Boone was the current farm manager). Elspeth loved nothing so much as building dams and water wheels in the several little streams that started above the Boone's or playing house in the nearby woods. There she was free from the constraints of her upbringing and the more circumscribed behavior demanded of her at home. Both Jamie and Elspeth enjoyed rather unique child-hoods, surrounded as they were by all varieties of people. They were able to partake of both the pleasures of the rural life, and the elegance and refinement of their other world in Asheville and beyond. They were also able to enjoy a father and mother who constantly concocted new and remarkable schemes to create fun. Jim was a very popular father in his children's eyes. Elfie was about three when he wrote: "We are enjoying a blanket of snow and today Elspeth went out in her Grandfather's little sleigh and after she had a long ride, she met us at the foot of the mountain as we came home from church. There a shift was made and Jamie was proudly pulled by the car all the way home on his Grandfather's sleigh . . . It is a surprisingly well-made affair" (James G. K. McClure, Jr. to the Stuarts, January 10, 1926).

By his tenth year, Jamie had moved up to the larger members of the animal kingdom on the farm.

The Spring fever has got the best of Jamie and he has decided to feed two calves to sell this fall. Each calf weighs 200 lbs. and neither have had a halter on, so the last week has been a hectic affair. In order to tame them, Jamie

Left: *Jamie and Elspeth on the pastures behind Ferguson, Spring 1929.* Right: *Mathilda Shorter.*

keeps them tied and leads them to water night and morning. We never knew whether a calf will shoot out of the barn with a muzzle velocity of 40 miles an hour with Jamie at the back end of the rope or whether Jamie will slowly emerge, pulling with all his might on a balky calf. It is a regular circus performance. (James G. K. McClure, Jr. to the Stuarts, March 19, 1929)

Elspeth remembers one summer afternoon when her brother Jamie came running around the corner of the porch shouting, "John's got a new wife! John's got a new wife!" They ran through the courtyard and there was Mathilda, all smiles, sitting on the bed in John Shorter's tiny house by the woodshed. Mathilda was from New Orleans. She had met John while working for a family summering in the mountains, and she could cook like a dream and care lovingly and dependably for children. She brought joy to Elizabeth. The couple were promptly set up in a little place down below the Huntleys, a rather sketchy house left over from the road builders that Mathilda soon made into a charming cottage. She was a natural artist and was blessed with an imagination to match Elizabeth's. She and John earned a position of greatest respect in the McClure household. Respect for people was one of the strongest of the virtues taught to Jamie and Elspeth by their parents. It was natural and easy for these children to grow up free of racial prejudice with men and women like John, Esther and Mathilda a part of their daily life.

All through the twenties Jim was becoming more and more involved in community activities, first in Fairview, then in Asheville, and before long at the state level. All his life he was loyal to the Republican party of his class and upbringing, despite moving into the Democratically "Solid South" and despite managing a Farmers cooperative that depended on the help of local and state government. Over the long haul, it was the politicians who would begin courting him, with his influence and, most of all, with his ability to draw a big crowd. Jim made light of his Republican affiliations when he fell into a serious political discussion on the train to Raleigh during President Harding's administration. ". . . I had a most interesting trip for a political dissension in the Democratic Councils had sprung up and was at white heat. The gentlemen with whom I went to Raleigh were in the thick of this and even tho I am known as a black Republican I sat in with them at their grave and warm councils" (James G. K. McClure, Jr. to the Stuarts, April 22, 1923). In the 1924 election, the Progressive Party was led by the highly respected Robert LaFollette of Wisconsin. Jim's conservative swing was complete as he joked about his brother Arch's predilection for the more left-wing candidate. "[E]lection day is not far off. I still fear that Alec [Arch] will secretly cast his ballot for LaFollette and I believe he ought to be watched at the Polls" (James G. K. McClure, Jr. to the Stuarts, October 19, 1924).

Jim tried always to take the higher view of politics. His real opponents were the corrupt and ignorant people who had, by deception, graft or whatever, come to hold offices of public trust. No one could demoralize the population more easily than crooked or selfish politicians, and therefore, in order to promote the Kingdom of God, a more altruistic political order would have to assume power. When Jim first came to Fairview, the local Republican party offered to support him in a local election. He was tempted, giving the matter considerable thought, but he declined, wisely, in that it might have jeopardized his ability to organize the Federation.

He did enter the shifting tides of Fairview politics, however, by becoming appointed to, and then actively seeking a seat in the powerful local school committee. His commitment to progressive education never wavered despite having to constantly wade against the strong current of self-interest. "The Fairview School year is now at the Commencement state and it is resting somewhat heavily on me as I am now a School Committeeman and the School Committee has to pick the teachers. In a community like ours where everyone has an ax to grind and everyone has a brother, daughter or niece who is a school teacher it is a riotous job" (James G. K. McClure, Jr. to the Stuarts, May 6, 1923). Two months later, elections were being held. Jim went into the community to stand squarely behind his proposal to centralize the primary and secondary education in the township into one consolidated school building. "In Fairview we are in the midst of a school election." he wrote to the Stuarts, "The campaign is becoming heated and I put in Friday and Saturday electioneering. Our voting day is not until Aug. 6th but we are in the midst of registering at present. Opposition develops on the most surprising grounds, one large faction being opposed because the new school will be on the highway and at least one hundred children per year will be killed by passing cars" (James G. K. McClure, Jr. to the Stuarts, July 15, 1923). His electioneering tactics were successful, and he became a committee member. The following June he reported a peculiar act of larceny carried on by him and the Committee on behalf of the school children of Fairview. "The Fairview School Committee executed a well planned raid into Yancey County during the week in an effort to run off with a particularly able school principal who is located in the fastness of Yancey. We made our getaway without having a shot fired at us and hope to get our man in the next week or two" (James G. K. McClure, Jr. to the Stuarts, June 8, 1924).

Although he remained a Republican, he was often appointed by the Democratic powers of the state to serve on committees for the public benefit, and Jim took these responsibilities quite seriously. By 1925, he became the natural choice to join the staff of the Bureau of Markets for North Carolina. The job entailed developing markets for the state's agricultural products, and was a paid political appointment. A year later he reluctantly resigned. "I hate to lose the salary," he wrote to Hetty and Doug, "but inasmuch as I have so much Federation business and so much personal business, and inasmuch as political jobs are very open to criticism, I feared that the Federation might be hurt by my hanging on longer to the salary" (James G. K. McClure, Jr. to the Stuarts, July 4, 1926). Jim was willing to sacrifice almost anything for the Federation.

Soon, however, he was appointed to the State Board of Conservation, a volunteer post he greatly relished and for which he worked hard. His first meeting, in January of 1926, was held in Raleigh.

> We met yesterday in the Governor's Office, the Governor being Chairman of the Board. The Board has under its jurisdiction the State Department of Forestry, the State Department of Geology, Water Powers, & the Development of Manufacturer's, Mines & Minerals. As the Governor is keen on the Development of the Resources of the state we have a big job on our hands & you will have to expect more hot air on North Carolina when next we get together. Out of the seven on the Board, three are Mac's so we should be able to look after the finances. (James G. K. McClure, Jr. to the Stuarts, 1926)

Jim was a sports hunter himself, as well as something of a conservationist in the Teddy Roosevelt mold of scientific soil and water management. He personally worked hard to create better hunting conditions by setting up game refuge areas and wild bird propagation projects. In two years, he could proudly show these concrete results of his work: "We created another game refuge in Macon County in the Nantahala National Forest of 10,000 acres, which is the project I had been working up . . . We also voted to operate a small quail farm in Randolph County . . . we will have something like $50,000 to spend on game propagation . . . this will enable us to do some good construction work" (James G. K. McClure, Jr. to the Stuarts, January 8, 1928).

By the end of the decade, Jim McClure's selfless efforts began to gain wider recognition. For once he received an honor that carried no new responsibilities or requirements on his part. A small Kentucky college, uniquely tied to the education of the Appalachian people, invited him to their graduation in 1929.

> James Gore King McClure, Jr., son of the Manse, student in the school of Christ: who, joining the seekers of health in the southern mountains, saw the poverty of our people, refused to be content with maudlin pity, romantic contemplation, pauperizing doles; who, with careful statesmanship, began to lay the broad foundations of a better economic life, and of a cooperative commonwealth among the individualistic farmers of the mountains:
>
> By the authority conferred upon me by the Trustees of Berea College, I bestow upon you the degree of Doctor of Science, with the certification and the hood appropriate to the degree.
>
> President Hutchins[31]

Of all the many accolades that would in time come to Jim McClure, this honor from Berea College always possessed special significance for him. The trustees of the school were the first to recognize the value of his work, and moreover, they held a special vantage point: the hope of the Federation's goals illuminated the very region to which Berea College had dedicated itself. The Appalachian people, with their traditions of resourcefulness, wanted to be able not just to endure, but to progress and to escape from inhibiting stereotypes. Jim McClure wanted to minister to a region, not only by preaching the gospel of progress, but also by building a new foundation for prosperity.

The twenties were such flush times that Jim, like many of his contemporaries, felt that modern economics had unlocked the secrets for a steady growth of wealth in the United States. His assurance in modern business practices gave him the confidence to start the Federation in the first place. With the door to wealth unlocked, the great challenge for America was to maintain its drive for spiritual excellence. Jim worried less about financial collapse than the swamping of the nation's moral fibre in the high waters of prosperity. He understood, like the brilliant writers of the age, that material success leaves one with an empty victory. But unlike Thomas Wolfe, Sinclair Lewis and F. Scott Fitzgerald, he did not respond with bitterness or cynicism: he refused to satirize *Homo Americana*.

In 1926 Jim McClure gathered his thoughts about the destiny of his country, and wrote a paper that he delivered before a distinguished group of intellectuals in Asheville known as the Pen and Plate Club. Dr. Pinckney Herbert had proposed him for membership, and throughout his life he made use of his opportunities to speak there to formulate his deepest convictions. The club's purpose was to stimulate and sharpen the intellect of the members and each paper was followed by a series of penetrating questions from the floor. To Hetty and Doug he confided his struggles in piecing together his first presentation. "My week has been miserable as I have to read the paper next week at the Pen and Plate Club, and I have had to snatch at it when I could. My subject is 'Has

Democracy fulfilled its economic purpose?,' and I am daily growing sorrier and
sorrier for the poor Pen and Platers" (James G. K. McClure, Jr. to the Stuarts,
February 14, 1926).

The following excerpts from the paper show the direction of Jim's ideas
during this period:

HAS DEMOCRACY ACHIEVED ITS ECONOMIC PURPOSE?

The impelling forces in human history have almost always been unconscious forces, and it has usually been decades or centuries after an event before
these unconscious forces could be rightly analyzed. In this paper I want to
make a study of those fundamental forces and hopes of mankind which have
created our American Democracy; of the realization of the promise of the
creators and of the future possibilities of this great experiment in human
co-ordination . . .

The great hope which has brought men to our shores can be divided into
three chief motives—the hope of Religious Liberty, the hope of Political
Liberty, and the hope of Economic Liberty.

Of the first, Religious Liberty, it is enough to say that it has been realized
to a surprising extent, considering our human frailties and prides and suspicions, and it is with reverence and gratitude that we realize that this hope of
religious liberty . . . [has] brought to our shores, as its first permanent settlers,
a type of man and woman of such strength of character that they fixed on this
great country a tradition of idealism, of fair dealing, of enduring morality and
of a God-given destiny which is, perhaps, its chief source of strength and hope
for the future . . .

The second great hope, Political Liberty and Equality, has also been realized to an extent almost beyond the dreams of the founders of this country.
Every man stands equal before the   , and casts his independent vote. The
people decide the issues and policic   ch their representatives carry out . . .

We have our political defects, so serious and so dangerous, that some voices
among us appear to be on the verge of despair, but we have achieved in theory
the political liberty and equality for which our forefathers fought.

The third great hope which has peopled our shores has always been the
hope of economic liberty and equality. And it is with our realization of this
dream that my paper will be concerned. Even those who first came to America
to achieve religious and political freedom, seem to have had also the hope of
economic betterment. And the great bulk of our immigrants have come with
this single purpose. The Promise of America has been a promise of economic
independence and prosperity.

"Neither race nor tradition," says Professor Hug Muensterberg in his volume on "The Americans," "nor the actual past, binds the American to his
countrymen, but rather the future which, together, they are building." From
the beginning the Americans have been cemented together by a vision of a
future. Most nations have their national tradition, built around the past of glory
or struggle, but with us in America it is, and has ever been, our future that
appeals even more strongly to our loyalty and imagination. And the dominant
note in this projected ideal is a future in which economic prosperity will be still
more abundant and still more accessible than it has ever been. It is this hope

Elspeth standing on south side of McClure home, "with bleeding heart and narcissus planted in the myrtle." [Elizabeth McClure's note.]

which invites the native American and the alien immigrant. Men come here because they hope to have a better chance and a fairer opportunity than the Old World can afford . . .

Our democracy, with its practical and proven faith in the equality of political and religious opportunity, has released the people of America from the millstone of social inhibition that has hung round the neck of all peoples of all times. This social inhibition has deadened ambition, stifled hope, and smothered energy. Ambition and hope are the parents of energy. Put ambition and hope into the heart of a young man, and they will drive him fast and far. He will extend himself. His power will develop as his pace increases. Energy will keep generating within him.

And the releasing of this chief driving power of human progress in the hearts and minds of these, the people of the United States, has given a momentum to social progress that can never stop.

The people of America are making more rapid progress toward this goal of economic equality and prosperity than they realize. Wealth is increasing at a rapid rate, and prosperity is becoming more and more diffused. We are approaching equality among occupations. The wages of manual labor have been going higher and higher, and as between the manual jobs and the white collar jobs of the mediocre sort, there is practical equality now . . .

. . . We all know that the carpenter and the plumber, and now even the unskilled laborer, rides to work in his car. The manufacturer recognizes this diffusion of wealth. His vision is to make goods that are universally used—to make goods so well and so cheap that they will be used in every home. Our manufacturers do not advertise "Purveyors to His Majesty," but instead, "A Million Satisfied Users. . . ."

. . . They say that we are so strong financially that the entire wealth of the Roman Empire could be passed through our bank clearing in a single day and only the statisticians would notice the bulge. This tremendous economic prosperity has come, I believe, because the democratic form of government which we have created has called forth the ambitions and hopes and energies and talents of the people. Democracy has fulfilled its economic promise, and its economic momentum is gathering strength each day.

This diffused prosperity has come to us, as we held to the ideal of economic freedom and liberty. It came to us as we were following the ideal. We can only retain it as we continue to follow the ideal. Wealth, when sought for itself, eludes the grasp or turns to bitterness when grasped. Unless America keeps her aims vitally idealistic, her doom is sealed. There is no life except as spiritual ideals are held to. We must carry out this idea of a more equable division of wealth.

And further, we have been so busy creating this wealth that we have had no time to think why we wanted it. We must now set ourselves to alchemize our newfound wealth and leisure into spiritual and intellectual gains; into those things that permanently satisfy the soul of mankind. [32]

The man who penned these words was describing the bedrock on which he based his optimism for the American future, the same future that he envisioned as the source of American national unity. Four years later, that faith would be severely tested by the Great Depression. As Jim advised here, each man or woman must constantly check his or her personal motivations and adherence to ideals. Asheville and Buncombe County in 1926 were the scene of the beginning of a colossal hysteria, a money-mad binge that would eventually leave both entities bankrupt. Real estate values increased so rapidly that nearly everyone who had a little money could join the delusion and create a paper fortune. The whole tottering structure would blow away like smoke in 1930, leaving behind countless examples of financial devastation. Soul searching would become the order of the day. Jim McClure did not escape this tragedy, but he understood what happened to men when their souls had lost their idealistic moorings.

By the end of the twenties, his own life had become a marvel of variety, a circus of activities and projects. His powers of inspiration and judgement were being constantly tested. He discovered, thankfully, that his own sermons were prophetic. If one but gave himself up to the powers of God, his maker would grant the wisdom and strength to accomplish the task. Jim's God had given him a wife who shared his ideals, and two children who gave his life a center and a refuge from all the pressures he had created for himself. He had learned how to relax, when to enjoy the restorative entertainments that came his way. The end of the decade, though, proved also to be the end of an era. Not only would the style of entertainment shift, but the very faith in progress and democracy that had helped to fuel the American economy, and the Farmers Federation, would be sorely tested by the ensuing depression. Jim's own financial stability would be sorely threatened as well, but his vision of a better future failed to crumble into cynicism. On the eve of this particular national disaster, the Federation was thriving, his family was bursting with enterprise, and he and his wife remained healthy. Even in the worst of times, these are gifts worthy of a man's thankfulness.

1. Interview with Elspeth McClure Clarke.
2. Interview with Mrs. James E. Davidson.
3. *Ibid.*
4. Interviews with Elspeth McClure Clarke.
5. James G. K. McClure, Jr., diary, May 30, 1921.
6. Elizabeth Cramer McClure, diary, September 26, 1921.
7. James G. K. McClure, Jr., diary, September 26, 1920.
8. *Ibid.,* April 30, 1918.
9. *Ibid.,* February 14, 1920.
10. James G. K. McClure, Jr., sermon given at Fairview Baptist Church, August 6, 1922.
11. Interviews with Elspeth McClure Clarke.
12. James G. K. McClure, Jr. Graduation address, Asheville School, date unknown.
13. Interview with Frances Herbert.
14. *Ibid.*
15. Interview with Lawrence Huntley.
16. *Ibid.*
17. Interview with Mrs. James Davidson.
18. James G. K. McClure, Jr., diary, April 1, 1922.
19. Elizabeth Cramer McClure, diary, April 21, 1922.
20. *Ibid.,* April 22, 1922.
21. *Ibid.,* November 9, 1922.
22. *Ibid.,* November 3, 1922.
23. Telegram from Mildred Burrage to Elizabeth and Jim McClure, February 4, 1923.
24. Interview with Elspeth McClure Clarke.
25. Interview with Mrs. James E. Davidson.
26. Elizabeth Cramer McClure, diary, October 18, 1923.
27. Elizabeth Cramer McClure, diary, October 31, 1922.
28. James G. K. McClure, Jr., diary,May 6, 1923.
29. James G. K. McClure, diary, April 23, 1923.
30. James G. K. McClure, Jr., diary, March 31, 1922.
31. Honorary Degree from Berea College, conferred June 1929.
32. James G. K. McClure, Jr., "Has Democracy Fulfilled its Economic Purpose?" paper given before the Pen and Plate Club, Asheville, North Carolina, February 18, 1926.

Chapter Sixteen
Hickory Nut Gap in the Depression

Whether Siddy and I can keep our place is a question—tho at present we can not sell it and as we are down to a cook only, we will live there as cheaply as anywhere . . . We will keep our house if we can but will try to sell any part of the farm that we may get an offer for. (James G. K. McClure, Jr., to the Stuarts, no date)

By 1929, Jim and Elizabeth McClure had become deeply involved in Western North Carolina. The Farmers Federation was expanding. Jim had begun his trips north to raise money for the development of new enterprises to help the mountain people. Elizabeth had put her heart and artistic gifts to work fixing up the old inn, planting boxwoods and flowering borders, and entering into the lives of her neighbors. As suddenly as a bolt of lightning the financial crash that heralded the Great Depression threatened everything they were working for. It was the real estate boom and bust that did the most harm to the economy of the mountains in general, and the McClures in particular.

Ownership of land had always been important in Western North Carolina, ever since the first settlers came over the Blue Ridge Mountains. Like those pioneers, Jim and Elizabeth had come with an independent spirit, seeking land of their own and freedom from outworn ideas. For the early settlers land and wealth were synonymous, for so it had been for as long as memory served back in their old countries.

There had been two mild land booms before and after the Civil War, but nothing in the past could have prepared the local citizenry for what happened during the twenties. A fit of real estate covetousness took hold in Western North Carolina, especially in Buncombe County. By the latter part of the decade, this fit had grown into a full-fledged delusion. All up and down Asheville's Patton Avenue real estate offices were scattered, each one filled with enthusiastic and urgent salesmen generating a faith in the never ending upward spiral of land values. Oftentimes the realtors would hire bands to play out on the sidewalks, creating a carnival air that promoted the general hysteria. Inside a realtor's office, one might enjoy a free lunch in exchange for glancing through a few brochures. Sharp real estate dealers, known as "binder boys," had poured into the mountains after a hurricane had wrecked their game in South Florida. They knew how to bind an imprudent person to one of their contracts, and Buncombe County seemed to have the right mix of wealthy tourists and beautiful undeveloped property to suit them. After all, Asheville was to the summer tourists what Miami was to their winter counterparts. The binder boys wanted to exploit the wealthy and glamorous people who had been attracted to the cool, beautiful mountains of North Carolina.

Author Thomas Wolfe, in *You Can't Go Home Again,* described the setting for this land boom and its focal point, Asheville, as he saw it when he returned after a long absence.

> The sleepy little mountain village in which he had grown up—for it had been hardly more than that then—was now changed almost beyond recognition. The very streets that he had known so well, and had remembered through the years in their familiar aspect of early-afternoon emptiness and drowsy lethargy, were now foaming with life, crowded with expensive traffic, filled with new faces he had never seen before . . .
>
> But what he noticed chiefly—and once he observed it he began watching for it, and it was always there—was the look on the people's faces. It puzzled him, and frightened him, and when he tried to find a word to describe it, the only thing he could think of was—madness . . . The faces of natives and strangers alike appeared to be animated by some secret and unholy glee . . .
>
> The real estate men were everywhere. Their motors and busses roared through the streets of the town and out into the country, carrying crowds of prospective clients. One could see them on the porches of houses unfolding blueprints and prospectuses as they shouted enticements and promises of sudden wealth into the ears of deaf old women. Everyone was fair game for them—the lame, the halt, and the blind Civil War veterans or their decrepit pensioned widows, as well as high school boys and girls, Negro truck drivers, soda jerkers, elevator boys, and bootblacks.
>
> . . . And there seemed to be only one rule, universal and infallible—to buy, always to buy, to pay whatever price was asked, and to sell again within two days at any price one choose to fix. It was fantastic.[1]

This fantasy world was built on easy credit, and encouraged the collusion of men who should have known better, but had neither the will nor even the desire to try to break the momentum of such wild speculation. Wolfe's description continued:

> The town was burgeoning rapidly and pushing out into the wilderness, people were confident of a golden future, no one gave a second thought to the reckless increase in public borrowing. Bond issues involving staggering sums were being constantly "floated" until the credit structure of the town was built up into a teetering inverted pyramid and the citizens no longer owned the streets they walked on. The proceeds of these enormous borrowings were deposited with the bank. The bank for its part, then returned these deposits to the politicians or to their business friends, supporters, allies, and adherents—in the form of tremendous loans, made upon the most flimsy and tenuous security, for purposes of private and personal speculation.[2]

One example of the boom spreading into the "wilderness" around Asheville occurred in the valley just below Hickory Nut Gap Farm. A development known as "Hollywood" was being platted and sold there by the quarter-acre. Busses came from Asheville, hauling prospective buyers to walk about on fields covered with the stubble of last year's corn crop. And yet the grandiose visions of lakes and golf courses, as described in the sales pitch, made believers of many.

During the late twenties, Asheville's real estate market began to resemble a large scale poker game, as the frenzied buying and selling took hold of the local psychology. Nearly everyone with a little money counted himself in on the stakes. People proudly bragged of their winnings, spurring on others to jump into the action. What was to happen to all this prosperity, and why?

By the late twenties many an American had made his bundle of money. The rich citizens of the era were able to glut themselves on the trinkets of the age—fine automobiles and grandiose homes, along with the new mass-produced gadgets that were the source of so many of these fortunes. Asheville itself had become something of a trinket, a place to enjoy a lavish summer at a resort hotel in the cool of the beautiful mountains. George Vanderbilt's choice of the area to build his great house, and the continuing presence of his widow in the exclusive suburb of Biltmore Forest (developed from a portion of the Vanderbilt estate), lent an aura of credibility to social Asheville.

But even these conspicuous consumers could not find enough goods and services to buy, and so turned increasingly towards investment as a haven for their cash. Inevitably, the market for stocks and real estate became dangerously overinflated. During the summer of 1929 the stock values began to sag, foreshadowing the collapse of a nation's investment portfolio. Investors, money managers and business executives began to feel concern, followed by desperation, then by panic. By late fall, the soaring values of stocks and bonds came crashing down and stayed down. On cue, like the midnight stroke in Cinderella, just as the decades shifted, the glitter of the twenties ball was turning into the rags of the Depression.

For Buncombe County the fantasy ended the morning the Central Bank and Trust Company failed to open its doors, November 20, 1930. The previous day Jim was on the train travelling towards Raleigh, perhaps to a Conservation and Development meeting. From some of his fellow passengers he heard a rumor that the Central Bank was in trouble, and even might close soon. The train always made a short stop in Greensboro. He jumped off and hurried to call Elizabeth. The next morning she set forth for town with John Shorter at the wheel of the Hudson. At the top of Coxe Avenue, they saw the line of cars reaching a mile down Patton Avenue to Pack Square, where the bank's doors were already shut forever.[3]

Behind the doors was not only an insolvent bank, but also almost all the financial assets of the City of Asheville and Buncombe County. Both had to default on their interest payments. A long line of people were filing past the bank as if viewing the open coffin of a close relative. Nearby, the mayor of

Asheville put a gun to his head, not willing to endure the shame of the disclosure of his illicit dealings with Central president Wallace Davis, who would himself spend time in the penitentiary. The mess was left for lawyers and the courts to sort out. But these events affected people all over the region. Only a few weeks before Elizabeth had persuaded their cook, the widow Edith Williams, to take her savings out from under her mattress and put them in the bank for safe-keeping.

As the house of cards came tumbling down in Buncombe County, the universal rule became: "Sell, *sell* at any price." But no one was buying now. The Hollywood development below Hickory Nut Gap grew up in scrub pines and blackberries. The unfortunates who had bought lots there would never see a golf course, and could hardly afford to build a house. As the chain reaction of failed banks spread through Western North Carolina, counties and munici-palities, businesses and individuals were ruined.

Months rolled into years and the situation worsened. Jim's lawyer ex-plained to him that Buncombe County owed more than $50 million, making the debt per $100 valuation work out to about $46, effectively reducing the market for local real estate to the vanishing point. To buy local property meant also to buy a portion of that debt. There is no doubt that this area was one of those hardest hit in the entire country. A number of responsible, community minded citizens, among them Jim's young friend, Julian A. Woodcock, Jr., set up a sinking fund to begin paying off this debt. He was in charge of the final liquidation party, celebrated in 1979.

Before the crash, Jim's assumption that his wife's share of the Skinner fortune would provide amply for the family's future was reasonable. As the two aunts, Elizabeth (Bessie) and Frederika (Freddie), declined in health with the years he had figured that future material needs would be cared for by their estates and that, as a good steward, he should invest the money at his disposal to bring the greatest return. Jim McClure believed in the local land game, and he jumped in with the hope that he could develop an investment income suffi-cient to allow him to work for the Federation without salary. And besides, he couldn't resist the excitement. He used Elizabeth's money, swelled by her legacy from Aunt Bessie, who died in 1923, and the money Aunt Freddie gave him to invest, to form the North State Corporation (Aunt Freddie had come to live in Asheville). By 1929, the company had amassed a long list of holdings. Lots in Asheville were a very liquid asset during the twenties, and Jim and his North State Corporation were fairly floating in this particular commodity. There were Amboy lots, Ardmion lots, Forest Hill lots, Roberts Street lots, Kimberly lots, Biltmore Avenue lots, and Takoistie Trail lots; not to mention three houses, three farms, and a store.

Outside of town, Jim owned an interest in a large tract of land in the Wayehutta section of Jackson County, an interest in 36,000 acres along the upper Pidgeon River in Haywood County known as Sherwood Forest, and a share in 14,000 acres along the headwaters of the Tuckasegee River in Jackson

County. Up in Yancey County, Jim invested $6,000 in a cyanite mining company. By the end of 1930, Jim and his company owned, or had an interest in, twenty-eight pieces of property, with taxes due in January of 1931.[4]

Jim McClure's motives for buying all of this property might have been more idealistic than some of the other local schemers, but the disastrous financial results of the crash hit him just as hard when the doomsday bell sounded. North State collapsed in the real estate debacle.

During the thirties, it was all Jim and Elizabeth could do to keep Hickory Nut Gap Farm. The figures tell the plight of the McClure family. At the end of 1931 the value of their assets still maintained a healthy lead over their liabilities, but a year later their assets were sinking much more rapidly than their liabilities. Moreover, the assets they had were mostly Buncombe County properties that were almost impossible to sell at any price. By 1933 the minus column surpassed the plus column by more than $10,000, creating great gloom up at Hickory Nut Gap. Elizabeth's inheritance, locked up in the Northern Trust Company of Chicago until the last of Ambrose Cramer, Sr.'s children should die, had ceased paying dividends.

Jim began taking a small salary from the Farmers Federation, as he could no longer afford to contribute his services as he had been doing, and he made every possible economy on the farm. He wrote soberly to Doug Stuart, "I know you are right about the necessity of my clearing up our situation, but it is a complicated matter to work out. I now wish I had taken your advice four years ago and let all the properties go" (James G. K. McClure, Jr. to Doug Stuart, exact date unknown). The number of farm hands was trimmed and those who remained received lower wages. For most of these families, cash was still something of a luxury and as long as they had a house and a garden place they could "make it." Jamie must have been eleven years old and Elspeth about eight when the financial troubles reached their depths. Elizabeth faced the necessary changes in their way of life squarely, with her customary humor and gallantry. One morning she made a special time to explain to her small daughter that she would be counting on her to help with many household chores. Elspeth remembers listening quietly, knowing this was serious business for the grown-ups. But secretly she was thrilled at the prospect of making beds and sweeping floors with her delightful mother, who always made a shared task fun. Jamie was equally eager to take on more farm chores; but being children they doubtless wearied of their duties soon and sometimes forgot them.

Mr. Will Boone became farm manager when James Davidson left. He was a direct descendent of Daniel Boone and a representatives of the independent tradition of the mountains. He had two daughters close to Jamie's age, Adeline and May, and a son, Richard, just a few months younger than "Sis," as Elspeth now liked to be called. Jamie was the intrepid leader of these children's many adventures. Elspeth remembers the joys of playing hide and seek in the old barn, prisoner's base in the special soft grass that grew in front of the Boone's house, and dodge ball in the dry, dusty backyard. With great labor, under Jamie's direction, they dug a pond in the pasture between the big house and the Boone's that actually filled with muddy water deep enough for swimming. One of the most distressing days she can remember was when a doctor, who had come to see her mother about occasional severe headaches, condemned the pond as a hot-bed of typhoid fever germs. Elizabeth was always careful about matters of health, and swimming in the pond was thereafter forbidden. After that it was remarkable how frequently people fell in.

The Huntley family moved to the farm several years later. Jamie used to go down to play the banjo with Frances, who played the guitar, while his little sisters Evelyn and Betty sang. Theirs was a musical family. It was whispered that Rev. David Huntley had been the best fiddler for miles around in his youth, but when he was called to preach he put his fiddle away and never touched it again. Now he wrote hymns, complete with music, to be sent off to the Stamps Baxter Company, which published the Paperback hymnals widely used in the country churches. When he drove Elizabeth to town he always put on a sober suit and composed hymns while he waited for her to do her errands.

Life went on happily at Hickory Nut Gap Farm, in spite of the loss of the upstairs and downstairs maids. Elizabeth never complained and made everyone around her happy with her enthusiasm for new ventures. They were "down to a cook only:" as Jim wrote to Hetty and Doug, but there was another figure in the household who helped Elizabeth hold it all together. Miss Agnes Paterson was a Scottish lady who was nurse, governess and dear friend from about 1928 right through the worst years of the Depression. Miss Pat was, as she herself put it, a "bright Christian," incredibly thin, a mere wisp of a woman, conscientious, thoughtful and gentle, but brave as a lion if she felt one of her charges was in danger. Elspeth remembers her rushing up the lawn and through the rock garden to stop the headstrong Shetland pony Neddy, who was running away with her down the steep gravel road to the barn. This in spite of the fact that she was physically fragile, and given to spells of lumbago (a dire pain in the back). Miss Paterson was able to take responsibility for the complicated household when Elizabeth had to be away during Aunt Freddie's last illness. Under Elizabeth's direction, she taught Jamie and Elspeth. She was a gentle influence in the rough farm world.

Miss Frederika Skinner lived gamely on through the first months of the debacle of the North State Company's fortunes, spending much of her time in bed recovering from a broken hip. She had given Jamie an electric train, which he had set up in the attic with an elaborate system of tunnels under magazines and loops around family trunks. Elspeth remembers Aunt Freddie riding proudly up in the dumbwaiter to the attic to witness the train in action. Aunt Freddie died in the fall of 1930. Jim was on a money raising expedition in Philadelphia, but rushed home when he received word that she was failing. He and Ambrose were the executors of her estate.

Miss Freddie's death marked the transfer of the Skinner estate from one generation to another. Elizabeth received the bulk of its worth, but it quickly

Left: *"Preacher" David Huntley*
Right: *Miss Agnes Patterson*

became apparent that this inheritance would prove a burden rather than the source of financial freedom for the McClure family. From the time Aunt Freddie died in 1930 to November, 1932, her estate lost $471,155 in value. It was in fact an empty treasure chest, and Jim and Ambrose had to spend long hours corresponding with institutions and individuals to whom Aunt Freddie had left legacies, including aged household helpers and a heroic Vermont poetess, Miss Salley Cleghorn. Finally they simply had to divvy up the list of worthless Buncombe County properties and send deeds to the various recipients. It would be one more lesson for Jim, as the whole affair settled in his mind, of the foolishness of putting one's faith in the material world.

When he saw how matters were going Jim wrote to Doug Stuart a letter, part plea and part apologetic explanation:

> Dear Doug,
> . . . Elizabeth and I had always "figured" that when Aunt Bessie's and Aunt Freddie's estates were divided up that her share would pay up all our indebtedness and that there would be about $250,000.00 principal left for

income. Due to the tremendous shrinkage of the two estates, the cash legacies took almost all of Aunt Bessie's. What was left for Siddy was applied on our debts with a few stocks of very little value still on hand. By the time some stocks . . . reached Siddy they were valueless.

Aunt Freddie's estate ended up with no cash at all but some properties came to Elizabeth and me, and also some debts come with some of them.

The final windup of the estates instead of leaving us out of debt and with a good income, finds us with a large indebtedness and a lot of property for which there is no market . . . As to your suggestion of letting properties go, this is just what I should like to do but it also presents difficulties . . .

If I can pledge the Cyanite stock and the Sherwood Forest stock in friendly hands, I can then let one or two of the creditors take a judgement and when they find they can get nothing, I think I can settle . . . at a low figure, provided I have the cash from the pledged stock to make the settlement. As to the Banks there is nothing to do but keep trying to sell some property and try to do this before interest and taxes eat us up . . .

I am doing everything I know how to do to get rid of this debt, and if you have any suggestions, I shall be only too glad to have them. (James G. K. McClure, Jr. to Douglas Stuart, no date)

This letter to Doug Stuart, asking him to become the "friendly hands" of his financial salvation, was difficult to write. Doug, who was financially secure, would help him out of course, because he and Harriet were loyal relations and friends, but not before questioning Jim's business judgement. The Quaker Oats executive had listened over the years to his brother-in-law's many social theories and his youthful anti-capitalist sentiments. Now Jim was financially prostrate and struggling to avoid the economic ruin that the collapse of land values had brought on. His investments must have seemed reckless to a competent and hard-nosed businessman like Doug Stuart. He thought Jim McClure's business notions tended to be over-optimistic; that his belief in the steady progress of prosperity was too sanguine. He loved and respected the man of vision, and he and Harriet backed him up from first to last. Nevertheless the present circumstances justified Doug's cautious business sense, and made Jim feel irresponsible. They both lived in a business culture, where every man stood before the world as a commercial success or failure. The pride of many men was based on their personal success in the marketplace. It was a mask worn at all the social functions of their kind. The shock of the Depression stripped many of these men naked; too often suicide became the alternative to facing up to one's contemporaries in the new role of "failure." Jim McClure's life was built on more enduring values, and although he faced a desperate financial situation, his faith carried him through. His identity was too rooted in the spiritual world to be shaken by material difficulties. But he must have been deeply worried about the future of his family. Doug Stuart did come to the rescue, by buying one-half interest in the Tuckasegee property and interests in some of the others, thus helping Jim and Elizabeth through this difficult period.

The education of Elspeth and Jamie became another burden for Jim and

Elspeth riding the "airplane" on the porch, February 1930.

Elizabeth during these years. They were both determined to give them "the advantages" that had meant so much in their own lives when they were growing up. Jamie was bright and tended to be opinionated, and they worried that life on the farm provided him too little companionship and left him too much by himself reading in his room. Dr. Emerson, a child specialist whom they respected, assured them that a slightly truculent son who did not want to take suggestions was quite natural and recommended a summer at Birch Rock Camp in Maine. He assured them that such an experience would give him an entirely different point of view, especially about home. Jamie did spend two summers there, soaking up the New England atmosphere his parents prized and learning to get along with boys his own age. He played baseball, learned to swim, which was difficult to do on the farm as there was no deep water for miles, and fought and made friends with other campers. At home on the farm two of Doug and Harriet Stuart's daughters, Anne and Margaret, were spending the summer, and he wrote to his sister: "How are you getting along without me? I am wishing I was with you every minute. From Mummy's letters I have heard that you and the Stuarts are having a fine time. Have you had a wrestling match with Margaret: If so, who won . . . ? There's a sailboat race in August, and several of us are engrossed in boatmaking" (Jamie McClure to Elspeth McClure, June 1930).

His interest in sailing, begun at camp, would be a lasting one for this land-locked mountain boy. The next year, on his way to camp, the indomitable Aunt Wiggy, now dean of women at Simmons College in Boston, met him between trains and sent back to Elizabeth a perceptive account of his short visit. She wisely took him to see an exhibit on engines, where she left him for a time to do an errand.

"Jamie, will you stay just here if I go down & telegraph?" "Why, Aunt Wiggy! What do you think. You couldn't get me away from here."

Jamie McClure.

... *always* he was most absorbed. I always had to talk to him to make him aware of my presence. At the Hudson (20th Century) interior I would find him consulting the chart, and then nipping back to the engine, simply enraptured— I never saw such a perfect—"dead to the world."..I succeeded in getting him away from the trains by getting him to come to select a model of the engine in which he was so interested ... We would be walking along and he would put his arm 'round *my shoulder* and saunter on talking, talking oblivious ... We got up to the Claremont [Hotel] a little ahead of time to his joy! as he wanted to watch "the shipping." I could scarcely get him in. It was boiling and he, at once, before one could wink, started to take off his coat. It was so funny! The waiter said you can't take off your coat and Jamie said "I should think comfort came before beauty!" but he kept his coat on. He ordered *just* the things he wanted and enjoyed supper hugely in both senses of the word. He

did seem to be very happy watching the ferries and eating at the same time.
(Martha Clarke to Elizabeth Cramer McClure, Summer of 1931)

The camp experience certainly served to smooth some rough edges for this
most enthusiastic and outspoken young man. He added his interest in sailing to
his fascination with Charles Lindberg's flight across the Atlantic to France.
Elspeth remembers the flying school he conducted with herself as pupil. At the
green table on the porch, where the family ate their meals all summer, she
learned the parts of a plane and learned to "fly" a tricycle made to look like an
airplane by pushing it up to the top of the rock garden and driving it fast down
the sharp angles of the path, to crash land in the box bushes at the foot of the
lawn. In the courtyard Jamie began building an airplane as large as the Spirit
of St. Louis out of beaverboard. She was as convinced as he that someday it
would soar over the farm.

School was of course an even more important question for these children.
Elizabeth herself had taught Jamie at first, using the Calvert method. The
Calvert School in Baltimore carried on a correspondence course that reached
worldwide, and was used by families in lonely areas. The emphasis was on art,
history and literature. Miss Paterson took over the daily teaching, but Elizabeth
always kept close to the school room.

Home teaching was not a permanent solution. Jamie was sent to a small
private school in Asheville, the Grove Park School, for fourth and fifth grades,
then to public school in Fairview. On the first day in public school he came
gleefully home announcing, "Eighteen boys in the class and I had a fight with
seventeen." He enjoyed his year, made some friends and was fortunate to have
an excellent teacher, Miss Sally Merrill. But his parents, sensitive to the mountain accent and determined on the best possible education for their precocious
son, sent him the next year to the Asheville School for Boys, a private boarding
school on the far side of Asheville. He had a scholarship and to save paying
board and keep Jamie in the family for a little longer, he lived at home. Father
and son left the house at 6:45 a.m. six days a week. Saturday was a school day.
This made such a long day for Jamie that the next year they let him board. Jamie
was growing up to be as inquisitive a young man as he had been as a boy.
Machines, engines, ships, locomotives and the rest continued to enthrall him.
He was neither a great athlete nor a smooth ladies' man, but remained enthusiastically bookish. He spent hours studying Jayne's *Fighting Ships,* the famed
authority of the navies of the world, and could recognize the profile of every
American naval vessel. Jane Raoul Bingham, then a young Biltmore Forest
belle, recalls attending a dance at the Asheville School that she had been anticipating for some time. The McClures and Raouls were old friends, but Jane's
heart sank when she met up with Jamie, who was several years younger. He
insisted on taking her over to view a room full of science exhibits, which he
thought much more stimulating than the fearful constraints of a boys' school
dance. Poor Jane dutifully followed her little friend, to see what were to her the

dullest objects imaginable. While he explained the beautiful order of science, she would hear the tantalizing strains of the dance music.[5]

As we have seen, the educational and religious traditions of New England meant much to both Jim and Elizabeth, so they decided the Hotchkiss School in Lakeville, Connecticut, was the place they wanted Jamie to go for high school if possible. They liked the values the school stood for and they respected the headmaster, George Van Santvoord, known to the boys as "The Duke." Jim wrote to him in November 1932, asking if the school could offer some scholarship aid.

> When this work [the Farmers Federation] first started in 1920 I contributed my time and this I was able to do for seven years. The Farmers Federation then started to pay me a small salary. Business conditions have swept away our entire income and resources except for this salary from the Farmers Federation. This salary is not sufficient to send Jamie to a good school and in fact it is with great difficulty that we are able to live at all. He is on a scholarship basis at The Asheville School.
>
> I feel that the work here must be carried on irrespective of financial inducement elsewhere and I shall not leave it. We are very anxious to have Jamie at Hotchkiss. Mrs. McClure and I were brought up in the North and tho the excellence of the Asheville School is unquestioned, we are eager that Jamie whose whole life has been spent in the Southern Mountains shall have the standards and influence of Hotchkiss and New England.
>
> I trust that Jamie will dedicate himself to a life of usefulness. It has been the tradition of our family and I hope that if you can see your way clear to granting him a scholarship that he may be of value and use to the school. I know that it will mean everything to him. (James G. K. McClure, Jr. to George Van Santvoord, November 1932)

Jamie was accepted at Hotchkiss with a scholarship and worked hard throughout his four years. At that time scholarship boys waited on tables, cleaned bathrooms and did other chores while paying students did not. He loved the school, and greatly enjoyed working on the newspaper. He made some good friends, especially Jack Butler, who spent his summers sailing on Cape Cod, an opportunity that he generously shared with his mountain roommate. Jamie loved everything about the ocean and sailing more and more. At Hotchkiss he was well prepared for his father's college and won the Yale Hotchkiss scholarship for his freshman year. But this is getting ahead of the story.

Back at Hickory Nut Gap, Jamie's pleasures continued to be his books, hunting and fishing, helping out with the farm work and, as he grew older, taking part in the work of the Federation. He was a fearless fellow, who entered into any activity from pitching hay to dancing at the country club with boundless enthusiasm. He was learning to play the banjo from "Pistol Pete" Taylor of the Farmers Federation String Band and loved to sing the mountain ballads, which were a delight to his mother, especially.

Some of the family's happiest times were spent at Tuckasegee, the one land interest saved from the crash. It was a glorious retreat. There the head waters of the Tuckasegee River gather together and are forced through gorges and over waterfalls to create spectacular sights. The property lies in one of the most remote and beautiful parts of Western North Carolina, in the recesses of Jackson County. It can be reached only by a narrow road, which was so bad in those days that if it rained you couldn't get back until the mud dried. The river was a paradise for trout and for fishermen. The churning, tumbling waters fall from 4,000 to 2,500 feet on this property alone, making as dramatic a landscape as North Carolina has to offer. At intervals tributary streams come rushing down the steep sides of the gorge. The lower gorge, called the Shut In because it is so difficult to pass through, begins where Bonas Defeat Cliff rises 500 feet from the stream bed. The cliff was named for a fabled hound named Bonas who chased a deer for three days until both were so exhausted they could only walk. Reaching the top of the cliff the deer gathered his strength for a final rush, whirling back to safety at the cliff's edge. Old Bonas matched the deer's rush, but was unable to stop and fell to his death on the rocks below.

The Tuckasegee property had been purchased in August of 1926 by four Asheville men, including Charles A. Webb, P. H. Branch and Jim Stikeleather, Sr., the latter a trustee of the Educational and Development Fund of the Farmers Federation. They bought the nearly 14,000-acre tract for a little over a quarter of a million dollars, or about eighteen dollars an acre. There were several small interior holdings, including a seventy-acre farm, along the most level section of the stream, above the old mill dam where the river plunged into a narrow defile. The owner, John Hamp Smith, lived in a simple two-story frame house that was suitable for a club house. He had no faith in a man's personal check, so George Ward of Waynesville, acting as agent, went up with $6,545.82 in gold and silver and counted it out to Mr. and Mrs. Smith as they sat by their hearth.

Jim Stikeleather interested Jim McClure in buying a share of the property. Cameron Morrison, a former governor of North Carolina, and others soon joined the group. These men dreamed of creating a retreat from the strains of civilization that many men endured in their pursuit of wealth. The Tuckasegee Rod and Gun Club brochures were printed early in 1929. One hundred memberships were to be paid at a stiff price of $7500 each. The bottom dropped out of land values just as the brochures were ready, and not even Jim McClure could sell a membership in this scheme. He and the others were saddled with an enormous property and its debts, at a time when it was hard to sell mountain land to anyone at any price.

Fortunately the headwaters of the Tuckasegee River lie in one of Eastern America's rainiest districts, and consequently the trees grow very rapidly. After Doug Stuart took over his half interest, Jim, acting as agent for the remaining owners, was able to arrange a long-term timber sale to the Gennett Lumber Company. A pall of gloom descended at Hickory Nut Gap at the thought of cutting the great trees, but careful arrangements were made with the company to stay 300 feet from the banks of the Tuckasegee and its major tributaries. Later, Jamie and his friends got a tremendous thrill out of riding the old engine, called the Black Satchel, which pulled the logging train, and the remains of the railroad lines served as walking and riding trails to remote parts of the property long after the rails were pulled up and the ties and trestles rotted away. The most important benefit was that the timber sales paid the taxes and the salary of the wardens for many, many years.

Both Jamie and Elspeth loved weekend trips to Tuckasegee, and their parents encouraged them to take their friends. Hetty and Doug Stuart did make a few a visits there, but they were soon absorbed in a ranch in Wyoming where they would spend all available free time.

Two of their daughters, Anne and Margaret, spent three summers at Hickory Nut Gap Farm. Harriet must have been pleased to have the girls come under the happy influence of her friend Elizabeth, and the McClures were delighted to have the girls and some other young people as well to be playmates for Elspeth and Jamie. Jim wrote to Hetty describing some activities of the first summer, 1930:

> Yesterday they spent the morning riding on the hay wagon which was hauling in the oats—and the day before they had a treasure hunt which was the most amusing thing I have ever seen. Siddy had instructions for them at different points, dragons had to be slain, a princess was found gagged and bound to a tree, invisible coats were worn during part of the hunt and all in all—I have never read more absorbing directions or seen a hunt carried out with more fervor—It took all morning and they came in exhausted but with the treasure in hand. Siddy even hid marbles in the sand pile, and the entire sandpile had to be dug over by hand before the requisite number were found. (James G. K. McClure, Jr. to Harriet McClure Stuart July 27, 1930)

One summer two of Arthur Page's sons, Arthur and Johnnie, and Jim's nephew, Nate McClure, joined the gang. The family employed a college student to lead the boys on camping trips and in farm work projects. Elizabeth gave art lessons, and wrote and directed a play about Sherrill's Inn in Civil War days. Anne, Margaret and Elspeth almost undermined a foundation wall in the basement trying to make a fireplace for the stage, until Elizabeth discovered them and showed them how to make a better fireplace with the cardboard boxes that had held canning jars. Nate McClure, an impulsive young man of good heart, sliced his finger in the bean frenching machine and had to have stitches. One Sunday he put all his summer's allowance into the collection plate when the extended family attended John and Mathilda Shorter's colored church on Brush Creek for a special preaching day. Miss Paterson somehow lived through these summers when her "little Elspie" became unruly with the support of her Stuart cousins. The children fought, teased each other, and had many beneficial experiences.

After the last and most exciting summer of visiting cousins and friends, it was discovered that Elspeth was "anemic." Her mother kept her in bed for breakfast and stuffed her with iron pills. Both she and Jamie used to have bouts of "acidosis," a childhood malady that no longer seems to exist. This was cured by spending a day or two in bed eating delicious chicken broth and rice. Her mother made staying in bed so delightful that Elspeth developed a taste for it. Elizabeth was a careful mother where health was concerned, but a firm family rule was that you *never* talked about illness outside the family, just as you never discussed money or the lack of it.

Hickory Nut Gap Farm was fairly isolated from the social doings of Asheville for two young people growing up during the Depression. Trips to town were expensive. Elizabeth did not drive and John Shorter or Rev. David Huntley had to be snatched from some necessary project to make such a journey possible. The bus could be flagged down at the top of the driveway, but the bus station was far from the houses of their friends. It cost ten cents to telephone Asheville and only necessary calls were made. Elspeth had school at home with Miss Patterson until fifth grade. It is not surprising that socializing did not come naturally to either of the McClure children. Fortunately they both enjoyed solitude, but Elizabeth kept encouraging their social life because she thought it was an important part of a person's development.

The McClure's friends the Heywoods, the Herberts and the Izards had children who remained faithful friends in spite of distance. Beckie Herbert and Mary D. Heywood, and later Mary Eleanor Smith, often came to stay on the farm for weekends. Beckie and Elspeth made up a game of "Brownies." They would sneak down to the kitchen even before the early-rising, ponderous Mrs. Williams came in, and attempt to make breakfast and do other household chores secretly, pretending to be invisible. Sometimes the invisible game went on all day, which meant rushing past any grown ups encountered, especially guests, so fast that they would not see you.

A great delight was joining the Boone girls and Richard at the fruit stand they operated for the farm, beside the famous spring on the curve of the road just below their house. Here they sold summer apples, cider and grapes. Beckie and Elspeth charged five cents to show off the Scotch Terrier Chug's tricks. Once they dressed as gypsies and offered to tell fortunes. This was frowned upon by their parents, but buying watermelons from passing trucks from Polk County for a nickel and selling them for a dime, or even a quarter, was encouraged. One summer Beckie and Elspeth, who both loved horses, formed the B. and E. Health Department and attempted to clean up the horse barn. Once again germs were suspected and the project was squelched. The Raoul family had given the McClures their black and white cob pony Circus, and Elspeth and Beckie or her friend Richard Boone could ride over the country and have memorable races with Circus and Neddy, the Shetland pony.

It was about this time that Elizabeth again had one of her painting fits. She decided to surprise Jim for Christmas with a portrait of Elspeth. The only place where Elizabeth could hide the project from Jim and have the necessary north

Elspeth, riding "Circus," and Becky Herbert with the two dogs "Wags" and "Chug," summer of 1933.

light was the basement; so amidst cobwebs and canning jars she set up her easel, with a big green door open to the little garden below the house. Elspeth, who was trying hard to be a tomboy, had to stop playing with her constant companion Richard Boone, dress in a white organdy dress, and spend hours sitting in a chair placed on a table. Fortunately Aunt Wiggy was visiting and read aloud during the sessions. As you look at the portrait, hanging today in the dining room at Hickory Nut Gap Farm, there is little to suggest an energetic little girl enduring long hours of posing. The child, sitting firmly but naturally, wears a summer dress so light that a hint of her shoulder is visible through the short sleeves. She holds a bowl of flowers and her dress is tied with a wide blue sash. Elizabeth wanted the portrait to fit in with the ancestors already hanging in the dining room of her Grandmother Skinner and Jim's great-grandfather Dixon, so she left off her daughter's freckles because, as she said, "Ancestors *never* have freckles." The young model was spared much posing time when Elizabeth did the finishing touches with a large pillow stuffed inside the dress and tied firmly with the sash. One can imagine Jim's delight at this surprise present.

During these years when Elspeth and Jamie were growing up, older members of the family were falling away from this world. Aunt Freddie's name lived on at Hickory Nut Gap. Ben Owenby, herdsman for the Herefords, named his twins Fred and Frederika after the grand old lady from Chicago. On the McClure side two devoted sons of Christ were taken home. Jim's beloved brother Arch, whose career in the Presbyterian Church was as full of promise as his father's was full of accomplishment, died unexpectedly in 1931 while undergoing an appendectomy. Arch and Jim were the closest of brothers, full of mutual admiration and his death struck Hickory Nut Gap with terrible sorrow. Within the year the family gathered once again to mourn the passing of Jim's able and widely beloved father. James G. K. McClure, Sr. was buried in Lake Forest in the winter snows of 1932. He left his children and grandchildren a challenge to Christian manhood as exemplified by his belief that Christ did not come to make life easy, but to make men great. His life had shown that putting ideals into practice often depends on long acquaintance with a community and the confidence and trust that friendships built over the years bring. Annie Dixon McClure, who had always been a loyal and gracious partner in his work, spent many of her remaining years in North Carolina with Dumont and Annie Clarke.

Elizabeth and Jim continued to take their family to Lake Forest for vacations. As well as the Stuarts, "Granny" Cramer was still living at Rathmore, Elizabeth's childhood home, although Ambrose Cramer, Sr. had died years before. Elizabeth's step-sister, Isabelle Ryerson, and her children, Joannie and Tony, were great favorites with the McClures. Isabelle was always called "Aunt Ginty," and was a thrilling figure: she rode to hounds, wore glamourous clothes, and had a mischievous sense of humor. Her husband, Donald Ryerson, was a brilliant man and had been a special friend of Jim's in Lake Forest. It was a great tragedy of the Depression when he committed suicide. Joannie and Tony often came with their mother to the farm and were adventurous pals for Jamie and Elspeth. In the summer of the Chicago World's Fair, the McClures drove to Lake Forest. The trip, complete with gas, meals and an overnight stop in a motel that boasted a restaurant shaped like a giant coffee pot, cost $14.50. Attending the World's Fair, with Aunt Ginty discovering the most exciting exhibits, was a thrill for the farm children. Jamie McClure was particularly excited by the submarine on exhibit. He took issue with the guide on a technical point, insulting that gentleman properly. After the tour they went together to some source of infallible information and Jamie, who was about fifteen, was proved right, which delighted his father. Jim and Elspeth were most inspired by the transportation pageant, "Wings of the Century." It was as dramatic as the Buffalo Bill Show he had seen as a boy, with whole Indian tribes moving across the stage, engines from east and west meeting for the driving of the golden stake when the transcontinental railroad was completed, and finally the appearance of the airplane. Surely this drama proved his theories of progress.

When the Ryersons came to visit the farm there were many adventures for the children. Once Jim and his brother-in-law Donald Ryerson staged a battle for the hayloft. The four children manned the fort in the old grey barn below the garden, spending days building tunnels in the hay and barricades at the front. Hay was then stored loose in the barn instead of in bales as it is today. When the day of battle came Jamie McClure and Joannie Ryerson had stirred up a secret weapon, a mixture of cotton seed meal and water that looked just like soft manure. But the men had a surprise, too. The farm truck filled with snow dug from the late-lasting snow bank at the top of the gap. The barn fight raged fast and furious until Miss Paterson, stationed where she could watch over the picket fence at the bottom of the garden, was suddenly stricken with lumbago and had to be carried from the field!

The children spent hours with sledge hammers and wrenches gradually taking apart a rusting rock crusher abandoned in the quarry at the top of the gap by the road paving crew. Jamie was planning to make a fortune from scrap metal. Other welcome visitors were Elizabeth's half-brother Corwith with his wife Laura and young son Cory, who was several years younger than Elspeth. After struggling to tag along with older cousins, Elspeth remembers it was fun to have someone younger to show around the farm. The two became great friends. Young Cory would spend many summers on the farm as he grew up because his father was a yacht salesman and the family lived on a succession of boats.

The Dumont Clarkes moved to Asheville in 1930, and there were frequent get togethers of the two families. Led by Jim, they all enjoyed vigorous outdoor activity, followed by voracious feasting. Elizabeth described one of these clan gatherings to Hetty. "Thanksgiving was a grand day as it was deliciously mild and the young climbed the peak in the morning & played touch foot-ball in the afternoon in spite of having cleaned up two twelve pound turkeys and 28 small mince & pumpkin pies not to mention drinking five gallons of cider. I truly expected them all to die of apoplexy" (Elizabeth Cramer McClure to Harriet McClure Stuart, December 2, 1934).

To this rising generation Jim McClure was both a man who loved fun and a stern model of moral rectitude. His example, both of self-discipline and of working idealism, brought him a natural respect from both his own children and his nieces and nephews. They all wanted to earn Jim's accolades.

Christmas on the farm often brought visitors from Lake Forest. One year both Aunt Ginty with her children and Uncle Ambrose ("Bowser") and his young wife Mary were on hand. Right after Christmas everyone, including Elizabeth was struck down with the flu, everyone except Jim. First he would don an apron and appear with trays for all hands, then slip into his Harry Lauder outfit, a pair of plaid undershorts with a tweed jacket, and come into each sick room with his concertina to cheer up the patients with Scottish songs. Later he would don a white coat and appear with thermometer and black bag to check on their progress. He managed to turn a disaster into a good time. Aunt Mary, who was so protective of her new husband that he called her his Banty Hen, spent hours chinking the open cracks of the "green room" with tissue paper. When Elizabeth recovered enough to creep out of bed and check on the comfort of her guests she looked in on the Cramers, saw a bit of paper at a window and began to pull, exclaiming that the room must not have been cleaned properly. Aunt Mary vows she pulled out every bit of the caulking before she finished cleaning up!

Midway through the Depression years there was a sad farewell for Miss

Paterson. She went to live with a family in Lake Forest, highly recommended by Elizabeth. Elspeth loved her dearly and it was a difficult parting, but the little girl was now nine years old and she was to go to Grove Park School in Asheville. Miss Pat had taught her at home for four years. The school, where Jamie had gone before her, was run by two high-minded maiden ladies whose great interests were moral instruction and dramatics. She remembers what fun she had driving to school with her father. He taught her many songs, including "Abdul Abulbul Amer," "Clementine," and "The Cowboy's Prayer," which he had learned on the roundup in Texas. She loved to hear stories of his days on the range and often wished he had taken up the old nester's offer to stay in Texas, so they could have worked on a ranch together. They used to plan a long camping trip by wagon, which never actually took place. Jim had never gotten the gypsy yearnings out of his soul. He had taught her to ride and now that the pony Circus was growing old they used to go out on one or another of the three farm horses when they were not occupied in the field. At last Jim bought a Tennessee Walker named "Adam." Elspeth promptly changed his name to "Fleetfoot," although Mr. Huntley stubbornly continued to call him "Adam" because he thought it was unlucky to change a horse's name. Then the three farm mares produced colts, a wonderful delight. Gypsy was Elspeth's own, and with her father's help she trained the little horse. When riding with her father, Elspeth remembers burying her fears with pride, for he was a man whose admiration you worked to gain. This eliminated the possibility of whimpering or complaining.

Education was such a high priority for the McClures that when several Asheville families started the Asheville Country Day School, which offered a conventional college preparatory curriculum, they joined with the Pinckney Herbert family to employ a teacher for their daughters, Beckie and Elspeth, who were in eighth and ninth grades respectively. The school only went as far as the seventh grade, but they arranged for a room in the building, an old house on Victoria Road, and the two girls took part in all school activities. Their teacher was Mrs. Millard Ward, a sensitive, intelligent New Englander. The McClures had hoped to send Elspeth to New England for high school, but after visiting around Elizabeth decided that Chatham Hall, in Virginia, was inspired by the traditions she respected and had the warmth and loving spirit she had missed as a girl at St. Timothy's. They were not disappointed and came to love the headmaster, Dr. Edmund J. Lee, and his wife Lucy, who had been missionaries in China. Jim even brought up the Federation's string band and put on a square dance for the girls, along with a talk about the Farmers Federation. Elspeth, after suffering terrible pangs of homesickness during her first year, loved the school so much that she later sent her two daughters there. The only thing that troubled Jim was that Chatham Hall was an Episcopal School. He arranged to have his daughter become a member of the Lake Forest Presbyterian Church one summer, just to make sure she didn't get any ideas in her head.

Going off to school, helping her parents entertain many visitors, and, especially for Elspeth, helping her father at the Federation picnics that he was now holding every summer, helped to cure her social shyness. Jamie was driving, and he soon taught his sister so they could join their friends more easily. By Christmas 1937 Elizabeth was writing to Harriet Stuart that " . . . Tryon, Flat Rock and Biltmore were all full of parties & Jamie—once the recluse, has now become the most pronounced kind of partyhound! He was resplendent in Doug's 'tuck' and 'tails' . . ." (Elizabeth Cramer McClure to Harriet McClure Stuart, January 11, 1938).

Jim described for his sister one of his son's first successful forays into the social domain, accompanied by his slightly older cousin. Jim McClure was a senior at Hotchkiss and his cousin Jamie Clarke was at Princeton. "We have had great fun this Christmas. Jamie McClure has picked up sufficient interest to attend three dances! He goes arrayed in Uncle Dumont's tuxedo and Jamie Clarke arrayed in mine. The first dance they attended Jamie Clarke split his pants in the middle of the dance floor and had to be escorted off the floor by an encircling body guard. The rest of the evening he had to move with the utmost caution . . ." (James G. K. McClure, Jr. to Harriet McClure Stuart, January 1, 1937).

Perhaps the contradiction as to the origin of Jamie McClure's "tuck" came because a mother is usually the arranger of borrowed tuxedos. The activities of all, Grandmother McClure as well, are recounted in this letter written by Jamie McClure to his Aunt Hetty.

> In spite of unpleasant weather, the vacation has been a lively one. Bert Lewis [husband of Phebe Ann Clarke], Jamie Clarke, and I have been together a lot, and the result is that much wood has been cut, to say nothing of the dissipations of the society whirl. The Clarkes have been in great force, and Grandmother is her usual amazingly lively self. She has become quite a figure in Asheville's older circles; is referred to quite solemnly, I believe, as Madame McClure! Jamie [Clarke] has just gone back to Princeton. He has to cover a couple of hockey games for the *Prince* [the college newspaper] (he's hockey Editor), as well as considerable studying to make up for time lost through journalistic activities. The new board of the *Prince* for 1938 has just been elected, and Jamie was named Secretary. This post goes to the Sophomore who leads the field on his board, and it puts him right in line for the chairmanship if he keeps up his present high standards. I hope he gets it. (Jamie McClure to Harriet McClure Stuart, January 2, 1937)

The work Elizabeth did for everyone's happiness at Christmas, quietly, almost secretly, was remarkable. Santa continued to appear for all the farm tenants and their children and there was always a beautiful Christmas Eve supper. One year Jim wrote to his parents "Siddy does get up the finest affairs with the table wonderfully decorated & old photographs as place cards. After dinner we sang Christmas carols, Jamie Clarke leading on his violin" (James

Jamie McClure and Jamie Clarke "Off for Mt. Mitchell," March 1935.

G. K. McClure, Jr. to his parents, December 26, 1930). On Christmas morning, when the family opened the door to the study, the spirit of her generosity emanated from every corner of the room, centered on the bulging stockings, each with a bright card or a tempting package decorating its top. There might be mostly new toothbrushes, nuts and oranges inside, but there were always one or two specially desired items in the pile of gifts.

The most triumphant Christmas surprise she ever arranged was a present of a new study for Jim. There was a little room off the main study, which opened only onto the porch and had no entry into the house itself. While Jim was away raising money for the Fund, Elizabeth directed Mr. Huntley in the construction of a secret book door connecting these rooms. Ambrose Cramer supplied the plans. When Jim came home the door was in place. For years this room had been used to keep potted plants in the winter and for the family's boots and overshoes. Elizabeth blocked the one window with an old garden hat and a lanky geranium plant so that the work in progress could not be seen from outside. One morning there was snow and Jim tried to open the locked door from the porch to find his galoshes. Elizabeth told him she had locked the door so no one would open it by mistake and let her plants freeze, and that she had lost the key. Surely she would find it by evening. Jim threatened to break the door down to find the missing overshoes, but somehow she dissuaded him and had a pair out for him when he came home. Each morning Jim would set some task for Mr. Huntley to accomplish that day, and each evening when he came home the task was not completed, because Mr. Huntley was spending every available moment making shelves and cupboards in the secret room. Finally he told Elizabeth, "Mrs.

McClure, we've got to tell him. I can't stand this deception no longer." Elizabeth had her work cut out for her to persuade the honest preacher to continue the deception a few days longer. Finally it was Christmas Eve. She still had to tack down the red checked oil cloth on the new shelves and she was afraid Jim would hear her hammering; so she asked Elspeth to turn on the record player. Jim was horrified with the loud jazz on such a sacred evening and reprimanded his daughter sharply. On Christmas morning all was in readiness. A letter from Santa Claus was sticking out of the book shelf, Mr. Huntley himself was in the "little study" jingling sleigh bells, and when Jim followed the instructions in the note to push on the wall he beheld a cozy little room with his father's high backed desk all ready for him.

Needless to say Elizabeth did not have much leisure for painting in the midst of all her other activities, but fortunately she did take time out to paint a special gift for Jamie on his seventeenth birthday—a portrait of his father. It hangs in the dining room of the old house today, opposite the portrait of Elspeth. Elizabeth said she could not paint Jim in the style of the "ancestors" as she had her daughter, because "he is such a modern man." Jim sits as though ready to speak, and step out into the room to take part in a family gathering. Old John Shorter put it best when he said, "When I build a fire in the dinin' room, I have to build it just right 'cause Mr. McClure's eyes - they follow me." Jim wrote to Hetty that "Siddy had painted my portrait during the past few weeks and gave it to him [Jamie] as a birthday present. Everyone thinks the portrait a masterpiece and I consider Siddy a genius" (James G. K. McClure, Jr. to Harriet Stuart, March 22, 1936).

Elizabeth painted only three portraits professionally after she married Jim. One was of her friend, Frances Herbert, commissioned by her children, one of another close friend, Harvey Heywood, and a third of Elizabeth "Ibby" Elkins, at that time married to Harry Hollins, who had come down from the North to run the Federation uniform plant as a service job. Each is an excellent likeness and a decorative success. "Ibby" adored Elizabeth and used to pounce on Jim to tell him he *must* make a place for her to paint and allow *time* for her. Perhaps partly because of this Jim did build a studio for Elizabeth at the back of the courtyard, beyond the spring house and the old fort. She was very excited about the prospect of a place to work where she would have a large north window and would not have to be constantly putting her painting paraphernalia away. But by the time it was built the second World War was coming on, in all its horror and tragedy. It was not to be a time for painting.

Throughout the thirties the McClures continued to enjoy the Asheville social rounds despite the hard times and the changed attitudes toward extravagance. Jim was asked to be the "general" of the Rhododendron Brigade of Guards, organized in 1934, and each year he donned his regalia as commander-in-chief during the Festival Week. He looked like something out of a Sousa band, with a tall hat and oversized golden buttons. He carried off his role with mock seriousness and felt that this gave him a good contact with Asheville's young businessmen. Elizabeth almost balked at being called the Countess of Pisgah, but the Rhododendron Festival was a civic event Jim relished. All the details were reported in the local newspaper:

> All members of the Rhododendron Brigade of Guards, including the 29 new ensigns to be commissioned at the annual Ensign Ball at Grove Park Inn tomorrow evening, have been ordered to report at the inn . . .
> An elaborate ceremonial will attend the commissioning of the new ensigns and Queen Myra [Lynch] in the Rhododendron throne room . . . Hod Williams and his orchestra have been engaged to play for the ball . . . Major-General James G. K. McClure, Jr., commander of the Brigade, will lead the ceremonials and will officially present the King's commission to Queen Myra, naming her honorary Colonel-in-Chief of the First regiment of the Guards . . .
> The Rhododendron Brigade of Guards . . . is colorfully uniformed and is considered one of the most important units of the general festival organization.[6]

For her part, Elizabeth gained a reputation as Asheville's most accomplished mimic during these years. At one party, given by a club known as the Bachelors and Benedicts, she dressed Jim up to look like Chief Justice Hughes. She knew one trick that made a Person unrecognizable, and so Jim remained throughout the evening. She raised his height with little lifts on his shoes. The party took place during the furor over Franklin Roosevelt's attempt to pack the Supreme Court with sympathetic New Dealers, and so she made a sign for him to carry that read "ain't they mean to the Court Supreme." But Elizabeth herself stole the thunder at that particular ball. She transformed herself so that she not only looked like Charlie Chaplin, whom she adored, but she adopted his mannerisms as well. She could shuffle and jerk just like the master. At one point, a young man who knew the McClures well, Pruden Smith, felt duty bound to give her a swift kick in the rear and a lecture for hanging about the entrance of the ladies' room. He was enormously embarrassed when he learned her identity. A few years later he took over a division of the Federation and the story was the subject of many jokes.

Much of Jim McClure's social life revolved around encouraging contributors to the Educational and Development Fund. During the mid-thirties, the tobacco heiress Mrs. Benjamin Duke became interested in his work. Jim wrote to Hetty: "Mrs. Duke is up here and threw a party for me and the fiddlers last night. It went big—I brought Jamie along and he played and sang with the fiddlers" (James G. K. McClure, Jr. to Harriet McClure Stuart, July 25, 1936). Jim nursed her interest in the Federation along to the point where she was ready to donate a million dollars to the Fund. The papers were all written up, awaiting her signature, when her sudden death ended this dramatic possibility.

All this time Jim was carrying a heavy load, directing the growth of the Federation through a difficult economic period. Yet he was also carrying on his father's tradition of public service, along with his full-time job. He had been a member of the State Board of Conservation and Development for some years and in Buncombe County his influence was broad, stretching across all sorts of social boundaries. Offers of committee positions frequently came his way, and he devoted himself to each one as a practitioner of the Social Gospel. He found time to serve as a trustee for Asheville's Mission Hospital, a director of the Blue Ridge Milk Producers Cooperative Association, a member of the Board of Directors of the Federal Home Loan Bank, and vice-president of the North Carolina Cooperative Council. In his own community he remained a member of the School Committee. In the twenties he had helped to consolidate the six small one-room structures in Fairview township into one larger building, and to start a high school. Previously only a few boys and girls had been able to continue their education beyond seventh grade by going to other towns. There were no politics quite as serious as school politics, and keeping public education on an even keel in the thirties was no easy task, since Buncombe County was bankrupt.

Jim became the subject of a minor controversy in the state when the governor failed to reappoint him to the Board of Conservation and Development in 1932. He had been a hard-working and useful member of this group and was influential in setting up game preserves and focusing the state's attentions on the conservation problems of its too often neglected western region. He took a keen interest in the responsibilities of his position, as a letter from an engineer he had worked with testifies. Mr. Thorndike Saville of Winston-Salem had heard that the governor was planning to appoint a member of his own Democratic party to the post. He wrote to Jim, "I have many times expressed to the Director and to other members of the Board that there was no member of the Board who had taken the trouble to inform himself and to evidence as intelligent an interest in the several activities of the Board as you have done . . . I am firmly convinced that it would be a calamity to the State if you were not reappointed for another term . . ." (Thorndike Saville to James G. K. McClure, Jr., July 16, 1932).

Governor Ehringhaus found this position too valuable a political appointment to fill with a "Black Radical," as Republicans had been called in North Carolina since Reconstruction days, no matter how conscientious and effective he might be. It must have been some consolation to Jim that the local papers stood up for him. W. K. Beichler wrote the following letter to the Asheville *Citizen*, which was printed in A. L. Banister's column, "Hunting and Fishing in Western North Carolina:"

> Editorials in both Asheville papers of this past week have supplied very excellent and pertinent comment upon the loss of Mr. James G. K. McClure, Jr. from the State Board of Conservation . . . Figuratively speaking, his has been for years a "voice crying in the wilderness" for the cause of conservation. He has done more than any other man in the western half of the state to overcome our sadly apathetic and do-nothing attitude toward the possibilities of this state as a commercial forest land and recreational area. For years he has advocated and worked for a comprehensive system of state-owned forest,

parks and game refuges. Not only that, he has presented definite plans to show that such a system can be acquired as a distinct investment, and not merely as a disbursement of public funds. It is not . . . generally known that he is directly and almost solely responsible for Western North Carolina's four great game refuges on National Forest lands. His was the idea for them, and his the accomplishment of working out with the Federal government the cooperative arrangement.[7]

Santford Martin, editor of the Winston-Salem paper, who had served with Jim, wrote a personal note to him during the controversy.

> Of all the members of this Board, I think the State could have spared any of them better than it can spare you. I have many times said behind your back that you were by all odds the best informed and best fitted for this type of service to the State of all the members of the Board. It is a tragedy . . .
>
> The more I see of the type of politics in the ascendancy in North Carolina, the more firmly I become convinced that the old mountaineer up in your country was right when he said, "Politics are a ass!" (Santford Martin to James G. K. McClure, Jr., August 8, 1933)

Jim wrote to Hetty, "The Governor did not reappoint me to the Board of Conservation . . . I have been on the Board for eight years and have enjoyed keeping in touch with the Resources of the State" (James G. K. McClure, Jr. to Harriet McClure Stuart, August 10, 1933). An Asheville *Citizen* editorial written in his behalf said, "Conservation work cannot prosper except as it is kept out of politics as far as possible. Experience is worth something. Zeal in the public service is not as common as to count for nothing when it is encountered."[8] The writer was an astute observer of Jim's work. His zealous promotion of the public good, in the face of an often overwhelming effort to push along partisan or regional interests, set this man apart. His combination of warmth and charm, his quick mind, his persistence and insistence on seeing results, made him ideally suited to the constraints of the board room. He actually liked meetings. Whether small and intimate or large and noisy, they usually brought out the best in him. Another trait that helped Jim was his skill, in making a disparate group of people first trust one another as friends, so that when it came time to make decisions, personal rivalries and competitions could be minimized.

As Jim continued to involve himself in local and state affairs, he was also asked to head up a national organization capable of considerable influence. Forestry was a science he pursued relentlessly during the thirties, both as the overseer of the Federation's Forest Products Division and as a private owner responsible for cutting timber on large tracts of mountain property. As a result, he first became a director of the American Forestry Association, and then served a term as president of the North Carolina branch for three years. In 1937 he was elected president of the national association. During his tenure, the efforts of members were directed by its president to support the Cooperative Farm Forestry Act of 1937, which authorized a federal appropriation of $2.5 million to assist the states in advancing farm forestry. At the end of his term as president of the association, Jim continued as a director for two years and then became vice president. His pursuit of good citizenship had involved him in politics, from Washington to Raleigh to Asheville and back home to Fairview. At each level, he brought a large vision and the courage to act.

As president of the American Forestry Association, Jim was in a position to observe the New Deal government at close range. Here was a government made up of people with a commitment to their convictions that Jim could admire. But his Republican outlook kept him from becoming swept up in the excitement. In a paper for the Pen and Plate Club, he sorted out his various reactions to the rapid political and economic changes brought in by Franklin Roosevelt. Jim McClure's views were quite astute for a man living in the midst of the era, and represent a critique that flowed directly from his own experience and philosophy.

> Here we come to March 1st, 1933, with our political creeds unchanged but with the country's industrial economic life paralyzed. The new administration takes charge in Washington. In one hundred days bills are passed in Congress that revolutionize the government of the United States . . . It almost seems as if the Senate and the House had been anesthetized. It almost seems as if they were not conscious of what they were doing. A revolution, perhaps the greatest revolution . . . that has ever occurred and yet . . . without the gathering of a single mob, or without the pressure of a single soap box orator, or a single riot, or a busted head . . . A program was put through Congress putting collectivism into action. In a world where individualism seemed to have failed a new national planning was inaugurated. The government is put in full control of agriculture, industry and business . . .
>
> . . . [As] I have thought about this new program, I must confess that from the idealist's point of view it has a strong appeal. One interesting fact connected with it is the almost religious fervor of the men who have worked out these ideas. They feel and believe that they are engaged in a crusade for the rights of the average man . . .
>
> This step, it seems to me, marks an era in the development of mankind. It is a step where mankind has adjusted himself to new conditions without a bloody social revolution . . .
>
> As to the outcome of these changes, no one knows. We do not even know whether these changes are temporary or denote a permanent change in our manner of Government. I happened to be in the gallery of the Senate the night the National Recovery Act was passed and the compelling argument for its passage was "Gentlemen these are desperate times and require desperate remedies." When we attempt to pass judgement on these great changes we must temper our idealistic hopes with practical experience. We have no precedent to guide us . . .
>
> The control of industry will involve an immense bureaucracy—and the hand of bureaucracy will deaden business . . . Let Federal agents go about inspecting the affairs of business men, and you will have a multiplication of the evils

and abuses, including bribery and blackmail, that we see in our municipalities
enforcing building codes, tenement house regulations, and so on.

We have failed to develop in this country a tradition of public office that
inspires us with any confidence . . .

Men go to any length to get into office and accumulate political debts which
they must pay out of the government pork barrel. My experience in government and state agencies has been that petty political considerations come first
in almost all decisions—and there even arises an inability to see or think
clearly on questions of efficiency and public good.

Our experience with Government Regulation of the railroad has not been
an inspiring one. The Interstate Commerce Commission has cost us millions
of dollars, . . .

Today we are faced with tremendously increased government control. It is
no longer a debatable question, it is an accomplished fact . . .[9]

Meanwhile, the Depression did little to dim the social life at Hickory Nut
Gap. Jim never needed frills to have a good time. He had his Santa Claus suit
for Christmas and he could always pick up a few firecrackers for the Fourth.
Jim's antics and parlor games never failed to entertain his guests. He could talk
the best dressed young man into placing a glass of water on his forehead, and
trying to rise from a prone position to a standing one in front of the howling
guests at a party. He could always feel when a certain heaviness began to hang
over a group of people and liked to take it upon himself to dispel the deadening
influence. He did this for his own family, too. Elspeth remembers him livening
up breakfast at a hotel one morning. He whispered to her that he would give her
a dollar if she could get a whole waffle into her mouth at once. Poor Elizabeth
was horrified, but it certainly lifted the family spirits. He still loved to play his
concertina, especially on trips; and this made Elizabeth quite nervous about the
possible effect on other guests!

Elizabeth continued to surround the old house with beauty. She and Aunt
Wiggy, who was a frequent summer visitor, and Elspeth formed the "groundhog
club" and spent happy hours uncovering rocks to enlarge the Rock Garden above
the house where several boulders already protruded. They planted snowdrops
and daffodils and blue Chinodoxia under the cherry trees, which made the place
a fairy land in the spring. Mathilda Shorter replaced Mrs. Williams in the
kitchen when the latter went off and got married (much to everyone's amazement). Mathilda would pack up a lunch in beautiful baskets, with fried chicken
and other delights, and Elizabeth and perhaps some guest would meander up
into the orchard and set up a picnic on Turkey Rock, where in April they could
gaze across a sea of apple blossoms to the Fairview valley below. During the
spring, when the smell of apple blossoms drenched the whole farm in their
subtle scents, her appetite for beauty came alive. She never failed to be renewed
by the appearance of the first snowdrops and crocuses, and then the forsythia
and daffodils that served their eternal notice that the harsh domination of winter
had once again passed.

Jim did not have Elizabeth's almost religious love of beautiful surroundings, painting and music; but he truly appreciated all she did. He wholeheartedly shared her passion for boxwood, and they were thrilled when they learned of an old couple living far up on a mountainside in a cabin who had several English box bushes they wanted to "get shet of." When they arrived with the farm truck and crew the old man had just chopped down the biggest bush to make it easier to get his first cook stove in the door. The McClures planted the remaining beauties along one side of the rock garden to screen it from the dirt road that led dowi to the barn. The bushes grew and grew until they are now a solid mass of green humps and bumps. Elizabeth carefully trimmed the American box and the hedges she had grown from cuttings, but English box never needs to be sheared, unless you want to get a new stove in a door. Its natural growth is close and slow.

In 1937, Jim found himself on the same podium as Roosevelt's Secretary of State Cordell Hull. Both men had come to New Haven to receive honorary degrees from Yale University. Hull, a native Tennessean, would have been much interested in Jim's work with the Federation. For Jim, the occasion was something of a triumphant homecoming. He probably made use of his time there trying to interest prospective contributors to the Fund, and he enjoyed the companionship and good will of a graduation ceremony. The New Haven paper recorded the event.

> Prof. William Lyon Phelps, university public orator, presented the candidates for honorary degrees, and President [James Rowland] Angell conferred the degrees. Professor Phelps: [said of Jim McClure]
>
> Farmer, Yale B.A. 1906. After graduation he studied theology at Edinburgh, Chicago, Tubingen, Jena, and Berlin. Thus being thoroughly grounded, he became a dirt farmer . . . In earlier days he worked with such vigor as pastor of a church in the Upper Peninsula of Michigan that his health gave way and he was required to rest. This breakdown, tragic as it seemed at the time, was beneficial; for in the mountains of North Carolina he became interested in working out plans to aid people to make a better living. He became the first president and general manager of the Farmers Federation . . . Mr. McClure is a multitudinous blessing and a first-rate illustration of applied Christianity. President Angell:
>
> Throughout long years of devoted toil, you have translated the spirit of the Gospels into a happier and richer life for thousands of your neighbors. In grateful recognition of this invaluable service your Alma Mater confers upon you the degree of Master of Arts, admitting you to all its rights and privileges.[10]

Along with Jim McClure and Cordell Hull, two other notables received honorary degrees that day: author Stephen Vincent Benét, and the Minister of Finance for China, H. H. K'ung. Mr. K'ung was a lineal descendent of Confucius, in the seventy-fifth generation, making Jim's claim to be descended from travelers on the *Mayflower* seem pretty insignificant. All of these men, the

Secretary of State, the patriotic writer, the Chinese official, and Jim McClure, sat together during the formalities of the occasion, enjoying each other's conversation. All of them were on the brink of a life shattering world-wide cataclysm that would alter each life markedly.

In the spring of 1939, when Elspeth was in her junior year at Chatham Hall, her family planned an operation to complete the straightening of her "turning eye." She had had the first operation several years before in Asheville, and the skilled Austrian ophthalmologist Dr. Sprinza Weizanblatt, a special friend of Elizabeth and Jim's, had succeeded wonderfully. But both she and Elizabeth thought it would be wise to have the final delicate work done at Johns Hopkins Hospital in Baltimore by Dr. Alan C. Woods, an outstanding specialist. This must have been a terrible expense for the McClures to face, but as usual there was no complaining. Elspeth's account of the trip follows.

> We arrived from the train at "The Little Inn," just across from the hospital, which "Aunt Jane" Heywood had recommended. When we were shown upstairs to our pretty room, my mother was so appreciative, as always, that she charmed the proprietor completely. Then he told us the rates. It was too much. She knew we couldn't swing it! But she hated to hurt his feelings so she went down to the desk and told him she had changed her mind and planned to stay with friends, called a taxi and had the driver go off round the block, then come slowly back so she could make discreet enquiries where she had seen a sign for boarders. She was good at spotting cheap places, for she had had so much practice on family trips. My father used to call us the "boarding party" when he sent us in to check out a place.
>
> The one she found was pretty dingy and down at the seams. The walls were painted pale green coated over with Baltimore soot and there was one bathroom for the floor. Those row houses stretched down the street opposite Hopkins—dingy brick with short steps going down to the street, where people sat on those hot summer evenings. It cost something like $2.00 a night—no meals. Next morning we went to see Dr. Woods. He wasn't keeping his appointments and we were told to return next day. Again he wasn't there. We were told it might be a day or two before he could see me as he had a fall from a horse. We would just have to wait. The days stretched to a week or more.
>
> My mother didn't want to tell my father she needed more money so she made a wonderful game of stretching it. We located a restaurant in the next block called "Bilgers," where we could get a plate of fish and boiled potatoes and beans for thirty-five cents. Breakfast was even less. We bought bread and tomatoes for lunch. We called our restaurant "Bulgers" and we looked forward intensely to each meal, for not only were we hungry but it was air conditioned! My mother was disappointed that her cousin Mark Skinner Watson and his family were away in Vermont. She and Cousin Mark had been great friends when he was a young man working on the newspaper in Chicago and now he was an editor of the Baltimore *Sun*. But she soon found the Baltimore Museum, and was delighted by the way the paintings and tapestries were shown, with large, open wall spaces and excellent lighting. It was so interesting and such fun to see the beautiful paintings and statues with my mother. We both forgot all about the absent doctor, our shrinking treasury, and the heat, and

were both carried away into a fascinating world. There were even *free* concerts! I learned that in any large city the museum is the place to go to have a
perfectly splendid time for almost nothing.

For a very special treat one night we went downtown to a cafeteria and then
to see a movie, "Four Feathers." But when we got to the ticket window we
found the tickets cost a few cents more than we had with us! I'm sure my
mother could see my disappointment. Extravagantly we got on the trolley back
to Hopkins, got the extra quarter needed. I can never forget the excitement of
the rush back to the theatre, or the wonderful movie with Errol Flynn as a
dauntless cavalryman who proved he was not a coward.

As I think back now on the complete material comfort and the many advantages my mother had been surrounded with when she was growing up, I
appreciate more and more her making these ten days when we were stuck in a
dreary boarding house in a hot city, with evaporating funds, waiting anxiously
to see a mythical doctor, one of the most interesting and happy times I can
ever remember. She was a magic person.

When Dr. Woods appeared at last he was gruff and bearish. He put off the
operation for a year, and directed me to wear a patch over first one eye and
then the other, alternating every two weeks, and taking Sunday off, for the
entire coming year at boarding school. The strange thing was that I did really
well academically at Chatham that year. It was a struggle to read during the
two weeks when I could use only my "lazy eye" and perhaps it was because I
had to concentrate extra hard that my grades were better than ever before. The
next June I was accepted at Vassar without having to take the last two college
boards. I was especially happy at graduation for I had made my parents and
Jamie proud. My mother and I went to Baltimore right after graduation for the
scheduled operation. My mother was an angel about reading aloud to me while
I had to lie still for several days with eyes bandaged. But we also listened to
the radio. This was June 1940, and what we heard was stark news of German
tanks rolling across France through the broken Maginot line as the French
soldiers retreated before them. This was terrible news for my mother. It was
good that she was staying with the Watson family, who were understanding
friends.

Dr. Woods disappeared again and the hospital bill kept increasing. Finally
my mother decided it was time to go. I got dressed and we just paid the bill
and walked out and took a taxi to the Watson's with no ill consequences! My
mother took the train home while I stayed a couple of weeks longer with the
wonderful Watson family so that I could have checkups and eye exercises at
the hospital. She was so glad to see Cousin Mark again. He was humorous,
kind, very intelligent, and a first rate writer. Cousin Susan, his wife, was a
hospitable, wise Southern belle and their daughters, Ellen and Susan, were
wonderful friends for me.[11]

When Elspeth returned from Baltimore, bringing the two Watson girls with
her for a visit on the farm, there was a tinge of sadness there. The terrible news
of the war affected both Jim and Elizabeth. They had both spent considerable
time in Europe and they felt anguish for the people torn by the war. Jim no
longer had any illusions about pacifism. Both of them had a vast admiration and
sympathy for Churchill and the British in their uphill battle against the horrors

of Nazi Germany. Jim was asked to head up the isolationist movement in North Carolina "America First," but he turned it down before Elizabeth even said a word.

He backed up the President in his aid to the British, but as the decade ended he had turned against Franklin Roosevelt and his New Deal. The notion that a government could spend money way beyond its revenues was abhorrent to him. Deficit spending by a nation was the way to court disaster, he was sure. He also wondered how such an unwieldy conglomeration of programs could be well-managed, knowing full well that many of them that he had dealt with were not. The fact that so many of Jim's northern friends and contributors to the Fund were wealthy and very conservative may have influenced his feelings about the New Deal. When Roosevelt ran for his third term, Jim began to think the man was simply power hungry. He compared his habits with those of Hitler and Mussolini. The McClure family dog, Trixie, expressed Jim's political views as well as any of his Pen and Plate Club papers. As a regular part of the Hickory Nut Gap visit, Jim would mention to Trixie rather casually, "Did you know Roosevelt was elected again?" The little white dog would immediately throw up her head and let out a series of mournful howls. He loved to tell New Deal jokes. One of his favorites came as the result of a scientific breakthrough—the cure for gout was discovered to be a medicine whose secret ingredient was the sweat of a WPA worker. A call went out immediately that a reward would be offered of one million dollars for each drop of that precious commodity. But the drive had to be abandoned, so the story went, due to the lack of donors. Perhaps Jim's best epitaph for the New Deal was scrawled in the margins of one of his papers. (NRA stood for the National Recovery Act).

> NRA'S PROGRESS
> 1933—Nuts Running America
> 1934—No Recovery Anticipated
> 1935—National Ruin Accomplished
> 1936—No Roosevelt Again[12]

Although Jim's personal life during the decade prior to World War II was marked by financial difficulties, he remained steadfastly on course. His leadership capabilities made him a powerful influence in all the varied facets of life that he touched. He translated the respect and confidence he had earned into new accomplishments, but with all his achievements he never became vain. Like his mountain friends, whom he realized had a great sense of a power above, he gave God the credit. People listened to him because his words squared up with his life.

He liked to speak of the present evils in the world: crime, the rackets, and the political illusions of communism and fascism. Repeatedly he stood before graduating seniors and a great variety of congregations delivering his message, especially to young people, of the importance and the joy of the useful life. "If

Jim McClure (right) and "Old Man" Parker, hunting at Sunburst, November 1935.

you catch a vision of usefulness—follow it as a hunter follows a bear. Track it to its lair and capture it—make it yours." "Pick out [a] place where you can best serve God & man—[your] powers will increase and develop." "Every compromise with the infinite value of the human soul leads straight back to the jungle." "If we are to build a better America—we must have better Americans." "How, the skeptic asks, can one weak man do anything against odds which are so overpowering? The amazing thing is that when we try to accomplish something beyond our ability, some power from above flows through and gives [us] strength." "God gave the children of Israel the promised land, but they had to take it themselves." "Communists 'are' ahead of us today in their teaching to endure hardship." "Let each man think himself an act of God. His mind & thought, his life a breath of God and let each try, by great thoughts and good deeds, to show the most of Heaven he hath in him." "If God is your master make your plans big." "Follow God's will and He will reveal His creed." Jim believed this last idea was very important for people who had trouble in accepting Christianity.[13]

To Jim McClure, faith was not a small and mean affair built on self-righteousness, but rather an act of courage that liberated one from fear and insecurity. Jim's seeming platitudes rang true because of the life that stood behind them. Prior to 1920, he had not been sure what God's purpose was for him, but by the outbreak of the second World War, the Farmers Federation was twenty years old and a testimony to one man's courage and devotion to an idea. He described for the graduates of Haw Creek School the same life of service that had fulfilled his own ambitions. "I am offering you a greater & more important call," he said. "I am calling you to dedicate your life to building this Commonwealth. It will take more patience, more hanging on, more dogged determination & more real grit & nerves than it would take to reach out tonight & fight an attacking army . . . If you are to carry on the torch, you must so live that your character is preserved not for your self but for your country. Give your life and your job to serve the Commonwealth."[14]

He spoke for the highest order of political integrity and individual behavior based on the Christian promise of freedom as the result of the submission to God's will. God's will, to Jim, meant pushing and shoving mankind along the way pioneered in the United States, where the ideal of individual liberty before the law had reached its greatest development. Jim wanted to add a strong dose of community involvement to balance against the American individualism that was so strong in the mountains. Over and over he asked in his sermons and speeches, why cannot men and women create a Christian movement with the impact of the Nazi Party or Bolshevism? How is it that these movements wield so much power over individual lives and can be so effective in remolding their societies, while Christians backed by the supernatural power of the Almighty and of the forces of goodwill in the Western World appear so impotent? It is a question worth pondering, and one that James McClure tried to answer. He wanted to inspire young people with Christian ideals to translate their idealism into bringing a better economic life to people in the mountains. In spite of all discouragement, he never ceased to believe this was possible.

1. Thomas Wolfe, *You Can't Go Home Again* (New York: Signet Books, 1966), pp. 90–91. The book was originally published by Scribner's in 1934.

2. *Ibid.*, p. 281.

3. Interview with Elspeth McClure Clarke.

4. Information about real estate holdings from family papers.

5. Interview with Jane Raoul Bingham.

6. Article in the Asheville *Citizen*, April 1934.

17. W.K. Beichler, letter to the editor, Asheville *Citizen*, August 13, 1933.

8. Editorial, Asheville *Citizen*, August 10, 1933.

9. James G. K. McClure, Jr., "The Recent Amazing Changes in our Government and Some Pros and Cons," paper given at the Pen and Plate Club, Asheville, North Carolina, March 1, 1933.

10. Article in the New Haven *Register*, June 23, 1937.

11. Interview with Elspeth McClure Clarke.

12. Comments written in the margin of early draft of paper written by James G. K. McClure, Jr. for the Pen and Plate Club, "Remaking Western North Carolina," 1939.

13. James G. K. McClure, Jr., excerpts from sermons, 1930–1939.

14. James G. K. McClure, Jr., Commencement address, Haw Creek High School, Asheville, North Carolina, May 1932.

Chapter Seventeen

The Farmers Federation
and the Depression

At a business meeting soon after the onset of the Depression former General Manager Guy Sales remembers: The President reported that the employees had a meeting immediately after the collapse of the Central Bank, in which they voluntarily agreed to reduce their salaries. Those receiving over $100 per month reducing their salaries by 20% . . . This action of the employees was commented upon most favorably by the directors, it being pointed out that it showed not only loyalty but a keen sense of sound business judgement, in sensing the situation and acting immediately.

(Interview with Mr. Guy Sales)

Dear Mr. McClure,

I like to tell you about the federation has meant to me. In 1930 I was about to lose my farm but the federation helped me sell enuf rhododender to pay off the Morgag and I have supported my family of 7 chilerden with out going on relief and helped my nabors by giving them work getting out rododendum this year. I have sold rodadendum and subbry thru the federation whitch brought me in $995 so you see why I will stand by the federation thru thick and thin

Yours truly

J. G. Taylor

(J. G. Taylor to James G. K. McClure, Jr., exact date unknown)

When the Central Bank and Trust Company of Asheville failed, three of its depositors were the Farmers Federation, the Educational and Development Fund and James G. K. McClure, Jr. The Farmers Federation did not collapse under the economic pressures of the Depression because member farmers and employees stood loyally behind it, while the President and directors could turn to the Educational and Development Fund for help in the worst times. As the chain reaction of failed banks spread through Western North Carolina, counties and municipalities, businesses and individuals were ruined. The Federation lost money in eight bank accounts and had to be tided over by loans from the Fund to stay in business.[1] Jim McClure's faith in progress would be sorely tested by the greatest adversity the Federation and his family had yet faced. Although farm prices had been weak throughout the twenties, no one could have guessed what would happen during the early thirties. As the banks tried to collect as many of their loans as they could, mortgages were foreclosed and businesses shut down. Jim's personal debts were considerable at the end of 1930 and included $129,000 he had signed for loans to the Federation.[2] Just after Christmas, he wrote to Hetty and Doug that "conditions thru the country here are at a low ebb. Eight banks in our Federation territory have sunk to the bottom of the sea, and as one native put it 'the people are raving'" (James G. K. McClure, Jr. to the Stuarts, December 28, 1930).

With so many local governments, banks and businesses busted, how could an idealistic farmers cooperative hope to survive? But the Federation not only weathered the storm, but spread to new counties, offered new services, opened new departments and initiated a program to reinvigorate the spiritual life of the area, the Lord's Acre Plan. The Federation kept going and the cooperative's vigor helped lift Western North Carolina out of the Depression. With the average mountain farm at least half in forest, Jim McClure reasoned that with proper management this asset could be turned into enough annual cash to at least pay the taxes, so in 1930 Forest Products and Shrubbery Departments were added to the Federation. Appalachian farmers could then more easily take advantage of the demand for pulpwood, acid wood (for tanning leather), locust for insulation pins and fence posts, or dogwood for cotton mill shuttles. They could cut logs for building and veneer, for telephone poles and railroad ties, and there was a growing market for all varieties of mountain shrubs. Big, burly Harry Rotha of Waynesville, an experienced forest products man, was hired to manage this enterprise. At the onset, in January of 1930, Jim prophesied in the Federation *News* that the Forest Products Department "will mean untold wealth for all W.N.C."[3]

At the same time, the Federation committed itself to managing a large-scale poultry business, opening three hatcheries, one each in Spindale, Sylva and Asheville, with a total capacity of 73,400 eggs. They were opened with typical McClure fanfare early in 1930, when other businesses in the area were struggling to stay solvent. Eggs and broilers had accounted for almost half of the total sales figures in 1929, and expansion of a successful venture seemed the logical move. The cool summers and limited cropland in the mountains made poultry a reasonable choice. Unfortunately, spreading financial troubles depressed the poultry market during the year, and the Federation found itself battling with large competitors at each stop of the railroad car. Jim explained the problems to readers of the Federation *News* in August 1930:

> Our poultry car business is $148,133.23 below last year's record. This is the only department of the Federation to report a reduction in business, and this reduction is due to three causes: First, the price of poultry has been so low during the year that we have advised farmers to hold their poultry and build up flocks. Second, the low price of poultry has reduced the dollar value of our shipments about thirty per cent. Third, the large poultry business we have built up has become known and large Poultry operators have come in and tried to take our business. For months these large operators placed a car beside ours whenever we started a car, taking advantage of our advertising and buying days. As we were building up this business for the farmer, we decided to hang

on. This competition cut our volume and also caused this Department to operate at a loss, the only department which operated at a loss last year. Our fear was that if we dropped out of the poultry marketing game, these large operators would then drop prices and this would discourage poultry production. We have, therefore, hung on and maintained our poultry car service . . .

At this writing this competition has withdrawn from the field, and we are operating over a wider territory than ever before, offering a market for poultry to the farmers in twenty five counties.[4]

Even though commodity prices continued to fall, each warehouse made a profit during 1930. Jim felt that, if the Federation could remain solvent, it would help the mountain area to weather the Depression. Agriculture in Western North Carolina had been depressed for at least a generation. Most of the families were quite used to "making do" on meager incomes. As long as they held title to their own land and could keep up with the taxes, they were probably better off than their blue-collar counterparts in the cities who had no way to garden or feed their families. Maybe the years were leaner than usual, but most mountain families would have noticed little difference. To most, the cataclysm in New York seemed as far away as China. Many farmers were actually able to improve their financial lot during the thirties as the Federation spread into new areas, bringing with it new markets, information and reliable farm supplies.

The Federation was Jim's destiny, his calling, and he had no intention of ever abandoning it. He never measured his success in profits, but by obstacles surmounted and people helped. Jim McClure summed up his reasons for keeping the Federation going, in spite of all discouragements, in an article for the "Yale Alumni Weekly."

The Federation markets chickens, eggs, Irish potatoes, sweet potatoes, corn, wheat, rye, vegetables, forest products . . . and other mountain farm products such as pottery and baskets.

It has survived fires, bank failures, and depressed business conditions. It has learned how to run the farmer's business successfully . . . The experience, gained in this way, is worth many thousands of dollars to the mountain farmers . . .

Some mountaineers have been able to pay the mortgage on their homes, others have put running water into their houses, women have been able to have a doctor at childbirth, many have been able to earn tax money, and particularly during the drouth year of 1930, many, through our forest products department, were able to have bread and meat in their houses and keep their children from starving. The people have earned every cent they have received. The Farmers Federation is building character and initiative and permanent self support.

. . . We believe that we are developing the economic and spiritual resources of the people themselves.[5]

The year 1932 brought new problems. When President Roosevelt declared the Bank Holiday, closing banks nationwide from March 6–10, the Federation printed up its own scrip, with a picture of Jim McClure in the center of each paper certificate.[6] At this time of crisis, Mr. Jim Cole, a loyal member farmer, came to see Mr. McClure in his office. When the door was shut he quietly handed Jim four thousand dollars in bills, to use while it was needed. Years later Jim would preach at Mr. Cole's funeral service, stressing the importance of the independent spirit of the mountaineer. Mr. Cole was a legend. No one knew quite where his money came from or where it went when he died, but it was pretty well known that his main source of income was corn liquor, manufactured in the recesses of his vast mountain tract.[7]

Despite all the facts and figures, and talk of new business ventures, Jim McClure maintained the point of view of a pastor tending his flock, a minister of the social gospel. His congregation met, most of them, in their own little churches, usually of the simplest construction. Often the fare served up behind the old fashioned altar each Wednesday evening and twice on Sunday was a fiery exhortation rivaling the best of Jeremiah. When Jim preached in these churches, as he was often asked to do, he preferred to stress good citizenship and community building. He preached the healing of Nehemiah.

It is essential, he reasoned, to build better schools and better churches, to make better homes. But it is also important, while doing so, not to stray from God's higher laws. The history of the Hebrew nation provided him with many texts and examples on which to build his themes. But religious preaching, he thought, was all too often just a veneer, a coating for the sake of respectability. For him, Christianity meant effective action.

Thomas Wolfe dreamed of a new America, "the real America," merging purified from the materialism of the Twenties.[8] Jim McClure, too, saw the hope of renewal rising out of the ashes of despair of the Depression. In the early 1930s Jim felt that the "real America" must come both from the entrepreneurial spirit that was nourished by American liberty, and the spiritual striving of a people who claimed the inheritance of the Christian church. The tension between these must be kept in balance. Without the spiritual influence he knew that selfish materialism would flourish. Without the business-like approach, he saw that hopes would die out, churches would decay, and education would be forgotten. He tried to pursue both goals, making every effort to increase the productivity of the mountain farms and at the same time emphasizing spiritual progress as an equal in importance.

Therefore, during the same months in 1930 when the financial pyramids of Buncombe County were teetering and the Federation was branching out into new endeavors, Jim McClure launched a bold new program that backed up his talk about the spiritual resources of the region with an agency designed to help them; the Lord's Acre Plan.

Jim had heard of the Lord's Acre Plan some years before. Back in 1927 he had broached the idea in the Federation *News:*

> An acre of potatoes, or corn for the Lord, on every farm in this section!
> What a spiritual awakening this would bring . . . A few years ago the members

of a church in Georgia all agreed to plant an acre of cotton for the church. The Lord's Acres of cotton did well, and brought in a rich harvest to the church, not only in money but also in enthusiasm and power . . . the pastor is the most important man in any community. His salary must be increased. He must have the money to get around and see people.

An acre of potatoes, or an acre of corn, or perhaps a steer to be fed for the church, or a tenth of the eggs, and the proceeds brought in to a church Harvest Day in October, would wonderfully help to raise our church budgets, and wonderfully bless the life of our churches.[9]

This early call for the Lord's Acre resulted in a small response that quickly petered out. There had to be someone to promote and sustain the project; to go to the churches, sell the idea, build up morale, and then push hard to maintain the momentum. Jim knew just the man for the job. The success of the idea was assured when he persuaded his old friend and brother-in-law, Dumont Clarke, to move to North Carolina and take on the work of building up the country church. Spearheaded by Dumont's unflagging determination and missionary zeal, the Lord's Acre Plan not only answered the needs of impoverished rural churches in Western North Carolina, but also came into use in many parts of the United States and even spread to the mission field world wide. The Religious Department made the Farmers Federation unique among American cooperatives. For Jim McClure it was a characteristic follow-up of a visionary idea with an organization to implement it. Dumont Clarke's career in the ministry had been continually frustrated by poor health, and Jim thought he knew why. Dumont needed, as he himself had, a project that would call forth all of his energy and devotion. Dumont's previous experience had been as the school minister at Phillips Andover Academy and the Lawrenceville School. He then became Assistant Pastor of the Mount Vernon Heights Congregational Church in Mt. Vernon, New York. In each position, bad health had demoralized him and interfered with his work.

Like Jim, Dumont had planned to devote his life to mission work, and had actually gone to India as a YMCA Secretary, but his health had broken in the Indian climate. Now both he and his brother-in-law felt Western North Carolina was in need of mission work. In the Depression years country churches in the mountains had very little money. Often they could afford to pay a preacher for only one or two Sundays a month. Dumont accepted the challenge without pay and made the Lord's Acre work something of great and lasting importance. The Educational and Development Fund underwrote the salary of a secretary and office expenses. He threw himself into the work, with the result that the Lord's Acre Movement spread like a mountain fire "let out."

Jim announced the new Federation program for the country church and endowed it with a statement of purpose in the Federation *News* in February 1930.

> The Federation has opened up another department, the Religious Department. Rev. Dumont Clarke of Manchester, Vermont is the Director . . .
>
> The country church is, in the opinion of many people, the most valuable institution in America. The country church has been the nursery for many of the most constructive movements of the past five hundred years and it has been a large factor in developing the strength of character of many of the leaders of the Anglo-Saxon civilization . . .
>
> The Present period of re-adjustment in the country church is difficult. Today in our mountains cash money is scarce. It is increasingly difficult for the country church to pay an adequate salary to the preacher, and the spiritual life of the communities is in danger . . .
>
> The farmer cannot subscribe much cash to the church, but he can subscribe an acre of corn or an acre of potatoes. He can subscribe a pig and grow it up or a calf and grow it up and his wife can subscribe a hen and raise a brood of chickens, and every child in the family can undertake some project; perhaps it might be to raise a few baby chicks. In this way it will be possible to quadruple the income of the country church.
>
> The Federation . . . is now in a position to offer [its marketing] service for the churches and for the first time the churches can look to a farmers organization that is capable of handling just about anything the church members will raise.[10]

There was nothing like the whiff of a new project to rekindle the inner fires of Jim McClure. He could not help but tell people about it, and throw himself into the promotional fray. Jim wrote to his sister Hetty about the progress of the Lord's Acre. "Dumont has stirred up so much excitement amongst the churches that it broke out into a movement to have a 5:30 a.m. meeting this morning in the Gap. At this I was scheduled to make a "talk." Jamie supported me. We arose at 4:30 a.m. I dropped in on Jamie to see how he was getting on with his dressing and found him leaning on the radiator fast asleep in his pajamas. All the rest of the family remained snoring in their beds. Well we had a fine sunrise meeting."

Jim went on to describe Dumont's Easter sermon and a Lord's Acre picnic beside the Pigeon River near Waynesville, and to list his many callers in regard to the new project. He finished Hetty's letter with: "How is that for a full day for the Director of the Religious Department? Remember that this followed a Saturday when he left at 8 a.m. for his office and then made a round of his six churches in the afternoon seeing all the preachers. He is doing a huge lot of work and seems to me better than ever" (James G. K. McClure, Jr. to Harriet McClure Stuart, April 20, 1930).

One of Jim's first converts to the Lord's Acre Plan had been a neighbor, Mr. Millard Edgerton, who rode into town with him one winter's day. He described the incident to Hetty:

> Yesterday morning I drove in with Millard Edgerton . . . & asked him how big a family he now had—He replied fifteen young 'uns but the Lord had blessed him and every time meal time came around there was something to

Dumont Clarke, Jim McClure's brother-in-law, promoting the Lord's Acre Plan.

eat. He said, however, that he was behind with his church dues, and had been fifty cents behind for some time and could not seem to pay it—I suggested D's scheme of setting aside an acre, putting all fifteen hoes to work & giving the proceeds to the church & told him I wanted to be present when each member of his family marched into church seventeen strong, each with a bushel of corn on his back. He was carried away with the idea and yesterday came to tell me that he had had it up with the family and every one was in for the idea. I think I will tell D of this 100 percent conversion to the idea. (James G. K. McClure, Jr. to Harriet McClure Stuart, January 24, 1930)

At one of the first churches Dumont visited, the Tweed's Chapel Methodist Church in Fairview, five boys signed up, each agreeing to raise a hog for their church. Jim explained later that: "These boys would not have been able to put 10 or 15 pennies in the collection plate during the course of the year, but by some hook or crook they fed their pigs, and you know, if any boy feeds a pig for the Lord twice a day, all summer, it is going to have a lasting effect on his character . . . And those pigs brought from $12 to $15 apiece, and that made a huge difference in the spirit and energy of the church superintendents."[11]

The six churches that signed up in 1930 were Tweed's Chapel Methodist, Avery's Creek Baptist, Fairview Baptist, Mills River Presbyterian, Avery's Creek Methodist, and Mill's River Methodist. These churches proved the plan. It really worked, raising both money and morale. The second year forty churches joined, and in 1932 the Lord's Acre Movement was one hundred churches strong. Jim liked to point out that very often it was the children and young people who shamed their elders into committing themselves.

Mr. Clarke went up to a church away back in the mountains which had a budget of $80 a year, but for three years had been unable to meet their budget and they were very much discouraged. He presented the idea of the Lord's Acre Plan of raising their budget. They took it up with enthusiasm and were going to present it to their church membership the next Sunday. Well, the next Sunday was rainy, so they put it off another week, and the next week they had arranged for some kind of a picnic so they put it off another week, and they gradually put it off until the planting season was over. Well, one day last August, the teacher of the primary department came in with her primary class. She had taken up the idea herself and begun it for her class, a class of thirty-three of these small children, and given each one of them a baby chick. Five of the baby chickens had died, but twenty-eight of the children appeared with a grown chicken, and they sold the chickens for enough to buy paper-backed hymn books for the adult members. That so shamed the adult members that they set to work and painted their church and built new seats for it. And that stirred them up.[12]

Dumont never resented Jim's leadership. He was a determined team player, who made his own way into the hearts of the mountaineers. He made friends with the preachers and their families, often having dinner with them after church, or spending the night. For the young people he had riddles and tricks,

JESUS CALLS US

Jesus calls us, o'er the tumult
    Of our life's wild, restless sea,
Day by day His sweet voice soundeth,
    Saying, "Christian, follow Me."

Jesus calls us from the worship
    Of the vain world's golden store;
From each idol that would keep us,
    Saying, "Christian, love Me more."

In our joys and in our sorrows,
    Days of toil and hours of ease,
Still He calls, in cares and pleasures,
    "Christian, love Me more than these."

Jesus calls us: by Thy mercies,
    Saviour, may we hear Thee call;
Give our hearts to Thy Obedience;
    Serve and love Thee best of all.

I WOULD BE TRUE

I would be true, for there are those who trust me;
I would be pure, for there are those who care;
I would be strong, for there is much to suffer;
I would be brave, for there is much to dare.

I would be friend of all, the foe, the friendless;
I would be giving, and forget the gift;
I would be humble, for I know my weakness;
I would look up, and laugh, and love, and lift.

HOWARD ARNOLD WALTER.

Above and following page: *Early promotional material for the Lord's Acre.*

like moving a penny from one finger to another. And he was a gifted speaker. His slide shows of Lord's Acre projects were a hit all over his circuit.

He drove many miles visiting churches throughout the mountains, and his well worn car became a welcome sight. Dumont believed in the power of memorized Bible verses. He had a special book rack built under the steering wheel in his car so that he could read passages and commit them to memory as he drove along. Some of his family questioned the safety of this practice, but Dumont's driving record remained unassailable. He would never pass a hitch-

He that is faithful in that which is least is faithful also in much; and he that is unjust in the least is unjust also in much.—Luck 10:16

Fairview Baptist Church,
     Rev. N. B. Phillips, Minister.

Tweed's Chapel Methodist Church,
     Rev. F. L. Setzer, Minister.

Mills River Presbyterian Church,
     Rev. W. S. Hutchinson, Minister.

Mills River Methodist Church,
Avery's Creek Methodist Church,
     Dr. O. B. Mitchell, Minister.

Avery's Creek Baptist and Union Church,
     Rev. Charles F. Owen, Minister.

Farmers Federation,
     Rev. Dumont Clarke, Director of Religious Department.

hiker, but demanded of each one a Bible verse from memory as payment for his ride. If the passenger failed the test Dumont determinedly taught him a verse.

Jim often preached on the Lord's Acre himself. At the height of the New Deal, he explained to a congregation: "In all [the] confusion of Gov't chaos one thing is certain—permanent civilization [is] only possible if built on the character of people—[The] country church [is the] great training ground of character—Most important institution in America . . ."[13]

He continued in this sermon to describe what he considered were two fallacious theories: first, if an individual is changed nothing else is necessary;

and second, that society can be saved without changing individuals. In the first instance he felt a person must get into action as well as having a change of heart. The second, he thought, was the philosophy behind the New Deal and socialism; that by social management and holding all property in common, by sharing the wealth, society will be changed. He argued that there would be no new society built by political and economic measures alone. There *did* have to be a change in the hearts of individuals. Jim felt the Lord's Acre could change hearts and involve people in the work of the church and of society. "Every time the Lord's hen and chickens come strutting through the yard they preach a little about the Lord."[14]

Jim McClure's vision was not unlike the one that had filled Thomas Jefferson with hope years before. Both of these men saw great moral fiber and strength in the lives of the small yeoman farmers: independent, close to nature, and undefiled by the temptations of urban life. Jim's symbol of corruption was Chicago. His notebooks were filled with reports of political payoffs, bossism and the evils of urban gangsters. Everyone who lived in the midst of such a world, he argued, found it difficult to maintain the highest moral standards. There were just too many daily degradations in the city. Like most of his contemporaries, he blamed the recent flood of southern and eastern European immigrants for the situation, and indeed Chicago was a checkerboard of such ethnic neighborhoods. He felt that these men and women had to be rescued from their own histories, and envisioned no group more capable of raising the moral climate of the United States than the thoroughly independent, Anglo-Saxon, Protestant Appalachian mountaineer. As they migrated to the cities, these internal immigrants could help to counteract, according to Jim, what he felt to be hypocritical in the teaching of the Roman Catholic Church. His Covenanter Presbyterian upbringing set his mind, and he fully believed the ideals of democracy were subverted by the authority of the priest and subservience to the Pope. For him it was the issue of indulgences all over again. How could the likes of Al Capone assuage the pangs of conscience with a few Hail Marys and regular confession? Jim argued that the country church was the source of strength in America, and the mainspring of democracy. When the country church faltered, the roots of liberty were threatened.

All of these thoughts Jim worked through in a paper he wrote during the early thirties, entitled "Rackets and the Public."

> One startling thought is that many city people seem to like [the rackets.] Capone is a modern Robin Hood. He is kind hearted, gives liberally to charity. The mixed population of our great cities, never Americanized, many of them brought up in European countries where things have always been more or less this way—seem to think it is the normal way of living. They do not recoil in horror from this racketeering. It seems to them a necessary evil and all they need do is adjust themselves to it . . . "American ideals! Can that stuff," is about all you get in the cities . . .
> The struggle for freedom is not as easy as that and unless we arouse our

people to a consciousness that the struggle is still on, we will wake up some fine day to find our free institutions gone and our American Government in the hands of people who knew not Joseph and who know and care not at all for the things of the spirit . . .

And while our native sons are busy piling up money, playing golf, riding to hounds and sending their sons to swell schools and colleges and bringing out their debutante daughters, who is running our cities? As an Englishman put it, "Just the usual hardboiled American gang of grafters, gamblers, bootleggers, vice merchants, police superintendents, friends of theirs, shyster lawyers and political bums . . ."

. . . The black hand, and the black shadow of graft, corruption and terrorism is stretched out over our great cities.

This is something that the finest American tradition can never tolerate. If America is to fulfill her promise, and if we are to cherish and develop the inner things of the Spirit, we must declare war to the death of this philosophy of the Rackets and all its brutalizing offspring.

We must clean them out, or they will clean us out![15]

These words are vintage McClure, but moral indignation begs for actions. Jim felt that the Lord's Acre Movement, by strengthening the influence of the country church on young people, was a positive force for combating the "Philosophy of the Rackets." "Something is moving in the countryside," he asserted. As Jim pointed out over and over again, the rural districts, especially in the South, were producing nothing if not children, and today's youth were tomorrow's America. Influence these young people through their churches, he argued, and future moral strength would be greatly enhanced. The rackets could be cleaned out by the infusion into the cities of confident men and women, willing to stand their ground with force of character.

But for this job to be done, the country churches would themselves have to be greatly strengthened to handle the task. Members of congregations would have to start working together. Preachers would need to be better educated, be more effective community leaders, and rely less on emotional froth to arouse their people. Sunday Schools would need good quality instructional materials. Most of all, though, Christians everywhere would have to be infused with a sense of purpose, a sense of destiny. In Jim's view, the need for Christian soldiers was never greater. Until a man or woman, boy or girl became dedicated to a larger cause or movement, Jim believed, he or she had not fully tasted the richness of life. The same human craving for belonging drew men into the rackets as into the church, and it was therefore the responsibility of Christian leaders to provide the bonds of identity, cemented with urgency of purpose, to draw the strength of America for good rather than evil.

By the fifth anniversary of Dumont Clarke's work, it was time for a special celebration. The practice of the Lord's Acre had succeeded in creating new excitement in hundreds of churches. For this special occasion, Jim and Dumont really wanted to beat the drum, and so they went after one of the great political celebrities of the day, Secretary of Agriculture Henry A. Wallace, and brought

him to Western North Carolina. Predictably, his appearance generated large
headlines in the Asheville newspapers and stirred Jim himself to heights of
excitement. Wallace had presided over some of the most controversial government farm programs in American history. Trying to decrease farm surpluses to
raise the price for the farmer, his department had supervised the destruction of
huge quantities of grain, paid farmers not to grow, encouraged the slaughter of
piglets, all in the midst of the unprecedented hunger of the Depression. Although Jim had not approved these practices, he admired the man. Henry Wallace, standing behind the pulpit of Asheville's Central Methodist Church, spoke
of the spiritual wealth in Western North Carolina. His address was entitled,
"The Necessity of a Socialized Spiritual Life in the Countryside."

> Great Spiritual power will eventually emanate from these mountains of
> Western North Carolina, which will influence the whole of the United States
> . . . You farmers here are, perhaps, among the poorest as to material wealth,
> but you have a very rich life, a life that is teeming with vital potentialities.
> Some of the most profoundly moving spiritual forces have had birth in very
> small and harassed areas.
>
> You people of this mountain section, who have not been affected by the
> capitalistic influences of industrial areas may have a fundamental influence
> upon the lifting of the shadows flung far and wide by capitalistic potentates.
>
> Progress has meant to many People in our country—more especially to
> nations across the sea—the building up of a faith in material things that is so
> intense that it borders upon the side of worship. This belief, this devout
> materialistic movement, spawned Communism, Fascism, Socialism and all the
> other "isms" now overlapping their purposes.
>
> Capitalism has influenced people to divorce their minds from spiritual
> things. Many city churches are under capitalistic rule. The Lord's Acre Plan
> carries us back toward pre-capitalistic days, to days when we had sympathy
> with better things.[16]

Out in the audience, absorbing this barrage of New Deal rhetoric, sat
Douglas Stuart. He was now Chairman of the Board of the Quaker Oats Company, and Chairman of the Industrial Advisory Board of the National Recovery
Administration. It was he who had actually persuaded Mr. Wallace to come.
The next day, Wallace, Jim and Doug attended the Laurel Pines Baptist Church
in Fairview, for a Lord's Acre rally. The Agriculture Secretary spoke and then
the men climbed up Ferguson's Peak behind the McClure home. One can only
wonder at the provocative discussions that bounced around between them along
that trail. Elspeth McClure, who went along on the climb, was twelve and
doesn't remember what they said, but she does remember cracking walnuts with
Secretary Wallace on the living room hearth. Henry Wallace, Jim McClure and
Douglas Stuart were confident men with strong ideas. Jim had also invited Mr.
R. W. Freeman, a local farmer and one of the founders of the Federation, to add
spice to the gathering. The next year, Dr. Toychiko Kagawa was the featured
speaker for the Lord's Acre annual meeting, and Jim used the occasion to

OUR CHURCHES
WITH THE LORD'S ACRE PLAN

IDEAL: THE SPIRIT OF JESUS IN OUR LIVES
THROUGH HIS WORDS AND HIS WORKS

TEND FAITHFULLY THAT WHICH YOU HAVE
DEVOTED UNTO THE LORD.

KEEP THE WEEDS OUT.

KEEP THE WEEDS OUT OF YOUR HEART
ALSO.

NO MAN HAVING PUT HIS HAND TO THE
PLOW . . . . .

Carry this folder with you — Memorize and
THOUGHTFULLY repeat the verses.

April-May, 1930.

Front of folder promoting the Lord's Acre Plan.

THE   LORD'S   ACRE   COVENANT

PLEDGE CARD FOR ALL PROJECTS

_____CLASS OR CHURCH GROUP

Recognizing God's goodness to us and His claim upon us and especially upon our farm life, because without His sunshine and His showers all our efforts would be in vain,

WE HEREBY AGREE TO BEGIN, TO DEDICATE TO THE LORD, AND TO TEND FAITH-FULLY IN 193___, THE PROJECT LISTED OPPOSITE OUR NAMES, AND TO GIVE THE PROCEEDS FROM EACH PROJECT TO_____CHURCH

Name	Project	Goal	Started	Inspected	Yield

Suggested projects: potatoes, corn, cotton, chickens, a pig, a calf, Sunday eggs, etc. Those working for wages may give dedicated hours of earnings; or, special business or craft projects may be carried out.

Extra lines on other side

Pledge card for the Lord's Acre Plan.

evaluate Secretary Wallace in a letter to Doug Stuart. "This year Uncle Dumont had a tremendous crowd out. The freak value of a real life Jap proved a better drawing card than the Secretary of Agriculture—tho I think anyone who knew them both would give the freak award to the Secretary" (James G. K. McClure, Jr. to the Stuarts, March 22, 1936).

At the same time that the Lord's Acre Movement was becoming established the Federation, with the aid of the Educational and Development Fund, spread to new towns and counties: Franklin in Macon County; Morganton in Burke County; Marion in McDowell County; Sylva in Jackson County; Tryon in Polk County; Murphy to serve Cherokee, Clay and Graham Counties; Bryson City in Swain County; Brevard in Transylvania County; Burnsville in Yancey County; and Lenoir in Caldwell County. The area serviced by the Federation, Jim McClure never tired of pointing out, was larger than the three states of Rhode Island, Connecticut and Delaware combined. At seven of the Federation's warehouses, the Federation operated feed mills to grind the farmer's corn and add the correct ingredients for whatever feed the grower needed. All of these warehouses had to be linked together by an efficient transportation system, and the State of North Carolina's highway building program was a key factor in making this possible.

The expansion process created its own color, lore and heroes. Whenever enough interest seemed to justify organizing in a new location, sufficient stock would have to be sold to capitalize the new business and to interest the farmers in the Federation operation. No one could sell stock like "Uncle Church" Crow-

Left to right: *James G.K. McClure, Henry Wallace, Dumont Clarke, and Doug Stuart. Photo property of the McClure Fund.*

ell. He had joined up with Jim McClure during the early days of the Federation, and stuck with him. He was prominent in mountain politics, having represented Buncombe County in the State legislature. He genuinely loved being thrown into a new section to sell stock to strangers. His humor and charm produced results, and a great many tales. He said he liked "to live off the land," stay in the homes and eat off the tables of those people he had come to sign up. Describing the organization of one new county, Jim McClure wrote in the *News*, "The year 1936 saw the Farmers Federation again expand. In the Autumn our Vice President, R. Church Crowell, together with a committee of McDowell County farmers campaigned in McDowell County and more than three hundred stockholders joined the Farmers Federation. It is said that Mr. Crowell gained twenty pounds during his stay in McDowell."[17] In a speech in New York, Jim McClure described in more detail the difficulties of selling stock in the mountains, and then told a story famous in Federation circles about Mr. Crowell.

When we expand into an additional county, we have a selling campaign to sell stock in our cooperative. We try to see every farmer in the county. It is a slow job selling the farmer stock. You have got to visit each one. It is a harder job to sell a farmer $10 worth of stock than to sell a $1,000 bond in New York. You have to go and talk with him the first time and he will tell you he will think

about it, then you have to go back and remember the names of his children, his dog and his pig. It takes three or four visits. We have one man who is extremely good at talking to the farmers—our vice president, Mr. Crowell—and I want to say that all the people running this enterprise are mountain people who have grown up with it. Three or four months ago, a woman, a widow, came to my office. Our people had been out on a stock-selling campaign in the county in which she lived. She said, "Mr. McClure, I have brought ten dollars to buy a share of stock and I want to get it right now. Mr. Crowell came out about three weeks ago and came to my house about eleven o'clock in the morning and started talking about the Farmers Federation. He stayed until dinner time and I had to ask him to sit down to eat dinner and he ate the biggest meal I have ever seen." Then she said, "He went away, but he came back about a week later and wanted to know if I had had time to study about it, and he again talked about an hour about the Farmers Federation. Then it got to be dinner time and I had to ask him to take dinner again, and he ate another tremendous big meal," and she said, "I want to pay my ten dollars before he comes back another time."[18]

After this speech, someone asked Jim a very pertinent question, "Can you succeed in getting practically all the farmers in?" He replied:

No, we get about 300 members in each county. Out of perhaps 1,500 farmers in a county, we get the best farmers. A great many of our farmers simply cannot get up ten dollars. We let them pay in eggs, chickens or any kind of produce. We deal with non-members as well as members, because the ones we want to do the most for are the ones that can't get up the ten dollars.[19]

But if a man had the cash, chances were that "Uncle Church" would get it for his Federation. Another story that circulated about him took place during the drive to sign up stockholders in Swain County.

[Uncle Church] . . . had a black Ford that used a quart of oil a day . . . He was driving along by himself one rainy day when he spotted a big fire burning by the side of the road. There were men working nearby, and Uncle Church, thinking that it was one of Swain County's WPA road improvement projects, stopped to warm himself and to inquire if there were any good prospects living nearby.

The Foreman greeted him cordially, "Step right up and take all the fire you can stand," he urged. "We'll be having lunch directly. Be glad to have you eat with us."

This sounded pretty good to Uncle Church, who was a big eater. "I don't want to take away you boys' dinner," he said. But the foreman was strong in his invitation.

"No, sir, we got a-plenty. You just wait about fifteen minutes."

Pretty soon the men came in from their various tasks, and they ate lunch

Opposite: *Members of the Lowell Pines Baptist Church (Fairview, N.C.) plant 1¼ acres of potatoes for their Lord's Acre Plan, 1938.*

and drank coffee around the fire. It was a dark day, and Mr. Crowell was unable to see clearly many of the four around him, but he decided to try selling a little stock to the group anyway.

"I've eat dinner off you boys," he said. "Now I'm going to give you something in return. I'm going to make you a speech about the Farmers Federation.

"Fine," said the Foreman. A speech about anything would brighten up life in this remote corner. So Mr. Crowell turned lose with a burst of oratory about the Federation. When he finished he said,

"Now, I want you boys to take some stock in the Farmers Federation. It'll be the best investment you've ever made. $10 a share, and its the only stock in North Carolina paying 6 percent."

"You can put me down for five shares," said the foreman.

"I'll take ten dollars worth," chimed in a man who looked like the assistant foreman.

"Give me two shares," came a voice in the back.

"That's fine boys, Fine," exclaimed Mr. Crowell. "Let me have your names and I'll put you down on this list . . . Now when are you going to pay me for this stock? I'll be glad to take it now, and that will leave you plenty of time to make more before Christmas. Your dividends begin as soon as you pay for your stock. On January 1st you'll get a green check from the Farmers Federation, Incorporated."

"Here's fifty dollars for mine," said the foreman, fumbling in his overalls for his wallet, which had a rubber band tied around it.

"I'll pay you my ten first of the month," the assistant foreman declared. "I just got through paying my taxes, and that likes to break a man."

"How about you, my good man?" Uncle Church asked the man at the rear of the circle who had subscribed for twenty dollars.

"Well," the man replied, "The state's got me for thirty years, but I'll pay you as quick as I can after that."

Uncle Church had sold to a member of the Chain Gang.[20]

Once the money was in hand on a stock drive, the warehouse was constructed, and a grand opening planned. In a letter to his son, Jim McClure describes the opening of the Brevard warehouse.

> Yesterday was a big day—Hitting Asheville about 8, the General Staff of the Federation including the high powered mayor of Bee Tree [Allan Coggins], the fiddlers, the Redoubtable Rotha, Senator Browning, Uncle Dumont and Guy Sales all entrained for Brevard, where at ten o'clock we had a rousing opening of our 17th warehouse. The place was crowded, and some 250 stood up under the barrage, the Senator pulling his well tried stories out of the bag—and all meeting with success—We elected a committee of 10, had lunch with them at 12 o'clock, loaded up again and set out for Fairview Siding. (James G. K. McClure, Jr., to Jamie McClure, date unknown)

Opposite: *"Uncle Church" Crowell and a group of boy scouts. They raised an acre of tomatoes which brought $145.45 to the Acton Church in Buncombe County in 1942.*

The purpose behind all of these efforts was, to use Jim's apt slogan to "Help the Mountaineer Help Himself." When raising money for the Educational and Development Fund he never failed to contrast his own programs, which created new wealth, with those of the federal government during the New Deal, which he felt were designed only to divide up existing wealth. His appeal to successful businessmen and their wives in the Northeast for contributions always stressed the independence and the hard-working nature of the mountaineer, traits that held a high place in the values of the American business community. Jim also emphasized the ancestral bond between the Anglo-Saxon Protestants of Western North Carolina and their counterparts up north. He implied that both groups had inherited the same qualities. Anglo-Saxon Protestants believed in the supernatural power of the Creator and in the ability of representative government to protect personal freedom. He convinced his audiences that if the mountaineer was only given the education and the opportunity he, too, would create an economic miracle. Jim was incredibly successful at raising money to develop productive schemes in the region, and to educate the farmers in the new agricultural ways of the twentieth century.

The Federation *News* remained Jim's primary educational tool. With time, the information became increasingly technical and complex, as the farmers learned the vocabulary of their occupation. O. J. Holler of Union Mills contributed a well-informed column for several years, one he unabashedly called "Master Farmer of Rutherford County." For more than thirty years, Professor S. C. Clapp of Buncombe County, originally the director of the state test farm in Swannanoa and later an officer in the Federation, contributed a knowledgeable column in each issue. After leaving the test farm, he was hired by the Federation as head of its Seed Department. Always, the information stressed scientific management, and the latest in agricultural studies. Reliable ideas were scarce in Western North Carolina, and the Federation aimed to make such knowledge readily accessible. The *News* also promoted the programs of the Federation, and included a column devoted to women and home economics by Tillie Rotha, a daughter of the Forest Products Department Manager. Elizabeth McClure contributed an anonymous column called "Garden Notes."

In 1935 a new and more direct form of education was launched by the Federation. Jim McClure had always wanted to operate a vocational school to train the most promising young men in the region in the business of cooperative agriculture. In many ways, the Farmers Federation Training School was a forerunner of the technical colleges the State of North Carolina would develop much later. The Training School could educate only a few boys at first. They received a thorough and practical education in both agriculture and business. In January of 1937, the members of the third class of the Federation Training School gathered to begin their year's course.

> The courses of study include business law, salesmanship, bookkeeping, and a study of the Farmers Federation and the farm cooperative movement.

In addition to these courses of study, the boys have lectures on many subjects, such as the ones listed below.

(a) Seeds, dealing with germination, purity, and sources of different kinds of seeds . . .

(b) Insecticides, covering a study of the insect pests, blights, and plant diseases.

(c) Marketing of different farm products.

(d) Demonstrations in setting up and servicing farm machinery.

(e) The religious aspects of the farm cooperative, with practical work in the Lord's Acre Movement.

In addition to these lectures, the boys will have practical work all during the year in the different departments of the Farmers Federation, half the time being devoted to study and half the time to securing practical experience . . .

This school is attracting wide attention, as it appears to be the first school in the State to train young men in the practical workings of a community service organization like the Farmers Federation.[21]

One of the young men in the class of 1939 was Don Ramsey, from Cherokee County, the western-most section of North Carolina. He remembers graduating from high school, and finding out that there just were not any jobs for an unskilled eighteen-year-old. He had heard about the interviews for the Training Schools and went down to the Murphy warehouse to find out if he qualified. All the candidates had to be farm boys with superior high school records. Don made the grade, and went to Asheville the following fall. The school was located in the Federation headquarters on Roberts Street, and all the boys roomed at "Ma" Ramsey's place nearby. Bed and board was $7 a week, which gobbled up most of the Federation check of $40 a month each received for the work that was part of the curriculum. The Federation hoped to train young men who would stay with the cooperative after graduating from the training school.[22] Don Ramsey became one of the most outstanding warehouse managers, and eventually took over the Federation operation in Murphy.

Each of the Federation warehouses competed directly with other feed, seed and hardware businesses. There was always a push to increase volume and profit. The Federation tried to maintain a price edge on the local competition, but oftentimes was out-maneuvered and lost customers. The Federation was well known for its quality seeds and liberal credit as well, and tried to make use of the yearly patronage refund for each customer's business total as an incentive to shop with the Federation. Don Ramsey felt that the reputation of fine seeds helped to draw in loyal customers. Jim McClure had worked with the North Carolina Extension Service and the State Department of Agriculture to make sure that the cooperative handled only the best seeds. Many times farmers were tempted to purchase shoddy seeds for a bargain price, and Jim McClure warned his readers about such false economy in the *News*.

There is only one kind of seed that it pays the farmer to sow and this is the best seed, with the highest germination and free from obnoxious weed seeds.

Low grade seed . . . will not only be followed by a poor and scattering crop
but may so infest a field with damaging weeds that it will take years of work
to remove the pests.

. . . Whenever seed prices are high, there always comes out of old cellars
and old storehouses a lot of low-grade seed which is offered cheap on the
market . . .

It has been our observation that the best farmers, the farmers who make
money year after year, are very particular to hunt for and buy the best seed
obtainable . . .[23]

It was not until 1937 that the Federation once again felt strong enough to
pay a patronage dividend to its customers. Jim McClure hoped that the resump-
tion of these payments would boost sales through the warehouses, and so asked
the farmers to redeem the coupons they had received at the time of each transac-
tion during the past year. Rather than pay out cash, the Federation gave each
customer credit towards a $10 share of stock. These patronage refunds had been
dropped after 1923, when the organization was facing a severe credit squeeze,
which was exacerbated by the central warehouse fire of 1925. With the announcement that the patronage refund rate would be 2 1/2 percent on business
done in 1937, Jim reminded everyone to keep their coupons.

No matter what incentives were offered to the customers, the balance
between success and failure at each warehouse was determined by the ability
of each manager and his assistants. The Federation had to push hard to make
use of its large buying power, its economy of scale, while at the same time
making each warehouse outlet as friendly as a family-owned feed and seed store.
A change of personnel was often a touchy operation. The management had to
gauge not only the business acumen of an individual, but also his popularity
among the patrons. The store in Hendersonville was one of the strongest links
in the business chain, and in 1938 its longtime manager, Mr. C. H. T. Bly,
decided to retire. Jim McClure worked out an advisory position for him in
Tryon, so that the Federation could give him a place to live and a small income
to live on. But among Mr. Bly's old customers, the plan did not sit well at all.
A groundswell of protest erupted until he was returned to Hendersonville to
placate those men and women who were accustomed to "trading" with him. The
results were explained in an article in the News. "When Mr. Bly's many friends
and customers in Henderson County learned of this proposed move they put up
a tremendous outcry against it. Requests that Mr. Bly remain in Henderson
County were so numerous that the Directors arranged to retain him at the
Hendersonville Warehouse. He will be relieved of the responsibilities of management, but Mr. Bly will be at the Warehouse and ready with his advice and
counsel, on which the people of the territory depend."[24] One could never under-
estimate the fierce loyalty the mountaineers felt for their favorite storekeepers.

In 1938, Jim McClure was relieved of his duties as general manager of the
daily operations of all the Federation warehouses by the appointment of Guy
Sales, a careful businessman, to this important position. He had been working

for the Federation since 1922, when he was first engaged as a bookkeeper. Mr. Sales was a thorough man who relied less on morale boosting and good will, and more on disciplined policies carefully carried out. No one understood the inner workings of the cooperative better than he did, having been the sole auditor for most of its existence. He watched as the poultry business grew from a black pot at the Fairview Siding into a million dollar enterprise. He understood the financial weaknesses and strengths of the Federation. For instance, he knew that money was to be made in selling feed to broiler producers, even if money was lost when the birds were marketed. The profits justified the losses. He knew the importance of cash management. Cash flow was often preserved, for instance, by delaying the payment of bills outstanding to the fertilizer and feed companies. "They'd holler a lot of times," he recalls, but the Federation account was one that was too large to drop. Guy Sales also had to try to hold down the flow of credit out of each store, and finally began charging excess amounts against the paychecks of the managers. He hounded the managers to collect those overdue bills from the customers. These hard-nosed policies made the Federation a healthier business enterprise, and Jim McClure was able to devote more effort and time to fund-raising, promotion and expansion.[25]

Jim's business abilities ran in the direction of creating incentives and devising innovative approaches. He loved contests and prizes, and each year would offer $100 in gold to the manager who could increase his sales percentage the most over a year's time. He also concocted little contests to keep up employee morale, such as the hot competition that grew up over which warehouse could unload a boxcar of fertilizer the fastest.

Jim had another vision for helping mountain people to a better life. He wanted to bring industries into Western North Carolina, so that one or two members of every family could earn some cash to supplement the farm income. He wrote men like Henry Ford, urging them to build plants in his district.[26] Two very large plants built by Champion Fibre and American Enka, were built and became the beginning of the industrialization of the mountains. Jim decided there was a need for small manufacturing projects and pushed ahead to start some, on his own, in order to create wages where they could not otherwise be earned. At the Fairview Siding, women were hired to make blouses, shirts, uniforms and even rag dolls in what was known as the Federation Sewing Room.[27] Later the "sewing room" spawned a uniform company known as "On Duty Clothes," under Federation management.

In Henderson County, the cannery operation came to employ between 50 and 150 people, nearly all women, during the harvest season (from July to October). Under the Carolina Sunshine label, the Federation marketed its most unique product, yellow tomato juice, along with canned beans, tomatoes and okra. There was even a brief attempt to can grits, but that product went the way of all bad ideas. The Educational and Development Fund helped to promote a small toy shop in Tryon for a brief period. Most of these projects struggled to show a profit, especially during the Depression. But Jim McClure kept trying to devise schemes for making money in the mountains, and his imagination and courage left few opportunities untried. His goal, largely realized today, was to provide enough opportunities to earn wages so that the families of Western North Carolina could remain on their farms, proud and independent.

By design, most of his employment ideas involved women. He felt great pity for them out on their little farms, trapped by the drudgery of their subsistence lives. Jim liked to explain the plight of the mountain woman with a story he told often and well.

> We are trying to find something that the mountain women can make in their homes and sell, because if these mountain women can earn a little money it will change their whole outlook on life . . . In certain ways, there is no more tragic figure on the American scene . . . The average mountain woman has to cook something like one thousand and ninety-five meals a year, and then when January 1st comes around she has to start right over again and cook another thousand and ninety-five meals. They never get away from home. We thought if we could get a little money in their hands it would mean a great deal to them. They tell a story about the mountain woman that illustrates better than I can tell you the condition of things. A mountain family received a letter from a lawyer stating that the family had been left a legacy of eight hundred dollars. They all gathered around the fire in their log cabin to decide what they would do with that money. The old man thought he would buy a new rifle, the oldest boy thought he would buy a bicycle and one of the boys was going to buy a victrola, the daughter thought she would take a trip to Asheville, she had never been there before; and when they decided what each member of the family would do, there was a pause. They heard the dishes rattling in the kitchen and they remembered their mother, who was doing all the work and washing up all the dishes, and they said, "What will we get for Maw?" They commenced to think, and finally one of the sons had a bright idea, and he said, "Let's get Maw a new axe."[28]

He liked to calculate not only the number of meals cooked, but also the number of miles a mother travelled in a year to carry water for her family. These figures spoke eloquently enough of the hard lives these women led. It was usually the mother who yearned for a more civilized, more prosperous life for her children. Jim felt that creating work for these mothers, outside or in the home, would open up new possibilities in the lives of the women and their families. He began, like many Northerners before him, to encourage the production and sale of mountain crafts. Knitters, basket weavers, hooked rug producers, and others, were brought together, given quality control guidelines, and put to work. These items usually brought in precious little money for the hours of work that went into making them, but at that time any money was better than none at all. More important, perhaps, was that these women came in touch with other people, both other craftsmen and those living far away who bought what they had made. Moreover, the money received represented self-esteem, and the chance to buy something for themselves more fitting than a new axe. The Federation eventually set up a Home Industries Division that would market everything from sorghum molasses to picnic baskets to corn meal to hand-knitted bed jackets. Jim wrote to Hetty urging her " . . . to buy sweaters from the English Knit Shop in Lake Forest. This is Helen Farwell's Shop. They are giving us a very nice business and I am suggesting that you go in and demand North Carolina sweaters and buy till it hurts, and then keep on buying!" (James G. K. McClure, Jr. to Harriet McClure Stuart, February 3, 1937). Jim had once more brought his old world and his new one in touch with one another.

In 1939, Jim steadied himself to gather together his thoughts. What were, realistically, the possibilities for future life in Western North Carolina? Armed, as usual, with reams of statistics, he argued in a paper for the Pen and Plate Club for the "remaking" of his mountain region. He believed that from the potentials of manpower and resources a new basis for civilization was possible in the area. He began by complimenting his fellow Pen and Plate Club members on their intellectual prowess, while simultaneously warning them that his address would be a great deal more prosaic than poetic.

> The subject I have selected for your attention this evening is "Remaking Western North Carolina." I bring this subject to your attention because it presents not only a local problem, but the type of problem that is facing all communities in the United States . . .
>
> In the development of America the time has come when we must turn to the improving or building up of our own communities. As we hear so frequently, the frontier is gone . . . Opportunity was unlimited, but it was always found by moving on. A pioneer could take up land, kill off the fish and game near his cabin, skim the fertility off the soil and then move on to the frontier again and homestead another tract of land . . .
>
> The frontier dominated American thinking and now the frontier has gone, and America finds herself faced with an entirely different task. That task is to develop our own communities with the same drive and energy and determination and daring, with which we have developed the unexplored frontier . . .
>
> To bring this matter right home to us I want tonight to talk about our own community—Western North Carolina . . .
>
> The people of Western North Carolina are chiefly rural people. The population of the 18 counties in 1930 was 390,359, of whom 73,516 were urban, which means that 81% of the population is rural . . .
>
> . . . During the past twenty years, changes have come . . . Excellent roads have opened up the entire territory, penetrating and connecting up even the most inaccessible sections. Tremendous improvement has been made in the State school system, and High School opportunity has been placed within reach of nearly all the boys and girls. Some new industries have come into this territory, bringing their life-giving pay rolls and followed by a higher standard of living . . . we really need thirty or forty times as many as we have.
>
> I also want to point out in considering our subject that we have in this mountain territory one asset of very high value. A few days ago I had the privilege of having lunch with General Wood, of Sears Roebuck, and Henry

Ford. General Wood spent some time in telling Mr. Ford that America's most precious resource was in the South. He referred to the young people under 21. North Carolina has roughly twice as many young people—under 21—as Illinois in proportion to population. And this mountain region is particularly rich in this precious asset of the human race—children . . .

Lest we think that good roads, industries, and schools have solved this problem [of farm income] during these years, I want to present to you recent figures. [1937]. These figures of income and outgo [are] an average of 59 TVA demonstration farms in one of our counties. These are taken as average farms, and careful accounts kept . . . the average of these 59 demonstration farms is 54 acres . . .

Of the 54 acres—11 will be in crops, 5 in meadow, 15 in open pasture, 21 in woods pasture and 2 in buildings, garden, roads, etc. The average livestock will be 1 horse or mule, a pig, 40 chickens . . .

The total income is $486.81. The total farm expense is $437.25, leaving net cash of $49.56 for the cash needs of a family of six for one year. Gentlemen, let your mind rest on that figure a moment, $49.56, for a family of 6 for a year. Why, a sickness, or a burial, would wipe it out in one day. What about books? What about subscriptions to a paper? What about a winter coat for the wife? What about a few toys for the children at Christmas? They are out, gentlemen, completely out.

May I remind you, in posing this problem, that these people in this territory are practically 100% the old American stock. It is one of the only areas in the South where there are few negroes—less that 10% of our population being colored and in the rural districts very much less than that . . .

Jim McClure proceeds to sort through the bewildering list of New Deal programs and their impact on Western North Carolina. By 1939, he was quite disillusioned with Franklin Roosevelt, and the federal debt that he had built up paying for his "alphabet" projects. But he was fair to point out the benefits of new roads, agricultural loan programs, low-cost fertilizer from the TVA, and the bold thrust to promote soil and water conservation. He then concluded with these remarks.

And now I want to revert to my subject, "Remaking Western North Carolina," and to the question I posed. Reminding you of our low income farmer with a net cash income of $49.56 per year, and reminding you of a lack of income so general that in Swain County 82% of the population are certified as needing relief. What can we do about this problem? How can it be solved? How can civilization be remade and opportunity of development created?

In the first place we must note that many of these Federal expenditures are only of a temporary nature. They cannot continue because they are expenditures of debt, not of income, and regardless of their merit they cannot continue on this scale. Those that are worth retaining can only be retained if we balance our national budget. This spending spree will be stopped by the people of the United States voluntarily and with courage, or it will be stopped involuntarily by our credit giving out . . .

In the second place the farm activities described are building up the soil, improving practices and improving conditions.

In the third place the emergency government programs are not building any permanent income. The money runs off as fast as the rain runs off our mountains.

In the fourth place in a section like ours, of low incomes and no capital, we must create markets, develop industries, and develop services for which money can be received. For these things we must accumulate capital. We must save up capital and invest it in our own enterprise and in our own communities. We have the population, but we have very few constructive enterprises being developed.

And what we need above all is men and women who will spend their lives developing our communities or developing a small industry—who will make that their life work.

And we must not forget to conserve the spiritual resources of this territory. No word of that in [the] Federal program, everything [is] on the material basis. In all this gigantic machinery of Federal spending in all its roar and confusion, we can hear scarcely a note of the spiritual, and it will always be true that "man cannot live by bread alone." It will be out of spiritual development and insight and motive that new life will come to this community.[29]

Despite Jim's personal ambivalence about many aspects of Roosevelt's New Deal, the Federation certainly benefited from the favorable climate for cooperatives that existed during these years. Public attitudes toward the idea of cooperatives swung back and forth, from the notion that anyone promoting such enterprises was tending toward socialism; to its opposite, that cooperatives provided a much superior business model when compared with traditional profit capitalism. After 1930, the pendulum swung decidedly towards the latter opinion. But general public acceptance was only one of the results that benefited Jim's work. Legislation on many levels provided specific aids and incentives to cooperatives. A bank was organized with government capital, designed specifically to loan money to operations like the Farmers Federation. The branch that served Western North Carolina, the Columbia Bank for Cooperatives, became a willing source of cash, and strengthened the financial position of the Federation immeasurably. Another institution, the Farm Credit Cooperative Bank of Washington, lent money as well. The crown jewel of the New Deal, the Tennessee Valley Authority, encompassed a large part of the Federation territory. The TVA assisted farmers through demonstration projects using low cost, high analysis fertilizers. These fertilizers are now widely used on a commercial basis. The Soil Conservation Service was one more federal agency that helped mountain farmers improve their land during these years. Jim McClure helped organize the Soil and Water Conservation District in his area.

Because farm commodity prices remained low during the thirties, the Federation's profits were scarce. Moreover, many of his Fund contributors were hit hard by the stock market crash, making that source of capital more uncertain. But Jim didn't quit trying. He wrote to Hetty, "Dumont and I are trying to take money away from the tight fisted money barons and economic Royalists of Wall St. D is a huge help, he has a campaign spirit on him that bids fair to high pressure Wall St. just as he has high-pressured the mountaineer" (James F. K. McClure, Jr. to Harriet McClure Stuart, October 10, 1936).

With help from these sources, the Federation did expand into new counties, and with new services. The tobacco and forest products projects remained healthy operations through the thirties, while Jim McClure worked to improve the income of dairymen through the Blue Ridge Milk Producers' Association. By the end of the Depression, the Farmers Federation's sales began to approach the million dollar mark, a figure that had been reached only once before, in 1929. Volume had increased steadily through the Depression years, but soft prices kept the dollar total low. Despite all the discouragements, year in and year out, Jim McClure never wavered in his determination to push the organization to the limits of its capacity in order to fulfill its destiny of "Helping the mountain farmers to help themselves."

1. Minutes of the Farmers Federation, Meeting held January 21, 1931, p. 95., Book no. 1, "December 9, 1926 through April 18, 1934."

2. James G. K. McClure, Jr., personal financial statement, January 1, 1931, his personal account book.

3. James G. K. McClure, Jr., Farmers Federation *News*, January 1930.

4. Farmers Federation *News*, August, 1930.

5. James G. K. McClure, Jr., *Yale Alumni Weekly*, December 30, 1932.

6. Interview with Mr. Guy Sales.

7. Interview with James McClure Clarke.

8. Thomas Wolfe, *You Can't Go Home Again* (New York: Scribners, 1934).

9. Farmers Federation *News*, March 1927.

10. James G. K. McClure, Jr., Farmers Federation *News*, February 1930.

11. James G. K. McClure, Jr., speech on the Farmers Federation, given September 10, 1935, and transcribed in "Proceedings of the New York Farmers, 1934–1935 Season," New York, 1935, p. 14.

12. *Ibid.*, p. 15.

13. James G. K. McClure, Jr., sermon, "Something is Moving in the Countryside."

14. James G. K. McClure, Jr., speech on the Lord's Acre, date and place unknown.

15. James G. K. McClure, Jr., "Rackets and the Public," unpublished paper written in the early 1930s.

16. Henry A. Wallace, quoted in the Asheville *Citizen-Times*, Sunday, February 24, 1935.

17. James G. K. McClure, Jr., "The Seventeenth Year," Farmers Federation *News*, August, 1937, p. 7.

18. *Op Cit.*, New York Farmers, p. 16.

19. *Ibid.*, p. 18. Question asked by Mr. James Henry Hammond.

20. James McClure Clarke, anecdote written in personal notebook.

21. James G. K. McClure, Jr., "News from the Front," Farmers Federation *News*, February 1937, p. 4.

22. Interview with Mr. Don Ramsey, March 20, 1981.

23. James G. K. McClure, Jr., "News from the Front," Farmers Federation *News*, February, 1937, p. 4.

24. James G. K. McClure, Jr., "News from the Front," Farmers Federation *News*, September 1938, p. 13.

25. Interview with Mr. Guy Sales.

26. letter from the Ford Motor Company to James G. K. McClure, Jr. 1922 (exact date unknown.)

27. Interview with Mrs. Ethel Williams, February 2, 1982.

28. *Op Cit.*, New York Farmers, p. 13.

29. James G. K. McClure, Jr., "Remaking Western North Carolina," speech given at the Pen and Plate Club, Asheville, 1939.

Chapter Eighteen
*The Picnics**

How do you do everybody, How are you?
It's the Farmers Federation greeting you.
Now we hope you're feeling fine,
And we'll have a great big time.
How do you do- do- do- do- do- do-?
(*Written and sung by Gaither Robinson*)

For more than twenty years, the Farmers Federation picnics were a joyful mixture of entertainment and education for countless people in Western North Carolina. A picnic was a day of friendship and goodwill, held once a year in a high school or courthouse in each county served by the Federation. The purpose of these gatherings was twofold: to educate people about the programs offered by the Federation, and to encourage the musical talent of the mountains, both string players and choirs and quartets from rural churches. Here was an outlet and an audience for many talented local performers in the days before organized recreation and television.

The idea for the picnics doubtless grew out of the Federation stockholders' meetings, which were held at night in each warehouse during early spring, just before planting time. Jim McClure and Guy Sales, the general manager, reported on the progress of business, and the Farmers Federation String Band played a few numbers. Usually only farmers who were seriously committed to supporting the cooperative attended, often with wives and children. These were small, cozy meetings, with chairs drawn up near the heater among the shelves of groceries, and baby chicks chirping from stacked up cages in the corner of the warehouse. Chicks were given as door prizes and made a great hit. After the business there was often a little buck dancing by male members of the audience before coffee and doughnuts were handed round. Jim wanted this kind of program available to larger audiences. Buck dancing was a traditional dance in the mountains done exclusively by men (at least in public). The steps have evolved into what is now called clogging.

The first picnic occurred in the early thirties. They gradually became large gatherings that anywhere from 800 to 1,000 people might attend, sometimes

*This chapter is written in cooperation with and with the invaluable assistance of James McClure's daughter, Elspeth McClure Clarke.

376

Gaither Robinson (banjo), Johnny Rhymer (fiddle) and "Panhandle Pete" playing for a Farmers Federation Warehouse meeting. Photo property of the McClure Fund.

even more. The Farmers Federation String Band was the mainstay of entertainment, but an amazing array of local performers always showed up. Every summer there would be three or four especially good acts, and these performers would be asked to attend some or all of the picnics the next year, while receiving a small stipend to cover expenses. Jim often talked about "the great reservoir of musical talent in the Southern mountains" and loved both the string music and the church singing with which he had become so familiar as he attended many different country churches. He used to say you never heard a sour note in the mountains.

A picnic began officially at ten o'clock. To reach places at the eastern edge of the Federation territory like Morganton and Lenoir, or far to the west like Murphy and Hayesville, the McClure family had to leave home by five thirty or six. Elizabeth was not an early morning person, but she got up gamely and Jim would cheerfully make breakfast, urging everyone all the while to hurry. The McClures usually carried a performer or two with them. Gaither Robinson, banjo picker and lead singer of the Farmers Federation String Band for many years, used to sit sideways on the back seat of the car and play and sing to while away the hours on the road. Jim would call for one number after another. It was a wonder Gaither wasn't hoarse before he ever reached the picnic.

There were always people gathered on the school grounds and even a few expectantly sitting in the auditorium or court room when the McClure's arrived. Two or three daughters of Federation employees greeted people as they entered the building, pinning on yellow picnic tags and urging them to come right up and take a good seat. In later years Jim's two granddaughters would help, too. Jim mounted the stage dressed in white shirt and "ice cream pants," his picnic uniform, to start the program. He was never late, except twice. Once he had two blowouts on the way over Soco Gap to Bryson City. And once he arrived at the Burnsville picnic, always held on the fourth of July to open the season, both a few minutes late and wearing dark pants. His four-year-old granddaughter Annie (now the wife of the author of this book), had been sick in his lap on the way. Her birthday was July third and the combination of birthday cake, firecrackers, mountain roads and the first picnic was hard on the digestion of such a small trouper.

Different musicians played in the Federation Band over the years, but Gaither Robinson was always there. Jim began the day by introducing the band and calling on Mr. Robinson to greet the audience with a song called "How Do You Do?" Gaither had springy white hair and wore steel-rimmed spectacles. He always looked newly scrubbed and earnest. His voice was high and distinct and he dead-panned the funny lines in such a way that all his songs became comic. The audience felt relaxed and cozy the minute he began to sing:

> How do you do everybody, How are you?
> It's the Farmers Federation greeting you
> Now we hope you're feeling fine,
> And we'll have a great big time.
> How do you do- do- do- do- do- do-?

The morning program featured string music interspersed with talks on farming and programs of the cooperative. Jim McClure and Dumont Clarke *always* spoke, as well as other officers of the cooperative and usually a local representative of the State Agriculture Extension Service. The Federation band started the program off with several numbers and remained in the wings ready to fill in if necessary, but many local performers always turned up in the course of the morning to register with Jim as he sat at a table on one side of the stage. As local worthies arrived he would interrupt the program to recognize them. "Here comes Mr. Winslow Burgin, one of our Farmers Federation directors," he would say. "We're all glad to see him and we want you to come right up here and sit on the stage." Or "Sheriff Hines, we know we'll have a good picnic today with you here to keep order. Step right up on the platform with us!" If he could not remember some name he would send out a runner to find out. Soon everyone in the audience felt they were a personal friend of Jim McClure's, and part of the show.

The membership of the string band changed occasionally. Pender Rector was fiddler until the early forties, a stocky little man with a big grin who always encouraged young performers. Johnny Rhymer followed him, himself one of the young performers Pender had encouraged, and he became a legend in the mountains, playing as fast in 1989 as he did in 1943. He played old English fiddle tunes like "Bonaparte's Retreat" or the latest tune from Nashville and he always got an audience into the swing.

Jim understood how important it is to keep a program moving, and since the possible performers were an unpredictable group, changing from picnic to picnic and from year to year, this required an imaginative approach and a sure feel for the mood of the audience. When Elspeth began to help at the picnics, her job was to line up performers and speakers in the wings of the stage ready to appear when he called them. In later years, when Jim's nephew Jamie Clarke ran the picnics, he, too, understood how important it was to keep speeches short. Once he surreptitiously sent one of his small sons, Dumont, to offer a speaker a cookie, which effectively checked him in the midst of an oratorical flight.

The picnic audience was a fluid mass. Everyone felt perfectly free to leave the auditorium when the spirit moved. People were constantly arriving to swell the crowd, while others were going out, not to leave the picnic, but to cool off outside, or talk with a friend perhaps not seen since last year, or to try to find a family member temporarily lost in the confusion. As people left their seats others came in to take their places in the hot, stuffy auditorium. Little girls would sit obediently with their mothers; but little boys moved in independent, unpredictable groups. Often they were dressed up in white shirts and clean bib overalls— "mean little ol' boys," Max Roberts, picnic director, and head of the Federation Training School, called them.

If people sensed the least threat of boredom in a speech, an exodus would begin. First a group of "little ol' boys" in the front row would leave, then a woman with a baby, soon followed by a mother with several children. A portly man would rise in the center of the hall and push his way out to stride up the aisle toward the doors, soon followed by a whole group of men and women, until the house was half empty. The unfortunate speaker droned hopelessly on, almost drowned out by the tread of heavy feet. Jim was a natural showman and he quickly learned to intersperse the educational parts of the program with audience-riveting entertainers.

"Next we're going to hear Johnny Rhymer play 'Home, Sweet Home' on the balloon," he would announce. "But just before he comes on we're going to hear a few words from Professor Smith, who knows more than any one in Western North Carolina about this new hybrid corn." The crowd squirmed a little, but no one wanted to lose a seat just before Johnny Rhymer came on. A "walk out" was always a threat, keeping the maestro on his toes.

When Jamie McClure, Jamie Clarke and later Elspeth were away serving in the Navy in World War II Elizabeth wrote letters to them describing the picnics. She could write very fast, describing the performances just as it was happening.

Audience at the annual Yancey County Picnic of the Farmers Federation, July 4, 1942.

"Darling Elfie," she began one such letter,

It's a lovely day—cool and crisp with floating whipped cream clouds and the countryside fresh and green after a good shower yesterday.

Corwith [Cramer] and Corwith's friend John Compton, . . . are here for the picnic season as lemonade boys," We are packed into the Buick with Betty Huntley, Daddy and I. Betty is playing, "Oh, what a Beautiful Morning," and the day looks promising, with picnickers streaming along the road towards Burnsville school house . . . I shall try to give you a running account of the picnic as the events of the day move along.

Mr. Wilson Edwards, who is the Chairman of the Farmers Federation in Yancey [County], has just opened up by turning the meeting over to "Mr. McClure." "Mr. Clarke [Rev. Dumont Clarke] is making a very fine prayer and now Daddy is introducing Norman Barnett [manager of the Burnsville warehouse] and the other members of the warehouse [team] . . . Now! Mr. Robinson [is] singing, "How do you do?" (He looks more immaculate than ever—simply shining).

Mrs. Elizabeth Anglin, a very sprightly young blonde on the plump side, is swirling through "The Old Age Pension Check Comes to Our Door."*

*Here are two verses of the song, very popular that summer:

When the old age pension check comes to our door
Then Grandma won't be lonesome any more
They'll be waiting at the gate,
Every night she'll have a date
When the old age pension check comes to our door.

... [Next] the Drake [Sisters] four teenage girls, part Indian, with black eyes and flashing smiles, always escorted and accompanied on the piano by their father. They were a "hit" [last year] and so were invited to attend several picnics with us ... A little speech from Joy (the oldest) who is introducing the different members. Joy has put up her hair and looks quite different but the singing is just as much of a knock-out as ever. Little Bunny's voice is even more tremendous! I think they sang a hymn but it was all expressed in very fine jazz time to which the ever ready toe of the audience lent instant tapping response. They are now giving an encore of "Comin' in on a Wing and a Prayer" with perfectly super harmonies and much feeling, a good slow tempo and much dragging of the key words. The audience is sitting pop-eyed. Now they are changing the tempo and doing some very complicated harmonizing, very fast and effective. (Mr. Drake at the piano is really something to see—slick and jaunty. He always has a slight air of the race track about him, to me!)

Betty Huntley in a green and white striped dress ... is singing, "Oh, What a Beautiful Mornin'." She has a truly, lovely voice and the song "suits it."

Next we are going to have the "Wabash Cannon Ball" sung by two Yancey County performers. The boy has sandy hair and a penetrating, tight mountain voice. Pender Rector is "helping" with the fiddle and the Cannon Ball is really going to town. People are coming in in streams. The building is already full—and the day only starting.

[Now] little Gene Boone is singing "Gro-u-nd Hawg"—a most wonderful version that he undoubtedly learned from his grandfather as he sings it in the traditional half singing—half talking fashion of the pioneer, with a wonderful drag and slur and melancholy whine to Gr-aa-o-und Haw-g that is just inimitable.**

Betty Huntley is at it again, singing "The San Fernando Valley" in the best radio style.

Mr. Bailey for the Farm Security organization is about to speak. There is a menacing movement from the rear which may or may not be a "walk out." Mr. Bailey is struggling to get en rapport with his audience. So far no luck. It's all copy book stuff. Yancey County is definitely bored. But it's over now. I'm afraid his message didn't grip. Now *another* Mr. Bailey is giving *another* message from the Farm Security organization which turns out to be a series of remarkable animal noises: an old hen, a superlative midnight cat, baby chicks at all stages of development, a rooster that was absolutely triumphant in his crowing. The crowd is just amazed. Now, Mr. Bailey is getting in a little farming stuff. He's good. Very direct and clear. "Produce more, on less

All the drug stores will go busted on that day,
And cosmetics they will all go out to stay,
Faded cheeks will be the rage,
And old maids will tell their age,
When the old age pension check comes to our door.

**Here comes Sal with a giggle and a grin,
Here comes Sal with a giggle and a grin,
Ground Hawg grease all over her chin.
Gr—o—u—nd Haw—g, Gr—oo—uu—nd Haw—g.

Claude Boone, Betty Jean Boone and Eugene Boone, Caldwell County Picnic, Kings Creek School, August 7, 1943.

ground." Now he's doing Bob White and Lady Bob White, the Song Sparrow, the Cardinal and now a Turkey hen calling her young, an old "house dog" greeting strangers, hunting a rabbit and "raring up bayin' at the moon" and now a few words urging us to "keep the birds and let *them* kill the insects and so save insecticides and money." Now, a Whip-poor-will followed by a squirrel and the most amazing whinny of an old horse out at pasture —wild applause . . .

. . . Uncle Dumont brought a sailor boy—a young man named McCurdy who is just about to speak on his experiences in Salerno . . . an impressive and interesting talk and should help the [war bond] sales. (Daddy announces) "All you singers come up and help us sing America," and now "All you singers break right into this—'When the Roll is Called up Yonder' —There's a few people in the house not singing!! Sing! Sing!—'When the Roll is called up yonder, I'll be there.'"

Daddy is now paying a tribute to the singing of Yancey County and Western North Carolina in general . . . (Elizabeth Cramer McClure to Elspeth McClure, July 4, 1944, from Burnsville, NC)

The picnics were a good combination of sacred and secular music. There was always a slight rift between the gospel singers and the string players. Some, like Betty Huntley, a preacher's daughter herself, were beginning to bridge the gap, accompanying both hymns and ballads on the guitar, but the gap was there—some lingering feelings that dance music and drinking went together and promoted sinful activities. Max Roberts, head of the Federation Training School and a devoted churchman, had to spend a lot of time making arrangements with string performers in his capacity of picnic director. Sometimes he found them undependable and often he could be heard muttering under his breath, "Musicianers are all low down and lazy." One string band that filled in for the Federation band one summer, when Johnny Rhymer was in the army and Pender Rector was working full time in a pawn shop, lived up to Max's worst fears. Sometimes they would not appear at the picnic until after noon, and then drag in looking pallid and hung over. But when they stepped onto the stage their smiles lit up like electricity, and the lead singer, Elmer, would belt into "Blessed Jesus, Hold My Hand." Every old lady in the audience would be wiping away tears by the time he finished. Gaither Robinson disproved all Max's theories about "musicianers," with his exemplary employment record as a bus driver and his solid life. The combination of both kinds of music at the picnics helped to dispel prejudice about string music. Elspeth remembers a minister who opened the afternoon session with prayer saying, "Thank you, Lord, for allowing us to forget ourselves." One of the most remarkable things about the picnics was that they brought all elements of a community together. The man who was known to take a drink too often would sit faithfully listening to a church choir. Solid, respectable farm families would be crowded cheek by jowl with the drifters and ne'er-do-wells. The socially approved and those they disapproved all seemed happy together for one day. Segregation or integration never came up. Who could be more eloquent than the Black preacher at Hayesville who always said the blessing over the truckload of watermelons?

To keep the audience attentive to his report on the various departments of the Federation and the new programs he wanted to emphasize, Jim adopted a plan of getting well known local figures to stand up in a line on the stage, each wearing a large placard labeled with the name of one of the departments. As he made his report on the progress of the cooperative he would have each man step forward to be introduced. Then he would speak about the activity his placard represented.

Elizabeth included snatches from Jim's talk in her letter from Burnsville in 1944:

We now have 13,000 members . . . All we did when we started out was to establish a beach head. We soon found we must develop specialists in all branches of farming. Little by little we have done this . . . We've developed a bunch of boys who have come up through our training school . . . Hard to get feed [This was because of wartime scarcities], but we've managed to keep feed . . . The biggest business ever this year—over three million dollars . . . want to remind you that you are now beginning to get control of your own business . . . When you trade with your own stores, every sale goes back into increasing the service of the Farmers Federation. Here, the egg price has never dropped below 27 cents. In many other parts of the country eggs dropped to 15 cents. Tennessee asked us to come over there and take charge of the egg situation which was desperate. We were able to do this in the Eastern section of the State . . . We need our own feed mills, our own sawmills, freezer lockers . . . Have a little patience . . . It's a tough time to do business . . . surely stick to the Farmers Federation as it is the one hope of your doing business:

The letter continued:

Mrs. Elizabeth Anglin is now singing, "I'll Die for the Red White and Blue," a dreary little song sung at top speed. Jack Gattis [head of the Federation Hatchery] is now at the loud speaker. There is something about the look and sound of him that makes for confidence. "Our incubators have a capacity of 462,000,900 chicks per week. We have resources here for growing the best poultry in the United States . . . Your money is staying right here at home when you trade with the Federation." [Now] Daddy is summoning the cacklers [hen imitators]. Frank Reed [manager of the Fairview warehouse] is in top form and [there is] a wonderful old guy who swoops and crows and must have spent his life in a hen house. "Now Mr. Harry Love will give a talk on tobacco." (The back of the room has 7 rows deep of people standing) . . . (a very interesting and quite astonishing statement on the possibilities of making money with tobacco [follows]). Mr. Love has impressed everyone.

While the audience is taking this in, a group of 4 young men have appeared with guitars and a part-song with wonderful slurs and harmonies and repeats. Thunderous applause. "We'll have them back again."

"How many of you read the Federation *News*?" Daddy inquires. (A big show of hands.)

"That's a good number. Now I shall introduce the Editor of the Federation *News*. Bob [Brown] is very dashing in a palm beach suit with a new hair cut.

We have some post cards here with a picture of a picnic truck." [Bob Brown tells the audience. The truck is crammed with people.] "The cards will he passed so that everyone can write a message to a boy or girl in the service. Then you may drop them at the Bond Booth and they will be stamped and mailed free.."..Some very fine yodeling is going on right now while the postcards are being passed. (Never fear, you will receive one!) . . . Mr. Nor-

Opposite: *Jamie Clarke, "Freezer Lockers"; Dumont Clarke—"The Lord's Acre"; and Jim McClure speaking, Burnsville (Yancey County) picnic, July 4, 1947.*

man Barnett [warehouse manager] is giving forth a . . . welcome to the picnickers and is telling the glad tidings of the watermelon feast in store.

And now, [a little grey speaker is rising to give some expert agricultural
advice.] The poor dear man has not uttered three words but the tramp, tramp,
is starting and there is a vast progression toward the door . . . The end has
come at last. We are now all stampeding toward the watermelons.

The noon hour, as far as we were concerned, was notable for the fact that
nobody had brought anything to eat so that our sandwiches and tomatoes just
melted away. Except for Mrs. Greenwood who had a superb pie and cake and
delectable sandwiches. No one else seemed to have brought anything . . . The
place was a complete shambles from the watermelon orgy and Corwith and
John and a crew of little boys toiled for a long time cleaning up; the races [sack
races, relay races] were "run off" and it was at length time to begin the
afternoon events.
    Perry Green [head of the Poultry department] opened up with a lengthy
discourse on chickens. Five fair maids of uncertain age were introduced as the
"egg handling crew" and received enthusiastic applause. (At this point, the egg
crew returned having to clamber over me . . . both exiting and entering.)
    They were swiftly followed by a very active [buck] dance given by a
number of old timers and "Little Bob Brown." [eight-year-old son of the editor
of the *News*.] Then four young men engaged in a very clever harmony-there
is a basso-profundo . . . "Kneel at the Cross" was wonderful . . . The bond
chairman has just reported $1600.00 in bond sales. Much enthusiasm.
    Now a Navy petty officer is speaking—a funny little guy from N. J. who
said a great many words all of which boiled down to a general appreciation of
the region. A little boy about 7 or 8 is singing "There's a Star Spangled Banner
Waving Somewhere." He has a piercingly true little voice, with a lovely cool
quality and the crowd liked him. It was his first [Public] appearance and he
was completely calm and unruffled.
    Little Cleo Owenby is now at the piano and Frank [Reed] is assembling his
cohorts for a big general sing. "We want to sing 'Revive Us Again'" (The
hymns and songs of the afternoon have been typed on sheets of paper distributed around for all to use.) Daddy is asking for "I Shall Not be, I Shall Not
be Moved." (How many great, good times that brings to mind.)
    Now Daddy is saying that if we want to maintain our freedom and liberty,
it must be done by maintaining the spiritual atmosphere of the rural home and
the rural church . . . Mr. Clarke is now being introduced and is making a fine
address. Everyone listens intently. (Elizabeth Cramer McClure to Elspeth
McClure, July 4, 1944)

Dumont Clarke attended every picnic to report on the progress of the Lord's
Acre Plan, which was spreading far and wide in the United States and even into
the mission field. He was tall and straight, with silver hair and a kind and
commanding presence, and the audience always gave him rapt attention. Although he spoke quietly, he was an orator and he was greatly loved by people
all over the mountains. He had probably spoken in every church from Murphy
in the west to Lenoir in the east, had dinner at someone's house afterwards, and

Left to right: *Charlie Ownby, Broadus Morrow, Boyce Moon, Lewis Kirstein and "Little" Cleo Ownby—The Fairview Quartette [sic], first prize winners at the Buncombe County Picnic, July 15, 1943.*

photographed young people of every church with their pigs, chickens, calves or crops dedicated to the Lord.

The contest for best choir and quartet followed Dumont's talk. Jim was very interested in the traditional "shaped note" singing of the mountains. The shape of the note, whether a square, a triangle, a circle, etc., indicated the pitch rather than its position on the staff. These hymns were fun to sing, with complicated parts and a fast tempo. The prizes offered at the picnics were new hymn books. Singers liked to get a new paperback set every year or two and learn new hymns.

We return to Elizabeth's letter as the singing contests followed Reverend Dumont Clarke's talk:

> The Swannanoa quartet is assembling—all older men. (While they are being introduced, all the members of the Big Ivy Choir are coming up to the stage -a huge crowd of all ages and sizes.) The Swannanoa quartet is doing a grand job, "Keep a Little Sunshine in Your Sky." Now, an encore, something very gay and foot-tapping—with a great emphasized rhythm.
>
> [Now the choir:] There are a vast number of girls singing—the men are all concentrated on the back line and there must be at least 16 or 18 girls. Now they are off again. "There's a Mansion up Yonder Just Waiting for Me."
>
> The Roberts family are now singing—two very pretty girls and a professional father who has a big bass voice. The song is one of the most compli-

cated—part-singing in the chorus dominated by the soprano—extremely clear and true. Loud applause from the crowd and an encore in prospect. A wild scurry at this point when the microphone took a stagger and almost fell into the expectant arms of the audience, but Mr. Drake (father of the singing sisters), by a sort of ju-jitsu caught it before it took a final spin. The Roberts never batted an eyelash but launched right into "The Cabin on the Hill"—very well done with a fascinating rhythm and a sort of counter point performance on the part of the singers.

"Next, I am calling on all the singers to come up and sing under Frank Reed in a big song."

Uncle Joe Pressley and Preacher Riley Corn are assembling their chorus. Now they are off, Uncle Joe's white head focussing the picture. Daddy is almost into the choir—just hanging onto the fringe! Frank is in his element and Uncle Joe can be heard all over the hall. A little bit of a girl is singing with all she's got. "I'm so happy singing Halleluyah, halleluyah! (I must say I've always thought Halleluyah was a lovely musical word, no matter *what* you do to it!)

Another quartet of four is now singing. Two long, lanky boys, a pretty girl with yellow curls and a little short, stumpy man. Two good songs from them, no piano accompaniment which is much the nicest with this kind of singing, I think.

Now a solo by Miss Bunny Drake, a wonderful song, "When they ask about you." Huge applause. Now all 5 sisters are singing, "Coming in on a wing and a prayer." (I miss Joy's curls terribly!) Deafening applause, shouts, yells, cat calls of enthusiasm. They will have to come back. Here they are, singing "Swing Low." Joy has the lead and Bunny replies. I should think that they might be snapped up by a Broadway Producer. "It's the only song we know how to sing backwards—would you like to hear us?" With that they all turned their backs and sang the last verse. The audience yelled! . . . (Elizabeth Cramer McClure to Elspeth McClure, July 4, 1944)

The picnic at Bryson City had a special character because a large part of the Cherokee Indian Reservation lived in Swain County, and many Indians attended. In July 1945, Elizabeth wrote about the Bryson City picnic, this time to Jamie Clarke and Elspeth when they were in the Navy in Washington, D. C. According to her report the family rose at the usual early hour, and

. . . Betty [Huntley] was waiting for us at her mail box and we picked up little Jean Kennickel at Fairview. She is a little bit of a thing—weighs about 90 lbs. and looks 12, with golden hair, lovely little features . . . She is 17 but so tiny that her accordion almost covers her up.

The picnic is now officially opening with a welcome from Frank Bird who is in charge of the warehouse here.

Now comes Frank Reed leading the "Old Rugged Cross" and then a good but *very* long prayer by a local "preacher." Daddy is reminding everyone that the Federation picnic today in Swain County is to be dedicated to friendship and goodwill. Now he is giving a brief recognition to all the boys in the fighting forces "whose wonderful achievements maintain the things we believe in." Uncle Jim is now urging everyone to keep in mind the need for food

Shirley and Irma Styles, 11 and 12 years old, daughters of Mrs. Ted Styles, who accompanies them on the piano, 1947.

production. The moment is come for Gaither [Robinson] to mount the rostrum and after the usual stupefying introduction he is singing "How do you do?"— He looks if possible even more dapper than usual.

. . . Betty [Huntley] . . . "There's a Happy Land Somewhere" . . . She looks very sweet and sings really beautifully

. . . The crowd likes it so she's at it again with "Don't Sing Aloha When I Go.."..Billy Owl, a small 8 year old Indian boy, is now singing "In the Halls of Montezuma." Mr. Robinson is helping with his banjo and the little Owl is a lusty singer, with more vigor than melody. Mrs. Leila Smart with a five year old and a six year old are now up to bat. The little girls have the softest little voices and are singing in perfect harmony, "Don't Fence Me In," while their mother accompanies them with the guitar—*huge* applause. As usual, the smaller and younger you are, the more the crowd loves the performance. A little 12 year old girl and two small brothers are now playing and singing a complicated, fast mountain hymn, with long drawn out wailing harmonies.

Guy Sales is up now looking very solid and impressive. His speeches get better and better—very direct and to the point and everyone seems to want to listen. He is explaining the cooperative movement and its significance—"A movement framed up out of necessity." He is explaining the assets in the co-op and the meaning it has for the people—how they can go to work and buy stock—just what services can be worked up that will make life easier and more abundant. Good applause. *No* walk outs . . .

A harmony trio, all "Breedloves," are at the microphone—two girls with white blouses and short black cotton skirts with white ruffles,—and a younger brother. They appear to be triplets—all the same size and shape—all redheads. It's surprising how much red hair and red gold hair there is in the mountains. I suppose it's the Scotch ancestry.

[Now Jim:] "We are very fortunate in having with us your County Agent"—a *very* warming little introduction by the President. The agent looks like a friendly, likeable person. [He boosted the seeds and fertilizer sold by the Farmers Federation and ended with an encouraging report of REA (Rural Electrification Administration)] . . . many benefits may be anticipated. Electricity for everyone. [Many farm families did not have electric power at this time.] (Elizabeth Cramer McClure to Elspeth McClure Clarke and Jamie Clarke, July 8, 1945)

Reverend Dumont Clarke was in charge of the next event—"Musical Chairs." He would call a group of well known local citizens up to the stage to take part. The Federation band provided the music. Johnny Rhymer was, and still is, a master of the sudden stop—it sent participants tumbling into the available chairs. The incongruity of large, serious men playing this children's game on stage never failed to delight the audience. Dumont's daughter, Phebe Ann Lewis, had suggested the game and it became a perennial hit. Elizabeth described how it went:

A group of solid leading citizens including the Sheriff [come on stage]. Mr. McClure with a most impressive manner is turning the program over to Uncle Dumont and "Musical Chairs" is now in progress with 10 Swain County worthies, a little dazed—The crowd is asked to "pick a winner"—The band starts up and the leading citizens are parading solemnly round! Casualties are beginning;— "Walt Jenkins is out!" Eight are left. The audience is loving it. The Sheriff is still in. Round and round they go to the strains of "Sourwood Mountain." Two more are left out. The situation grows more tense. Several more casualties. "The Sheriff is out!" Only two are left—Harry Breedlove wins—"the best looking man in the audience!"

The game is over but many of the players have joined the group sitting on the stand, making a lively back drop for the performers. Now Slim Nanny is singing "Rosy" to the sturdy and somewhat monotonous accompaniment of his band. It's a combination wail and yodel—a "lonesome" plaintive melody.

After a pause to discuss the tobacco market, the show went on.

Alex Houston, the little ventriloquist, is now about to appear—[This talented boy with his talking dolls, Elmer and Katy, was a regular picnic performer for several years] . . . He is a frail creature looking scarcely more than ten though I believe he is actually twelve. He has a new line that is very snappy and delights the crowd. Elmer is more convincing than ever and Alex seems even more extraordinary . . . Katy sings a duet with Elmer in a high soprano . . . Elmer whistles like many wild birds and does a little puppy dog that brings down the house.

Now, "Mr. McClure" is about to give a little talk on the poultry program—inheritance, livability, etc.—a slight tendency to walk out—Suddenly from behind the scenes emerges . . . the finest rooster and hen you ever did see . . . [Frank Reed and Bob Brown] The hen lays an egg-ostrich size—yells of delight—the few who walked out are hurrying back . . . "Look at what big eggs and then think about the Farmers Federation baby chicks." . . . I am still agog myself over the costumes. Some genius in Asheville made them. They would do justice to the Russian Coq d'Or—immensely effective and realistic and hugely decorative . . . "This kind of hen will make money for you."

. . . The Harmony Trio is now up—Then a talk about a big turkey program that the Fed is going to launch next year . . .

"The next number will be Miss Neil Anne Allen of Canton who will do an acrobatic act"—a pretty little slim thing—tall—incredibly lanky—immensely graceful, is now performing in the most startling . . . manner—"fish flops"—somersaults and unbelievable bends and gyrations. The crowd is goggle eyed with surprise and amazement—Never have they seen anything like *this!*

. . . It's a lovely day—the mists have all risen and its cool and delicious—Time now to close the morning session and get to the business of watermelons and lemonade. Many Indians on hand standing around in little knots. The strange [white] preacher to the Indians—"Mr. Smith," is on hand, looking more of an anomaly than ever. One Indian woman has a huge fat baby strapped on her back, papoose fashion—The lemonade boys are very smart and efficient this year . . . Betty Jean and I sliced tomatoes and made sandwiches under the big trees at our usual stand and fed dozens of little grabbing boys who looked half starved and would have eaten joyfully pieces of blotting paper if we had buttered it.

. . . In front of me is an Indian family—an old Indian in a very clean white shirt and his old wife in a snappy black and white print—a great contrast to the other old Cherokees who all have bright red and yellow turbans around their heads, vivid blue and orange scarves and a gaiety of prints . . .

Jim McClure made a point of recognizing anyone present from the armed forces at the picnics during World War II, and there were usually some account of the war from an officer or two, and some patriotic songs included in the program.

At Bryson City the singing contests had their own special quality, according to Elizabeth's account.

Now for the choir contest—

Echota and Rock Hill—with no piano—A group of eight Indians—The Rock Hill Choir, singing a strange mournful melody—almost a chant with

Corbert Reed as the Rooster, Frank Reed as the Hen, Clay County Picnic, Hayesville, N.C., July 11, 1947.

queer minors and a background of repetitive singing that is a little like the music in the Russian Church. Very restrained and all in Cherokee—beautiful. Now they are doing another one, faster and very rhythmic—the voices are softer and fuller than the white chorus—with a fine depth and resonance in the bases and a very pleasing balance and unity of effect.

Now for the Echota Choir—four Indian [men] and two old Cherokee women. A long drawn out, solemn cadence with great stressing of the harmonies and a lot of almost antiphonal singing. Very dignified and impressive— Lots of minors—and really beautiful harmonies—unexpected and surprising— Another song in exactly the same key—more antiphonal singing—a lovely background of harmony that has almost an organ quality. I don't see how the judges will *ever* decide!

Now the Cold Spring Choir led by Elspie's friend "Mr. Smiley." (Uncle Jim at this point has suddenly decided that a well known agricultural expert should be recognized.) This expert is now somewhat hurriedly making his little talk with a nervous eye on the advancing choir and on the audience that is weighing a speech against their yearning to listen to the singers.

. . . Another quartette—Soco Valley—No piano, which makes it so much more effective—Rather slow impressive harmonies and a nice tenor who is the leader . . . These people are good,—all Indians except for the strange preacher Smith who is part Cherokee anyway. Soco Valley wins the prize for the "best quartette.."..A burst of good congregational singing, "Farther Along" and "When the Roll is Called up Yonder"—Then a startling change in tempo as the young acrobat comes on [again] she leaps and plunges and twists in serpentine gyrations—a bent whalebone could not be more pliable. She looks just like an animated long legged rag doll— the kind that debutantes used to twist around bed posts . . . Shrieks, cat-calls, yells— particularly from the masculine element.

The afternoon program always ended with "the contests"—for the largest family present, the most recently married couple and the couple married longest, and at the end, the bald-headed contest. Sometimes a man would attend several picnics to win this coveted honor.

Mr. Roberts is calling for the youngest married couple—so far no responses to his pleas which have been unavailing— "Evidently, people around Bryson just don't get married." Finally a pair married three years have been discovered. Now for the oldest married—a neat, tidy little pair, married forty years, have come forward. The old gentleman at the mike says he hopes he "will live to see another picnic."

A family of eleven is now approaching the stage. Mr. Roberts is proposing that they all sing a song—(one boy is in the service making twelve)—Bob is about to take their photographs—The three girls are embarking on "Don't You Cry Over Me"—This dreary ditty for some reason brought down the house—another one about "Remember I Died for the Red, White and Blue." The girls have piercing voices—"Keep your chin up and be brave for me, little darling"— More whistles and howls of pleasure—Wow-w!

Frank is announcing that "Echota Choir" is *first*, "Coldspring" next, and "Rock Hill" last. Truck drivers are counting their loads [of people]. One man brought eighty-five—oh boy! Another truck carried seventy-two.

The bald headed contest is on—The judges will decide by the fervor of the clapping as to who wins. Elspie's friend Mr. Smiley is up—he seems to have plenty of admirers as the racket is prodigious. Other contestants in order—so far, Mr. John Breedlove seems to draw forth the most blood curdling yells—but even more deafening is the roar that greets [a] Mr. Marr who brought the largest truck load—A tie between Mr. Marr and Mr. B.— the clapping and shouting is terrific; Times Square on election night could not *possibly* equal the din for Mr. B.— forty seconds of uproar. Mr. Marr steps up—his supporters out do themselves—the testimonial to Mr. B. fades to nothing in comparison—I only fear that it will quicken the sluggish Cherokee blood and produce the hidden tomahawk! Mr. Marr wins!! And the 1945 Bryson County picnic is over.

Well, my pets, if you have gone this far with me I congratulate you—I don't think you can read a word but I really had to "step on it" as things move fast here.

. . . I forgot to say that many Indians asked for Elspie and sent messages of greeting.

Elspeth and her father had worked up a "fox chase" act, managing between them to sound like a pack of hounds and a little yipping Feist dog. The Indians particularly liked this number and a man asked Jim once, "When your daughter bark?"

After the Bryson City picnic the troupe moved even further west for more

Top: *Truck leaving the Haywood County Picnic.*
Bottom: *Elspeth and Jim McClure performing their "fox chase" act.*

picnics, spending the night in Murphy, county seat of Cherokee County. In 1942, when Elizabeth was writing to Jamie, there was a tornado in Murphy just before they arrived. Two cars had been demolished, the electric power was out and picnic director, Max Roberts' hat blew away just as they stepped out into the street. She wrote,

> Nothing daunted, the Federation "Talent" gathered in the living room of our small lodging house and sang, played and danced until all hours to huge pleasure of the landlord. All done by the light of one feeble and expiring lamp! Next morning we were off again to Hayesville ... where a crowd of some four or five hundred gathered. The great event of the day was the group of little girls—nine sisters from 21 years to 18 months—the "Martin sisters," who appeared all dressed alike, all pretty and all more or less the same size except for the baby who was carried by the oldest sister and who was as good as gold and dressed just like all the rest in cute little flowered organdy dresses with black velvet ribbons. The mother had died of pneumonia last winter and the father was in attendance to chaperone his crowd, in addition carrying one very, very small baby brother and shepherding another about 4 years old! Eleven children! It was spectacular though I am mindful of the man with 24 at the Burnsville picnic who knew he had "2 sons in the Navy" but didn't know how many "might be in the Army." And the nonchalant old boy who said to Daddy "T'ain't no surprise to have 24 children, I done got 22 myself." (Now how's that!)
>
> Daddy made a special plea to have the Martin sisters come to the Franklin picnic next week but Mr. Martin was a little doubtful. "I ain't sure as I can be there," he said, "Seems like they cain't make it iffen I cain't be there to fight the young 'uns (by this he meant the two small boys, who definitely had to be beaten down at intervals). Mr. Martin didn't seem to regard himself as unduly burdened with responsibility. He just coped with what came along as best he might!
>
> We had dinner at Dillsboro at the hotel there and were much entertained by mine host who had a huge red nose and was a character out of Dickens. We ate enormously—wonderful ham and other delicious country tit-bits. Home by midnight and never did bed seem more desirable. (Elizabeth Cramer McClure to Jamie McClure, 1942)

As a true artist Elizabeth had a deep appreciation for the picnics. Every year new performers would turn up and some you had hoped to see again would have disappeared. One of the greatest entertainers at the picnics was "Pan Handle Pete," who first appeared several years after Elizabeth's death. A big man, with a broad red face, he stomped into a picnic one day with an enormous drum strapped on his back, a pair of cymbals lashed to his ankles, his guitar hanging around his neck, and a harmonica somehow wired in place. Altogether he carried seventeen different instruments, including a horn form a Model T Ford, and he was singing "The Chew Tobacco Rag," with appropriate spitting noises. The audience went wild and they continued to go wild as long as Howard Nash appeared.

Panhandle Pete (Howard Nash).

He was a natural clown as well as a gifted musician and his fierce exterior covered a gentle heart. With his side kick Steve Ledford, an old time mountain fiddler from Little Rock Creek on the side of Roan Mountain, he would spellbind the crowd with "The Audience Song."

"I see a lady a sittin' by the aisle—" He and Steve would stop playing and peer into the crowd.

Then Pan Handle would leap from the stage and walk around staring at first one lady and then another.

"I see a lady a sittin' by the aisle—" Many giggles and much blushing. Finally he would sit down beside the chosen woman, always of mature years and solid figure.

"If she'll stick around I'll see her after awhile. There'll be a hot time in the old town tonight!"

The next verse might be "I see a lady, her teeth so pretty and white—"
Loud laughter from Pan Handle and Steve.

"Just like the stars, they come out every night. We'll have a hot time in the old town tonight!" Shrieks erupted from the audience!

To focus attention on the poultry program he, Pan Handle, would lurk about in the rear of the auditorium in the policeman's uniform until everyone was looking uneasily over their shoulders, then rush toward the stage to arrest the innocent Gaither Robinson in mid banjo chord, and triumphantly drag him off as a "chicken thief." Corny stuff perhaps, but it was real audience participation and brought joy to people whose days were filled with toil. Pan Handle's humor, like that of all true comedians, was always kindly.

Jim would announce a fiddling contest. Pan Handle and Steve would leap forward, each claiming to be the best. Each tried to out do the other's tricks until at the end Pan Handle was half lying on the stage, playing his enormous "bull fiddle" under his back. When he was acclaimed the winner amidst the shouts of the crowd, Steve would protest angrily that the prize should have been his and a fight would erupt. Steve would get hold of Pete's shirt and start to pull, and pull and *pull* until the shirt extended right across the stage, like a banner, with Farmers Federation emblazoned in large letters.

The entire picnic program, over all the years, had the charm of the unexpected, both for those who watched and those who ran the show. You never knew what might turn up. There was the cowboy whose rope tricks sometimes failed, but still left little boy's eyes popping. A bag piper was so foreign to our mountains that a Federation director at Franklin called for another number on "that Italian instrument." And there were countless others.

What was it that made the day special? The joy of the music, of old friends meeting over the watermelons and lemonade at the noon hour, of singing "The Old Rugged Cross" together in the packed auditorium after lunch, of thumping your feet to the strains of Pan Handle Pete's One Man Band? Whatever it was, the appeal was universal,for the program seemed to be as much of a hit at the Waldorf Astoria in New York as in the Blue Ridge Mountains of North Carolina. Thomas J. Watson, founder of the IBM Corporation, was much interested in Jim McClure's work and sponsored Federation picnics at the Waldorf. Picnic troupers went north for several of these occasions. Sam Queen and his famous Maggie Valley square dance team, the Federation String Band, Pan Handle Pete, Herman Jones from Sylva, singing "I'm on the Battlefield for My Lord" at the top of his voice. Jamie McClure sang at the first New York picnic. He came down from Yale to sing "John Henry," the ballad of the old steel driving man, in the old mountain way his mother loved to hear. One year Betty Huntley sang "Silver Haired Daddy of Mine" in honor of Jack Bierworth, President of National Distillers, who was a staunch supporter of the Federation.

Jim McClure was a master at reading the mood of an audience and adjusting the program accordingly. He also had the trouper's conviction that the show must go on. He told Jamie Clarke that just before the first picnic at the Waldorf he lost his voice completely. He went into a small room and sat quietly for ten minutes, and it came back in time to start the program.

Jamie Clarke helped Jim run the North Carolina picnics for ten years after World War II. As his family grew he even began to win the prize for largest family present occasionally. Jim got a great kick out of having his grandchildren attend picnics. Once he stepped outside the Columbus Courthouse, where the Polk County picnic was always held, to get a breath of fresh air and was surprised to see a toddler tied by a long string to a tree. He took a close look to see if the little fellow was all right, and found it was his own grandson (and namesake) Jim! He was a very active crawler and his mother had secured him temporarily while doing some errand.

Because Jamie Clarke was familiar with the picnics he was able to carry right on after Jim died in 1956, continuing as long as he was with the Federation. These gatherings brought together the finest elements of the Appalachian tradition in order to promote the progressive development of the region. But no matter how they were justified, the picnics were about as much fun as people are allowed to have in this world, and entertained an entire generation in an age when recreation was scarce.

Chapter Nineteen

The War Years

When the Farmers Federation was born in 1920, the neighbors said he was a weak child and couldn't be raised.

But the child has grown by leaps and bounds. He has now grown to be a real giant embracing twenty counties of Western North Carolina, waving his magic wand . . . influencing, for good, the economic, political, moral and religious thinking of the best people on earth, who grace the hill-tops and valleys of the God favored country of ours. (*John Henry Biggs of Mill Springs, N.C., quoted in Farmers Federation* News, *August, 1943, p. 5*)

This terrible war reaches its fingers right into our hearts. (*James G. K. McClure, Jr. to Harriet Stuart, May 1, 1943*)

What fascinated Jim McClure about war was its power to change people. Here was an enterprise that could draw together whole nations of individuals into a spirit of common purpose to risk everything for abstract loyalties and beliefs. Vast amounts of untapped human energy would be brought to bear against the common foe, and men and women stood willing to sacrifice for a cause much larger than themselves. And yet all of these energies of war were marshalled with the intent to kill and destroy, to demolish the basis of the enemy's civilization. The spiritual fruits of war demoralized whole generations of people. It was all too easy to be corrupted by army life, and all too difficult to respect life after one had grown bored with death. For Jim, the question was always the same. What was the source of this power of war to redirect and motivate people? Why could not the compassionate and constructive potential of Christianity draw out the same dedication and persistence in men, to build rather than destroy? There had been moments in the history of the church when this force gathered strength. It was the potential for the power of God, unleashed in the world, that had originally drawn Jim into the ministry; and the search for its motive force that moved him through the struggles of his life.

In 1920 Jim McClure had declared war not only on poverty, but also on apathy, hopelessness, poor education, weak churches, and deficient stewardship of the land. He thrived on a sense of purpose. He wanted to lead men and women on toward a promised land, to infuse their lives with a sense of intention that brought out in them efforts and satisfactions that would surpass any material gain that might have been won along the way. The Farmers Federation promoted change, progress, and purpose as an approach to living. It opposed lifeless routine, habits of superstition, and spiritual death. Although the means toward the end were in the realm of the material—fertilizer applications, corn clubs, erosion control, sweet potato yields and so on—what Jim McClure was working towards was the spiritual regeneration of a demoralized region of Appalachia. For him, the fruits of the spirit were measured, not just by the fervor of Sunday worship, but by the sense of self-esteem felt by the farmer and his wife as they sat together on their front porch after a week of hard work.

Jim wanted each family in the mountains to sense that a better future was possible, and to motivate them to self-sacrifice in order to pursue that hope for their community.

He understood that the basis of the American democratic faith rested with the morale of each of these families, and that this faith in the political and economic ideals of the nation were sorely tested during the Depression. Franklin Roosevelt's political gifts enabled him to prop up this faith, but it was not until militant fascism began to march across Europe and Asia that the American spirit escaped from the doldrums of self-doubt and launched a war machine that surpassed any other in the history of man. The war stimulated a sluggish economy as well, and set in motion forces that would transform Western North Carolina.

The Second World War, much more than its predecessor, drew out of the mountain cove, and hollows young soldiers who would meet people and see places that would change their view of the world. Thrown in barracks and ships with blue-collar workers of the North, Californians, prosperous farm boys of the Midwest and their brethren from across the South, these mountaineers would return home, if in fact they did return, much different people than when they left. These were the same men that Jim McClure had been grooming to reignite American democratic faith. He had kept his eye on the large population bulge that had been growing up in the mountains and had designed the Lord's Acre primarily for the benefit of these young people. He had strengthened their schools, and spoken at their graduations. Now they were sent out to become a part of the American war machine, and Jim McClure knew that many of them would exhibit the same strength of character as the great mountain hero of World War I, Sergeant York.

Long before Pearl Harbor, the European war began to stimulate the economy of the United States, especially the agricultural markets. The Farmers Federation felt the push of new prosperity after 1938. Beginning in 1939, the number of dollars that passed through the organization expanded rapidly. The figures speak for themselves:

Dollar Volume: Federation Business

Year	Volume*
1939	$1,077,991.58
1940	1,261,506.26
1941	1,501.858.52

1942	1,940,306.33
1943	3,063,955.86
1944	3,588,137.04
1945	3,967,641.08

(These figures do not include the hatchery operation and the tobacco warehouse receipts, both of which were managed by the Federation.)

When the government began ordering food for the troops, the Federation was in an ideal position to benefit. Its marketing operation had become efficient and its department heads were trusted. The New Deal administration was sympathetic with cooperatives in general, and the Federation in particular. The farmer was in a position to plant and harvest all he could grow, and to find a good market for nearly everything. Army life even helped to stimulate the cigarette industry, increasing the demand for burley tobacco. By 1945, the Federation had built a new tobacco warehouse, complete with special lights to show the leaf to its best advantage. The shady practices endemic to this market made the dependability of the Federation operation all the more appreciated by growers.

The expansive financial outlook encouraged Jim and the other directors to try out several innovations during these years. Genetics had always been one of Jim's favorite farm subjects. and so the program to build up the quality of the local mule and horse population continued. Walter Jeffords of Philadelphia, a contributor to the Fund, sent down Warcraft, son of the racehorse, Man O'War, from his own farm. This fine stallion joined the Percherons and jacks already employed to service the mares of Western North Carolina. The cross of a thoroughbred with an ordinary mare often produces a work animal of size and stamina. But after the war, horses and mules would give way to tractors, and Jim was studying other projects for the Fund that would have a more lasting impact. One of these, artificial insemination of dairy cows, would have to wait until after the war.

Another was the sexing of baby chicks. This practice, too, was affected by the coming of war. Male and female chicks look just alike for the first weeks of life to the untrained eye, so a farmer who purchased day old chicks could expect roughly half of them to be roosters, to be sold as broilers, and half to be pullets, to be raised for egg production. But the Japanese had developed the ability to identify male and female birds as soon as they were hatched. This skill was a great advantage for the poultryman, as he could concentrate on the kind of production he chose. When war came between Japan and the United States, Japanese chick-sexers went home. But Jack Gattis, hatchery manager, announced in the Federation *News* that he had American experts who had learned to perform this complex job and there was a good supply of sexed chicks ready for sale.

The war created other scarcities Jim tried to turn into opportunities for Western North Carolina. He even promoted the cultivation of silk worms, an idea that failed to appeal to the mountaineer. Mica and feldspar, two locally abundant minerals, were used extensively in the war industries, and Jim asked farmers to bring samples to the picnics to be inspected by experts. One unusual shortage that had little to do with the war effort sent mountain folk out into the woods looking for old and gnarled mountain laurel bushes. It was announced in the Federation *News:* "A plant to manufacture pipe blocks is being started by the Farmers Federation in the cannery building at Hendersonville. Nearly the entire supply of briar, which was formerly imported from Europe, has been cut off; and pipe manufacturers find that the close grained mountain laurel is the best substitute available.[1]

Before Jim realized what was happening he was in trouble with many of his wife's garden club friends. Staunch conservationists that they were, they were horrified at the prospect of thousands of large laurel shrubs being uprooted to support a questionable habit. Criticism began to pour in, and he set out to answer the accusations in the following issue of the *News.* Only in rare instances, he explained, a lumpy growth called a burl is caused by disease on the root of a laurel bush. Such shrubs are usually found in remote, boggy places, and when roots bearing burls are removed, fresh growth quickly springs up. Federation horticulturists had studied the matter thoroughly and felt that the beauty of the mountains would not be affected if the burls were secured under supervision . . . and there is the opportunity to bring in income that will be a blessing to many mountain families."[2]

The pipe block enterprise was a part of the Federation's effort to bring small industries into Western North Carolina. For the eighteen months of its existence, ninety people drew wages there. Jim wisely thought that such industries would offer employment to one or two members of a farm family, which would supplement the small income from mountain farming and enable the family to continue living and working on their place. He explained, in the *News* some of the specific enterprises the Federation had implemented.

> The great objective of the Farmers Federation is to develop facilities and services that will enable the farm people of Western North Carolina to increase their own incomes and in this way build a finer civilization. Part of our program is to encourage and develop small industries. The Farmers Federation will be glad to work with individuals or groups in any county toward this end. We have a dream of helping to establish one or two small industries in every township in Western North Carolina.
>
> The Farmers Federation has an active interest in the Biltmore Company, the Appalachian Textile Company, the Swannanoa Textile Company, the Treasure Chest Mutual, Inc., and the Farmers Federation Handicraft Mutual, Inc. This last is a cooperative of knitters. All these enterprises are creating new wealth in Western North Carolina. We trust that our members and committees will keep constantly working toward the end of creating more wealth in this section.[3]

The war had reverse effect on one project. The Hendersonville Cannery, the first Federation small industry, suspended operations because the demand for fresh produce left no need to preserve a surplus. As the Federation expanded, the Lord's Acre was keeping pace. By the fifteenth anniversary of the plan, Rev. Dumont Clarke was making tours throughout the United States and Canada promoting the idea. He often spoke on radio programs and in 1941 enjoyed a big promotional windfall, which he described in his regular column in the *News:* "Wide publicity, entirely prepared by publishers interested in constructive activities of our time, has been given the Lord's Acre Movement," he wrote. "The April issue of *Christian Herald,* which is read largely by church members, carried an illustrated article . . . entitled 'Harvesting the Lord's Acre.' This was reprinted in the "Readers Digest" with its 4,100,000 circulation."[4] From Dumont Clarke's office in Asheville, all sorts of Lord's Acre packets, buttons and pamphlets were mailed across North America and various foreign mission groups. For a congregation with a persistent pastor and lively members, the Lord's Acre Plan brought in both material and spiritual fruits. Of all the churches who were helped by the program, the Dana Baptist Church of Henderson County became the standard by which all other programs were judged.

> The Lord's Acre program of Dana Baptist Church for 1940 was brought to a close with a remarkable total of $2,071 in hand. The largest single item was $553.75 from the group potato project. A second large item was $117 from an apple project. There were many individual projects, and the total includes gifts of labor on the new parsonage and some cash donations.
>
> In four years time the Lord's Acre program of the Dana Church has yielded $8,000. A beautiful brick veneer church has been erected and a parsonage adjoining the church is nearly complete . . .
>
> The Lord's Acre plan has made it possible for a comparatively small congregation to achieve really great things. The members of the church and Sunday School have been engaged almost 100 per cent, year after year, in substantial Lord's Acre projects. This has developed a very strong spirit of cooperation and has made possible results which otherwise could not have been attained.[5]

The Federation picnics also created cooperation and a positive spirit. Attendance kept growing, and although the purpose was education, the results were spectacularly entertaining. Perhaps people needed the picnics more than ever during these tragic and serious times. As always the program was dominated by Jim McClure's canny showmanship. During the war he used these great gatherings to sell war bonds and stamps. Jamie McClure, Jamie Clarke and Elspeth all pitched in to help out. In 1941, after graduating from Yale, Jamie McClure wrote to his Aunt Harriet Stuart that he had made lemonade and cut watermelons " . . . for crowds that have ranged from 800 to 2500 . . . you never know just what sort of 'musicianers' or other forms of entertainment are likely to turn up, and the way Daddy runs his meetings make them the big event of the year to most of the people who attend" (Jamie McClure to Harriet Stuart, July 23, 1940).

Jamie looked forward to the time when he could work with his father in the Federation. While at Yale he had investigated the theory of cooperatives and for a senior paper wrote a description of his father's work, entitled "Frontier Civilization in the Blue Ridge Highlands." The conclusion echoed Jim McClure's thoughts: "The most effective way of helping these people toward a higher level of income is to give them a means of working out their own economic salvation. The practical possibilities of this approach are already being demonstrated in Western North Carolina, and it is my firm belief that with careful long range planning the co-operative exploitation of mountain farming holds promise of a new future for the Southern Highlander."[6] Another of Jamie's Yale papers traced the history of cooperatives, going back to the origins with the Rochdale Pioneers in England. He wrote, "Thus from a dingy basement hole-in-the-wall sprang the English Consumer Cooperatives, the largest single business in the British Isles."[7]

After working his way through Yale in the Student Pressing Agency, which he managed his senior year, Jamie went with the Yale Glee Club on a tour of South America. Elizabeth sold the pearls the Skinner Aunts had left her to help finance the trip. He returned to Hickory Nut Gap, only to set out on a hitchhiking adventure to California and back. After years of school the freedom of the open road felt wonderful. In the fall he started work in the tobacco warehouse. The Federation had been assigned to administer the government's price support program and a majority of farmers selling tobacco on the Asheville market had to contribute a dollar to the program. Jamie McClure and his cousin Jamie Clarke were assigned the task of signing up farmers. It was a tough job to locate and make friends with a man, then persuade him to part with a dollar in the cold and confused atmosphere of a tobacco warehouse. But the boys succeeded.

Jamie Clarke, Dumont's son, had been as impressed as his cousin with his Uncle Jim's work in the Farmers Federation. Jim McClure began to train both young men for eventual leadership in the organization. These two cousins and friends, raised in the atmosphere of Christian service, stood ready to carry on the McClure tradition of a life of usefulness. Neither sought to become ministers as their fathers had done, but both of them nonetheless were willing to devote themselves to a lifework that pursued the larger vision of brotherhood. Jamie Clarke graduated from Princeton in 1939, two years before his cousin finished at Yale. He, too, had worked hard, as chairman of the *Daily Princetonian,* and he went off for a well-earned trip to Europe with his roommate Fred Fox, who would become an influential Presbyterian minister. It was the eve of war, August 1939, and they were lucky to get safely back across the Atlantic on the *Athenia.* Her sister ship was sunk by a German submarine. Early in 1940 he went to work at the Hendersonville Federation warehouse, relinquishing the glories of college leadership and accepting his new lot as a store clerk. His uncle Jim wanted him to learn the business of the Federation from inside out, and put him under the charge of Bill Francis at one of the biggest volume warehouses in the Federation system. He later joined the Navy, and had time to write down some of his experiences on the job, creating a vivid picture of the daily pace of a Federation warehouse.

> The first day I went to work an old employee named Cecil Jones and I were sent to deliver a new power sprayer to a hardbitten old landowner, "Old Man Hill" of Edneyville. The sprayer was heavy, and we had a good deal of trouble unloading it. I wasn't being of much use, which was brought home sharply when Old Man Hill said, "You've never done any work before. You must have been raised in the city."
>
> The work really got tough after the first week. Spring planting season was upon us, and carload after carload of fertilizer rolled in to be unloaded at our storage warehouse across the tracks. Fertilizer is packed in 200-pound bags, which are difficult for one man to lift by himself. My chief fellow worker was a 225-pound Carolina boy, Lloyd Rhodes. He had been working at this job for a year and was a powerful chap.
>
> The procedure was to roll our two-wheeled warehouse truck into the box car and then each man would pick up one end of a bag and we would load it on the truck ... Most people wheeled only four bags, but Lloyd always wanted to take five, which made 1,000 pounds.
>
> This was a heavy load for one man to wheel on that type of truck and at first I had a hard time. Bridging the gap between the boxcar and the unloading platform was a heavy flat piece of steel which served as a sort of gangway. The second time I tried to wheel 1,000 pounds of fertilizer over the flat plate I slipped and the truck went skidding out of my hands ...
>
> Seed potatoes were being shipped into our warehouse from Prince Edward Island in Canada ... I remember one morning having to wheel about 100 of these sacks from a commercial truck ... there had been a party in Asheville the night before ... and at 7:30 a.m. my strength had not returned. The trucker was a loud-talking fellow named Jim and with mouth loaded with tobacco. He was in a hurry and was impatient. All of this made for a rough two hours.
>
> Bill Francis, the manager, was a dandy storekeeper. He was on the job at 7 a.m. and never left before 7 p.m. He never walked—he always ran. Farmers and farmer's wives from far out in the country appreciated his friendly "Hello, Mrs. Hooper, be with you in a minute."
>
> The trust these people had in him sometimes made it hard for us to put through sales.
>
> "Where's Bill. I want to talk to Bill," was often asked us.
>
> This experience of having to wait on people, humoring them and being friendly no matter how you felt inside was good for me. I believe that it would be helpful to thousands of our college boys and girls who tend to get the idea that the world should wait on them. After going through it you begin to understand the feelings of the other man behind the counter and become more considerate of him.
>
> Charley Drake, a ... colored man of remarkable sense who used to clean up the warehouse for us, admired Bill Francis' skill in dealing with people. He once told Lloyd Rhodes and me that "Mr. Francis he'll sell it to them whether he's got it or not."

Family bringing chickens to sell at a Federation Warehouse.

North Carolina is a hay importing state. Our Federation warehouse at Hendersonville handled ten or 15 [railroad] cars of hay a year. The bales weighed between 40 and 60 lbs. and were usually handled by sharp hay hooks. One afternoon when Charlie Drake and I were piling the bales up high in a dark part of the storage warehouse, my hook missed the bale and went through the loose skin underneath Charley's chin. "You nearly got me that time, Mr. Jimmie," he said good humoredly. It bled rather badly and worried me . . .

An old, old couple, Mr. and Mrs. Hubbard, used to come in every week or two from Jumpoff Mountain on a sled pulled by steers . . .

We had a mill next to the Hendersonville warehouse. Farmers brought in their corn on Saturday morning and left it at the mill to be ground up.

The miller would take out one-seventh of the resulting corn meal as our "toll." Big Rob, the assistant miller, surprised me one day by telling me that his stomach had been cold for the past 20 years! He let me feel it and sure enough, it was really cold. He attributed it to a case of double pneumonia he had had without, apparently, being able to get to a doctor . . .

The first big rush at Hendersonville came at Irish potato planting time. Then there was a short lull, followed by heavy activity as the corn planting time drew on. I never expect to be with a harder working group of men. In three months we unloaded 35 cars of fertilizer alone, which is over two million pounds . . .

I sold some nails to a gentleman from way back in the hills and as I was wrapping them he said "You'd better double-poke them, son."

What he wanted was a real mystery until he came behind the counter himself and carefully took two paper bags and placed one inside the other . . .

We had our fun at the warehouse every day. Boys of the age of Troy Downs, the bookkeeper, Lloyd Rhodes and myself, would call into us as they went by, "Farmers Ruination."

Lloyd was easily perturbed, and Troy and I used to make out charge tickets for him for things he had never bought. Bill Francis would collaborate in this and tell Lloyd he must hurry and pay up. Lloyd retaliated by always picking his end of the fertilizer sack up first.

This makes it much harder for the man on the other end than if both ends came up simultaneously.

When pretty country girls came in to sell their eggs, Troy used to count them out one by one taking as long as possible. The girls loved it. Troy was a very good looking boy anyway. One of the girls at the Fassifern School in Hendersonville used to escape at night, jump the fence and go to the movies or to one of Hendersonville's numerous dances with him.[8]

Jamie Clarke remembers his time at the Hendersonville warehouse as a chance not only to learn the Federation business, but also to learn about and appreciate his fellow workers and the patrons of the cooperative. Later, as the editor of the Federation *News,* he learned more about the art of salesmanship from the Federation's star feed salesman, Blake Greenwood of Leicester. In order to meet Federation customers and get pictures of their farms and livestock, he would occasionally spend a day traveling with Blake in his yellow truck. Blake taught Jamie that you never went directly into your sales pitch. First he would greet his prospective customer cheerfully, spend time talking about his particular concerns, admire everything on his farm and eat anything that was offered to him. Only then would he get out his pad and pencil to take down the order, which never failed to come through.

One day they stopped to see Blake's Aunt Lily, on her farm up on Big Ivy. The water system was out of order, but she asked them to dinner and Blake, knowing there was no water to be had, urged Jamie to "try some of those fine peppers." These were red hot peppers, which Jamie had never seen. Blake kept watching him but his pupil kept right on eating politely and praising the food. He didn't get cooled off until they stopped at a spring![9]

Blake really entered into the lives of his customers. Once he stopped to see Mr. and Mrs. Charlie Shepherd, who had a dairy at Democrat. Mr. Shepherd had the flu. He had come up to the house after milking without cleaning the barn and he told Blake he had felt too bad to clean it the night before as well. As Blake stepped onto the porch he saw the dairy inspector, Miss Chick, who was one of the first woman inspectors and very tough, driving into the barnyard. He rushed back in the house and told Mr. Shepherd to jump into the bed quick and pull the sheets up over his clothes. Then Blake talked to Miss Chick. The little lady was persuaded to overlook the sick dairyman's dirty barn since he was so sick; but Mrs. Shepherd never forgave Blake Greenwood for the manure from Mr. Shepherd's boots on her clean sheets. It was people like Blake who made the difference in developing business.[10]

By 1940, the Farmers Federation was successfully entering its third decade, primarily as the result of Jim's persistence and idealism. As new honors and recognition came to him he liked to think that these honors helped to certify in the minds of potential supporters that the work was worthy of their interest. In 1941, he received an honorary master of arts degree from his college rival, Harvard University. He was still able to wear his wedding morning coat, and the porter asked him as he stepped off the train if he was going to be married! The following June, the University of North Carolina invited him to Chapel Hill for a similar honor. He found that the solemn event could become the highest entertainment when the vagaries of nature gave his afternoon of honor the drama of uncertainty. He wrote to his son Jamie:

> This finds Mummie, Elspie and me in a crowded day coach on a hot ride back to the mountains . . . All the graduating class, their girls, their mothers, and a large sprinkling of army and navy boys made a simultaneous rush for the two coaches as they came into the station—Elspie & Mummie with their famous ability somehow snared a seat and here we sit surrounded by mounds of baggage. We had a big day yesterday—We first were taken [on] a tour of the University, then we attended the Alumni Luncheon which was a huge affair and most interesting. A state University (or maybe it is just North Carolina) has a sense of mission or responsibility for the state that is missing at many private institutions . . .
>
> Mummie was a knock out & Elspie was in great form . . . We all went to President [Frank] Graham's for an early supper & thence to commencement which was in the stadium. The stadium is a sunken bowl with trees and woods all around it, and a beautiful place—
>
> Clouds were gathering and growing bigger & blacker as the exercises began—the college & post graduate degrees are given out individually—and it takes hours for the 800 or 900 to file by, have their names read & get their sheepskin & Bible. They are all given a $3.00 Bible!
>
> Well as they kept filing by, it got more threatening, and then drops began to fall. The result was that by the time the Honorary degrees came along, it was a soggy downpour,—and so as the last act on the program, the five Honorary Degrees were conferred in almost a deluge-Mummy & Elspie stuck it out to the end & were soaked— . . .
>
> (James G. K. McClure, Jr. to Jamie McClure, June 10, 1942)

Two years later, in 1944, the National Institute of Social Sciences awarded him their gold medal. "Siddy and I are going to New York to attend the dinner which I told you about of the National Institute of Social Sciences," he wrote to the Stuarts. "The other recipients are Bernard Baruch and Mrs. Henry P. Davison. It is a huge pleasure for me to be there at the same time as Mrs. Davison because she has been such a tower of strength in our whole enterprise" (James G. K. McClure, Jr. to the Stuarts, sometime in 1944). In receiving the award, Jim spoke of his own life, the work of the Federation, and his thoughts about the importance of providing opportunities for the low-income citizens within a democracy.

Mr. Chester, Mr. Hall, Members and Guests of the National Institute of Social Sciences.

I am quite overwhelmed, and just about rendered speechless by the presentation of this medal. What I have done in the Appalachian Mountains has been made possible by those who have supported our educational fund and by the people in the mountains who have enthusiastically supported our cooperative movement.

This award is a very great honor, and I accept it with gratitude and much humility, as I do not at all feel that I deserve it. I am, however, particularly happy to have the type of work in which I am engaged recognized in this outstanding way. It is, in a way, a new approach to one of the basic problems of Democracy.

. . . Some 25 years ago, because of overwork, the doctors advised me to get out of doors for a few months. We took this opportunity to locate a spot that might become a permanent vacation headquarters. We bought a farm in a gap of the Blue Ridge Mountains near Asheville, N. C. The countryside is beautiful and as we were fixing up the farm, we got acquainted with the people. One man on the farm was a lineal descendent of Daniel Boone. The people sang the oldest of English ballads, used Elizabethan and even Chaucerian English, and had the characteristics that enabled the pioneers to conquer the wilderness; resourcefulness, independence and humor, and they also had the qualities which have created liberty and freedom, the consciousness of a power above and outside themselves and a reverence for individual human personality . . .

The idea with which we started our enterprise was a very simple one. The idea was to try to create markets for the things the people could raise so that they could increase their income by their own efforts. Our idea was to enable the people in the mountains to create wealth. In other words we acted on the theory that if a good market was available the people would respond by greatly increasing their production. To create such markets was a rather slow and laborious procedure and I can best illustrate it by the difficulties encountered in the development of a poultry industry . . .

The mountain country is ideally adapted to the growing of poultry and if every mountain farm could have a flock of a 100 hens it would tremendously increase the income of the region. When we started out there was practically no poultry production in the mountains. The poultry population averaged 12 or 15 chickens per farm. There was no market for poultry. We had the idea that if [we] should create a market the people would respond by greatly increasing poultry production, so we started operating live poultry cars stopping at each point in the mountains and paying cash at the car door and then running these poultry cars up to the great markets in New York and Philadelphia. In other words we created a cash market for poultry every day in the year. After operating these poultry cars for some years we discovered that the poultry population was no larger than when we started and that our theories just had not worked. We analyzed the situation and found the difficulty to be that the quality of the poultry in the mountains was so poor that it did not pay to increase that kind of poultry. The average hen in the mountains lays only 60

Top: *Elspeth, Jamie and Elizabeth McClure in front of the porch at Hickory Nut Gap.* Bottom: *Annual dinner of the National Institute of Social Sciences.* Left to right: *Bernard Baruch, Mrs. Henry P. Davison (early Fund supporter) and James G.K. McClure, Jr. Waldorf-Astoria, New York City, May 1944.*

or 70 eggs a year. This is not enough to pay for her feed, consequently the more hens a man had the poorer he became, so we turned around and started on an entirely different tact. We decided that we must make available and distribute a type of hen that would lay a lot of eggs. We got incubators, we persuaded farmers to have supply flocks for the hatchery and we maintained rigid requirements for these supply flocks. The hens had to be individually blood tested to eliminate inheritable diseases. The chief requirement was that every cockerel must come from a hen with a record of laying 250 eggs a year. That is, the chickens which we distributed would have the inheritance to lay a lot of eggs. It took some time to get this idea accepted—it took a great deal of patient field work first to start and oversee the supply flocks, then it took a great deal of patience, [and] personal field work to persuade individual farmers to venture into establishing a flock of one or two hundred hens, but little by little this has grown. When the great demand for war production of poultry came following Pearl Harbor we were like a runner poised and ready to go . . .

It seems to me that one of the great problems which we face in our Democracy is the problem of the low income group. In a Democracy we must somehow offer equal opportunity to all . . . Neither a dole nor public works solves this problem. The creative way, the American way, is to create the opportunity for these people to help themselves, to somehow develop the productive capacity of the people in the low income group so that they can increase their own earnings by their own efforts. This is the task to which we have set ourselves, translating as well as we can the findings of science, such as genetics in the practical action on the farm, discovering new uses for the products, discovering new outlets for the things people can make and thereby calling forth their own creative efforts. In this way we are trying to develop the capacity and the ability of a people in this low income bracket . . .

I cannot close without saying a word here about our Lord's Acre Movement. As we were organizing our cooperative we hoped to develop improved material conditions. We felt however that improved material conditions are not worthwhile unless spiritual improvement comes at the same time. We have seen so many examples of material improvement with no spiritual development and we always find that this material development ends up in a smash so we decided to try to back up the one organization in the mountains which concentrates on Christian character, which has been tough enough to survive, and that is the country church. We organized a Religious Department in our work and we suggest to the churches in the mountains that each member of the church and of the Sunday school have some kind of a project for their own church. A boy or a girl could set a hen and raise chickens, could raise a pig, could raise a calf, a man could set out a patch of potatoes or an acre of corn and we called it the Lord's Acre Movement. The greatest thing we did was to secure Dumont Clarke to head up this Movement. He has worked untiringly . . . It has kept on rolling along until today there are some 2500 churches in the mountains and some 2500 churches outside the mountains using this method to supplement their budget. It has spread to every state in the Union. It has given new life and vitality to country churches everywhere.[11]

Jim never missed an opportunity to preach his message. Mrs. Davison had listened since 1926 to the McClure gospel of the Farmers Federation, and one only wonders about the thoughts entertained by Bernard Baruch, the world

renowned economist, after hearing about poultry production in Western North
Carolina. Jim himself was the proud father of his Federation. He had realized a
dream of putting his ideas to work, and what he had to show for his quarter
century of struggles was an organization that allowed a region's people to hope
for a better future.

Jim McClure became more and more caught up in the web of his community. His many interests each made demands on his judgement and time. He
remained an executive of the American Forestry Association. He was also once
again elected to the advisory committee of the Farm Security Administration.
He wrote to his son,

> I was on this Committee when the F.S.A. started, we drew lots for the 1
> yr., 2 yrs., and 3 yrs. term and I drew the 1 yr. term, and as members cannot
> succeed themselves I was out in a year—July 1st my 2 yr. exile was over and
> I was reappointed, and this A.M. I was elected Chairman of the Committee. I
> am quite pleased as it gives the Farmers Fed high standing with all the Farm
> Security people in Western North Carolina—and Farm Security has a supervi-
> sor and ass't supervisor in every county about like the county agents.
>
> Well, we met all day, and it is very interesting. It is almost like a well
> trained farm management and financing corporation for the very poorest farm-
> ers, and it is putting them, a lot of them, on their feet. James G. K. McClure,
> Jr. to Jamie McClure, September 4, 1942)

Jamie Clarke left the Hendersonville warehouse to become the editor of the
Farmers Federation *News* in 1940. A hard working young man, he wanted to
please his uncle by making the most of the *News*. He ran contests and games to
increase reader interest, and made much more use of pictures than any previous
editor. Despite an unassuming and quiet nature, young Jamie Clarke made a
strong impression on his Uncle. But in December 1941, the Japanese attack on
Pearl Harbor broke harshly into the lives of all Americans. In February of 1942
Jamie left his desk at the Federation to join the U.S. Navy. Elizabeth wrote to
her son, Jamie McClure:

> Daddy asked Mr. Searle at the Miller Press [which printed the Federation
> *News*] how things were going without Jamie Clarke. He answered, " . . . I
> never saw such a fellow as that Jamie. He always got what he wanted done
> but in such a way that nobody minded change or criticism on his part if you
> could call it that . . . Jamie always seemed to keep perfectly relaxed and to
> make everybody else stay that way. He was always so simple and unassuming
> and unpretentious about everything he did, that I didn't really half realize
> what immense things he accomplished."
>
> Knowing Jamie, I thought this would interest you . . . Jamie never came
> worrying Daddy with anything . . . no fuss or feathers anywhere . . .
>
> I really think that Jamie is a natural for politics. I think he has the vote
> getting quality. He somehow inspires confidence. I believe that after the war
> if he chooses to continue with the Federation *News,* he will find it a natural

take-off for a political career. It might be very useful to the Fed to have Jamie in Washington as Senator Clarke for N.C.!!!!

You may think me more or less cracked, but it wouldn't be the first time(!). Jamie has a wonderful human touch. Great intelligence and a liking for human beings just as human beings. All that can easily spell success in politics. (Elizabeth Cramer McClure to Jamie McClure, May 24, 1942)

As usual Elizabeth McClure was a sharp judge of a person's possibilities. Many years later Jamie Clarke would serve three terms in the North Carolina Legislature, and then become the U.S. Congressman from the Eleventh Congressional District.

Jamie McClure made up his mind to enter the fight after Pearl Harbor. Like his father prior to World War I, Jamie had been anti-war, but the unprovoked Japanese attack changed his feelings and he desperately wanted to join the navy. His love of the ocean and knowledge of naval ships and history made this a natural choice; but he was very near-sighted, like his mother, and he could not pass the military physical examination. The best way for him to contribute to the war effort seemed to be to take a job in an IBM munitions plant. To his surprise he was assigned to a cannon plant in Poughkeepsie, New York, near where his sister and several of his friends, including his current girl, were in college at Vassar. His father had taught him never to complain, never to express envy or disappointment and he wrote jokingly to his Aunt Harriet Stuart:

I have had a draft classification of 1-B for some time on account of my eyes, and in spite of excellent connections, it seems absolutely impossible for me to get into either of the armed services in any capacity whatsoever at the present time. However, I did find an opening in a small airplane-cannon plant (through Mr. Watson of the I.B.M. which controls the plant) in which I think I can make use of such practical experience as I have had to greater effect than anything I have yet encountered . . . you'll get a laugh out of the location of the plant—its at Poughkeepsie! I think when some of my friends get wind of my move, I'm going to hear a lot of cracks about war profiteering . . .

I hope it works out, as I believe the job is as close as I can get to the shooting without actually using a gun, and perhaps, from a thoroughly impersonal point of view, I can make my training count far more in that position than in uniform. At least we can try to think that as long as they won't let me have a uniform. This current move will not, I hope, have any effect on my plans for keeping on the Federation, but I feel pretty strongly that winning the war is a job that must be cleaned up first. (Jamie McClure to Harriet Stuart, January 10, 1942)

Jamie put in long hours, sometimes working an eighty-hour week. Two maiden ladies, Miss Jennie and Miss Elise Kinkead, already friends of his sister Elspeth, befriended him. They fed Jamie many meals, held birthday parties for him and Elspeth and their friends, and made him feel at home in their beautiful Victorian house above the Hudson River. They also had a dairy farm outside

Poughkeepsie and Jamie could go out on Saturdays to pick apples or plow in the spring. But life in a munitions plant, lonely meals in the local diner, and knowing that most young men his age were in military service would often leave him demoralized. When his girl to whom he was so devoted told him she preferred a young Navy lieutenant, dashing in his blue and gold, Jamie sank to a new low. Fortunately he and Elspeth were close friends, and she was nearby to support him as best she could.

His mother sensed his need for special support at this time and both she and Jim wrote to him often. Spring had returned again to Hickory Nut Gap.

It has been one of these unbelievable days here-a cathedral blue sky—apple blossoms everywhere so that each gust of wind from the orchard carried the most heaven sent fragrance—all the white cherries clouds of white loveliness, violets in rivers of colour everywhere you stepped and the little rock garden just overflowing with blue bells and primroses and white snowdrops . . . Just as we finished supper who should drop in but Ernst Bacon from Spartanburg (who was on the faculty of the music department of Converse College there). He said he needed rest and change and just headed this way so we kept him for the night and were rewarded with Mozart and Chopin and Pappa Haydn while we listened with only candles and firelight. What a genius the man is, and what feeling and imagination he has and what supreme modesty. Absolutely unegotistical and a delightful fellow to talk to on any subject.

This afternoon we took cushions and the radio out into the courtyard and sat there in the midst of wisteria and purple violets and fluttering white butterflies and waving shadows and listened to the Philharmonic and the 2nd Brahms Symphony. It all seemed incredible and unreal and like people in a dream it was so beautiful. These ravings will make you smile but it was just one of these days that you prize forever and ever and ever. The music seemed to come from the trees or the sky. (Elizabeth Cramer McClure to Jamie McClure, April 19, 1942)

In another letter she told him how gas rationing had cut off the usual stream of spring visitors to Hickory Nut Gap, and surely she would accomplish a great deal, including extra plantings of vegetables to help supply nearby army camps.

. . . [John Shorter] is much pleased. He is absolutely inspired this year. He has "patches" out in every direction and is a perfect slave to the business of keeping down the weeds. I don't think he sleeps nights! His cold frames are bulging with tomato and celery plants and he has enough lettuce on hand to feed an army. The "victory garden" slogan has gotten under his skin and into his fingers and you've just never known such a fury of effort!

. . . We hear little or nothing about the German and Jap Diplomats who are lodged in the Grove Park Inn. Rumor hath it that the ladies make frequent shopping pilgrimages escorted by a heavy guard and that Miss Perkinson's and M. V. Moore's [two select Asheville stores] are just going great guns . . . (Elizabeth Cramer McClure to Jamie McClure, May 24, 1942)

Jamie had decided to join a small Presbyterian church in Pleasant Valley, near the Kinkead's farm. In two letters Elizabeth told him how happy she was about this step, and why she thought church membership was tremendously important. Elizabeth was not a preachy person who vaunted her religious beliefs before the world, but here she shared with her son her deep conviction that it is only as we follow the principles of Christ that we can hope to better the world.

> I am so glad you are going to join the church at Poughkeepsie. I think it will make a great difference to you to feel that you are part of a great organization the world over that stands for the Christian way of life and all that it means in these dark days. The church needs you, needs your support, your keen mind, your brave outlook, your eagerness to serve. There is no doubt at all that we each one of us need all the help and strength we can get, and belonging to the church does give one strength and help. There is something about sharing in the Communion service (when you have earned the right to share in it by acknowledging openly, and freely, that you mean to do your best to live according to Christ's teaching) that is wonderfully uplifting and renewing. However critical we may often feel about what the church does, or does not do, there is no getting away from the fact that we need it more than ever before,—for leadership in the Christian way of life in which we all so fervently believe, in these terrible times.
>
> I don't think any of us are strong enough to stand alone. We must all march together, shoulder to shoulder, with a common purpose in our hearts. (Elizabeth Cramer McClure to Jamie McClure, May 17, 1942)

And in the second letter she wrote:

> I am hoping that this will reach you on Sunday . . . my dearest love and to tell you how much I am thinking about you especially during the morning service.
>
> There is an old hymn by George Neumark that was I think Grandfather McClure's favorite. One verse of it goes like this and I send it to you for today:
>
> If thou but suffer God to guide thee,
> And hope in him through all thy ways
> He'll give thee strength what e'er betide thee
> And bear thee through the evil days.
> Who trusts in God's unchanging love
> Builds on the rock that naught can move.
>
> These are truly evil and terrible times, but if we can dedicate our lives anew, each one of us, to carrying out the principles of Jesus Christ, something new and glorious and fine will grow out of all the misery and horror and I am convinced that we will be able to build a finer and better world.
>
> I am glad that you have waited until now to join the church. Because, now, you do so with a full understanding of the responsibilities and privileges that should come to him who truly and sincerely seeks to live the Christian life. We have such need now in the world of strong young men who are convinced

that Christ's way of life is the only one that makes for service and brotherhood and permanent happiness

I know that it will be a great source of strength to you and a revitalizing of your own spiritual life to join with all those who like you have felt a need to band together to work for the Kingdom of God.

There is a verse in Joshua that I think of so often—"Be strong and of a good courage; be not afraid, neither be thou dismayed"—(and in these times how often we are dismayed—"for the Lord thy God is with thee whither so ever thou goest."

Bless you my darling. And may Christ in his infinite love and majesty guide you and keep you all the days of your life. (Elizabeth Cramer McClure to Jamie McClure, June 5, 1942)

As always, May became June and the heat of the summer began to pour down on Hickory Nut Gap. John Shorter's peas would bear, and then brown out. The sun would be good for the tomatoes and okra, green beans and corn, but it sure made the chubby old black man sweat as he cut the weeds with his hoe. Elizabeth could not be kept from her flower beds, but as she weeded and planted and nurtured along, her thoughts were quite often carried away to Jamie. His father tried to keep him cheered up as well, and to keep him abreast of the Federation happenings. He portrayed his own life as a great adventure, not wishing the struggle to show through to anyone, even his own son.

This finds Guy [Sales] and myself on a Southern day coach travelling from Columbia to Asheville . . . As there is no diner on the train and as the News Butcher has no eats we are slowly starving, but I tell Guy it is good for him . . . We went down to see the Columbia Bank for Co-ops, as we felt that additional working capital would enable us to take advantage of cash bargains in seeds and fertilizers. After explaining our need and suggesting that we had some properties we could offer as security, the bank President said they were more interested in our record than in our security, and they asked if it would be satisfactory if they gave us a line of credit of $200,000.00 which we could use as we needed!! Guy and I nearly fainted, but they evidently meant it seriously. So that is how it wound up—interest rate 2 1/2%. In other words they said they would finance us to the extent that we need financing from time to time. This certainly is great, and will enable us to buy up lespedeza, soybeans, clover seed, etc. at harvest time and carry over until the season comes to sell it. (James G. K. McClure, Jr. to Jamie McClure, May 27, 1942)

In July he wrote to Jamie that things continued to go well:

Hugh Toland [the Federation's accountant] has just about completed our June 20th statement. The statement looks mighty good with a net profit after liberal reserves of $48,000. The Hatchery under the fiery leadership of Jack Gattis shows a profit of $6,000 and we are buying a new 66,000 capacity incubator giving us a capacity of 237,000. Lexington Avenue [a new ware-house in Asheville] crashed through with a profit. Usually we make our years profit in the spring months and only hold these gains during the fall and that may happen again this year as we are able to secure less and less hardware and implements and sales will fall off. (James G. K. McClure, Jr. to Jamie McClure, July 29, 1942)

Up in Poughkeepsie Jamie kept hoping to find a way to take a more active part in the war. He heard that the Coast Guard "Temporary" Reserve was easier to enter than other services and wrote his parents he was going to try for it. He also had good news to report on his job. His father replied:

> Well, we are all mighty proud of your "raise." You certainly deserve it, but it is very pleasant to have them spring it on you unsolicited. The Coast Guard opening seems just down your alley. I trust nothing will come to prevent your getting in. I expect I.B.M. Plant No. 4 will be sorry to see you go, but you have found a spot for which you are fitted. I am sure you will make a point of getting around and saying your Good Byes to all the people in the plant and elsewhere who have coached you along . . . (James G. K. McClure, Jr. to Jamie McClure, July 29, 1942)

In August, 1942, Jamie enlisted in the Coast Guard Reserve without a physical exam. Jim wrote to Hetty, "Siddy left by bus Thursday at 7 A.M. . . . . She took a notion that she must see Jamie before he goes into the Coast Guard— She had saved up her money for a trip up to see him and off she went" (James G. K. McClure, Jr. to Harriet Stuart, August 10, 1942). The premonitions of mothers are a well known if disputed phenomenon, and Elizabeth had a deep emotional attachment to her son.

His duty was to patrol the coast of Maine on one of the converted sailing yachts the Coast Guard used for this purpose. They were especially useful because their wooden hulls could not be picked up by German sonar. The CG-26 was fifty-four feet over all, a tight fit for nine men. Jamie was Boatswain's Mate 2nd Class, and terribly proud of his sailor's uniform and his ocean-going duty. The CG-26 had an open cockpit and the Maine winter made their voyages rugged, but he was an enthusiastic crew member. When the "Temporaries" were transferred to the regular Reserve several months later, he memorized the eye chart and somehow managed to squeak through the physical.

Back in North Carolina Jim threw himself into extra war jobs. In addition to selling war bonds at the picnics, he organized rallies at each school in Buncombe County, getting the children to go to see everyone. He was district chairman of the United War Fund of the state, an agency that raised funds for local social agencies, the USO, the War Prisoners Aid and the United Seaman's Service. His sense of duty forced him to stretch his limited time to the utmost. He pushed his farm work force, now headed by Mr. J. R. Riddle, a good boss and a great trader, to make as much from the land as they could. Farm prices were up, but he was motivated by patriotism as well as profit, for he was well aware that war in the Twentieth century had become as much a battle of economics as of armies. German prisoners of war were garrisoned nearby and were

Jamie McClure in his Coast Guard uniform.

sent to farms when the owners requested help. Several came to help fill the silo at Hickory Nut Gap and Jim enjoyed trying out his previous grasp of the German language. One young man was from a town where he had studied years before, and the boy knew some of his old friends.

Just before Christmas great news came from Maine. The CG-26 was being winterized and Jamie was coming home for Christmas! "Talk about your luck!" he wrote. "We did plenty of griping when we had to stay on patrol through November with no heat and an open wheel, but it was that very lateness that kept us under repair through the holidays. You couldn't have held me down with a 100-lb. anchor when our C.O. asked me, quite out of a blue sky, if I wouldn't like ten days over Christmas . . ." (Jamie McClure to the Stuarts, January, 1943).

Jamie Clarke, too, had leave from his Navy Photo Interpretation Squadron. The McClures had a square dance for all the young people. Mathilda made a cake, crowned by a little sailor-boy and a gold braided officer to represent the two cousins. Elizabeth always used all her creative powers at Christmas to provide a meaningful occasion for her family and friends, never losing the spiritual quality of the Savior's birth. She made a special effort this year, although she could not know it would be their last Christmas together.

After Christmas Jamie returned to Biddeford Pool, Maine, and spent the rest of the winter on the icy waters of the Atlantic. In February the CG-26 encountered a great storm. When the sails had to be brought in Jamie was the crew member who walked out on the icy bowsprit to tend the ropes. They were blown a thousand miles off their course and finally limped into Gloucester, Massachusetts. The little boat was beaten past repair and the crew was reassigned. Jamie was given command of a small patrol boat that was being put in shape at Biddeford Pool.

Perhaps it was one of those unbelievable April days at Hickory Nut Gap, with "a cathedral blue sky" and "apple blossoms everywhere," when Jim and Elizabeth received a telegram that Jamie was in the Biddeford Hospital. He had been overcome by carbon monoxide gas, from the coal stove, while asleep on his boat. He died before they could reach Maine, travelling by slow, crowded war-time trains. Elspeth had come from Poughkeepsie and was at his bedside, but he never recovered consciousness.

From the hour of birth a parent is frequently reminded by the series of accidents and near catastrophes that befall a child just how fragile is the grasp of life over death. At frightening intervals, death seems to jump out of the shadows to threaten the very ones through whom your own life has been given meaning, without whom existence would be unimaginable. The senseless, accidental quality of Jamie's death made it even harder to accept. Both Jim and Elizabeth bore up bravely, supported by Elspeth, but life could never be the same. Elizabeth's painting friend from France, Mildred Burrage, lived close by in Kennebunkport. She and her sister "Bob" took the devastated family in. They had been family away from home for Jamie for the past nine months.

Elspeth has always been glad that she went to Maine twice to see her brother, once in the fall when she and a classmate, Mel Black, had enjoyed a rousing welcome from the crew of the CG-26 and a lobster dinner on board, and again just before Jamie's death. He had had a forty-eight-hour pass and they had gone skiing at North Conway to celebrate his birthday.

Now Jim and Elizabeth's Lake Forest families closed ranks to support their brother and sister. In this time of tragedy Lake Forest seemed like home. Jim telegraphed Harriet Stuart to ask if Jamie could be buried near his grandfather, and they made the trip to Chicago with their son's coffin. Dumont Clarke conducted the funeral service in the Lake Forest Presbyterian Church. Summing up the life of a young man whose full potential would never be realized on this earth, he said:

We come together in loving memory of this gallant boy. He was unflinching in his courage and in his devotion to duty. He was thankful that he could put all his enthusiasm and ability into the service of his country.

All his life he had responded to the inspirations that had touched him and he went about the business of preparing for coming responsibilities in a thorough and patient manner. He realized that visions must be translated into action in a practical way, and he was never dismayed or discouraged by obstacles or blows. In every new circumstance, he immediately started to learn and to master the problems involved. He weighed every situation carefully, concentrating on the best elements and attacking the difficulties with enthusiasm and zest. He went amongst us with gaiety and a glad heart and a great desire for usefulness.

His young life was lighted from within by ideals of service and he was, to a rare degree, without thought of self. His independence of action was based on long and careful consideration of the problems involved. Once his course was determined he was fearless and unswerving in his allegiance.

His family and friends meant everything to him; he had the strongest loyalty to all those whom he loved and it was his greatest happiness to serve them in any way.

In a surprising fashion, he stirred the minds of those with whom he came in contact, and his eager interest in all manner of subjects stimulated the imagination and intellects of those about him.

Young as he was, he was a constructive force in the world. He was always bent on definite accomplishment and in the words of one of his friends, "Somewhere beyond our ken he will keep right on doing things."

In this time of peril and world disaster, he leaves us a heritage of courage and high purpose. He lived and worked during his brief years of maturity in such a way as to add, now, to the store of integrity and valor that we so desperately need in facing the uncertainties of the future. He would have us "carry on" and march forward.

There is a verse in Joshua that was to Jamie an unfailing source of strength and inspiration and guidance:

"Be strong and of good courage; be not afraid, neither be thou dismayed: for the Lord thy God is with thee whithersoever thou goest."[12]

Elizabeth, Jim and Elspeth took the train home the next day. Her mother quietly wrote something and passed it to Elspeth during the journey. It read:

He who died at Anzim sends
This to those who were his friends.

****

Sweet friends, what the woman lave,
For the last sleep of the grave,
Is a hut which I am quitting,
Is a garment no more fitting,
Is a cage from which at last
Like a bird my soul hath passed.
Love the inmate, not the room,
The wearer, not the garment

the eagle, not the bars
That kept him from the shining stars.

****

He who died at Anzim sends
This to those who were his friends.

This poem, here freely remembered by Elizabeth McClure, was written by Edwin Arnold (1832–1904) and titled "Death in Arabia." It certainly expressed Elizabeth's feeling about death. She was sure Jamie was on important business in God's universe. It was harder for Jim to talk about his feelings. Once that summer Elspeth was with him at Tweeds Chapel Church in Fairview. The preacher spoke a great deal about Jamie, and it was hard for him to keep back tears. Afterwards he said, "Well, Pet, it's pretty tough."[13] The best way for him to handle his loss was to keep on the light side. After the funeral he wrote to thank his sister for all her help.

> It was a great comfort to have Elspie with us, and she and Elizabeth have been wonderful as we have sought to re-establish ourselves. We have been somewhat overwhelmed by the deluge of letters. It seems as though every one whose life Jamie touched has written. We are now facing the task of answering 600 letters . . .
> You and Doug were so generous about the tickets. It was a huge help to us. We had sold a mule and a mare and I had the money in my pocket when the night call reached us—and somehow with this and the help of the Coast Guard, and the big lift by the Stuarts, we reached home without borrowing. (James G. K. McClure, Jr. to Harriet Stuart, April 16, 1943)

Frances Herbert, Elizabeth's close friend, recognized how thoroughly jolted she was by the death of her son. As a little girl Elizabeth had been wrenched by the death and absence of her mother, and now her sensitivities were strained by another broken bond. A government hospital had been built on the site of the old State Test Farm, where the early Federation picnics had been held. The hospital was used to care for the casualties of the war. Elizabeth decided these young soldiers could use her gift of beauty to aid in their recovery, and undertook to build up and care for a flower garden there. Frances Herbert remembers her gathering up hoes, spades and rakes and boarding the bus for Asheville at the top of her driveway. She hated to take John Shorter or Mr. Huntley away from duties on the farm to drive her for the day to Moore General. In Asheville, she lugged her implements to another bus that would carry her out to Swannanoa. Many times Frances Herbert would meet her out there. "She just really couldn't stop working," said Mrs. Herbert later. "I used to take my yardman out with me, and he would be worn out. She worked like a day laborer."[14] She felt there was something obsessional about this gardening project, an attempt to cope with Jamie's death by helping the sons of other mothers. In one of her "Picnic" letters to Elspeth and Jamie Clarke she wrote: "Gaither

Robinson is up singing "John Henry"—(but no one will ever sing it as our dear Jamie McClure used to do it—with a feeling of suspense and drama and imminent tragedy and yet a kind of coziness about it all that made you think of covered wagons and camp fires and the vast romance of the West always opening up). A wonderful haunting melody, with all the queer slides and drags that make it so completely mountain" (Elizabeth Cramer McClure to Elspeth and Jamie Clarke, July 8, 1945).

Jim, too, was determined "to carry on and march forward." Not only did he continue all his duties as president of the Federation and community good citizen, he kept right on raising money for the Educational and Development Fund. This must have been particularly difficult after the loss of his son because his success depended so much on his charm and personal magnetism. People gave to help his projects because they liked and had confidence in him. He had to be always at his best. Each fall, reluctantly at first, he boarded the train for the annual campaign. He soon got into the spirit of the effort and mapped out each year's drive as a grand game, setting his goal almost unrealistically high, and pushing hard to reach it. He remembered names and a little something about each man or woman that was of importance to them. His daily tallies were kept in a little black book, with a running total he could compare with his progress from the last year. He would carry his cocktail all evening without taking a sip, moving from one conversation to another, introducing people to each other, always managing to turn the conversation towards the problems of his friends in the Southern mountains. He studied the Social Register and even plucked the names of successful people he hoped to reach out of magazines and newspapers. Special friends organized luncheons or dinners where he could speak. Sherman Pratt, of the Standard Oil family, had made a movie of the Federation and the people it served, and this was very successful in arousing interest.

Many of Jim's innovative projects depended on his money-raising efforts. During the war years the Educational and Development Fund was pumping nearly $60,000 annually into the picnics, the Training School, the Lord's Acre, and projects to improve the genetic quality of the dairy herds and poultry flocks of the mountains. Jim was so successful as a fund raiser that he could never replace himself. Each year he worked up a promotional pamphlet "The Forgotten Pioneer, A New Chance for the Mountain People." He included figures such as, " . . . for each dollar donated to date, the Fund has put $22.84 in the pockets of our farmers. We are helping the mountaineers to help themselves." He wrote sister Hetty, "I enclose our new circular. I have to raise my Budget on it—Do you think it has chex appeal?" (James G. K. McClure, Jr. to the Stuarts, June 20, 1936).

Each pamphlet had on the cover a large photograph chosen to impress his contributors with the proud and honorable people of North Carolina who were trying to pull themselves out of a hopeless economic inheritance. The pictures exhibited the quaintness of life there: the mules and oxen or the simple log homes that had earned for the region its reputation for backwardness. And yet

Picture of the "Forgotten Pioneer." Jamie McClure took this picture of Dave Sharp.

Jim chose fine faces for these covers, with great strength and fortitude. The October 1941 issue showed "The Forgotten Pioneer" riding on his ox sled with a bag of flour. In 1945, a pretty young woman leads two mules out into her family's pasture. The 1947 issue featured three cheerful bare foot boys, sitting on the porch holding their hoes. Jim liked to remind his audiences of the great number of children in the mountains, and how important their lives were to the future of the United States. He would then introduce the work of the Lord's Acre, very popular among the Protestants of the North. In 1943, the picture was a studied contrast between the pride and optimism of a young soldier, and the mountain cabin he was leaving behind. Of all the photographs, one he used in May 1941 was his *tour de force*. Way up on the side of a high mountain ridge, a man stands upright and proud next to his field of corn. In the distance, three mountain ranges, row after row, are plainly visible. The man appears to see beyond the beautiful landscape at his feet to the better future for his grandchildren. Jamie McClure took that picture of Dave Sharp.

Open up one of Jim's pamphlets, and there were more pictures that give visual expression to the work of the Federation. One featured two parents planting their garden, followed by three small children hoeing and pulling the dirt back over the seeds, standing over the heading "FOUNDATIONS OF AMERICAN DEMOCRACY: The Family." Jim asked rhetorically, in large print, "Who Are These Mountain People?" and "Are They Worth Helping?" On the back cover, he would list the prominent citizens who were backing him up. Mrs. Henry Davison was still with him, as the Chairman of the Women's Committee in New York. Arthur Page remained a strong captain in the efforts. Angier B. Duke, Thomas J. Watson, Henry P. Luce, Mrs. J. C. Penney and several Fords and Biddles were some of the famous names that stood behind Jim McClure's efforts.

The high point of the Fund drive became the annual "mountain picnic" held in the Grand Ballroom of the Waldorf Astoria in New York. Jim McClure treated his supporters and their friends, a sophisticated crowd, to an evening unlike any other in the city. The Federation String Band set the tone and rhythm, performing buck dances, singing old ballads, and playing the Tennessee Waltz. Jim and Elspeth found that their "fox chase" imitation was as popular in New York as it was with the Cherokee Indians. Just as in North Carolina, local performers turned up to take part in the program: Mr. Watson's son "Dick" (Arthur K.) Watson yodeled; Madame Novatna from the Metropolitan Opera performed; Jimmy Van Alan, who invented the tie-breaker rules for tennis, sang a song he had composed about Jim. The song was sung to the tune of "The Old 97."

> When Jim McClure hit the Southern mountains
> In the year one nine one six,
> It was common belief that the North and South land
> Could never, never mix.
> Then Jim McClure smiled that smile that's loosened purse strings
> That never were loosed before . . .

The guests took part in musical chairs with as much enthusiasm as the players in Yancey County, while the New York audience collapsed with laughter. Dinner was served, and the more adventurous barely hesitated to try out the delicate and indelicate staples of the mountain diet. One typical menu included Potlikker soup, wild strawberry jam, cornbread with sorghum molasses oozed on top, all followed by a slice of blackberry pie. Slices of Federation turkey would likely as not be the centerpiece of the meal, raised, everyone was reminded, with the help of contributions made to the Fund. Waldorf waiters were stuffed incongruously into bib overalls, and Jamie Clarke remembers the confusion in the vast basement when he delivered white Southern cornmeal, sweet potatoes and several lively calves to help create a country atmosphere. Jim was himself master of ceremonies and IBM's Thomas J. Watson paid for the entire evening. In 1941, Mr. Watson made this introduction of the evening's principal speaker.

Waldorf-Astoria Federation Picnic, 1954 or 1955. Max Roberts (on far left), Jim McClure (center) with his famous white pants, and Elspeth McClure on the far right.

You all know that back of everything worthwhile are two things: an idea and a personality. The idea back of the Farmers Federation is to improve the conditions and raise the standards of living of the community in Western North Carolina mountain country. The personality back of this worthwhile proposition is Mr. McClure . . .

The point I would like to have all of you remember in regard to this work is that Mr. McClure has never given a dollar to a farmer, nor loaned him any money, but he has given him an educational institution. I consider it the finest type of agricultural college I have ever seen. He has taught these people how to produce more from their soil, and he has found markets for their products . . .[15]

Jim wooed his audience with an address he had refined and polished over the years. He liked to begin with a tale or two he had picked up through the years.

Away back in the Smoky Mountains, a man lived in a small cabin, alone except for his dog. Well the winters there are long and lonely, and so this man decided to teach his dog to play checkers. One day he was sitting in front of the fire playing checkers with his dog sitting in the opposite chair—when he heard a knock on his door. It was a New Yorker, lost in the mountains, and he entered when the mountaineer yelled for him to come on in. "Well, what do you want stranger?"

"Nothing. I just want to watch the game." The dog made a move, the

mountaineer studied a while and made his move. The dog thought a while and
moved again. In a few more moves the dog won—

The stranger said, "Will you let me take you and that dog to New York.
Why you can get more money in one night in New York than you will make
in ten years on this farm. People will pay big money to see that dog play
checkers.

The mountaineer hesitated and thought it over. "Stranger, he's really not
as good as you might think. I reckon I win somewheres of three games out of
every five."[16]

With such a story, Jim brought his audience down to North Carolina. The
isolation, the poverty and honest naivete of the mountaineer were described in
a way that would catch the attention of his contributors, and give him a spring-
board into describing the work of the Federation. Jim always kept his speeches
short and soon brought the Federation band back to liven up the spirits of the
crowd. Several similar events were held at the Barclay Hotel in Philadelphia,
where George Munson and Clare McCoy, publisher of the *Evening Bulletin*,
steered Jim's fund raising activities. The purpose of the evening was to arouse
the interest of these people, to give them an unshakable curiosity about life in
Western North Carolina, so that their generosity might be cultivated for the
benefit of the work in the mountains. A rousing square dance went on late into
the evening, with occasional breaks to auction baby chickens, a pony or a piglet,
which created a great stir. These picnics were a curious blend of the two worlds
of Jim and Elizabeth, and exhibited once again the skill with which he could
combine fun with purpose in order to enlist the help of all sorts of people.

The best part of these forays to New York, Philadelphia or Detroit was
getting back to Hickory Nut Gap, sometimes as late as December. Jim wrote to
Elspeth at college once at the end of a campaign, "Tomorrow I head back to
Heaven and the Heaven keeper!"[17] Back at the farm John and Mathilda Shorter
were still the main props at the house along with Rev. David Huntley, whose
children were fast growing up and moving successfully out into the world. Betty
was the capable and willing secretary to Mr. McClure in his capacity as the
president of the Federation.

Elspeth and some of her Vassar classmates spent the summer of 1943
working on the farm. As in World War I, extra vegetable crops were planted to
help feed soldiers in nearby army camps. Sis Rice received a proposal from her
husband-to-be while weeding the asparagus patch. Jess Rattray almost collapsed
while picking endless lima beans in the boiling heat, and Virginia Osborne
stayed all summer to help tend and dust green beans, hoe corn, and pick
tomatoes with the farm hands and their families. Clinard Settles and his brother
John Scott Settles were the heart of the work force, under the able and humorous
leadership of Mr. J. R. Riddle. Nannie Settles, John's strong wife, was the
fastest bean picker. Several acres of yellow tomatoes were struck by a blight
that was new to the mountains. As the girls and their co-workers washed the red
clay off the fruits in a great tub, it was hard to tell which tomatoes were a ripe

yellow and which were rotten. Jamie Clarke's letters from Guadalcanal were read over and over, but they could give little hint of what was happening in the far Pacific. The girls also attended every picnic with Jim. Elspeth helped her father line up the program and wrote the articles for the paper. Virginia Osborne sat gallantly in the blazing sun, selling war bonds and stamps with Mr. A. C. Reynolds.

Elspeth planned to follow her brother into military service after graduating from Vassar on the accelerated plan in the spring of 1944. Her parents came up for the graduation ceremonies, and while they were having breakfast with the Misses Kinkead, who had been so good to their children, the telephone rang. A harassed Vassar official asked for James McClure. President Roosevelt had been scheduled to make the graduation address, but had to cancel at the last minute. Could Jim work up a speech in time? Miss Elise remembers his response. "Do you think we can do it in two hours?" he asked Elizabeth. With her lovely smile she jumped up and "Yes. Jim—let's try!"[18]

How he loved a crisis. The speech was enthusiastically received. It was vintage McClure, a call to arms to the best and brightest in the nation. The Poughkeepsie newspaper reported:

> Tracing American ideals, the speaker, whose daughter, Elspeth McClure, was a member of the graduating class, reminded that "The hope of the world lies in our purpose to carry these ideas forward. It will take fresh understandings and new research and original effort and keen penetration to discover afresh the great power that lies in these American ideals . . .
>
> General Smuts has said, "mankind has struck its tents and is on the march." In the world which is so rapidly changing today there lies ahead of the class of 1944 a period of unparalleled opportunity.
>
> You are finishing your preparation on the eve of the invasion of Europe, for which the free people of the world are waiting.
>
> Our success in arms must be followed through by America's entry into world citizenship. There is no escape from it. It is the destiny of America. The world is fluid and your generation will make the patterns and determine the moulds of the immediate course of mankind. Success in a shot in golf depends on the follow through. The same will be true of our entry into world affairs. You will be the ones to follow through.
>
> And so today, I want to talk to you of the Creative Power of American Ideals and of how the ideas which made America can restore us here in America and promise hope to the world. Freedom and liberty have enabled mankind to develop abilities in a remarkable way under democracy."[19]

His speech was an adaptation of one he had delivered before the Pen and Plate Club in Asheville entitled "The Springs of Democracy." He concluded his remarks at Vassar by challenging the class of 1944, and their parents and friends. In so doing, he verbalized the motive force in his own life. He said, "Everyone here, today, instinctively believes in the things that have made America, we believe so strongly that we will fight for them on every battle front in the world . . . It will be a tough assignment to put these ideals into practice. I am not offering a life of ease but instead a life that will call for all your energy and all your ability. It is a great challenge which will require a peculiar quality of mind and spirit."[20]

In essence Jim McClure believed that it would be possible to export ideas like the Farmers Federation and the Lord's Acre to foreign lands, and raise up the incomes and the spiritual resources of developing nations as he had done in the Southern Appalachians. He actually admired the way Adolph Hitler had transformed millions of Germans from inertia to action by offering them hope and pride. But the energy Hitler roused was directed to evil and destructive purposes. Why could not the energies of the American people be utilized to conquer the world in the name of human progress? Jim's World War I ethic that peace could be achieved by nonintervention had been replaced by the belief that America must actively promote the values of democracy. A few years later he talked about the possibility of sending out young men and women to Third World countries to work for a year or two, an idea very similar to John F. Kennedy's Peace Corps.

Now his own daughter was going into the Navy and he was proud of her. After graduation she was accepted for WAVE Officers Training School. Soon she was marching in formation all over the campus of Smith College in Northampton, Massachusetts, learning Navy communications. There was universal support for the war against the dictators and young people all over the country were enlisting in military service. The scarcity of manpower in Western North Carolina put many women behind the wheels of their husband's tractors, making for delightful cover photographs for the Federation *News*. To a serviceman overseas, one picture of a pretty girl was worth much more than many thousands of words. Bob Brown, editor of the *News*, started a contest for a Burley Tobacco Queen of Western North Carolina and Miss Ophelia Cole, the first winner, graced the cover of the December tobacco issue. Barefooted and smiling, she stands in front of the crop she helped to grow, wearing what appears to be nothing but a skirt and blouse of tobacco leaves. Pauline Smith, another candidate, received two trunks full of letters from homesick servicemen after her picture was in the *News*. She was shown watching a tobacco bed being burned near Barnardsville School, wearing the shortest of shorts. One ship's crew made her their pin-up girl and asked for large pictures. Dumont Clarke must have been dubious about this promotional stunt. Already he cringed at the thought of the Federation's support of tobacco. But he was so busy spreading the Lord's Acre plan far and wide that he hardly had time to complain.

With Elspeth away the farm would have been lonely that summer, but Elizabeth's nephew, Corwith Cramer, Jr., came to work on the farm and at the picnics, bringing his school friend, John Compton, son of the nuclear physicist, Dr. Arthur Compton. Cory had already spent much time at the farm, for his father's boat business kept him moving about. Elizabeth, Jim and Elspeth all loved him, and in many ways he was like Jamie McClure. He had the same brilliant mind and energy, and he was learning to play the banjo and sing mountain ballads. He and John worked on the farm and at the picnics and it meant a great deal to Jim and Elizabeth to have him there.

Just when Elspeth finished her WAVE training at the end of August 1944, Jamie Clarke arrived home on leave, after eighteen months in the Pacific, with long duty on the island of Guadalcanal. Elspeth had loved Jamie for a long time. She had grown up during the nearly two years since they had seen each other, and Jamie discovered he felt the same way. They were cousins, so it took some careful thought and research into the genetics of the situation. The related side of their families was the strong McClure side, which was in their favor. With Elspeth stationed at the Navy Yard in Charleston, South Carolina, and Jamie at the Navy Department in Washington, they had to do some long distance considering, but at last all the obstacles were worked out.

Elizabeth and Jim planned to spend Christmas with Elspeth in Charleston. They were offered an apartment in the old part of the city by Jim's cousin, Cornelia Cogswell Sage, and a WAVE friend of Elspeth's helped her set up a Christmas tree in a pot of earth sneaked from St. Phillips churchyard. Just a day or two before they were to leave Elizabeth was running down the steps to the garden to gather some greens for the Garden Club's Christmas wreath project, when she slipped on the ice and broke her arm. With one arm in a cast she kept right on with Christmas preparations, tieing up packages with one hand and her teeth. On Christmas Day Elspeth had "the duty" at the Navy Yard Communications office. That evening she told her parents, who already knew what was in the wind, that she and Jamie were indeed engaged. They were delighted and supportive. Elspeth and Jamie had pooled Navy resources to buy her mother a fur coat for Christmas, something she had not had since she was a young girl. Somehow, in spite of her broken arm, she cut branches of forsythia and yellow jasmine ("Spring Candlelight," she always called it) and forced them into bloom for the February 17th wedding in the Presbyterian Church in Asheville, where there was room for their many friends. Elspeth had a hard time getting the ten days leave to be married, which was guaranteed to WAVEs, from her crusty commanding officer, and reached home the day before the wedding. Young Corwith Cramer, his father, Uncle Ambrose, and Tommy DeBevoise, son of a New York supporter of the Federation, who had spent the winter working for the coop and living at the Clarke's, were ushers. Jamie's contemporaries were all away in the service. Elspeth's childhood friends, Beckie Herbert and Mary D. Heywood, were able to take part, and her roommate from Vassar, Farley Walton, was maid of honor. The day before the wedding Jamie's mother Annie took Elspeth aside and told her that Jamie had never given her a moment's worry.

Elizabeth and Jim went to stay with Annie and Dumont after the wedding, leaving Hickory Nut Gap as a peaceful haven for the new couple. Elizabeth even arranged to send groceries out on the bus to Mathilda, as gas rationing limited driving severely. The newlyweds had no cares, save for getting lost in

Miss Ophelia Cole, 16, of Newfound, Tobacco Queen for the 1943–44 season.

a fog on Big Bearwallow Mountain above the little town of Gerton. They wandered down the wrong side of the ridge, ending up twenty miles from home at a little country store, where they telephoned to John Shorter to pick them up, along with the three little white farm dogs! While they waited they enjoyed in silence the muttered comments of an elderly male customer "That boy ought to be in the army!"

Elspeth and Jamie had been closely observed by neighbors as they started their walk earlier in the afternoon. When they got back to Gerton they learned that loyal friends had organized a search party! John dreaded wasting more precious gas, but Elspeth thought they must try to notify them that the lost were found.

"That's the—ah worry," the old man sighed wearily as he drove up the rough Bearwallow Road. Half way up they found Uncle Mouse Freeman's son, Filmore, Deputy Sheriff of Gerton. At once he blew a tremendous blast on a siren attached to the roof of his car and answering whistles and shouts came from the mountainside.

When the ten days were over the newlyweds returned sadly to their posts in Charleston and Washington. But Elspeth had been scheduled to attend Communications School in Washington in a few weeks, and the WAVE District Personnel Officer had offered her hope for a transfer to Washington. The East-

Opposite: *Dumont Clarke prays with a group of Lord's Acre participants.*

Wedding of James Clarke and Elspeth McClure. Left-right: Mary D. Heywood, Farley Walton, Rebecca Herbert, Phebe Ann Lewis, Dumont Clarke, Annie McClure Clarke, James McClure Clarke, Elspeth McClure, Elizabeth Cramer McClure, James G.K. McClure.

ern Seaboard Naval installations were dropping personnel as the war with Germany drew to a close.

In Washington Jamie, with brave optimism, answered an ad for a house. Housing was very scarce, but his sentimental telegram melted the heart of the landlady. She chose his application over hundreds of others because she was about to get married herself. Elizabeth's brother Ambrose, who was heading up Lend-Lease for the United Kingdom, and his wife Mary, invited him to live with them until Elspeth arrived. The Communications School made a happy break in their separation, and Jamie had the little house filled with daffodils when Elspeth arrived. By the end of May the transfer came through and they were able to get settled. Elspeth worked Navy watches round the clock, changing every two days, in the big Navy code room while Jamie had regular hours as editor of *Naval Aviation* magazine, but they were so happy together in their pretty little house in Georgetown that it didn't matter at all. Elizabeth visited them and resolutely cooked artichokes in the dish pan, for they had no large sauce pan. She even sent them rooted boxwood cuttings for their pocket-sized garden![21]

When the war was over the one thing Jamie Clarke wanted to do was get back to Asheville to help with the Farmers Federation. Late in the fall they both were out of the Navy and able to move into the cottage behind the spring house. Jamie went straight to work.

On V-J Day, Jim McClure was sixty years old and the time was coming when he would have to pass the torch of his work on to the young. Jamie Clarke was a hard worker, capable and willing. But the founder was a very special man, most would say indispensable. The Federation was in his head, and it was hard to learn all the angles.

The war years had been a great mixture of blessings and difficulties. Nothing could compensate Jim for the loss of his son. But the business of the Federation was making great strides forward. Soon Jamie and Elspeth would bring back the sounds and duties of little children to Hickory Nut Gap. Jim did not remove himself from the struggle. He could never retire, because he loved the working and fighting too much. The Lord had indeed equipped him with the strength to carry a heavy load.

1. Farmers Federation *News*, November 1940, p. 7.
2. Farmers Federation *News*, December 1940, p. 10.
3. Farmers Federation *News*, August 1940.
4. Dumont Clarke, Farmers Federation *News*, May 1941, p. 19.
5. Dumont Clarke, Farmers Federation *News*, May, 1941.
6. Jamie McClure, "Frontier Civilization in the Blue Ridge Highlands, unpublished paper, written for a course at Yale University, no date.
7. *Ibid.*
8. James McClure Clarke, unpublished recollections, 1947.
9. Interview with James McClure Clarke.

10. *Ibid.*

11. James G. K. McClure, Jr., address given before the National Institute of Social Sciences, New York City, May 24, 1944.

12. Dumont Clarke, address at the funeral of Jamie McClure, Lake Forest, Illinois, April, 1943.

13. Interview with Elspeth McClure Clarke.

14. Interview with Mrs. Frances Herbert.

15. Thomas J. Watson, speech quoted in *Business Machines,* the IBM company newspaper, January 16, 1941.

16. Paraphrased from a speech by James G. K. McClure, Jr.

17. Interviews with Elspeth McClure Clarke.

18. *Ibid.*

19. "U.S. Must Join in World Affairs, Speaker Tells Vassar Graduates," Poughkeepsie *New Yorker,* April 19, 1944, p. 1.

20. *Ibid.,* p. 4.

21. Interviews with Elspeth McClure Clarke.

Chapter Twenty
Last Years

So long as our lives individually strive to embody the spirit that comes of God, our souls seeing renewal always in the source of all life must then meet, and of necessity become one, since in God there is no separation. That which is you and that which is I must then perforce unite and become eternally part of one another just as two rivers meeting, henceforth mingle and become one stream that continues on its way until it is merged in the great sea . . . (*Elizabeth Cramer to James G. K. McClure, Jr., February 8, 1916*)

By March, one can expect in the Southern Appalachians a fair number of the most delightful warm days. All across the region, the sun begins to work its miracle of drawing out the world's most diverse variety of wild flowers and blooming shrubs. Each mountain homestead, almost without exception, has its well-tended beds of transplanted wild azaleas, lady slippers and phlox. In spring a woman will find time each day to study these sacred little patches, watching for the first shoots of daffodils or iris. About the same time, her husband manages to swing by for a look at his bee gums, to see how the colonies fared over the winter as they respond to the warming rays of sun.

Elizabeth McClure rejoiced each year in this renewal of spring, and loved to wander about and rediscover the hidden beauties that lay scattered about her home in the mountains. Trailing arbutus, the first herald of the new season, is the shyest of the ephemerals, signalling the pure white drifts of Sarvis trees in the leafless forest. Quickly come great beds of trillium, showy orchids, dutchman's breeches and blood root, followed by punctatium (the earliest, small leafed Rhododendron), dogwood, and flame azalea with great splashes of color in the newly greening woods. For Elizabeth, this seasonal show was holy revelation enough to prove the existence of a loving Creator.

In late March of 1946, Elizabeth and Jim had been married for thirty years, and had spent almost the entire time at their beloved Hickory Nut Gap. For all that time Elizabeth had been working in partnership with the fecund Blue Ridge soil, with proud mountain men who were amazed to find themselves working with "pretties," and with assorted small boys in faded overalls, to surround the old house with beauty. Throughout the three growing seasons, native plants and those chosen with care from her array of catalogues made a succession of changing colors against the ever growing backdrop of glossy green boxwood. Many of these she and Jim had planted as scraggly shrubs bought from unappreciative owners. Jim and Elizabeth set some of these at the boundary of the rock

garden above the house, where they slowly grew into veritable giants, shoulder-
ing each other in undulating waves. Elizabeth rooted countless cuttings and set
them out to grow into hedges. She trimmed them faithfully over the years, using
a string line to keep those all important straight lines that she carefully planned
to melt into the looseness of a large, untrimmed bush, or to lead the eye into the
green woods beyond the garden. By 1946 Hickory Nut Gap had become a happy
combination of architecture and landscape and a wonderful botanical adventure.
Elizabeth was the conductor of a floral symphony that played a different movement in each season of the year, to the delight of her guests and family.

That spring, the paths and courtyards of Hickory Nut Gap were for Jim and
Elizabeth filled with memories of their children. Twenty-five years before, little
"Punie" would have enjoyed the warmth of March crawling about the lawn
pulling at the dandelions. It would take only a glance at the sandbox to remind
her of the treasure hunts she used to organize for little Elfie and her Stuart
cousins from Chicago. In the spring of 1943, she had lost Jamie altogether to
this life. Now Elspeth was beginning her own family at Hickory Nut Gap.

Elizabeth and Jim were now members of an older generation, and they
wore their dignity with the kind of confidence men and women possess when
their lives have stood for a glorious purpose. With the one exception of their
son's death, the sorrows and disappointments that were allotted them had been
dispelled by the courage and the vision both shared when they were married
back in 1916. Their works had matched their faith, and they were surrounded
by the variety of their friendships.

For March 29, 1946, Elspeth and Jamie planned a surprise anniversary
party, secretly inviting a number of these oldest friends including, of course,
Annie and Dumont Clarke, who had been in on the courtship from its beginning.
Everyone was asked to come in the costume of the time of their own marriage,
and to bring a photograph. Elspeth persuaded her mother to go off with Jim on
an overnight trip to Tennessee, which gave her time to decorate the studio at the
back of the courtyard with the photographs of the guests and to set up tables for
supper with Betty Huntley's help. Meanwhile, Mathilda prepared the feast. Jim
and Elizabeth had only just returned when the first guests arrived. Elizabeth was
even more startled than Jim, but they both entered right into the spirit of this
celebration of friendship and love.

Even at this stage of their lives, though, there was little time for reminis-
cing. Jim continued to manage the Farmers Federation, whose business raced
along during the post-war period. The summer picnics were now a mountain
tradition, a holiday that thousands anticipated. And Jim continued to make his
autumn pilgrimages up north to gather together loyal contributors and treat them
to his charm and the revised pitch of "What we are doing about the mountain
farm." He threw himself as well behind the great efforts to build new schools
in Buncombe County and to introduce symphony music to Western North Carolina.

The region was changing; industry was building up in the mountains, stemming the out migration of young families to the mill towns of the Piedmont and elsewhere. Young soldiers returning home brought with them new aspirations, and a hankering for their piece of the American Dream. Fewer would remain satisfied with the rigors of subsistence agriculture or its meager economic rewards. Everyone wanted an automobile, and many once prim and well-kept mountain yards became the shrines of a generation of self-taught mechanics. Petunias and asters had to compete with old transmissions and discarded bumpers. Very few farms would escape at least one or two junkers out in the yard, with a V-8 engine dangling from the old oak shade tree. The jacked-up car of the whiskey runner was added to the moonshine legend. In fact, the curves through Hickory Nut Gap became the "Thunder Road" for many aspiring blockaders who liked to refine their road handling skills by squalling and screeching up and down the mountain on a Saturday evening.

But it was roads such as this one, and new ones besides, that opened up the region to the national economy. Not only were manufactured goods readily available in Western North Carolina, but the families themselves enjoyed new mobility and sources of income. Jim McClure's dream of a wage earner in every home appeared possible. Manufacturers discovered the capabilities and the willing spirit of the mountain worker, who appreciated his earnings and wanted nothing more than to go home after work to do a little tinkering, hoe in the garden or play ball with his children.

The new economic order in the mountains meant a new role for the Farmers Federation. In many areas farming remained the main source of livelihood, but in others conditions were changing. With the war over, Jim McClure began to formulate new ideas and projects for the Federation. In the Twenty-sixth anniversary issue of the News (1946), he laid before the membership a bold new plan of action.

A GREAT PROGRAM AHEAD

The Farmers Federation is developing a great, constructive program which will build solid foundations for a better civilization in Western North Carolina . . . We are planning to build a solid foundation of markets which will mean the prosperity of the towns.

Poultry and Eggs: We already have started a new modern poultry-processing plant on Valley Street in Asheville. This will have zero storage rooms for frozen poultry; cold storage rooms for eggs, apples, and potatoes; it will have lots of space to take care of these farm products. We are planning this building to be a solid foundation for the marketing of poultry, eggs, apples and potatoes in Western North Carolina.

Turkeys: We are launching a campaign for turkey production . . .

Freezer Lockers and Frozen Foods: Great strides will be made within the next few years in the processing and use of frozen foods. The Farmers Federation plans to keep right abreast with this movement. We already have four locker plants in operation and another one just about to be built at Brevard. Campaigns for locker plants are going forward at Marion and Spruce Pine.

The Farmers Federation stands willing to go ahead with any community in the erection of a locker plant if a survey shows that the installation can be operated at a safe margin. These locker plants will enable the farmers to get started in the frozen food business; and also, in the processing of meat . . .

Milk: We are already at work building a cooperative dairy plant. The directors of the Farmers Federation feel that this will establish a solid foundation for the marketing of milk and milk products in Western North Carolina . . .

High Production: The program of the Farmers Federation will call for high production in every branch of agriculture. You all know the standards we have set in our hatchery: Every baby chick has the inheritance behind it for 250 eggs. We have the Dairy Improvement program, also based on genetics, designed to increase the average production of dairy cows to ten or twelve thousand pounds a year . . . the bull barn for an artificial insemination program is now being built.

Spiritual Resources: The Religious Department plans to go even further in backing up and trying to help strengthen the country Sunday Schools and churches. The Lord's Acre Movement has given new vitality and strength to our country churches and Sunday Schools.

We now plan to add to that service a church and Sunday School recreation service so that wholesome recreation can be used through the Sunday Schools in developing the kind of Christian character that we need for this new atomic age into which we are coming. The strength of America has always been in the country districts. We want to develop the type of strong Christian character in our rural sections that will keep America marching forward into a better day.[1]

The first rays of that "better day" were already shining in the North Carolina mountains. In all measurements of economic activity, the region still lagged behind the rest of the nation, but the opportunities of 1946 were vastly different from those of 1916 when Jim and Elizabeth first came to the South. The effects of two wars, the TVA, better highways, more tourists, more industry, and better access to national markets were remaking the lives of the mountaineers. The Federation was playing a leading role in the development of the region, raising up the level of skills and the hopes of the men and women and their children who lived in its territory. As Jim McClure often said, "A rising tide raises all boats." By his hammering on the facts of scientific agriculture, in cooperation with the County Agricultural agents, a generation of farmers had ready access to the most current techniques of farming. And with the *News* and the picnics, Jim made the information better than accessible, he made it understandable and downright fun. The habits of progressive farming spread, with the obvious results that the members who followed these procedures grew more food, and made more money for their families.

In a less obvious way, these men and women learned to think in a critical, problem-solving manner. Sociologists have noted the difficulties traditional societies face when trying to mesh with the ways of the modern industrial system. A large part of the adjustment involves a new philosophical approach, an acceptance of the scientific method of critical thinking. In Western North Carolina, the Federation helped to promote this approach to problems, and therefore contributed to the remarkably smooth transition the region experienced in shifting away from the habits of its traditional culture.

Jim McClure chaired an endless number of committees and meetings that involved the farmers in their own business. He taught by example organizational rules and etiquette, and how to arrive at an acceptable joint decision after several opinions were expressed. The farmers involved learned about minutes, and treasurer's reports, and how to elect people to positions correctly and with a minimum of hard feelings. The policies of the Federation were set by two directors elected by the membership of each county. These were usually leading farmers. Warehouse committees helped to manage the policies of each of the Federation stores. Market news taught the mountain farmers how to think in terms of supply and demand, world commodity markets, government policies, and all the other factors that determine crop prices.

If the Federation was something of a large-scale school, its central purpose remained to put cash in the pocket of the mountain farmer. Jim McClure had always used his powers of imagination to create money-generating schemes. With the aid of the Fund he had been able to try out many of them. The Federation created, promoted and maintained a wide variety of programs. Ironically its very success would eventually contribute to the demise of the organization. After the war, the Federation expanded into new areas such as freezer locker plants, the sale of home appliances, a modern poultry dressing plant, a cooperative dairy plant, artificial insemination and other programs. The expertise and energies of the management became more dispersed just at a time when agriculture nationally experienced a burst of specialization.

For example, the Federation committed itself to building up a modern poultry business. From the earliest days of the cooperative, Jim McClure had felt that Western North Carolina was an ideal region for chickens. The cool summer climate, along with the requirement of mountain farmers to raise a crop that did not need rich bottom land, made poultry and turkeys very promising. The business did grow and continue to put cash in the pockets of farmers, from the days of the black pot out in front of the Fairview warehouse for scalding and plucking chickens through the era of the live poultry railroad car, and finally to the building of the Federation's own hatchery and dressing plant. Over the years the officers of the Federation learned a lot about the fickle nature of the chicken business, overcoming diseases and fighting a series of marketing difficulties; but Jim always remained sure that the Federation could prevail and provide for its region a stable and profitable poultry enterprise.

An improved hatchery was built to ensure a supply of healthy baby chicks, with the best inheritance for rapid development in the case of broilers or high production in the case of laying hens. Chicks sold to farmers were repurchased by the Federation and processed at the dressing plant in Asheville, where they were scientifically killed, plucked, gutted, packaged and marketed. A modern plant was begun in 1946 and completed the next year at a cost of $130,000. The Educational and Development Fund assisted in launching this new project. At the May 1948 meeting of the Fund Trustees the completion of the plant was noted and the immediate support of the Fund requested.

> . . . [T]he modern poultry processing plant of the Farmers Federation . . . is in operation. This plant was necessary as a marketing foundation on which to build a poultry industry in the mountains, but this plant cannot develop volume enough to pay its way in the fiscal year . . .
>
> Since these fine facilities were built and put into operation to further the development of agricultural production in the mountain territory and since time is needed to develop volume of business to the point where they will be self-sustaining, a motion was made that the Budget be amended to include an item to cover interest and depreciation on these buildings . . . amounting to $36,278.07 . . . This motion was seconded and duly carried.[2]

Spread over the next decade, over $300,000 of Fund money was spent promoting and maintaining the hatchery, the dressing plant and various other poultry related enterprises.

It had always been the objective of the Federation to spread the poultry business out among many small farmers to help them increase cash income. Fred Moffitt was one of the first to be "in chickens" with the Federation in Clay County, a sparsely populated and remote county at the far western tip of North Carolina. He had a supply flock, furnishing eggs for the broiler breeds to the Federation hatchery in Asheville: Rhode Island Reds and Domineckers. Each week a yellow Federation truck would pull up to the Moffitt farm, pick up the eggs, and leave the correct amount and mix of feed. During periods of tight money, the Federation would allow a dependable man like Fred Moffitt to build his credit up a bit. For his part, he was sure that the Federation poultry business was the "best thing going at the time." In truth there were then few other opportunities in Clay County. All over Western North Carolina chicken houses began to spring up and there was a feeling of excitement and optimism as the profits started to come in.

It wasn't long, however, before large feed companies began to see the advantages of creating their own poultry operations to stimulate the sale of their products. They would go so far as to build large chicken houses for the farmer, on credit, advance him the birds, and then pay for raising them. Very quickly, for both layers and broilers, the scale of profitable operation grew larger and larger. The tremendous expansion of the broiler business in particular, with large-scale credit extended by the feed companies, resulted in overexpansion of the industry and heavy losses to the companies and to the farmers. Many big chicken houses still stand empty in Western North Carolina as a monument to this overexpansion and excessive credit.

Fred Moffitt had started out with what seemed a large enterprise at that time—200 hens and 20 roosters. But he "went out" when the modern, large scale company-owned birds "came in." He understood that "Today a farmer must raise seven to ten thousand birds to make it."[3]

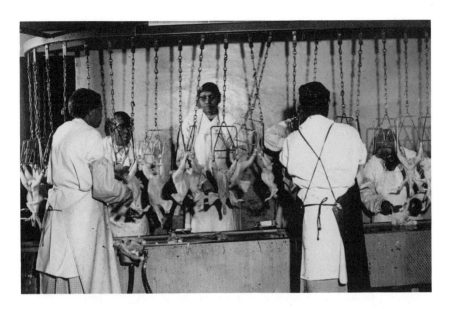

Farmers Federation poultry processing plant, built in 1948.

Jim McClure's dream of a poultry industry geared to raise the standards of living of the small farmer in the North Carolina mountains ran head on into the post-war drive of big business entering the agricultural field. His 1950 report in the Federation *News* reflects the way this development was beginning to affect business.

Perhaps the highlight of the year just passed, when we look back at it, will be the development of the broiler industry. This was an instance of turning a near disaster into a solid achievement. The baby chick business took a decided slump all during the fall of 1949, and early spring of 1950. Eggs dropped in price. No one wanted baby chicks. We even had to shut down the hatchery. Jack Gattis, the manager of the hatchery for some years, resigned and it took us some time to find his successor . . . There was no market for baby chicks. It takes a lot of broiler houses on farms to develop a broiler industry in any section. One of the chief obstacles to developing a broiler industry in our mountain section has been the individual farmers have had in financing broiler houses. It takes about one square foot per broiler, and you can readily see it's expensive to build a 5,000 square foot broiler house . . .

Instead of closing the hatchery, we decided to put on a real campaign to get out the broilers. If we closed the hatchery, our supply flocks would necessarily have no market and we would lose all that we have built up in the past few years . . .

We hope that this year, which has been so tough on the hatchery, will result in building a solid foundation for a great broiler industry in the mountains. Our hatchery is coming through the 12 months with a loss. This loss should be a permanent gain to the farm people of Western North Carolina because of the development of a real broiler industry.[4]

The "solid Foundation" crumbled four years later, in the summer of 1954, when disaster struck the Federation's poultry business. Within a six-month period, the market price for broilers dropped 29 percent, and egg prices dropped 34 percent. The Fund was forced to cover some of these unexpected losses, helping the Federation through a particularly rocky situation.

Jim was always proud of the multiplication factor by which the Federation increased the power of the contributor's dollar, but clearly from a business standpoint he had failed to create a self-sustaining poultry, turkey and egg industry in Western North Carolina.

The efforts by the Federation to provide freezer space through its territory faced a similar predicament. Jamie Clarke led the stock campaigns to provide capital for these freezer locker plants. Patrons would rent lockers to preserve their meats and vegetables for family use or for sale.

> The Farmers Federation has now in operation eight Frozen Food Locker plants. These plants offer a twofold opportunity for the mountain farmers, first to develop a frozen food industry in the mountains and second to develop a better diet through using the potential of the freezing process. Research and experiment should be carried on to see what fruits, vegetables and meats will best lend themselves to the development of a frozen food industry. For the second part of this program, every effort should be made to acquaint the mountain farmer with the possibilities of saving and of diet improvement made possible by the freezing process.[5]

Western North Carolina did not develop a significant frozen food industry for two reasons. First, large established food processing companies took control of this business. Second, soon after the freezer locker plants were built, home freezers came on the market. The entire project gradually became another drain on the resources of the Federation.

The Skyline Cooperative Dairy, a subsidiary of the Federation, was organized in order to return to the dairy farmer more of the profits he earned in his barn. Jim McClure had long been interested in the problems of the dairymen of Western North Carolina. Since the thirties, the Blue Ridge Milk Producer's Association had worked to secure fair prices and practices for dairymen from the commercial dairies in the area. In the Craggy section northwest of Asheville the Association owned a small processing plant, the Dairyman's Creamery. The objective of the association was to insure that other dairy plants that bought farmers' milk classified the milk fairly.

In 1946, the Federation merged with the Milk Producers' Association and took over the operation of the little Craggy plant. The new joint organization was called the Skyline Dairy Cooperative. Immediately, plans were drawn up and resources gathered to build a large plant, with the capacity to compete with the other processors in the region. The new facility was built on Tunnel Road, east of Asheville, and opened in August 1947.[6] Jim McClure provided the fanfare. He described the plant as:

> . . . fitted with the very latest and most modern equipment. The equipment that goes into a modern dairy plant is what might be called a mechanical miracle. Can washers, bottle washers, bottle fillers operate in an almost miraculous way. After this plant gets a little straightened out, we hope our members will all visit it. It was all night work for everyone the night the boys moved into this plant. We saw three of them drink 12 quarts of coffee for breakfast after this all-night job.[7]

Ten years later the Skyline Cooperative Dairy was still operating, but on a starvation diet of profit. The plant proved to be a heavy drain on the Federation's management and capital resources. Twice Jim McClure sent his assistant, Jamie Clarke, to run the dairy plant for several months to stop losses. Each time he managed to turn loss into profit. Competition of larger dairies was growing. After Jim's death Jamie Clarke arranged for the Federation to sell the plant to Coble Dairy Products Cooperative, which continued to provide a market for local dairy farmers.

Innovation was always the strong suit of the Farmers Federation, and Jim was now ready to use the research that had been carried out by E. Parmalee Prentice, at Mount Hope Farm in Williamstown, Massachusetts, to implement the first artificial breeding station in the Southeast. Prentice was a cousin of Elizabeth's, and the McClures had often visited his farm. He made the amazing discovery that the genes for increased milk production come not primarily from the cow, as had been supposed for hundreds of years, but from the bull. To be certain a bull had this property, the milk production of a number of his heifer calves must be compared with that of their dams. Once a bull's ability to transmit significantly higher milk production is established, he is called a "proven sire." Through the system of artificial insemination, such a bull could increase the milk production of a great number of cows. Another advantage of artificial insemination was that it eliminated the need for keeping a bull on individual dairy farms. Dairy bulls tend to be much more savage that those of the beef breeds and Jim knew many a dairy farmer who had been severely gored or even killed by his bull.

Parmalee Prentice was a brilliant man of unwavering principle. He discovered through painstaking research that some crossbred bulls, belonging to no recognized breed, might have the magic ability to transmit higher production. He then made up his mind that the entire system of dairy breeds was pointless and should be scrapped. The production of purebred dairy cattle was big business and his attack on the purebred principle infuriated breeders all over America so much that they discounted the whole idea of the proven sire.

Parmalee's son, Rockefeller Prentice ("Rocky" to his friends), appreciated

Southeastern Artificial Breeding Assoc., January 9, 1948. Left to right: George Lewis, herdsman holding Guernsey bull; Dr. Elliott, N.C. State College specialist in artificial insemination; Joe Wells, Buncombe County Inseminator; Riley Palmer, Buncombe County Farm Agent.

his father's remarkable discovery, but realized it could only be put into practice by working *with* rather than against the purebred breeders. He established a stud farm in Madison, Wisconsin, with purebred bulls of various established breeds who were also proven sires. His father was furious at what he considered a dilution of his scientific discovery by his own son, but Rocky persisted. Jim McClure had followed the situation, through both the son and his parents. When Rocky ran short of funds and his father refused to help him, Jim loaned him money to continue. (The loan came from a gift his mother, Mrs. Prentice, had given to the Educational and Development Fund!) In time Rocky would repay every penny to the Fund. After the war Jim visited the stud farm in Madison. He reported back to the Federation officers that it was a good operation. A month later, plans for the Southeastern Artificial Breeding Association were finalized. They included the installation of " . . . a battery of eighteen proven bulls, six registered Guernseys, six registered Holsteins and six registered Jerseys, on the farm owned by the Educational Fund . . . near the Fairview Warehouse of the Farmers Federation . . . [A] series of meetings is being held to develop county breeding rings. No bull will be placed in this stud unless it has been proven by the records of his daughters that this bull transmits high milk production."[8] Parmalee Prentice had recently died. Jim went straight up to see his widow, Alta Prentice, who was a sister of John D. Rockefeller, and suggested that this project would be a fitting memorial to her husband. She agreed, and the business was set up with her son Rocky in charge. Jim was thrilled with the results of his negotiations, and wrote to Hetty that "We built the Barn, Laboratory, sheds, etc. with Fund money which Alta had given—and then by a wonderful maneuver, we leased everything to J. Rockefeller Prentice trading as the Southeastern Artificial Breeding Association. Rocky operates the association. The standards are very high and it is the greatest thing that has happened in the Dairy industry in the South since the first cow was milked in 1760" (James G. K. McClure, Jr. to Harriet Stuart, February 1, 1948).

Jim's enthusiastic prediction proved to be true. At that time the average production of milk per cow in North Carolina was approximately 3,500 pounds a year. The bulls bought by the new stud farm had the capacity to transmit production of up to 10,000 pounds a year to their daughters. The Federation and the Fund promoted artificial breeding in Western North Carolina. Field men were sent into the barnyards to convince dairy farmers that the offspring from this system of breeding would have only one head and not over four legs. Many a stubborn mountain skeptic hung on to his pet bull rather than have his cows serviced with semen produced somewhere else. But Joe Wells of Leicester set a record by being the first association technician to breed 10,000 cows on the first breeding service, having first talked these farmers into trusting him. His work and that of others like him followed the efforts of Jim McClure and the Fund to pioneer in the South a procedure that has revolutionized the dairy industry. When the technology for frozen semen became practical in 1954, the American Breeders Service closed down the Fairview barn and the entire Southeast was served with semen shipped by air from bulls in Indianapolis.[9] By 1983, the average yearly milk production per cow in Western North Carolina was more than 14,000 lbs., quadruple the figure for 1950.

Jim had already helped to bring in burley tobacco, the leading cash crop in the mountains. Since 1930, when the first warehouse was built in Asheville for burley, it had been a dependable crop. Demand increased rapidly for tobacco products during and after World War II. As a result, the Federation opened up a second warehouse, and both of them were profitable operations set up to offer the farmer a place to sell where he could be sure of an honest settlement. "Bring the Children With You—They Will Want to Hear the Auctioneer IMPORTANT Do Not Sell Your Tobacco . . . to 'Pin-Hookers' on Your Way to the Warehouse. Display Your Tobacco on the Sales Floor and Get the Highest Possible Dollar." advised an ad in the Federation *News*.[10] In the parlance of the tobacco market, a colorful institution that still flourishes in Asheville, the "pinhooker" was a sly trader who would buy a man's tobacco from him so that he would not have to wait until the time of the auction for his money. Unscrupulous pinhookers were known to pull off a "hand" of tobacco here or there, drop it on the floor, and sweep them up together and sell them for some easy money. The other tobacco auctions often attracted patent medicine salesmen and other hucksters, and since the warehouses were usually cold, bottles of spirits were frequently passed from hand to hand. But Jim McClure made every effort to insure the honesty of the Federation warehouses, and many farmers traded there because of the organization's ethical reputation.

Those people who understand the intricacies of this market best remember Jim McClure above all for one accomplishment: bringing a second set of buyers to the Asheville market. Having two buyers from each of the tobacco companies put the Asheville market on an equal footing with its competitors in Eastern Tennessee. Two sets of buyers made it possible to have sales in two warehouses on the same day. This shortened the long lines of farmers' trucks waiting to be unloaded and made it possible for growers to get quick sales. Faster sales meant not only less waiting by the farmers, but also less chance for the perishable crop to dry out and change color while waiting in the warehouse. More tobacco sold in Asheville helped the banks, where the farmers deposited much of their cash; the local merchants, who made big sales during the tobacco marketing season at Christmas; and the warehousemen themselves. Jim worked for five years before the second buyers came to Asheville. In 1949, he enlisted North Carolina congressmen and senators for an all-out assault on the problem. He went to Washington to meet with Secretary of Agriculture Brannon, who promised to help out. When the latter failed to keep his word, Jim unloaded his frustrations in the Federation *News*. " . . . Mr. Brannon went off to South America before this assistance came through."[11] But Jim did not give up. He worked through individuals in the tobacco companies themselves. The 1954 market had been open just a few days when a second buyer from one company appeared, next day another and then the full set. Jim McClure's persistence had once again paid off handsomely for the mountain farmer.

The Federation was involved in mountain tobacco in two other ways as well. Each year, the Farmers Federation was designated by the federal government to administer the price support program for the Asheville, Boone and West Jefferson burley markets. If a man's tobacco failed to bring the minimum price set for each grade, the Farmers Federation, as the agent for the Commodity Credit Corporation, would purchase it at the support price. It was then dried and stored and later resold, hopefully when off-season prices had risen.[12] The second effort by the Federation was to promote the growing of Turkish aromatic tobacco, a high-priced imported variety that was suited to Western North Carolina. This crop was even more labor intensive than burley, because the leaves matured at different times and were much smaller. But the prices for Turkish tobacco were high, and farmers were not restricted by government allotments as to how much they could grow. The Fund hired field men to teach the mountain farmers how to cultivate this new crop, but in the end Turkish tobacco proved to be too much work for the return, a sign that the new economic opportunities in the mountains had raised the value of the farmer's own time.

Even though Turkish tobacco did not take hold in the mountains, it showed that Jim McClure was not allowing his imagination and drive to lapse with his increasing age. A more successful idea he implemented with Fund money was to develop a cut flower industry in Western North Carolina. He brought Charles Tillinghast, a Harvard horticultural graduate, down to experiment with large scale gladioli culture. Mr. Tillinghast helped prove that there was money to be made in the business, and gladioli have been grown in the mountains ever since.

For most farms, specialty crops would be the wave of the future. Large quantities of grain staples could be grown more cheaply in the Midwest, where the geography was more conducive to highly mechanized and capitalized farming. During the fifties, the average acreage cultivated by the American farmer skyrocketed, sending ripples of change down to Western North Carolina. At the same time, industrial jobs became more and more available throughout the region, and agriculture became more of an after work occupation than a source of principal livelihood for a family. The Farmers Federation, originally formed to devise ways to bring cash to the small independent farmer, increasingly found its traditional role undermined by the new economic world of post-war America. By the time of Jim McClure's death in 1956, his successor and son-in-law, Jamie Clarke, recognized the need to trim out many of the Federation's unprofitable operations, and three years later to find a merger partner to place the business in a viable financial position.

One facet of the Federation absorbed all of these changes in a much different way. Dumont Clarke continued to promote the Lord's Acre Movement, which after twenty years had now spread around the globe. In North Carolina, the new sources of wages increased the ability of church members to tithe cash rather than produce, and so Dumont added a new wrinkle known as the Lord's Hour to his program. Each worker was to pledge the first hour each week for his Creator, donating that money to his church. In reporting to the Federation stockholders at the annual meeting in 1951, Dumont expressed his belief that the work had "come of age."

> More churches than ever before took part in the Lord's Acre work in 1950. Reports have again come from Maine on the Atlantic to Oregon on the Pacific, with many fine ones in Western North Carolina . . .
>
> The Lord's Acre Movement . . . is bound to grow. The need for it has never been greater. It is becoming increasingly obvious that the only way to overcome the forces which are destroying moral and spiritual life is through a far more thorough Christian training. By this I mean training our church people, young and old, really to discipline themselves . . . for the fulfillment of every Christian duty . . .
>
> One of the most notable comments which was made last year was by the newly-elected head of one of the important denominations in America, who is also a missionary about to return to Africa. Upon working for hours with others harvesting a Lord's Acre field of potatoes in Farmers Federation territory, he said, "I go back to Africa, where I have spent the last 25 years as a missionary,

Top: *Lord's Acre Sunday School Project.* Bottom: *The Lord's Hour.*

with a new method and a new inspiration. The Lord's Acre will fit like a glove Africa's need for bringing Christ into all of life."[13]

In an era where fears of communism set the national tempo, the work of Dumont Clarke was seen as a constructive bulwark for freedom, democracy and Christianity. In 1949, "Progressive Farmer" magazine awarded him its highest honor, "The Man of the Year in North Carolina Agriculture." In 1951 he was both the "Rural Minister of the Year in North Carolina" and "Man of the Year in Service to Southern Agriculture." The venerable editor, Clarence Poe, who had written one of the books on which Jim based the Farmers Federation, wrote this about Dumont Clarke. "It is our hope that this "Man of the Year" recognition of the incalculable values of the Lord's Acre Movement, so long promoted by the man whom we now delight to honor, will cause many another Southern church to start a successful Lord's Acre plan in 1952."[14] In 1955, the twenty fifth anniversary of the Lord's Acre, Princeton University presented him with an honorary degree for his work. The two brothers-in-law, back in 1930, had dreamed of an organization that would breathe life into the rural church, raising a generation of men and women strengthened both by their rural upbringing and the Christian virtues. The hope was that as these people moved to towns or cities, or organized their own communities, the values implanted by the Lord's Acre program would be manifested in their new surroundings.

Dumont's son and Jim's daughter, Jamie and Elspeth, moved out to Hickory Nut Gap when they were released from the Navy in the Fall of 1945. Elspeth presented her father and mother with their first grandchild on December 3, 1946. Susie Skinner Clarke, named for Elizabeth's mother, was the first of eight children born to these two cousins. The sadness of the sudden death of Jamie's mother, Annie Clarke, came just three days after the joy of Susie's birth. Annie had been a cheerful and game helpmeet to Dumont, and her going left the big white house at 392 Charlotte Street very empty for Dumont and Monty, his older son, who worked at the Federation Garden Shop.

Elizabeth adored having the baby, Susie, in the house and described her as " . . . jolly and cute and good natured with a dimple in each cheek and very blue eyes" (Elizabeth Cramer McClure to Harriet McClure, February 12, 1947). In the spring Jamie and Elspeth moved into the house just across the garden, which Elizabeth had helped them design. The lumber was a gift from Hickory Nut Gap Farm.

During the winter of 1947 Jim had a hernia operation, his second, at the urging of his close friend Dr. Pinkney Herbert. While he was recovering, his ever generous sister Hetty sent along a check to cover all the medical expenses. He thanked her by replying:

> It is the established rule at the Mission Hospital that they will not let a patient go home until his bill is paid—
> Just as I was worrying myself into a relapse, as to how I could ever get out

of the Hospital, your air mail letter arrived this morning—as a consequence I have had the best day I have enjoyed at this hospital.

Hetty—it is a huge check—and you never should have done it. But it is such a welcome check—you just can't imagine. It is not only the immediate relief but the easing up for some weeks ahead, of Realizing that the horrible Bill is Paid. I had two operations and have had to have a nurse much longer than I expected, so my gratitude is very, very keen . . .

It now looks as if I might have to remain at the Hospital until Friday—I am tip top, but my age is not what it once was, and the Doc wants to take no chances— (James G. K. McClure, Jr. to Harriet Stuart, February 26, 1947)

Not long afterwards, Elizabeth too was laid up in the hospital. She had been in the attic, and was crossing a platform that bridged the stairway, her arms full of boxes, when she slipped. Elspeth found her mother in a heap at the bottom of the steep steps. Jim wrote to Hetty, "Darling Siddy had a bad fall on Weds the 21st, falling from the attic down those stairs, the result is that she is still in the Hospital with five cracked and broken ribs. Luckily Elspeth was in the house at the time . . . [T]here are no internal injuries, they say, and it is just a matter of time, but she has been very uncomfortable, because every move of any kind has been painful, even a cough or a laugh" (James G. K. McClure, Jr. to Harriet Stuart, February 11, 1948).

Again Hetty helped her brother with a check to cover the hospital expenses. Elizabeth's recovery was quite slow and painful, although the stoic in her rarely allowed the discomfort to pierce through to worry others. Hetty and Doug sent another check so that she could spruce up the farm for spring, to lift her spirits. The first check came to clean up the boxwood nursery. Mr. "Coon" Reed, a local Fairview favorite, was hired then and there to complete that chore. Then a second check arrived to redecorate the living room, a project Elizabeth had been pining to accomplish. "Siddy has already sent for samples—It is many long years since the living room was dressed up" (James G. K. McClure, Jr. to Harriet Stuart, April 5, 1948). Preparations were also underway for a second grandchild, due later in the summer. But in spring, Elizabeth had her flowers as the strongest tonic of all.

The Shorters, John and Mathilda, were slowing with age, but they remained at Hickory Nut Gap as beloved and devoted servants. Mathilda's health removed her from the kitchen post, a gastronomical disaster for the McClures, but John toiled faithfully on. Jim and Elizabeth employed a lively young woman with a fourteen-year-old daughter, Elzina and June Gibson, to take Mathilda's place. John Shorter kept up his daily round of chores, hand-milking the two cows down at the barn, weeding the various gardens, and repairing and mending in the workshop. His presence in the kitchen was so fixed that the table there was always referred to simply as "John's table." After milking, he would emerge from the dairy barn carrying the pails of steaming milk, and walk them up the hill to the spring house. He always wore big boots that were rarely tied, so that as he passed through the porch to the old kitchen he could slip them off and head for his table in stocking feet. Rev. David Huntley, a most deliberate and careful man, had taken over John's chauffeuring chores. He, too, was growing older, but remained a faithful member of the household.

The end of April 1948 loomed ahead as a particularly hectic time for the McClures. Elizabeth was still recovering from her attic fall of the past February, but she was not the kind to make any request to curtail their busy schedule. On May first, the newly created North Carolina Symphony was coming to Asheville for its spring concert. The idea of a state orchestra supported by both public and private funds was a novel one, and helped to give credence to the idea that North Carolina contained the South's most progressive citizenry. Jim stood behind the symphony with the resources of the Fund, his personal influence, most importantly, with his talent for "chex appeal." No one looked forward more to these performances than did Elizabeth, who had had her regular diet of fine music severely curtailed since moving to Western North Carolina. She knew the state symphony would be a new source of beauty for the people of North Carolina, a beauty that would be a curative balm to the routine frustrations and calamities that drained the spirit. The symphony came to play for the school children as well, so that this particular expression of divinity could become a natural part of their education. A dinner honoring the orchestra and its local supporters was largely a McClure arrangement, and was to be held that year on April 30, the night preceding the concert.

That same evening, two friends of Ambrose and Mary Cramer's were arriving at the Asheville railroad station. The new kitchen help, Elzina and June, had chosen this moment to take a vacation, and needed a ride to the bus station. So on the night of the symphony dinner, David Huntley drove Elzina and June, Elizabeth and her pregnant daughter Elspeth into Asheville from Hickory Nut Gap. The schedule was a bit tight, but there was never any hurry to Mr. Huntley. Once in town, Elspeth switched cars with her father to run June and Elzina on to the bus station, from whence she was to proceed down to the railroad station to meet her mother and pick up the Cramer friends. Then there was to be a big rush over to the symphony dinner. In all the hurry, Elspeth slid through a stop sign on her way to the station, and another car crashed into her.

Elizabeth, a stanch supporter of the "slow and easy" school of pregnancy, had her worst fears confirmed when news finally reached the station as to why her daughter was so delayed in meeting her. Elspeth was virtually unharmed after the impact, but Elizabeth found it difficult to suppress a growing anxiety about her prospective grandchild. Her own doctor had, after all, forbade motoring altogether when she was pregnant. Nevertheless, the plans for the evening were eventually carried out, and everyone returned to Hickory Nut Gap exhausted by all the excitement.

Early the next morning, with her help off on the bus jaunt, Elizabeth slipped out of bed to prepare breakfast for her brother's friends. She called Elspeth to see if she was quite all right, and then asked if Betty Huntley, who was helping on Saturdays with the baby, might come up to give the guests their breakfast trays. With characteristic sensitivity she did not want them to think she had gone to any trouble for them. Betty remembers that morning.

> . . . [W]hen I walked into the old kitchen door, she didn't say anything. I called to her, and I just turned around to hang up my sweater. I heard her come into the old kitchen, and when I turned around I saw something was wrong, and I understood her to say, "If I could just get the coffee." She made it back in the kitchen [where] she slumped over, and I caught her from behind around the waist. I laid her over the shelf until I could reach out my foot and pull a chair up.[15]

Jim was at that moment talking on the telephone, telling someone about Elspeth's accident. Betty hurried to tell him what had happened. He dropped the receiver and rushed to his wife's side. She was already unconscious and Betty ran down to the barn to tell John Shorter, who was milking the cows. He came hurrying up, as fast as an old man with his boot laces all untied can go. Jamie Clarke was bringing in the wood for a cheery breakfast fire. He dropped the wood and ran to the kitchen. They carried Elizabeth into the study and laid her on the sofa where Elspeth found her, and Mathilda, too, hurried up from her house. Dr. Herbert was out of town, and Dr. Charles Hensley rushed out to Fairview. Elizabeth never recovered consciousness and died before the ambulance arrived. She had suffered a cerebral hemorrhage that morning in her kitchen, leaving behind her husband and daughter quickly and painlessly.

Elizabeth Cramer McClure died on May first, the old festival day honoring the beauty of flowers and the mystery of creation. The grace with which she infused her life had nurtured Jim's talents for more than thirty years, just as his own exuberance continually stimulated her imagination. She balanced his impetuous bustle with her calm elegance, reminding him by her presence of the pursuit of excellence. She was never the stiff society girl, bound up by the rules and regulations of proper behavior, but nevertheless exhibited in her daily activities the spirit of grace that is the source of such a code. Her wisdom and humor, her perception and quest of beauty made her the sort of woman others are drawn to emulate. Her sudden death was a dreadful shock for Jim.

He and Elspeth went into the dining room to make plans. Both of them agreed that she should be buried nearby, because they could not bear to have her grave far off in Lake Forest. The immediate family had to be contacted. Hetty and Doug left Chicago almost immediately. They offered to purchase the stone and the plot for Elizabeth, which they did. Rocky Prentice and his wife Abby drove all night to reach the farm. Hickory Nut Gap soon filled with friends and admirers of Elizabeth. Her friends in the Garden Club made a blanket of laurel in bloom for the casket. The funeral ceremonies were the celebration of the accumulated wealth of one woman's friendships, and her legacy of excellence.

A flood of letters poured into Hickory Nut Gap, and Jim and Elspeth waded into the mountain of replies by trying to describe the qualities that had filled Elizabeth's life. Jim wrote many variations of a letter that went like this:

> Elspie and I thank you from the bottom of our hearts for your kind message of sympathy. Your letter brings comfort and strength to us.
> Elizabeth enlarged our lives with her radiant personality, and opened our minds to the sources of beauty in the life around us. She had the extraordinary quality of somehow creating life and warmth wherever she went. She lived with no retarding thought of self. She lived with such freshness and faith and gaiety that unconsciously she added to the world's store of courage and stead-fastness. What she was and is bears witness to a goodness in life that enriches it forever.
> We have been wonderfully blessed by her life and will strive to go forward as she would have us . . . (James G. K. McClure, Jr., May 28, 1948)

Going forward had always been Jim's reaction to adversity, but after thirty-two years of marriage, being suddenly without Elizabeth's counsel and without her eagerness to hear about his daily adventures, the readjustment in his life was overwhelming. Elspeth and Jamie moved across the garden to the big house the day the last relatives left, to do whatever they could to keep the place going. New life continued to replace the old. In August, Elspeth had a son, James Gore King McClure Clarke. If the name was a bit cumbersome, it nonetheless honored the memory of a distinguished line of men.

The momentum of Jim's life kept him busy. He remained the president of the Farmers Federation, continuing to travel north each year on behalf of the Educational and Development Fund. At home he was asked to come on one committee after another. Mrs. Edward Dameron, a remarkably capable woman who had been an executive at Lord and Taylor in New York, had come to Asheville, and Jim hired her on as a public relations assistant. For many years following she was a tremendous help to Jim and later to Jamie Clarke.

In 1949, at the request of Governor Kerr Scott, Jim served as Western North Carolina Chairman for passage of a $20 million State Bond issue for construction of rural roads. The bond issue passed largely due to the big majority it received in the Western counties. Although Jim was a lifelong Republican, Democratic leaders frequently turned to him for help.

The same year, the Buncombe County Commissioners asked him to serve as Chairman of a Citizens Committee for Better Schools. The challenge was enormous. Ever since the bankruptcy of the county in 1930, school construction had practically come to a halt. In twenty-two years, only one new school had been built. Since the county essentially dropped its financial responsibilities for capital improvements for schools, many local groups had tried to raise money on their own. The result was a patchwork quilt of tax districts. The school buildings themselves, for the most part, were crumbling edifices under the control of highly partisan local committees, which exercised the primary powers of hiring and firing personnel. The results were predictable. More often than not, bitter factions had grown up vying for control of the school and its patronage jobs. Teachers and principals, even janitors and cooks, were necessarily caught up in the rivalry and forced to bend to the arbitrary rules of these committees, or lose their jobs. In 1949, these schools, often with obsolete structures and poorly qualified personnel, were poised on the edge of the greatest influx of children the county had ever witnessed, the post-war baby boom. The tasks of public education were enormous, but first the in-fighting had to be curtailed to permit constructive planning.

With characteristic thoroughness, Jim McClure became absorbed with the subject of public education. He delivered his Pen and Plate Club paper that year on the subject, "A Look at the Public Schools of the United States." He began by tracing the national passion for education back to its colonial roots, and then challenged his listeners to a new vision of the scope of public education. "It may be that character education is more important than intellectual education . . ." he said. "Almost nothing is being done along the line of character education. There are reservoirs of human strength which, it seems to me, are practically untapped by our educational system. The driving force which is generated by dedication to a purpose is something that we have hardly commenced to get hold of in our educational system. The development of character and purpose and initiative have been scarcely touched."[16] Although Jim went to work to build school buildings, he never lost sight of the ideals and purpose of education. His Citizens' Committee was formed to study the needs of the Buncombe County Schools. He conscientiously sifted through the muddle of school districts and financing schemes. His committee resolved unanimously to attack the most glaring problems facing local public education. He announced in his report that the county should assume all of the outstanding debts in the various school districts and establish a uniform county-wide tax rate to pay off this indebtedness, and that the citizens of Buncombe county should be offered the chance to vote in a five and one-half million dollar bond issue for immediate construction. With one bold stroke, the county could reassert its authority over the schools, face the expansion that was imminent and place the school system on a firm and progressive financial base. But would the voters back such a plan?

"Debt" was a word laden with anxieties to the generation who had grown up during the thirties, as was the notion of increasing the public debt in a county that was still trying to pay for its failure of 1930. The consolidation of all the high school students into six schools meant the loss of the older students to numerous local all grade schools. Shifting community identity would be a severe jolt to Buncombe's citizens. Opposition to the Citizens' Committee was fierce. and the political contest created its share of rancor. The "no" crowd had only to conjure up the old fears. But new schools were desperately needed, and the PTA, the League of Women Voters, local industries, and the educational community all pulled together with the Citizens' Committee to win the vote.

The Asheville morning paper reported that:

The Challenge Is Met

> By a decisive margin Buncombe County has voted in a new day for public education—a new day of safe and sound buildings, more room for more children and more teachers, school equipment which will equalize opportunity for every child in Asheville and Buncombe.
>
> This is what the consolidation of the debt and the approval of the $5.5 million bond issue mean . . .
>
> From the very beginning the Citizens' Committee for Better Schools kept faith with this undertaking. Representative citizens worked long months . . . on a plan which would be submitted to the voters. No two men worked harder than Mr. J. G. K. McClure, the chairman, and State Senator Frank M. Parker. When they became convinced of the worthiness of the program they carried their convictions to the people in countless forums and in tireless measure. They . . . are owed a debt of gratitude by the people of Buncombe.[17]

The campaign in Buncombe County received wide attention across the country, because nearly every American community faced the same demographic circumstances. As the result of his victory, Jim McClure was invited to join the National Citizens Commission for Public Schools. This group published a booklet entitled "How Can Citizens Help Their Schools?" In it the committee chose to describe the tactics Jim had employed in Buncombe County, right down to the PTA parade the day before the election.

After the election was over, Jim kept the fire hot. The Citizens' Committee was made permanent, and invited ninety-two additional people to join it. He wanted to maintain the progressive momentum that he had helped to build up. The numerous members were divided up into committees, such as special education, visual and audio-visual aids, spiritual emphasis and character building, health, corrective speech, and recreation. As the direct result of all of these efforts, Asheville was named one of eleven All-American Cities for 1951, for its example of "citizen teamwork in government." The presentation of the award swelled local pride, and 3,000 people were on hand for the ceremony in the city auditorium. Jim McClure really enjoyed a good fight, and rarely in his life was the public acclaim so resounding. Roy Larsen, the president of Time, Inc. and the chairman of the National Citizens Commission for the Public Schools, came to present the award. He admitted in his speech that the visit was also " . . . an opportunity . . . to visit another man whom I have long admired and have had the privilege of working with for several years, your Chairman, Jim McClure."[18]

Jim could count many such friendships, and in a real sense the work of his life was his friends. From his earliest days in theological school, he knew he possessed a rare gift of influence, and felt the best use of this gift would be to draw people together to pursue worthwhile goals. As a leader, he would define the purposes, design a promotional appeal, and then seek out the most influential or "strongest" men and women, as he liked to put it, to carry out the plan. Whether it was building a warehouse in Clay County, or raising money in New

York, he built his work on the basis of friendships. These relationships were important to him, and he worked hard to keep them sincere. Each of his efforts was built up by a sense of camaraderie not unlike the *esprit de corps* he admired in a successful athletic team. To him, success was the result of the spiritual sense of unity that develops in a group of people who have a shared purpose. Jim lived for that sweet emotion of shared victory after the struggle that comes when men and women are committed to each other to endure and win.

In 1954, Jim McClure turned seventy. The same year, one of his oldest friends and supporters, Thomas J. Watson, turned eighty. Jim's letter to him on that occasion reveals this sense of friendship.

Dear Tom:
Your 80th birthday presents an opportunity to me to tell you how much your 80 years has meant to the world and to me personally. The world is a better place because you have lived in it, and I personally have tried to be a better man because of the inspiration of your life.

At all times and everywhere you have eternally kept on striving to improve the material and the spiritual condition of mankind. You have done this in a big and organized way, and at the same time in a remarkable way you have kept a constant realization of the individual needs of thousands of people whom you know. Your influence has always been for good. You have carried your immense responsibilities and burdens lightly, and at all times have added a creative touch for the solution of any problem presented to you.

Your leadership has brought blessings in many, many different fields. I just want to point out that your willingness to back up and sponsor our movement here in the Blue Ridge Mountains of North Carolina has brought a new power of accomplishment and a new strength of purpose to thousands of mountain people whom you have never seen and whom you do not know. This is the kind of contribution which you have made in many areas.

Your generous, creative, staunch life has added to the reservoir of good in the world and helped lift mankind to a higher level.

I send you my warmest congratulations on your 80th birthday. (James G. K. McClure, Jr. to Thomas J. Watson, February 2, 1954)

In Tom Watson's simple reply, one senses the importance of friendship in the methods of Jim McClure.

Dear Jim:
Your deeply touching and cordial letter on the occasion of my eightieth birthday helped to make the day a very pleasant one, and I send my best thanks to you for this thoughtful expression of your friendship.

Your letter prompted many happy memories of our friendship during the past 30 years and the many pleasures which this friendship has brought to the members of the Watson family.

Yours has been a life of Christian endeavor which has benefitted countless numbers of people. In the unselfish devotion you have given to the cause of underprivileged peoples, you have erected a monument which will stand for all time.

The members of the Watson family are grateful for your friendship and we join in sending you our affection and warmest wishes. (Thomas J. Watson to James G. K. McClure, Jr., March 8, 1954)

Jim's new status as a widower, a very charming and handsome one at that, made him a much sought-after companion. There are never enough widowers to go around and Jim enjoyed the close friendship of several women. Elizabeth Izard, a lovely woman and a longtime family friend, understood and appreciated the people of the mountains as he did. She arranged for the Federation's Handicraft Department to be largely taken over by the Biltmore Country Market, which she had founded with the help of other members of the French Broad River Garden Club. This business brought together talented mountain women, standards of high quality, and a successful marketing outlet.

Helen McDonald, in New York, had helped generously in the work of the Fund. As Jamie Clarke was able to take over more of the day-to-day operations of the Federation Jim had a little more time for vacations, and Helen enticed him down to the Bahamas several times. Peggy Hitchcock, widow of the noted polo player Tommy Hitchcock, was another friend with whom Jim had great fun. Once he visited her at Beaumaris in Canada, and they drove down to visit the American Ambassador in Ottawa—the Honorable Douglas Stuart and his wife, Harriet. Jim was very proud of the recognition given to his brother-in-law, and the way his sister managed her new responsibilities.

Both Helen McDonald and Peggy Hitchcock visited Hickory Nut Gap Farm and attended Federation Picnics. They were good sports travelling in crowded cars with Elspeth and the children, and riding the farm horses.

Occasionally Jim had to dodge an admirer. The summer after Elizabeth's death Harriet and Doug Stuart invited him to go on a European trip. They looked up a Belgian lady who had been kind to their son Bob during the war. She was reported to be enormously wealthy and Jim thought she might be a prospect for the Fund. He turned on the charm and Madame DuBosque took a great fancy to him. Before long she turned up in America and came to visit "Jeem" on his farm. A dark, striking woman, she wore rustling black taffeta, cinched at the waist by a money belt. Jim drove her around to see the Federation enterprises, always taking care to have Jamie's brother, Monty, accompany them as chaperone. Whenever Mr. Dave Snelson, a director from Leicester, saw Jim after that he would mockingly drawl, "How's that Belgian woman?"[19]

Jim had intended in his life to forgo the pleasures of wealth, and he was left in his last years with only a small salary from the Federation and the Fund. Elizabeth's inheritance had begun to pay dividends, but this money was willed to Elspeth and she used it to keep house at Hickory Nut Gap. Doug and Hetty Stuart, understanding the situation, sent him a monthly check to help defray his personal expenses. He confided to Jamie Clarke that he gave this money regularly to the Federation to reimburse the cooperative for a loss its hatchery had sustained in a disputed settlement with the Quaker Oats Company relating to diseased hatching eggs. Of course Doug and Hetty had no idea that he was doing this. Doug Stuart always remained a loyal friend and after Jim's death he made a generous addition to the Lord's Acre endowment. Jim's letters arrived frequently in Lake Forest full of tales of mountain life, to be savored by the Stuarts. "We have a skunk under the house and the country people tell us that when a skunk takes up with you under the house—no one in the house has a cold. For that reason we are debating whether to try and trap him or keep him, and all at the moment favor being hospitable to our winter visitor" (James G. K. McClure, Jr. to the Stuarts, February 18, 1954).

The redoubtable Dottie Settles (Clinard's sister) had returned after many years away to manage the kitchen at Hickory Nut Gap, and her husband Claude Hall took over many chores that John Shorter could no longer perform. Dottie and Claude approved of the skunk. They had once kept a deodorized pet skunk in their house, and loved all their animals—dogs, cats and goats. But they loved Elspeth and Jamie's children, too, and put their best efforts into entertaining guests at Hickory Nut Gap.

Jim's public life remained full and varied during these last years. He wrote, "Yesterday we had our 17th picnic and last county picnic of the season— Tomorrow we have an employees' supper and picnic—This is employees & families and last year over 700 turned up. Then Tuesday a chicken supper for the school principals & their families & then we are through our schedule" (James G. K. McClure, Jr. to the Stuarts, August 15, 1954). Each fall, in cooperation with the North Carolina Extension Service, Jim hosted a 100 Bushel Corn Luncheon for the most successful corn growers in Western North Carolina. The next month he was entertaining a large crowd at the Waldorf Astoria farmer's picnic.

> . . . [A]t the moment we have 104 tables reserved so it looks like 900–1000 people. Also we decided to have a Picnic at Philadelphia as the Fiddlers will come up that way—so on Friday, Nov. 10 we have the Philadelphia Picnic at the Barclay Hotel and that appears to be a sell out—all this is a lot of trouble to raise some money, but since I have no alumni it seems about the only way . . . Marjorie Lloyd-Smith has suddenly decided to get a pony and give it as a floor prize. (James G. K. McClure, Jr. to Harriet Stuart, October 29, 1950)

In the meantime his daughter's progeny had increased to five, two girls and three boys. Susie, nine, and little Jim, eight, were special allies of their grandfather. All these children kept Hickory Nut Gap lively, and Jim enjoyed teaching the two oldest to ride horseback. Though he was now seventy, he urged Jamie and Elspeth to take a January trip to England and Scotland, just the two of them. He volunteered to look after the children, with Mathilda and John's faithful help. He gloated about his success to Hetty. "I had the greatest luck with the children. They kept well the whole time—25 days times 5 children—125 child days and not a sniffle!" (James G. K. McClure, Jr. to Harriet Stuart, January 31, 1955). As these children grew older the McClure era of Hickory Nut Gap

MERRY CHRISTMAS AND BEST WISHES FOR THE NEW YEAR

Top: *100 bushel corn lunch, 1956.* Bottom: *Family Christmas card, 1953. Left to right: Jim, Annie, Jim McClure; Dumont, Elspeth, Susie and Jamie Clarke.*

began to fade away. No one single man epitomized the old order more than
John Shorter. It was during the summer of 1955 that his enlarged heart finally
gave out.

> John Shorter died last Thursday afternoon, passing away peacefully with
> no pain after a heart attack about noon. Fortunately—Elspie called me—and I
> got home about a half hour before he died. The funeral was Sunday afternoon
> at 2 o'clock and what a funeral: Preacher Huntley made an extra good talk. I
> paid a tribute to John, as you know he was the finest kind of man—honest
> through & through—no short cuts—kind, good—all Christlike qualities—the
> little church was jammed with colored and white—It was very touching—John
> had been with us 39 years. (James G. K. McClure, Jr. to Harriet Stuart, June
> 22, 1955)

Earlier that spring Jim had made the decision to slow down a little himself,
and one afternoon in May he started home early to go for a ride with his
granddaughter, Susie. On the way, he thought he must have dozed off for a
minute. Whatever the cause, his car ran off the road, and although it did not
overturn it struck a boulder with such violence that some vertebrae in Jim's
back were broken. Dr. Herbert put him in a cast from his hips to his neck. In
the hospital Jim confided to Elspeth that Dr. Herbert had found a weakness in
his heart years before, when Jim was in his thirties, and had advised him then
to slow *way* down and take care of himself. Even now, in his cast, Jim hardly
slowed down. He insisted on attending all the picnics, only conceding the
afternoon program to Jamie Clarke so that he could rest half the day. Betty
Huntley, his secretary, drove him to and from the picnics and remembers how
painful the curving mountain roads were for him. In the fall he went north on
his campaign and raised the largest total ever, with some help from Jamie
Clarke. The Educational and Development Fund was now well endowed.

Back home for Christmas with the family, Elspeth was expecting a sixth
child, and early in January the doctor told her it would be twins. This news
considerably startled the prospective parents and they decided to keep it a secret
from all but the family until the safe arrival of the babies. A few days before the
due date Elspeth went to Asheville to buy some last supplies. Every other person
she met exclaimed about the expected twins! The news was too exciting for Jim
to keep! He loved to tell people that Elspeth and Jamie had moved in to keep
him company and now he "was hanging on by his eyelashes!"[20]

Ambrose and William ("Bobo and Billy") did arrive safely, brown eyed,
healthy and identical. Jim went off to the Bahamas, minus his brace, and
returned refreshed to a new round of meetings. Luther Hodges, the governor of
North Carolina, was coming to address the annual Federation stockholders meeting and Jim was putting on a dinner for him afterwards. The big yearly meeting
of the Citizen's Committee for Better Schools soon followed. Then Jim went
to New York to attend a dinner given by Arthur Page, for so many years
Chairman of the Trustees of the Educational and Development Fund, for the

"people he worked for." When Mr. Page had retired from the Bell Telephone Company, he had opened a consulting office and many famous people availed themselves of his remarkable wisdom. This was Jim's last trip. When he returned to North Carolina it was Dumont Clarke who first noticed that there was something different—something wrong with him. He sent out the alarm to Hetty.

> My dear Harriet:
> You will wish to know this, I am sure . . . Jim has been looking badly; especially following his recent visit to New York and to you in Canada (although he has since received some very encouraging contributions . . . his condition seems *physical* rather than one of mental anxiety).
> He had planned to go to the Mission Hospital for his third operation for hernia on this Wednesday the 9th, but he has come down with a rather severe case of bronchitis and was sent to the hospital this morning. It looks as though he would be there—recovering from his operation till the 26th or 28th [of May]. We are much concerned for him, and trust that he will regain a full measure of strength. (Dumont Clarke to Harriet Stuart, May 7, 1956)

A week later, Dumont's prognosis was even more discouraging.

> Dear Harriet:
> This is strictly confidential so far as Asheville people, or others outside of the family are concerned. I saw Jim this morning for one minute with regard to a possible successor. He looks very badly. His vision is blurred. He can speak only with great difficulty. Notwithstanding this, Elspie says that Dr. Crow states that Jim's heart is in "good" condition. I think you will wish to know this, and to be kept posted. (Dumont Clarke to Harriet Stuart, May 14, 1956)

Jim suffered a series of small strokes on the following day at the hospital. Elspeth spent all possible time with him and loyal friends, among them Elizabeth Izard, Mr. H.A. Haseltine, principal of a private school, and Claude Hall from the farm, came to read to him. Harriet and Doug Stuart hurried down to see him after Dumont's second letter. Everyone tried to keep up an optimistic front but Jim was failing fast. As his heart wound down, he slowly lost the remarkable powers of his personality, those powers which he had used to faithfully serve his Creator and to build up a whole region in a way that emphasized the highest spiritual values.

Jamie Clarke took his three oldest children to Riverdale, New York, for the exciting wedding of his father, Dumont, to Elizabeth Dodge Huntington, a friend from his youth, whose husband had died some years before. Just after Jamie returned Jim McClure died, June 6, 1956. Dumont and his bride, honeymooning in Maine, hurried south so that he could conduct the funeral service in the Presbyterian church in Asheville, attended by throngs of people from all over Western North Carolina. His death was a shock. He had always seemed younger than his years.

Jamie Clarke was elected president by the Directors of the Federation and wrote in the *News:*

> Mr. McClure spent his life in building the Farmers Federation. It was his single-minded devotion to the interests of the Federation which, more than any other one factor, was responsible for its growth and the wide range of its help to the people of the mountains.
>
> The great message he would leave with us—leave to employees, directors, members and patrons—is to carry the Farmers Federation forward . . . "Others have labored, and ye have entered into their labors."[21]

An editorial in the Asheville *Times* concluded by proclaiming, "All who were privileged to know Mr. McClure honor and mourn him today for his many great achievements and for his noble character."[22]

These statements were public acknowledgements of the devotion of Jim to the good works of citizenship. But the real mourning took place in the hearts of many people, of all social standings: black, Cherokee, mountaineer, and privileged, who counted Jim as their friend. One of the latter, Charles Goodyear, sent this eloquent testimony to Hickory Nut Gap on hearing of the death of a very old friend.

> When Jamie's telegram was received Sunday afternoon it was such a shock that it is still hard for me to realize that Jim is no longer here. That is because he was such a definite personality and meant so much to me. I have lost my best and dearest friend whom I have known for half a century.
>
> Jim and I not only had many happy times together, beginning when we were roommates at Yale, but he always was such a help to me as he was to others during times of trouble. *I never knew a more loyal friend. He was tolerant of the frailties of others. He never made it obvious that his character and Christian life had influence on so many people. I have often said that Jim was my ideal of a true Christian.* (Italics in original) (Charles Goodyear to Elspeth Clarke, June 19, 1956)

Jim's character had been developing through his nearly seventy-two years on earth. That character and its power to influence other people is what Jim always meant when he complimented others for building up the stores of courage within the human community. Character is achieved through personal struggle, and Jim had won this spiritual battle. As Jim had said of others, he, too, built up the stores of courage within the human community. But he would have been the first to admit that the strengths of his own family, the Dixons, the McClures, and most of all the influence of Elizabeth were all greatly responsible for whatever he might have accomplished. He hoped to pass on to others in his family and community the historic strengths he had inherited and that had so inspired his own life. Jim McClure always believed men and women should be judged by how they managed their own birthrights, and whether they had, in the accounting procedures of life, accumulated or squandered the spiritual resources given freely by the grace of Almighty God. Death is never a neat, clean separation from life, and with Jim many loose ends and emotional connections were rudely severed, but in the larger matters of his own conscience, the peace of Jim McClure's death reflected the victory of his life.

1. James G. K. McClure, Jr., "A Great Program Ahead," Farmers Federation *News,* August 1946, p. 6.

2. Minute book of the Farmers Federation Educational and Development Fund, May 10, 1948, p. 72.

3. Interview with Mr. Fred Moffitt.

4. James G. K. McClure, Jr., "The Farmers Federation's 30th Year," Farmers Federation *News,* August 1950, p. 5.

5. Minutes of the Fund, December 12, 1949, p. 4–5.

6. James G. K. McClure, Jr., "The Farmers Federation's 26th Year," Farmers Federation *News,* August 1946, p. 10.

7. James G. K. McClure, Jr., "News from the Front," Farmers Federation *News,* September 1947, p. 4.

8. Minutes of the Farmers Federation, August 7, 1947, p. 210.

9. James G. K. McClure, Jr., "News from the Front," Farmers Federation *News,* April 1954, p. 3.

10. Advertisement in the Farmers Federation *News,* December 1955.

11. James G. K. McClure, Jr., "News from the Front," Farmers Federation *News,* December 1950, p. 3.

12. James G. K. McClure, Jr., "News from the Front," Farmers Federation *News,* December 1954, p. 3.

13. Dumont Clarke, presentation made at the annual meeting of the Farmers Federation, Farmers Federation minutes, March 31, 1951.

14. Clarence Poe, "Clarke is Recognized for Lord's Acre Work," February 1952, p. 23, quoted from "The Progressive Farmer," January, 1952.

15. Interview with Mrs. Betty Huntley Beard.

16. James G. K. McClure, Jr., "A Look at the Public Schools of the United States," speech given at the Pen and Plate Club, Asheville, NC, August 18, 1949.

17. Asheville *Citizen,* April 20, 1950.

18. Roy Larsen, "The Importance of Schools to a Community," speech given in Asheville, NC, April 3, 1952, reprinted in pamphlet form.

19. Interviews with Elspeth McClure Clarke.

20. *Ibid.*

21. James McClure Clarke, "News from the Front," Farmers Federation *News,* July, 1956, p. 3.

22. Editorial, Asheville *Times,* June 18, 1956.

Epilogue

The Shorters, the Huntleys, the Davidsons, along with the McAbees, the Boones and the Riddles no longer inhabit the cottages of Hickory Nut Gap Farm. Their children and grandchildren live in a vastly different world, where the opportunities for making money, for spending it, for entertainment and education divide the generations from one another. Few of them farm, except on the side, although most retain a fascination for the soil, hoeing faithfully during the hot summer months between their rows of corn and beans.

The Farmers Federation died with the passing of the age. The patient remained terminally ill into the sixties, generating in its weakening condition a fair share of vindictive hatred. It was not a painless death. But the passing of the Federation was a victory. The dream of Jim McClure had been fulfilled. There was no need for the farmers to band together for survival anymore. He had helped steer an entire region through the rocky straits of underdevelopment into the larger waters of economic integration with the nation. His efforts helped to transform Western North Carolina almost painlessly from one economy to another, a remarkable sociological case study. Jim McClure appreciated the traditional culture while building for progress, and that, simply put, was the secret of his success.

When I talk with the grandsons and granddaughters of Federation members, most tell of a sense of nostalgia for the old ways described by their grandparents, but most are realistic enough not to miss the drudgery and poverty that were endemic to that life. The federal government and the private business sector have worked together to create favorable conditions for the hundreds of manufacturing plants that are scattered now throughout the old Federation territory. The Appalachian Regional Commission has financed a fine system of roads that has ended, finally, the isolation of Western North Carolina. Federal money has helped to build the water and sewer systems that are a prerequisite to industrialization. American businessmen have discovered that the "independent" mountaineer can be as fine a workman as there is anywhere in the country. The Southeastern United States has enjoyed the benefits of a rapidly burgeoning economy since the early sixties, and this time the Southern Appalachians were not left out. So, for better and for worse, the American cultural heroes of sports and television, fast foods, and consumerism are found as readily in the mountains of North Carolina as they are in Southern California.

All of these factors contributed to the cause of death for the Farmers Federation. With the passing of Jim McClure in 1956, Jamie Clarke was elected president by the directors. He was determined to place the Federation on a sound financial foundation. He began to prune out unprofitable enterprises, trying to discover a mix that could save the business. He continued to go north each year, and succeeded in getting contributions for the Educational and Development Fund. He knew, though, that the Federation had to be weaned from its dependence on contributions. For the cooperative to survive into the future, it would have to be built on the same business values as any other commercial organization. The spirit of desperation that had pushed his uncle in 1920 into forming a cooperative was now gone, and with it the values of self-sacrifice and unity.

There were other problems for the new president as well. With the death of Jim McClure, the founder and president for thirty-six years, management infighting broke out. Some of the older employees had hoped that they might be promoted to the top, and so resented Jamie Clarke's new stature. There were rumors of contrary death bed commitments from Jim McClure, which made the rounds of the Federation's central office. These festering resentments helped to sap the creativity of the management during these last years, just when the challenge for survival was greatest. In June of 1957, Guy Sales resigned as the General Manager. He had worked for the Federation almost from its birth. He had been a tireless taskmaster under Jim McClure, emphasizing always the need to tighten up the business practices of the cooperative. Much of the success over all of these years can be attributed to the daily efforts of Guy Sales. Charles W. Davis assumed the position of General Manager. He was an outstanding poultry farmer who had been involved with the Federation for about twenty years. He became a capable manager, and remained loyal to Jamie Clarke throughout all the troubles ahead.[1]

The foundation of these troubles was economic. After World War II, agriculture began to decline in comparative importance with other livelihoods in Western North Carolina. What serious farming remained tended to become more specialized. Many growers of single crops organized their own cooperatives, such as the tomato growers and the apple growers. The Federation had always been willing to sell or market nearly anything, but increasingly specialized competition was growing up and beating them out. These trends were at the same time the fulfillment of the goals of the Farmers Federation and the reason for its demise.

Jamie Clarke spelled out the problems of the Federation in the Farmers Federation *News* in February 1959.

> For some time, there has been apparent a rapid trend toward bigness of agriculture. The growth of the broiler business has been accompanied by large-scale financing and the process called "vertical integration" whereby large companies own their own feed mills, hatcheries, and poultry dressing plants, and finance all broiler and turkey flocks and often hogs and cattle in the field . . .
> Your company has been troubled for some time by lack of operating capital and increasing competition from all sides. We are also hampered by the condi-

tion of the freezer locker and poultry business, both of which have become
impossible for us to carry on.

Furthermore, we are at a competitive disadvantage-because we do not own
an adequate feed mill or fertilizer mill.

The difficulty about this is that the record of the Federation's earnings over
the past 15 years is not good enough to justify . . . borrowing.

We know of no banking institution which would lend . . . to us.[2]

The profits squeeze exacerbated management infighting. Jamie Clarke
wanted to implement a satisfactory pension plan for the workers, but was unable
to do so as long as business suffered. By 1959, he and a majority of the directors
decided bold action was imperative, that the Federation needed a merger partner
in order to survive. The Farmers Cooperative Exchange (FCX), a much larger
North Carolina Agricultural Cooperative, was interested in expanding into the
western end of the state. Negotiations between the Federation and FCX were
completed early in 1959, and then the fate of the Federation rested with the will
of some 7500 stockholders.

Under the laws of North Carolina, a vote to dissolve the Farmers Federation
had to be conducted differently from the Rochdale plan of one man, one vote.
Each stockholder, both holders of common stock and preferred stock, held one
vote for each share he or she owned. In order for the Federation-FCX merger
to be completed, a favorable two-thirds vote of the shares was required. Opponents to the plan had only to persuade the owners of one-third of the stock to
vote nay or not to vote at all. A stockholders meeting was scheduled for February 26, 1959, in a Buncombe County courtroom. For six weeks, the plan was
discussed (and cussed!) throughout the coves and hollows of Western North
Carolina. Opposition to the proposal centered around a group of management
personnel dubbed "the upstairs gang" by General Manager Charlie Davis (a
Clarke ally).[3] This group was led by Joseph Higdon, manager of the central
office; Katherine Bach, his secretary; and 0. J. Holler, a director of long standing from Rutherford County. Mr. Holler probably felt disgruntled after being
passed over for the presidency when Jim McClure died. No doubt the jealousies
within the management helped to fuel what became a rancorous battle over this
issue. Unquestionably, many of these men and women thought they might lose
their jobs if the Federation merged with FCX, and they could look forward to
almost no pension for their long years of work.

The "upstairs gang" staged a series of meetings throughout the Federation's
territory, lining up farmers to vote against the merger. They accused Jamie
Clarke and the other proponents of the plan of mismanagement and duplicitous
dealings, while hinting at enormous payoffs from FCX. They exploited the fact
that the owners of common stock would receive FCX stock " . . . only after all
monies due the Federation are collected and all debts paid and would probably
lose some money," while preferred stockholders would receive equal 10-year
four percent debentures in FCX dollar for dollar."[4] These preferred stocks had

been purchased at a premium, with the legal requirement that the owners would have first access to the assets of the cooperative.

By February 26, the emotions surrounding the issue precluded any real dialogue. A last-minute shift from the courthouse to the city auditorium due to the unexpectedly large turnout (about 350 stockholders attended) left groups muttering on the courthouse steps, "declaring the last-minute change in location disqualified the Auditorium session altogether."[5] The following account of the meeting is taken from an article by reporter Doug Reed of the Asheville *Citizen*.

> The meeting was opened by the Rev. Jack Waldrep who asked that there be "no discussion out of prejudice and temper." The meeting thereafter rapidly proceeded into both realms . . .
>
> [The Federation directors] heard themselves branded a "rubber stamp" board that did the bidding of administrative officers . . .
>
> The furious opposition to the sale, charging large scale mismanagement and a "sell-out" to FCX, burst into flame as soon as the meeting was called to order . . .
>
> The gathering was, in some respects, much like the famed Federation picnics where everybody had his say. There was no band, but it is unlikely it would have found a harmonious note to strike in an air thick with accusations.
>
> With Higdon and Attorney Henry C. Fisher bringing sharp rebuke to Federation President Clarke for attempting to limit each speaker to five minutes talking time, a floor motion overwhelmingly granted Fisher all the time he wanted to state his case.
>
> Fisher . . . declared that "I can't do it in five minutes and I don't intend to stop in five minutes and you can put your objection in the minutes."
>
> The plan, he said, is "not a sale, but a giveaway, with a $500,000 gift wrapped to it."
>
> Value of Federation's assets far exceeds in many instances, he said, the book value shown . . .
>
> Fisher branded several Federation enterprises in recent years as wild dreams and charged that poor management was to blame for reported losses . . .
>
> The stockholders, he said, weren't "attending a merger, you are attending a funeral."
>
> "You've got a good business that's in the hands of management that cannot and will not make a success of it," Fisher said, adding " . . . all you'll get is an IOU due in 10 years."[6]

Federation creditors were on hand, arguing on behalf of the merger. Oscar Mooneyham, president of Security Bank of Rutherfordton, said he was afraid common stockholders stood to lose either way, but "if we sell, I think we have a chance of getting some of our money back. The other way, I doubt if we'd get a penny."[7] Mr. Mooneyham's assessment turned out to be prophetic.

Virginia Dameron, loyal assistant to Jamie Clarke; Betty Huntley, who grew up at Hickory Nut Gap and was a favorite singer at the picnics; and Carolyn Frady, Mr. Clarke's secretary, remember well the bitterness of that meeting. Mrs. Dameron recalls "My sisters were so afraid of what might happen

ATTENTION
ALL STOCK HOLDERS
In The
FARMERS
FEDERATION!

Don't be misled by the information appearing in an article in the Asheville Citizen on February 20th, 1959 and in the Farmers Federation News Issue for February 1959 on the proposed give away of Farmers Federation to FCX.

There is nothing wrong with our Farmers Federation except mismanagement or the lack of management that has allowed us to fall into a poor position with relation to cash available, to bills payable. We have the resources to overcome this. **Don't let your own Farmers Federation vanish. "It can survive."** The Future looks good under a reorganization plan for the Farmers Federation. We are not poverty stricken now. We have good farm to market roads, well kept farms with high quality cattle, and the latest in farm machinery. We have been civilized and progressive for more than One Hundred years here in Western North Carolina. Our children are well clothed and we are loved and respected by our fellow man. Let's keep it that way and reorganize our own Farmers Federation. If you can not attend the meeting on February 26, 1959, sign the proxy which appears below, cut out and mail to Box 7585, Asheville, North Carolina. **DO IT TODAY!**

February 25, 1959   *Asheville Citizen*

ATTENTION
FARMERS
FEDERATION
STOCKHOLDERS!

BE SURE to attend the Farmers Federation stockholders meeting on the Fourth Floor of the Buncombe County Courthouse, Asheville, N. C., at 10 A. M. tomorrow to get FULL facts on the proposed sale to the Farmers Cooperative Exchange.

Since a two-thirds majority of all preferred and common shares is required to approve the sale, failure to vote or to send in your proxy constitutes a vote against the proposal.

Executive Committee of the Board of Directors of Farmers Federation Cooperative

> James McClure Clarke, President
> Charles W. Davis, Vice-President
> R. Alex Crowell, Secretary
> H. Arthur Osborne
> Walter K. Pike
> D. M. Snelson
> Joe R. Wells

Above and left: *Ads appearing in the Asheville* Citizen, *February 23, (*left*) and February 25, 1959.*

that they came to the meeting to lend support."[8] After the meeting was over, these three women laboriously counted each vote, one for nearly all of the 133,347 voting shares of stock. For four days they counted, while the voting box remained under constant armed guard. By the next Tuesday, Jamie Clarke had to concede that ". . . the final vote would fall short of the percentage needed."[9] Carolyn Frady remembers being almost in tears as the voting trends became clear. General Manager Charlie Davis urged her to "Just go ahead and cry."[10] Tears were the only reasonable response to the acrimony created out of a cooperative Jim McClure envisioned as a bond of brotherhood among the people of Western North Carolina.

Sixty per cent favored the merger with FCX, just short of the two-thirds vote needed to carry the sale. On March 7, the Directors, both those who had supported the merger and those against it, met at the Federation Freezer Locker Plant to pick up the pieces. They passed a resolution that included the following:

> . . . AND WHEREAS, it now appears that the Stockholders and Directors of this Corporation desire new management. NOW, THEREFORE, BE IT RE-SOLVED that James McClure Clarke, President, Charles W. Davis, Vice President . . . are requested to individually and collectively resign their said offices forthwith."[11]

There was nothing else for Jamie Clarke and Charlie Davis to do. Their resignations were accepted, and a slate of officers was proposed to replace them. O. J. Holler became the new president and Joe Higdon the vice president and general manager. Mr. Holler, an elderly farmer, was never more than a figure-head. Joe Higdon ran the business.

Jamie and Elspeth had eight children by this time and he had to find a job. Julian Woodcock, Jr. (always called Jack) was a loyal friend. He suggested the Asheville *Citizen-Times,* and recommended Jamie as an editor. This was a natural choice, with his considerable experience in journalism. But before he went to work at the newspaper, he and Elspeth decided a trip was in order. She had never been to Europe and they decided to take their three older children, Susie, thirteen; Jim, nearly eleven; Annie, nine; and their friends' son Sandy Colburn, twelve. The trip included England and Scotland, Ireland (where Elspeth had Somerville relatives), and as much of the continent as time and money allowed. They stayed in bed-and-breakfasts, ate picnic lunches, rode bicycles in Holland, and generally saw so many wonders and had such fun, along with the normal logistical difficulties of taking such a family through several countries, that Jamie could not dwell on the problems of the Federation.

But the fight was not over back in Asheville. When they returned the new administration of the Federation demanded that Jamie turn over the Educational and Development Fund to them immediately or face legal proceedings. They argued that Jim McClure had raised the money as an aid to the work of the cooperative and that the money should be controlled by the officers of the

Headlines from the Asheville Times *(from top): February 26, February 27, February 28, 1959.*

Federation. Jamie Clarke, who had helped to raise this money, knew that it was to help the people of Western North Carolina. He was convinced that the present management of the Federation would not use it wisely, was determined that the Fund should be preserved for the purposes Jim McClure had intended. The new officers of the cooperative realized that the Farmers Federation was not a viable business without the aid of that money. Jamie was certain that they would pour all of it into the sinking ship, and he staunchly refused to capitulate. The trustees, headed by Jim's loyal friend Arthur Page, backed Jamie up. Joe Higdon wrote him on September 17, 1959: "Since the date of your resignation . . . you have neglected, failed or refused to resign as a Trustee and Executive Secretary of the Fund, in favor of Mr. O. J. Holler, your successor . . ." (Joe Higdon to James McClure Clarke, Sept. 17, 1959).

The letter threatened action after ten days of noncompliance. Jamie Clarke and the trustees did not hand over the Fund, and in 1961 the whole matter landed in the courts. It was a bitterly contested suit. The issue revolved around the pivotal point of whether the Educational and Development Fund was legally tied to the Farmers Federation, or whether it was a completely separate and independent entity. In actual practice, the two were thoroughly interwoven. Salaries were commonly shifted from the Federation to the Fund, for example. But legally the two were just as clearly independent. In 1944 Jim McClure had had the Fund incorporated, clearing up any ambiguities that might have left the contributions of his friends unprotected.

The case dragged on as the Federation's management fruitlessly stalled for time, trying to figure a way around the legal facts. Finally, in January of 1963, the plaintiff "announced its desire to submit to the Judgement of Voluntary Non-Suit . . ."[12] The Fund would survive.

Three weeks later, the Federation went busted once and for all. All through the mountains, the treasured stock certificates that had been purchased with so much hope became worthless. For most, it was the only form of business investment they would ever make. Had the merger with FCX passed, the value of these stocks would have been preserved. But the James G. K. McClure Educational and Development Fund, so named in June 1959, continues the tradition of good works in the name of the man who had a great vision for Western North Carolina. Thousands of deserving mountain students have attended college as the result of this money. In many instances, the money received has made the difference between attending college and missing the chance altogether. Arthur Page remained the President of the Trustees of the Fund during all the times of trouble, and he helped to map out new directions for it in light of the faltering state of the Federation. He wrote a personal letter to all the contributors, summarizing the origins of the Fund and describing the new circumstances in the mountains:

> As President of the Educational and Development Fund I want to report to you concerning a change your Trustees are making in the spending of the money you contribute.
>
> The Educational and Development Fund has graduated from its elementary task to a higher one.
>
> Jim McClure's ambition was to bring opportunity and a good life to the mountain people.
>
> Now a good life and a good living are not necessarily the same thing, but a good living is a very handy and helpful base on which to construct a good life.
>
> The mountain farmer didn't make a good living. There were several reasons for that. But perhaps the most obvious one at that time was that he had no good market for his products and, therefore, little incentive to exert himself. If, in the local phrase, a man grew enough to do him and his family there was little else he could accomplish. And growing enough to do himself provided a very meager living.
>
> So Jim set about to create markets. He created the Farmers Federation with its warehouses which could act as collection points for the farmer's produce and which could in return sell him his blue jeans, fertilizer and so forth . . .
>
> But markets are not the whole story by any means. Some 13% of the American people grow enough food for our population and enough to create a serious problem of oversupply. The technological advances and the reduction of many hours in farming have been as fast or faster than those in industry. Education—general and vocational—is the basis of this revolutionary change. There is now far more prospect for improving life in the mountains by aiding education than there is in looking for new markets. It means that there will be

fewer people on the farms but greater output—more brains and less muscles, more chemistry, more apparatus and more profit.

Happily, the excess people who will be displaced from the farms will not have to leave home, for a considerable amount of industry has come into the mountains and this provides not only jobs, but a local market for farm produce.

All these changes are behind the decision of the Fund to change emphasis from markets to education, to hospitals, to nursing and things which directly add to the good life.

When this decision was made it was apparent that regular commercial competition not only had grown enough to make more or less adequate markets but that it had made inroads on the business of the Federation. The ordinary operations of the Federation were not doing too well financially. This led Mr. Clarke to suggest a merger of the Federation with the larger Farmers Cooperative Exchange which operated in other parts of the State. It has more buying power and more managerial experience than the Federation.

To consummate this merger it was necessary to have a favorable vote of the stockholder owners of the Federation. A majority voted for the merger. But the North Carolina law requires a two-thirds vote. Had everyone voted, there would probably have been a two-thirds majority. But those who voted "no" and those who did not vote at all made up more than one-third of the total, so the merger was lost.

Mr. Clarke resigned as President of the Federation to devote himself entirely to the Fund.

The Federation is under other management. It has its own program, which does not include any project financed by the Fund, for the kind of projects the Fund contemplates, now that marketing is out, do not fit with the Federation's operations.

At this point I think it is appropriate to recall that from the very beginning Jim McClure was as interested in the things of the spirit as he was in material well being.

The Lord's Acre is an example . . .

One of Jim's major interests was education.

He was Chairman of the Buncombe county Citizen's Committee which persuaded a county that thought it had no money and hadn't built but one school in 22 years to spend $6 million to tear down many of the old buildings and create a new consolidated school system, properly housed . . .

There is no question that in this day and time, good will and good back muscle are not enough.

Education is opportunity. The valuable part of a man is his brain and it is better when exercised young by education.

With the coming of better high schools it should be possible to open the doors of opportunity in the colleges to the bright young boys and girls of the mountains by scholarships. Mr. Clarke's program this year begins this enterprise . . .

The better part of thirty years I worked on the Fund with Jim McClure. His enthusiasm for human betterment never wavered. His main objectives stayed the same. But the means of attainment shifted rapidly as changes in conditions occurred.

The changes in conditions which have motivated our change were develop-

ing before Jim died and had he lived, by now, I am clear that he would have
suggested changes, either what we have done or something more or less like it.

And I think he would view the future, as I do, as being as full of good
possibilities as there were at any time in the past.[13]

While the assets of the Fund would find new and productive use, there
lingered an unmistakable sadness at the death of the Federation. It had always
been more than a business; it was an organization that had stood for high values
of honesty. And it had drawn so many people together for a purpose. Doug
Reed, the Citizen reporter, tried to express the sense of loss felt all across
Western North Carolina.

> For nearly 40 years mountain farmers have felt no need to specify.
> "The Federation" was enough.
> But . . . the dream of a Chicago-born Presbyterian preacher will almost
> surely vanish.
> And the Farmers Federation Cooperative, the creature of its maker, will be
> no more.
> It began without capital and so it apparently will end—broke, harassed by
> competition and unable to find the money it needs to survive . . .
> In 1920, when James G. K. McClure—minister, educator, promotor and
> businessman—viewed Western North Carolina he saw quagmire roads, run-
> down farms, scrawny cattle, lame horses, broken plows, barefoot children and
> leather-skinned women. About the only thing standing up for the whole lot
> was the dirt farmers who waded the roads, worked the farms, cursed the cattle,
> beat the horses, swore at the plow, caned the children and loved the women.
> He had no money and no one would lend him any. He couldn't sell what he
> grew and he frequently wouldn't grow what he could sell.
> He was poverty-stricken, but McClure turned that into an asset, winning the
> pity and the purse of influential financiers.
> With the kind of talk he understood, McClure showed the mountaineer
> farmer how to wipe the tobacco juice off his beard and market it around the
> world. He set up stores where a man's produce was taken and cash money
> paid. Men stopped sawing pine trees for firewood and started shipping it for
> paper.
> Over the years, the Federation branched out . . . It spread its network of
> familiar yellow, clapboard stores into 21 towns in 15 counties.[14]

And then, all of a sudden, the Federation was gone. But people still remember,
they sure do. Just ask around about the picnics, or mention James G. K.
McClure's name. They remember the Lord's Acre as well, and will tell you
what a wonderful friend Rev. Dumont Clarke was to them and to their children.

The Fund continued to support the Lord's Acre Movement. Dumont Clarke
retired from his post the year of Jim McClure's death. He had married Elizabeth
Dodge Huntington and moved to Riverdale, New York. He chose Reverend
Jack Waldrep as his replacement. Dumont Clarke said farewell in his familiar
editorial space in the Farmers Federation *News* in the October 1956, issue.

It was nearly twenty-seven years ago, in December, 1929, that God led me to become director of the Religious Department of the Farmers Federation. During these years I have had a wonderful privilege of establishing a very large number of Christian fellowships in North Carolina and in many other States. Therefore it is with much regret that, having lessened endurance for field work, I must now sever my active connections with Farmers Federation, and cease my visits to country churches, with all their cherished associations . . .

To all who have encouraged me with their friendships and cooperation, I give most hearty thanks. I shall miss the friendly welcome of country church people in many counties. My prayerful good wishes go to you. May God bless, everyone.[15]

Rev. Jack Waldrep worked tirelessly to carry on the spirit of the Lord's Acre both at home and abroad for seventeen years, until the Trustees of the Fund decided that there was no longer a need in Western North Carolina for those methods of raising cash and morale. Now the income from the endowment for the Lord's Acre is used to help rural ministers to further their education. Dumont Clarke spent his last years writing a book on Scripture Prayer and promoting its use. His full and useful life ended in 1960.

The job of Executive Secretary of the McClure Fund is only part-time, and Jamie Clarke was also editor of the Sunday Asheville *Citizen-Times* and associate editor of the daily *Citizen* for eight years. He then became assistant to the President of Warren Wilson College. His father's old friend, Arthur Bannerman, was president of the college at that time, and Jamie worked with him until his retirement. He then continued as assistant to President Reuben Holden. During this time he also served as Chairman of the Buncombe County School Board for eight years, and served in the North Carolina State Legislature for three terms. In 1982 he resigned from Warren Wilson College to run for the United States Congress. When he was elected, he resigned as Executive Secretary of the McClure Fund. The author, John Curtis Ager, was chosen as his successor by the trustees. Virginia Dameron assisted in the many charitable activities of the Fund until she retired in 1980. She passed away in 1987.

Life at Hickory Nut Gap Farm, still the home of Elspeth and Jamie Clarke, retains all of the warmth and hospitality with which Jim and Elizabeth McClure endowed it. Although it is a working dairy farm and apple orchard, it also is devoted to people, and each summer old John Shorter's vegetable garden feeds (and works) many visitors, guests and helpers, who arrive from all points and for a wide variety of reasons. Square dance music, under the direction of one of the Federation's star picnic attractions, Johnny Rhymer and his Bear Creek Ramblers, is a frequent accompaniment to a summer evening at Hickory Nut Gap. Sixteen great-grandchildren (at last count) of Jim and Elizabeth McClure are growing up on the same farm that cast its spell on the newlyweds when they first drove the Honeymoon Hudson up the curving mountain road. These children like nothing better than dressing up in clothes from the attic and acting out

"Mr. and Mrs. McClure plays." Their favorites are the courtship scenes, culminating in the buggy ride around Central Park.

The visitor to Hickory Nut Gap Farm who has a keen eye and ear would find a great deal of Jim and Elizabeth still there. The gardens and boxwoods, the landscaping and interior design, are all obvious contributions of Elizabeth's. Her murals depicting Sherrill's Inn and the portraits of Jim and Elspeth in the dining room are all works of her genius. Less tangible, but no less real, is the extraordinary hospitality that draws strangers together there. Throughout his life, Jim McClure loved nothing so much as being able to orchestrate a diverse collection of people into a happy gathering. Whether before the warm fire of the dining room in winter or amidst the summer breezes on the porch, a dinner at Hickory Nut Gap retains a charming conviviality quite suited to the old mountain inn. The talk is easy and relaxed, full of old stories and the friendly needling that grows up among the current group of people who have spent the day working on their tasks together. The serious talk runs to politics, as Jamie Clarke has devoted himself more and more to public service. The family has retained its Presbyterian base and one is as likely as not to discuss the tenets of the Christian faith while picking raspberries in the garden. Sons of Elspeth and Jamie, especially Mark and Douglas, have spent time working on and managing the farm. Both their daughters, Susie and Annie (wife of the author), live nearby with their families and are always ready to help with farm projects. Susie's husband, Dr. Will Hamilton, is the family doctor for the area. A lawyer son, Billy, his wife Sinclair, and their four children also live nearby. Another lawyer son, Dumont, and his wife Shirley Linn, come as often as they can from Charlotte to keep in touch. The oldest son, called Jim like his great-grandfather, works in Kannapolis, North Carolina, but he and his wife Francine come when he can escape the pressures of his accounting work with Cannon Mills.

Dogs and children, kittens, sheep, chickens, horses and pigs all appear to have the run of the place. Life at Hickory Nut Gap Farm has nothing to do with the search for a utopia, and everything to do with the acceptance and enjoyment and encouragement of people in all their variety. It is a community based on the family traditions exemplified by Jim and Elizabeth McClure.

At the end of this book, one feels the need to try to somehow pull together the meaning of Jim's life, but it would be the futile exercise of a biographer's conceit. By his own reckoning, he would want to be judged by how his spiritual pursuits translated into tangible results. There was a great courageousness to Jim McClure, that much is undeniable. Since he was unafraid of other people, he felt free to befriend them. He also stood ready to make decisions, to choose his course of action, and then to pursue the results he imagined possible. He also had the courage to fail, and to admit when his plans faltered, and to go on undiscouraged. The Christian ethics taught him by his father and mother were the axis on which his life turned. He sought the spiritual challenge, and rewards, of Christian service, and as such consciously set himself apart from his contemporaries. Jim McClure devoted his life to creating a business that made profits for others. His life is a rich mine of ideas and impulses, some fruitful and some stillborn. But most of all he was a man with many friends, whom he loved to join together for useful ends. These friends wanted to remember this man, to be reminded of how much he loved his life, his wife, his children and them. To all these people, I commend the life of James G. K. McClure, Jr.

1. James McClure Clarke, "News from the Front," Farmers Federation *News,* July 1957, p. 3.

2. James McClure Clarke, Farmers Federation *News,* February, 1959.

3. Interview with Mr. Charles Davis.

4. Doug Reed, "Federation's Fate Hangs on Proxy Vote's Outcome," Asheville *Citizen,* February 27, 1959, p. 1, 5.

5. *Ibid.*

6. *Ibid.*

7. *Ibid.*

8. Interview with Mrs. Virginia Dameron.

9. Doug Reed, "Votes Need for Sale of Federation FAll Short," Asheville *Citizen,* March 4, 1959, p. 1.

10. Interview with Carolyn Frady.

11. Farmers Federation Minutes Book, March 7, 1959.

12. Farmers Federation Cooperative vs. McClure Fund, Superior Court of North Carolina, January 21, 1963.

13. Arthur Page, letter to contributors to the McClure Fund, November 1, 1959.

14. Doug Reed, Asheville *Citizen,* February 15, 1963.

15. Dumont Clarke, "The Country Church With the Lord's Acre Plan," Farmers Federation *News,* October 1956, p. 27.